Between State and
Essays on Charities Law and Policy in Canada

Between State and Market surveys and critiques the existing literature on charities law as well as the laws themselves. The authors offer policy prescriptions for the future of an increasingly vital sector of Canadian society.

After an overview of the charitable sector in Canada, the first section of the book contains a sociological review of altruism in different societies, a discussion of altruism in various philosophical and religious traditions, an economic analysis of "rational voluntarism," and an assessment of the relationship between the charitable sector and the welfare state. The second section contains five papers on the legal definition of charity, both general (the jurisprudence of the Federal Court of Appeal and a proposal for rethinking the concept of "public benefit") and particular (the politial purposes doctrine, religion as charity, and a commentary on the recent Supreme Court decision on the meaning of charity). The third section deals with the tax status of charities: two papers evaluate the current tax credit system and one deals with the administration of charities by the Canada Customs and Revenue Agency. The final section contains essays on charities and commercial enterprise, on the regulation of fund-raising, and on needed reforms in non-profit corporation law. At a time when the federal government is about to embark on a wide range of policy initiatives to assist and regulate the non-profit sector, these essays are necessary reading for anyone concerned with the future of the charitable sector in Canada.

JIM PHILLIPS and BRUCE CHAPMAN are professors of law at the University of Toronto. DAVID STEVENS is professor of law at McGill University.

Between State and Market

Essays on Charities Law and Policy in Canada

Edited by

JIM PHILLIPS,

BRUCE CHAPMAN, AND

DAVID STEVENS

Published for the Kahanoff Foundation –
Non-Profit Sector Research Initiative
by
McGill-Queen's University Press
Montreal & Kingston · London · Ithaca

ISBN 0-7735-2096-1 (bound)
ISBN 0-7735-2112-7 (paper)

Legal deposit second quarter 2001
Bibliothèque nationale du Québec

Printed in Canada on acid-free paper

McGill-Queen's University Press acknowledges the financial support of the Government of Canada through the Book Publishing Industry Development Program (BPIDP) for its activities. It also acknowledges the support of the Canada Council for the Arts for its publishing program.

Canadian Cataloguing in Publication Data

Main entry under title:
Between state and market: essays on charities law and policy in Canada
Papers originally presented at a conference held in Toronto, Ont., 1999.
Includes bibliographical references.
ISBN 0-7735-2096-1 (bound) – ISBN 0-7735-2112-7 (pbk.)
1. Charitable uses, trusts, and foundations—Canada.
I. Phillips, Jim, 1954- II. Chapman, Bruce III. Stevens, David
IV. Canadian Policy Research Networks Kahanoff Foundation.
Nonprofit Sector Research Initiative.
KE3542.Z85B48 2001 346.71'064 C00-900899-3

Typeset in 10/12 Baskerville by True to Type

Contents

Tables and Figures

TABLES

FIGURES

Acknowledgments

Our principal debt of gratitude is to the Non-Profit Sector Research Initiative of the Kahanoff Foundation, which provided funding for this research, for a conference at which authors presented preliminary versions of the papers, and for this publication. The Non-Profit Sector Research Initiative, established by the Kahanoff Foundation, promotes research and scholarship on non-profit–sector issues and seeks to broaden the formal body of knowledge on the non-profit sector. The initiative works to increase understanding of the role that non-profit organizations play in civil society and to inform relevant public policy.

The conference at which these papers were first presented was an integral part of our project, and we would like to thank the law firm of McCarthy Tétrault in Toronto for assisting us with the costs. We owe a particular debt of gratitude to Jennifer Tam of the Faculty of Law, University of Toronto, for her very able organizing of that event.

We also wish to acknowledge our debt to our contributors, who have been a pleasure to work with and who have, we believe, admirably carried out their assigned tasks.

Finally, our thanks to the University of Toronto Law School, and especially to its dean, Ron Daniels, who also supported this project.

Bruce Chapman
Jim Phillips
David Stevens

Contributors

NEIL BROOKS is professor of law at Osgoode Hall Law School, York University, and the author of numerous works on tax and tax policy.

CARA CAMERON is completing her BCL and LLB at the Faculty of Law, McGill University.

BRUCE CHAPMAN is professor of law at the University of Toronto. He has written extensively on law and economics, legal theory and torts, and he prepared a background study for the Ontario Law Reform Commission's project on the law of charities.

KEVIN E. DAVIS is assistant professor at the Faculty of Law, University of Toronto. His teaching and research are concentrated in the areas of commercial law, white-collar crime, and law and development.

ABRAHAM DRASSINOWER is assistant professor at the Faculty of Law, University of Toronto, where he teaches principally intellectual property law. He holds a PhD in political science and an LLB, both from the University of Toronto. In 1998–99 he served as a law clerk at the Supreme Court of Canada.

DAVID DUFF is assistant professor at the Faculty of Law, University of Toronto, where he teaches tax law and policy.

RICHARD JANDA is associate professor of law at McGill University and past director of McGill's Centre for the Study of Regulated Industries.

WILL KYMLICKA is professor of philosophy at Queen's University. He specializes in political philosophy and is the author of *Contemporary Political Philosophy* (Oxford, 1990) and of *Multicultural Citizenship* (Oxford, 1995).

ANDRÉE LAJOIE is professor of law at the Université de Montréal and a research fellow at the Centre de recherche en droit public. She is a member of the Royal Society of Canada.

MAYO MORAN is associate professor at the Faculty of Law, University of Toronto. She teaches trusts and torts, and has an interest also in constitutional law.

CHARLES-MAXIME PANACCIO has completed his LLB and BCL at the Faculty of Law, McGill University, and is currently clerking for Mr Justice Charles Gonthier at the Supreme Court of Canada.

JIM PHILLIPS is professor at the Faculty of Law, University of Toronto, and is also appointed to the Department of History and the Centre of Criminology. Principally a legal historian, he has also written a number of articles on the law of charity and is a member of the editorial board of the *Philanthropist.*

JANE ALLYN PILIAVIN is a social psychologist and professor of sociology at the University of Wisconsin – Madison. She has written extensively on altruism and helping behaviour, most recently on blood donation and volunteering.

DAVID SHARPE is a lawyer with the Office of the Attorney-General of New York State. He has an LLB from the University of Toronto's Faculty of Law and after graduation clerked at the Supreme Court of Canada. He is the author of *A Portrait of Canada's Charities* (1994)

LORNE SOSSIN is an assistant professor at Osgoode Hall Law School, York University, where he teaches administrative law. He is cross-appointed to the Department of Political Science at York, where he teaches a course on democratic administration. He has published several articles on tax administration.

DAVID STEVENS is professor of law at McGill University, where his subjects include tax, corporate and commercial law, and trusts. He has published in a variety of areas and is the author of the Ontario Law Reform Commission's *Report on the Law of Charities* (1996).

JEN-CHIEH TING is a post-doctoral fellow at the Academia Sinica, Taiwan. He received his PhD from the University of Wisconsin – Madison under the supervision of Professor Piliavin and has published on religion, altruism, and helping behaviour. He is currently researching new religious organizations in Taiwan.

Between State and Market:
Essays on Charities Law and Policy in Canada

1 Introduction

BRUCE CHAPMAN, JIM PHILLIPS,
AND DAVID STEVENS

In the last few years the role of the charitable sector in Canadian society has become an increasingly important subject.[1] Federal and provincial governments have begun to study the sector and to ask how they can best facilitate its workings,[2] newspapers devote much more attention to it than they ever have,[3] and it has engaged the attention of the scholarly community in a way unthinkable just a decade or so ago. Long content just to get on with its tasks, the sector itself has also turned its mind to a highly publicized exercise in self-study and lobbying.[4] The reasons for all of this interest are not difficult to discern. Principally, the contraction of the welfare state has meant that much that was previously done by government agencies is now done by charities or other non-profit groups. Often this is occurring at the same time as cut-backs in government spending are diminishing charities' resources. In addition, the enhanced role of the voluntary sector has led to more scrutiny of it, more demands for accountability in all areas from program delivery to fund-raising.

The growing role of the sector has, as noted, led to new academic interest in it, and the sixteen original essays in this volume are just a small part of that initiative. Their genesis lies in research sponsored by the Non-Profit Sector Research Initiative of the Kahanoff Foundation, organized principally at the University of Toronto Law School, and carried out by (mostly legal) scholars from six universities. All but one of the papers included here were first presented at a conference held at the University of Toronto's Law School in January 1999 and then revised for publication.[5]

David Sharpe sets the context (chapter 2) for the volume by providing us with crucial background data on charities in Canada. Focusing on registered charities (because it is only these for which the Canada Customs and Revenue Agency, or CCRA – formerly Revenue Canada – keeps records), Sharpe first presents us with details on the current (1999) breakdown of charities by general sector (religion, welfare, education, health, and benefits to the community) and more specific category (assigned by the CCRA to capture more specific activities within a sector – for example, hospitals within health and disaster funds within welfare) and with a picture of how this breakdown has been changing over the last decade. Sharpe also lays out the finances (revenues and expenditures) of charities by type of charity. Second, he provides invaluable data on the activities of donors and volunteers within each province and by demographic groupings. Cautious in the conclusions that he draws from these data, Sharpe offers, third, some recommendations on how the CCRA might increase the comparability of the data across different classification schemes and how it might better monitor the data that it collects.

From the outset the focus of this research project was to be the legal aspects of charities' status and operations, but also from the beginning we wanted to infuse the legal analyses with broader perspectives. Hence the four chapters of Part I are either empirical or theoretical in nature, or some combination of the two.

The same problem of comparability of data examined by David Sharpe in chapter 2 plagues any attempt at careful cross-cultural assessment of altruism in different countries, according to Jen-Chieh Ting and Jane Allyn Piliavin, authors of chapter 3, which opens Part I. For example, we need to break down further the altruistic notion of "helping others" into assisting others "within one's group" and helping others, including strangers, more generally. The sociological literature surveyed in this essay suggests, for instance, that Americans may be more helpful or altruistic to others in general than are, for example, the Chinese or Japanese but that the latter are more altruistic to "in-group members." Also, within the broader concept of the "civil society," with which Americans have so closely associated themselves since de Toqueville's discussion over 150 years ago, and which is closely linked with the vitality of the charitable sector, it is important to distinguish between volunteering (in the sense of helping others) and joining a voluntary association. Despite the Americans' historical reputation for being great "joiners" of voluntary associations, more recent data show, for example, that Canadians equal or surpass them on certain measures of membership in such organizations. However, this difference largely disappears when one drops union affiliation, a not-altogether-charitable activity, from the analysis. Also, while in studies of Canada, the United States, and western Europe the United States consistently shows the highest percentage of volunteers in the population, this ranking falls somewhat when one eliminates religious volunteering. Whether one should construe religious participation more as associated membership or as volunteering is a difficult question, but whatever the answer, Ting and Piliavin make it clear that this is one factor among many that makes comparison of altruism across cultures very difficult.

The next two essays in Part I are more theoretical. Will Kymlicka (chapter 4) delves deeply into two contrasting understandings of altruism and seeks to lay bare their different assumptions. The first, based in modern secular conceptions of social justice, sees charitable giving as the fulfilment of an obligatory duty on the part of the donor, something that the recipient can demand as a matter of entitlement and for which a potential donor, on failing to give, can be deemed blameworthy. The second, which Kymlicka claims is rooted in older religious conceptions of ethical virtue, sees altruism as exemplified in a praiseworthy voluntary gift, the stuff of free, supererogatory donation. Kymlicka argues that these two contrasting understandings explain how differently people see charitable institutions – indeed, even reveal how much normative room there is for such private organizations as opposed to the public institutions of government. Kymlicka argues that the older religious conceptions of charity, focused traditionally on the donor's pursuit of self-perfection through altruistic giving, have now given way to a more modern idea that such giving provides to the recipients only what they can rightly demand as a matter of justice.

Chapter 5, by Bruce Chapman, offers a theoretical account of rational voluntarism and suggests what this might mean for the regulation of charities and their internal organization. Chapman criticizes both the economist's model of the calculating, self-interested rational actor and the sociologist's account of the unthinking player of social roles. Instead he offers a description of *homo socioeconomicus*, a somewhat more complicated sort of being, who often sees herself, at least presumptively, as part of a team or larger social enterprise, though not so much that all calculative regard for self-interest disappears. Chapman argues that we can see traces of homo socioeconomicus throughout the charitable sector and in the way it is regulated. Specifically, we can better understand the need to keep the charitable sector separate from the political process, the unusually high impact of the tax subsidy on a charitable donor's willingness to give, and the propensity for charitable institutions to organize as non-profits and at some distance from commercial activity, Chapman says, if we look at rational voluntarism through the eyes of homo socioeconomicus.

Part I ends with Neil Brooks (Chapter 6) on the role of the voluntary sector in a welfare state. In a wide-ranging tour of political and economic theory and empirical observations, Brooks argues that while a dynamic charitable sector has much to offer society, it cannot be an effective substitute for the welfare state. Brooks traces the rise of interest in the so-called third sector over the past three decades and links it to a desire among some to dismantle the post-war welfare state. He then takes on the arguments of those who contend that the sector is indispensable – even more than good government – to the proper functioning of society. While he acknowledges the major role that it plays, he again asserts that it must complement, not replace, government. Building on these arguments, two further sections of the chapter argue that the sector cannot, as a practical matter, substitute for the full range of public social services and, ironically, that attempts to have it do so will not only devitalize it but also make it effectively part of government.

Part II begins our more detailed examination of legal issues facing charities in Canada. Here no question is more important than the threshold one of what constitutes "charity" in law. Common law rules on this question go back hundreds of years and today in Canada operate principally to determine whether an organization can achieve the status of "registered charity" with the CCRA and thereby issue donation receipts.[6] Much dissatisfaction has been expressed in a variety of quarters with the current legal definition of charity for purposes of the Income Tax Act,[7] although some critics do not offer much analysis of why the law is inadequate. The chapters in Part II represent a collective and sustained analysis and critique of many aspects of the current law. Three of them look generally at the legal meaning of charity. Jim Phillips (chapter 7) reviews the jurisprudence of the Federal Court of Appeal, the court which hears appeals from refusals to register by the CCRA and that therefore sets the parameters for what is charitable. He argues that although one early case demonstrated a willingness to adapt the legal definition to Canadian circumstances, the court has generally shown too much adherence to a traditional and English-derived definition and been unwilling to search for a modern and appropriately Canadian definition. It has also hampered itself by an approach to statutory interpretation that places too much emphasis on the particular activities of a charity and too little on its general purposes.

Phillips is principally concerned with advocating a different process for deciding whether an organization is charitable and does not offer specific prescriptions for the content of a new legal definition. Mayo Moran's paper (chapter 8) takes on that task and is in some ways a companion piece to Phillips's; it seeks to point the way to the future, while his decries the past. Moran suggests that the courts ought to look to the values in the Charter of Rights as emblematic of what should be "charitable" at the end of the twentieth century. In part that means that charitable organizations that in some way offend the Charter should lose their status. Here she offers an extended discussion of the now well-known case, albeit a case about a charitable trust decided under provincial law, in which discriminatory provisions were struck down.[8] More important for the long-term development of the legal definition, she also discusses what she calls the "expansive effect" of the Charter on the law of charity. She argues, for example, that any purpose that seeks to ameliorate the conditions of disadvantage of groups singled out for protection by the equality rights in the Charter should be charitable. More admittedly controversial is her suggestion that the political purposes doctrine may find it hard to survive in a Charter world. Not all will agree with some of the prescriptions advanced in this paper; few seriously interested in the legal definition of charity are likely to be able to avoid the questions that Moran poses.

Two authors mentioned above also provide (chapter 11) a commentary on the Supreme Court of Canada's 1999 decision in *Vancouver Society of Immigrant and Visible Minority Women v. Minister of National Revenue.*[9] For the first time the Supreme Court has made a major statement on the meaning of charity, and Moran and Phillips are critical of the majority of the court's refusal to take an expansive approach. The court largely reaffirmed existing categorizations of, and approaches to determining, charity. It also, however, the authors concede, cleared up some areas of uncertainty in the law.

The other two papers on the legal meaning of charity look in more detail at particular aspects of it. Abraham Drassinower (chapter 9) takes on a difficult and controversial subject – the rule that a political purpose cannot also be a charitable purpose. Some criticize this rule as overly restrictive on charities' activities, while others support it as delimiting a fundamental difference between what it is to do "charity" as opposed to "politics." Drassinower seeks to throw new light on the debate by coming at it from a different perspective. He argues that the conceptual underpinning of the rule – that the courts cannot decide whether a political purpose is for the public benefit – is incoherent as it now stands. It can be made coherent only if an exception is made for those political purposes that seek to attain what he describes as the "minimal conditions of human dignity." Drassinower's analysis will win the approval of those who do not like the political purposes doctrine in any form and of those who think the notion essentially sound but are troubled by how an organization such as Amnesty International, or the purpose of freeing political prisoners and ending torture, can somehow not be charitable.

Jim Phillips's examination (chapter 10) of religion and the Charter of Rights does not take on directly the normative question of whether religious activity ought to be charitable. Rather, it suggests that some of the distinctions made by charities law between different religions, and between religions and other forms of ethical belief, offend the Charter of Rights. If the courts ultimately vindicate his interpretation there will be profound consequences for the law of charity in Canada. Such a decision would mean that the centuries-old English law on which our law is based would have to acknowledge an evolving legal and cultural context. Such an event might well be a harbinger of its also recognizing a changed social, economic, and political context.

As we noted above, much of the contemporary concern about the legal definition of charity revolves around access to registered charity status under the Income Tax Act. Tax policy and the CCRA's administration of the registration process are the foci of Part III of this volume. Lorne Sossin (chapter 12) first provides a detailed study of the CCRA's charities division. After summarizing the process and the manner in which the division operates, he stresses the extent to which it, like all bureaucracies, has considerable discretionary authority and argues that one can find both inconsistency and incoherency in its exercise of that discretion. His prescription for better administration is simple to state, even if it will prove difficult to put into practice: the division must receive better guidance on the purposes behind registration and regulation of charities. And the best way to achieve this, he suggests, is through a clear statutory definition of charity, one that will perhaps eliminate some of the problems, discussed in Part II, caused by continuing reliance on the common law definition.

The other two papers in Part II focus on the system of tax benefits for charities. After extensively reviewing the history of the Income Tax Act's treatment of donations to charity, and laying out how the current system works, David Duff asks (chapter 13) why charitable donations should receive any kind of favourable treatment. He reviews different kinds of tax measures against the goals often alleged to be achieved by them – tax equity, rewarding generosity, encouraging donations, and promoting pluralism. He comes out squarely against a simple deduction as achieving none of these purposes adequately and applies this criticism to the current Canadian provision, which he sees as "a deduction masquerading as a credit." He then argues that a new system, one based on a tax credit with a declining rate, would be more equitable and would more fully achieve at least the goals of encouraging donations and promoting pluralism.

In this conclusion Duff is somewhat at odds with Neil Brooks, who in chapter 14 argues for repeal of the tax credit for charitable deductions. First, he suggests that none of the rationales usually offered for the credit – that it promotes pluralism, altruism, and innovation and that it contributes to the independence of the charitable sector – actually holds true. Indeed in some respects, he argues, the tax credit achieves the opposite. Second, he argues that the credit directs government funds to the wrong places or at least not to the places where they are most needed. Third, he maintains that the credit represents a government spending program that is not subject to any of the criteria of control, accountability, and transparency that should, and normally do, accompany such programs. Finally, he suggests that while the research on the issue is somewhat equivocal, on the whole the tax credit is not an effective method of raising funds for the charitable sector – certainly not as effective as taxation-derived grants would be. Brooks concludes with an argument not often heard these days – that progressive taxation promotes citizenship and social cohesion in a way that charitable tax privileges can never do. Not all readers will agree with the arguments made and the conclusions offered here; but no serious discussion of the issue can ignore either.

The contributions in Part IV, on the associational and regulatory law of the sector, strike out in new and original directions. It is common enough in the writing on the sector to encounter inquiries into the sector's accountability to its patrons. Usually the focus is on accountability to patrons and the community at large through disclosure and monitoring. Using the fund-raising efforts of McGill University as a backdrop for his study, Richard Janda and his colleagues (chapter 15) ask a different question: what effect does such fund-raising have on the integrity of charitable entities' own projects? Might there be too much responsiveness to donors and patrons when gifts are solicited for purposes that respond to donors' demands and are donated on conditions dictated by donors? Along the way Janda et al. engage another equally compelling set of questions: what is the relationship between distributive justice and charity, and what is the relationship between the welfare state and charitable activity? They address these issues against the remarkable transformation of Quebec society over the past 40 years from church-centred charity to state-centred social welfare and now back with the retreat of the state in the face of limited finances and the inherent limitations of law as an instrument of social development.

Kevin Davis (chapter 15) examines the legal regulation of commercial activities of charities with a view to contributing to our understanding of "social enterprise." After a short review of the legal situation in Canada, Davis evaluates that regime against three values that he suggests ought to be applied to it: the intrinsic value of charity, efficiency, and fairness. His argument is that any proper understanding of the legal regulation of social enterprise ought to enhance the pursuit of charitable purposes, be in accord with the fundamental purposes of commercial law, and be fair in the sense that similarly situated actors ought to be treated alike. Using these three perspectives, Davis examines the benefits and the dangers of social enterprise with a view to identifying appropriate objectives for regulation. On the positive side of the ledger, he argues that social enterprise facilitates charitable activity when it provides goods and services at below-market price and when it allows a disadvantaged group to work. He also notes that social enterprise is an efficient mode of supplying goods and services in situations where information asymmetries require the extra trust that the non-distribution constraint ensures. The negative side of the ledger includes the claims that charities compete unfairly when they use their tax subsidy, that charities compete inefficiently because they do not have residual claimants ensuring that the fiduciaries are producing effectively, and that the commercial activities of charities simply lead them astray. Davis's chapter ends with some suggestions about the direction in which any law reform should go.

David Stevens (chapter 17) starts with the general question: "What can or should the state do in respect of charities and other non-profits?" He suggests that the state's primary role in regard to charity is to do what it can to facilitate it. He claims that the principal means of facilitation is to provide an appropriate set of associational laws. Oddly, he observes, the state in Canada has performed its responsibilities in this domain very poorly. Stevens takes the central case of failure – the lack of an appropriate non-profit corporation law – and suggests reasons why Canada has virtually ignored the project of designing an appropriate corporate law. He then sets out to identify the main elements of a good design, all of which rest on the observation that the first task is to understand the purposes that these associations pursue, since these purposes shape the instrument. Stevens does not offer specifics of a new statute; he does, however, identify how such a valuable reform of the law should proceed.

NOTES

1 We use the term "charitable sector" here because the book is largely about organizations that are legally "charities." There is much current interest in the "voluntary sector," by which people generally mean more or less the same thing as "charitable sector" and which is probably roughly coterminous with it. They are not precisely the same, however, for some of the voluntary sector is not legally charitable and much of the charitable sector is not voluntary; indeed it includes multi-million-dollar enterprises such as universities and hospitals. The charitable sector is, of course, part of the much wider "non-profit sector," which includes mutual assistance organizations, political parties, and a host of other, not legally charitable organizations. For an excellent review of the difficulties of defining the "third sector" (not government, not the market), see L.M. Salamon and H.K. Anheier, "In Search of the Non-Profit Sector: The Question of Definitions," *Voluntas* 3 (1992), 125.

2 See Ontario Law Reform Commission (OLRC), *Report on the Law of Charities*, 2 vols. (Toronto: Government of Ontario, 1998); and Canada, *Report of the Joint Tables: Working Together: A Government of Canada/Voluntary Sector Joint Initiative* (Ottawa: Privy Council Office, 1999).

3 See in particular the series of long articles by André Picard which appeared in the *Toronto Star* in 1998.

4 See Panel on Accountability and Governance in the Voluntary Sector, *Building on Strength: Improving Governance and Accountability in Canada's Voluntary Sector* (1999)

5 The exception is M. Moran and J. Phillips, chapter 11 in this volume. This is a commentary on a major Supreme Court of Canada decision that was not released until after the conference. In addition, Neil Brooks presented one paper at the conference which we thought more suitable for publication as two (chapters 6 and 14).

6 We are aware that the law originally gave a specific meaning to "charity" in order to determine whether a trust to achieve certain purposes was valid; it was so only if the purposes were charitable. This is still part of the law of trusts, but for charities lawyers such issues have been substantially eclipsed by questions of tax law.

7 For critiques of the law in addition to those in this volume, see, among others, Panel, *Building on Strength*, 51–4, and A. Drache, "Charities, Public Benefit, and the Canadian Income Tax System: A Proposal for

Reform," Working Paper, Non-Profit Sector Research Initiative, Kahanoff Foundation, 1998. The OLRC's *Report on the Law of Charities,* in contrast, generally supports the structure of the current law.

8 See *Re Canada Trust and Ontario Human Rights Commission* (1990), 74 OR (2d) 481 (CA).

9 [1999] 1 SCR 10.

2 The Canadian Charitable Sector: An Overview

DAVID SHARPE

This chapter offers an overview of Canada's charitable sector, looking at, first, the sectors and categories of charitable organizations, their size, and their financies; second, the donating behaviour of Canadians by region and other characteristics; and third, future directions for research and classificatory schemes.

When we discuss charities in Canada, we must distinguish between registered and unregistered charities.[1] We can speak with some confidence about those that are registered because the Canada Customs and Revenue Agency (CCRA) maintains records on them.[2] About the unregistered we can say little with any certainty. Indeed, beyond the realm of registered charities, there is a whole world of organized non-profit activity in Canada about which we know very little. There are no doubt many unregistered charitable organizations in Canada – organizations that operate according to the basic definition of charitable activity but which simply have not registered as charities with the CCRA. There are also a large number of non-profit organizations that pursue a range of objectives, some of which may be charitable. Estimates of the number of non-charitable non-profit organizations in Canada range as high as 100,000.[3] Yet it is only registered charities that are monitored and measured in any systematic way.[4] This paper therefore focuses on registered charities.

Data sources on the charitable sector are far from ideal. Different sources tend to use different classification systems for charities. Thus, when two sources offer what appear to be comparable estimates – for example, of charity revenues – they often do so using different classi-

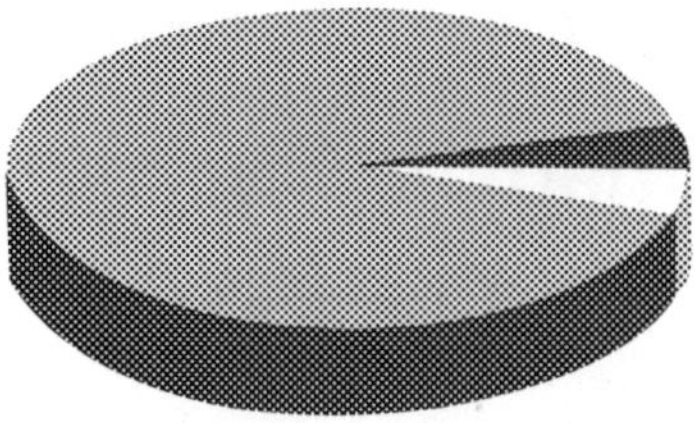

Figure 2.1
Registered charities, by CCRA designation, February 1999
Source: CCRA, T3010.

fication systems. This makes it difficult to compare the data in anything but a general way. As a result, one must take each report, each table, each breakdown, on its own terms.

The CCRA regulates the charitable sector in Canada. Consequently, its system for classifying charities provides the overall analytical structure for this section of the analysis. The broadest distinction is between charitable foundations (which provide funding) and charitable organizations (which deliver programs).[5] Charitable foundations can be either private or public, depending on how they are managed.[6] Thus there are three designations within the CCRA's system: charitable organization, private foundation, and public foundation (see Chart 2.1).

CHARITY POPULATION STATISTICS

Charities According to the CCRA's Sector/Category Classification

The term "charitable sector" usually refers to the charitable sector as distinct from the business sector and the public sector. For the CCRA, "sector" has a more specific meaning – it refers to each of the six broad types of activity in which charities engage – Benefits to the Community, Education, Health, Religion, Welfare, and Other.[7] Within these sectors, the CCRA assigns a "category" code according to the more specific type of activity to which the charity is committed. Charities are assigned to a category when they are first registered, and the category code is part of the charity's unique registration number, which appears on all official receipts.[8] There are 47 categories, some of them extremely specific (for example, Disaster Funds) and others very broad.

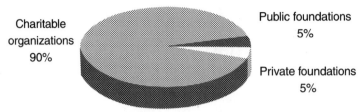

Table 2.1 presents a detailed breakdown of the charitable sector according to the CCRA's sectors and categories. Each statistic or cell in the table includes charitable organizations, public foundations, and

private foundations. The largest sector is religion, with 41 per cent of all registered charities. Next is welfare (18 per cent), followed by education (17 per cent) and benefits to the community (15 per cent). The single largest category is "Other Denominations," with 12 per cent of all charities. The only other category with more than 10 per cent is "Welfare organizations not elsewhere classified," with 10.3 per cent. The most prominent of the others are Roman Catholic parishes and chapels (6.3 per cent), support for schools (5.2 per cent), and community organizations, etc. (5.1 per cent).

While the Religion sector is the largest, its place within the general charitable sector is declining over time. Table 2.2 shows the relative size of each sector and category in late 1991 and early 1999. The charitable sector as a whole grew, between 1991 and 1999, by 26.4 per cent. This is almost twice the rate of population growth in this period. Religion declined from 45.2 per cent of the broader charitable sector in 1991 to only 40.8 per cent in early 1999. This is because the number of religious charities grew at only half the rate of the charitable sector as a whole. The fastest-growing sector was welfare (which grew by 45.7 per cent), followed closely by benefits to the community (39.6 per cent) and education (38 per cent). Health grew by only 20.5 percent.

Some of the most striking statistics have to do with the growth and decline of specific categories. The number of hospitals, for example, shrank by 38.2 per cent – from 1,092 in 1991 to only 675 in early 1999. The only other category to show a decline in absolute numbers was employee charitable trusts, within the "Other" sector (down 16.6 per cent). Important relative declines (growth that was less than the average) occurred in virtually all places of worship – for example, Anglican parishes (only 2.1 per cent growth in 7½ years), Salvation Army temples (0.7 per cent), and Roman Catholic parishes and chapels (2.4 per cent). With such a large segment of the charitable sector – places of worship – showing such weak growth, we inevitably see stronger-than-average growth in almost all other categories.[9] Some of the largest increases took place in charitable trusts and corporations. Welfare charitable corporations, for example, grew by 62.8 per cent, health charitable corporations by 54.8 per cent, and health charitable trusts by 61.8 per cent. The number of community charitable trusts grew by a startling 106.1 per cent, from 82 in 1991 to 169 in 1999. While places of worship lost ground, the number of religious charitable corporations showed strong growth: 92.6 per cent during the period. Strong growth was also seen in disaster funds, which increased from only 26 in 1991 to 64 in 1999 – a growth rate of 150 per cent.

Table 2.1 Canadian registered charities, by sector and category, February 1999

Sector	*Category*	*Category code*	*Number*	*Share of Sector (%)*	*Share of all charities (%)*
Welfare	Care other than treatment	1	3,256	23.2	4.2
	Disaster funds	2	64	0.5	0.1
	Welfare charitable corporations	3	1,923	13.7	2.5
	Welfare charitable trusts	5	738	5.3	0.9
	Welfare organizations n.e.c.	9	8,045	57.4	10.3
	Subtotal		14,026		18.0
Health	Hospitals	10	675	12.2	0.9
	Health services other than hospitals	11	2,713	49.0	3.5
	Health charitable corporations	13	1,022	18.4	1.3
	Health charitable trusts	15	254	4.6	0.3
	Health organizations n.e.c.	19	877	15.8	1.1
	Subtotal		5,541		7.1
Education	Teaching institutions	20	2,996	23.2	3.9
	Support for schools	21	4,015	31.1	5.2
	Culture and arts promotion	22	3,576	27.7	4.6
	Education charitable corporations	23	893	6.9	1.1
	Education charitable trusts	25	419	3.2	0.5
	Education organizations n.e.c.	29	1,013	7.8	1.3
	Subtotal		12,912		16.6
Religion	Anglican parishes	30	2,256	7.1	2.9
	Baptist congregations	31	2,171	6.8	2.8
	Lutheran congregations	32	1,067	3.4	1.4
	Mennonite congregations	34	661	2.1	0.9
	Pentecostal assemblies	36	1,456	4.6	1.9
	Presbyterian congregations	37	1,107	3.5	1.4
	Roman Catholic parishes and chapels	38	4,912	15.5	6.3
	Other denominations	39	9,399	29.6	12.1
	Salvation Army temples	40	406	1.3	0.5
	Seventh Day Adventist congregations	41	356	1.1	0.5
	Synagogues	42	253	0.8	0.3
	Religious charitable corporations	43	286	0.9	0.4
	United Church congregations	44	3,053	9.6	3.9
	Religious charitable trusts	45	153	0.5	0.2
	Convents and monasteries	46	525	1.7	0.7
	Missionary organizations	47	2,026	6.4	2.6
	Religious organizations n.e.c.	49	1,666	5.2	2.1
	Subtotal		31,753		40.8

Table 2.1 (continued)

Sector	*Category*	*Category code*	*Number*	*Share of Sector (%)*	*Share of all charities (%)*
Benefits to the Community	Libraries and museums	50	1,936	16.4	2.5
	Military units	51	166	1.4	0.2
	Preservation of sites	52	1,087	9.2	1.4
	Community charitable corporations	53	523	4.4	0.7
	Protection of animals	54	488	4.1	0.6
	Community charitable trusts	55	169	1.4	0.2
	Recreation, playgrounds, camps	56	3,012	25.4	3.9
	Temperance associations	57	492	4.2	0.6
	Community organizations n.e.c.	59	3,963	33.5	5.1
	Subtotal		11,836		15.2
Other	Service club charitable corporations	63	178	10.6	0.2
	Service club 'projects'	65	86	51.1	1.1
	Employee charitable trusts	75	532	31.6	0.7
	Registered amateur athletic associations	80	14	0.8	0.0
	Miscellaneous organizations n.e.c.	99	99	5.9	0.1
	Subtotal		1,683		2.2
Total			77,751		100.0

Source: CCRA, T3010. Note: Percentages may not add to 100 because of rounding.

Charities by Province

The concentration of charities varies by province, as shown by Table 2.3. All other things being equal, one would expect a province with, for example, 12 per cent of Canada's population to have approximately 12 per cent of its charities. Ontario is home to 38 per cent of the nation's population and 35 per cent of its charities; British Columbia is home to 13 per cent of the population and 13 per cent of all charities. Another way to look at concentration is to measure the number of charities per 1,000 people. Nationally, this figure is 2.6. In Ontario, it is 2.4, and in British Columbia, 2.5. But there are several striking departures from the average. In the Northwest Territories, Quebec, and Newfoundland, there are only 1.8, 2.0, and 2.1 charities per 1,000 people, respectively. At the other end of the spectrum, Yukon and Saskatchewan have 5.3

Table 2.2 Changes in composition of Canada's charitable sector, by sector and category, 1991–99

Sector	*Category*	*Category code*	*Share Dec. 91 (%)*	*Share Feb. 99 (%)*	*Growth 1991–99 (%)*
Welfare	Care other than treatment	1	4.1	4.2	28.3
	Disaster funds	2	0.0	0.1	150.0
	Welfare charitable corporations	3	1.9	2.5	62.8
	Welfare charitable trusts	5	1.0	0.9	16.0
	Welfare organizations n.e.c.	9	8.5	10.4	53.4
	Subtotal		15.5	18.0	45.79
Health	Hospitals	10	1.8	0.9	–38.2
	Health services other than hospitals	11	3.5	3.5	25.4
	Health charitable corporations	13	1.1	1.3	54.8
	Health charitable trusts	15	0.3	0.3	61.8
	Health organizations n.e.c.	19	0.9	1.1	66.3
	Subtotal		7.6	7.1	20.5
Education	Teaching institutions	20	3.7	3.9	31.2
	Support for schools	21	4.3	5.2	51.3
	Culture and arts promotion	22	4.5	4.6	29.0
	Education charitable corporations	23	0.9	1.1	53.1
	Education charitable trusts	25	0.5	0.5	51.3
	Education organizations n.e.c.	29	1.3	1.3	29.2
	Subtotal		15.2	16.6	38.0
Religion	Anglican parishes	30	3.6	2.9	2.1
	Baptist congregations	31	3.3	2.8	5.9
	Lutheran congregations	32	1.7	1.4	3.2
	Mennonite congregations	34	1.0	0.8	7.1
	Pentecostal assemblies	36	2.1	1.9	10.6
	Presbyterian congregations	37	1.7	1.4	6.2
	Roman Catholic parishes and chapels	38	7.8	6.3	2.4
	Other denominations	39	11.6	12.1	31.5
	Salvation Army temples	40	0.7	0.5	0.7
	Seventh Day Adventist congregations	41	0.5	0.5	15.2
	Synagogues	42	0.3	0.3	21.6
	Religious charitable corporations	43	0.2	0.4	92.6
	United Church congregations	44	4.8	3.9	2.3
	Religious charitable trusts	45	0.2	0.2	62.8
	Convents and monasteries	46	0.8	0.7	0.6
	Missionary organizations	47	2.8	2.6	16.6
	Religious organizations n.e.c.	49	2.1	2.1	31.7
	Subtotal		45.2	40.8	13.9

Table 2.2 (continued)

Sector	*Category*	*Category code*	*Share Dec. 91 (%)*	*Share Feb. 99 (%)*	*Growth 1991–99 (%)*
Benefits to the Community	Libraries and museums	50	2.4	2.5	33.4
	Military units	51	0.2	0.2	21.2
	Preservation of sites	52	1.1	1.4	57.9
	Community charitable corporations	53	0.5	0.7	76.1
	Protection of animals	54	0.5	0.6	68.3
	Community charitable trusts	55	0.1	0.2	106.1
	Recreation, playgrounds, camps	56	4.0	3.9	21.4
	Temperance associations	57	0.5	0.6	47.3
	Community organizations n.e.c.	59	4.4	5.1	46.0
	Subtotal		13.7	15.2	39.6
Other	Service club charitable corporations	63	0.2	0.2	49.6
	Service club 'projects'	65	1.3	1.1	10.5
	Employee charitable trusts	75	0.1	0.7	–16.6
	Registered amateur athletic associations	80	0.0	0.0	250.0
	Miscellaneous organizations n.e.c.	99	0.1	0.1	106.1
	Subtotal		2.6	2.2	6.1
TOTAL			100.0	100.0	26.4

Source: CCRA, T3010.
Note: Percentages may not add to 100 because of rounding.

and 4.6, respectively. Thus, in the average town in Saskatchewan, there are more than twice as many registered charities as there are in a similar-sized town in Quebec or Newfoundland.

If Quebec and Newfoundland have few charities compared to other provinces, their proportions of places of worship differ markedly. While well over half of all registered charities in Newfoundland are places of worship (56 per cent), this figure in Quebec is 24 per cent. (The national average is 35 per cent.) The only provinces in which places of worship have anything close to the profile that they have in Newfoundland are New Brunswick (45 per cent) and Saskatchewan (44 per cent). Combining what we know about the overall concentration of charities and the share of charities that are places of worship, we can make a striking comparison. In a typical Quebec town of 50,000 people, we would find 24 places of worship; in a town of the same size in Saskatchewan, we would find 101.

Table 2.3 Charity concentration and places of worship, by province, 1999

	Charities per 1,000 people	*Places of worship as proportion of provincial charities (%)*
Newfoundland	2.1	56
Prince Edward Island	4.0	40
Nova Scotia	4.0	36
New Brunswick	3.5	45
Quebec	2.0	24
Ontario	2.4	36
Manitoba	3.9	35
Saskatchewan	4.6	44
Alberta	2.8	42
British Columbia	2.5	31
Yukon	5.3	35
Northwest Territories	1.8	43
Canada	2.6	35

Sources: Statistics Canada; CCRA, T3010.

Similar disparities are found in the distribution of charities within each province and across provinces (see Table 2.4). While Manitoba accounts for only 4 per cent of Canada's population, it has almost 6 per cent of its hospitals. British Columbia, with 13 per cent of national population, has 17 per cent of the country's teaching institutions. Quebec, with 24 per cent of the population, has 31 per cent of all welfare charities. In fact, welfare charities account for 29 per cent of all charities in Quebec, while they represent only 18 per cent of all charities nationally.

A number of other distinctive characteristics emerge from the data. More than a quarter of all charities in Nova Scotia are classified as "Benefits to the community," when the national figure is only 15 per cent. Nationally, teaching institutions represent 4 per cent of all charities, but this figure ranges from a high of 9 per cent in the Northwest Territories to a low of 1 per cent in New Brunswick. In addition, we know from more detailed charity statistics that Newfoundland is home to 25 per cent of all Salvation Army temples in Canada.

Finances: Revenues

Table 2.5 presents data on the distribution of revenues by type of charity. The charitable sector in Canada is dominated by a small number of very large institutions – principally Canada's hospitals and

Table 2.4 Registered charities, by province and major category, February 1999

	Nfld.	*PEI*	*NS*	*NB*	*Que.*	*Ont.*	*Man.*	*Sask.*	*Alta.*	*BC*	*NWT*	*Yukon*	*Canada*
Welfare	102	62	463	399	4,330	4,532	746	707	992	1,670	18	17	14,038
Hospitals	6	4	24	30	175	266	39	27	31	68	4	1	675
Other health	72	38	245	146	910	1,721	269	277	449	722	13	5	4,867
Teaching institutions	23	15	75	37	595	979	227	158	351	520	15	4	2,999
Other education	120	62	444	270	1,992	3,711	526	415	936	1,405	22	16	9,919
Places of worship	628	217	1,347	1,166	3,628	9,861	1,548	2,042	3,401	3,145	59	51	27,093
Other Religion	29	17	114	108	944	1,951	238	184	449	613	2	3	4,652
Benefits to the comm'ty	136	121	969	426	1,731	3,483	737	818	1,465	1,902	33	22	11,843
Other	6	7	38	23	544	771	57	37	63	136	1	0	1,677
Total	1,122	543	3,719	2,605	14,849	27,275	4,387	4,665	8,137	10,181	167	119	77,763
Horizontal percentages													
Welfare	1	0	3	3	31	32	5	5	7	12	0	0	100
Hospitals	1	1	4	4	26	39	6	4	5	10	1	0	100
Other health	1	1	5	3	19	35	6	6	9	15	0	0	100
Teaching institutions	1	1	3	1	20	33	8	5	12	17	1	0	100
Other education	1	1	4	3	20	37	5	4	9	14	0	0	100
Places of worship	2	1	5	4	13	36	6	8	13	12	0	0	100
Other religion	1	0	2	2	20	42	5	4	10	13	0	0	100
Benefits to the comm'ty	1	1	8	4	15	29	6	7	12	16	0	0	100
Other	0	0	2	1	32	46	3	2	4	8	0	0	100
Total	1	1	5	3	19	35	6	6	10	13	0	0	100
Provincial share of national population	1.9	0.5	3.1	2.5	24.5	37.7	3.8	3.4	9.4	13.0	0.1	0.2	100.0

Table 2.4 (continued)

	Nfld.	*PEI*	*NS*	*NB*	*Que.*	*Ont.*	*Man.*	*Sask.*	*Alta.*	*BC*	*NWT*	*Yukon*	*Canada*
Vertical percentages													
Welfare	9	11	12	15	29	17	17	15	12	16	11	14	18
Hospitals	1	1	1	1	1	1	1	1	0	1	2	1	1
Other health	6	7	7	6	6	6	6	6	6	7	8	4	6
Teaching institutions	2	3	2	1	4	4	5	3	4	5	9	3	4
Other education	11	11	12	10	13	14	12	9	12	14	13	13	13
Places of worship	56	40	36	45	24	36	35	44	42	31	35	43	35
Other religion	3	3	3	4	6	7	5	4	6	6	1	3	6
Benefits to the comm'ty	12	22	26	16	12	13	17	18	18	19	20	18	15
Other	1	1	1	1	4	3	1	1	1	1	1	0	2
Total	100	100	100	100	100	100	100	100	100	100	100	100	100

Source: CCRA, T3010.

Table 2.5 Distribution of charitable-sector revenues, by charity type

Charity type	*% of all charities in Canada*	*% of all charitable-sector revenues*
Places of worship	34	6
Hospitals	1	30
Teaching institutions	4	28
Other charitable organizations	(51)	(30)
Welfare	15	10
Health	7	6
Education	9	6
Religion	5	3
Benefits to the community	13	5
Other	1	0
Public foundations	5	6
Private foundations	5	1
All charities	100	100

Sources: CCRA, T3010 for February 1999; David Sharpe, *A Portrait of Canada's Charities: The Size, Scope and Financing of Registered Charities* (Toronto: Canadian Centre for Philanthropy, 1994, Table 5.
Note: Percentages may not add to 100 because of rounding. "0": between 0 and 0.5 per cent.

teaching institutions.[10] Because of their size, these institutions have a significant effect on all of the financial statistics for the charitable sector. Thus, when reading reports on the revenues or expenditures of the charitable sector, or on the degree of government support provided to the sector, one should realize that, more probably than not, these figures include hospitals and teaching institutions. The organizations that most people think of when they think of charities are receiving far less, and spending far less, than the aggregate statistics would suggest. Hospitals account for only 1 per cent of the number of registered charities in Canada, yet they receive almost one-third of all the revenues flowing into the sector. Similarly, teaching institutions represent only 4 per cent of charities but receive over a quarter of all revenues.[11] The corollary of this fact is that the majority of registered charities in Canada are very small. Of these, the largest single charity type is places of worship. These account for over one-third of all registered charities, yet they receive only 6 per cent of all revenues.[12]

Finances: Sources of Revenue

In 1994, the Canadian Centre for Philanthropy conducted a survey of registered charities.[13] Combining the results of its survey with data from the CCRA, the centre arrived at estimates of charity revenues, by source, for each of what it called charity type. As we can see in Table 2.6, charities as a whole rely on governments for well over half of their overall budgets (57 per cent). This reliance on government funding was, not surprisingly, most pronounced among hospitals (66 per cent) and teaching institutions (70 per cent), but "Other Charitable Organizations"[14] also showed a heavy dependence (49 per cent). The charities least reliant on government were places of worship (2 per cent). Private foundations reported receiving 20 per cent of their revenues from government sources.

Donations were the largest source of revenue for places of worship, accounting for 62 per cent of all income. Hospitals and teaching institutions relied the least on donations (1 per cent and 2 per cent, respectively). Investment income accounted for only 4 per cent of revenues for all charities but was reported as a major source of revenue for private foundations (25 per cent).

The two largest sources of funding to the charitable sector are governments and donations. The Canadian Centre for Philanthropy estimated that, in 1993, governments at all levels transferred $48.9 billion to registered charities, with the bulk of this going to either hospitals (35 per cent) or teaching institutions (34 per cent). The majority of donations come from individuals, and only one-eighth from corporations. Individuals donated an estimated $8.2 billion.[15] Table 2.7 presents the centre's estimates of how these two flows of funds were distributed within the charitable sector. It shows that particular types of funding are clearly tied to particular types of charities. Three-quarters of all individual donations go to either places of worship (45 per cent) or other charitable organizations (33 per cent). Governments, in contrast, provide most of their support to hospitals (35 per cent) and teaching institutions (34 per cent). Corporations, which gave an estimated $1.2 billion in receipted and unreceipted donations to registered charities in 1993,[16] tend to support other charitable organizations (36 per cent) and public foundations (29 per cent), with a modest share (16 per cent) going to teaching institutions.[17]

Charity Expenditures

Table 2.8 shows the breakdown of registered charity expenditures by type of expenditure and by charity type – the classification system developed by the Centre for Philanthropy based on Canada's system.[18] Overall, registered charities responding to the centre's survey reported spending 65 per cent of their budgets on programs, 16 per cent on administration, and 1 per cent on fundraising costs. Gifts to

Table 2.6 Dependence on sources of funding (%)

Source of revenue	*Places of worship*	*Hospitals*	*Teaching institutions*	*Other charitable organizations*	*Public foundations*	*Private foundations*	*All charities*
Government							
Federal	1	3	8	10	2	2	6
Provincial	1	62	60	34	37	17	48
Local	1	1	2	6	8	1	3
Subtotal	2	66	70	49	46	20	57
Receipted donations							
Individuals	58	0	1	8	17	25	8
Corporations	0	0	1	1	6	12	1
Other	4	0	0	2	2	3	1
Subtotal	62	1	2	11	25	39	10
Unreceipted donations	11	0	1	4	4	3	2
Gifts from other charities	8	1	1	4	4	4	2
Gifts in kind	0	0	0	2	0	0	1
Investment income	7	1	3	4	8	25	4
Net capital gains	0	0	0	0	0	0	0
Net related business income	0	1	0	2	1	1	1
Fees	1	0	11	6	3	2	5
Other income	8	31	12	18	9	6	19
Total revenue	100	100	100	100	100	100	100

Source: Sharpe, *Portrait*.

Note: Percentages may not add to 100 because of rounding; "0" indicates a figure between 0 per cent and 0.5 per cent.

Table 2.7 Distribution of principal revenue sources: governments and donations (%)

Source of revenue	*Places of worship*	*Hospitals*	*Teaching institutions*	*Other charitable organizations*	*Public foundations*	*Private foundations*	*All charities*
Government							
Federal	1	15	34	48	1	0	100
Provincial	0	40	35	21	4	0	100
Local	1	6	16	61	16	1	100
Subtotal	0	35	34	26	5	0	100
Receipted donations							
Individuals	45	2	5	33	12	4	100
Corporations	2	4	16	36	29	13	100
Other	24	2	13	48	10	4	100
Sub-total	38	2	7	34	14	5	100
Share of total revenues	6	30	28	30	6	1	100
Percentage of all charities	36	2	4	50	5	4	100

Source: Sharpe, *Portrait*.

Note: Percentages may not add to 100 because of rounding; "0" indicates a figure between 0 per cent and 0.5 per cent.

Table 2.8 Proportion of charity expenditures going to each type of expenditure, by charity type (%)

Source of revenue	*Places of worship*	*Hospitals*	*Teaching institutions*	*Other charitable organizations*	*Public foundations*	*Private foundations*	*All charities*
Programs	58	69	65	65	51	31	65
Administration	15	13	17	17	14	13	16
Fundraising costs	2	0	0	3	4	1	1
Fees to consultants	0	0	0	0	0	0	0
Political expenditures	0	0	0	0	0	1	0
Gifts to qualified donees	16	1	1	4	25	48	4
Accumulated with permission	1	0	0	1	3	2	0.4
Other expenditures	8	17	18	10	3	4	14
All expenditures	100	100	100	100	100	100	100

Source: Sharpe, *Portrait.*

Note: Percentages may not add to 100 because of rounding; "0" indicates a percentage between 0 per cent and 0.5 per cent.

qualified donees – essentially the transfer of funds between charities – accounted for only 4 per cent of all charity expenditures but, not surprisingly, accounted for 25 per cent of public foundations' expenditures and 48 per cent of private foundations' expenditures.

According to the CCRA, charitable organizations and foundations must meet certain requirements in terms of their spending on programs and gifts to qualified donees.[19] The centre's survey suggests either that charities are not meeting these requirements or that they experienced some confusion as to how to report their expenditures on the survey questionnaire.

INDIVIDUAL CHARITABLE BEHAVIOUR

Donating

Traditionally, researchers have had to estimate donations using a limited number of data sources. Some of these, such as taxation statistics, are reliable but reveal only part of Canadians' donating behaviour. Other sources attempt to measure all donating behaviour but are, for one reason or another, less reliable. The most reliable source historically has been the T1 Individual Tax Returns. Both the CCRA and Statistics Canada analyse these data on a regular basis and release summary statistics. T1 statistics, however, tell us nothing about donations to registered charities that are not claimed or about donations to unregistered charitable or other non-profit organizations.

Occasionally, Statistics Canada has included questions relating to donating behaviour in one or other of its regular surveys, such as the Family Expenditure Survey. These reports have allowed researchers to say how much Canadians donated, whether or not they claimed those donations. But these reports, like all reports based on surveys of individuals, suffer from various deficiencies. First, they tend to rely on respondents' ability to remember accurately how much they donated in the previous year to particular kinds of organizations. Second, respondents may for a number of well-known reasons either under- or over-report their donations.[20]

Donations Claimed by Tax-Filers

Because the T1 statistics, despite their limitations, are so reliable, I present them in some detail. In 1997, almost 5.3 million Canadian tax-filers claimed donations on their T1 individual tax returns. Together, they claimed a total of $4.3 billion. While the number of tax-filers claiming donations dropped 3.1 per cent from 1996 to 1997, the total amount claimed increased by 7.7 per cent, with the average personal donation increasing from $728 to $808.[21] Table 2.9 shows aggregate T1 donations statistics for the period 1984–97.

The pattern in recent years of a declining rate of tax-filer donors coupled with strong growth in the amounts claimed could be related to recent changes to the tax treatment of charitable donations. For many years, the maximum amount that could be claimed in charitable donations by any individual tax-filer was 20 per cent of his or her personal income for the year. This limit was raised first to 50 per cent and in 1997 to 75 per cent. While this does not necessarily explain the levelling off in the number of tax-filers claiming donations, it does help to explain why the total amount being claimed has continued to increase.

Tax-Filer Donations, by Province, 1995 Taxation Year

Table 2.10 shows provincial variations in the basic donating characteristics of Canada's "tax-filer donors" in the 1995 taxation year. The first column shows the proportion of all tax-filers in the province who claimed charitable donations supported by official donation receipts.[22] The highest rates of tax-filer donors were among tax-filers in Ontario, the Prairie provinces, and Prince Edward Island. The lowest rates were among Newfoundland and Quebec tax-filers. The median amount claimed by tax-filers in 1995 was highest in Newfoundland, at $250. Newfoundland tax-filer donors also ranked first when the median donation was measured as a percentage of donors' median donation.[23] The typical Newfoundland tax-filer donor claimed 0.9 per cent of his or her personal income in donations. The province with the lowest median donation as a percentage of median income was Quebec, at 0.3 per cent, matched by tax-filer donors in the two northern Territories. The median donations in the two territories were considerably higher, however, than the median donation for Quebec.

Table 2.11 reveals other interesting provincial characteristics of Canada's charitable sector. The most striking relate to Quebec. In 1995, it was home to 25 per cent of the national population and 23 per cent of all Canadians who claimed donations on their tax returns. Quebecers who claimed donations, however, tended to claim much smaller amounts than taxpayers in other parts of Canada. Quebec therefore accounted for only 12 per cent of all donations claimed through the tax system in 1995. Ontario, in contrast, accounted for 41 per cent of all tax-filer donors and 46 per cent of all donations claimed on T1 tax returns, even though it is home to only 38 per cent of the

Table 2.9 Aggregate T1 donations, 1984–97

Year	*Tax-filers*	*Tax-filer donors*	*Increase over previous year (%)*	*Tax-filer donor rate (%)*	*Donations claimed ($000)*	*Increase over previous year (%)*	*Average donation ($)*
1984	15,522,181	3,984,548		26	1,826,887		458
1985	15,864,486	4,357,811	9.4	28	1,994,046	9.1	458
1986	16,538,060	4,671,150	7.2	28	2,172,933	9.0	465
1987	17,071,350	4,972,490	6.5	29	2,441,136	12.3	491
1988	17,579,870	4,989,380	0.3	28	2,638,348	8.1	529
1989	18,132,050	5,253,250	5.3	29	2,884,917	9.3	549
1990	18,758,730	5,538,220	5.4	30	3,076,369	6.6	555
1991	19,050,830	5,598,340	1.1	29	3,192,483	3.8	570
1992	19,437,070	5,596,760	0.0	29	3,283,558	2.9	587
1993	19,829,240	5,512,260	–1.5	28	3,368,592	2.6	611
1994	20,153,510	5,397,680	–2.1	27	3,379,400	0.3	626
1995	20,514,590	5,478,940	1.5	27	3,515,773	4.0	642
1996	20,251,190	5,451,860	–0.5	27	3,969,171	12.9	728
1997	20,566,381	5,285,560	–3.1	26	4,273,085	7.7	808

Sources: M.H. Hall and S.L. Bozzo, "Trends in Individual Donations: 1984–1996," in Canadian Centre for Philanthropy, *Research Bulletin* 4, no. 4 (fall 1997), 2, Table 1; Statistics Canada, *Daily*, Thursday, 3 Dec. 1998.

Table 2.10 Donors' behaviour, by province: T1 statistics for 1995 tax year

Province	*Tax-filer donor rate (%)*	*Median tax-filer donation ($)*	*Median tax-filer income ($)*	*Median tax-filer donation as % of median tax-filer income (%)*
Newfoundland	23	250	27,100	0.9
Prince Edward Island	32	220	26,900	0.8
Nova Scotia	27	190	31,400	0.6
New Brunswick	26	220	30,200	0.7
Quebec	25	100	33,000	0.3
Ontario	30	170	36,100	0.5
Manitoba	31	170	30,400	0.6
Saskatchewan	30	220	29,300	0.8
Alberta	28	160	34,700	0.5
British Columbia	25	160	35,200	0.5
Yukon	19	130	44,100	0.3
Northwest Territories	16	170	56,600	0.3
Canada	27	150	34,100	0.4

Source: Statistics Canada, *Tax Statistics on Individuals: 1997 Edition, Analyzing 1995 Individual Tax Returns and Miscellaneous Statistics.*

Table 2.11 T1 statistics for 1995 tax year

Province	*% of national population*	*% of all tax-filer donors*	*% of national personal income*	*% of claimed donations*
Newfoundland	2	2	2	1
Prince Edward Island	1	1	0	1
Nova Scotia	3	3	3	3
New Brunswick	3	2	2	3
Quebec	25	23	23	12
Ontario	38	41	41	46
Manitoba	4	4	3	5
Saskatchewan	3	4	3	4
Alberta	9	9	10	11
British Columbia	13	12	13	14
Yukon	0	0	0	0
Northwest Territories	0	0	0	0
Canada	100	100	100	100

Source: As for Table 2.10.

Note: Percentages may not add to 100 because of rounding; "0" indicates a figure between 0 and 0.5 per cent.

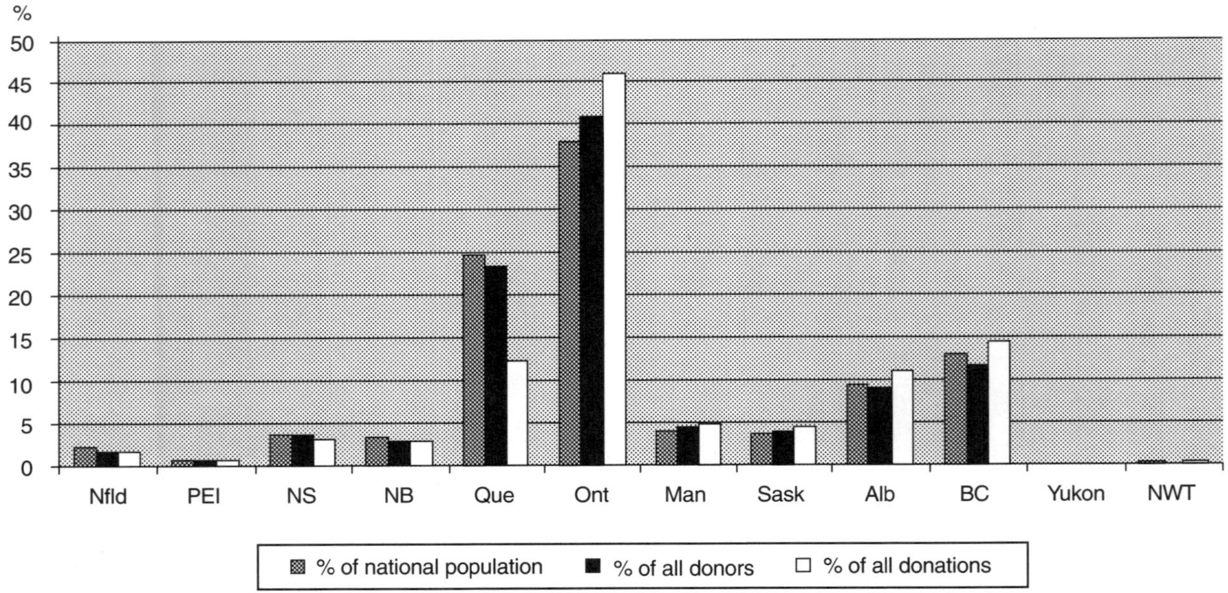

Figure 2.2

Donating behaviour, by province: share of population, donors, and donations (T1 claims, 1995)

Source: Statistics Canada; CCRA, *T1 Individual Tax Returns for the 1995 Taxation Year.*

Table 2.12 Donors' behaviour, by province: T1 statistics for 1997 tax year

Province	*Tax-filer donor rate, 1997 (%)*	*Median tax-filer donation, 1997 ($)*	*Increase in median donation, 1995–97 (%)*
Newfoundland	21	270	8
Prince Edward Island	28	260	18
Nova Scotia	25	230	21
New Brunswick	24	260	18
Quebec	23	100	0
Ontario	28	200	18
Manitoba	30	210	24
Saskatchewan	38	250	14
Alberta	26	190	19
British Columbia	20	200	25
Yukon	19	160	23
Northwest Territories	14	180	6
Canada	26	170	13

Source: Statistics Canada, *Daily*, Thursday, 3 Dec. 1998.

population. For all other provinces and territories, the share of donors and donations is more or less equal to the share of national population. Chart 2.2 illustrates these patterns.

Tax-Filer Donors by Province, 1997 Taxation Year

In the 1997 taxation year, there was a slightly smaller percentage of tax-filers claiming donations than in 1995, while the median donation for the country rose from $150 to $170. Table 2.12 shows noticeable differences in provincial figures. There were pronounced declines in the tax-filer donor rate in British Columbia and in Prince Edward Island, with drops of 5 per cent and 4.2 per cent respectively. Tax-filers in Newfoundland and the two territories were the least likely to claim donations (21 per cent, 19 per cent, and 14 per cent of tax-filers, respectively), while those in Manitoba, Ontario, and Saskatchewan were the most likely (30 per cent, 28 per cent, and 28 per cent, respectively). The highest median donations were among tax-filer donors in Newfoundland ($270), Prince Edward Island ($260), and New Brunswick ($260), while the lowest was in Quebec, unchanged from 1995 at $100.

Individual Donating as Reported in Surveys

In late November and early December 1997, Statistics Canada conducted the National Survey of Giving, Volunteering and Participating

Table 2.13 Comparing two reliable data sources

Source	*Donors covered*	*Flow of donations measured*	*Amount estimated*
Statistics Canada, 1997 Analysis of Individual Tax Returns	Tax-filers: 5.3 million	Donations to registered charities claimed on T1 returns	$4.3 billion
Statistics Canada, 1997 National Survey	All Canadians: 18.6 million	All donations to charitable and non-profit organizations	$4.51 billion

Sources: Statistics Canada, *Daily*, Thursday, 3 Dec. 1998; Statistics Canada, *Caring Canadians, Involved Canadians.*

as a supplement to the Labour Force Survey. It asked respondents about their donating and volunteering behaviour during the period 1 November 1996 to 31 October 1997. The survey used a representative sample of 18,301 Canadians aged 15 and over, based on a response rate of 78.4 per cent. The results indicated that "direct financial support to charitable and non-profit organizations" from Canadians aged 15 and over totalled an estimated $4.51 billion.[24] (Table 2.13)

The survey and statistical methods that Statistics Canada employs are recognized the world over, and yet this figure appears surprisingly low. We know from the CCRA that in the 1997 tax year Canadian taxpayers claimed $4.3 billion in donations to registered charities (see Table 2.13). This is the amount for which charities issued official receipts. It does not include either donations to registered charities that were not claimed through the tax system or donations to non-profit organizations not registered with the CCRA. When the Centre for Philanthropy conducted its survey of registered charities in 1994, responses suggested that charities issue receipts for only 80 per cent of all donations they receive.[25] If this figure is accurate, one would expect a reliable estimate of all donations to registered charities and to non-profit organizations to exceed the $4.51-billion figure emerging from Statistics Canada's survey.

If, however, both the CCRA's T1 statistics and Statistics Canada's survey results are equally valid, one reaches a surprising conclusion. The survey says that 18.6 million Canadians donated $4.51 billion to registered charities and non-profit organizations. The CCRA tells us that 5.3 million claimed $4.3 billion in donations to registered charities. This leaves 13.6 million Canadians who together donated only $210 million. Thus, if both sources are to be believed, Canadians who claimed their donations to registered charities gave, on average, $811 each to registered charities, while those who did not claim their donations gave, on average, only $15 each to both registered charities and non-profit organizations.

Despite these puzzling discrepancies, we should accept the national survey as reliable, subject to the standard cautions concerning survey and response bias.[26] Statistics derived from the T1 individual tax returns are inherently less valid as measures of the donating behaviour of all Canadians because of the special characteristics of tax-filers who submit receipts to earn tax credits. For a number of reasons, these individuals are not representative of all Canadians who donate. A rigorous survey of a scientifically selected random sample of over 18,000 Canadians is clearly more reliable for these purposes.

Assuming the accuracy of the 1997 survey, here are the results. More than three-quarters of all Canadians – 18.6 million – gave a total of $4.51 billion in direct financial contributions to charitable and non-profit organizations during the survey period. A third of these donors reported giving $39 or less, a further third reported giving between $40 and $149, while the final third reported donations of $150 or more. This last third accounted for fully 86 per cent of all donations.

Table 2.14 presents what we know about the links between demographic characteristics and donating. Women are more likely than men to make a donation, but it appears that the men who donate give larger amounts. This is clear from the higher average donation for men ($243) than for women ($236). However, women's median donation is higher than men's. This suggests that the "typical" female donor (more accurately described using the median figure) donates more than the "typical" male donor. The median statistic measures the middle amount – the amount that divides the group into those who give less and those who give more than this figure. The median is not sensitive to the very large amounts being given by the most generous donors. The fact that the average donation is roughly three to four times the amount of the median donation (for both men and women) suggests that there is a small number of very generous donors in both groups. That men reported a higher average donation than women, even though the median amounts were reversed, indicates that the small number of very generous men donated significantly more than the small number of very generous women.

Age plays a significant role in both the tendency to donate and the amount donated. If a person is going to make donations, he or she is probably already doing it by the age of 35. That is when the donor rate reaches its peak of 84 per cent. Beyond 35, those who give tend to give larger amounts. Both the median and the mean donation continue to

Table 2.14 Donating behaviour, by major demographic characteristic, 1997

Characteristic	*Donor rate (%)*	*Average donation ($)*	*Median donation ($)*
Age			
15–24	59	79	20
25–34	78	159	55
35–44	84	258	83
45–54	83	291	105
55–64	83	313	108
65 and over	80	328	140
Sex			
Male	75	243	73
Female	81	236	83
Marital status			
Married or common law	85	261	92
Single, never married	63	162	35
Separated, divorced	73	200	70
Widowed	76	302	121
Education			
Less than high school	68	156	50
High school diploma	76	198	75
Some postsecondary	78	177	60
Postsecondary diploma	84	240	82
University degree	90	473	168
Labour force status			
Employed	83	253	81
Full-time	84	242	65
Part-time	79	297	85
Unemployed	64	103	29
Not in labour force	72	227	78
Household income			
Less than 20,000	63	134	40
20,000–39,999	77	182	60
40,000–59,999	81	221	80
60,000–79,999	86	255	91
80,000 or more	90	455	150
Total	78	239	76

Source: Statistics Canada, *1997 Survey*, Chapter 1, Table 1.1.

rise through to the last age group. Canadian donors aged 65 and over contribute an average of $328 per year to charitable and non-profit organizations. The other two demographic characteristics besides age that are strongly correlated with both the tendency to donate and the amount donated are education and household income. The more educated a person and the more he or she earns, the more likely he or she is to donate and the larger the amount he or she is likely to donate. Among those with household incomes of $80,000 or more and those with a university degree, 90 per cent reported making a donation. They also reported generous donations: average total donations of $455 and $473, respectively. Those working full-time tend to donate less than those working part-time. Those who are married or living common-law are more likely to donate than those who are single, separated, divorced, or widowed, and they also make generous contributions. They are outperformed, however, at least in terms of amounts donated, by widows and widowers.

Volunteering

The most recent statistics on Canadians' volunteering behaviour appeared in Statistics Canada's National Survey on Donating, Volunteering and Participating (1997). It is the first comprehensive survey of its kind since the National Survey of Volunteer Activity in 1987 and provides detailed findings as well as reliable demographic analysis, based on a large survey sample. The survey found that 7.5 million Canadians volunteered their time and skills to groups and organizations across Canada between 1 November 1996 and 31 October 1997.[27] They contributed a total of 1.1 billion hours during this period – the equivalent of 578,000 full-time, year-round jobs (assuming 40 hours per week for 48 weeks).[28]

Table 2.15 presents the survey's principal findings by demographic characteristics. The highest rates of volunteering were among Canadians aged 35–54 – the age group most likely to have children of school age.[29] Canadians who are married or living common-law are more likely to volunteer their time than those who are single, separated, divorced, or widowed. While older Canadians are less likely to contribute time to charitable and non-profit organizations, those who do tend to contribute more hours. Women are more likely than men to volunteer, but the men who do volunteer contribute a higher average number of hours.

The likelihood of volunteering increases with household income. Almost half of all Canadians in the wealthiest households volunteer at least some time. People working part-time are significantly more likely to volunteer than those who are unemployed (44 per cent compared to 29 per cent). It also increases with education. Each stage of education brings with it a higher rate of volunteering: only 21 per cent of

Table 2.15 Volunteering behaviour, by major demographic characteristic, 1997

Characteristic	*Volunteer participation rate (%)*	*Average hours volunteered*
Age		
15–24	33	125
25–34	28	133
35–44	37	142
45–54	35	157
55–64	30	160
65 and over	23	202
Sex		
Male	29	160
Female	33	140
Marital status		
Married or common law	33	151
Single, never married	31	133
Separated, divorced	29	186
Widowed	20	157
Education		
Less than high school	21	126
High school diploma	29	159
Some postsecondary	36	153
Postsecondary diploma	34	149
University degree	48	159
Labour force status		
Employed	34	138
Full-time	32	138
Part-time	44	139
Unemployed	29	121
Not in labour force	27	176
Household income		
Less than 20,000	22	148
20,000–39,999	29	163
40,000–59,999	33	150
60,000–79,999	36	144
80,000 or more	44	136
Total	31	149

Source: Statistics Canada, *Highlights*, chap. 2, Tables 2.1 and 2.2.

those with less than a high school diploma reported volunteering, while almost half of all Canadians with a university degree reported at least some volunteer hours. Based on these findings, we can imagine the kind of Canadian most likely to volunteer at least some time to a charitable or non-profit organization. That person is female, middle aged, married, with a university degree, working part-time, and living in a household with an annual income of at least $80,000.

If there is one kind of Canadian more likely to volunteer, there is another who is more likely to volunteer a high number of hours. Though not the most common among volunteers, this type of person tends to give more hours than others. This person is male, older, probably over 65, retired, and either separated or divorced. He has at least a high school diploma and lives on a modest annual income. Canadians living in wealthier households, though more likely to volunteer at least some time, are not the most generous in terms of the number of hours they give. It is Canadians in middle-income households – between $20,000 and $59,999 – who volunteer the highest average number of hours.

The survey found another characteristic quite strongly associated with a tendency to volunteer: religious affiliation. Those who identified themselves as having a religious affiliation were more likely to volunteer (33 per cent) than those who did not (28 per cent). Still more likely to volunteer were those who said that they attended church every week (46 per cent, compared to 28 per cent). Finally, those who consider themselves "very religious" are more likely to volunteer (44 per cent) than those who do not (30 per cent). The same patterns surfaced for number of hours volunteered.[30]

The survey devoted considerable attention to what prompted people to become involved in volunteering. For each volunteer event that a respondent reported, the survey asked how that person became involved. The answer in 44 per cent of all cases was that someone in the organization asked him or her to volunteer. The next most common response (29 per cent) was that he or she approached the organization.[31]

More than half of all volunteers (57 per cent) said that they volunteer for only one organization. Only 7 per cent volunteered for more than three organizations. Those who volunteered were then asked which types of charitable activity they supported.[32] Three-quarters of all volunteer events and more than three-quarters of all volunteer hours related to five types of charity. Social service organizations accounted for 21 per cent of all volunteer events and 21 per cent of all hours. The other four principal charity types were other recreation and social clubs (16 per cent and 17 per cent), religious organizations (14 per cent and 18 per cent), health organizations (13 per cent and 10 per cent), and sports organizations (11 per cent and 11 per cent).

The survey found some noticeable shifts in the patterns of volunteer activity between 1987 (when the last comparable survey of volunteer activity was conducted) and 1997. There was a pronounced increase – roughly 125 per cent – in the number of people volunteering for charities devoted to the environment and wildlife. Other types of charity benefiting from a shift in volunteering activity were arts and culture (roughly 90 per cent) and health (75 per cent).

Corporate Donating

A Portrait of Canada's Charities, published by the Canadian Centre for Philanthropy in 1994, estimated that corporate donations accounted for 1 per cent of all registered charity revenues, far outweighed by government funding and individual donations. But the role of corporate donations varies according to type of charity. For some types of charity, corporate donations are much more significant. In the summer of 1995, the centre conducted a survey of over 1,500 Canadian charities (excluding religious charities and private foundations) that reported revenues of $1,000 or more in 1993.[33] The purpose of the survey was to learn more about the fund-raising behaviour of charities, and the results shed light on the importance of corporations' donations to the sector as a whole, as well as the types of charities that they tend to support.[34] The centre found that corporations tend to donate to much larger charities: over half (55 per cent) of all of their donations went to charities with annual revenues of over $1.5 million. The types of charities most often supported by corporations are social services (26 per cent), other (23 per cent), and education (20 per cent). The largest median corporate donation went to hospitals ($18,000), followed by education ($15,000) and health ($11,000). The type of charity receiving the smallest median donation was arts and culture ($5,000).

FUTURE RESEARCH AND CLASSIFICATION

Future Research

This chapter alludes to a number of problems with the various data sources on the charitable sector. The three most important sources of information on the sector – the CCRA, Statistics Canada, and the Canadian Centre for Philanthropy – use different systems for classifying charities. It would be of great benefit to those who share an interest in the charitable sector if all data, statistics, and reports were based on the same terms, definitions, and categories. A number of countries have already adopted the system of classification developed by the Johns Hopkins Comparative Nonprofit Sector Project. The system has a foothold in Canada because of its adoption in 1997 for the National Survey of Donating, Volunteering and Participating. This is an encouraging development. I outline the principal classification schemes below.

Whether or not a new classification system is developed, more work needs to be done to ensure that financial information submitted by registered charities on their T3010 Registered Charity Information Returns is accurate and complete. The Centre for Philanthropy learned, for example, that it is not uncommon for charities to submit returns on which they enter figures in thousands of dollars, such that $5 million appears as $5,000. Thus, for some charities, particularly the larger ones, every figure on the T3010 should have an additional three zeroes at the end, and yet data-entry personnel at the CCRA simply enter the amounts into the T3010 database as they appear on the form. A related problem is the lack of generally accepted definitions and standards for the reporting of financial information by registered charities. While every charity must fill out the same form, there is no guarantee that they all interpret the terms in the form in the same way.

Until these problems are addressed, researchers will be able to rely on the T3010 with confidence only as a source for statistics on charity population. Financial information will have to come from surveys of selected samples of registered charities.

With regard to individual donations, we need more information about the flow of unreceipted and unclaimed donations. Understanding why individuals do or do not ask for official donation receipts, retain them, and submit them with their tax returns would help us to understand the extent to which tax incentives play a role in individuals' donating behaviour.

The Need for a New Classification System

When preparing *A Portrait of Canada's Charities,* I discovered serious problems in the financial reporting of many registered charities. Many simply left the financial sections of the T3010 blank. Others entered specific revenue and expenditure items but left the totals lines blank. Still others entered figures in all appropriate places but made arithmetical errors. The most serious problem, however, involved the "three zeroes." Because of these problems, the T3010 is a reliable data source only for charity population. Even then, there are problems with the CCRA's classification system. Some categories are very specific in the activities that they describe. For example, there are separate categories for disaster funds, registered amateur athletic associations, and convents and monasteries, while there are no category codes for international relief, human rights advocacy, and housing. Additional detail is sorely needed. When over half of all welfare charities are classified as "Welfare organization not elsewhere classified," there is clearly a problem.

A Portrait of Canada's Charities proposed an alternative to the CCRA's system for classifying Canadian registered charities. It was not a new system; the centre was forced to work, in the short term, within the constraints of the CCRA's system. Using designation, sector, and category, the centre reorganized the existing components of the charitable sector and presented them according to what it called charity types. The centre decided to modify the CCRA's classification system to minimize the risk of double-counting and to reveal hidden characteristics of certain types of charities. First, there is a risk of double-counting whenever one presents financial statistics based on the T3010 according to sector or category. These variables do not distinguish between charitable organizations and charitable foundations. Any funds received by a public foundation and then disbursed to charitable organizations in the same year will appear as revenues for both the foundation and the charitable organization. To separate out the flow of funds from foundations to charitable organizations while at the same time identifying particular types of activity, it is necessary to divide charities initially by designation and then by category.

Second, three CCRA sectors – religion, health, and education – contain categories – places of worship, hospitals, and teaching institutions, respectively – that skew any aggregate statistics about those sectors. Places of Worship deserve separate treatment both because they are so numerous and because they receive almost all of their revenues from individual donations. Hospitals and teaching institutions, while far less numerous, dwarf the rest of the charitable sector in financial terms and, unlike most other charities, receive a clear majority of their funding from governments.

The centre first listed public and private foundations (designations A and B) separately. This left designation C: charitable organizations. It then broke these up into four broad classes: places of worship (particular categories within the religion sector), hospitals, teaching institutions, and other charitable organizations. It listed the first three separately because of their special characteristics.

While the "charity type" approach was in some respects an improvement on the CCRA's system, it does not provide a fully comprehensive analytical framework for high-quality research. This requires a wholly new system – one that is not built from the components of the existing one.

If the CCRA were to consider overhauling its classification system – perhaps as part of a comprehensive review of its regulatory approach

Table 2.16 International Classification of Non-Profit Organizations (ICNPO), revision 1

Major activity group	*Subgroup*
Culture and recreation	Culture and arts
	Sports
	Other recreation and social clubs
Education and research	Primary and secondary education
	Higher education
	Other education and vocational and technical schools
	Research (including medical, science and technology, social sciences)
Health	Hospitals and rehabilitation
	Nursing homes
	Mental health and crisis intervention
	Other health
Social services	Social services
	Emergency relief
	Income support and maintenance
Environment	Environment
	Animal protection
Development and Housing	Economic, social, and community development
	Housing
	Employment and training
Law, Advocacy, and Politics	Civic and advocacy
	Law and legal services
	Political organizations
Philanthropic intermediaries and voluntarism	
International	
Religion	
Business and professional associations	
Groups not elsewhere classified	

Source: Statistics Canada, *Highlights of the 1997 National Survey*, Appendix A; see also L.M. Salomon and H.K. Anheier, *In Search of the Nonprofit Sector II: The Problem of Classification*, Johns Hopkins Comparative Nonprofit Sector Project, Working Paper No. 3 (Baltimore: Johns Hopkins, 1992).

to the charitable sector – it could do much worse than to adopt the system developed by researchers at the Johns Hopkins project. Lester Salomon and Helmut Anheier, both at Johns Hopkins, have overseen the design of a comprehensive classification system for non-profit organizations. It has now been adopted by several countries and therefore provides the basis for reliable international comparisons. It divides non-profit activity into twelve major activity groups and then subdivides these into 24 sub-groups: see table 2.16.

NOTES

1 A registered charity is a charitable organization, private foundation, or public foundation, as defined in the Income Tax Act, that is resident in Canada and was either created or established in Canada; or a branch, section, parish, congregation, or other division of an organization or foundation as described above that is resident in Canada and was either created or established in Canada and that receives donations on its own behalf.

2 Every year, registered charities must submit to the CCRA a Registered Charity Information Return and Public Information Return, known as the T3010. It contains sections on receipts and disbursements, assets and liabilities, remuneration to employees and executive officers, and volunteers. There are also sections where the charity states its charitable purpose(s) and activities, lists its gifts to other charities, and names its executive officers. All of this information is available to the public.

3 K.M. Day and R.A. Devlin, *The Canadian Nonprofit Sector* (Ottawa: Canadian Policy Research Networks, 1997), 27.

4 Since 1993, the CCRA has required larger non-profit organizations – those with annual revenues of more than $10,000 or assets of more than $200,000 – to file Form T1044. See ibid., 26. The CCRA does not require charities to register. It simply requires that any organization that wishes to issue official donation receipts (which a donor may then use to claim a tax credit or a tax deduction) must first register. In addition to being able to issue official donation receipts, a registered charity is exempted from paying taxes. An organization may obtain these benefits by registering, or it may choose to operate without these benefits. Exactly how many organizations have chosen not to register is unknown.

5 A charitable organization is one that may or may not be incorporated and which devotes all of its resources to its own charitable activities – that is, those activities under its direct control. None of its income may be payable to or otherwise available for the personal benefit of any proprietor, member, shareholder, trustee, or settler of the organization. A charitable foundation is a corporation or trust set up and operated exclusively for charitable purposes which is not a charitable organization. None of its income is payable to or otherwise available for the personal benefit of any proprietor, member, shareholder, trustee, or settler of the organization.

6 A private foundation is a charitable foundation of which 50 per cent or more of the directors or trustees do not deal with each other and with the other directors and trustees at arm's length; or a person or group of persons who do not deal with each other at arm's length and contribute more than 50 per cent of the capital. Such a person does not include a

government, a municipality, another registered charity that is not a private foundation, or a non-profit organization. A public foundation is a charitable foundation of which 50 per cent or more of the directors or trustees deal with each other and with each of the other directors or trustees at arm's length or; a person or group of persons who do not deal with each other at arm's length and have not contributed more than 50 per cent of the capital. Such a person does not include a government, a municipality, another registered charity that is not a private foundation, or a non-profit organization.

7 This general taxonomy derives from English common law definitions of charitable activity. These are generally considered to date from the Statute of Charitable Uses (1601) – the so-called Statute of Elizabeth – but the leading definition of charitable uses or purposes in Anglo-Canadian law is the case *Commissioners for Special Purposes of the Income Tax v. Pemsel*, [1891] AC 531 at 583 (HL). In that case, Lord MacNaghten said: "'Charity' in its legal sense comprises four principal divisions: trusts for the relief of poverty; trusts for the advancement of education; trusts for the advancement of religion; and trusts for other purposes beneficial to the community, not falling under any of the preceding heads." See generally Ontario Law Reform Commission, *Report on the Law of Charities* (Toronto: Commission, 1996), chap. 7.

8 From time to time, charities may be reassigned to a different category, usually in response to a request submitted to the CCRA. There is no systematic monitoring the CCRA of charity activity in light of category status to ensure proper classification.

9 "Places of Worship" are charitable organizations within the religion sector within the following CCRA categories: 30 (Anglican parishes), 31 (Baptist congregations), 32 (Lutheran congregations), 34 (Mennonite congregations), 36 (Pentecostal assemblies), 37 (Presbyterian congregations), 38 (Roman Catholic parishes and chapels), 39 (Other denominations), 40 (Salvation Army temples), 41 (Seventh Day Adventist congregations), 42 (Synagogues), and 44 (United Church congregations).

10 Category 20, "Teaching Institutions," includes not only universities and colleges but also public school boards, separate school boards, private schools, vocational schools, and a range of other educational institutions such as Bible colleges.

11 David Sharpe, *A Portrait of Canada's Charities: The Size, Scope and Financing of Registered Charities* (Toronto: Canadian Centre for Philanthropy, 1994). These figures are from estimates of charity revenues in 1991. When the centre embarked on its analysis of data from the CCRA's T3010 files, it discovered that the financial information being reported each year was far from reliable. In an attempt to remedy this problem, it conducted a

survey of registered charities, asking them, among other things, about their finances. Unfortunately, the survey did not use a scientific sample, and its results should therefore be treated with some caution: see ibid., Appendix 1, "Data Sources and Methodology."

12 It was because of the tendency of the CCRA's categories to mask this imbalance between the number and financial heft of charities within each category that the Canadian Centre for Philanthropy decided to present data in ibid. using a different classification system. Table 2.5 uses the breakdown developed by the centre. In a report analysing Registered Charity returns for 1995, the Charities Division of the CCRA adopted a similar breakdown. Hospitals and teaching institutions are separated out and treated separately. See *Working Together: A Government of Canada/Voluntary Sector Joint Initiative: Report of the Joint Tables* (Ottawa: Government of Canada, 1999). The full report can be found at http://www.pco-bcp.gc.ca/volunteer/vstf_e.htm.

13 See Sharpe, *Portrait.* Because the response rate from charities that received the survey was low – the number of usable responses was only 6 per cent – the results of this survey are of limited value. However, the survey was not used to produce the actual dollar amounts of revenues and expenditures for the charitable sector as a whole. Instead, the report accepted the aggregate amounts reported to the CCRA by charities on their T3010s (with a number of adjustments to improve reliability) and used the results of the survey only to estimate the proportion of those aggregate figures accounted for by each charity type.

14 This charity type consists of all charitable organizations (therefore excluding funding foundations) that are not places of worship, hospitals, or teaching institutions. It therefore contains the kinds of charities that come closest to what most people think of as a registered charity.

15 Statistics Canada estimated this amount to be $4.51 billion. Statistics Canada, *Highlights of the 1997 National Survey of Donating, Volunteering and Participating.* (Ottawa: Statistics Canada, 1998).

16 Sharpe, *Portrait.*

17 Perhaps the best-known public foundation is the United Way.

18 Table 2.8 does not present actual dollar amounts because the centre's report gave estimates of 1993 expenditures. Nevertheless these percentages provide a reasonable indication of the relative importance of different categories of expenditure for each charity type.

19 This required spending is the "disbursement quota." The quota differs for each category of registered charity. A qualified donee is an entity to which a Canadian resident can make a tax-deductible donation. Such donees include: registered charities; registered Canadian amateur athletic associations; housing corporations constituted exclusively to provide low-cost accommodation to the elderly that are resident in Canada and

exempt from tax; Canadian municipalities; the United Nations or agencies thereof; universities outside Canada prescribed to be universities, the student body of which ordinarily includes students from Canada; charitable organizations outside Canada to which Her Majesty in Right of Canada has made a gift during the taxpayer's taxation year or the 12 months immediately preceding that taxation year; Her Majesty in Right of Canada; and Her Majesty in right of a province.

20 Surveys based on questionnaires usually suffer from what is known as "response bias". This can take several forms. The most relevant for our purposes are social desirability (giving the answer that is perceived as socially acceptable or desirable), prestige (providing an answer that will enhance the image of the respondent in the eyes of others), and auspices (answers dictated by the image or opinion of the sponsor of the survey rather than the actual question): see generally P.L. Alreck and R.B. Settle, *The Survey Research Handbook* (Homewood, Ill.: Irwin, 1985), 112.

21 Statistics Canada, *Daily*, Thursday 3 Dec. 1998.

22 Individual tax-filers earn a tax credit for their donations equal to 17 per cent of the first $250 claimed and 29 per cent of any amount beyond $250 up to a maximum amount of 75 per cent of personal income. In the 1995 tax year, the value of all charitable donations tax credits was $968 million, or 27.5 per cent of the total amount claimed as charitable donations by tax-filers ($3.5 billion). See CCRA, *Tax Statistics on Individuals: 1997 Edition*, which analyses individual tax returns for 1995.

23 The median is often used instead of the average, or mean, as the most representative statistic. It is the middle amount, meaning that precisely half of all donors gave less than the median and half gave more. The mean, in contrast, is calculated by dividing donations by the number of tax- filer donors. This statistic is susceptible to inflation because of a small number of very large claims. The median is preferable to the mean whenever there are unusually large amounts at the upper extreme, as is usually the case with donations.

24 Statistics Canada, *Highlights*, 14.

25 See Sharpe, *Portrait*, 28–30.

26 See note 20, above.

27 In Sharpe, *Portrait*, the Canadian Centre for Philanthropy estimated that Canada's registered charities relied on a volunteer base of 4.5 million Canadians. As for the discrepancy, the centre surveyed registered charities, while the 1997 National Survey asked Canadians about the time they contributed to charities and non-profit organizations. However, the centre's survey was far less reliable than Statistics Canada's survey, and we should treat the figure of 4.5 million with some caution: see Sharpe, *Portrait*, Appendix 1.

28 Statistics Canada, *Highlights,* 27.

29 An important demographic variable commonly included in such surveys is the number of children living in the household. Statistics Canada (ibid.) did not include this variable.

30 Ibid., 32.

31 Ibid., 33.

32 The survey used the classification system developed by the Johns Hopkins Comparative Nonprofit Sector Project: see Appendix.

33 Sharpe, *Portrait*; M. Hall, *Charitable Fundraising in Canada* (Toronto: Canadian Centre for Philanthropy, 1996).

34 The centre did not survey places of worship, religious charities, or private foundations. The survey used the following classification of charitable activity: arts and culture, community benefit, education, health, hospitals, social services, and other.

PART ONE

Empirical and Ethical Perspectives

3 Altruism in Comparative International Perspective

JEN-CHIEH TING
AND JANE ALLYN PILIAVIN

Human beings are dependent on each other throughout life. However, human societies differ greatly in the ways in which family relationships, formal organizations, and states are structured to meet human needs and to encourage humans to discharge their obligations towards each other. Social psychologists who study the various ways in which individuals contribute to each others' well-being use the general term "prosocial behaviour" to refer to such actions. Within this very general realm, they use more specific terms, such as "altruism," "co-operation," and "helping." In this chapter, we review what is known about cultural (largely cross-national) differences in prosocial behaviour. For reasons to be explained below, we focus on helping behaviour towards strangers, the development of moral judgment, socialization into prosocial behaviour, and formal volunteering and donating.

We begin with an example that underscores the complexity of this topic. Four recent studies in western Europe examined social participation of various kinds: membership in voluntary organizations (excluding churches and unions), volunteering, willingness to give money to "Third World" countries, and blood donation.[1] Table 3.1 presents the data from these studies, indicating the percentage of individuals polled who participate, or say they are willing to participate, in each of these activities. Note that there is little or no consistency among societies across the various actions. The "best" country for blood donation, France, is the "worst" in willingness to give money for the support of the Third World. The highest-ranked country for volunteering, Norway, is near the bottom in giving blood. The Nether-

Table 3.1 Social participation of four types in western Europe

	Blood donation		*Volunteering*		*Membership in voluntary organizations*		*Donations to Third World countries*	
Country	*%*	*Rank*	*%*	*Rank*	*%*	*Rank*	*%*	*Rank*
Belgium	20	10	29	4	25	6	46	11
Denmark	34	3	27	6	–	–	56	9
France	44	1	23	8	20	7	39	12
Great Britain	32	4	12	10	31	4	66	7
Greece	38	2	–	–	–	–	78	1
Ireland	27	7	28	5	26	5	74	3
Italy	21	9	24	7	18	8	70	5
Luxembourg	14	12	–	–	–	–	76	2
Netherlands	28	6	37	2	44	1	70	5
Norway	16	11	38	1	40	2	–	–
Portugal	16	11	18	9	–	–	53	10
Spain	24	8	–	–	17	9	70	5
West Germany	30	5	32	3	32	3	61	8

lands is consistently in the top half of the distribution; Portugal is consistently near the bottom. But beyond these outliers, the numbers demonstrate that we cannot make any strong statements regarding comparative altruism – even when defined as public participation of these four kinds.

Before proceeding further, we define some terms and provide a brief history of the scientific study of prosocial behaviour. First, prosocial behaviour is generally defined as actions that are "defined by society as generally beneficial to other people and to the ongoing political system."[2] Paying taxes, following traffic laws, giving to charity, and giving directions on the street could all fall within this general definition. What most social psychologists claim to have studied is helping behaviour – "action that has the consequences of providing some benefit to or improving the well-being of another person."[3]

Altruism is "a helpful act that is carried out in the absence of obvious and tangible rewards."[4] Some authors further limit behaviour that may be counted as altruistic – for example, to that motivated by concern for the welfare of the other or requiring some self-sacrifice by the helper. A goodly proportion of prosocial behaviour and helping does not qualify as altruistic by such definitions.

The great majority of research on altruism, helping, and volunteering has been carried out by experimental social psychologists in the United States. Darley and Latané began research in the area in the

1960s in an attempt to understand theoretically the lack of intervention on the part of bystanders in New York City to a vicious criminal attack on a woman named Kitty Genovese.[5] Doubtless because of these origins, most studies have focused on responses to momentary problems or emergencies occurring to strangers, either in laboratory or field settings. The second largest area of research has examined the development of moral reasoning and prosocial behaviour in children; in this area, similarly, the focus is on understanding general processes of development. Only recently has there been any real attention to more institutional forms of helping, such as volunteering. Similarly, there have been few systematic attempts to compare such phenomena across cultures or between countries.

We thus look at those few major topics with enough cross-national comparison to permit us to draw some, albeit tentative, conclusions. We discuss them in descending order of similarity, from those topics in which cross-cultural similarities appear to predominate to those in which the most differences appear. We then discuss a cultural distinction that may lead us to a more general understanding of the source of cross-national differences – namely, the broad distinction between individualist and collectivist societies. We end with a specific comparison of Canada and the United States.

Before we examine the specific topics, however, we raise one more caveat – that the literature on comparative differences in altruism is not voluminous. There are two related reasons for this. First, researchers, who mainly emphasize testing of theories, have paid little attention to the influence of culture. They may thus have ignored, trivialized, or explained away many differences between cultures by reference to differences in method. Indeed, the inattention to cultural difference is in part the result of method; most investigators of helping behaviour are theoretically oriented experimentalists, who use rigorous procedures and measurement tools but are relatively unconcerned about representative sampling. Western researchers, especially psychologists, are interested principally in finding general patterns of psychological mechanisms and not in "culture" as such. Thus the nuances of how different cultures may foster different forms of behaviour has largely been ignored, as Sinha notes:[6] "The cultural, philosophical, and historical matrix in which the individual benefactor or recipient operates has been only generally taken into account. When different cultural groups have been compared with regard to different aspects of helping behaviour, cultural factors have been considered more or less in a blanket fashion without analysis of discrete aspects of a given culture that are directly related to altruistic behavior. In comparisons of different samples drawn from diverse cultures, only certain similarities and differences have been highlighted with very little effort to interrelate them with the cultural, philosophical, and religious traditions of these societies."

Non-Western scholars, as is evident from this quotation, have quite a different perspective and have argued for the importance of cultural differences in civic participation, rates of volunteering and other forms of social participation, and particularly in the development of moral reasoning and socialization into helping behaviour. These are all topics in which the process or behaviour being examined occurs over a much longer period of time, and less rigorous methods are typically used to investigate them.

A second reason why cultural differences have not played a large role in research in this area is that in some contexts they indeed do not seem to matter much. The concept of "weak" versus "strong" situations is useful here.[7] An emergency provides a "strong" situation, one in which the stimuli are so compelling and people must act so quickly that personality differences, in contrast to the "pull" of the situation, have little effect on responses. Cultural norms and expectations may operate in the same way as personality differences; the situation may need to be less compelling for cultural considerations to override the power of the situation. Clearly there is something about an emergency that arouses a very primitive, perhaps even an instinctive, response, either to aid or to flee. Volunteer opportunities, in contrast, do not have such a strong emotional aspect.

Sinha has further argued that a good strategy for studying helping behaviour in cultural contexts would be "to analyze a particular culture in terms of prescribed norms, values, and socialization processes and then draw out specific hypotheses regarding prosocial behavior in that culture as against other cultures with different norms and practice ... [I]t would be advisable to analyze cultures with regard to the relative emphasis placed on aiding, helping, and sacrificing one's own good for the sake of others or of the community, and then identify the pattern of prosocial behavior in that culture and compare it with patterns from cultures with different or somewhat contrasting norms. Since cultures may vary in the extent to which they emphasize interrelatedness and mutuality among human beings and thereby foster concern and obligation toward others, it is essential to ascertain that factor in designing one's studies."[8] Unfortunately, we are aware of no research in which this excellent and sensible strategy has actually been pursued.

In the remainder of this chapter we proceed from that area of research in which it appears that culture has the weakest effect – helping behaviour towards strangers in momentary difficulty – through to that area in which culture plays the greatest role – civil society. We report our assessment of the role of culture based on the existing research, but the literature, for the most part, has not been designed for these comparisons, and variation in methods and measures renders them difficult to make systematically.

HELPING BEHAVIOUR TOWARDS STRANGERS

As we have noted, there is a large volume of research concerning the response of individuals (often college students in laboratory studies) to the occurrence of apparent emergencies or momentary problems of strangers. These events occur rapidly, and a response must be made – if one is to be made – quickly, without the opportunity for much reflection. Some of this research has involved the "real world." Experimenters have feigned collapses, dropped groceries, pencils, or sheafs of papers, asked directions, requested change, pretended to be blind, deaf, or lame and in need of help, or even stranded themselves on highways. Various independent variables have been investigated, including the sex and attractiveness of the person in need.

The first published work to explore cross-national differences is the pioneering study by Feldman, who compared the help offered to strangers in cities in three countries – Boston, Paris, and Athens. He found a number of significant cultural differences, but the results differed with the context and the nature of the favour being asked. One consistent finding emerged: in Athens foreigners who asked a favour received more help than did natives; the reverse was true in Paris and Boston – foreigners were treated less well than natives. Post hoc, he explained the findings by reference to the "ingroup versus outgroup" concept and particular historical developments in each of the countries, most specifically the "hospitality" norm in Greece.[9]

Feldman's work aside, the issue of cultural differences in helpfulness to strangers has largely been ignored. Only one variable has been explored in enough countries that we are able to make cross-cultural comparisons: the urban–rural distinction. Indeed, it is one of the more robust findings of social psychology in recent years that there is less helpfulness in urban than in non-urban environments. There have now been more than 60 comparisons of the level of helpfulness observed in urban and non-urban settings, and despite some variations,[10] recent reviews have been all but unanimous in confirming this behavioural characteristic of the urban environment.[11]

There appear to be two kinds of possible explanations for a rural–urban difference: dispositional variables (that is, urban people are just different from rural people)[12] and situational variables (that is, there is something about living in the urban environment that leads to less helpfulness). Research has consistently demonstrated more support for the latter than for the former. Yousif and Korte summarize the literature: "The best supported explanation is Milgram's input overload hypothesis, which sees the unhelpfulness shown toward neighbors and strangers in urban settings as an inevitable adaptation to a situation of excessive demands. This has been confirmed in several studies, which have shown that the level of helpfulness declines as a direct function of increasing levels of environmental inputs (e.g., sights, sounds, demands). Other analysts have argued for the explanatory role of specific community characteristics such as crime rate, salience of deviant subcultures, prominence of tourism, and neighborhood norms. Yet, except for crime rate, these community variables have not been shown to be related to observed levels of helpfulness."[13]

This is an area in which cross-cultural research would greatly increase our understanding. Yousif and Korte put it as follows:[14] "Our present state of knowledge about urban unhelpfulness seems to be that it is a fairly reliable finding but with only limited evidence in support of the various explanations for it. One type of evidence that would seem quite relevant to the explanation of this phenomenon is its cross-cultural generality. If urban conditions produce reduced sociability and helpfulness, and that reaction is evident across a variety of cultural settings, then urban unhelpfulness would appear to be the result of processes intrinsic to urban environments such as adjustment to input overload or deindividuation."[15] If, in contrast, the urban unhelpfulness effect proved less reliable in other cultural settings, then such a finding would strengthen arguments that explain helpfulness in terms of culture, community, and norm variables.[16]

What work has been done suggests that the urban–non-urban difference is fairly consistent cross-culturally. A review of the research on six countries (Australia, Canada, Israel, the Netherlands, Turkey, and the United States) found the difference significant in all these countries except the Netherlands.[17] Indeed, the Netherlands seems to be exceptional among developed Western countries in this regard, with helpfulness equally high in all city districts and in rural areas. This phenomenon has been attributed to a strong norm of "civility" in Dutch society.[18] But whatever its cause, the finding does suggest that cultural differences can matter.

Perhaps more important, the broad similarities among Western countries are arguably not reproduced in some less Westernized societies. Yousif and Korte note that "several analyses of cities in the developing world have argued that the Western model of urban social behavior and urban social characteristics does not apply to such settings, where cultural norms and strong social organization prevent the impersonality, distrust, alienation, and unhelpfulness often associated with urbanity ... The limited amount of relevant cross-cultural data presents a somewhat mixed picture."[19]

This "mixed picture" is shown, for example, in data from Papua–New Guinea, where buyer–seller interaction appears to be less positive in the urban settings, but no urban–non-urban differences emerged in the helpfulness shown towards tourists.[20] Also, although less helpfulness was found in Turkish cities than in smaller towns, helpfulness in the urban squatter districts of the cities was equivalent to that found in the towns. In fact, the variation in helpfulness within the urban settings was equivalent to that between city and town.[21] In contrast, the authors of two recent studies comparing the Sudan and the United Kingdom suggest that "[t]he Islamic culture of the Sudan is quite different from Western cultures, and the fact that urban size, urgency, and cost differences in helpfulness in the Sudan were comparable to those found in the United Kingdom suggest that the same processes may govern the decision on whether or not to help in the type of situations investigated."[22]

The complexity of findings suggests that the predictable urban–rural differences found in the West may not apply straightforwardly to the developing world, where cultural factors may intervene to change the outcome. Data from more cultures than those that have been examined would be invaluable in suggesting the answer to when we do and do not find the "urban unhelpfulness effect."[23] Following Sinha's suggestion for a research strategy,[24] cultures where the effect does not obtain would be very illuminating and should be examined to see what is different about those cities (or those cultures) that makes them an exception to the usual pattern. Among Western countries this suggests the need for an intensive study of the Netherlands, the outlier, which has been found to be different from other Western countries in other respects also.[25]

MORAL DEVELOPMENT

The study of how children develop patterns of moral reasoning has also been widely examined cross-nationally. By moral reasoning, we mean "the principles people use when they make ... decisions about what is the right way to act."[26] The psychological study of the development of moral reasoning started with Jean Piaget, a psychologist whose academic training was in biology. Given his background, it is not surprising that he proposed that cognitive abilities develop according to a sequence of culturally invariant stages. That is, he saw cognition, including moral reasoning, as a universal biological process in the human species, which develops in the same way and on the same timetable everywhere. Kohlberg later modified and extended Piaget's developmental model. The model involves three stages: pre-conventional, conventional, and post-conventional morality. In the first stage, the person sees actions as right or wrong depending on whether they bring rewards or punishments. In the second, the person determines morality by whether the actions receive social approval or are in conformity with rules and laws. In the final stage – which most people never reach – internalized personal moral standards are the basis for moral decision-making.[27]

Even within Western culture, the theory has been extensively researched and critiqued. Specifically, Kohlberg has been criticized for his apparent theoretical bias in favour of males. Carol Gilligan has emphasized gender differences in moral reasoning and has argued that females in American society develop an interpersonal "caring-based" morality rather than the abstract morality of justice favoured by males.[28] However, comprehensive reviews of empirical studies on moral reasoning have suggested that structural gender differences in moral judgment tend to be rarely prevalent in early and middle adolescence[29] and frequently favour female respondents over males.[30]

Claiming invariance naturally brings attempts at cross-cultural replication; Kohlberg's claim has been subjected to considerable scrutiny and has been shown to be valid for a number of societies.[31] Even very recent research supports his general development patterns of moral reasoning. Two recent studies, for example, compared adolescents in the United States and children and adolescents in Brazil on the correlates of prosocial moral reasoning (PMR). It was found that the "underlying structures of moral reasoning and its relationship to helping in both the U.S. and Brazil's adolescents are similar" and that "[i]n general, age and gender differences in PMR were similar for both Brazilian and U.S. adolescents."[32] The study concludes: "Overall, the present findings extend our prior understanding of individuals' thinking of care-based, interpersonal-oriented social dilemmas. There was further evidence that prosocial moral reasoning is linked to prosocial behaviors in some Western cultures. Specifically, self-focused, hedonistic concerns were negatively associated with helpfulness and generosity, whereas abstract, other-oriented internalized concerns were positively associated with helpfulness and generosity. Furthermore, femininity was correlated with approval-oriented and internalized prosocial moral reasoning in a theoretically expected manner and consistent with findings from U.S. samples."[33]

Thus, both across cultures and across genders, there seems to be some invariance in moral development. When considering this and most other studies, however, we must remember that we are essentially comparing only different Western cultures.

It is also possible that the lack of differences found cross-culturally may result from problems in measurement. Some observers have argued that the instruments usually employed – those developed by Kohlberg – are simply insensitive to existing cultural (and gender) differences.[34] Their central point is usually that the instruments simply assume the universal, justice-based form of moral reasoning and thus do not allow respondents to display a more interpersonal, relationship-based moral reasoning.

A second issue strikes at the heart of cross-cultural differences. Piaget and Kohlberg do assume that the individual's development of moral reasoning requires some commerce with a social environment that challenges his or her views; this allows, then, for possible differences in the ages at which children reach different stages. As Comunian and Gielen point out, research has shown that "participation in prosocial activities stimulates and is stimulated by the development of mature and autonomous forms of moral reasoning. Exposure to diverse social experiences and to the needs, values, and viewpoints of others seems to contribute to the development of a more mature, broad-based socio-moral perspective, reflected by a higher state of moral reasoning."[35]

However, allowing that social experiences can differ across cultures leaves open the possibility that cultures that provide greater, or different, exposures to prosocial situations may have different sequences, or even different endpoints, to moral development from those in the Western societies within which the theories were developed. As Eisenberg and Mussen have noted, "[c]hildren in different cultures differ ... in the reasons they give when they explain why someone should assist or not assist another in hypothetical situations." And as an example they offer the fact that "in their moral reasoning, children from an Israeli kibbutz focused more on internalized norms or values related to helping and on the importance of human beings than did urban Israelis and American children. Such reasoning is consistent with the ideology of the Kibbutz."[36]

There has been relatively little research conducted on moral development in non-Western cultures, especially on explicitly communal cultures such as those in South and East Asia. One study assessed the effect of interpersonal relationships on two aspects of Japanese university students' moral judgment: manner of application and the content of helping norms. It concludes: "Female Japanese students showed strong relation-based morality on these two dimensions" and "tended to make judgments without reference to the principle of universality or justice even when they knew the principle." This, the study argues, "suggests a relation-based moral orientation rather than a justice orientation."[37] Similarly, a recent review of research on moral development in Japan suggests that studies show that Americans tend to analyse problems in more abstract terms than the Japanese, who "saw life embedded in human networks." The author argues as a result for new ways of thinking about "principled moral reasoning in a culture where relationships are emphasized," including "relationships to others, society, the 'life-world,' and the universe."[38]

Research comparing Indian and American samples reveals similar cultural differences in moral reasoning. In the work of Miller, Bersoff, and Harwood, researchers presented scenarios to second- and sixth-grade children and college students in which the person requesting help was a close relative, friend, or stranger, and the need was extreme, moderate, or minor. In the case of extreme need there were no cultural differences; everyone said that they would help.[39] But in the case of minor need, the differences were substantial. For example, the minor need–friend scenario involved asking a friend for directions to a store; the friend refused to interrupt reading an exciting book and thus did not help. 93 per cent of the Indians thought the friend had an obligation to help, but only 33 per cent of the Americans thought so. In the case of strangers requesting help, the difference was 73 per cent (Indians) and 23 per cent (Americans).[40]

Miller summarizes this research cogently:

> There exists not one universal morality of caring contrasting with the morality of justice but, rather, alternative types of interpersonal moralities that reflect the meaning systems emphasized in different cultural groups. Both the supererogatory view of interpersonal morality held by Lawrence Kohlberg and the morality-of-caring framework developed by Carol Gilligan are shown to be culturally bound. Research conducted among American and Hindu Indian populations supports the claim that an individually oriented interpersonal moral code develops among Americans, stressing personal freedom of choice, individual responsibility, and a dualistic view of individual motivation. In contrast, a duty-based interpersonal moral code develops among Hindu Indians, stressing broad and socially enforceable interpersonal obligation, the importance of contextual sensitivity, and a monistic view of individual motivation.[41]

SOCIALIZATION INTO PROSOCIAL BEHAVIOUR

Children receive socialization for prosocial behaviour in addition to simply developing moral reasoning. Long ago Margaret Mead argued, in regard to socialization in general, that "human nature is almost unbelievably malleable, responding accurately and contrastingly to contrasting cultural conditions."[42] Mead compared two tribes in New Guinea, describing one, the Arapesh, as gentle, co-operative, generous, and responsive to the needs and feelings of others, and the other, the Mundugamor, as ruthless, aggressive, uncaring, and lacking in generosity and co-operation. Others have similarly argued for significant cultural differences in attitudes towards others. Turnbull, for example, compared the hostile Ik and the gentle, humane Hopi.[43] More recently, Robarchek and Robarchek contrasted the Waorani people of the Amazon (warlike) and the Semai Senoi, an Aboriginal people of the Malaysian rain forest, who enjoy a much more harmonious existence.[44] Other studies have highlighted the fact that both traditional societies and more modern socialist countries (for example, the Soviet Union at the time) value co-operation, social responsibility, and consideration for others as personal qualities.[45]

Some research suggests that one explanation for differences in the development of prosocial behaviour can be found in children's early experiences and responsibilities in their societies. Whiting and Whiting, for example, studied children aged 3 to 11 in six countries (India, Japan, Kenya, Mexico, the Philippines, and the United States). From numerous five-minute field observations of groups of children interacting in unsupervised settings they found considerable cross-cultural differences in helpfulness. Filipino, Kenyan, and Mexican children scored highest on the scale of prosocial behaviour, while U.S. children scored lowest. The Indian and Okinawan children were in a middle range.[46] Helpfulness was least likely in communities where children competed in school and were seldom assigned responsibilities for family farming or household chores. Prosocial behaviour was most common in cultures where children must co-operate with other family members in performing many chores and, in particular, where older siblings shared in the care and raising of other children. These researchers' interpretation of their findings is consistent with social learning theory: children learn both from what they observe others doing and from their own actions. Also supportive of a social learning interpretation is research on parents and teachers on Kibbutzim, showing that they reinforce each other in inculcating co-operative values and orientations and in discouraging competition among children.[47]

The work of Stevenson seeks to bring these comparisons into a larger context by discussing Eastern and Western ways of socialization and the merits and disadvantages of each system for the development of prosocial behaviour.[48] He analyses how three societies – China, Japan, and Taiwan – foster the development of children's prosocial behaviour. These societies are very different from Western nations and are of special interest here because they place extraordinary emphasis on children's socialization into prosocial behaviour. Stevenson argues that while the Asian concept of altruism is similar to that of the West, "Asian considerations differ from those in the West because of their conception of the role of the individual in relation to family and society."[49] He summarizes his findings about the differences between Eastern and Western ideas on socialization as follows: "Chinese parents focus primarily upon their child's moral development and academic achievement ... There is little concern for personality development ... Parents are considered to be successful if their child has a high moral character as reflected in proper conduct, good manners, humility, and respectfulness – and receives good grades at school ... [S]upreme among the typical Chinese and Japanese citizen's goals for society is the preservation of order and harmony ... The Asian orientation, then, is consistently directed toward the group. The individual is typically defined through participation in family, school, community, company, and the nation."[50] He later concludes: "Children's attitudes and behavior reflect what is valued by the societies in which they live. The emphasis in Asian cultures on group harmony, with the accompanying concern for prosocial behavior, stands in sharp contrast to the individualism of the West.... [I]t is evident that strong, explicit efforts are made in Chinese and Japanese societies to transmit positive attitudes about group loyalty and participation and about the critical role of prosocial behavior for the advancement of members of these groups."[51]

THE INDIVIDUALISM/COLLECTIVISM PARADIGM: THE CORE CONCEPT FOR COMPARATIVE ALTRUISM?

To this point we have considered a variety of social and cultural differences and how they may affect aspects of, and the level of, prosocial behaviour in different societies. But since Hofstede's *Culture's Consequences*[52] appeared in 1980, the principal focus of cross-cultural research in regard to altruism and prosocial behaviour has been the distinction between individualist and collectivist societies. As we saw in the section on socialization above, most Western nations tend to value individualism, with an emphasis on personal responsibility and achievement. Collectivist societies such as China stress the obligations of children to their families and of citizens to their community, valuing loyalty, trust, and co-operation. These cultural orientations have consequences for socialization, leading to an emphasis on self-reliance for the individualist cultures and on social conformity for the collectivist.

The importance of a collectivist ethic has been stressed by research on socialization in the Israeli kibbutz, probably the most prominent example of conscious collectivism in an individualist nation. That research suggests that the kibbutz does indeed promote co-operation to a larger extent than do the mainstream cultures of North America or Europe. Indeed, kibbutz children appear much more like those from "traditional" societies.[53] In contrast, the children of one of the leading individualist cultures, the United States, are regarded by some observers as "singularly deficient in prosocial development."[54]

What are the implications of the individualism–collectivism distinction for adult social behaviour? Are the differences as clear there as in the research on children? Some research suggests that this is the case. Work that preceded Hofstede, which did not specifically use the concept of individualism–collectivism, concluded that Chinese subjects were more likely to imitate the behaviour of a helping model than were Americans.[55] It argued that the Chinese tradition of caring for aged relatives and others might suggest that the norm of social responsibility is stronger in China than in the United States, where there may be an implicit norm of looking out for oneself.[56]

It would, however, be too simplistic to generalize that Americans necessarily show less prosocial behaviour than people in other cultures. For example, a laboratory study of students playing decomposed "prisoner's dilemma–type" games found no significant differences in social motives between the United States and the Netherlands.[57] Stevenson, in his article on differences in socialization between East and West, says: "[C]ultures of the East may help the West to gain insight into some of the problems of individualism. At the same time, there are many contradictions in a society's efforts to foster prosocial behavior. These efforts are often accompanied by problems: The ethnocentrism that often accompanies strong identification with a group, the lack of individual initiative that occurs when advancement of group has greater priority than individual achievement, the frustration that exists at viewing the conflict between the ideal behaviors of the mores and the realities of everyday life, the conflicts that arise between ingenuity and obedience to rules and authority, and the tension produced by pressure for individual achievement and the simultaneous need to work for the advancement of the group."[58]

Most commonly, consistent with Stevenson's comment on ethnocentrism, research suggests that prosocial behaviour is distributed differently between individualist and collectivist societies. Bond criticizes Western social scientists, "steeped in an unconscious philosophy of individualism," for seeing altruism as all-or-nothing behaviour, for assuming that "an altruistic person ... will be generous towards beggars, colleagues, spouses, tourists – the lot." In consequence, he argues, "Western social scientists place great emphasis on measuring individual dispositions." This approach contrasts with the way of thinking in a collectivist society, which "is dramatically different" and "pays close attention to the target of a person's social behaviour and the context of the interaction, historically and socially."[59] The author of another study argues that in Chinese society, "with strangers one ensures that there is a constant ratio between both parties' inputs and gains. With family members, however, one does whatever is needed. In other words, resources are allocated according to need, not fairness."[60] In other words, we might expect not overall more "altruism" or helpfulness in collective cultures, but rather different patterns of helping in the two kinds of societies.

A good deal of research bears out this expectation, making a particular distinction between assisting outsiders and helping the "in-group." One study, comparing India and the United States, found that Indians showed an overall lower level of helping, although Brahmins (a high caste) showed more helping towards other Brahmins.[61] To similar effect, a study of Chinese and Japanese subjects found that they gave more help to those whom they perceived to be insiders than Americans did, but less to those whom they saw as outsiders.[62] Moghaddam states that "[c]ross-cultural comparisons suggest that under some conditions people in the United States tend to be more helpful than people in traditional societies toward outgroup members." He attributes this to "the higher mobility and individualism of U.S society," which make Americans "interact more with outgroup members and be both dependent on and helpful toward strangers generally." In contrast, in "less mobile and more collectivistic societies, interactions with outsiders are less frequent, and less help is offered to them."[63]

These findings, and a good number of other studies,[64] suggest that, particularly in cross-cultural comparisons, it is essential to distinguish between help given to in-group and to out-group members. As Triandis states, "[i]n all cultures people are more likely to help an in-group member than an out-group member. However, the difference in the probability of helping in-group versus out-group members is larger in the case of collectivist than in the case of individualistic cultures."[65]

There is also some evidence that the nature of altruistic actions themselves becomes more collectivistic in collective societies, involving groups rather than individuals. Drawing on the work of the economist

Albert Hirschman, for example, which described grassroots development projects involving very poor people in six Latin America countries,[66] Moghaddam suggests: "Perhaps the most important benefit of people helping one another was the dispelling of isolation and mutual distrust and the emergence of stronger, healthier social networks." And he notes similar processes elsewhere: "The same kinds of patterns emerge in some aspects of Western life, such as among the grassroots organization that have grown in response to the AIDS epidemic. This indicates that changes in circumstances are associated with different patterns of altruism."[67]

The dimension of need may also evoke different responses in collective and individualistic cultures. A study of willingness to give money to hypothetical recipients, comparing India and the United States, shows that "Indian respondents distributed more on the basis of need and less on the basis of merit or equality than did the American respondents." But within this tendency there were gender differences: "the Indian males and the American males and females distributed more to the needy recipient and less to the meritorious recipient when money cutbacks rather than rewards were involved."[68] Indian females, in contrast, gave most to the needy in all cases. The authors conclude that "culture does seem to have a significant impact on how individuals evaluate the fairness of different allocation plans. Indian respondents tended to favor need much more than did the Americans who tended to favor equality or equity."[69]

Although these authors offer no conclusions, they suggest two possible explanations. Perhaps when the level of resources is low, need becomes more salient as an allocation strategy. Alternatively, collectivist and individualist societies may place different emphases on need; allocating on the basis of need may predominate in a more collectivistic society because of the greater stress placed on interdependence. "Members of a more individualistic society such as the U.S. ... may be less apt to favor need as a distribution strategy because of the cultural importance of independence and self-sufficiency."[70]

The collectivist–individualist paradigm also reminds us that social relationships are quite important in any discussion about helping behaviour. Several studies show the role of social relationships in the more interactive and dynamic sense, and Moghaddam summarizes this literature: "A cultural perspective leads us to view helping behavior as part of a larger moral system binding individuals together in social relationships. Reciprocity becomes more than just give-and-take between individuals, because the help exchanged has to be appropriate for a given context. The goal of exchange becomes much more than just maximizing material rewards because the value of help is not just material.... This is clearly shown by research in Sweden, Japan, and the United States demonstrating that people appreciate help more when there is an opportunity or obligation for them to reciprocate.... If the goal of such exchange was to maximize material rewards, it should not matter if reciprocity is impossible or if the donor is a rival – but it does."[71]

The extensive role that helping plays in establishing social relationships becomes clear in Yang's lengthy field study of *guanxixue* ("doing favours for people") in China. Guanxixue involves "the exchange of gifts, favours, and banquets, the cultivation of interpersonal relationships and networks of mutual dependence, and the manufacturing of obligations and indebtedness. What informs these practices and their native descriptions is the conception of the primacy and binding power of personal relationships and their importance in meeting the needs and desires of everyday life."[72] These practices have survived the enormous political and social changes of the twentieth century; as another study notes, "[d]espite official opposition, quanxixue continues to thrive in China and seems destined to outlive communism."[73]

Thus we can say that in Eastern cultures, especially the Chinese, collectivism appears to be specific to role relationships:[74] "Chinese culture places strong emphasis on altruism and the maintenance of harmony, values presumed to be conducive to integrative social organization."[75] The Confucian ideas of maintaining personal harmony and social order among persons situated in hierarchically structured relationships are still operating.

CIVIL SOCIETY AND VOLUNTEERISM

The extent to which members of a society exhibit a commitment to "civil society" may also vary greatly across cultures. Civil society is a difficult term to define. We use it here to mean those aspects of society "standing between the market and the state, embodying neither the self-interest of the one nor the coercive authority of the other ... a place of transition from the realm of particularism to that of the universal."[76] The components of civil society include "families, communities, friendship networks, solidaristic workplace ties, voluntarism, spontaneous groups and movements."[77] Wolfe argues that "[i]f there is one underlying theme that unifies the themes in sociology – such as organic solidarity, the collective conscience, the generalized other, sociability, and the gift relationship – it would be the idea of civil society."[78] The term can stand for a broader sense of altruism in the society, for individuals' willingness to join together and help others voluntarily.

Within this broad concept researchers usually study participation in voluntary organizations – churches, unions, political parties, charitable organizations, clubs, sports teams, musical groups, the PTA. In our discussion, however, we distinguish, as many writers have not, between membership in voluntary associations and volunteer work. Many voluntary associations have little if anything to do with providing social services, raising funds for charities, or otherwise attempting to improve society. Putnam's now well-known article "Bowling Alone" uses as an example of voluntary association an activity – participating in bowling leagues – that has nothing to do with helping others.[79] A society could easily have high rates of membership in voluntary associations but low levels of volunteering in the sense of helping, although it is difficult to see how a society without a tradition of voluntary associations could be high in volunteer activity.

In the United States there are long traditions both of "rugged individualism" and of the development of social movements and associations. Both have roots in the broader cultural templates discussed over 150 years ago by de Tocqueville and more recently by Bellah and others in *Habits of the Heart*.[80] Tocqueville wrote that "Americans of all ages, all conditions, and all dispositions" were inclined to "constantly form associations,"[81] and recent research has borne out this assessment. In both local and national surveys, relatively large proportions of respondents (50 per cent or more) reported memberships in one or more voluntary associations.[82] None the less, some argue, like D.C. Swift, that "[t]here has been a sharp decline in a sense of community and an increase in selfish individualism" and that "[i]ndividualism has triumphed over the equalitarian ethos, with corrosive privatism and the deterioration of community values."[83] We do not enter into this argument regarding the purported deterioration of civic participation or consider its causes[84] or solutions to the problem.[85] Suffice it to say that there is good evidence for (for example, the decline in voting) and against (the increase or at least stabilization of volunteer activity). Our interest here is in comparative questions.

As Curtis long ago noted, "the observation that Americans are joiners is a comparative statement."[86] Perhaps surprisingly, however, there has been little comparative research on rates of association membership.[87] What is the evidence for cross-cultural differences in such membership? Some of the best research is now more than 30 years old and is reproduced in Table 3.2.[88] It suggests that Americans are indeed more likely to be joiners than are citizens of other countries. More recent data from a Canadian national survey suggest that Canadians equalled or exceeded Americans on certain measures. That is, 64 per cent of Canadians reported belonging to at least one volun-

Table 3.2 Organization membership in five countries

	% of population belonging				
Number of Organizations	*USA*	*UK*	*Germany*	*Italy*	*Mexico*
1	25	31	32	24	23
2	14	10	9	5	2
3	9	4	2	1	0
4 or more	9	2	1	–	–
Total – multiple memberships	32	16	12	6	2
Total – all memberships	57	47	44	30	25
Number	(970)	(963	(955)	(995)	(1,007)

tary association, compared to 57 per cent of Americans. The percentages in the two countries were virtually identical, however, when union affiliations were removed from the analysis, and the percentages of respondents who reported multiple memberships were similar in both nations.[89]

We must make two other significant qualifications to the data contained in Table 3.2.[90] First, the differences between countries were greatest in membership in religious organizations, with 19 per cent of respondents belonging to them in the United States but only between three and six per cent in the other countries. Thus the "ranking" of American society drops substantially if such church affiliation is excluded.[91] Second, the U.S. ranking drops even further for active memberships: "In these instances, people from several countries, including Canada, Australia, the Netherlands, Northern Ireland, Norway, and Sweden, equal or surpass the membership levels of Americans."[92] Why are Americans more likely to join but less likely to be active in organizations? One possible answer is simply that the large number of organizations in the United States means that there is much greater opportunity for membership, and people simply join without any real intention of active participation.[93]

The analysis of various cross-national data conducted by Curtis et al. also found that some expected relationships did not occur. Protestant countries are not necessarily higher in involvement than Catholic countries. Levels of industrialization and urbanization also are not consistent determinants of civic involvement; Japan, France, and Germany are high on these variables and comparatively low in involvement; Austria is low in urbanization, but involvement there is also low. The authors suggest that centralized government control may account for France, Japan, and Spain's low involvement.[94] Curtis et al. conclude: "While each interpretation merits some consideration, none provides a complete explanation for the pattern of national rankings in association membership.... [A]ll of these factors may have predictive importance for joining behaviour. In addition, unique features in the cultural and historical backgrounds of countries may be more significant than any of these influences in explaining levels of association involvement."[95]

VOLUNTEER WORK

Volunteer work has been taken as a prototypical instance of non-spontaneous helping behaviour,[96] or even of altruism. Psychological research, however, suggests that volunteering is motivated not totally by the helper's concern for the recipient but also by a desire to express values or gain social experiences, and a number of other needs.[97] Sociologists also understand the performance of volunteer work as determined heavily by one's location in the social structure. Wilson and Musick, for example, present an "integrated theory of volunteer work," based on the premises that "volunteer work is (1) productive work that requires human capital, (2) collective behavior that requires social capital, and (3) ethically guided work that requires cultural capital." They operationalized human capital with measures of income, education, and functional health, social capital with number of children in the household and informal social interaction, and cultural capital with religion. Using panel data from the United States, they found "that formal volunteering is positively related to human capital, number of children in the household, informal social interaction, and religiosity."[98]

A detailed analysis of this kind – of motives and social location – has not been done cross-nationally. There are, however, data on volunteering rates for a number of countries over time. Studies of western European countries, the United States, and Canada for both 1981 and 1990 show that the United States consistently had the highest proportion of volunteers in the population (47 per cent), while the United Kingdom and Portugal had the lowest. The Scandinavian countries and the Netherlands had relatively high percentage rates, in the high 30s. In only three countries was there statistically significant change over time: Austria showed a decline of 7 per cent, and there were increases in Canada (6 per cent) and the United States (10 per cent). In the United States, this increase was strongest among post–Second World War cohorts, including the supposedly selfish "Generation X."[99]

These figures, however, tend to overstate the level of U.S. volunteering because of one aspect of American "exceptionalism." As with membership in voluntary organizations, when one eliminates religious volunteering, "American rates (34 per cent) fall somewhat beneath those of Canada (38 per cent) and Sweden (38 per cent) and are virtually equal to those of Norway (34 per cent), Iceland (35 per cent), and the Netherlands (33 per cent)."[100] Analysis of the factors positively associated with volunteering makes the same point. Across countries, education (human capital) is positively related to volunteering, as is religiosity (cultural capital). Greeley delineates the relative importance of these and other factors: "[A]ge, sex, income, and education account for 36 percent of cross-national variation in volunteer rates. Adding secular organizational membership accounts for 11 per cent more.... Finally, adding the two religious items – church attendance and membership in religious organizations – reduces the unexplained variation to 15 per cent. Thus even after the social structural variables are taken into account, 38 per cent of the differences among the countries in propensity to volunteer is attributable to religious activity. When all of these are taken into account, significant differences exist between the United States on the one hand and only four other countries – Britain, Northern Ireland, Denmark, and Iceland."[101] Religious involvement also fuels participation in secular volunteering. In short, Greeley argues, "Religious structures generate social capital that motivates people to volunteer, especially those who already have idealistic orientations."[102]

BLOOD DONATION

There is only one piece of cross-cultural research on blood donation of which we are aware.[103] It seeks to explain differences in the frequency of blood donation across 13 countries of western Europe in terms of the organization of the blood collection system. Across countries, donation is associated with being male, being middle-aged rather than old or young, being better educated and in the top quartile on income, and knowing someone who has received a donation – all findings that confirm U.S. research.[104]

Despite these similarities, there are significant differences among nations in the frequency of donations, and the study argues that "institutional factors are an important part of what determines rates of blood donation, over and above individual characteristics."[105] Rates were consistently higher in the three countries where the state health service collects blood than in either the four countries where the Red Cross does so or the six that use blood banks. Type of collection system also interacts with the characteristics of individuals in complex ways. The only hint (unmentioned) of a truly "cultural" effect is that the gender effect is particularly strong in most Mediterranean countries, where gender norms are still the most traditional. It is clear, then, that national differences reflect not only "culture" but, perhaps more important, differences in the organizational structure of collection. Thus we might not expect cross-national differences in blood donation to be similar to those in membership in voluntary associations, volunteering, or donating. This is, perhaps, another example of a "strong situation" overwhelming cultural propensities.

CANADIAN–U.S. COMPARISONS

Those aspects of the research discussed above on differences in joining voluntary associations and doing volunteer work that specifically involve U.S.–Canadian comparisons challenge the theories and empirical conclusions offered by the most influential commentator on the two countries, Seymour Martin Lipset. Lipset has argued that Canada's "counter-revolutionary" past led to the adoption there of more "collectively oriented" values than exist in the United States.[106] That is, Canadians, like the British, are "more disposed to rely on the 'state' for solving community problems, and thus less likely to emphasise voluntary activity."[107] But the data on volunteering do not bear this theory out, especially once we take religious organizations out of the equation.

Similarly, the data on charitable donation do not suggest large Canadian–American differences. A number of surveys have been carried out in both countries over the past decade or more,[108] and while differences in elements such as questions and sampling plans inhibit precise comparisons,[109] they are similar enough for us to draw some general conclusions. Overall, 78 per cent of Canadians sampled and 68.5 per cent of Americans reported having donated to charity in the previous 12 months. In both countries, respondents under the age of 34 gave least, and there was a slight decrease in giving after age 64 in Canada and 74 in the United States. Also in both societies married respondents gave more than the previously married, and singles gave least. Education and income are monotonically related to donation in both countries, and women were more likely to give than men. Full-time employed people give most, the unemployed give least (but 64 per cent of them in Canada give, and 61 per cent in the United States), and part-time and "not in the labour force" individuals place in between.

More distinctions emerge in destinations of donations (Table 3.3). The coding schemes used for recipient organizations, however, differ

Table 3.3 Types of organizations receiving donations, Canada and United States

Organizational type	*Canada 1997*	*USA 1995*
Religious	51	58
Health	17	8
Education and research	4	9
Social services	11	13
Philanthropic	6	2
Arts and culture	3	4
Environment	2	2
International	3	2
Other	2	2

*Figures are percentages of all donations made.

notably; we have tried to equate them, but it is essentially impossible to do so. The largest disparities in the table appear to be in health and in education and research. We are sure, however, that this is the result of coding. In the Canadian data, "research" is put in with health; in the U.S. data, with education. When they are added together, the disparity is quite small. The only other large difference is in religion – a consistent theme in the literature on civil society. Americans declare themselves to be very religious, and here they appear to put their money where their mouths are.[110]

These surveys also examined volunteering activity, again with coding problems. Most critically, the U.S. survey included as "volunteering" the category of "informal helping" – in our opinion an entirely different category of behaviour; it is not "volunteering" in the sense of giving time to a formal organization. Thus the finding that 49 per cent of U.S. respondents, but only 31 per cent of Canadians, "volunteered" in the most recent survey year is not very meaningful. And it is impossible to disaggregate the U.S. data to remove these individuals. Since 13.5 per cent of the hours given went to such "informal helping," we can correct the figures for the average number of hours per volunteer, which are initially given as 149 for Canadians and 218 for Americans. When the correction is made, the U.S. figure is reduced to 189 hours. There is another complication, however – there is a category of "sports" in Canada, in which 11 per cent of the volunteer hours appear; there is no such category in the U.S. survey (there is a "recreation" category, but it is clearly indicated as volunteering.) If this means that participating in sports counts as volunteer activity in Canada, we have a similar problem in the other direction, and a subtraction might be in order. Thus here again we have a confusion between participation in voluntary associations and volunteering in the sense of doing good for others.

Regardless of these problems, we indeed find the same pattern of relationships between demographic factors and volunteering in both countries that we discovered for charitable donation. It is, however, essentially impossible to do the sort of comparison across types of volunteering that we attempted for charitable donation. The only really interesting finding here is that the percentage of total hours volunteered (with all the problems of what is considered "volunteering") that is devoted to religious organizations is essentially identical in the two countries: 18 per cent in Canada and 17.2 per cent in the United States.

In short, the great gulf that Lipset once saw between the "conservative," more collective, and more European perspective of Canada – that government should provide social services – and the more rebellious, individualistic, and privatized, uniquely American perspective seems to have narrowed. Even in the dimension in which the United States has been seen as exceptional – the prevalence and importance of religious participation – the difference no longer appears in the giving of time, although it remains in the giving of money.

CONCLUSION

Even in the "global village," then, we still find cultural differences between the West and the East – and where communal forms of social organization exist, as in the kibbutz. How do we understand these differences? About thirty years ago, pioneers Latané and Darley argued that norms – a major element of a cultural analysis of differences in altruism and helping – could not explain the kind of helping at which they looked. Why not? They argued: "Norms ... seem to contradict one another. The injunction to help people is qualified by strictures not to accept help, to look out for yourself, and not to meddle in other people's business. In any specific situation it is hard to see how norms will be of much help to an undecided bystander.... A second problem with norms is that, even though contradictory, they are usually stated in only the most vague and general way."[111] Of course, Latané and Darley studied only responses to momentary problems or emergencies. We do not expect norms to have a strong effect in such circumstances, and we find no consistent cultural differences there.

These authors, however, are experimental social psychologists. We are sociologists, and after our review, we find that it is too simple to trivialize or explain away the influence of culture on helping behaviour more generally. Thinking more seriously about culture thus broadens our understanding of comparisons of human behaviour. As Miller and Bersoff argue, "A cultural perspective leads us to view helping behavior as part of a larger moral system binding individuals together in social relationships."[112] Thus such an approach may be useful in relationship to considered, habitual helping and prosocial behaviour more generally.

We need to explore in more detail two aspects of this matter: how the patterns of prosocial behaviour may differ among cultures, and the nature of the process by which culture may influence helping behaviour. In addition, we should examine the cultural factor more broadly and in a more elaborated way. We should consider not only social norms, but also sociopolitical background (elements such as civic participation), principles of social interaction (such as individualism versus collectivism), and possibly unique cultural climates (such as that of the Netherlands). All these issues should be explored intensively in the future. Finally, to relate this chapter to the focus of the volume, we note that our academic concern about the influence of culture on helping behaviour has a quite pragmatic implication: namely, how might we increase the altruistic orientation of human beings in general? We may be able to learn, by comparing and contrasting helping behaviours in different cultural contexts, the limitations and advantages of each culture in fostering helping behaviour.

Sam and Pearl Oliner have written extensively on the lessons to be learned from those who helped individuals and groups in the Holocaust.[113] In *The Altruistic Personality* they argued that they had discovered a personality trait – extensivity – that they believe more likely to be present in rescuers than in those who did not help. They define this concept as "the tendency to assume commitments and responsibilities toward diverse groups." Extensivity has two dimensions – attachment "which ranges from alienation or extreme detachment at one pole to love at the other," and inclusiveness "which ranges from exclusion of all others except the self at one pole to the inclusion of the universe at the other."[114] As a two-dimensional trait, extensivity thus can explain both why those who are highly "attached" and have great capability for altruistic behaviour could shut their doors in the face of supplicant Jews and why those who are intent on saving all humankind but are disconnected from real people may limit their options and become inured to the suffering of those around them.[115]

In their most recent book, the Oliners have offered eight lessons on how to improve people's helping behaviour.[116] All these could be thought of as cultural mechanisms. The eight lessons are intended to increase either attachment or inclusiveness. For attachment, the lessons include bonding, empathizing, learning caring norms, and practising care and assuming personal responsibility. For inclusiveness, the lessons involve diversifying, "networking," resolving conflicts, and "making the global connection." Looking at cultures that we have called individualist – Western cultures – we suggest improvements along the attachment dimension. The more collective cultures – the cultures of the East – may need to focus more on fostering inclusiveness.

In short, prosocial behaviour and altruism are found in all cultures. The forms they take vary from culture to culture. Furthermore, there are types of helping situations in which culture matters more and others in which it matters less. Future research needs to zero in on cultural institutions related to civil society; cultural practices, such as socialization; and cultural contents, such as normative injunctions. Only thus can we come to understand the wide variations in prosocial behaviour that we find across societies and across types of prosocial action.

NOTES

1 On membership in voluntary organizations, see J.E. Curtis, E.G. Grabb, and D.E. Baer, "Voluntary Association Membership in Fifteen Countries: A Comparative Analysis," *American Sociological Review* 57 (1992), 139. On volunteering, see A. Greeley, "The Other Civic America: Religion and Social Capital," *American Prospect* (1997), 68. On willingness to give to Third World countries, see J.-C. Ting, "Experience, Interest, Modeling, and Being Asked to Help: A Four Factor Model of International Helping," master's thesis, University of Wisconsin–Madison, 1992. On blood donation see K. Healy, "Embedded Altruism: Blood Collection Regimes and the European Union's Donor Population," *American Journal of Sociology* 105 (2000), 1633.

2 J.A. Piliavin, J.F. Dovidio, S. Gaertner, and R.D. Clark III, *Emergency Intervention* (New York: Academic Press, 1981), 4.

3 D.A. Schroeder, L.A. Penner, J.F. Dovidio, and J.A. Piliavin, *The Psychology of Helping and Altruism: Problems and Puzzles* (New York: McGraw-Hill, 1995), 16.

4 Ibid., 19–20.

5 See J.M. Darley and B. Latané, "Bystander Intervention in Emergencies: Diffusion of Responsibility," *Journal of Personality and Social Psychology* 8 (1969), 377–83, and *The Unresponsive Bystander: Why Doesn't He Help?* (New York: Appleton-Century-Crofts, 1970).

6 D. Sinha, "Community as Target: A New Perspective to Research on Prosocial Behavior," in E. Staub, D. Bar-Tal, J. Karylowski, and J. Reykowski, eds., *Development and Maintenance of Prosocial Behavior: International Perspectives on Positive Morality* (New York: Plenum), 445–56.

7 See, for example, D. Snyder and W. Ickes, "Personality and Social Behavior," in G. Lindzey and E. Aronson, eds., *Handbook of Social Psychology* (New York: Random House, 1985), 805–82.

8 Sinha, "Community as Target," 449.

9 R.E. Feldman, "Response to Compatriot and Foreigner Who Seek Assistance," *Journal of Personality and Social Psychology* 10(1968), 202. See also R.E. Feldman, "Honesty toward Compatriot and Foreigner: Field Experiments in Paris, Athens, and Boston," in W.W. Lambert and R. Weisbrod, eds., *Comparative Perspectives on Social Psychology* (Boston: Little Brown, 1967), 231–5.

10 For example, the urban–non-urban difference shows up only when the interaction involves strangers or neighbours; providing aid to family and friends does not seem to vary: see P. Amato, "Urban–Rural Differences in Helping Friends and Family Members," *Social Psychology Quarterly* 56 (1993), 249. In addition, "urban unhelpfulness" appears to relate to spontaneous and informal types of helping rather than to planned and formal versions of the behaviour: see P. Amato, "The Helpfulness of Urbanites and Small Town Dwellers: A Test between Two Broad Theoretical Positions," *Australian Journal of Psychology* 35(1983), 233.

11 See, among other things, Amato, "Urban–Rural Differences"; C. Korte, "Urban–Nonurban Differences in Social Behavior and Social Psychological Models of Urban Impact," *Journal of Social Issues* 36 (1980), 29; N. Steblay, "Helping Behavior in Rural and Urban Environments: A Meta-Analysis," *Psychological Bulletin* 102 (1987), 346.

12 See this argument advanced in L. Wirth, "Urbanism as a Way of Life," *American Journal of Sociology* 44 (1938), 1.

13 Y. Yousif and C. Korte, "Urbanization, Culture, and Helpfulness: Cross-Cultural Studies in England and the Sudan," *Journal of Cross-Cultural Psychology* 26 (1995), 476. The principal work reviewed here is S. Milgram, "The Experience of Living in Cities," *Science* 167 (1970), 1461; C. Korte and N. Ayvalioglu, "Helpfulness in Turkey: Cities, Towns and Urban Villages," *Journal of Cross-Cultural Psychology* 12 (1981), 123; C. Korte, I. Ypma, and A. Toppen, "Helpfulness in Dutch Society as a Function of Urbanization and Environmental Input Level," *Journal of Personality and Social Psychology* 32 (1975), 996; C. Fisher, *The Urban Experience* (New York: Harcourt Brace Jovanovich, 1984); J. House and S. Wolf, "Effects of Urban Residence on Interpersonal Trust and Helping Behavior," *Journal of Personality and Social Psychology* 36 (1978), 1029.

14 Yousif and Korte, "Urbanization," 476.

15 Festinger, Pepitone, and Newcomb introduced the concept of "deindividuation" to refer to a process in which antecedent social conditions lessen self-awareness and reduce concern with evaluation by others, thereby weakening restraints against the expression of undesirable behaviour.

One of those social conditions can be crowds in urban environments. See L. Festinger, A. Pepitone, and T. Newcomb, "Some Consequences of De-individuation in a Group," *Journal of Abnormal and Social Psychology* 47 (1952), 382. See also P. Zimbardo, "The Human Choice: Individuation, Reason, and Order Versus De-individuation, Impulse, and Chaos," in W. Arnold and D. Levine, eds., *Nebraska Symposium on Motivation* (Lincoln: University of Nebraska Press, 1969), 237–308.

16 See Milgram, "Living in Cities."

17 Steblay,"Helping Behaviour."

18 See Korte, Ypma, and Toppen, "Helpfulness in Dutch Society."

19 Yousif and Korte, "Urbanization," 476. This assertion draws on J. Abu-Loghod, "Migrant Adjustment to City Life: The Egyptian Case," *American Journal of Sociology* 67 (1961), 22, and P. Hauser, "Application of the Ideal-Type Constructs to the Metropolis in the Economically Less-Advanced Area," in P. Hauser and L. Schnore, eds., *The Study of Urbanization* (New York: John Wiley, 1965), 503–18.

20 P. Amato, "The Effects of Urbanization on Interpersonal Behavior: Field Studies in Papua New Guinea," *Journal of Cross-Cultural Psychology* 14 (1983), 353.

21 See Korte and Ayvalioglu, "Helpfulness in Turkey."

22 A. Hedge and Y.H. Yousif, "The Effect of Urban Size, Cost and Urgency on Helpfulness: A Cross-Cultural Comparison between the United Kingdom and the Sudan," *Journal of Cross-Cultural Psychology* 23 (1992), 114; Yousif and Korte, "Urbanization."

23 Yousif and Korte, "Urbanization," 476.

24 Sinha, "Community as Target."

25 See R.J. Taormina, D. Messick, S. Iwawaki, and H. Wilke, "Cross-cultural Perspectives on Foreign Aid Deservingness Decisions," *Journal of Cross-Cultural Psychology* 19 (1988), 387, and J.C. Ting, "Analyses on Euro-Barometer 28: Relations with Third World Countries and Energy Problems," unpublished ms., University of Wisconsin, Nov. 1987.

26 Schroeder et al., *The Psychology of Helping*, 133.

27 J. Piaget, *The Construction of Reality in the Child* (New York: Basic Books, 1954); L. Kohlberg, *The Psychology of Moral Development: Essays on Moral Development*, 2 vols. (San Francisco: Harper and Row, 1984).

28 C. Gilligan, *In a Different Voice: Psychological Theory and Women's Development* (Cambridge, Mass.: Harvard University Press, 1983).

29 K.S. Basinger, J.C. Gibbs, and D. Fuller, "Context and the Measurement of Moral Judgment," *International Journal of Behavioral Development*, forthcoming, 2000.

30 S. Thoma, "Estimating Gender Differences in the Comprehension and Preference of Moral Issues," *Developmental Review* 6 (1986), 165; L.J. Walker, "Sex Differences in Moral Reasoning," in W.M. Kurtines

and J.L. Gewirtz, eds., *Handbook of Moral Behavior and Development: Volume Two – Research* (Hillsdale, NJ: Erlbaum, 1991), 334–64.

31 J.C. Gibbs, K.S. Basinger, and R. Fuller, *Moral Maturity: Measuring the Development of Sociomoral Reflection* (Hillsdale, NJ: Erlbaum, 1992); L. Eckensberger, "Moralische Urteile als Handlungsleitende Normative Regelsysteme im Spiegel der Kulturvergleichenden Forschung" (Moral Judgments as Action-Orienting, Normative Rule Systems in the Mirror of Culture-Comparative Research), in A. Thomas, ed., *Kulturvergleichende Psychologie. Eine Einfuhrung* (Gottingen: Hogrefe, 1993), 259–95; C.P. Edwards, "The Comparative Study of the Development of Moral Judgment and Reasoning," in R.H. Munroe and B.B. Whiting, eds., *Handbook of Cross-Cultural Human Development* (New York: Garland, 1981), 501–28; U.P. Gielen and D.C. Markoulis, "Preference for Principled Moral Reasoning: A Developmental and Cross-Cultural Perspective," in L.L. Adler and U.P. Gielen, eds., *Cross-Cultural Topics in Psychology* (Westport, Conn.: Praeger, 1994), 73–87; J. Snarey, "The Cross-Cultural Universality of Social Moral Development: A Critical Review of Kohlbergian Research," *Psychological Bulletin* 97 (1985), 202 and 232.

32 G.S.H. Carlo, S.H. Koller, N. Eisenberg, M.S.D. Silva, and C.B. Frohlich, "Cross-National Study on the Relations among Prosocial Moral Reasoning, Gender Role Orientations, and Prosocial Behaviors" *Developmental Psychology* 32(1996), 231.

33 Carlo et al., "Cross-National Study," 238–9. Similarly, based on the moral reflection measure–short form (SRM–SF) developed by Basinger et al, "Moral Judgment," another study found that: (a) the SRM–SF could provide reliable and valid estimates for the development of moral judgment in Italian adolescents and adults; (b) there were no significant gender differences; (c) cultural differences between northern and southern Italy did not affect the results; (d) the age differences were like those in American samples; and (e) in general, their results indicated that moral reasoning is cross-culturally very similar, both within Italy and between Italy and the United States: A.L. Comunian and U.P. Gielen, "Moral Reasoning and Prosocial Action in Italian Culture," *Journal of Social Psychology* 135 (1995), 704.

34 For varieties of this critique see Comunian and Gielen, "Moral Reasoning," 700; A.L. Comunian and G. Antoni, "Il Sociomoral Reflection Measure–Short Form: Uno strumento per la misurazione del ragionamento morale" (The Sociomoral Reflection Measure-Short Form: An Instrument for the Measurement of Moral Reasoning), *Bollettino di Psicologia Applicata* 25 (1993), 25; U.P. Gielen, R.A. Ahmed, and J. Avellani, "Perceptions of Parental Behavior and the Development of Moral Reasoning in Students from Kuwait," *Moral Education Forum* 17 (1992), 20; A. Colby et al., *The Measurement of Moral Judgement: Volume 2 –*

Standard Issue Scoring Manual (Cambridge: Cambridge University Press, 1987).

35 See Comunian and Gielen, "Moral Reasoning," 700. Also reviewed here are A. Colby and L. Kohlberg, *The Measurement of Moral Development: Volume 1 – Theoretical Foundations and Research Validation* (Cambridge: Cambridge University Press, 1987); M.G. Mason and J.C. Gibbs, "Role Taking Opportunities and the Transition to Advanced Moral Judgment," *Moral Education Forum* 18 (1993), 3, and "Social Perspective Taking and Moral Judgment among College Students," *Journal of Adolescent Research* 8 (1993), 103; U.P. Gielen, A.L. Comunian, and G. Antoni, "An Italian Cross-Sectional Study of Gibb's Sociomoral Reflection Measure–Short Form," in A.L. Comunian and U.P. Gielen, eds., *Advancing Psychology and Its Applications: International Perspectives* (Milan: FrancoAngeli, 1994), 125–34. M. Hollos's unpublished data also show that isolated Lapp children, who have few playmates, were delayed in their development of conventional morality relative to Norwegian city children.

36 N. Eisenberg and P.H. Mussen, *The Roots of Prosocial Behavior in Children* (New York: Cambridge University Press, 1989), 53–4. For other work on which these conclusions are based, see N. Eisenberg, *Altruistic Emotion, Cognition and Behavior* (Hillsdale, NJ: Erlbaum, 1986); N. Eisenberg, K. Boehnke, P. Schuhler, and R.K. Silbereisen, "The Development of Prosocial Behavior and Cognitions in German Children," *Journal of Cross-Cultural Psychology* 16 (1985), 69; I. Fuchs, N. Eisenberg, R. Hertz-Lazarowitz, and R. Sharabany, "Kibbutz, Israeli City, and American Children's Moral Reasoning about Prosocial Moral Conflicts," *Merrill-Palmer Quarterly* 32 (1986), 37.

37 R. Ibusuki and T. Natio, "Influence of Interpersonal Relationships on Helping Norms among Japanese University Students," *Psychological Reports* 68 (1991), 1119.

38 T. Natio, "A Survey of Research on Moral Development in Japan," *Cross-Cultural Research* 28 (1994), 44–5. See also, in particular, T. Natio, R. Ibusuki, and W. Lin, "Interpersonal Relations and Helping Norms among University Students of Japan, Taiwan, and Korea," *Psychological Reports* 69 (1991), 1044, and N. Iwasa, "Post-Conventional Reasoning as a Basis for Moral Education: A Japan–United States Comparison," paper presented at the 15th Annual Conference of the Association of Moral Education, University of Notre Dame, Notre Dame, Indiana.

39 Note again here the apparent influence of a "strong situation": see Snyder and Ickes, "Personality and Social Behavior."

40 J.G. Miller, D.M. Bersoff, and R.L. Harwood, "Perceptions of Social Responsibilities in India and the United States: Moral Imperatives or Personal Decision," *Journal of Personality and Social Psychology* 58 (1990), 33.

41 J.G. Miller, "Cultural Diversity in the Morality of Caring: Individually Oriented Versus Duty-Based Interpersonal Moral Codes," *Cross-Cultural Research* 28 (1994), 3.

42 M. Mead, *Sex and Temperament in Three Primitive Societies* (New York: Morrow, 1935), 191.

43 C.M. Turnbull, *The Mountain People* (New York: Simon & Schuster, 1972).

44 C.A. Robarchek and C.J. Robarchek, "Cultures of War and Peace: A Comparative Study of Waorani and Semai," in J. Silverberg and J.P. Gray, eds., *Aggression and Peacefulness in Humans and Other Primates* (New York: Oxford University Press, 1992), 189–213.

45 See N.B. Graves and T.D. Graves, "The Cultural Context of Prosocial Development: An Ecological Model," in D.L. Bridgeman, ed., *The Nature of Prosocial Development* (New York: Academic Press, 1983), 243–64 (re the Polynesian people on the island of Aitutaki); R.P. Rohner, *They Love Me, They Love Me Not* (New Haven, Conn.: HRAF Press, 1975) (on the Papago Indians in Arizona); A. Tietjen, "Prosocial Reasoning among Children and Adults in a Papua New Guinea Society," *Developmental Psychology* 22 (1986), 861 (about the Maisin in Papua–New Guinea); U. Bronfenbrenner, *Two Worlds of Childhood: U.S. and U.S.S.R* (New York: Russell Sage Foundation, 1970).

46 B.M. Whiting and J.W. Whiting, *Children of Six Countries: A Psychological Analysis* (Cambridge, Mass.: Harvard University Press, 1975). See also B.B. Whiting and C.P. Edwards, *Children of Different Worlds: The Foundation of Social Behavior* (Cambridge, Mass.: Harvard University Press, 1988).

47 E.C. Devereux et al., "Socialization Practices of Parents, Teachers and Peers in Israel: The Kibbutz versus the City," *Child Development* 45 (1974), 269; A. Nadler, E. Romek, and A. Shapiro-Friedman, "Giving in the Kibbutz: Pro-Social Behavior of City and Kibbutz Children as Affected by Social Responsibility and Social Pressure," *Journal of Cross-Cultural Psychology* 10 (1979), 57.

48 H.W. Stevenson, "The Development of Prosocial Behavior in Large-Scale Collective Societies: China and Japan," in R.A. Hinde and J. Groebel, eds., *Cooperation and Prosocial Behavior* (New York: Cambridge University Press, 1991) 89–105. Stevenson also draws quite extensively on Ho's work: see D.Y.F. Ho, "Traditional Patterns of Socialization in Chinese Society," *Acta Psychologica Taiwanica* 23 (1981), 81, and "Chinese Patterns of Socialization: A Critical Review," in M.H. Bond, ed., *The Psychology of the Chinese People* (Hong Kong: Oxford University Press, 1986), 1–3.

49 Stevenson, "The Development of Prosocial Behavior," 90.

50 Ibid., 92.

51 Ibid., 103–4.

52 G. Hofstede, *Culture's Consequences* (Beverly Hills, Calif: Sage, 1980).

53 F.M. Moghaddan, D.M. Taylor, and S.C. Wright, *Social Psychology in Cross-Cultural Perspective* (New York: W.H. Freeman and Company, 1993). See especially 117–8: "Children from kibbutzim continued to cooperate and help each other on a task, even when individual achievement was rewarded. However, children raised in cities in Europe, America, and even Israel tended to compete in ineffective and maladaptive ways." The authors draw here also on other work: see especially Devereaux, "Socialization Practices," and A. Nadler, "Help Seeking as a Cultural Phenomenon: Differences between City and Kibbutz Dwellers," *Journal of Personality and Social Psychology* 51 (1986), 976; L. Mann, "Cross-Cultural Studies in Small Groups," in H.C. Triandis and R.W. Brislin, eds., *Handbook of Cross-Cultural Psychology: Volume 5 – Social Psychology* (Boston: Allyn and Bacon, 1980), 155–210.

54 D.G. Perry and K. Bussey, *Social Development* (Englewood Cliffs, NJ: Prentice Hall, 1984), 234. See also P.B. Smith and M.H. Bond, *Social Psychology across Cultures: Analysis and Perspectives* (London: Harvester Wheatsheaf, 1993), especially 70–1.

55 See especially L.C. Huang and M.B. Harris, "Conformity in Chinese and Americans: A Field Experiment," *Journal of Cross-Cultural Psychology* 4 (1973), 427. This work and others were influenced by F.L.K. Hsu, *American and Chinese: Passage to Differences* (Honolulu: University of Hawaii Press, 1970).

56 See also J.M. Innes, "The Semantics of Asking a Favor: An Attempt to Replicate Cross-Culturally," *International Journal of Psychology* 9 (1974), 57, and J.M. Innes and S. Gilroy, "The Semantics of Asking a Favor: Asking for Help in Three Countries," *The Journal of Social Psychology* 110 (1980), 3.

57 W.B.G. Liebrand and G.J. Van Run, "The Effects of Social Motives on Behavior in Social Dilemmas in Two Cultures," *Journal of Experimental Social Psychology* 21 (1985), 86.

58 Stevenson, "The Development of Prosocial Behavior," 103–4.

59 M.H. Bond, *Beyond the Chinese Face* (Hong Kong: Oxford University Press, 1991), 48.

60 K.-K. Hwang, "Face and Favor: The Chinese Power Game," *American Journal of Sociology* 29 (1987), 944.

61 A. L'Armand and A. Pepitone, "Helping to Reward Another Person: A Cross-Cultural Analysis," *Journal of Personality and Social Psychology* 31 (1975), 189.

62 K. Leung and M.H. Bond, "The Impact of Cultural Collectivism on Reward Allocation," *Journal of Personality and Social Psychology* 47 (1988), 793.

63 F.M. Moghaddam, *Social Psychology: Exploring Universals across Cultures* (New York: W.H. Freeman and Company, 1998), 315.

64 See, for example, H.C. Triandis, *The Analysis of Subjective Culture* (New York: Wiley, 1972). See also a recent study comparing college students from Australia, Egypt, Korea, Taiwan, the United States, and Yugoslavia, on a measure of past helping behaviour directed towards strangers, acquaintances, and co-workers. Scores are significantly higher in a small town U.S. sample than in an urban U.S. sample and in all the other countries. The South Korean and Taiwanese samples report the least past helping and are significantly different from the Australian, Egyptian, urban U.S. (Honolulu), and Yugoslavian samples, which do not differ from each other. The scale has a number of problems (for example, a large number of items refer to incidents involving automobiles, where opportunities to engage in the behaviour may differ across societies). However, as the authors point out, such problems would suggest that Egypt would be lowest on the scale, and it is not: R.C. Johnson, G.P. Danko, et al., "Cross-Cultural Assessment of Altruism and its Correlates," *Personality and Individual Differences* 10 (1989), 855.

65 H.C. Triandis, *Culture and Social Behavior* (New York: McGraw-Hill, 1994), 221.

66 A.O. Hirschman, *Getting Ahead Collectively: Grassroots Experiences in Latin America* (New York: Pergamon Press, 1984).

67 Moghaddam, *Social Psychology*, 320.

68 The design of the study involved two conditions: in one, the amount of money for all recipients was presented as being reduced, while in the other it was being augmented. The pattern of distribution differed as a function of this distinction.

69 V. Murphy-Bermank, P. Singh, A. Pachauri, and P. Kumar, "Factors Affecting Allocation to Needy and Meritorious Recipients: A Cross-Cultural Comparison," *Interpersonal Relations and Group Processes* 46 (1984), 1267.

70 Ibid., 1270.

71 Moghaddam, *Social Psychology*, 317. The work that he is reviewing includes principally M.A.C. Castro, "Reactions to Receiving Aid as a Function of Cost to Donor and Opportunity to Aid," *Journal of Applied Social Psychology* 4 (1974), 194; M.S. Clark, C.C. Gotay, and J. Mills, "Acceptance of Help as a Function of Similarity of the Potential Helper and Opportunity to Repay," *Journal of Applied Social Psychology* 4 (1974), 224; K.J. Gergen, S.J. Morse, and K.A. Bode, "Overpaid or Overworked? Cognitive and Behavioral Reactions to Inequitable Rewards," *Journal of Applied Social Psychology* 4 (1974), 259; E. Searcy and N. Eisenberg, "Defensiveness in Response to Aid from a Sibling," *Journal of Personality and Social Psychology* 62 (1992), 422.

72 M.M. Yang, *Gifts, Favors, and Banquets: The Art of Social Relationships in China* (Ithaca, NY: Cornell University Press, 1994), 6.

73 Moghaddam, *Social Psychology*, 318. For a similar finding for other countries that have undergone profound change, see F.M. Moghaddam and D. Crystal, "Reductions, Samurai, and Revolutions: The Paradoxes of Change and Continuity in Iran and Japan," *Journal of Political Psychology* 18 (1977), 355.

74 Contrast this with the Western conception, which assumes altruism to be associated with personality functioning. That is, we speak of altruistic or non-altruistic individuals.

75 D.Y-F. Ho and C-Y. Chiu, "Component Ideas of Individualism, Collectivism, and Social Organization: An Application in the Study of Chinese Culture," in U. Kim, H.C. Triandis, C, Kagitcibasi, S-C. Choi, and G. Yoon, eds., *Individualism and Collectivism* (London: Sage, 1994), 155.

76 See A. Wolfe, *Whose Keeper? Social Science and Moral Obligation* (Berkeley, Calif.: University of California Press, 1989), 16.

77 Ibid., 20.

78 Ibid., 17.

79 R. Putnam, "Bowling Alone: America's Declining Social Capital," *Journal of Democracy* 6 (1995), 66.

80 A. de Toqueville, *Democracy in America* (New York: Knopf, 1961); R.N. Bellah, R. Madsen, W.M. Sullivan, A. Swidler, and S.M. Tipton, *Habits of the Heart: Individualism and Commitment in American Life* (New York: Harper & Row, 1985). Note also Weber's description of the United States as "the association-land par excellence": M. Weber, "Deutscher Sociologentag" (German Sociology Today) *Verhandlungen* 1 (1911), 53.

81 Toqueville, *Democracy in America*, 141.

82 J. Curtis, R. Lambert, S. Brown, and B. Kay, "Affiliating with Voluntary Associations: Canadian–American Comparisons" *Canadian Journal of Sociology* 14 (1989), 143.

83 D.C. Swift, *Religion and the American Experience* (New York: M.E. Sharpe, 1998). See also Bellah et al., *Habits of the Heart.*

84 Swift argues that "the serious deterioration of community and excessive emphasis upon individualism probably began with the market revolution in the early nineteenth century; these tendencies were accelerated by subjecting much of life to the demands of the marketplace. The tendencies toward egoism and diminished community are inherent in classical liberal thought; the market revolution unleashed them and accelerated their growth. Bellah and his associates correctly indicate that the resolution of these problems lies in large measure in strengthening the culture's ties to its two taproots, Jeffersonian political thought and the nation's religious heritage. It is argued that devotion to the nation's religious heritage and Jeffersonian egalitarianism can diminish human antagonisms and serve as a basis for community and a sense of mutual

responsibility. Without these, there can be no long-term sociopolitical order or economic productivity." Swift, *Religion and the American Experience,* 289.

85 The so-called neo-Tocquevilleans have focused on how to increase civic engagement for American citizens or in general for democratic systems. Their answer has been to increase participation in voluntary associations: see Bellah et al., *Habits of the Heart*; J.S. Coleman, "Social Capital in the Creation of Human Capital," *American Journal of Sociology* 94 (1988), 95; R. Putnam, "The Prosperous Community: Social Capital and Public Life," *The American Prospect* 13 (1993), 35. This suggestion stems from the conviction that "[t]he norms and networks of civic engagement also powerfully affect the performance of representative government": Putnam, "Bowling Alone," 66.

86 J.E. Curtis, "Voluntary Association Joining: A Cross-National Comparative Note," *American Sociological Review* 36 (1971), 872.

87 An exception is Curtis et al., "Affiliating with Voluntary Associations," which used national samples from the United States, Canada, and several other countries.

88 The table is from G.A. Almond and S. Verba, *The Civic Culture* (Princeton, NJ: Princeton University Press, 1963), 320.

89 See Curtis et al., "Voluntary Association."

90 See ibid. for both these points.

91 It has been suggested that the comparatively high U.S. levels of membership in religious organizations probably result in part from extensive sectarianism, which may in turn cause "the comparatively aggressive 'marketing' of religion": see Curtis et al., "Voluntary Association,"145. The argument is drawn from R.W. Bibby, *Fragmented Gods: The Poverty and Potential of Religion in Canada* (Toronto: Irwin, 1987), 218–9.

92 Curtis et al., "Voluntary Association," 139–40.

93 This is suggested by ibid., 149. J. Grube and J.A. Piliavin, "Role Identity, Organizational Experiences, and Volunteer Performance," *Personality and Social Psychology Bulletin* (2000), 1108, report considerable conflict on the part of volunteers between their obligations to the various charities for which they work. They may solve these conflicts by giving just a little time to each of many organizations.

94 They draw here on A.M. Rose, *Theory and Method in the Social Sciences* (Minneapolis: University of Minnesota Press, 1954), 98–103.

95 Curtis et al., "Voluntary Association," 149–50.

96 See Schroeder et al., *The Psychology of Helping.*

97 See E.G. Clary and M. Snyder, "Functional Analysis of Altruism and Prosocial Behavior: The Case of Volunteerism," in M.S. Clark, ed., *Prosocial Behavior* (Newbury Park, Calif.: Sage Publications, 1991), 119–38. See also E.G. Clary et al., "Understanding and Assessing the Motivations

of Volunteers: A Functional Approach," *Journal of Personality and Social Psychology* 74 (1998), 1516.

98 J. Wilson and M. Musick, "Who Cares? Toward an Integrated Theory of Volunteer Work," *American Sociological Review* 62 (1997), 694.

99 Greeley, "The Other Civic America," 70.

100 Ibid., 71.

101 Ibid., 71.

102 Ibid., 73.

103 Healy, "Embedded Altruism."

104 See J.A. Piliavin, "Why Do They Give the Gift of Life? A Review of Research on Blood Donors since Oswalt (1977)," *Transfusion* 30 (1990), 444, and J.A. Piliavin and P.C. Callero, *Giving Blood: The Development of an Altruistic Identity* (Baltimore, Md.: Johns Hopkins University Press, 1991).

105 Healy, "Embedded Altruism," 24–5.

106 Seymour Martin Lipset presents these ideas variously in *The First New Nation* (New York: Basic Books, 1963); "Canada and the United States: A Comparative View," *Canadian Review of Sociology and Anthropology* 1 (1964), 173; *Revolution and Counterrevolution* (New York: Basic Books, 1968); "Canada and the United States: The Cultural Dimension," in C.F. Doran and J.H. Sigler, eds., *Canada and the United States* (Engelwood Cliffs, NJ: Prentice-Hall, 1985), 109–10; "Historical Traditions and National Characteristics: A Comparative Analysis of Canada and the United States," *Canadian Journal of Sociology* 11 (1986), 113; and *Continental Divide: The Values and Institutions of Canada and the United States* (New York: Routledge, 1990).

107 Lipset, "Canada and the United States," 141. This great attachment to British traditions is also said to characterize Australia: see Lipset, *The First New Nation*, chap. 7.

108 Every two years since 1987 the organization Independent Sector has done a survey in the United States asking about donation and volunteer behaviour. Statistics Canada carried out similar surveys in 1987 and 1997. We do not have access to the 1997 U.S. survey, so we are comparing the U.S. results from 1995 with the Canadian data for 1997. However, the variation among the 1987, 1989, 1991, 1993, and 1995 U.S. figures is not very large, and we have no *a priori* reason to believe that there have been major changes since 1995.

109 For example, the Canadian sample begins with age 15, the U.S. sample at 18. Also, the U.S. survey sampled households and asked about contributions by household, although the analysis then breaks respondents down by individual characteristics. The Canadian publication does not indicate how sampling was done. The U.S. reports break down donation by race (72.6 per cent of whites donated to charities,

as compared to 51.8 per cent of non-whites), but the Canadian surveys do not do this.

110 The differences, however, are smaller than in prior years.

111 Darley and Latané, *The Unresponsive Bystander*, 20–1.

112 J.G. Miller and D.M. Bersoff, "Cultural Influences on the Moral Status of Reciprocity and the Discounting of Endogenous Motivation," *Personality and Social Psychology Bulletin* 20 (1994), 592.

113 S.P. Oliner and P.M. Oliner, *The Altruistic Personality: Rescuers of Jews in Nazi Europe* (New York: Free Press, 1988); S.P. Oliner, "Introduction: Part Six," in P.M. Oliner, S.P. Oliner, L. Baron, L.A. Blum, D.L. Krebs, and M. Zuzanna Smolenska, eds., *Embracing the Other: Philosophical, Psychological, and Historical Perspectives on Altruism* (New York: New York University Press, 1992), 363–8.

114 Oliner, *The Altruistic Personality*, 373.

115 See the examples given in Oliner, "Introduction," 374.

116 P.M. Oliner and S.P. Oliner, *Toward a Caring Society: Ideas into Action* (Westport, Conn.: Praeger, 1995).

4 Altruism in Philosophical and Ethical Traditions: Two Views

WILL KYMLICKA

In his novel *Tom Jones,* written in 1749, Henry Fielding observes that

> the world are in general divided into two opinions concerning charity, which are the very reverse of each other. One party seems to hold that all acts of this kind are to be esteemed as voluntary gifts, and however little you give (if indeed no more than your good wishes), you acquire a great degree of merit in so doing. Others, on the contrary, appear to be as firmly persuaded, that beneficence is a positive duty, and that whenever the rich fall greatly short of their ability in relieving the distresses of the poor, their pitiful largesses are so far from being meritorious that they have only performed their duty by halves, and are in some sense more contemptible than those who have entirely neglected it. To reconcile these different opinions is not in my power. I shall only add that the givers are generally of the former sentiment, and the receivers are almost universally inclined to the latter.[1]

Two hundred and fifty years later, I think that we can observe the same basic division of attitudes. Like Fielding, I make no attempt here to reconcile these competing views. What I try to do instead is to describe some of their philosophical roots and assumptions.

Fielding suggests that these two attitudes towards charity are rooted in self-interest and social position: rich people favout the view that charity is a praiseworthy voluntary gift; poor people tend to see charity as an obligatory duty. There is no doubt some truth in this (rather uncharitable) observation about human nature. But from a philosophical point of view, the situation is more complicated. The historical roots of these two views lie not so much in self-interest and social position as in competing moral and religious traditions and worldviews. To oversimplify, I suggest that the former view is rooted in older religious conceptions of ethical virtue, and the latter in modern secular conceptions of justice.

I first explore the relationship between charity and justice in modern secular theories of justice. I try to show that most modern theories of justice tend to subsume charity under a broader conception of our obligations of justice and to cast doubt on the value of charitable acts that are not subsumable under the requirements of justice. Second, I examine older religious traditions – specifically the three monotheistic religions (Judaism, Christianity, Islam) – which more clearly distinguish charity from justice and attribute to it a value and purpose quite separate from that of justice. In the process, I hope to explore the question of how, or whether, charity can be seen as a moral virtue and/or as a moral obligation in a modern secular society.

One terminological point. My main focus here is on charity in the form of donating property (typically money), rather than, for example, volunteering time or physically assisting the injured. Moreover, not all financial donations constitute acts of "charity." We give gifts and offer help to friends, family, colleagues, neighbours, and others with whom we have face-to-face relationships. We also give donations to organizations that reflect and promote our own particular identity or way of life, such as organizations that promote our preferred form of leisure (for instance, opera, gardening clubs) or our ethnocultural heritage (folk-dancing) or religious creed (proselytizing missionaries) or that speak out for our preferred causes (the gun lobby). We can call these "philanthropy," as distinct from charity more narrowly conceived.[2] Some of these philanthropic gifts are defined as "charity" for the purposes of the law, but they are not my interest here. My concern rather, like Fielding, is with donations to anonymous others in need. In several places I extend the discussion to examine these broader forms of altruism, but to keep the topic manageable, I focus on the narrower issue of donating resources to anonymous others in need.

CHARITY AND MODERN THEORIES OF JUSTICE

Very few modern political theorists discuss the idea of charity, which has been almost totally eclipsed by the idea of justice. As Douglas Den Uyl puts it, "While the virtue of charity may still be alive among private individuals, it is moribund among theoreticians."[3] This is not an accidental oversight, but rather stems from the very logic of modern political thought.

Most pre-modern societies saw political and economic inequalities as "natural." Some people were by nature fit to govern, and others, to be ruled; some people were by nature fit to own land and other forms of wealth, and others, to be slaves, serfs, or labourers. People were born into these preordained social strata or "estates," and the inequalities between them were seen as natural, and hence in no need of moral justification.

Moderns, by contrast, see people as by nature "free and equal": no one is born with the right to rule over others, or to command the labour of others, or to claim an unequal share of the world's resources. Any political and economic inequalities are the result of social rules and conventions regarding the acquisition and transfer of property or the acquisition of political authority. We know that these rules and conventions vary from place to place and from time to time, rather than being natural or God-given, and that different systems of social conventions lead to different distributions of political power and economic resources.

As a result, the first task of modern political theory is to choose among competing sets of social rules and conventions, each with its own resulting pattern of distribution. And this choice must then be justified to citizens – in particular, to those who are less well off than they would be under some other set of social rules. We need to be able to explain why people – who are born free and equal – should accept a set of social rules and conventions that put them in a position of economic or political inequality.

What sort of a justification could this be? The answer, for most modern political theorists, is a theory of *justice* or fairness. We need to explain why the preferred set of social conventions, and its resulting distribution of economic resources and political power, is fairer than alternative sets of conventions. Of course, this just pushes the problem back a level: what sort of justification could there be for saying that the distribution that results from one particular set of rules is fairer than another? Perhaps the most common and most obvious way to explain the fairness of a set of rules or conventions is to say that the inequalities that it produces are the result of people's own choices and decisions. Where inequalities are traceable back to people's own choices, then those who have more can be said to deserve or merit their advantages, and those who have less can be said to be responsible for their status.

Some such idea underlies the prevailing justification for economic distribution in our society, which is based on the idea of "equality of opportunity." According to this standard view, inequalities of income and prestige and so on are fair if and only if there was fair competition in the awarding of the offices and positions that yield those benefits. It's acceptable to pay someone $100,000 when the national average is $20,000 if there was fair equality of opportunity – that is, if no one was disadvantaged by race, or sex, or social background. This seems fair to many people in our society because it ensures that individuals' fates are determined by their choices, rather than by their circumstances. If I am pursuing some personal ambition in a society that has equality of opportunity, then my success or failure will be determined by my performance, not by my race or class or sex. If I fail, it will not be because I happened to be born into the "wrong" group. Our fate should not be privileged or disadvantaged by such morally arbitrary factors as the racial or ethnic group into which we were born. In a society where no one is disadvantaged by social circumstances, then peoples' fate is in their own hands. Success (or failure) will be the result of their own choices and efforts. Hence whatever success they achieve is "earned," rather than merely endowed. In a society that has equality of opportunity, unequal income is fair because success is "merited" – it goes to those who "deserve" it.

People disagree about what is needed to ensure equality of opportunity. Some believe that legal non-discrimination in education and employment is sufficient. Others argue that affirmative action is required for economically and culturally disadvantaged groups, if their members are to have a genuinely equal opportunity to acquire the qualifications necessary for economic success. But the central motivating idea in each case is this: it is fair for individuals to have unequal shares of social goods if those inequalities are earned and deserved by the individual – that is, if they are the product of the individual's actions and choices. But it is unfair for individuals to be disadvantaged or privileged by arbitrary and undeserved differences in their social circumstances.

Surveys show that most citizens in Canada, and in Western democracies generally, find this an attractive view of justice.[4] Partly for that reason, many theorists of justice take it as their starting point. However, most have found a deep problem inherent in this view, for it ignores another source of undeserved inequality. It is true that social inequalities are undeserved, and hence it is unfair for that undeserved inequality to affect a person's fate. But the same thing can be said about inequalities in natural endowments. No one deserves to be born handicapped, or with an IQ of 140, any more than they deserve to be born into a certain class or sex or race. If it is unjust for the latter factors to influence people's fate, then it is unclear why the influence of the former factors is any more justifiable. The injustice in each case is the same – distributive shares should not be influenced by factors that are arbitrary from the moral point of view. Natural endowments and social circumstances are both matters of brute luck, and people's moral claims should not depend on brute luck.

For this reason, many political theorists argue that, as John Rawls puts it, the prevailing ideal of equality of opportunity is "unstable," for "once we are troubled by the influence of either social contingencies or natural chance on the determination of distributive shares, we are bound, on reflection, to be bothered by the influence of the other. From a moral standpoint the two seem to be equally arbitrary."[5] In fact, Ronald Dworkin says that the undeserved character of natural assets makes the prevailing view not so much unstable as "fraudulent."[6] The prevailing view suggests that removing social inequalities gives each person an equal opportunity to acquire social benefits and hence suggests that any differences in income between individuals are earned, the product of people's effort or choices. But those with natural handicaps do not have an equal opportunity to acquire social benefits, and their lack of success has nothing to do with their choices or effort. If we are genuinely interested in removing undeserved inequalities, then the prevailing view of equality of opportunity is inadequate.

The attractive idea at the base of the prevailing view is that people's *choices* – the decisions they make about how to lead their lives – should determine their fate, not the *circumstances* in which they happen to find themselves. But the prevailing view recognizes only differences in social circumstances, while ignoring differences in natural talents (or treating them as if they were one of our choices). This is an arbitrary limit on the application of its own central intuition.

Faced with this "instability" in our everyday views of justice, we have two choices. To put it crudely, we can move to the left, or we can move to the right. The left-wing option is to adopt a stronger form of egalitarianism, which seeks to eliminate *all* forms of involuntary disadvantage, including those that result from differences in natural talents. This is often called the left-liberal or "liberal egalitarian" view of justice. The right-wing option is to reject the initial premise that involuntary disadvantages as such are unfair, even if they are the result of social class, race, or gender. This is the right-liberal or "libertarian" view of justice.

Which of these two options we take will profoundly influence our idea of charity. Let me start with the left-liberal view, which claims that all involuntary inequalities, whether the result of social position or natural talents, are unjust.[7] Such a theory does not seek to eliminate *chosen* inequalities. It allows and expects that individuals will make different choices regarding the trade-off between work and leisure, for example, or regarding the trade-off between current consumption and long-term savings. If one person (call her Saver) chooses to forgo current consumption in order to save for old age, she will have more resources later in life than someone (call him Spender) who consumes more now and saves less for the future. But this inequality is not unjust, according to the left-liberal view, since it simply reflects the differing preferences among individuals about how to lead their lives. Similarity, legitimate inequalities can arise as a result of people's voluntary choices about the trade-off between work and leisure or about whether or when to engage in risks.

All of these choices may lead to inequality over time, but if they are made under conditions of equal circumstances, then they are not unjust, according to the left-liberal view. To simplify things, imagine that Saver and Spender have comparable talents and social background – so that their circumstances are similar – but they make differing choices about consumption and savings. The resulting inequalities are not unjust, it is argued, because both people had the same options to either save or consume, and both chose the option that they preferred.

The same would apply to differing choices between work and leisure. Imagine two people who have the same option of working full-time or part-time, and one prefers to work full-time, acquiring greater income with less leisure, while the other prefers to work part-time, acquiring greater leisure with less income. Perhaps one wants to buy an expensive house and so chooses to work full-time, whereas the other wishes to develop a time-consuming but inexpensive hobby and so chooses to work part-time. Since both chose the option they preferred, the inequalities in income that arise are not illegitimate.

A preference for current consumption or for leisure is an example of what is often called "an expensive taste" – i.e., to satisfy it leaves one little resources for other goals in life. There is nothing wrong with expensive tastes, of course, but people must be willing to pay for the costs of these choices. Assuming that both people had the same option, then to tax Saver to support Spender, or to tax the full-time worker to support the part-time worker, would be unfair. Rawls observes:

> [A]s moral persons citizens have some part in forming and cultivating their final ends and preferences. It is not by itself an objection to the [theory] that it does not accommodate those with expensive tastes. One must argue in addition that it is unreasonable, if not unjust, to hold such persons responsible for their preferences and to require them to make out as best they can. But to

argue this seems to presuppose that citizens' preferences are beyond their control as propensities or cravings which simply happen. Citizens seem to be regarded as passive carriers of desires. [The left-liberal theory of justice,] however, relies on a capacity to assume responsibility for our ends. This capacity is part of the moral power to form, to revise, and rationally to pursue a conception of the good. Thus, in the case we are discussing, it is public knowledge that the principles of justice view citizens as responsible for their ends. In any particular situation, then, those with less expensive tastes have presumably adjusted their likes and dislikes over the course of their lives to the income and wealth they could reasonably expect; and it is regarded as unfair that they now should have less in order to spare others from the consequences of their lack of foresight or self-discipline.[8]

As Rawls emphasizes, this view of justice rests on certain strong assumptions about people's capacity to form, reflect on, and adapt their plans of life. It assumes not only that people are capable of making such choices but that they value having these choices. Neither Spender nor Saver would have preferred to live in a society in which there was a single rate of savings that was imposed on all individuals, regardless of their own beliefs about the good life. Both value the facts that they can make their own choices about when to save and when to consume and that society views them as responsible agents capable of making these choices. Similarly, neither the full- nor the part-time worker would have preferred to live in a society in which there was a single rate of work imposed on all individuals, regardless of their plans of life. They both value their right to work more or less, so as to achieve their aims regarding consumption or leisure. This conception of individuals as responsible agents is indeed what makes this theory a *liberal* form of egalitarianism.[9]

This is a (simplified) sketch of the liberal-egalitarian conception of justice. It combines a strong commitment to eliminating unchosen disadvantages (i.e., distributions should equalize circumstances) with an equally strong commitment to respect inequalities that result from people's choices about the good life (i.e., distributions should reflect people's differing ambitions in life). Under such a theory, the only legitimate inequalities are those that are genuinely "earned" or "merited," since they reflect the differing choices that responsible adults make about effort, savings, and risk. These sorts of inequalities can be justified even to those who are less well off, since they are the result of people's own choices, for which they are responsible, and since people value having these choices.

What role, if any, can charity play in such a conception? At first glance, one might think that charity will play a key role. After all, we are very far from a just society as conceived by a left-liberal theory of justice. Some of our institutions make a half-hearted attempt to eliminate involuntary disadvantages; this is clearest in the case of health care and primary and secondary education. But in general, our existing institutions make little attempt to eliminate involuntary disadvantage, and so it can be only through voluntary charity that we can come closer to achieving justice. If justice is to be achieved in a world where institutions ignore or even create unjust inequalities, it can be only through the voluntary actions of individuals. This theory, then, provides a powerful motive for people in our society, with its numerous and myriad forms of involuntary disadvantage, to engage in charity.

Yet in another sense, charity plays only a very secondary and derivative role in the left-liberal theory. At best, it is a second-best response to injustice. The main obligation is to change institutions so that they treat people justly, rather than trying to rectify institutional injustice through private alms. This is partly a matter of efficiency: private charity is likely to be patchwork and unreliable, helping those who are near to hand or those who belong to religious or ethnic groups with strong systems of mutual aid, while ignoring others entirely. Moreover, certain norms of justice require institutional co-ordinating mechanisms that may not exist in the case of private charity. As John Stuart Mill puts it, to focus on charity is to make "the great error of reformers and philanthropists ... to nibble at the consequences of unjust power, instead of redressing the injustice itself."[10]

But efficiency is not the only objection to private charity. The main problem, rather, is that justice is a pre-condition for the legitimacy of public institutions. Since no one can claim the right by nature to command the resources or liberty of others, public institutions cannot legitimately claim authority over citizens unless they can justify their rules and conventions to all those subject to them. If institutions ignore or create injustices, then individuals have no moral obligation to comply with those institutions.

This is why the main goal of a left-liberal theory is to identify the appropriate set of social procedures and institutions for distributing (or redistributing) resources. In a well-functioning society, principles of fairness are implemented by the operation of collective institutions, in particular by social policy and the welfare state. Justice, in other words, is a requirement for the legitimacy of public institutions. Indeed Rawls says that justice is "the first virtue of social institutions."[11]

Where just institutions exist, the main obligation of individuals is to obey and uphold the rules. But if they do not yet exist, then we have what Rawls calls a "natural duty of justice" to bring them into existence. He calls this a "natural" duty precisely because it exists prior to social institutions: it is not the duty to comply with just social institutions, but rather the duty to create such institutions in the first place.[12]

In some times and places, there may be nothing that an individual can do to help create just institutions: imagine an oppressive regime where the state suppresses any attempts to mobilize politically for greater justice. In such circumstances, private charity may be the best the citizen can do to fulfil the natural duty of justice. But in a democracy, where it is possible to press for just institutions, people have an obligation to do so. Giving private charity would not relieve them from this natural duty to oppose unjust public institutions.

It would be wrong, therefore, on this left-liberal view, for someone to give charity to the poor while opposing redistributive policies that would eliminate poverty in the first place. More obviously, it would be wrong to give private charity to the poor while simultaneously pushing for cut-backs to public welfare for the poor. Even if the private charity helps to remedy an involuntary disadvantage, such behaviour would not be virtuous; it would be a violation of one's natural duty of justice. And, to repeat, the reason it would be wrong, according to liberal egalitarians, is not simply that private charity is less efficient in rectifying injustice than are public policies, but that justice is a pre-condition for the very legitimacy of the public institutions that exercise power over people who are born free and equal.

In this sense, the quotation from Fielding with which I begin this essay is quite apt: according to the left-liberal point of view, for the rich to give alms while opposing institutional reforms is "so far from being meritorious that they have only performed their duty by halves, and are in some sense more contemptible than those who have entirely neglected it."

Charity is not only second-best as a practical response to injustice, it is also secondary or derivative in terms of moral principles. While there may be times and places where giving charity is the best that a person can do to rectify injustice, none the less the content and justification for such charitable actions are defined by principles of justice. That is to say, in identifying appropriate acts of charity, we invoke our criteria of justice to identify who should be giving charity, to whom it should be given, and how much should be given: put simply, those who have more than their fair share (i.e., those who benefit from undeserved advantages in their circumstances) should give to those who have less than their fair share (i.e., those who suffer from undeserved disadvantages in their circumstances), up to the point where each person has their rightful share (ie., where the only inequalities are the result of people's choices).

Now if charity takes this form – i.e., as one possible (albeit second-best) mechanism for giving people what is rightfully theirs – then it is not really "charity" as traditionally understood. For the virtue of charity, as traditionally understood, is distinct from that of justice. The very idea of charity typically assumes that people are rightfully entitled to their resources and that charity involves giving something that one could rightfully keep to people who are not rightfully entitled to it. (This indeed is what makes charity praiseworthy.) But on the left-liberal view, in so far as "charity" reduces injustice, then it involves surrendering resources to which you have no rightful claim and giving them to those people who do have a rightful claim. And so, rather than saying that charity is praiseworthy, we would rather say that failure to give charity is blameworthy.[13]

In this way, justice crowds out charity on the left-liberal view, both in practice (since institutional reforms are superior to private charity) and in theory (since the virtue of charity is derived from the more basic virtue of justice).

Of course, there is nothing in the left-liberal view that precludes people from making gifts beyond what justice requires. But the moral status of such altruistic acts not rooted in justice is ambiguous. Consider two situations in which non–justice-based altruism might occur. First, imagine that we lived in a world where just institutions were in place and everyone had their fair share. Most inequalities – and in particular, most of the involuntary inequalities that elicit charity – would be eliminated, so there would be little if any need for charity. There would still be certain voluntary inequalities – as between Saver and Spender or between part- and full-time workers – but it is far from clear that there is any *moral* reason to remedy these inequalities, which simply reflect differing views about the good life. Indeed, to accept as a general ethical principle that such inequalities should be remedied (even if as a matter only of private charity rather than of institutional justice) would be to encourage irresponsible behaviour: it would imply that people who adopt expensive preferences can expect others to pay for the costs of their choices.

To be sure, there would still be lots of giving in a just society, even though the recipients already have their fair share. But it would not be "charity" as traditionally conceived. For example, we would continue to make gifts and offer help to friends, family, colleagues, neighbours, and others with whom we have face-to-face relationships. The willingness to give freely such kindnesses is part of what it means to have friends, family, colleagues and neighbours. Giving and sharing are part and parcel of the special relationship that we develop with particular people: gifts and assistance help to constitute, and to confirm, the bond between us.

We would also make gifts or donations to organizations that reflect and promote our own particular identity or way of life. We might, for example, support organizations that promote our favourite forms of art or leisure (such as opera, art galleries, local history groups, gardening groups), that advance our own ethnocultural identities (such as heritage-language groups and folk-dancing) or religious beliefs (religious publications, missionary proselytizing), to which we have personal loyalty (such as our alma mater), or that advocate our preferred public policies (such as environmental groups, the Monarchist League, the gun lobby). All these are donations to the projects, hobbies, and causes that define our vision of the good life.

Being able to make such donations – to friends and to cherished projects and causes – is part of the point of having a fair share of resources: it enables us to pursue our conceptions of the good in community with others who share our views, and to promote our views more widely. These are donations to people or organizations directly connected to our conception of the good life – they enhance the relationships or goals that we see as worth having and achieving. If we come to view these relationships or organizations as not worthwhile – if we come to change our view of the life worth leading – then we would cease to make such donations. So these two cases – gifts for relationships and for projects – are not relinquishing our fair share, but rather ways to spend our fair share – on the people and causes we care about.

We can call some of these gifts "charity" if we like, and the law defines some of these gifts as "charitable donations." But none of this is charity as traditionally conceived, which is directed to anonymous strangers who may not (and probably do not) share our personal causes and projects, rather than to people with whom we have face-to-face relations.[14] This is clear in the traditional catalogue of the objects of charity as defined by the major monotheistic religions. For example, the Koran says that the appropriate objects of charity are the poor, the needy, those in bondage and in debt, and the wayfarer;[15] the Torah commands particular concern for the sick, widows, orphans, strangers, the distressed, the captive, and the poor; and the seven traditional acts of mercy for Christians are feeding the hungry, giving drink to the thirsty, clothing the naked, harbouring strangers, visiting the sick, ministering to prisoners, and burying the dead. These prototypical forms of charity all focus on helping individual strangers who are unlikely to have any ongoing role in a person's life and who are unlikely to share his or her particular projects or beliefs.

Would this sort of charity – donations to anonymous others – be a virtue in a just society? The anonymous others are not likely to be in material need, and while some of them may have fewer resources than others, this is likely to be the result of their own decisions about how to lead their lives. So the usual motives for charity would not be present. One could still imagine someone's choosing to give up part of his or her fair share in order to increase the resources of anonymous others in the community, even though they are already as well off as he or she. Imagine someone who volunteered to pay more than his or her fair share in taxes, so that others – no worse off – could pay less. There is nothing wrong with such gifts, of course, but is it virtuous – is it the "right thing" to do?

There is reason to doubt this. To say that it is virtuous implies that we should encourage and educate others to adopt the same attitude, so that they too volunteer to pay more than their fair share of taxes. But this won't work: in a community where everyone altruistically offered to pay more than their fair share of taxes, the result would be in the end that everyone paid precisely their fair share. This example illustrates what Jon Elster calls the paradox of altruism: as an altruist, I give up my fair share to help you achieve your projects, but you are also an altruist, and so you give up your fair share to help me achieve my projects, and we end up in an endless cycle of giving to each other, with no one actually benefiting from the gifts. Thus the whole idea of altruism makes sense only if people have non-altruistic interests and projects and are willing to use the gifts they receive to satisfy these interests and projects.

So if it is a virtue to believe that one ought to accept less than one's fair share, it cannot be a *generalizable* virtue. It can work only if some people feel an obligation to give, while others receive without feeling any obligation to give back. One could imagine a society that tried to codify such a division of moral labour: for example, it could encourage and educate women to give up part of their fair share and encourage and educate men to accept these gifts and to enjoy more than their fair share. But this is hardly an admirable society.

This suggests that the willingness to accept less than a fair share is perhaps best seen as an individual idiosyncrasy. It is a distinctive, and often charming, feature of particular individuals that they are unconcerned with material resources. But for society to try to codify this as a virtue is problematic: if it educates everyone to think this way, it confronts the paradox of altruism. And if it tries instead to educate some people to give, and others to receive, then it is institutionalizing inequality.

This raises a second problem with viewing non–justice-based altruism as a virtue. From an impartial point of view, each person's interests are as important and worthy of concern as any others. There is no moral basis for saying, in general, that the interests of the recipient are more worthy of satisfying than those of the giver. Why then should I think that the right thing to do is to give up my fair share of resources – limiting my ability to pursue my interests, relationships, and projects – so that someone else, who already has their fair share, can better pursue their interests, friendships, and projects? Should morality not tell us that we all matter equally, rather than saying that, in general, my interests matter less than someone else's?[16]

This is perhaps even clearer in a second situation of non–justice-based altruism. Imagine we live not in a just society, but in a deeply unjust society, in which some people have far less than their fair share. According to the left-liberal conception of justice, the well-off have a duty of justice to give up their undeserved advantages. But what about the disadvantaged? To take the extreme case, consider the most disadvantaged person in society. It is clear that he or she has no obligation of justice to give up any resources that he or she has to help others, all of whom are already better off. But would it none the less be virtuous for a poor person to donate what little he or she had to charity?

As we see in the next section, charity in this situation is indeed encouraged by some religious traditions. But here again, we can question whether such giving really is a virtue. If it is a virtue, we should encourage and educate poor people to give to charity. Yet there is something potentially worrisome about inculcating the belief that a person with less than his or her fair share ought none the less to give up some of what little he or she has for those who are better off. Could this not encourage or reflect a false moral belief – namely, that one's own life and interests are worth less than others? To claim *more* than one's fair share is clearly a vice: it is the vice that Aristotle calls *pleonexia* (grasping, overreaching), which typically is the result of arrogance, thinking higher of oneself than is justified. But as William Galston notes, claiming less than one's share can also be a vice if it reflects an undervaluation of one's worth – a failure to recognize that one too is a human being whose life matters and matters equally, equal in rights and dignity to all other human beings.[17]

Here again, indifference to material well-being may be a charming idiosyncrasy of individuals. And there is nothing wrong with someone's choosing to undertake a vow of poverty, if he or she believes that material possessions distract him or her from what is truly important in life. These are morally valid choices for individuals to make, in pursuit of the life that they find most satisfying or rewarding. But to define this as a virtue – as something that every morally good person should do – is more problematic.

I have examined two cases of "charity" that are not reducible to, or defensible in terms of, the requirements of justice: charity given to people who already have their fair share and charity given by people with less than their fair share.[18] In each case, it is far from clear whether such non–justice-based altruism is a virtue.[19] There is nothing wrong with such gifts if they are done out of personal inclinations and attachments, but there is no reason to see this giving as a virtue: i.e., as an act that morally good people would or should do to avoid being morally blameworthy.

In short, if we accept the left-liberal conception of justice, there seems to be little room for a distinctive virtue of charity. As Den Uyl puts it, left-liberalism tends to divide "the moral landscape into issues of justice on one side and matters of personal preference or supererogatory conduct on the other."[20] For the left-liberal, acts of charity can fit into one of these two categories: either they are subsumable under obligations of justice, or they are reducible to personal preference. Some voluntary donations can play a useful role in promoting justice; but if so, their content and value are entirely derivative from the deeper obligations of justice. We identify the content of charity (i.e., how much we give, and to whom) by reference to principles of justice, and we engage in such acts of charity in order to promote justice. Any form of giving to anonymous strangers that is not subsumable under our obligations of justice is, on the left-liberal view, a legitimate personal preference, but not necessarily a moral virtue.[21] In sum, charity as a virtue distinct from justice, but not reducible to personal preference, seems to disappear entirely from the left-liberal "moral landscape."[22]

One possible response to this dilemma is to question the implicit left-liberal assumption that the state is capable in principle of achieving justice.[23] Left-liberal theories of justice typically assume that public institutions and public policies are indeed capable of ensuring distributive justice. If significant injustices exist in society, the explanation must be that citizens have failed to identify or support the right institutions and policies. But there is good reason to think that states are inherently imperfect and that even the best-designed public policies cannot remedy all of the forms of involuntary disadvantages that inevitably arise in modern societies. Even when public policies are motivated by a sincere commitment to justice, they can achieve only so much: coercive laws and impersonal bureaucratic regulations are often simply unable to identify and rectify the real sources of disadvantage facing specific people in specific contexts.

If we accept the inherent imperfection of the state, then we might be able to find a more positive role for charity within a left-liberal framework. Charity would no longer be a regrettable second-best approach but might instead be the best and only way of dealing with certain important forms of disadvantage. We could try to develop a theory of the imperfect state that would enable us to decide which claims of justice should be dealt with by the state and which can best be left to charity. This would be a promising line of inquiry. However, it has not yet been done by any of the prominent left-liberal political philosophers, perhaps because it would be seen as playing into the hands of neo-conservative critics of the welfare state. While they may acknolwedge in passing the imperfections of the state, left-liberals have not yet developed a *theory* of the imperfect state and hence have no systematic account of how charity can help remedy these limitations in the state's ability to achieve justice.[24]

Let me turn now to the other possible response to the apparent inconsistency in our prevailing notions of equality of opportunity. As we saw above, left-liberals respond to this inconsistency by becoming more consistently egalitarian, but one could move in the opposite direction and adopt a more radically right-wing or "libertarian" conception of justice. The libertarian view denies that there is any connection between injustice and involuntary disadvantage. If there is nothing wrong with people benefiting from their undeserved natural talents, as our everyday view supposes, so too, the libertarian argues, there is nothing wrong with people benefiting in an undeserved way from their race, gender, or social class. The fact that these natural and social inequalities are "morally arbitrary," unrelated to anyone's merit or desert, is irrelevant. On the libertarian view, people are entitled to whatever they acquire, either by gift or by market exchange, so long as there was no force or fraud in the process. There is no requirement or expectation that the inequalities in what people acquire in voluntary transactions are correlated with the merits of their choices or that people have an equal opportunity to acquire these gifts or market earnings.[25]

For libertarians such as Robert Nozick, Milton Friedman, and Ayn Rand, it may be regrettable that people are disadvantaged by factors beyond their control, but to try to equalize people's circumstances would require violating people's entitlements and would hence be unjust. These libertarians make no attempt to argue that people deserve their disadvantaged situation. Rather, they argue that people are entitled to keep whatever they acquire, so long as it is not acquired by force or fraud, even if they have done nothing to merit or earn greater resources than others. This libertarian view radically curtails obligations of justice, compared to the left-liberal view. The duty of justice, according to libertarians, is not to try to remedy inequalities in people's life-chances, but simply to avoid force and fraud in relations with others.

Libertarianism is sometimes said to be a selfish theory, lacking in compassion, since it allows people to enjoy their (undeserved) advantages while ignoring the undeserved suffering of others. And indeed there are a few libertarians who trumpet the virtues of selfishness while disputing the value of compassion. Ayn Rand, for example, argues that compassion is a vice, that selfishness is a virtue, and that the good person will not respond altruistically to the predicament of others.[26] However, most libertarians explicitly deny that their view is opposed to compassion. On the contrary, they insist that it is one of the strengths of their theory that it can make room for genuine compassion for others, unlike the *compelled* contributions required by the welfare state. Rose and Milton Friedman, for example, argue that the welfare state "poisons the springs of private charitable giving."[27] Similarly, Murray Rothbard notes: "It is hardly charity to take wealth by force and hand it over to someone else. Indeed this is the very opposite of charity, which can only be an unbought, voluntary act of grace. Compulsory confiscation can only *deaden* charitable desires completely, as the wealthier grumble that there is no point in giving to charity when the state has already taken on the task. This is another illustration of the truth that men can become moral only through rational persuasion, not through violence, which will, in fact, have the opposite effect."[28] Similarly, some Christians claim that the welfare state has extinguished genuine Christian charity. As Gordon Graham puts it: "We can force people to hand over part of their wealth or earnings which we may pass on to the poor, but we have not thereby forced them to give to the poor. It is precisely because they will not give that we have taken it from them. Needless to say, still less have we forced them to follow Christ's recommendation. In short, their relation to the poor has no religious value whatever."[29]

Needless to say, this is a radically different conception of justice and charity from the left-liberal view. The left-liberal view inflates justice to such an extent that it leaves little room for charity, and any forms of charity that go beyond the requirements of justice are of ambivalent moral value, particularly if they involve encouraging some people to subsidize the expensive tastes of others. By contrast, the libertarian radically curtails our obligations of justice, thereby creating ample room for voluntary acts of compassionate charity. And these acts of charity are clearly virtuous, even though they go beyond the obligations of justice, since they typically assist the involuntarily disadvantaged. In a libertarian world, there will be many people deserving of charity, and so it is a virtue to help them, although libertarians deny that their deservingness gives them any right to the property of others.

The fact that libertarianism provides more scope for the virtue of charity is, for some, a point in its favour. But it remains a minority viewpoint among members of the general public and among political theorists. The connection between injustice and involuntary disadvantage is simply too strong in our everyday moral consciousness, and few people are willing to entirely sever the connection between justice and remedying undeserved inequalities. Or put another way, we are likely to reject this deep intuition about fairness only if we are given some very powerful argument to do so. Yet libertarians have, I believe, failed to provide such an argument: they tend simply to assert, rather than to defend, the notion that we have an entitlement to whatever we inherit (as natural endowments or social advantages) and to whatever we receive through gifts or exchanges.

It is important to recall the justificatory burden that modern political theory faces, discussed above: its task is to show why people who are born free and equal should accept the legitimacy of social institutions that subject them to the political and economic power of others. In particular, it is necessary to justify these institutions to those who are disadvantaged by them and who can point to alternative sets of rules in which they would not be similarly disadvantaged. In the case of libertarianism, then, what sort of justification can its supporters give for adopting rules that allow individuals to acquire unrestricted property entitlements over vastly unequal shares of the world's resources, unrelated to effort, choice, or merit, rather than adopting alternative rules regarding the acquisition and transfer of property?[30] The task for libertarians is to show why their preferred set of property rules is fairer than any other. But this is, I think, a hopeless task: libertarianism provides fairness neither in the procedure to acquire property nor in the resulting distributions.[31]

It is easy to accept gross inequalities when these are viewed as "natural," and when some people are viewed as fit by nature to be lords or landowners and others as fit by nature to be serfs or workers. But once we recognize that inequalities are the result of mutable social rules and conventions, then we demand a justification for them. And it must be a justification that treats us as free and equal citizens, whose lives matter and matter equally. Only certain sorts of justifications can meet this test. Intuitively, the most obvious way to show that a particular inequality is fair is to show that it is somehow chosen or deserved. Another, closely related, view is to show that certain inequalities actually benefit the less well-off (who would therefore voluntarily accept them). These two sorts of justifications can be given to and accepted by free and equal citizens. Under these conditions, some people will have fewer resources than others, but they have no legitimate grounds for complaint against these socially sanctioned inequalities, which are the responsibility of, or in the interests of, the less well-off.

Libertarians, however, want to defend inequalities that cannot be justified by such considerations. They want to defend inequalities that are not the result of merit and which do not serve the interests of the less well-off. It is difficult to see what sort of reason can be given for the less well-off to accept social institutions that systematically disadvantage them in access to resources and opportunities in ways that are undeserved and not in their interests.[32] This perhaps explains why most contemporary work on justice is located broadly in the left-liberal tradition.

Much more can be said about the relative merits of left-liberalism and libertarianism. And, of course, there are many other accounts of justice that are worth examining.[33] But let me step back and summarize the main point of this section. As I see it, most modern theories of justice share a number of features that tend to diminish the significance of charity as a principle and as a practice. First, they see justice primarily as an institutional virtue: justice concerns not just fulfilling promises and repaying debts but also, and more important, the fairness of the social rules regarding acquisition of economic resources and political power. Second, as a result, inequalities that are the product of social institutions need to be justified to citizens. And in the modern world, the best way – and perhaps the only sure way – to justify such inequalities persuasively is to show that they are somehow deserved or merited as a result of the choices and efforts that individuals make.

If we accept this basic framework of modern justice, the practical and theoretical space for charity dwindles. Charity is effectively subsumed by, and grounded in, the prior duty of justice. We can preserve more space for charity by adopting a libertarian theory, which radically curtails our obligations of justice. But this is not an intuitively attractive theory of justice – indeed, it is not attractive even to many of those people who admire charity. Is there no way of giving charity a central role other than by moving to the far right of the political spectrum? Is there no way to give charity a positive role other than by radically curtailing our conception of justice? I believe that there is indeed another approach, but we need to look elsewhere to find it. We need to look, in particular, to older religious conceptions of morality and virtue, to which I now turn.

ALTRUISM AND RELIGIOUS VIRTUE

Charity plays a very different and more prominent role in the three major monotheistic religions – Christianity, Islam, and Judaism – than in modern secular theories of justice. For example, the New Testament says: "And now abideth faith, hope, charity, these three; but the greatest of these is charity."[34] Charity is also a basic obligation in Islam and Judaism as well. It is one of the five basic pillars of Islam (along with confession of faith, ritual prayer, fasting, and pilgrimage) and is one of the basic *mitzva* (commandments) in Judaism.

Within all three religious traditions we can find two distinct sorts of contributions – an obligatory (and sometimes legally enforced) system of mutual aid and support for the church and (b) more voluntary forms of charity, particularly for the poor. In Islam, for example, *zakat* is the regular and obligatory contribution in an organized Muslim community – usually 2.5 per cent of merchandise and 10 per cent of fruits of the earth – while *sadaqah* is alms more generally given in Allah's name. Similarly, Judaism distinguishes the obligatory *ma'aser* – 10 percent of the fruits of the earth – from the voluntary *tzedaka.* And many Christian communities have distinguished obligatory "tithing" from more voluntary forms of charity and almsgiving. In all three traditions, the obligatory contribution – the *zakat, ma'aser,* and tithe – has sometimes been legally enforced by religious or state authorities. Indeed, the tithe remained part of the law in England until the modern era.[35]

In this section, I am interested primarily in the religious conception of voluntary donations, rather than the obligatory contributions. These voluntary donations are most relevant for modern debates about charity, not just because they are indeed voluntary, but also because they tended to be directed primarily to helping the poor, whereas the obligatory contributions were also used for supporting religious personnel and maintaining religious property.

The sort of voluntary donations encouraged by these religious traditions is similar to modern secular conceptions of charity in their focus on the poor. But this similarity is potentially deceiving, since the *motivation* for charity is very different. In modern secular views, it is assumed that the motivation for charity is humanistic: to help those in need. Within the religious traditions, however, the motivation for charity is religious: that is to say, to achieve personal salvation. All three traditions see the hoarding of wealth as a sure route to divine punishment and charity as facilitating admission to the kingdom of heaven. As Jesus says in the New Testament: "Verily I say unto you, that a rich man shall hardly enter into the kingdom of heaven. And again I say unto you, it is easier for a camel to go through the eye of a needle than for a rich man to enter into the kingdom of heaven."[36] Likewise the Koran tells people to "spend in charity for the benefit of your own souls. And those saved from the covetousness of their own souls – they are the ones that achieve prosperity."[37] The Koran repeatedly denounces the habitual impiety of rich men,[38] stressing the "uselessness of wealth in the face of God's judgement and the temptation to neglect religion that wealth brings."[39] Those who give charity "will have their reward with their Lord: On them shall be no fear nor shall they grieve."[40] By contrast, those who hoard wealth are told: "On the Day when it will be heated in the fire of Hell, and with it will be branded their foreheads, their flanks, and their backs: 'This is the treasure which ye hoarded for yourselves.'"[41] Similarly, an old Jewish proverb states: "Charity saves from death."[42]

This should not be seen as simply the price one has to pay for entry into Heaven. Indeed, the New Testament emphasizes that charity given in such a spirit is without value: "And though I bestow all my goods to feed the poor, and though I give my body to be burned, and have not charity; it profiteth me nothing."[43] Charity is rather a way of getting closer to God, by renouncing those things (such as material wealth) that distract people from God and by sharing God's love of the world. As Matthew puts it, "Ye cannot serve God and mammon,"[44] and charity is one of the ways to strengthen a commitment to God rather than mammon.

In other words, while the object of charity may be the poor, the goal of charity is the giver's relationship with God. As Thomas Aquinas observed: "by charity I mean the movement of the soul towards the enjoyment of God for His own sake."[45] It is therefore "an act of self-perfection" that is concerned only indirectly with the sentiment of benevolence or with relations with others.[46] Other people enter the picture as a component of this process of self-perfection, but they are not its driving principle. Indeed, Aquinas emphasizes that since the poor can be sinners or enemies, charity requires only that we love their human essence (i.e., their capacity for improvement and salvation), while as individuals they may be appropriately the objects of hate.[47]

Since it is concerned with the achievements of the self, this religious conception of charity is (in Den Uyl's words) "supply-sided," whereas the modern secular conception that views charity as fulfilling duties towards others is "demand-sided."[48] In religious traditions, the focus is on the agent's character, and the "beneficiary" of ethical conduct is the agent himself or herself. While Aquinas viewed almsgiving as obligatory, "it is critically important to understand that we have this obligation not because we owe it to the other, as in justice, but because we owe it to ourselves; that is, such actions are a sign of our self-perfection (i.e., our love of God)."[49] Giving alms is an act of mercy, not justice.[50]

The fact that religious conceptions of charity are typically "supply-sided" – focused on the giver, rather than on the recipient – has a number of profound implications. First, on the modern secular view, where the motivation to give to the poor is a humanistic concern, we might think that it is a virtue not just to give some of our wealth to the poor, but also to use our talents to create that wealth in the first place. If our motive is self-perfection, however, and if wealth is seen as a distraction from God, then we might think that it is a virtue not only to give away wealth, but not to create it in the first place. And indeed we find strands of thought, particularly within the Christian and Islamic traditions, which argue that the ideal life – the most perfect way of directing the soul to God – is to renounce material wealth altogether, both its production and possession.

Christ told his would-be disciples that they should give up their jobs and give away their possessions to follow in his footsteps. When his disciples asked how then their needs for food and clothing would be met, Christ responded: "And why take ye thought for raiment? Consider the lilies of the field, how they grow; they toil not, neither do they spin; And yet I say unto you that even Solomon in all his glory was not arrayed like one of these. Wherefore, if God so clothe the grass of the field, which today is, and tomorrow is cast into the oven, shall he not much more clothe you, O ye of little faith? Therefore take no thought, saying What shall we eat, or What shall we drink or Wherewithal shall we be clothed ... For your heavenly Father knoweth that ye have need of all these things. But seek ye first the kingdom of God, and his righteousness, and all these things shall be added unto you. Take therefore no thought for the morrow, for the morrow shall take thought for things of itself."[51] This has often been taken as an instruction to Christians that it is desirable to devote themselves entirely to a life of true piety, even if this means living off the alms of others.

In other words, while giving charity to the poor is clearly a virtue in the Christian tradition, it is also a virtue to choose to become an *object* of charity: voluntarily to make oneself dependent on the charity of others. This is not a paradox, since the reason why giving charity is a virtue is not primarily because it relieves the suffering of others but rather for self-perfection, and the very reason that makes charity a virtue (namely, renunciation of material wealth and servitude to God) also makes becoming an object of charity virtuous. For someone voluntarily to become the object of charity may reduce the amount of resources available to help the (involuntarily) poor: it both reduces the amount of wealth created and requires this reduced wealth to be spread among more people. But this is no objection on the religious view, since the aim of charity is not to minimize poverty, but to maximize self-perfection.

This rather extreme view was strongest in the early Christian communities and in the medieval period among Muslims.[52] In other times and places, there was a reaction against this sort of extreme renunciation of wealth. Indeed, the Koran explicitly calls for a measured degree of generosity, without either miserliness or prodigality: "And render to the kindred their due rights, as also to those in want and to the wayfarer: But squander not you wealth [in charity] in the manner of a spendthrift.... Make not thy hand tied (like a niggard's) to thy neck, nor stretch it forth to its utmost reach, so that thou become blameworthy and destitute."[53]

Similarly, Judaism has rarely encouraged this extreme form of renunciation, although there is a hermetic strand in the Jewish tradition.[54] Indeed, Jewish law forbids giving up more than 20 per cent of one's income to charity, precisely to ensure that it does not become necessary for one to rely on the charity of others.[55]

So the three religions have varying views about the virtue of voluntarily becoming an object of charity. Still, that this is even conceivable – that the reasons for voluntarily giving charity could also be reasons for voluntarily becoming dependent on charity – shows how far removed these concepts are from the usual assumptions of modern secular debates.

The fact that religious views of charity are supply-sided has a second, related ramification. Since the main motivation for charity is the self-perfection of the giver, rather than the claims of the recipient, there is less concern in the religious traditions with determining the "deservingness" of the recipient of charity. In principle it can be as virtuous – that is to say, as self-perfecting – to give alms to an irresponsible spendthrift who has wasted his or her inheritance as to give alms to a responsible and hard-working person who was born into poverty. It can be just as self-perfecting to help those who deserve their disadvantages as to help those who are poor through no fault of their own.

As we saw in the first section, it is a preoccupation of modern secular theories of justice to distinguish the deserving from the undeserving poor. This is true even on the left-liberal view of justice. Yet the New Testament goes out of its way to encourage charity towards the "undeserving" poor. Recall the parable of the prodigal son. It begins with the very model of left-liberal egalitarianism: the father divides his wealth equally among his sons, who are then free to make their own choices about how to lead their lives. The elder son is frugal, works hard, and saves his money; the younger son consumes it in the city. Yet when the younger son returns, the father insists (in effect) on re-equalizing their resources. The elder son complains, but the father insists that the younger son's regret is sufficient justification for re-equalizing their resources.[56]

If our focus is on the recipients of charity – on the merits of their claims to resources – we might (with the left-liberals) see this as unfair. The responsible son bears all the sacrifices (he forgoes leisure and consumption and then has to share his hard-earned savings), while the prodigal son gets all the benefits (he enjoys leisure and consumption and then gets to share in the savings that his brother has worked hard to set aside). But if we look at the giver rather than at the recipient of charity, we may see assisting the prodigal son as a particularly striking way of moving the soul towards God.

A third, related implication of the fact that religious conceptions of charity are supply-sided is that the obligation to give charity applies equally to the poor and the rich. Since the principal aim of charity is the self-perfection of the giver, rather than the neediness or deservingness of the recipient, there is nothing paradoxical about expecting even the poorest of the poor to give alms. And here again the New Testament makes it explicit that this is a virtue. Consider the story of the poor widow at the temple. Jesus watched many rich people contribute large sums to the church treasury, but when a poor widow threw in her two mites, he called his disciples and said: "Verily I say unto you, That this poor widow hath cast more in, than all they which have cast into the treasury: For all they did cast in of their abundance; but she of her want did cast in all that she had, even all her living."[57] Similarly, the Koran insists that people should give "whether in prosperity or in adversity,"[58] and the Jewish Talmud insists that "Even a poor man who lives off *tsedaka* must give *tsedaka*."[59]

As we saw above, left-liberal theories have trouble seeing it as a virtue for the poor to give up their resources for others: why should the poor give up what little they have to help others who are less needy and less deserving of resources? But this left-liberal attitude is "demand-sided" – it is focused on the needs or merits of the recipient of the charity – whereas the religious attitude is supply-sided, focused on the giver, and his or her need to develop his or her character and his or her relationship with God. And from a supply-side perspective, the need to give charity is just as strong for the poor as for the rich.

There is yet another interesting implication of the fact that religious conceptions of charity are supply-sided: namely, they tend to put great weight on the anonymity of charity. A "demand-sided" view of charity is often concerned with preserving the anonymity of *recipients*, so that they are not stigmatized by their dependence on alms. But the religious traditions equally demand that the *donor* remain anonymous. For someone to publicize his or her charity reveals that the motive is not to come closer to God, but to achieve worldly honour, and worldly honour can be as much of a distraction from God as worldly goods. Anonymity helps to ensure that the gift is truly religiously self-perfecting.[60]

Thus Jesus says: "Take heed that ye do not your alms before men, to be seen of them: otherwise ye have no reward of your father which is in heaven... When thou doest alms, let not thy left hand know what thy right hand doeth."[61] Similarly, the Koran says that it is better for donations to be anonymous and tells people to "cancel not your charity by reminders of your generosity."[62] And several Talmudic sources condemn the practice of publicizing charity and say that it is only by anonymous giving that *tzedekah* saves people from unnatural death.[63] Indeed, the question of whether it is permissible to publicize donors remained a source of controversy in Judaism well into the nineteenth century, when it finally become more or less accepted practice.[64]

This preoccupation with the anonymity of donors makes sense on a supply-sided view of charity, where the concern is with the self-perfection of the donor, but is unnecessary and perhaps counter-productive on a "demand-sided" view. If publicizing the names of donors (while preserving the anonymity of recipients) elicits more contributions – or if it shames those who have not given into doing so – then it can be seen as making charity more effective, rather than eroding its original purpose.[65]

So the fact that the conception of charity within Christianity, Islam, and Judaism is "supply-sided" has a number of important ramifications. This view of charity is not a feature just of Western monotheistic or revealed religions. Indeed, it is perhaps even more evident in various Eastern religions, such as Buddhism, which view charity as part of the sought-after transcendence of self.[66]

What are we to make of these religious conceptions of charity? The introduction of "supply-side" considerations is surely a useful addition to the debate. Modern secular theories tend to look just at the recipient of charity and so to ignore the importance of charity for the giver. As I argued above, this focus on recipients means that in left-liberal theories the requirements of justice leave little room for charity. But by concentrating on the importance of charity for the giver, perhaps we can give charity a more prominent and positive role. The religious arguments described above do not depend on any particular conception of justice and could in principle be accepted by those on both the left and right.

But are these ancient religious traditions really relevant to modern secular societies? There are two obvious problems with relying on such religious traditions in our society. First, in a multi-ethnic and multi-faith society, we cannot base public policy on particular religious doctrines. We need therefore to be able to find a secular interpretation of the supply-sided, self-perfecting account of charity. But is such an account possible, or does the belief in the self-perfecting nature of charity ultimately depend on assumptions about God and salvation? Second, even if we can give a secular interpretation of the self-perfecting argument for charity, will the enforcement of modern conceptions of justice by public institutions not tend to squeeze out any room for charity?

Let me take these two questions in turn. Several writers have argued that the Christian belief in the self-perfecting quality of charity cannot be divorced from a belief in salvation through Christ. According to Den Uyl, for example, "In the absence of a theology which promises eternal rewards for such conduct, there is nothing especially self-perfecting about the mere act of aiding those in need."[67] Similarly, Gordon Graham claims that "isolated from Christian theology, there does not seem a great deal to commend the Christian ethic."[68]

Christians believe that giving charity brings people closer to God and helps to ensure eternal salvation. But if we set aside this theological reason for charity, is there any other way in which charity can enhance life? On a secular conception of the good life, giving away resources to anonymous others is likely to be seen as limiting, rather than as enhancing, access to the good things in life. To be sure, even a secularist can accept that the mindless pursuit of material wealth is often a distraction from the activities and relationships that are truly fulfilling and rewarding in life. But the alternative to the mindless pursuit of wealth is not necessarily charity, but rather the thoughtful use of wealth – for example, to help friends and family, to learn about the world, to engage in hobbies, and to promote worthwhile causes.

So it is not clear whether we can find a plausible secular defence of the claim that giving away resources is in general self-perfecting. Of course, even on the religious view, it is not the act of giving itself that is truly valuable, but rather the underlying spirit that motivates the act. We can define this underlying spirit as "the general outlook of cooperation, good will, or moral optimism."[69] According to Den Uyl, it is this general outlook that is self-perfecting: possessing such a spirit of good will and "moral optimism" makes it possible for people to find and enjoy the good things in life. If we are chronically distrustful and pessimistic, we are unlikely to find the will to form the sorts of relationships and projects that make life worth living.

We can call this general outlook one of "charity," since it involves taking a charitable view of other people and of their potential. I believe that charity in this broad sense – thinking charitably about others – is indeed necessary for self-perfection, even on a purely secular account. But charity in this broad sense is only loosely connected to charity in the narrow sense of giving resources to anonymous others. It is far from clear that thinking charitably entails making charitable gifts.

However, let us assume for the sake of argument that acts of charity are indeed self-perfecting on a secular view. This would give people a reason to engage in acts of charity even if they are not required by justice (for example, it explains why we should give to the prodigal son and why even the poor should give charity). But this immediately raises an interesting question: do such supply-side considerations concerning the spiritual needs of the donor generate a *moral* argument for charity or merely a prudential one? Even if charity in either the broad or the narrow sense plays a role in our conception of self-perfection, does this generate a moral obligation to engage in charity or simply a personal desire to do so? One could argue that if our basic reason for engaging in charity is self-perfection, rather than justice, this is ultimately a prudential motive for charity, not a moral motive. Indeed, isn't talk about self-perfection simply a rather elaborate and old-fashioned way of talking about our personal well-being – i.e., about how to have a more satisfying and rewarding life?

Religious believers see the obligation to engage in self-perfecting acts of charity as rooted in a deeper and prior obligation to God and typically see this obligation to serve God as a "moral" obligation. But on a secular view, it seems puzzling to say that we have a moral obligation to engage in self-perfection. To whom do we owe such an obligation? The obvious answer is that "we owe it to ourselves." But that is hardly a *moral* reason. We have a prudential reason for engaging in self-perfection: it enhances the quality of our life and makes it possible for us to have satisfying and rewarding relationships and projects. Self-perfection in this sense is something that we pursue naturally, as part of our conception of the good life. And so we should engage in acts of charity if and to the extent that they contribute to our good. That is a prudential, not a moral, reason for charity. If charity is truly self-perfecting, then someone who fails to give charity will miss out on some of the rewarding aspects of life, but he or she would not be exhibiting a moral failing.[70]

Indeed, the very idea that supply-sided considerations can generate moral obligations is arguably incoherent in a secular context. Outside a theological context, supply-side arguments are by definition prudential arguments: they tell us how to improve the quality of our lives. The religious traditions may give us some clues as to why charity is often one of the personal desires or projects that many people have. It may help explain why charity is not simply an eccentric or idiosyncratic taste that some people have. But it cannot explain why charity is a moral virtue rather than a prudential good. In this respect, the supply-side argument for charity is in the same position as the left-liberal theories discussed above: unless acts of charity are independently justified by the requirements of justice, they become matters of personal goals rather than moral virtue or moral obligation.

Of course, some acts of charity may indeed be independently justifiable as requirements of justice. But this raises the second major problem about the modern relevance of religious traditions: why do the requirements of modern conceptions of justice not supersede and displace charity? It might well benefit the donor to give charitably of his or her largesse to the disadvantaged, but don't the requirements of modern justice tell us that the disadvantaged have a rightful claim to those resources? And if so, shouldn't public institutions effect that transfer by taxation or other enforced rules, rather than by relying on voluntary acts of charity?

This raises an important question about religious conceptions of charity. As we saw above, they are primarily supply-sided, emphasizing the religious self-perfection of the donor. But of course they are not entirely indifferent to demand-sided considerations: there is some genuine concern to relieve the suffering of the poor. Relief of suffering is seen as an intrinsic good, not simply an instrument or mechanism by which donors engage in self-perfection.

But why then have these religions not insisted that reducing involuntary disadvantage is an obligation of justice, rather than an act of charity? The answer, I think, is that these religious traditions historically have had no real conception of social justice. There is, to be sure, some notion of divine justice, in which the undeserved inequalities of the world are somehow equalized in heaven. This is reflected in the parable of Lazarus and the rich man. The rich man "fared sumptuously every day," while ignoring Lazarus the beggar at his door. But when they died, Lazarus "was carried by angels into Abraham's bosom" in heaven, while the rich man was sent to hell. When the rich man asks for a momentary respite from the horrors of hell, Abraham says: "Son, remember that thou in thy lifetime receivedst thy good things, and likewise Lazarus evil things, but now he is comforted and thou art tormented."[71]

But there was no expectation or obligation to rectify undeserved inequalities in "evils" and "comforts" here on earth. On the contrary, as I noted above, inequalities between castes or estates were seen as "natural" until the modern era. None of the scriptures challenges the basic assumption that society will be divided into rich and poor, slave and free, landowners and tenants, or challenge the rules of inheritance that create these castes.

Justice in the scriptures, in short, is not about evaluating these basic social institutions; it is much more modest. Justice is largely a matter of paying debts, avoiding usury, and avoiding abuse of the helpless. It is not unjust that there are propertyless people, even slaves, in society, but one may not "abuse" them.[72] In this respect, religious conceptions of charity share a major feature with libertarianism: they both make space for charity by radically curtailing obligations of justice.

Consider the Islamic tradition. According to most Muslim traditions, justice requires equality before the Divine Law – that is to say, officials and judges should apply divine law without fear or favour. However, this sort of "equality" does not challenge "the distinctions between free men and slaves, landowners and tenants, rich and poor." On the contrary, these "irreducible residue of inequality" are seen as "inevitable" and do not "encroach, except in cases of 'abuse', upon the only sort of equality that a state could achieve in this world."[73] As Maxime Rodinson puts it: "Justice in economic matters consists for the Koran in forbidding a type of gain that was particularly excessive, *riba* [usury], and in devoting part of the product of the taxes and gifts collected by the head of the community to helping the poor, to hospitality, to the ransoming of prisoners, perhaps to grants or loans to the victims of certain disasters or circumstances of war. It is really a matter of mutual aid organized within the community... It does not affect the differentiation in social conditions, which is being conceived as being willed by God, natural."[74]

Indeed, the Koran specifically states that inequalities should not be challenged: "And in no wise covet those things in which Allah hath bestowed His gifts more freely on some of you than on others: to men is allotted what they earned."[75] One commentator explains this passage by saying: "Men and women have gifts from Allah – some greater than others. They seem unequal, but we are assured that Allah has allotted them by a scheme by which people receive what they earn. If this does not appear clear in our sight, let us remember that we have no full knowledge but Allah has. We must not be jealous if other people have more than we have – in wealth or position or strength or honour or talent or happiness. Probably things are equalized in the aggregate or in the long run, or equated to needs and merits on a scale which we cannot appraise."[76]

Rodinson claims that it would be anachronistic to criticize the Koran for not having "challenged the privileges or deprivations bound up with belonging to a particular 'estate,' which conferred a specific status upon a man from birth, such as nobility or slavery,"[77] since such a challenge emerged as a general movement only in the eighteenth century. However, whether we criticize it or not, we must recognize that "[n]either the justice conceived by the Koran nor that conceived under its influence by the Muslims of the Middle Ages [is] what the modern ideal calls justice."[78] And the same is arguably true of the Christian or Jewish traditions.

This pre-modern conception of justice – as paying debts and avoiding usury and abuse – was acceptable to people over a millennium ago, but it is not widely accepted today. Citizens today demand a modern conception of social justice: one that recognizes that the distribution of property is not natural but conventional and which therefore requires justification.

Some contemporary theologians in all three traditions have tried to construct such a modern conception of social justice. The Christian liberation theologian Juan Luis Segundo interprets the gospels' commandment to "love all men" to mean "seek first justice, before all else, and universal brotherhood." Similarly, J.P. Miranda argues that "to give alms" in the Bible should be interpreted as "to do justice."[79] There are also many contemporary Muslims who seek to find in the Koran evidence for a modern socialist conception of distributive justice.[80] And some Jewish authors argue that *tsedaka* should be seen as a requirement of justice: since the poor person has been "disinherited from his patrimony in the world's goods... he is then no object of mere pity. He is a man denied his rights, among them that to an adequate livelihood."[81]

Attempts to read modern notions of social justice into ancient scriptures are rather strained, since these scriptures clearly accept the division of society into the propertyless and the propertied. But even if we can (re)interpret these scriptures to generate a modern conception of social justice, this simply returns us to our original problem – namely, that such a modern conception of justice is likely to displace charity. Even if charity is self-perfective, this is not a sufficient justification for tolerating institutions that permit or create involuntary disadvantages. Once we accept a modern conception of social justice, our first obligation must be to ensure that social institutions fulfil principles of justice. And then for the reasons discussed in the first section, justice will crowd out charity, both in theory and in practice. It is only by radically curtailing obligations of justice that earlier religious traditions were able to make significant space for charity.

Indeed, it seems to me that religious conceptions of charity in the end face the same basic dilemma confronting modern secular theories of justice. Recall that on the left-liberal view, charity as a distinctive moral virtue almost disappears from the moral landscape, reduced on the one side to the requirements of justice and on the other side to merely optional personal goals. For left-liberals, charity is a moral obligation, but only if it is derived from, and reducible to, obligations of justice (i.e., if charity is done to meet the rightful claims of the recipient). Any act of charity that is not derivative of justice is not morally obligatory but rather is reducible to personal preference (i.e., if charity is done to promote the conception of the good of the giver). The only way to give charity a more positive role is to adopt an intuitively unattractive libertarian conception of justice that reduces our obligations of justice to those of merely refraining from force and fraud in our relations with others.

So far as I can tell, the religious accounts examined above do not rescue us from this dilemma. Their proponents face the same basic options. They can try to construct a modern conception of social justice out of religious foundations, as Christian liberation theologians or Islamic socialists do. But such a robust conception of justice will dramatically reduce the scope for charity, and any acts of charity that go beyond obligations of justice are essentially matters of the prudential pursuit of personal well-being (or self-perfection) rather than of moral virtue. We can try to give charity a more central role by reverting to a pre-modern conception of justice as paying debts and not abusing the vulnerable. But this is not intuitively attractive to citizens of modern societies.

In short, for all their profound differences, it seems to me that both the secular and religious accounts of charity confront the same basic set of difficulties. Religious and secular defenders of charity face a similar challenge in explaining whether or how charity can be a distinctive moral virtue or obligation in modern societies: they both have to explain why charity is something less than (or other than) the requirements of justice, but more than (or other than) the prudential pursuit of personal well-being.

I started this chapter by quoting Den Uyl's complaint: "While the virtue of charity may still be alive among private individuals, it is moribund among theoreticians."[82] I have tried to show that there is a reason why charity has become theoretically "moribund." There is indeed a very active practice of charity, but if we examine the principles or values underlying it, we see that they often seem to be reducible to more basic principles of either social justice or prudence. The distinctive moral virtue of charity is surprisingly elusive.

NOTES

I would like to thank Idil Boran for excellent research assistance and Jim Phillips for helpful comments on the paper.

1 H. Fielding, *Tom Jones* (1749).

2 For a related discussion of the distinction between charity and philanthropy, see Ontario Law Reform Commission, *Report on the Law of Charities* (Toronto, 1996), 145–6.

3 D. Den Uyl, "The Right to Welfare and the Virtue of Charity," in E.F. Paul, F.D. Miller, and J. Paul, eds., *Altruism* (Cambridge: Cambridge University Press, 1993), 224.

4 For reviews of people's beliefs about distributive justice in western democracies, see A. Swift et al., "Distributive Justice: Does It Matter What the People Think?" in J. Kluegel et al., eds., *Social Justice and Political Change* (New York: Aldine de Gruyer 1995); D. Miller, "Distributive Justice: What the People Think," *Ethics* 102 (1992), 555; T. Tyler et al., *Social Justice in a Diverse Society* (Boulder, Col.: Westview Press, 1997).

5 J. Rawls, *A Theory of Justice* (London: Oxford University Press, 1971), 74–5.

6 R. Dworkin, *A Matter of Principle* (Cambridge, Mass.: Harvard University Press, 1985), 207.

7 Perhaps the best-known exponent of this view is Ronald Dworkin: he calls his theory the "equality of resources" conception of justice, since the aim is to equalize the resources and capacities available to people, while allowing inequalities to arise as a result of people's voluntary choices about how to deploy these resources: R. Dworkin, "What Is Equality? Part I: Equality of Welfare; Part II: Equality of Resources," *Philosophy and Public Affairs* 10 (1981), 185 and 283. This basic approach has been developed and refined in various ways. See, in particular, Richard Arneson's account of "equality of opportunity for welfare" in R. Arneson, "Equality and Equal Opportunity for Welfare," *Philosophical Studies* 56 (1989), 77, and "Liberalism, Distributive Subjectivism, and Equal Opportunity for Welfare," *Philosophy and Public Affairs* 19 (1990), 159. See also G.A. Cohen's account of "equality of access to advantage"; G.A. Cohen, "On the Currency of Egalitarian Justice," *Ethics* 99 (1989), 906; "Incentives, Inequality and Community," in G.B. Peterson, ed., *The Tanner Lectures on Human Values*, vol. 13 (Salt Lake City: University of Utah Press, 1992), and "Equality of What? On Welfare, Goods, and Capabilities," in M. Nussbaum and A. Sen, eds., *The Quality of Life* (Oxford: Oxford University Press, 1993)), 9–29; Amartya Sen's account of "equality of capabilities" in "Equality of What?" in S. McMurrin, ed., *The Tanner Lectures on Human Values*, vol. 1 (Salt Lake City: University of Utah Press, 1980), 195–220, and "Rights and Capabilities," in T. Honderich, ed., *Morality and Objectivity* (London: Routledge and Kegan Paul, 1985); Erik Rakowski's account of "equality of fortune" in *Equal Justice* (Oxford: Oxford University Press, 1993); and John Roemer's account of "equality of access/opportunity" in "A Pragmatic Theory of Responsibility for the

Egalitarian Planner," *Philosophy and Public Affairs* 22 (1993), 146, and *Theories of Distributive Justice* (Cambridge, Mass.: Harvard University Press, 1996)). All the authors share the underlying intuition about eliminating unchosen inequalities, while providing space for inequalities that result from choices for which individuals are responsible.

8 J. Rawls, "Social Unity and Primary Goods," in A. Sen and B. Williams, eds., *Utilitarianism and Beyond* (Cambridge: Cambridge University Press, 1982), 168.

9 One can imagine an even more radical form of egalitarianism, which rejects the legitimacy of any form of inequality. Some Marxist theorists argue that the only just distribution is one that is fully egalitarian and that there can be no defensible justification for allowing (socially sanctioned) inequalities among people who are (by nature) free and equal. But such a radical view has little support among the general population or among political theorists, since it denies any role to human agency, choice, and individual responsibility. For a discussion of such views, see W. Kymlicka, *Contemporary Political Philosophy: An Introduction* (Oxford: Oxford University Press, 1990), 184–5.

10 John Stuart Mill, *Principles of Political Economy*, in *Collected Works* (Toronto: University of Toronto Press, 1965), 3: 953.

11 Rawls, *A Theory of Justice*, 3.

12 See the discussion of "mediating duties" in H. Shue, "Mediating Duties," *Ethics* 98 (1988), 687.

13 Some people argue that justice requires us only to do our *fair share* in creating just institutions and that we are therefore obliged only to make sacrifices for justice if others are willing to do the same. This is sometimes called the idea of "reciprocity." If we accepted this claim (which I do not), then it would constitute a praiseworthy (supererogatory) act of charity to give more than others, even if a person were left with more than his or her fair share, and to refuse to do more than others would not be blameworthy.

14 Indeed, these traditional forms of charity are often doubly anonymous: givers do not know on whom their gifts are bestowed, and the recipients do not typically know from whom the gifts are received. As we see in the next section, such anonymity has often been seen as the ideal form of charity. With friends, family, and colleagues, by contrast, such anonymity has little place. One can have an anonymous benefactor, but not an anonymous friend: friendship requires knowing what we do for each other.

15 Koran 9:60.

16 I am focusing on forms of charity that involve assistance to individuals, as befits the traditional focus of charity, and I argue that such individual-directed donations are not necessarily a virtue in a just society. However,

there are also donations to support various public or collective goods: consider the extensive system of public libraries throughout North America funded by Andrew Carnegie. It is difficult to distinguish this category of philanthropy from gifts intended to promote preferred causes, but at least in some circumstances the benefactor has no expectation that the money will be spent in a way of which he or she personally approves. (Imagine a benefactor who loves opera and despises hockey but none the less donates money to a local community to build either an opera house or a hockey rink.) Even in a just society, such communal-directed donations may be virtuous if they enable collective goods to be realized in communities that would otherwise lack the resources to support them on their own.

17 W. Galston, "Cosmopolitan Altruism," *Social Philosophy and Policy* 10 (1993), 126. See also J. Hampton, "Selflessness and the Loss of Self," in Paul et al., *Altruism.*

18 William Galston calls this the "justice-based" standard for altruism, so that "you could be said to act altruistically whenever, and to the extent that, you claim less than [your fair share] for yourself and are willing to surrender the remainder to others": Galston, "Cosmopolitan Altruism," 125–6. For more on the connection between the virtues of justice and charity, see A. Buchanan, "Justice and Charity," *Ethics* 97 (1987), 558, and J. Waldron, "Welfare and the Images of Charity," *Philosophical Quarterly* 38 (1986), 463.

19 I am focusing on sacrifices made for anonymous others, rather than on donations to friends and family or to causes in which one believes. There is nothing wrong with poor people making *these* kinds of gifts. On the contrary, as I said above, part of the whole point of justice is to ensure that everyone has a fair share of resources that they can use to promote the interests of the particular people whom they love and the causes that they cherish. However, the worry about inequality can arise even in the case of family and friends. There would be something quite worrisome about a family or friendship in which the person in greater need made most of the sacrifices in the relationship. See Hampton, "Selflessness," for a discussion of how altruism in intimate relationships becomes a vice, not a virtue, when it involves "loss of self" – i.e., loss of the recognition that a person's self and interests are as worthy of concern as others'.

20 Den Uyl, "The Right to Welfare," 202.

21 I am concentrating on charity in the form of donating property, typically money. There are other forms of charity involving personal care-giving that would still be valuable in a just society – for example, the actions of a "Good Samaritan." This suggests that principles of justice need to be supplemented, not so much with charity in the form of financial donations as with a duty of care that would encourage people to provide per-

sonal care to those in (non-monetary) need, such as the sick, the injured, the young, and the elderly. The best work on this topic has been done by feminist theorists of an "ethic of care." However, it would be important to ensure that this sort of caring work is itself fairly distributed in society. See C. Gilligan, "Moral Orientation and Moral Development," in E. Kittay and D. Meyers, eds., *Women and Moral Theory* (Totowa, NJ: Rowman and Littlefield, 1987), and Kymlicka, *Contemporary Political Philosophy*, chap. 7.

22 I have focused on one particular left-liberal theory of justice: the equality-of-resources view advanced by Ronald Dworkin. There are other left-liberal theories of justice that are worth mentioning.

The "compensatory justice" view argues that inequalities in resources are legitimate if they compensate for differences in the burdens that people face. For example, people whose work involves special risks or hardships are entitled to greater pay than those whose work is safe and enjoyable. The aim, on this view, is to achieve an equal distribution of both benefits and burdens: see J. Dick, "How to Justify a Distribution of Earnings," *Philosophy and Public Affairs* 4 (1975), 248–72. This account obviously generates the same restrictions on charity as Dworkin's theory. In so far as economic inequalities compensate for non-economic burdens, then it is difficult to see the virtue in giving charity to those with fewer material resources: this would be like asking Saver to subsidize Spender. Indeed, under reasonable market conditions, compensatory justice is likely simply to collapse into Dworkin's equality of resources: the former's account of "burdens" is really just the flip-side of the latter's account of "expensive preferences," both of which are determined by market mechanisms under conditions of equal resources; J. Carens, "Compensatory Justice and Social Institutions," *Economics and Philosophy* 1 (1985), 39–67.

Another popular left-liberal view of justice, associated with John Rawls, may seem to offer more scope for charity. This theory argues that inequalities that improve the well-being of the worst-off are legitimate. For example, inequalities may provide incentives for talented people to contribute to society in ways that benefit everyone, including the least well-off, so that the least well-off would be even worse off without these inequalities. Inequalities that simply allow the talented or privileged to exploit their undeserved advantages without helping the less well-off are unjust: see Rawls, *A Theory of Justice.* This theory seems to allow some scope for praiseworthy charity, since Rawls denies that the rich deserve their resources: it is, he says, just a matter of brute luck who has natural talents, and hence brute luck who gets to benefit from the incentives needed to elicit the use of these talents.

But here again, G.A. Cohen has argued that this theory collapses into the Dworkinian model. For why are the incentives needed in the first place? Why aren't the talented willing to develop and exercise their talents to help the less well-off without demanding additional income? The most reasonable answer is that the incentives are needed to compensate for unequal burdens involved in the development or exercise of these talents (such as extra training, extra stress, extra risk). In other words, this incentives argument is compelling only where it tracks the compensation argument: if incentives do not compensate for unequal burdens, then it is simply economic blackmail by the talented: see Cohen, "Incentives."

If so, then the theories of equal resources, compensatory justice, and incentives all tend to converge on a similar account of justified inequalities and so tend to converge on a similar account of the limits of charity.

23 See Janda et al., chapter 16 in this volume.

24 There are of course several analyses of the inherent limitations of state policy by sociologists and political scientists: see, for example, N. Glazer, *The Limits of Social Policy* (Cambridge, Mass.: Harvard University Press 1988). But this literature has not yet permeated the philosophical debates. One looks in vain in the corpus of the major left-liberal political philosophers – Rawls, *A Theory of Justice*; Dworkin, *A Matter of Principle*; Cohen, "Egalitarian Justice," Incentives," and "Equality of What?"; Roemer, "A Pragmatic Theory" and *Distributive Justice*; Arneson, "Equality" and "Liberalism"; and B. Ackerman, *Social Justice in the Liberal State* (New Haven, Conn.: Yale University Press, 1980) – for a discussion of the extent to which the state can or cannot fulfil the principles of justice that they endorse and of the possible role of charity in remedying the imperfections of state action.

25 Because the libertarian emphasis is on entitlements, rather than on either merit or equal opportunity, it is often described as an "entitlement theory." The best-known exponent of this view is R. Nozick, *Anarchy, State, and Utopia* (New York: Basic Books, 1974). For a recent survey of libertarian thought, see D. Boas, ed., *The Libertarian Reader: Classic and Contemporary Writings from Lao-tzu to Milton Friedman* (New York: Free Press, 1997).

26 A. Rand, *The Virtue of Selfishness* (New York: New American Library, 1964). This rejection of the very idea of compassion received its strongest formulation in Nietzsche, who felt that it was ethically depraved or degrading for the strong to feel compassion for the weak.

27 M. Friedman and R. Friedman, *Free to Choose: A Personal Statement* (New York: Harcourt, Brace, Jovanovitch, 1980), 120.

28 M. Rothbard, *Power and Market: Government and the Economy* (Menlo Park, Calif.: California Institute for Humane Studies, 1970), 164. Similarly, Robert Nozick insists that his theory does not valourize selfishness. He agrees that charity is morally desirable: it is an excellent way in which a

person can exercise his or her rights. He simply denies that anyone can legitimately be compelled to give up their property: Nozick, *Anarchy*, 265–8.

29 G. Graham, *The Idea of Christian Charity: A Critique of Some Contemporary Conceptions* (Notre Dame, Ind.: University of Notre-Dame Press, 1990), 93–4.

30 The usual answer is to invoke a principle of "self-ownership," but G.A. Cohen offers a decisive critique of the claim that self-ownership leads to unequal claims over the ownership of the world's natural resources: see "Self-Ownership, World-Ownership, and Equality," in F. Lucash, ed., *Justice and Equality: Here and Now* (Cornell University Press: Ithaca 1986), and "Self-Ownership, World-Ownership and Equality: Part 2," *Social Philosophy and Policy* 3 (1986), 77.

31 I do not have the space here to defend this rather bald assertion. But see Cohen, "Self-Ownership," for a decisive critique of Nozick's defence of libertarianism, and see Kymlicka, *Contemporary Political Philosophy*, chap. 4, for a more general survey of the problems with existing defences of libertarianism.

32 Indeed, at key points in their arguments, libertarians often implicitly revert to arguments about responsibility for choices, compensation for unequal burdens, or mutually beneficial incentives – i.e., the sorts of arguments which imply that inequalities are after all deserved by, or beneficial to, the least well-off. (These are the sorts of arguments that left-liberals invoke to show that some inequalities are justified: see Dick, "How to Justify a Distribution," and Carens, "Compensatory Justice"). Libertarians imply that differences between the rich and poor are somehow the result of some individuals' effort or willingness to take risks and that there are no feasible alternative set of rules that would not leave the least well-off even worse off. This shows how difficult it is to avoid appealing to our deep intuitions about the link between injustice and involuntary disadvantage. While the official libertarian view is that people are entitled to their resources even if they are unrelated to merit or to benefiting the least well-off, many libertarians feel compelled to show that a libertarian world would (miraculously) meet these left-liberal criteria of justice.

33 For a survey of recent work on theories of justice, see Roemer, *Distributive Justice*. For a collection of some of the major recent writings on justice, see W. Kymlicka, ed., *Justice in Political Philosophy*, 2 vols. (Brookfield, Vt.: Edward Elgar Publishing, 1992).

34 1 Corinthians 13:2–13.

35 The biblical commitment to give a "tithe" or tenth of the fruits of the land was first made by Abraham (Genesis 14:20), reaffirmed by Jacob, who said: "Of all that thou [God] shalt give me, I will surely give the tenth unto thee" (Genesis 28:22), and defined as an obligation for all

Jews in Deuteronomy 12:11. This obligation, sometimes enforced by Jewish religious or state authorities, is for the assistance of priests and Levites, as well as for the poor, widows, orphans, and strangers within the gate (Dueteronomy 12:29). A form of tithing is still the practice among Orthodox communities in Israel. There is no explicit passage in the New Testament that requires Christians to continue such tithing, but the tithe none the less became a general law in AD 900 in England, and this remained in partial effect until relatively modern reforms to land tax legislation: see J.D. Derrett, "Tithe," in B. Metzger and M. Coogan, eds., *The Oxford Companion to the Bible* (Oxford: Oxford University Press, 1993), 745; E.A. Livingstone, *Concise Oxford Dictionary of the Christian Church* (Oxford: Oxford University Press, 1996), 516; and L. Glinert, *The Joys of Hebrew* (New York: Oxford University Press, 1992), 133.

36 Matthew 19:23–24.

37 Koran 64:16.

38 Koran 34:37/34 ("Never did We send a Warner to a population but the wealthy ones among them said: `We believe not in the Message with which Ye have been sent'. They said: `We have more in wealth and in sons, and we cannot be chastised' ... It is not your wealth nor your sons that will bring you nearer to Us in degree: but only those who believe and work righteousness – these are the ones for whom a multiplied Reward for their deeds, while secure they reside in the dwellings on high!").

39 M. Rodinson, *Islam and Capitalism*, trans. B. Pierce (New York: Pantheon Books, 1973), 14, 24. See also the Koran 8:28 ("And know ye that your possessions and your progeny are but a trial: And that it is Allah with whom lies your highest reward") and 63: 9/10 ("Let not your riches or your children divert you from the remembrance of Allah").

40 Koran 2:277; cf. 4:162; 2:110; 57:18.

41 Koran 9:35. There is some dispute about whether this passage applies to Muslims, or just to Christians and Jews: see Rodinson, *Islam and Capitalism*, 25.

42 Glinert, *The Joys of Hebrew*, 250.

43 1 Corinthians 13:3.

44 Matthew 6:24.

45 Aquinas, *Summa Theologiae*, ed. T. McDermott (Westminster, Md.: Christian Classics, 1989), II-II, Q23, A2.

46 Den Uyl, "The Right to Welfare," 204.

47 Aquinas, *Summa Theologiae*, II-II, Q26, A6, 8 and 9.

48 Den Uyl, "The Right to Welfare," 205.

49 Ibid., 207. This is, I believe, the predominant view, both in the gospels and in subsequent Christian tradition. However, it is difficult to reconcile with the passage in Matthew 25:31–46. In this passage, Jesus is portrayed

sitting in heaven dividing the damned from the blessed, and he says to the blessed that they will enter heaven because they fed and clothed Him when He was hungry and naked. The blessed are puzzled by this, saying that they do not remember seeing Jesus hungry and giving Him food. Jesus responds: "Verily I say unto you Inasmuch as ye have done it unto the least of these my brethren ye have done it unto me." In this passage, the donors seem quite unaware that they are serving the Lord through their gifts and seem motivated solely by relieving the distress of "the least of these" in their community. (Of course, the point of including this passage in the gospels is presumably to make readers more conscious of the way in which charity is a means of serving and approaching God).

50 To be sure, there are other views in the Christian tradition. St Gregory defended the opposite view: "When we give the poor what is necessary to them, we are not so much bestowing on them what is our property as rendering unto them what is their own; and it may be said to be an act of justice rather than a work of mercy," quoted in Den Uyl, "The Right to Welfare," 209, n. 31. As I show below, this approach has been revived recently by some Christian thinkers (as in liberation theology).

51 Matthew 6:28–34.

52 Rodinson, *Islam and Capitalism*, 25.

53 Koran 17:31/29. cf. "Those who, when they spend [in charity], are not extravagant and not niggardly, but hold a just balance between those extremes" (Koran 25: 67).

54 M. Steinberg, *Basic Judaism* (New York: Harcourt, Brace Jovanovich, 1975), 82–4.

55 It also discourages disinheriting one's family in favour of charity to others, partly to ensure that one's children do not become dependent on charity: see A.M. Silver, "Inconsistencies and Misinterpretations: A Response to the Mishna Concerning Disinheritance and Charity," *Tradition: A Journal of Orthodox Jewish Thought* 29 (1995), 90–3, and "May One Dishinherit Family in Favor of Charity? Halakhic Conclusions to the Ethical, Moral, and Legal Issues Involving Inheritance," *Tradition: A Journal of Orthodox Jewish Thought* 28 (1994), 79.

56 Luke 15:11–32.

57 Mark 12:41–44.

58 Koran 3:134.

59 Quoted in Glinert, *Joys of Hebrew*, 250.

60 This is a reason why charity for the poor may be preferable to philanthropic gifts to operas or art galleries even on a purely supply-side approach. There is of course a demand-side reason for preferring charity over philanthropy – namely, the need for food and housing is more basic and urgent than the need for art and opera. But from a religious perspective, such demand-side reasons are secondary to considerations of

the spiritual health of the donor. From a supply-side perspective, charity is preferable to philanthropy because it tends to be anonymous, whereas philanthropic gifts tend to be publicized and indeed often involve naming an event or institution after the donor. In so far as anonymity is important, charity is better (more self-perfecting) for the donor than public philanthropy.

61 Matthew 6:1–3.

62 Koran 2:271; 2:262/264.

63 "What kind of charity is that which delivers a man from an unnatural death? ... When a man gives without knowing to whom he gives, and the beggar receives without knowing from whom he receives": Baba Batra 9b–10a, quoted in D. Ellenson, "Tzedakah and Fundraising: Communal Charity and the Ancient Spirit of Jewish Teachings: A 19th Century Response," *Judaism* 46 (1996), 391.

64 See Ellenson, "Tzedakah and Fundraising," for an extended discussion.

65 A related question concerns the appropriateness of providing tax breaks for charitable giving. From a demand-side perspective, they may be an efficient way of encouraging help for the poor (although Neil Brooks disputes this claim in chapter 6 of this volume). However, from a supply-side perspective, providing worldly benefits for charity (whether in the form of public honour or financial credit) corrupts its proper motive. This is indeed what some people argued during the parliamentary debates when charitable deductions were first introduced.

66 See P. de Silva, "Buddhist Ethics," in P. Singer, ed., *A Companion to Ethics* (Oxford: Blackwell, 1991), 61. See also H.H. Dubs, "The Development of Altruism in Confucianism," *Philosophy East and West* 1 (1951), 48–55, and P. Bilimoria, "Indian Ethics," in Singer, ed., *Companion to Ethics.*

67 Den Uyl, "The Right to Welfare," 221.

68 Graham, *Christian Charity*, 8.

69 Den Uyl, "The Right to Welfare," 221.

70 As Den Uyl puts it, once God is gone from the picture, it leaves "the satisfaction of desires to constitute the good for the self. Yet the satisfaction of desire is something one pursues anyway. Consequently, our relations with others would have to come to claim the central focus of normative theory and become the object of charity": ibid., 208. He argues, at 210, that this shift to the modern (demand-side) view of charity had occurred by the time of John Locke, whose discussion of charity makes no mention of "the perfective qualities of such actions with respect to the benefactor." See also E. Andrew, *Shylock's Rights: A Grammar of Lockian Claims* (Toronto: University of Toronto Press, 1988).

71 Luke 16:19–25.

72 "You shall not wrong or oppress a resident alien, for you were aliens in the land of Egypt. You shall not abuse any widow or orphan. If you do

abuse them, when they cry out to me, I will surely heed their cry; my wrath will burn, and I will kill you with the sword, and your wives shall become widows and your children orphans." Exodus 22:21–24; cf. Deuteronomy 10:19.

73 Rodinson, *Islam and Capitalism,* 27.

74 Ibid., 21.

75 Koran 4:36/32; cf. 16:73/71.

76 *The Holy Qu'ran: English Translation of the Meanings and Commentary* (revised and edited by the Presidency of Islamic Researches, IFTA, King Fahd Holy Qu'ran Printing Complex, Al-Madinah 1405 AH), 218, n. 542.

77 Rodinson, *Islam and Capitalism,* 21–2.

78 Ibid., 27.

79 See Graham, *Christian Charity,* 95–6; see also R. Preston, *Religion and the Ambiguities of Capitalism: Have Christians Sufficient Understanding of Modern Economic Realities?* (London: SCM Press, 1991).

80 See Rodinson, *Islam and Capitalism,* 19–27; see also M.A. Muradpuri, *Conflict between Socialism and Islam* (Lahore, Pakistan, 1970); M.I. Hamza, *Muslim Socialism and the Western Theories of Socialism* (Cairo: Supreme Council of Islamic Affairs, 1964); M. Abdul-Rauf, *A Muslim's Reflections on Democratic Capitalism* (Washington, DC:: American Enterprise Institute, 1984).

81 Steinberg, *Basic Judaism,* 81–2, who notes that *tzedeka* has the same etymological root as "righteousness" or "justice."

82 Den Uyl, "The Right to Welfare," 224.

5 Rational Voluntarism and the Charitable Sector

BRUCE CHAPMAN

THE NEED FOR AN ACCOUNT OF RATIONAL VOLUNTARISM

Economics is characterized more aptly as a method of analysis than as a subject matter. The days are long gone when economists focused on that most paradigmatic of economic subjects – the market – perhaps straying only reluctantly to the workings of certain fiscal or regulatory institutions when these "imposed" themselves on what was otherwise deemed to be free market exchange. Now one can find economists applying their methods to voting rules and political institutions, to the machinations of bureaucracy, to the decisions of judges and the workings of the courts and legal rules, and, most recently, to the social impact of cultural norms.

What is it, then, that economics characteristically brings to the study of such a broad array of very different institutions? The short answer is *homo economicus*, or the rational actor – that person who, armed with a healthy set of ordered preferences, seeks so far as possible to choose that alternative which, given institutional constraints, he or she most prefers, or is most conducive to his or her own "self-interest." The phrase is often construed as synonymous with "selfish," but that is not strictly accurate. The preferences of the rational actor can be determined by any number of factors, including the interests of others. Thus, odd as it may sound, there would appear to be no methodological reason why one could not usefully apply the model of the rational actor to the analysis of charity and charitable institutions, where it is usually thought that the interests of others, in contrast to self-interest, motivate key participants in this sector. One can, it seems, take a perfectly healthy interest in the interests of others and seek rationally to maximize that self-interest in the consistent choice of most-preferred alternatives.

Nevertheless, even though the rational-actor model can apparently accommodate the virtue of altruism, in this chapter I suggest some reservations about using the model in its purest form in the study of charity and charitable institutions. For while the rational actor is not exactly a knave,[1] thinking only selfishly about how the choice of certain alternatives might affect him or her, there is nevertheless something persistently *asocial* about him or her. He or she thinks, I argue, too reductively about collective action – that is, too individualistically – which can ultimately countervail the very interests of others in which he or she is said to be taking an interest.

Now this might suggest that we need here that other denizen of the social sciences sometimes trotted out to do theoretical battle with homo economicus – namely, *homo sociologicus*. This is a person who, without much rational or calculative regard to self-interest at all, simply does "the done thing" – that is, complies with whatever cultural norms, social roles, or habitual schemes are required of him or her. In other guises he or she sometimes appears as the Kantian who, without much regard to consequences, and certainly without any regard to the consequences for his or her own self-interest, does his or her duty for duty's sake.

But such an unthinking[2] paragon of socially required conduct surely strains our credibility as much as the rational actor of economics. While it seems at least partially true to say of the self-interested rational actor that "people are not really like that," it seems wrong to take this to mean that "people are not *at all* like that." For that broad exclusionary claim is precisely what seems so strained in homo sociologicus. It is surely more accurate to offer a more narrow exclusionary claim in response to the economist's rational-actor model – namely, "Not all people are like that," or even "People are not entirely like that." In other words, what we need is a more nuanced and heterogeneous account of people's motivations and their choices, either for people in general or for someone in particular, than what is provided for in the simple caricatures of both homo economicus and homo sociologicus. What we need, we might say, is an account of homo *socio*economicus.

However, such an account must have some real structure to it, something that has enough purchase and precision genuinely to inform our institutional choices. It is not enough to say, vaguely, that homo socioeconomicus is someone who is "in between" the other two sorts of beings, whose motivations are some sort of integration of the motivations of the other two, without saying very much that is specific about how this integration is to be achieved. In this chapter I aim to develop the beginnings of a structured account of homo socioeconomicus and to show the precise relevance of this account for our understanding of the charitable sector in general and for the regulation and organization of charitable institutions more particularly.

The charitable sector seems to be an appropriate place to begin looking for our new sort of actor. As I suggested above, the very notion of charitable conduct already strains the credibility of the self-interested rational actor. It seems more likely that the sort of being that is lurking here is something other than homo economicus, whatever the accommodating method of rational-choice theory might try to suggest. But there is also reason to believe, or so I argue, that those who participate in the voluntary sector reveal a commitment to the interests of others that is somewhat more contingent, or more subject to rational revision, than what the more absolute social commitments of homo sociologicus suggest. The challenge is to develop an account that allows for this possibility of rational revision of social commitments without having that possibility reduce at once to the full-blown and pervasive calculus of the rational actor. I hope to provide such an account in my characterization of homo socioeconomicus and to show that the charitable sector is regulated, and charitable institutions are organized, with this more complex sort of being in mind.

The argument in the chapter proceeds as follows. In the first section I provide a more detailed account of the motivational structure of homo socioeconomicus. I work with a general characterization of what it is to see oneself acting collectively and then, using the "prisoner's dilemma" game for purposes of illustration, show more specifically how the rational voluntarism that characterizes homo socioeconomicus differs from the motivational structures of both homo economicus and homo sociologicus. The second section shows some of the implications of this account of rational voluntarism for our understanding of the charitable sector. The three subsections of the section address: first, why homo socioeconomicus should be kept apart from the competitive pressures of politics; second, why homo socioeconomicus shows such a high degree of responsiveness to tax subsidies in his or her charitable donations; and third, why homo socioeconomicus would choose to organize charities as non-profits and otherwise seek to limit the commercial activities of charities. All of these implications, I suggest, follow from the motivational complexity of rational voluntarism and are much harder to comprehend within the more conventional models of homo economicus and homo sociologicus.

THE MOTIVATIONAL STRUCTURE OF RATIONAL VOLUNTARISM

We can usefully derive the beginnings of a possible motivational structure for homo socioeconomicus from an analysis of that game form which is still so much at the centre of the economic analysis of institutions – the prisoner's dilemma. While the invocation of this game might seem to beg the question in favour of the economic approach, and homo economicus, this model of strategic interaction remains intriguing for the economist (and others) precisely because it shows how economic theory *fails* to capture the possibility of social co-operation where we do in fact observe it (or at least partially fails to capture it – the question will often be whether the glass is half empty or half full when we observe what is typically something less than complete co-operation). Morever, the prisoner's dilemma is also frequently used to model the problem of supplying a public good or benefit through purely voluntary contributions. This also makes it relevant to our understanding of participation within the charitable sector. The notion of "public benefit" is crucial to the most general part of the historical definition of charity, and the more specific categories of charity typically listed within this definition are all public goods in the economic sense of that term.

According to economic thinking, a public good is a good which, once it is made available to some individuals, is equally available to others, regardless of whether these other individuals have made any contribution to provide for these goods. Standard textbook examples of such public goods include national defence, clean air, and the availability of a radio signal. But another example is the relief of poverty, something which is paradigmatic of what charities do.[3] Once this relief is provided for, it is there for everyone to enjoy (at least if they have an interest in the interests of others), regardless of whether they have made any charitable contribution of their own. But, according to the economist, it is the inability to exclude non-contributors that can generate a problem for the supply of public goods; if individuals cannot be excluded from consuming the public good even though they have not contributed to it, then each, as a rational actor, will choose not to contribute, and the good will not be adequately supplied.

This argument is typically represented as a prisoner's dilemma. Let there be a representative individual *i*, who is contemplating whether to make a voluntary contribution of some (unspecified) "fair" share to

Figure 5.1 The public goods problem as a prisoner's dilemma game

Individual i	*Everyone else*	
	1. Contributes (public good provided)	2. Does not contribute (public good not provided)
1. Contributes	*x*	*z*
2. Does not contribute	*w*	*y*

the public good. In the matrix (Figure 5.1), he or she is contemplating whether to choose row 1 or row 2. The columns 1 and 2 represent what everyone else does. In column 1 everyone else contributes their fair shares; in column 2 no one else contributes. Since, by assumption, individual *i*'s contribution is small, or insignificant, in terms of the whole cost of the public good, the good is provided in column 1 and not provided in column 2, regardless of what individual *i* actually does (i.e., regardless of which row, 1 or 2, he or she chooses). Thus, from *i*'s point of view, there are four possible social outcomes: everyone contributes, except *i* (social outcome *w*); everyone contributes, including *i* (*x*); no one contributes, including *i* (*y*); and no one contributes, except *i* (*z*).

Now suppose that *i* is the paradigmatic rational actor who, while taking an interest in the public good (for example, "the interests of others") being provided, nevertheless prefers not to contribute if everyone else does (for then the public good is provided for in any case). And, if no one else contributes, he or she feels that there is really little point in doing so (for then the public good is not provided in any case). Thus, *i* prefers *w* to *x* and *y* to *z*. However, *i* does consider this public good to be one worthy of contribution, even if this means contributing a fair share. (This, of course, requires that everyone else contribute as well). So *i* prefers *x* to *y*. Thus *i*'s ordering of the four social outcomes is (in order of preference from left to right): *w, x, y, z*.

Now consider *i*'s decision to contribute or not. Individual *i* knows that his or her contribution is too small to influence what everyone else does. Therefore, *i* simply takes everyone else's behaviour as given, or independent of *i*'s own. Of course, *i* does not know what everyone else will do. However, *i* reasons that if everyone else does contribute, he or she does best not to contribute, thus securing his or her most preferred social outcome. That is, *i* chooses *w* over *x*. However, if no one else contributes, and if *i* were to contribute, this would be the worst of all possible worlds, *i*'s having spent something for nothing. So *i* also chooses *y* over *z*. Thus, no matter what everyone else actually does, *i* chooses not to contribute. Alternatively, we can say that *i* has a *dominant* strategy to choose row 2. Moreover, since *i* is a representative individual, everyone else has this same incentive. Therefore everyone else chooses not to contribute (chooses column 2), and the social outcome that prevails is *y*, or the status quo, "no contribution" alternative. This is the case even though all the individuals, like the representative *i*, would have preferred getting to social outcome *x*, where all contribute their fair shares.

Now those who would propose homo sociologicus rather than homo economicus as a more appropriate model of individual behaviour will suggest that the difficulty with the prisoner's dilemma, or the reason that it fails to explain the fact that people *do* voluntarily contribute to public goods even though they have a dominant strategy to "free ride" on the contributions of others, is that it works with too impoverished a view of human nature.[4] Most people make these contributions, the argument goes, because they feel that it is their duty or because they otherwise deem it normatively appropriate. Anything less, it might be said, would be to do less than "one's part" – less than what it is properly to do the "done thing."

Economists also sometimes attempt to explain voluntary giving by suggesting that individuals derive some satisfaction, or "warm glow," just from the act of giving, even if the gift has almost no consequential effect on the provision of the public good in question.[5] In the economic account of the prisoner's dilemma, of course, this pure taste for giving has no role; there the rational actor looks only at the consequences of his or her own giving and, if the gift makes no real difference to the amount of public good provided, will choose not to make it.

But a taste for pure giving seems just as unlikely as the idea that we are all, unambiguously, free riders on the contributions of others. Whereas the free rider has a dominant strategy of never contributing in any circumstances (since such giving is so inconsequential), the contributor who is motivated purely by a taste for giving gives without any regard to consequences at all – that is, just out of the pure love of giving and regardless of whether the public good is actually being provided as a result. Where we might say the free rider is too consequentialist in his or her reasoning, asking only whether his or her gift makes a real difference to the public goods outcome, we must surely also say that the individual motivated by a taste for pure giving is too *non*-consequentialist and insufficiently attentive to whether his or her preferred outcomes are actually being achieved. Indeed, we might even see some special irony in the altruistic motivations of the pure giver, since he or she seems selfishly to care only about his or her own giving and not at all about whether it is actually helping others.[6]

Furthermore, the economist's account of "warm glow" giving fails to capture the subtlety of what it is to do "one's part" within a larger scheme of social co-operation. Indeed, one could also say the same of the more simple-minded caricatures of homo sociologicus, at least when these accounts contemplate individuals' acting co-operatively (or choosing row 1 in the prisoner's dilemma) in only a somewhat unreflective way. For doing one's part, or doing the "done thing," presupposes that there is already in place a co-operative venture, or *whole*, of which it can sensibly be said that one's own contribution is only a *part*, or, alternatively, *from* which one can determine the standard for the "done thing." In terms of the prisoner's dilemma, it presupposes that the representative individual who is choosing *between* the rows can know (or at least can reasonably expect) that he or she is choosing *within* column 1. But the economist's account of "warm glow" giving does not require that the individual be much concerned about whether there is any such co-operative venture in place. This is what makes that account so agnostic about actual consequences; the warm glow simply attaches to one's own giving. And the unreflective homo sociologicus co-operates just as unconditionally. While he or she might speak of "doing (his or) her part," if he or she never actually attends to whether others, who share the same conception of the public good, are doing their parts within the co-operative scheme (that is, never thinks about whether he or she is in column 1 or column 2), then this motivation, while absolute, seems purely formal – the stuff of thoughtless and empty commitment.[7]

What we need under the idea of "doing one's part" therefore is some possibility of a more conditional co-operation.[8] In particular, what we require is a co-operative motivation that can account for the feeling that one is obligated to co-operate if others are doing so (if the representative individual finds himself or herself in column 1), but not, if they are not (column 2).[9] The first part of this conditional cuts against the free-ride strategy of homo economicus, who is non-cooperative regardless of what others are doing; the second part, against the co-operative absolutism of either the "warm glow" giver or homo sociologicus, each of whom is co-operative regardless of what others are doing. But the strategy that co-operates conditionally – that is, only if others in one's co-operative venture are also co-operating, and otherwise not – would appear to differ from both. It is tempting to think that we might find the definitive strategy for homo socioeconomicus here.

However, that would be an overly hasty conclusion. For while some version of conditional co-operation will inform the motivation of homo socioeconomicus, there is a logical problem with the purest version of this strategy. More significantly, the logical difficulty reveals a deeper substantive requirement for our account. There is still something reductive and overly individualistic in the purely conditional co-operator, a character trait inherited from the ancestor homo economicus. What we need, rather than a mind perfectly open to, or rationally impartial in its treatment of, the differing conditions for co-operation and non-co-operation, is a more unthinking presumption in favour of co-operation. While this might sound like a retreat to the motivations of homo sociologicus, it is not. Because the presumption in favour of co-operation is less than absolute, being open *at some point* to rational revision, we now see that it is much more like the complex integration of motivations that we are looking for in homo socioeconomicus.[10]

The logical difficulty in a strategy of purely conditional co-operation is that it cannot generalize for all representative individuals without becoming paralysingly self-referential.[11] Each representative individual, seeking to condition his or her choice of a co-operative strategy on whether others are co-operating, must wait until those others reveal their choices. But those others, being equally representative individuals, are likewise waiting for him or her (and others like him or her) to reveal the conditions on which they can base *their* choices. Thus, in infinite regress, each representative individual is suspended in a kind of strategic limbo, unable to make any strategic choice until the other (equally representative) individuals have determined their strategic choices first.

Now there are several ways out of this problem. One is to avoid the strictly logical problem of self-reference by allowing a representative individual's decision to co-operate to condition not so directly on another such individual's own decision to co-operate but, rather more indirectly, on his or her receiving from the other individuals some sort of publicly observable message saying that these others will co-operate if they receive like messages from him or her (and others like him or her). This surprisingly small adjustment in the rules of the game avoids the logical difficulty of self-reference. However, some economists will continue to be sceptical unless one also assumes some unlikely degree of transparency, or honesty, in the messages being sent between representative individuals in such stategically charged situations.[12]

Another approach comes closer to some of the themes already discussed in this chapter. Each representative individual can escape strategic limbo by working with a simple presumption that other representative individuals will co-operate. This presumption allows each and every individual to begin with co-operation and, on observing the like-motivated co-operation of others (who have begun with the same presumption), to carry on co-operating with equanimity.

However, the introduction of a working presumption in favour of co-operation will strike the sceptical economist as just a little too convenient. Does the presumption not simply assume what needs to be shown? Do we not have to ground the presumption *in*, or explain it *by*, some sort of rational motivation, rather than the other way round – that is, we cannot structure our account of rational motivation around a given presumption. While we might expect this objection from anyone weaned on the rational-actor model, it is not at all obvious that the sceptical economist can raise it comfortably. For, in the absence of such presumptions, there will be no way to achieve some of the efficiencies, dear to the economist, that are present in even the most simple situations calling for social co-ordination. Yet these efficiencies seem to be easily attainable if individuals can be induced to think more collectively and less individually and, as a result, to presume in favour of certain co-ordinating actions rather than others.

To see this last point, consider the simple two-person co-ordination game called "matching pennies."[13] Each person, without consulting the other, must turn up either "heads" or "tails" on his or her own coin. If each person turns up "tails" – a match – then each will win another penny from the pot. However, if each turns up "heads" – another match – then each will win one hundred dollars from the pot. In the absence of a match, each wins nothing. What should each person do?

It seems obvious enough that each person in the game is motivated to match the other and moreover should turn up "heads" and walk away with the larger winnings. And it seems easy to predict that this is exactly what will happen if two players are reasonably well adjusted socially. But it is surprisingly difficult for two individually rational actors to get to this result. Why? For exactly the same reason that it was difficult for the two conditional co-operators to get to the mutually co-operative outcome in the prisoner's dilemma. The representative person could sensibly co-operate there, it will be recalled, only if the others had already resolved to co-operate and so had laid down the basis for the representative person's conditional co-operation. But the others were likewise waiting for him or her (and others like him or her). Hence the strategic limbo.

In the game of matching pennies, the problem is exactly the same for the rational actor. It makes sense for either one of the players to turn up "heads" only *if* the other person is turning up "heads"; otherwise, despite the larger winnings, it makes more sense to turn up "tails." However, both persons are reasoning in this way (and, moreover, it is common knowledge that they are), so that neither can really find a determinative way to get to "heads" and the larger winnings that go with that strategy. It seems that, in theory at least, two individually rational players can end up choosing in this game so that there is a non-trivial chance that any one of the four possible strategy combinations is the final outcome. Yet we can surely doubt that in the real world two reasonable players would have this problem.

What this suggests is that we need to purge homo economicus of more than his or her propensity for unconditional non-co-operation (in the prisoner's dilemma) if we are to explain how individuals do, sensibly, co-operate with one another. That first step takes us only as far as conditional co-operation but still leaves individuals uncertain how mutually to condition their conditionals. I have suggested that the reasonable way to proceed is to assume that conditional co-operators work with a presumption in favour of co-operation, which involves purging homo economicus further of the propensity to think *too* conditionally about co-operation – in particular, to think from the very beginning that he or she should co-operate only *if* others are doing so. While thinking conditionally about co-operation makes sense of the idea that one is "doing one's part" in some larger sort of collective action – something that neither homo economicus nor homo sociologicus (for quite different reasons) can really do – thinking too conditionally about the prospect of co-operation – that is, without even an initial presumption in its favour – serves only to reproduce the same sort of individualistic or non-collective thinking so characteristic of homo economicus that we hoped to avoid in homo socioeconomicus. To some extent at least, homo socioeconomicus must not be tempted by the question "What should *I* do?" and should substitute the more collective version of that question "What should *we* do?"[14] The former question, even if it can accommodate the more conditionally motivated structure of homo socioeconomicus, and therefore make some sense of the idea of "doing one's part" within a collective enterprise, still encourages the individual to think too much (that is, too immediately or too pervasively) about what he or she should be doing in contrast to what others similarly situated, might be doing. This is what exposes him or her to the difficulty of a purely conditional "co-operation strategy" – namely, that he or she (and other like individuals) should co-operate in the collective enterprise only if the others are doing so.

The more collective question "What should we do?", in contrast, encourages the individual to think about the overall profile of strategy choices that the individuals as a group should adopt and then identifies the choice for each individual as the one that simply (categorically) has that individual "doing (his or) her part" within that overall profile. Someone who has framed a strategy choice in this more collective way does not have to consider whether the other players are themselves doing their parts as components of this profile of strategies in order to identify and justify his or her particular choice.[15] Rather, in response to any question about why he or she was doing what he or she was doing, the first reaction would be only to say: "This is simply what we do when we do strategy profile *S* as best" or, perhaps, "This is simply what *I* do when we do strategy profile *S* as best."

I emphasize this response as a *first* reaction – that is, as something that he or she might say immediately about what he or she is doing. But while the individual characterizes and motivates his or her conduct in a *categorically* co-operative way – that is, as simply *what it is* to be a part of some overall collective strategy *S* – the individual need not view himself or herself as *absolutely* committed to co-operation under strategy *S*.[16] For while a co-operative strategy cannot be purely conditional (this not making any sense of collective action to begin with), it cannot end with a purely *un*conditional or absolute commitment either, since this makes nonsense of attending to whether there is really any social "whole" of which one's own individual choice is only a part. Thus, at some point, and more particularly at that point (still unspecified) where there are too few fellow co-operators, the first reaction must give way to a rational revision of what one is doing, to allow for not co-operating when others are not co-operating as well. This is a presumption in favour of co-operation, but not an absolute presumption.[17]

But, since collective action implies both the initial presumption in favour of cooperation *and* the defeasance of that presumption in the presence of countervailing non-co-operation, then the conjoining of these two ideas is not merely an ad hoc or convenient conglomeration of unrelated elements but rather, under the aspect of a single idea, a rational integration of these elements into the complex motivational structure that makes up homo socioeconomicus.

Before we examine the implications of this motivational structure for the organization and regulation of the charitable sector, we should summarize briefly what we have learned about the motivations of homo socioeconomicus. There seem to be three essential and quite general characteristics, and one broad organizing principle.

(1) There is conditional co-operation. In contrast to both homo economicus and homo sociologicus, who in the prisoner's dilemma play their respective strategies of non-co-operation and co-operation unconditionally, homo socioeconomicus co-operates conditionally, co-operating when like individuals are doing so and (subject to the qualifications below) not co-operating when others are not.

(2) There is a collective frame. Homo economicus, in a situation calling for either co-ordination or conditional co-operation, continues

to frame the strategic question individualistically as "What should *I* do?" Homo socioeconomicus, in contrast, frames the question in a collective way as "What should *we* do?" and then identifies the appropriate individual choice as that which has him or her doing his or her allotted part within the overall strategy profile chosen as best for the group.

(3) There is a non-absolute presumption. In further contrast to homo sociologicus, who adopts the collective frame absolutely, homo socioeconomicus takes it up presumptively, or non-absolutely, and reveals a willingness to revise the presumption if an insufficient number of other like individuals are actually co-operating.[18]

Finally, there is what we may term the broad organizing principle – "rational voluntarism," or "doing one's part." The three preceding points of contrast follow as implications of the single idea of rational voluntarism – namely, that *homo socioeconomicus* is the sort of reflective being that is motivated to do his or her allotted part within a collective enterprise. Neither an unconditional strategy (in either its co-operative or un-co-operative versions) nor a purely conditional strategy (that is, one without any sort of collective frame favouring co-operation) can make sense of the (both logical and ontological) priority of the collective enterprise that such a motivation, rationally construed, must presuppose.

With these summary points to guide us, we are now ready to see whether there is any real evidence that homo socioeconomicus is at work within the charitable sector. In the next section I argue that the evidence for homo socioeconomicus exists in the various ways in which our charitable institutions and their regulation conjoin concern for the three different possible pairs of the three general characteristics of homo socioeconomicus that together constitute rational voluntarism. One of these three possible pairs provides the focus for each of the three subsections in the third section.

First, there is, I suggest, some recognition of the motivational complexity of homo socioeconomicus in the fact that regulators of the charitable sector are keen to keep charities apart from politics. Such a regulatory posture shows that the regulators are aware that institutional environments that are more competitive than co-operative severely test the predisposition that homo socioeconomicus has to co-operate. This calls for a strategy that attempts to separate out, or screen,[19] the species' co-operative predisposition into the charitable sector, where his or her *non-absolute yet conditional* predisposition to co-operate can do its work. Thus, this subsection focuses on the conjunction of characteristics 1 and 3 above.

Second, I find further evidence of the predisposition to co-operate if others are doing so in the fact that donors reveal a highly elastic response to the tax subsidies that are offered on charitable donations. These high elasticities (with values higher than one) are hard to account for on the more conventional models of homo economicus, even when these models allow for conditional co-operation, and the subsidies themselves are unnecessary on the model of homo sociologicus. Thus use of these subsidies suggests that the taxing authorities are acutely aware that they are dealing with homo socioeconomicus in the charitable sector – that is, with a predisposition to co-operate that is conditional yet (presumptively) collective, or a conjunction of characteristics 1 and 2 above.

Third, and finally, I argue that rational volunteers themselves recognize that their commitments to co-operate are less than absolute. This explains their propensity to organize charities as non-profit organizations. It also explains, I argue, why a regulator might be concerned about their potential ability to earn unrelated business income. Again, this explanation calls on the motivational complexity of homo socioeconomicus. Where homo economicus shows too little commitment to any particular common cause to make sense of his or her choosing the non-profit form of organization to begin with, homo sociologicus shows too much commitment to the common cause to require his or going on with it in a non-profit form. Thus the choice of a non-profit form manifests the collective yet non-absolute commitment to co-operation that is peculiar to homo socioeconomicus and the conjunction of characteristics 2 and 3 above.

RATIONAL VOLUNTARISM IN THE CHARITABLE SECTOR

Rational Voluntarism and Political Debate

One of the most influential accounts of the charitable sector is that offered by Burton Weisbrod.[20] He views the sector as a kind of "add on" to whatever the political sector determines are the appropriate quantities of public goods that are to be provided out of general tax revenues. Some individuals, Weisbrod argues, will feel that these amounts (amounts determined, at least in the usual analyses of majoritarian voting, by the preferences of the median voter[21]) are inadequate and will naturally turn to the private sector to have the quantities supplemented. This, Weisbrod has argued, is the role properly played by the charitable sector, which acts largely in concert with, or as a supplement to, the political sector.

While this analysis is intriguing, nothing in it would appear to require that those in the charitable sector be prohibited from coming back to the political sector to lobby for policies favourable to their charitable organizations. Yet those charities that engage in such political activities are typically in danger of losing the very charitable status that allows them to attract tax-subsidized voluntary contributions.[22] Now it might be true that charitable groups would not be much expected under Weisbrod's analysis to return to the political sector, since the politically decisive preferences of the median voter would already have been exhausted. But it is not clear why, as a regulatory matter, there is any reason on his account actually to *prohibit* charities from any access to the political sector. After all, it is the essence of his theory that charitable groups view the political and the private voluntary sectors as merely complementary methods for achieving their goals.[23]

However, a quite different perspective on the relationship between the two realms follows from our understanding of homo socioeconomicus – a perspective that can make some sense of why we might want to keep them apart. Homo socioeconomicus, we recall, is someone who is prepared to do his or her part within some larger co-operative scheme, at least in so far as there is some substantial amount of co-operation already resolved upon by other like-minded co-operators. However, in the face of substantially countervailing evidence of non-co-operation, or in the absence of a common enterprise to begin with, homo socioeconomicus is also inclined to be less co-operative. This suggests, to the extent that we are relying for the production of public goods on the predispositions of homo socioeconomicus to be co-operative, that we will want to keep him or her isolated from any public forum that disputes rather than accepts a given conception of the public good or common enterprise. Such controversy, while understandable in politics, has the appearance of non-co-operation and may undermine the presumption in favour of co-operation that animates homo socioeconomicus.

Why should the production of public goods within the charitable sector be any less controversial than their production within the political realm? Is there not the same diversity of views to be accommodated in either case? Such questions ignore the fact that different institutions respond to this diversity of demand in different ways. In competitive markets for private goods, for example, various individuals buy different quantities of the goods at the same competitive prices. Indeed, the fact that they can and do do so is what allows them to bring their marginal rates of substitution for the different goods into equality with one another, so that efficient aggregate consumption results.

However, in politics, where public goods are supplied, and where everyone must therefore consume, the same quantities of the public goods so provided, these variable demands at the same prices cannot be accommodated by quantitative variations in individual consumption. Thus, the diversity of demand continues to show itself as a range of political disagreement that must somehow be resolved collectively – by majority voting, for example. In principle, of course, one could reduce the range of this political disagreement or conflict perhaps by having various individuals pay *different prices* for the *same quantity* of public good. Indeed, it should be possible in theory to use price discrimination across individuals with different demands for the public goods and to achieve thereby the same efficiencies in consumption of public goods as the market achieves vis-à-vis private goods.[24] However, such a scheme is impracticable, especially among diversely motivated individuals who realize that their higher demands for certain public goods will produce higher tax prices. In such conflictual circumstances, an individual, acting competitively, would appear to have every incentive to misrepresent his or her high demands as lower than what they actually are. Thus the political realm cannot resolve the range of disagreement across individuals about quantities of public goods by supplying the same quantities at different tax prices but must continue to resolve them collectively in the supply of the *same quantities* of public goods to be consumed at the *same tax prices.* We have reason therefore to worry about the high levels of disagreement about public goods that will manifest themselves politically.[25]

However, in the charitable sector, no group of individuals can impose its collective will on some other group at some given tax price but must instead consume the public good in both varying quantities and at varying prices (according to the magnitude of each individual's voluntarily chosen contribution to the collective enterprise of which he or she chooses to be a part). There is accordingly less conflict over (albeit the same diversity in) the supply of these same public goods. After all, why should group A care much at all about what public good group B chooses to provide? So long as there are no tax implications for the members of group A in the provision of a public good to the members of group B, the accommodation of difference between the individuals in these two groups takes on more of the appearance of the same sort of accommodation that we saw when the market supplied private goods in varying quantities to individuals.[26]

I emphasize the word "appearance" here. For readers will object immediately that this analysis ignores, in at least two important respects, the reality of how charities are funded. First, in a way still to be described and analysed, voluntary donations to charitable institutions attract certain forms of advantageous tax treatment, both for the donor and for the organizations themselves. It is common (though not universal[27]), for example, for donors to receive either a deduction from their taxable income or a credit against their tax liabilities according to how much they donate. And charities often receive tax breaks on the incomes that they earn or the taxes that they are obliged to pay as organizations. Second, whatever one might want to say about private donations to charities, by far the greater part of the funding of charities continues to come from general tax revenues.[28] Thus, the argument goes, to think of the charitable sector as involving "private decisions" is largely illusion.

I have more to say below about the tax advantages that charities enjoy, but here I want to focus on the suggestion that these tax advantages help to characterize the sector as public rather than private and thus render suspect any attempt to keep this sector apart from politics. The important point for my argument is not so much where the funding ultimately comes from, but rather what sort of decision-making is combined with what sort of funding. Just as collectively imposed (for example, majoritarian) decision-making can be combined with public funding in a non-divisive way if tax prices are variable for individuals (such variability serving to temper the destabilizing diversity that might otherwise be present within a broader range of political disagreement[29]), so public funding from general tax revenues, or even variable matching public funds by way of tax credits or deductions, can be combined without difficulty with the manifestation of a group will that is not collectively imposed. A non-collective manifestation of a group will is what occurs when charities are identified and funded by an aggregate of individual donors' decisions that are co-ordinated only under the aspect of some larger group enterprise or purpose. While each individual voluntarily does his or her part within the group enterprise, there is no moment of collective imposition of that group will on others. The tax revenues that come from matching deductions and credits are merely the further public implications of these individual decisions.

However, because they do not share a particular and public moment, these tax implications do not have the sort of political salience that might call for a reply from some other group. It is this sort of reply that can be destabilizing, both for the political sector in general *and* for the specialized sense of common enterprise that informed the co-ordinated action of the different volunteers to begin with.[30] Equally, while the approval of public funding from general tax revenues does seem to call for a genuinely collective decision, even that decision, in that it targets a charity that has been privately identified and (at least on initial donations) privately funded, is less self-consciously political than a decision that both originates in, and is completed by, public debate. Thus it too represents a lesser danger both to what is stable within politics and to what conduces to rational voluntarism within the charitable sector.

This reply might suggest that the only real concern for charities (and charitable status) is that some particular public good has been pursued as a political *activity*. That is, it might seem that the only real issue is whether the public good has either been identified as a matter of collective decision-making and in a way that might attract a political response, or has itself engaged in some overtly political activity that, equally, might call for a countervailing political move by some competitive group.[31] But, while this might be the more usual sort of concern, it is not the only one. Some charitable *purposes* can be sufficiently controversial to attract a political or regulatory response by a rival concern, even if they are not pursued as a political activity. For example, a group devoted to preventing the gratuitously cruel treatment of animals might not be controversial if it were organized as a private charity and there were no salient political moment that called for its funding out of general tax revenues. Everyone might not share the same enthusiasm for this cause, but few (or at least not so large a number as to be politically decisive and destabilizing) would believe that the charitable purpose was really bad (or worth organizing against) either. But the same group might become controversial, even in the absence of any political activities, if it began to organize the private sector against animal experimentation to the point where certain medical advances became jeopardized. And this controversy might well attract a decisive countervailing political response.

While this last sort of private activity should clearly be permitted, it is at least arguable that it should not be permitted *for a charity*.[32] The point of producing public goods within the charitable sector, unlike producing them politically, is that they can be produced without manifesting the controversy that endangers both political stability and the spirit of co-operation that is conducive to rational voluntarism in charities. However, to allow charitable status and, more specifically, the tax subsidy that goes with it to a charitable purpose that is itself politically controversial, may, rather than reducing political conflict as intended, actually exacerbate it. The result may be the reproduction of the original political instability that we sought to avoid, this time as a kind of regulatory overlay on the now tax-subsidized activities of (controversial) private initiatives. This is not an altogether coherent political result. The best way to avoid the problem, or at least the worst manifestations of it, would be to restrict charitable status, and its tax-subsidy advantages, to those groups whose activities are unlikely to appear to other groups as actually promoting some public *bad* and, therefore, as requiring some politically salient response. This analysis should also rationalize and inform a requirement that we typically observe of organizations seeking charitable status – namely, that they promote a genuine "public benefit" in their declared purposes and activities.[33]

I mean these arguments to show why it is so important to keep charitable institutions away from overtly political activity. Too close a relationship is bad, both for the politics that can otherwise unite us under broader social understandings and for the achievement of those more particular and common charitable purposes that distinguish us into groups and help to give different (and richer) meaning to our individual lives. An overly diverse range of public goods, at least when pursued in an exclusively political and competitive way, can mean a divisive and unproductive politics, the stuff of instability and stalemate. And when charities engage in political activity, the activity brings out what is non-co-operative in us and thereby undermines the achievement of the various public goods that serve to group each of us as part players within larger collective enterprises.

Moreover, these insights are available to us only if we believe in something like homo socioeconomicus. The homo sociologicus account cannot comprehend the danger that exists for charities themselves in politically competitive behaviour. Homo sociologicus is simply too (absolutely and implausibly) committed to his or her co-operative role for this sort of conflictual environment to undermine his or her disposition to co-operate. Homo economicus, in contrast, is no stranger to competitive behaviour; for him or her the puzzle must continue to be why there is any co-operation or voluntary giving at all. But if there is, and charitable institutions exist, then he or she too cannot comprehend why the sort of competitive being that he or she is should be kept apart from the competition that is politics. Only homo socioeconomicus, whose motivations to co-operate, while non-absolute, are sufficiently conditional on there being a surrounding environment of like-minded co-operators, can understand why voluntarism must be rationally and exclusively pursued within the more quiet waters of the charitable sector.

Rational Voluntarism and the Donor's Tax Subsidy

In my discussion above of a representative individual's motivation to contribute to some public cause, I suggested that to postulate a taste for pure giving, or so-called warm-glow giving, was as implausible as postulating a pure free rider. Certainly, the very fact that individuals do make charitable contributions at all does suggest that something is amiss with the free-rider analysis and the account of homo economicus that it presupposes. But is there any analogous reason for doubting the idea of "warm glow" giving, or the analogous idea, derivable from the account of homo sociologicus, that someone might give unconditionally just because that was the right thing to do?

The notion of "pure giving," whether it is motivated by tastes or explained by ethical commitments, does seem to be inconsistent with the empirical data on charitable contributions. Consider a warm-glow giver who, out of a pure desire to make his or her own contribution to some charity, is poised to make a gift of ten dollars. Consider now what would happen if he or she learned that he or she was to receive back from the government fifty cents on every dollar contributed to this charitable cause. Such a government subsidy would effectively reduce the cost, or price, of charitable giving by half. How should this change his or her behaviour? If all else remains the same, he or she should now be willing to contribute twenty dollars. Such a contribution, combined with the government subsidy of ten dollars, brings him or her back to a net personal contribution to the charity of ten dollars – the same gift that he or she wanted most to provide before the government subsidy was introduced. Thus the government subsidy allows the individual to continue to indulge a taste for giving ten dollars personally by giving twenty dollars *gross* less the ten-dollar government rebate.

The sort of behavioural response just described implies that the charitable giving of an individual who is motivated only by a pure taste for giving would exhibit a negative price elasticity equal to one. That is, a one per cent decrease in the price of charitable giving would, for such an individual, result in a one per cent increase in charitable donations. Some think that such a price elasticity has normative significance because it means that if a tax subsidy can reduce the price for charitable giving in this way, then the increased expenditures by taxpayers on charitable goods will exactly offset the forgone tax revenues. However, in a long series of papers, the economist Martin Feldstein and various collaborators have shown that in the United States this negative price elasticity of charitable giving actually exceeds one, suggesting that increased charitable contributions will *more* than offset any government tax subsidy.[34] This suggests that charitable donors are indulging something more than a mere taste for giving.

Economists, puzzled by Feldstein's results, would probably agree with this conclusion, suggesting that a charitable donor possesses both a taste for pure giving *and* a desire to consume more private goods. But such mixed motivation would normally suggest a negative price elasticity for charitable giving of *less* than one. The following comments by Hood, Martin, and Osberg on Feldstein's results are typical: "Feldstein's findings, however, imply that when marginal tax rates are reduced [i.e. government subsidies increased] individuals will give away to charity even more than the amount of their tax saving, thereby ending up with less [sic] consumption goods than they had previously. This the authors find somewhat odd. An elastic demand may be a reasonable finding for many goods, but when the 'good' in question is in fact consumption by others, it strains credulity.... It seems more reasonable to believe that when tax rates are cut people keep some and give some away."[35] Thus, even when the economist admits the possibility that a potential donor or volunteer, in addition to being concerned about his or her own consumption of public and private goods, might also be concerned about his act of giving to others, the economist does so in a way that cannot fully explain the empirical data.

However, homo socioeconomicus might well show a negative price elasticity greater than one for charitable giving. For recall that such a person reveals a commitment to personal giving and co-operation that varies with the level of giving and co-operation that is shown by others. Now consider how such an individual might react to a price reduction on charitable giving, as provided, for example, by some government or tax subsidy. He or she will not be like the individual who has an unwavering commitment to personal giving and who, therefore, increases his or her giving by one dollar for every dollar in tax subsidy received (a negative price elasticity of one). Nor will he or she be like the purely self-interested contributor whose (mixed) motives are still enough like those of the free rider that he or she cuts back on public-good contributions when others are providing matching contributions – for example, through taxes (a negative price elasticity of less than one).[36] Rather, the government subsidy positively affects contributions by homo socioeconomicus, because it reduces the price of charitable giving not only for him or her, *but also for others – something that gives him or her greater assurance that others like him or her will give.* This last fact probably encourages him or her to give even more than he or she might otherwise have done if he or she were concerned only about his or her own levels of giving, and certainly more than if his or her concerns about the giving of others were of the sort traditionally assumed by the economist. Thus it is reasonable to expect that the negative price elasticity of demand for charitable giving that is revealed by homo socioeconomicus will be larger than one.[37]

It is in this way, therefore, that Feldstein's results make good sense. Under the tax subsidy provided by a deduction or credit for one's donation, homo socioeconomicus not only faces a lower price for the contribution; he or she is also more assured that fellow co-operators, upon whose behaviour his or her own is conditional, will also make some sort of contribution for the same reason. Given the nature of his or her motivations, particularly his or her presumption in favour of an initial contribution, this should induce yet a further contribution. Moreover, there should be further, recursive second-order effects beyond these presumptive and first-order interactions. This, at least, is what Feldstein's high (greater than one) negative price elasticities suggest.

Rational Voluntarism, the Non-profit Form, and Commercial Activity

The most influential explanation of the non-profit form of economic organization is probably still that of Henry Hansmann,[38] who develops his account of the non-profit sector in relation to what he describes as the more usual way of providing private goods and services in a market economy – namely, through for-profit firms. For-profit firms, Hansmann argues, supply goods and services at a quantity and price that represent maximum social efficiency only if certain conditions are satisfied. Three of the more important of these conditions are, first, that consumers can make a reasonably accurate comparison of the products and prices of different firms before they make a decision to purchase; second, that consumers can reach a clear agreement with the chosen firm concerning the goods or services that it is to provide and the price to be paid; and, third, that consumers can determine subsequently whether the firm has complied with the resulting agreement and can obtain redress if it has not. These three conditions point to possible problems of contracting in the market, and the failure of any one of them might suggest "contract failure."

Hansmann identifies three basic forms of contract failure that might require, in his view, the existence of non-profit firms as a solution.[39] One of these, which he calls the "separation between the purchaser and the recipient of the service," most obviously applies to charitable donations. Indeed, he illustrates the problem with the example of CARE, a charitable organization devoted to distributing food and other supplies to needy individuals in the Third World. Hansmann argues that if CARE were organized for profit, it would have a strong incentive to "chisel" on the goods or services that it has promised to provide, since any savings thereby achieved accrue to it as its residual claim, or profit. The geographical separation between the donor-purchaser and the location where the donated goods are received and consumed is what makes this chiselling possible. Given such a monitoring problem,

Hansmann argues, a donor is likely to choose a non-profit over a for-profit firm to provide this service, because, while a non-profit still has the same capacity to chisel the donor, it has less incentive to do so, since it no longer captures any of the cost savings as extra profit. Other examples, according to Hansmann, of problematic separation between purchaser and ultimate consumer include day care facilities (where the young child is unable effectively to monitor the quality of the service provided and report any discrepancies back to the parent) and nursing homes (where there are analogous difficulties for an ageing relative).

The second form of contract failure occurs when firms provide public goods, which Hansmann defines in the usual economic fashion, focusing on the problem of non-excludability (where the good, once provided, is equally available to all) and the consequent problem of free riders. His examples include radio signals and television broadcasts – a not altogether happy choice for his purposes, since so much of the radio and television sector is dominated by for-profit rather than non-profit firms. However, Hansmann suggests that these firms have overcome the problem of the free rider by effectively selling audiences to advertisers rather than by selling television or radio to audiences, thus effectively converting the problematic public-goods situation into the more usual one of supplying private goods (in that access to advertising spots is available only to advertisers who pay).[40] Nevertheless, some people, Hansmann suggests, do not like the radio or television that is provided in this way and indicate a willingness (despite the free-rider problem) to buy a different sort of product. However – and this is Hansmann's essential point – they are more likely to take their unsatisfied demands for commercial-free radio or television to a non-profit than to a for-profit firm because, given that the product is a public good, if they buy it from a for-profit firm, they can never be sure that their contribution has had any marginal impact on the product provided. Their contribution might just as easily have gone to higher profits on the *same* level and quality of output; that, at least, is where the incentives lie for a for-profit firm. Thus consumers of public radio and television are much more inclined to support non-profits, which have no such profit-seeking incentive. By doing so they can be more sure that their contribution has had a marginally beneficial effect on the quantity or quality of the product provided to them. After all, with only fixed claims coming out of the firm, and no residual claim in the form of profit-taking, where else can the marginal contribution go except into the production process?

Hansmann's third form of contract failure centres around personal services that are inherently complex and therefore difficult for the consumer to assess. Health care and education are his examples. Once more the problem is the consumer's inability to monitor the purchase adequately – a fact that again lends itself to possible chiselling by the seller. Hansmann argues that the non-profit form that is commonly observed in education and health care shows that consumers think that this risk is smaller for non-profits for reasons that, by now, should be familiar.[41]

Of these three forms of contract failure, only the first, invoking the separation between purchaser and recipient, would seem to involve donative activity or charitable giving. And even here the connection to the non-profit form is not immediate. I can also send a gift through a for-profit firm, as I do when I ask a department store to send a wedding gift, or a florist to send flowers, to a friend. But Hansmann's rejoinder is that in such cases the separation of the purchaser from the recipient is less great and that, as a consequence, delivery of the gift or donation is more easily monitored.[42] I can and do easily check to see if my flowers have arrived at their destination, and I look forward to the usual "thank you" note confirming the receipt of my wedding gift. Thus Hansmann argues quite convincingly that the presence of for-profit firms in these particular cases of gift giving is actually supportive of his theory rather than contrary to its predictions.

However, one striking feature of Hansmann's analysis obscures the possible considerable overlap between altruistic or charitable activity and the non-profit organizational form.[43] All of his examples are driven by *demand*-side analysis. In the case of CARE, for example, donors decide that they would rather trust a non-profit than a for-profit firm to deliver foreign aid to some faraway place, and the suppliers of that aid, who (like florists, it seems) could just as easily have been organized for profit, simply respond to that demand. In the case of public broadcasting, consumers dissatisfied with commercial broadcasting look elsewhere, to non-profits in particular, for quality radio and television; again, the producers simply react to this demand for a non-profit institution.[44]

However, it is difficult to look at the usual list of non-profits, which includes social service agencies, providers of health services, religious organizations, arts and cultural groups, and educational institutions, without finding some sort of charitable motivation, or commitment to a public cause, operating on the *supply* side as well. These are all public services or, to use an old- fashioned term, public "callings," where for-profit motivation seems somehow out of place.

Why "out of place"? It is not because "profit" is a nasty word, but rather because the non-profits, as suppliers of these services (even when they are commercial non-profits supported by sales revenues earned in the market; more on this below), are making transfers of very specific goods to (often) specifically targeted individuals. That is, they are making so called transfers in kind.[45] They will therefore both seek to control the price at which the good is sold – choosing often something less than the profit-maximizing price to encourage the transfer – *and* focus more often on the special qualities of the good that is delivered. These concerns, which are more ideological than profit-maximizing, provide ample supply-side motivation for their decisions.

The point is not that the very idea of taking profits undermines the possibility of a charitable transfer to others.[46] One could, for example, if one were homo sociologicus, simply make charitable transfers, or transfers in kind, to targeted recipients via for-profit firms. This may require that one not always choose those opportunities elsewhere that better maximize one's profit, but that should not be a difficulty for the likes of homo sociologicus, whose commitment to the common cause is absolute. Thus, there is no obvious reason why homo sociologicus need organize the delivery of charitable goods in non-profit form.

Rather, the point of the non-profit form of organization – a point that only homo socioeconomicus could foresee – is to remove the temptation within a for-profit firm to defect from supplying goods identified as appropriate to the common cause or transfer in kind that links him or her with fellow co-operators. After all, such action might lead to higher profits. But the ideologically motivated volunteer does not want, at least presumptively, to become the sort of investor who is interested more in profits, whatever the source, than in the specifically identified transfers in kind that originally informed his or her collective purpose and co-ordinated his or her particular contribution with the contributions of others. Furthermore, he or she does not want fellow investors to be able to sell out to such profit-oriented investors, who would probably seek to appoint managers of the charity that would be interested only in profit.[47] Thus homo socioeconomicus, aware that his or her presumptive commitment to the common cause is more fragile (less absolute) than that of homo sociologicus, seeks to remove these supply-side temptations by organizing the enterprise as a non-profit and, further, by restricting the transfer of ownership in the non-profit firm.

The same sort of worries about what is sometimes called "mission drift," or drift away from the public cause chosen for the firm, can extend to how the organization, once formed as a non-profit and subject to restrictions on transfer of ownership, might afterwards be managed. First, to control managers' "free cash flow," and the managerial discretion that goes with it,[48] there is good reason to have a regular obligation to make disbursements of the kind imposed on charities by, for example, Canada's Income Tax Act.[49] This rule disciplines managers to the common cause by forcing them to return regularly to their ideologically motivated investors and donors.

Second, and also related to free cash flow, there should be limits on both the investments that charities can make and the sorts of "unrelated business activities" in which they can engage. Moreover, this last restriction should continue even if management says that the money so obtained would go to charitable purposes. The idea is not to subsidize just *any* charitable purpose, but rather the one that motivated the original investors under a common cause.

Even if charities were permitted to earn unrelated business income,[50] it would not follow, because of their charitable status, that they should receive any kind of special tax relief on the earning of this income. Such tax relief may be appropriate for donated income, since donors would not be much encouraged by a tax subsidy on donations if they perceived that the donation was only to be taxed later in the hands of the very collective enterprise that was their reason, or common cause, for giving it. But tax relief is not appropriate on income from unrelated business activity, since, again, the idea is to aid not just any sort of charitable activity, even one chosen by the managers of the charity in question, but only that selected by, and collectively motivating, particularly organized and focused donors and investors.[51] Thus there is a need for a tax break only on donated income; anything broader is in danger of, first, undermining the motivational impact for homo socioeconomicus of having a *single* common cause and, second, subsidizing the managers of charities in their "altruistic" use of other people's money.[52]

Finally, nothing in the argument so far requires that income from "related business activity" be non-taxable. This last recommendation is different from some prevailing views *and* from current legal practice.[53] Nevertheless, it is a common criticism that the current tax subsidy on related business income operates as an unfair government subsidy of non-profits in their competition with for profit firms.[54] The analysis presented here would allow this subsidy to be removed, although it would not require it. One of my points is that there can be a charitable transfer in kind in selling a good (or providing a certain quality in the good) in a commercial market at *less* than its market price. But if that is so, there is no donation in the price that *is* charged and, therefore, no charity in the income that is received commercially. Thus, at least on the argument presented here, there is no need to exempt a charity's related business income from corporate income taxation.

CONCLUSION

In this chapter I have tried to provide an outline of the complex motivational structure of homo socioeconomicus and to present some evidence for the existence of this more complicated sort of being in the way in which our charitable institutions are organized and regulated. I have also referred to "rational voluntarism" as the phenomenon that this more complicated sort of motivation makes possible. Each of the terms in this phrase serves to displace one of the two simpler models of human behaviour that we see in homo economicus and homo sociologicus. That there is any voluntarism at all, for example, is a problem for the model of homo economicus. Homo economicus is not much inclined to volunteer, preferring instead that the other fellow make the requisite contribution to the public good. Thus the mere fact that we have a vibrant voluntary sector must mean that we are not all like that.

Or perhaps it means only that we are not all like that all of the time. For I have also stressed the vestigial rationality in the voluntarism that we do observe, which is hard to accommodate in the model of homo sociologicus. Homo sociologicus avoids the paradoxes of collective action that plague homo economicus only by postulating an absolute and somewhat unreflective commitment to social role or norm-guided behaviour. But this also seems contrary to what we observe in the charitable sector and its regulation. The strongly virtuous being that is homo sociologicus would have no use for the strategy of institutional separation that seeks to shelter a more fragile co-operative motive from both political competition and commercial temptation. Yet we find both forms of this strategy at work in the regulation and organization of charities. Furthermore, there would appear to be no need to encourage or sustain such a virtuous commitment to co-operation by offering it anything like a tax subsidy. The tax subsidy should at best make no difference to homo sociologicus; at worst, it might undermine social co-operation as a virtue because it would tend to frame it as something to be bought.[55] Again, however, we not only observe the tax subsidy working on voluntary donations in the charitable sector, but we also see it working in a supportive rather than counterproductive way.

The three subsections of the third section each served to illustrate, in differing combinations, the three general characteristics of homo socioeconomicus, namely, that his or her co-operation is conditional, collectively framed, and non-absolute. The separation from politics allows our less-than-absolute charitable instincts to get a more secure, albeit conditional, purchase on the co-operative behaviour of others than would be provided in a world of political competition. And the separation from the profit motive protects this merely conditional presumption in favour of the collectively framed co-operation from falling prey to the temptation that comes with anything less than absolute commitment. The success of the tax subsidy for charitable donations shows both the (presumptively) collective frame and the conditional nature of co-operation at work. All three subsections together, therefore, demonstrate the full range of homo socioeconomicus and the full effect of his or her rational voluntarism.

NOTES

I am grateful to Susan Rose-Ackerman for her very thoughtful comment on this paper at the conference. I was also much helped by comments from Kevin Davis, Abraham Drassinower, Ed Iacobucci, and Jim Phillips on an earlier draft.

1 David Hume is often cited for the idea that it is wise, at least in the design of governmental institutions, not to assume too much of persons. In his essay *On the Independency of Parliament*, in K. Haakronssen, ed., *Hume's Political Science* (Cambridge: Cambridge University Press, 1994), he remarks: "In constraining any system of government and fixing the several checks and controls of the constitution, every man ought to be supposed a knave and to have no other end in all his actions than private interest." This may be a wise strategy for the design of governmental institutions, where there is a large concentration of power and the possibility of its abuse, but as a more general assumption for understanding institutions it is overly narrow and encourages theorists to overlook some opportunities for better institutional design. On this last point, see G. Brennan, "Selection and the Currency of Award," in R.E. Goodin, *The Theory of Institutional Design* (Cambridge: Cambridge University Press, 1996), 258.

2 I should register some reservations here about implicating Kant as an "unthinking" paragon of virtue, since so much of his argument turns on the freedom that goes with being a rational self *exercising* that rationality over given predispositions. For Kant an action has no moral worth if it is merely done "in accordance with duty" but not "out of duty," for example. Nevertheless, there is in Kant, and many Kantians, the idea that one should do the "right thing" regardless of what others do, and it is this lack of attention to others' conduct that I am characterizing as "unthinking" here.

3 The relief of poverty may be paradigmatic of what charities do *as* charities, but it is arguable that it is not typical of what most organizations reg-

istered as charities actually do. For example, according to D. Sharpe, chapter 2 in this volume, Table 2.1, the number of registered charities in Canada's so-called welfare sector is second to the number in "religion." Furthermore, in terms of revenues, the welfare sector is third after hospitals and teaching institutions (Table 2.5).

4 For a good critique of these sorts of game-theoretic accounts of voluntary giving, see R. Sugden, "On the Economics of Philanthropy," *Economic Journal* 92 (1982), 341, and "Reciprocity: The Supply of Public Goods through Voluntary Contributions," *Economic Journal* 94 (1984), 772. The prisoner's dilemma does not arise simply from an individual's being "selfish," in the sense of giving exclusive weight to his or her own interests. Pure altruists, who give exclusive weight to the interests of others, will also confront the prisoner's dilemma. Indeed, it is possible to construct a prisoner's dilemma for any agent who gives any sort of *unequal* weighting to the interests of the players. It is only if all the individuals weigh the interests of all the players equally in their choices, in the manner of the classical utilitarian, that the prisoner's dilemma can be avoided. For discussion, see J. Tilley, "Prisoner's Dilemma from a Moral Point of View," *Theory and Decision* 41 (1996), 187. Of course, this should not be altogether surprising, since then all such individuals will have identical rankings of all the various social outcomes.

However, for these utilitarian individuals there will still be the problems of co-ordination, to which I refer below – a problem effectively analysed in D.H. Hodgson, *Consequences of Utilitarianism* (Oxford: Clarendon Press, 1967), and in D. Regan, *Utilitarianism and Cooperation* (Oxford: Clarendon Press, 1980). All of this suggests that the problems that begin with the prisoner's dilemma are not to be solved by manipulating interests, and the weights we give to them, but rather require some rethinking of what it is to make a rational choice in the face of these interests. This is the spirit in which I offer the arguments in this chapter.

5 See J. Andreoni, "Impure Altruism and Donations to Public Goods: A Theory of Warm Glow Giving," *Economic Journal* 100 (1990), 464.

6 I am grateful to Kate Kempton for raising this point. However, there is still some ambiguity here. It is clear that the warm-glow giver will rank outcome x in the prisoner's dilemma as best of the four and outcome y as worst. Thus, however he or she ranks the other two outcomes, w or z, he or she will have a dominant strategy to contribute to, or co-operate in, the provision of the public good. But if the warm-glow giver ranks the four outcomes in the order x, w, z, y, then it would seem that he or she ranks the consequence of the public good actually being provided by others in outcome w as higher than his or her own inconsequential contribution in z, something that belies a motivation focused purely (and selfishly) on his or her own giving. It is only if he or she ranks the four

outcomes in the order *x, z, w, y* that we can say with some confidence that he or she is concerned only about his or her own giving regardless of the consequences. Of course, as the notion of dominance suggests, these differences in the overall preference orderings of the warm-glow giver will not be observable in the choices made.

7 Again, there is room for some ambiguity here (compare the previous note). If homo sociologicus ranks the four outcomes in the prisoner's dilemma in the order *x, z, w, y*, then his or her commitment to doing his or her part does seem to be thoughtless and empty. However, if his or her ranking is *x, w, z, y*, then he or she would appear to be somewhat sensitive to the general idea that "doing one's part" makes more sense when there is a whole (*w*) of which his or her own contribution can be deemed a part (*x*); this is what induces him or her to rank *z* as only a third-best outcome. The problem is that by continuing to rank *z* ahead of outcome *y*, he or she does not carry this insight into his or her behaviour in a thoroughly consistent way. The result is that he or she continues to have the same dominant strategy of co-operating, or of contributing to the public good, as does the more thoughtless version of homo sociologicus.

8 The idea of conditional co-operation has been much discussed under the aspect of David Gauthier's theory of a "constrained maximizer," someone who has developed for prisoner's-dilemma situations a disposition to co-operate with another co-operator, but not otherwise. (A "straightforward maximizer," by contrast, is someone who would not co-operate, even with a fellow co-operator – the sort of unconstrained maximizing behaviour that we saw in the prisoner's dilemma as originally presented.) Gauthier has argued that it is in the interest of individuals to develop this sort of disposition, at least if the disposition can be made somewhat transparent to others. See D. Gauthier, *Morals by Agreement* (Oxford: Clarendon Press, 1986).

In this chapter the idea is more that a conditional form of co-operation is logically implied by the notion of "doing one's part," a motivation that need not be grounded in self-interest, although it does involve seeing one's behaviour *rationally* – that is, as *organized* under some *categorical* (and collective) sense of "*what it is* that *we* are doing."

9 If we were working with preferences to explain this sort of thinking, then we would have substituted what Sen calls an "assurance game" for the original game of prisoner's dilemma; see A. Sen, "Choice, Orderings, and Morality," in S. Korner, ed., *Practical Reason* (Oxford: Blackwell, 1974). In an assurance game, a representative individual ranks the above four possible outcomes in the order *x, w, y, z*. But here I am retaining the original prisoner-dilemma preferences and suggesting a rational motivation for playing that game which would induce an individual to behave

as if he or she had assurance-game preferences. Sen also suggests this "as if" connection but does not suggest a comparable sort of motivation.

The sort of principled motivation I am attempting to articulate here is very like Sugden's principle of "reciprocity"; see Sugden, "Reciprocity." However, Sugden locates the motivation for the principle of reciprocity in a sense of "fairness" between individuals rather than in the idea of "doing one's part" in some collective enterprise. Sugden's more individualistic approach has the somewhat extreme consequence that an individual has to reciprocate only an amount of co-operation equal to the minimum amount of co-operation shown by any other fellow co-operator. Thus the non-co-operation of any one co-operator can justify the non-co-operation of any or all others. The idea of doing one's part within a (largely, but not completely) successful collective scheme does not have this extreme implication.

10 I have argued elsewhere that a rational individual is someone who follows a rule presumptively, but only in a defeasible (non-absolute) way, and that this account of rational behaviour might help us to avoid certain difficuties in the theory of games. See B. Chapman, "Law Games: Defeasible Rules and Revisable Rationality," *Law and Philosophy* 17 (1998), 443.

11 See G. Den Hartogh, "The Rationality of Conditional Cooperation," *Erkenntnis* 38 (1993), 405.

12 I have suggested that an obligation on the sender to provide reasons for his or her message can make these messages at least partially transparent to other players, so that misrepresentation of preferences is a less accessible strategy; see B. Chapman, "Rationally Transparent Social Interactions," in M. Streit, ed., *Cognition, Rationality, and Institutions* (Berlin: Springer, 2000), 189–204.

13 For an analysis of this game, and the problems that it presents for conventionally rational actors, see R. Sugden, "Rational Co-ordination," in F. Farina, F. Hahn, and S. Vanucci, eds., *Ethics, Rationality and Economic Behaviour* (Oxford: Clarendon Press, 1996), 245–62; and in R. Sugden, "Rational Choice: A Survey of Contributions from Economics and Philosophy," *Economic Journal* 101 (1991), 751, 774–8.

14 Michael Bacharach refers to the more collective version of this question, "What should we do?," as operating in the "we-frame," contrasting it with the more conventional game-theoretic question (involving the usual Nash conjecture), "What should I do?," which operates in the "I/he frame"; see his "'We' Equilibria: A Variable Frame Theory of Cooperation," paper presented at the Seminar on Cooperative Reasoning, St John's College, Oxford, 1997. I discuss the implications of Bacharach's variable frame theory for play in the prisoner's dilemma in Chapman, "Rationally Transparent Social Interactions." For philosophical accounts

of the "we-frame" idea, see R. Tuomela and K. Miller, "We-Intentions" *Philosophical Studies* 53 (1988), 367; and G.J. Postema, "Morality in the First Person Plural," *Law and Philosophy* 14 (1995), 35.

15 Compare Robert Sugden's characterization of "team reasoning" in his "Thinking as a Team: Towards an Explanation of Nonselfish Behavior," *Social Philosophy and Policy* 10 (1993), 69, 86: "To act as a member of a team is to act as a *component* of the team. It is to act on a concerted plan, doing one's allotted part in the plan without asking whether, taking other members actions as given, one's own action is contributing to the team's objective."

In my "Law Games," I have also argued that the prisoner's dilemma game might be played by those who can see themselves as being in either an individualistic- or a collective-choice frame and that the non-simultaneous availability of these two different frames might give rise to a defeasible conception of rational choice – that is, a conception that makes one's choice under a rational strategy conditional on what the other (otherwise identical and symmetrically placed) player happens to choose. This argument combines features of Sugden's team reasoning and Bacharach's variable frame analysis; see Bacharach, "'We' Equilibria."

16 See Chapman, "Law, Incommensurability, and Conceptually Sequenced Argument," *University of Pennsylvania Law Review* 146 (1998), 1487, 1507, on the difference between the *categorical* and the *absolute* within the sequenced structure of a defeasibly rational or reasoned choice. Also see Chapman, "Law Games," 455, for the application of this idea to rational choice within games.

17 In Tuomela and Miller, "We-Intentions," 374–8, the presumption in favour of co-operation is captured in the idea that the agent has an "unconditional" intention to co-operate. But the agent must be able to expect in some broad way that his or her co-actors are (probably) going to co-operate – an expectation that would obviously be severely tested if the (probable) level of such co-operation gets too low.

18 My account of homo socioeconomicus is very similar to, and much inspired by, Philip Pettit's notion of a "virtually self-interested rational actor"; see P. Pettit, "Institutional Design and Rational Choice," in R.E. Goodwin, ed., *The Theory of Institutional Design* (Cambridge: Cambridge University Press, 1996), 54, 68. However, in Pettit's theory, the defeasance of a prior motivation to cooperate in "role play" seems to come about almost only because the sacrifice in the satisfaction of self-interest gets large enough that a "red light" goes on for the agent. Up until that point the presence of self-interest is only "virtual," not actual. In my account, the idea need be less about self-interest and personal sacrifice. It could simply be that it is harder to "frame" one's behaviour col-

lectively as there become fewer fellow cooperators. Thus the problem is about the use of concepts rather than a test of personal preferences or self-interest – something that Pettit has characterized elsewhere as "inference theoretic" rather than "decision theoretic" concerns; see P. Pettit, *The Common Mind: An Essay on Psychology, Society and Politics* (Oxford: Oxford University Press, 1993), chap. 5.

Indeed, some of these more conceptual concerns arise even for Pettit when he speaks (in "Insitutional Design," 78–85) of certain features of institutional design. For example, when we become focused on deterrence or deviance, Pettit argues, we raise the profile of non-co-operation in a way that does not happen when we see institutions from a more "compliance centered" point of view. This can undermine co-operation. But it is not clear that anything has changed for the actor in terms of self-interest; only the conceptual frame that supports, or gives profile to, co-operation has changed. I make use of a more compliance-centered strategy to support charitable contributions in the first two subsections of the third section of this chapter. (It may well be, however, that the argument in the third subsection relies more on something like Pettit's "virtually self-interested rational actor.")

19 For interesting discussion of this screening strategy, and a claim that theory of institutional design has too much neglected it, see Brennan, "Selection," and Pettit, "Institutional Design."

20 B.A. Weisbrod, "Toward a Theory of the Voluntary Nonprofit Sector in a Three-Sector Economy," in S. Rose-Ackerman, ed., *The Economics of Non-Profit Insitutions* (New Haven, Conn.: Yale University Press, 1986), 21–44.

21 On the median-voter result, see D.C. Mueller, *Public Choice II* (Cambridge: Cambridge University Press, 1989), 67–73. This result assumes that there is some single and decisive continuum of judgment along which all voters can assess all the alternatives for public choice. Movements towards the alternative that the median voter most prefers will always receive majority support, and movements away from this point will obtain only minority support. Thus the median voter's most preferred outcome on the continuum is the majority voting equlbrium outcome. When there is no such general agreement on a single decisive continuum for judgment, a majority voting equilibrium is much harder to achieve. For discussion of the significance of this last point for the regulation of charities and their political activities, see B. Chapman, "Between Markets and Politics: A Social Choice Theoretic Appreciation of the Charitable Sector," *George Mason Law Review* 6 (1998), 821.

22 For more on the so called political-purposes doctrine in the law of charities, see Drassinower, chapter 9 in this volume.

23 Weisbrod's approach is quite conventional in this respect. The idea is to postulate that people in different institutions are more or less the same,

and that they simply react differently to different institutional constraints. The idea that different sorts of people might be attracted to different institutions, which informs the "screening" hypothesis of both Brennan, "Selection," and Pettit, "Institutional Design," or the related idea, developed here, that different institutions might bring out systematic differences in people's motivations, is viewed by economists with suspicion. One economist, Harold Demsetz, has even labelled this as "the people could be different" fallacy, his argument being that it is naive, for example, to assume that those within the public sector are somehow more "other-regarding" than those in competitive markets. See H. Demsetz, "Information and Efficiency: Another Viewpoint," *Journal of Law and Economics* 11 (1969), 1.

24 This would be the effect of charging what are called Lindahl prices; see J. Buchanan, *The Demand and Supply of Public Goods* (Chicago: University of Chicago Press, 1968), chap. 7. For how the market accommodates variable demand by having variable quantities of private goods consumed at given competitive prices, how the political sector could theoretically solve the same problem by permitting the identical consumption of a public good at variable prices, and how the charitable sector might even be seen as achieving something of the latter, see B. Chapman, "The Governance of Nonprofits," in R. Daniels and R. Morck, eds., *Corporate Decisionmaking in Canada* (Calgary: University of Calgary Press, 1995).

25 For argument that this might result in the sort of majority voting paradox that forms a principal subject of concern for public choice theory, see Chapman, "Between Markets and Politics," 845–53.

26 When individuals in group A and group B must come together and, politically, decide the relative quantities of public goods A and B that are to be provided by them as a whole, the reference group for their collective deliberations is, correspondingly, groups A *and* B. But this larger group has, by hypothesis, (internal) differences of opinion rather than a common cause. It is this potential for conflict around a moment of collective choice, rather than a mere diversity of opinion across groups each in pursuit of its own common cause, that undermines the disposition to co-operate in homo socioeconomicus. I am grateful to Susan Rose-Ackerman for encouraging me to clarify this point.

27 In the United Kingdom, for example, there is no tax deduction or tax credit for charitable donations.

28 For a statistical summary of the funding sources of charities in Canada, see Sharpe, chapter 2 in this volume.

29 See ibid., n 25.

30 Sugden suggests that the same sort of concern would attach to his account of charitable giving under the notion of "reciprocity"; see Sugden, "Reciprocity," 783.

31 On this view, the sort of argument that was used against allowing an ancillary-activities doctrine in *Scarborough Community Legal Services v. The Queen*, (1985) 17 DLR (4th) 308 (FCA), may make some sense. The worry is not that certain political activities, if merely ancillary, might be used to mischaracterize an organization's overall charitable purpose. Rather, it is that a bona fide charitable organization, if active politically, can attract a political response that is both destabilizing as a political matter and undermining of the commom purpose that induces co-operative and charitable behaviour to begin with. For a more sympathetic view of the ancillary-purposes doctrine, and for a critique of the *Scarborough* case that rejected the use of this doctrine in the case of charitable organizations, see Phillips, chapter 7 in this volume.

32 For some indication of how this particular example might be treated in the English law of charities, see *National Anti-Vivisection Society v. Inland Revenue Commissioners* [1948] AC 31 (HL).

33 The fourth and most general head of the common law categorization of charitable purposes is "other purposes beneficial to the community"; see *Commissioners for the Special Purposes of the Income Tax* v. *Pemsel* [1891] AC 531 (HL). Purposes that are controversial as goals within the community are less likely, it seems, to be construed as generally beneficial. Thus political controversy, if directed at charitable organizations that otherwise have no political salience because they are not politically active, evidences a purpose that is not for the public or general benefit and therefore is, while perhaps legally permissible, not charitable.

While some purposes might be controversial in fact, they attend to such a broad range of interests that they *should* not (reasonably) be controversial. The protection of universal human rights – something that is presupposed in the effective pursuit of any set of interests, no matter how partial or private – might be an example. Thus, it is not clear that the activities or purposes of Amnesty International should be viewed as so political as to be non-charitable. For further discussion of this sort of example, as well as more general issues, see Drassinower, "The Doctrine of Political Purposes."

34 See Feldstein, "The Income Tax and Charitable Contributions: Part I – Aggregate and Distributional Effects," *National Tax Journal* 28 (1975), 81; Feldstein and Clotfelter, "Tax Incentives and Charitable Contributions in the United States: A Micro-econometric Analysis," *Journal of Public Economics* 5 (1976), 1; Feldstein and Taylor, "The Income Tax and Charitable Contributions," *Econometrica* 44 (1976), 120; and Boskin and Feldstein, "Effects of the Charitable Deduction on Contributions by Low Income and Middle Income Households: Evidence from the National Survey of Philanthropy," *Review of Economics and Statistics* 59 (1977), 351. For a good survey of the price elasticity for charitable contributions

which shows that Feldstein's results are generally accepted, see Clotfelter and Steuerle, "Charitable Contributions," in Aaron and Pechman, eds., *How Taxes Affect Economic Behaviour* (Washington, DC: The Brookings Institution, 1981). Some research has suggested that the negative price elasticities for charitable giving in Canada are less than they are in the United States (and, on average, less than one). See G. Glenday et al., "Tax Incentives for Personal Charitable Contributions," *Review of Economics and Statistics* 68 (1986), 688; Hood, Martin, and Osberg, "Economic Determinants of Individual Charitable Donations in Canada," *Canadian Journal of Economics* 10 (1977), 653. However, in their recent summary of the U.S. and Canadian empirical work, Scharf, Cherniavsky, and Hogg have concluded as follows: "Price elasticities of giving in the United States have largely been estimated to be greater than one in absolute value, indicating that not only do tax concessions garner more dollars per dollar of concession, but they are also cost-effective from a revenue point of view. The same conclusion holds generally for Canada, with two exceptions [citing the above two Canadian studies].": K. Scharf et al., *Tax Incentives for Charities in Canada*, Canadian Policy Research Networks, Working Paper No. CPRN 3 (Ottawa, 1997).

35 Hood et al., "Economic Determinants," 660–1. This idea that the increased contributions by others should lead to a *reduction* in the contributions of any one individual is also part of Howard Margolis's theory of altruism. See his *Selfishness, Altruism and Rationality* (Chicago: University of Chicago Press, 1982). This should not be surprising, since Margolis admits that his theory of giving can be interpreted as akin to the economist's familiar notions of diminishing marginal rates of substitution, here applied to substitutions between spending in the group interest (for example, the pure utility of giving) and spending in self-interest (for example, the usual free-rider motive). See ibid., 42.

Thus we can think in the following way of the differences between the free rider, the mixed-motive contributor modelled by both the economist and Margolis, and the contributor whom the economists critique in Feldstein's work. Where the free rider cuts back dollar for dollar on his or her own potential contributions, in the light of the contributions of others, this is analogous to not spending *any* of the additional dollars received on public goods if he or she suddenly and unexpectedly became richer. To see this, observe that the free rider is trying to achieve an outcome where, for example, he or she enjoys $10 worth of the public good *and* keeps $10 worth of his or her own wealth. He or she can do this *either* by free riding once he or she knows that others will make the $10 contribution *or* by making the $10 contribution when others do not *and then* becoming $10 richer. In the latter case, the additional, unexpected $10 does not result in any additional contributions to the public good. It is therefore in this sense that the free rider does not spend any additional dollars of his or her wealth on public goods.

However, those economists (together with Margolis) who believe in some marginal rate of substitution between spending on the public good (perhaps because of the warm glow that one gets) and private goods (the return from free riding) would suggest *some* increased expenditure on public goods as one becomes richer, though *not* so much as an increase of a dollar or *more* for every dollar of increased wealth. It is the latter possibility that Hood et al. are criticizing in Feldstein's high-price elasticity results (lower prices, after all, are one way to increase everyone's real wealth or income).

36 See Feldstein, "The Income Tax"; Feldstein and Clotfelter, "Tax Incentives"; Feldstein and Taylor, "The Income Tax"; Boskin and Feldstein, "Effects"; Clotfelter and Steuerle, "Charitable Contributions"; Glenday et al., "Tax Incentives"; Hood et al., "Economic Determinants"; Scharf et al., *Tax Incentives*; Margolis, *Selfishness.*

37 Strictly speaking, what the account of homo socioeconomicus predicts is that the effect of a tax (positive or negative) on any one individual will be reinforced or magnified *for that individual* by the same effects that the tax will have on other like-minded individuals. Feldstein's empirical results, where the price elasticities of voluntary giving are greater than one, are merely one possible manifestation of this. Of course, increasing income tax rates on individuals, so that the price of charitable giving drops (there now being a greater tax advantage in the charitable deduction) can have both a substitution effect (towards charitable giving and away from other "spending") and an income effect (away from spending altogether). If the income effect dominates the substitution effect, so that the taxpayer responds *negatively* to a more advantageous charitable tax deduction (i.e., an increase in the tax rate) then the homo socioeconomicus account would suggest an elasticity of *less* than one. The general point, therefore, is that under the account of homo socioeconomicus the divergence of elasticities will be larger than that expected by the more simple theory of homo economicus. Feldstein's results only provide some corroboration (on one of the two extremes) for the homo socioeconomicus account.

38 Hansmann, "The Role of Nonprofit Enterprise," *Yale Law Journal* 89 (1980), 835.

39 Although these three forms of contract failure appear in ibid., the three-part classification appears most clearly in his article "Reforming Nonprofit Corporation Law," *University of Pennsylvania Law Review* 129 (1981), 497.

40 Hansmann, " Role," 850.

41 For some effective criticism of Hansmann's account of the non-profit form, see A. Ben-Ner and T. Van Hoomissen, "Nonprofit Organizations

in the Mixed Economy: A Demand and Supply Analysis," in A. Ben-Ner and B. Gui, eds,. *The Nonprofit Sector in the Mixed Economy* (Ann Arbor: University of Michigan Press, 1993), 27–58.

42 Hansmann, " Role," 847.

43 This point has been suggested by another of Hansmann's commentators; see R. Atkinson, "Altruism in Nonprofit Organizations," *Boston College Law Review* 31 (1990), 501.

44 The fact that the non-profit suppliers are largely passive in Hansmann's theory, or at most merely reactive to the demands of consumers, also may explain why Hansmann seems to think that they would not be opportunistic against consumers when organized as non-profits. But it is difficult to think why homo economicus would not seek, just as much as in the for-profit firm, to chisel a larger (albeit now fixed) return out of consumers who cannot adequately monitor (against the money contributed) the quality or quantity of product that is ultimately delivered.

45 This point is much emphasized in the economics literature to explain what otherwise looks like inefficient behaviour. Normally, it is more efficient to supply subsidies in cash than in kind; this method allows recipients, who are normally the best judges of their own interests, to make their own choices. However, in charitable giving the *donor's* interests are also important, and the donor often wants the recipient to consume some specific good. See, for example, D. Johnson, "The Charity Market: Theory and Practice," in T. Ireland and D. Johnson, eds,. *The Economics of Charity* (London: Institute for Economic Affairs, 1973), 85–90.

46 This is Atkinson's claim; see Atkinson, "Altruism," 550.

47 For analysis of the non-profit form as a device to control these sorts of agency costs, where managers might otherwise, in pursuit of profitable opportunities, drift away from the non-profit mission, see R. Fama and M. Jensen, "Agency Problems and Residual Claims," *Journal of Law and Economics* 26 (1983), 327, 341–5.

48 See M. Jensen, "The Agency Costs of Free Cash Flow: Corporate Finance and Takeovers," *American Economic Review* 76 (1986), 23. He argues, for example, that the declaration of a dividend, or the substitution of debt for equity, commits management to reducing its holdings of cash and therefore reduces the possibility of managerial opportunism that would otherwise exist with respect to earnings retained on investments funded through an equity issue. Management, after paying a dividend or the interest on debt, must go back to the capital market so as to be able to continue funding its strategic investments. This capital market promises a way to monitor and discipline management should it stray from the interests of shareholders. Thus the declaration of a dividend, or the substitution of debt for equity, can be associated with a positive effect on a firm's share price, something that is difficult to explain on many other theories.

49 Income Tax Act, RSC 1985, c. 1 (5th supp.) [as amended] s. 149.1(2).

50 Charities can earn income from unrelated business through their passive investments in other organizations that are not themselves charities. It is hard to see how things could be otherwise; charities are not expected to keep donated income tucked away in mattresses. Needless to say, it is often difficult to distinguish between passive business investments (which are permitted to charities) and active investment in an unrelated activity (which is not). For some sense of the litigation on this issue, see *Church of Christ Development Co. Ltd. v. MNR*, [1982] CTC 2467 (FCA).

51 This differs from the position advocated by Atkinson, "Altruism," 616ff. Atkinson's view is that all favourable tax treatment for charities is to be understood as a tax subsidy for altruism, the sort of thing we want to see encouraged. Thus Atkinson sees little point in distinguishing how the subsidy is provided – a tax break on donated income, on passive investments, or on unrelated business activities – so long as the extra money ends up being used for charitable purposes. However, if the point is not just to encourage altruism in the abstract, but rather the particular forms of altruism that the donors themselves have selected, and which gives them common cause, then only a tax break on donated income is justified.

52 The idea of a cross-subsidy suggests that it will often be difficult to separate those situations in which the managers are using only new sources of income (for example, unrelated business income or even income from new donors) to fund new charitable purposes from those situations in which the managers are (to some extent at least) using old (original-donor) sources of income to fund these new purposes. Arguably, only the latter involves a malign form of mission drift. For an argument that it is possible to keep these two situations apart and therefore that unrelated business activities should be permissible for charities, see Davis, chapter 15 in this volume.

53 See, for example, Income Tax Act, RSC 1985, c. 1 (5th supp.) [as amended], s. 149.

54 For discussions of this criticism, which has the effect of sharply limiting its scope, see S. Rose- Ackerman, "Unfair Competition and Corporate Income Taxation," in Rose-Ackerman, *The Economics of Non-Profit Organizations*, 394–414; and Davis, " Regulation."

55 Peter Singer has effectively made this point against Kenneth Arrow. In "Gifts and Exchanges," *Philosophy and Public Affairs* 1 (1972), 343, 350, Arrow had queried Richard Titmus's argument in *The Gift Relationship* (London: Allen & Unwin, 1971) that the presence of a market for blood would affect the motivation to donate blood altruistically. Arrow wondered why the "add on" presence of a market for blood would prevent a donor from continuing to donate blood if that was what he or she wanted to do. But Singer argued that the character of the gift would now

be different. Before the advent of the market, he or she effectively gave the "gift of life," since the recipient depended on the gift and could not otherwise get blood; after the arrival of the market he or she would only save the recipient a few dollars, the cost of the market alternative. See P. Singer, "Altruism and Commerce," *Philosophy and Public Affairs* 2 (1973), 312, 316.

6 The Role of the Voluntary Sector in a Modern Welfare State

NEIL BROOKS

This chapter presents a general review of the role of the voluntary sector in a modern welfare state. Its central argument is that voluntary organizations should complement government activity, not substitute for it. Calling on the voluntary sector to replace government services threatens the characteristics that provide its strengths and that constitute its unique attributes as a form of social organization, such as flexibility, responsiveness to local and minority interests, the capacity to innovate and initiate new ideas, and the ability to oversee and monitor the exercise of power by the state and other dominating institutions in society. Financing of the provision of basic public goods and services that further collective social goals should come from taxes, not from donations or other forms of private funding. If governments continue to cut back on social services and to shift them to the voluntary sector, not only will they jeopardize the provision of these services and the social goals that they serve, but also they will produce a voluntary sector that will be largely passive and irrelevant, instead of being vital and innovative. Furthermore, the apparently increasingly prevalent view that "downsizing" government and increasing the presence of voluntary organizations can revitalize civil society is profoundly wrong. An active and vibrant democratic government is a prerequisite for a flourishing civil society. The greatest threat to civic engagement and social cohesion is the increasing inequalities in income and wealth, a problem that can be addressed only by revitalized government action.

In addressing this general theme I divide the rest of this chapter into four related sections. The first section notes the increased attention paid to the voluntary sector from many sources over the last couple of decades and the recent recognition of it as a third sector of the economy. Instead of reflecting the outcome of benign social forces, I argue, the rise of the voluntary sector is attributable to the shift in public philosophy from what might be described as pluralist welfare liberalism to elitist neo-conservatism. Its rising importance is an integral part of the neo-conservative campaign to dismantle the welfare state and constrain democratic decision-making.

Neo-conservatives contend that over the past 30 years there has been a dramatic decline in personal morality and social cohesion and that welfare states have been largely responsible for this social disruption by causing an erosion in personal responsibility and encouraging anti-social choices of lifestyle. Drawing on the work of Robert Putnam and others on the role of civil society, they contend that a reinvigorated voluntary sector is essential for fostering civic renewal and a sense of social cohesion. In the second section I suggest that the social disintegration that neo-conservatives seem to see was in large part the product of the economic policies that they supported and that social cohesion will be restored only if we return to the values and commitments that gave rise to the welfare state.

A related and equally persistent thread in neo-conservative thought is that the welfare state has suppressed charity and the voluntary sector and that once we roll back the boundaries of the state, the voluntary sector will once again emerge to provide a helping hand to vulnerable people and families. Accordingly, in the third section I look at the effects of government downsizing on the voluntary sector. Contrary to the neo-conservative claim, there is compelling evidence that a strong voluntary sector actually needs a strong state and extensive government support. Far from being antagonistic, the two sectors appear to enjoy a positive relationship. Moreover, not surprisingly, the impulse to provide for others through government seems to be linked to the impulse to provide for them through charity.

The fourth and final substantive section looks at the consequences of contracting out public services to the voluntary sector. Although such arrangements have a long history in public administration, over the past 15 years or so, as a result of the popularity of the movement to "reinvent" and privatize government, it has become a major strategy. Some argue that this is a positive change, that instead of simply downsizing and hoping that, or being indifferent to whether, the voluntary sector will fill the gaps, governments are right to delegate functions to the voluntary sector by contracting with them to provide services. That is, governments should become purchasers of services instead of providers. I argue that such a move brings with it a serious danger that the government and the voluntary sector have entered into a Faustian bargain, in which each may lose its soul. The government will be "hollowed out" and lose its ability to govern and ultimately its legitimacy, while voluntary organizations will lose the distinctive qualities that make them a unique and valuable form of social organization. To prevent these consequences, those voluntary organizations that accept long-term contracts from the government for the delivery of social services should effectively become part of the government sector.

REWRITING THE SOCIAL CONTRACT: THE RISE OF THE THIRD SECTOR AND THE DEMISE OF THE WELFARE STATE

The Rise of the Third Sector

I make a straightforward claim in this section. We can best understand the elevation of voluntary organizations to a third sector in Western economies, alongside the government and the market, as an integral part of the larger agenda that dominated public policies in the 1980s and 1990s – namely, the rolling back of the economic and social borders of the state.[1] This agenda got its support from an ideology that began emerging in the late 1960s and became a powerful political force by the early 1980s – neo-conservatism.[2] Its central project is the reduction of the role of government in the economy and increased emphasis on the role of individual choice, markets, and non-governmental associations in allocating resources.

It hardly seems necessary to document the increased attention paid to the voluntary sector over the past 25 years. Claims of an "associational revolution" and of the virtues of the voluntary sector abound in academic journals, newspaper headlines, and the platforms of political parties. However, a brief review of recent developments in the United States, the United Kingdom, and Canada underlines its hegemony.

In the United States, it was not until the early 1970s that academics, or even those involved in philanthropy, began thinking of voluntary organizations as constituting a unified third sector of the economy. The genesis of the idea is usually traced to the Filer Commission,[3] which published its influential report in 1975. During the 1950s and 1960s there had been an increasingly hostile public reaction against charities – in particular, against private foundations and the tax concessions that they received. The Filer Commission, a privately funded body, was formed, largely as the result of the initiative of John D. Rockefeller III, to study "the voluntary, 'third' sector of American society" and to make recommendations "concerning ways in which the sector and the practice of private giving can be strengthened and made more effective."[4] In addition to its report, the commission published six massive volumes of scholarly studies on the voluntary sector. Following on its work, in the late 1970s Yale University established a Program on Non-Profit Organizations. The program has published more than 250 working papers and has sponsored many of the leading monographs and texts relating to the voluntary sector.[5]

In the late 1970s, various associations representing the interests of voluntary bodies formed a national organization – the Independent Sector – to represent the interests of all U.S. charitable organizations. In addition to its advocacy functions, it attempted to facilitate and encourage research on the sector, and by 1988, in part because of its efforts, there were over 20 research centres at several universities.[6] Reflecting increasing academic interest was the launching of the Johns Hopkins Comparative Nonprofit Sector Project in 1990. It is an ambitious endeavour of comparative research devoted to the collection and analysis of data on voluntary organizations in 12 countries.[7] There are now two scholarly journals wholly dedicated to publishing research on the sector; each is published by an association of academics specializing in such research.[8]

Most of the recent academic interest in the U.S. voluntary sector[9] received financing from voluntary organizations. It appears that few scholars have shown an interest in the sector as a matter of pure intellectual curiosity. This sponsorship raises questions of intellectual independence. In 1987, Yale's Program on Non-Profit Organizations published a *Research Handbook.*[10] In his review, historian Barry Karl anxiously expressed his concern about the study of philanthropic organizations being funded by those very bodies and about the confusion between research and advocacy. Noting that philanthropy needed advocates to defend itself against its critics, he suggested: "The use of the term 'research' as an umbrella that would cover the various aspects of advocacy without drawing critical attention to the process has been a stroke of genius."[11] A number of comments appeared in the late 1980s dealing with the potential conflict of interest that arises when grant makers and related organizations are the object of the studies that they fund,[12] but interest in the issue appears to have subsided.

Throughout this period of increasing academic interest, the voluntary sector was growing exponentially in the United States as the Republican government downsized and contracted out social services. President Ronald Reagan championed the sector as being morally superior and less costly than government provision. George Bush promised in his inauguration speech in 1989 that "it is the ambition of my Presidency to make these thousands points of light [acts of volunteerism] to shine brighter than ever before." House Speaker Newt Gingrich, in his *Contract with America*, promised to renew the United States by "replacing the welfare state with an opportunity society" featuring market incentives and "volunteerism and spiritual renewal." One of President Bill Clinton's first major acts in office was to hold a National Summit for America's Future – essentially a meeting about reinvigorating volunteerism and voluntary organizations. Texas Governor George W. Bush, in his first policy speech as a candidate for the Republican presidential nomination, given in July 1999, proposed spending $8 billion on tax incentives designed to stimulate contributions to nonprofits and religious groups and undertook that, "[i]n every instance when my Administration sees a responsibility to help people we will look first to faith-based institutions, to charities and to community groups that have shown their ability to save and change lives."[13]

Prior to the 1980s, numerous studies had been undertaken in the United Kingdom on the voluntary sector.[14] As an indication of how much the sector had grown and changed in that country over the previous 25 years, in the mid-1990s, in reflecting back on the Wolfendon Report of 1978 on the voluntary sector, David Wilson observed that its context was almost unrecognizable: "This was a state-of-the-art report produced fifteen years ago, but the picture it portrayed of voluntary organizations as partners, gap-fillers, and providers working alongside Government agencies is virtually unrecognizable today in the enterprising, professionalized and contracting out 1990s."[15] This change was in large part the result of the policies of Margaret Thatcher. Her government turned the delivery of many social services over to the voluntary sector and constantly extolled its virtues.

In 1995 Britain's National Council for Voluntary Organizations set up the Commission on the Future of the Voluntary Sector (the Deakin Commission), which reported in 1996.[16] Partly as a result, the government and the voluntary sector entered into an agreement setting out what should be the relations between the two sectors.[17] It is not legally binding, but it does acknowledge that "the voluntary and community sector has a vital role in society as the nation's 'third sector', working alongside the state and the market." In his introduction, Prime Minister Tony Blair states: "The work of the voluntary and community organizations is central to the Government's mission to make this the Giving Age."

In Canada, several reviews of the voluntary sector have taken place over the past 25 years, mirroring U.S. developments.[18] Canadian governments have also been supportive of the sector. As early as 1976 the government's working paper "The Way Ahead" cited as one of the areas of social responsibility meriting further consultation and consideration "[m]echanisms to encourage the further development of cooperatives and voluntary organizations." It made reference to the need for finding the appropriate balance between the public and private sectors in meeting social costs. It spoke of "an emerging middle way" for the responsibility or role of goverment, a view adhered to by the government, which argued "that it is both possible and desirable to seek substantial reductions in the rate of growth of government expenditure and direct government intervention, and to search for alternative strategies – less expenditure oriented – to serve the legitimate social concerns of government, and in fact to better serve society."

Brian Mulroney expressed his commitment to the voluntary sector in a speech to the Progressive Conservative Party shortly before he took office in 1984: "One of the major priorities of my government will be a complete revision of social programs in order to save as much money as possible. One way of meeting that objective is to encourage the voluntary sector to participate more in the implementation of social programs. Volunteer work is the most efficient method of work in Canada." Much of his agenda while he was in office came from the report of the Macdonald Commission, which in 1985 issued an unambiguous and comprehensive verdict in favour of neo-conservatism. It recommended "the continuing devolution of responsibility for delivering social services to the community level and to nonprofit associations,"[19] largely on the grounds that they are "less bureaucratic and therefore potentially more responsive, structures"[20] than government departments.

The current Liberal federal government has continued to devolve responsibility to the voluntary sector. In the program reviews initiated in 1994, it sought to identify the core roles for government by subjecting each program to six tests, including, the "Partnership Test: What activities or programs should or could be transferred in whole or in part to the private or voluntary sector?"[21] In recognition of the importance of the voluntary sector, in each of its first three budgets the Liberal government enriched and liberalized the tax credit for charitable contributions. In early 1999 it entered into a joint initiative called "Engaging the Voluntary Sector," intending to form a long-term partnership with a view to improving the voluntary sector's ability to provide public services. Three so-called joint tables were established to deal with the regulatory framework of the voluntary sector, to devise mechanisms to strengthen its capacity to deliver services, and to build a new relationship between government and the voluntary sector. The joint tables were to present their recommendations over the course of 1999.[22]

In Ontario in 1995 the newly elected Conservative government almost immediately began downloading responsibilities to the voluntary sector by announcing a 21 per cent cut in welfare payments. In the government's first throne speech on 27 September 1995, the lieutenant-governor announced a number of initiatives "to support and nurture the spirit of the voluntary action in Ontario." Among other things, the government set up an Advisory Board on the Voluntary Sector. In its report, the board noted that the change in relations between government and the voluntary sector "calls for a new partnership between government and the voluntary sector, with government acting to enable and enhance voluntary action rather than directing and controlling it."[23]

The Demise of the Welfare State

It might appear that benign social and economic forces lie behind the rise of the third sector and the increased attention being paid to it by academics, politicians, and the press – forces such as the need to deliver public services more efficiently, or increased virtue. To the contrary, although there is no question of the sincerity of the many thousands of people who work in the sector, the effort to elevate it to a major form of social organization in the collective lives of citizens is an integral part of the efforts by business interests, wealthy individuals, and neo-conservative governments to rewrite the prevailing post-war social contract.

Every society possesses a social contract that establishes the obligations that its members assume towards each other. Indeed, a society or culture is defined by its social contract. It reflects how the nation balances government, market, and community responsibilities. Each sector emphasizes different values and operates according to different norms. One of the most important components of the contract is the relationship between the private and the public sectors. The emergence during the 1940s in most industrialized countries of a social contract that has become known as the Keynesian compromise has been told countless times and does not bear repeating here in any detail.[24] After the Great Depression, in which it became obvious to almost everyone that the capitalist system left on its own could wreak enormous havoc on the majority of the population, and in particular after the Second World War, in which the great majority of people sacrificed so much, it became clear that workers would no longer tolerate a society in which only the rich prospered and everyone else lived in economic insecurity. Therefore an implicit deal emerged between business interests and other groups in society about the respective roles of the public and private sectors. Although most private goods and services would continue to be produced in the private sector, and be allocated via the price system, governments would stabilize the economy, provide workers with a degree of economic security, guarantee open and universal access to services essential to human development, and foster a high degree of social equality. This implicit social contract resulted in the modern welfare state.[25]

Obviously not everyone was satisfied with the Keynesian compromise. The right expressed concern about government restrictions on "freedom" and the disincentive effect of taxes and transfers; the left worried about capitalism's alienation of workers and the effect of welfare state programs in fracturing working-class solidarity and in submerging class conflict, but basically the centre held – until the early 1970s. Then, concerned about declining profitability, economic uncertainty, the power of labour, and the increasing size of democratic governments, business interests decided to attempt to rewrite the contract. The main features of these events are familiar. Business set about trying to shore up profits by lowering wage costs and public expenditures and by changing public opinion about the respective roles of private and public institutions. To this end, leading corporate executives organized themselves, formed new vehicles to develop the "business outlook," funded "think tanks" to provide the (pseudo-) intellectual foundations for their agendas, revived near-dormant "trade associations," and worked to modernize political partics that would adopt neo-conservative policies.

As a result, since the mid-1970s, the welfare state has been under an intense and sustained ideological and political assault from business interests and neo-conservative governments. The main lines of attack on the welfare state reveal why the idea of a major third sector that can fulfil collective social and economic goals was so attractive to those on the right and so congruent with ideas of neo-conservatism.

The neo-conservatives launched an array of economic arguments against the welfare state. They argued that the seemingly high taxes needed to finance it reduced economic output by diminishing the desire of rich people to work, lessening their incentive to save, and impairing new sources of private investment. Moreover, the deficit and debt "crises" indicated that the state had apparently reached its fiscal limits. Globalization and the increasing mobility of skilled labour and capital became trump cards in this argument. The welfare state's social programs were also alleged to have adverse economic effects. Unconditional cash transfers reduced the incentive of their recipients to work, and labour regulations "rigidified" the labour market.

Another group of claims made by neo-conservatives against the welfare state were plainly moralistic in tone. The welfare state was based on a concept of citizenship that assumed that people had rights and social entitlements derived solely from their status as citizens. This implied that individuals should be able to exercise their right to physical and mental health and the development of personality independently of the marketplace, family fortune, or private connections. The neo-conservatives postulated that this concept of citizenship ignored corresponding responsibilities and duties. Society is entitled to demand some form of reciprocity from those who rely on public provision. The idea of absolute social rights, they argued, was morally corrosive.

The welfare state was designed to prevent people from being exploited in their relationship with others, whether in market exchanges, in family relations, or in civil society, by providing them with the means to exist separate from these relationships. Those attacking the welfare state first denied that people entering into consensual arrangements could be exploited and second, by turning this argument on its head, claimed that the welfare state fostered dependence on the state.

The welfare state assumed a notion of community and solidarity that entailed a belief that the risks and vicissitudes of social and physical life (birth, sickness, unemployment, and ageing) can be most fairly and effectively met through schemes of collective provision. It presupposed relationships in which benefit entitlements were disconnected from the size of one's contributions. Community was rooted in principles of equity and need. Neo-conservatives, by contrast, believe that the source of community lies not in collective protection against risk but in the shared commitment to moral precepts and values. Further, they argue that social life must be held together by "mediating" institutions, including families and community organizations, outside the mandates and force of law implicit in government programs.

The welfare state also rested on the assumption that social equality was not only important in building a sense of community but was worthy in its own right. A society in which there was great social distance between people was unlikely to be cohesive; moreover, it was unjust. The neo-conservatives argue that the inequality in the distribution of income is in large part the result of people's efforts and merit and that so long as everyone has a minimum level of subsistence inequality is not a matter of social concern.[26]

Two further, related arguments against the welfare state, which are not so much moral as social-psychological, are that it undermines self-reliance and disempowers the institutions of civil society. Neo-conservatives hypothesize that the revitalization of voluntary organizations is the key to reinvigorating individual responsibility and community, which in turn will produce salutary results for the economy.

A final assault on the welfare state was the attack on government bureaucracy. Over the last 25 years the public service, which once enjoyed widespread support, came under attack from all sides. The force of this attack cannot be overstated. Government bureaucracies were accused of being bloated, inflexible, inefficient, and out of touch with the people whom they served. These pathologies could not be cured, and therefore government services had to be privatized and contracted out.

These attacks on the welfare state have blunted instruments of government policy in many countries over the past 20 years, with government regulation of industry, health and safety, and the environment weakened or repealed; government assets and business sold to private owners; tax systems rendered less progressive; labour relations and labour standards rolled back; universal social programs targeted; social welfare payments slashed; unemployment benefits restructured; restrictions on international trade and investment "liberalized"; and the delivery of services contracted out. Most of these changes are referred to compendiously as "privatization." They shift decision-making about the allocation and distribution of resources in society away from the public sector and democratic institutions to the private sector, including markets, the family and voluntary organizations.

Why were the neo-conservatives so successful in shrinking the welfare state? Some would undoubtedly argue that it reflects the force of good ideas.[27] Others would say that the demise of the welfare state was inevitable, given the forces of technological change and "globalization." Undoubtedly, a range of factors explain this sea change in public philosophy. However, in Canada, a major explanatory variable is the increasing political power of business and the influence of its neo-conservative philosophy.

The remarkable rise of the non-profit sector is part of this shift in the élite's worldview. It is an integral part of the rewriting of the social contract by business interests. The present move to download and delegate responsibilities to the voluntary sector constitutes a crucial part of a coherent policy to weaken and dismantle the welfare state.

CIVIL SOCIETY, SOCIAL CAPITAL, AND THE VOLUNTARY SECTOR

Sorting out the Debate

In recent years, the need for thriving voluntary organizations has assumed significance beyond simply enriching the social lives of their participants, engaging in political representation, or delivering public services. It is argued that in more subtle ways the voluntary sector is essential for sustained prosperity and a vibrant democracy. Although there are countless variations, the basic claim goes something like this. By participating in voluntary organizations, individuals establish networks of friends, become embedded in a web of social relations, internalize norms of appropriate social conduct, develop a sense of reciprocity, and acquire feelings of solidarity with, and a sense of trust in, others. This socialization process gives rise to social capital that facilitates economic transactions and hence prosperity by reducing transaction costs and results in more efficacious democratic institutions by encouraging co-operation. Although this argument reflects the traditional interest of sociologists in the voluntary sector, it has been taken up by economists and political scientists and has assumed new twists and greater urgency.

Over the past decade there has been a swirl of debate in universities, government departments, think tanks, and the media relating to the associated concepts of civil society (or sometimes, and perhaps more appropriately, civic society), social capital, social cohesion, citizenship, and community capacity. The debate started in the early 1990s with a pervasive sense that modern society was becoming inflicted with alienation, excessive greed, social disintegration, erosion of public morality, and political indifference. Hence there was an urgent need to take steps to reglue society. The debate has been sustained in the academic community, where it is encompassed by fashionable intellectual currents such as communitarianism and because it raises perplexing theoretical and challenging empirical issues. Conservative think tanks and the popular business-owned media have fixed on the issue, since it complements neo-conservatism and can be used as yet another battering ram against the state. By any measure, reviving local organizations and communities and promoting good manners appear preferable to the coercive actions of the state and intrusive bureaucracies. Liberals too, however, have been concerned about the issue. A decline in civic engagement may directly harm the quality of public life and indirectly erode support for the provision of public goods by the state.

The terms used to carry on this debate are not consistent. The term "civil society" has a long history in political philosophy. Indeed, disentangling its meaning and uses among the political classics has become an intellectual cottage industry on its own in recent years.[28] As an analytical concept it appears to have slid into obscurity for most of this century while social scientists concentrated on attacking and defending the welfare state. Then in the late 1970s and the 1980s left intellectuals revived its use during the crises and collapse of communism in eastern Europe, which has been characterized as "the revolt of civil society against the state."[29] More recently, it frequently refers to the voluntary sector writ large – voluntary associations, interest groups, social movements, and informal gatherings. It also sometimes includes families and neighbourhoods and even the values and beliefs underlying a country's public philosophy and culture. Even more encompassing, it occasionally means all aspects of social and economic life outside the government sector.

The term "social capital" sometimes refers narrowly to "the ability of actors to secure benefits by virtue of membership in social networks or other social structures"[30] or, more broadly, and in the most frequently quoted reference, as "features of social life, such as trust, norms, and networks, that can improve efficiency of society by facilitating coordinated actions."[31] Although it is a function of individual-level actions and attributes, usually "social capital" is described as a community-level attribute and is commonly measured in attitudinal surveys with questions about the respondent's level of trust in others or in institutions. It is "capital" because it is a resource on which society can draw.

"Social cohesion" is a term that refers sometimes to an even broader analytical category than "social capital." In a widely quoted definition, the government of Canada's Policy Research Sub-Committee on Social Cohesion defined it is as "the ongoing process of developing a community of shared values, shared challenges and equal opportunity within Canada, based on a sense of trust, hope and reciprocity among all Canadians."[32]

In line with my theme of defending big government and disparaging the voluntary sector, I argue here that the voluntary sector, or civil society, is not as central in generating social capital and cohesion as many commentators have implied. Much more important is government policies that promote social equality, reduce economic inequality, and ensure equal and effective political participation. However, before we look directly at the suggestion that voluntary organizations can have an unintended but positive benefit on democracy and the economy, I would note the somewhat-related line of inquiry often associated with this claim and frequently put forth as a separate strand of the argument. This is the position that modern society's illnesses call primarily for a moral revival, not necessarily civic renewal. I briefly mention this claim in part to delineate the issues but also because it provides me with another opportunity to emphasize the role of government action and the near-irrelevance to the nation's general well-being of civic associations that are not involved in political activity.

Moral Revival

While not holding identical views, an odd mix of influential academics and public intellectuals – communitarians, social conservatives, and "third-wayers" – concentrate more directly on the moral development of citizens than on the reinvigoration of civil society. By placing emphasis on the adjective "civil," they treat the expression "civil society" as being a goal, not the description of a sector of society. They are concerned primarily with developing a society of well-behaved, hard-working, civil and moral individuals who are prepared to accept personal responsibility for their actions and their station in life.[33] The American historian Gertrude Himmelfarb argued: "It is not enough ... to revitalize civil society. The more urgent, and difficult, task is to remoralize civil society."[34]

These social commentators point to the deteriorating social conditions in most of the industrialized countries as measured by rising crime, divorce, illegitimate births, declining fertility, a loss of personal trust and confidence in social institutions, and generally a decline in moral cohesion and public civility. All these trends appear to have begun around the mid-1960s and are alleged to threaten the social fabric of liberal democracy. In his most recent opus, Francis Fukuyama refers to the period as "The Great Disruption."[35] He treats these trends as interconnected symptoms of a single process – a decline in "social capital" or the set of informal values that enables human beings to co-operate to their mutual advantage.

Although the groups advocating moral revival do not all agree on the causes of the breakdown in civility and morality, in almost all accounts government action bears a large portion of the blame. They allege that policies such as welfare assistance to single mothers have led to family breakdown and other social pathologies and, more generally, that government tolerance for so-called "lifestyle choices" and "cultural relativism" has brought permissiveness and a shirking of personal responsibility. The social conservatives also blame the decline in morality on the shift from tradition and religion to secular humanism, and the communitarians blame it on the decline in civic engagement. However, most advocate, in addition to government policies that penalize immoral conduct and reward virtue, the need to strengthen civil society, particularly the family and community organizations, which institutions are alleged to build character.

This perspective on the structure of social relations is deeply troubling.[36] Among other things, as advocated by social conservatives, communitarians, and even proponents of the third way it has a strong authoritarian tone.[37] But the only point I want to make here is that those who argue that there has been a decline in morals and civility since the mid-1960s, and that governments should therefore seek ways to strengthen the voluntary sector, are profoundly wrong in both their diagnosis of, and prescription for, our social ills. When I went to law school in the late 1960s, apparently at the outset of the great social disruption, my classes contained predominantly white males – few, if any, women, Native Canadians, visible minorities, openly gay or disabled persons. What kind of a moral order tolerated the exclusion of the majority of the population from institutions that train the economic élite and whose missions are central to democratic governance? Should we really be looking back on this period nostalgically as one when people were civil and moral? Throughout the following period of supposed moral decline, all these groups have made significant progress in claiming the most basic rights of citizenship. At the law school at which I now teach, about one-half of the students are women, and visible minorities, Native Canadians, and students with disabilities attend in some number. Social engagement in voluntary organizations did not bring about these changes. They were primarily the result of the actions of social movements and reform of public policy.

Civic Renewal

The importance of voluntary organizations for democracy has been asserted for years. Indeed, in some ways the current preoccupation with civil society reflects the concerns of pluralists in the 1950s and 1960s. Pluralism's central project was explaining how private interests could be organized and expressed without destabilizing the politics of social class. Private desires, the theorists of pluralism said, are aggregated by interest groups and voluntary organizations and represented to appropriate government élites for adjudication and compromise. The traditional democratic defence of voluntary organizations by the pluralists applied primarily, if not exclusively, to representational groups.[38] However, in recent years, the literature expounding the concept of social capital has implicated the entire voluntary sector in the maintenance of a vibrant democracy and a prosperous economy. The concept of social capital was developed by sociologists.[39] However, at the centre of the current debate over the value of civil society and social capital is the work of Robert D. Putnam, a political scientist and director of the Center for International Affairs at Harvard University.

In a widely acclaimed book Putnam presents the results of his 20-year, quasi-experimental study of the subnational governments of Italy.[40] In 1970, in an effort to decentralize the state, Italy established 20 regional governments. Putnam set out to examine the levels of effectiveness between these various regional governments and the factors that might account for any variation. The key question that guided his research was, "What are the conditions for creating strong, responsive, effective representative institutions?"[41] He concluded that, on the whole, regional government was more efficient and productive in the north than in the south and that the most notable correlation with high-quality democratic government was membership in "horizontally ordered groups" such as sports clubs, co-operatives, mutual aid societies, and cultural and voluntary associations. He contrasted the abundance of these groups in the north with the more hierarchical social structures in the south. He explained the comparative efficacity of regional governments in the north by hypothesizing that voluntary organizations create social capital.

More recently Putnam has pursued a study of the revitalization of American democracy. Initially he argued that, contrary to conventional economic models, the capacity for trust and co-operation has historically been a key determinant of economic growth and prosperity.[42] Then, in a cleverly titled article, "Bowling Alone," which created a sensation in the U.S. media and caused great concern among the non-profit sector, he proposed that Americans' social connectedness and civic engagement had declined in recent decades.[43] As evidence of decline he cited the drop in membership in such voluntary organizations as the Boy Scouts, the Federation of Women's Clubs, and various service clubs; most pointedly, he noted that fewer people were joining bowling leagues but instead bowling alone with families and friends. Most recently he has argued that of all the explanations for the decline in civic engagement in the United States, and therefore for the destruction of social capital, the most probable appeared to be increased television viewing.[44]

Putnam's work on civic engagement and social capital has sparked an ongoing debate both in the popular media and in academic journals.[45] The debate has been fuelled by two other best-selling books. In 1995 Jeremy Rifkin wrote eloquently of the need to "empower" the third sector in order to foster participation and social capital.[46] His central argument is that the structural unemployment created by technological advances and globalization will be overcome only by creation of more employment in community development: "Now ... that the commercial and public sectors are no longer capable of securing some of the fundamental needs of the people, the public has little choice but to begin looking out for itself, once again, by reestablishing viable communities as a buffer against both the impersonal forces of the global market and increasingly weak and incompetent central governing authorities."[47] Another popular book on social capital, was the work of Francis Fukuyama, also published in 1995.[48] His central finding is that societies with strong intermediate institutions, such as voluntary organizations, which encourage association and the formation of trusting relationships outside the family, are likely to be economically developed and prosperous.

As a result of these studies, and others, social capital and social cohesion have become a pressing matter for academics, policy institutes, and governments around the world. In part, the concern has grown out of recognition that the implementation of neo-conservative economic polices in many of the advanced industrialized countries has created greater income inequality, persistently high unemployment, economic insecurity, and more social exclusion. In December 1996, the Organization for Economic Co-operation and Development (OECD) held a one-day conference on societal cohesion and the globalizing economy. The foreword to the published collection of the papers presented at the conference acknowledged that the neo-liberal economic strategies advocated by the OECD have given rise to serious social problems and a lack of social cohesion.[49] It notes: "The diffusion of this malaise threatens to undermine both the drive towards greater economic flexibility and the policies that encourage strong competition, globalization and technological innovation."[50]

Many analysts and groups are calling for the revitalization of the voluntary sector, or civil society, as the way to promote social cohesion and social capital. In the United States, in response to Putnam and others, both major political parties are championing the voluntary sector, and most major foundations are supporting research on civil society. Two of the larger commissions released reports last year that are now being debated in the United States. Although there are many similarities, the two reports reflect the two divergent streams of argument in that country. As I mentioned above, one stream focuses on the nation's culture and moral underpinnings; the other, on the civic life of the country. The Council on Civil Society, which is sponsored jointly by the University of Chicago Divinity School and the Institute for American Values and co-chaired by Jean Betke Elshtain, took the need for moral renewal as its starting point. It concluded that the nation's civic crisis is primarily philosophical and moral: "American civic institutions are declining," the report said, "because the moral ideas that fueled and formed them are losing their power to shape our behavior and unite us." The report argued that "the qualities necessary for self-governance are the result of moral ideas about the human person and the nature of the good life" and that when we ignore the moral grounds of our existence, "all that is left is power."[51] For the National Commission on Civic Renewal, the overriding objective is to promote civic works through voluntary organizations, not necessarily to inspire a moral or cultural renewal.[52]

The premise underlying the recommendations of these reports and their calls for civic renewal is that voluntary organizations should be encouraged because membership in them builds trust, solidarity, and reciprocity – qualities necessary for a prosperous and democratic society. Most people find that a dense network of social relations, which is often found in voluntary organizations, helps overcome isolation and makes life more satisfying. However, to go beyond this and argue that the pressing social problems of our times have been caused by a decline in social engagement and that therefore voluntary organizations must be encouraged is problematic on a number of grounds.

First, it is not clear that social engagement has declined. The forums in which people engage socially are likely to shift as demographics change, as women enter the workforce, as workers experience heightened pressure on their time, and as families become more mobile. The fact that fewer people join clubs does not necessarily indicate a decline in social engagement, which may just have found other venues.[53] As Putnam himself noted, although Americans are bowling less in leagues, they in fact are bowling more, but informally, with family and friends. Perhaps this kind of social engagement increases social capital more than does participating in formal organizations.[54]

Second, discussions about the creation of social capital assume that voluntary organizations teach people to work together to resolve the dilemmas of collective action and become more community-oriented. However, in many cases, joining such bodies fosters exclusion and demands for conformity.[55]

Third, assuming that participation in voluntary organizations creates networks of civic engagement and trust, it is not yet clear whether this trust in fact results in "social" capital. That is, although the trust among members of a particular voluntary organization might increase, that does not include greater trust of others or of other collective organizations such as government. It seems likely that in many cases the trust that develops in a group depends in part on specific norms of reciprocity between members, the possibility of sanctions against defectors, and the fact that members may acquire a good deal of information about others in the group. Whether there is a connection between membership in voluntary organizations and generalized trust is an empirical question that has not yet been satisfactorily answered.

Fourth, if there is a correlation between a rich associational society and effective democracy, the direction of causation is also not yet clear. Does civil society shape the nature of government, or is the nature of civil society the result of public policies? I suggested at the outset of this chapter that the nature of civil society is intimately connected with government policies and that it is profoundly misleading to try to conceptualize it apart from political power. In a telling critique of Putnam, Theda Skocpol has noted that even in the United States throughout the nineteenth and twentieth centuries it was largely state activity that encouraged and even organized the voluntary organizations that make up civil society.[56]

Fifth, on a related point, many of those who look to civil society to deal with problems of modern society view it as if it were somehow apart from the economy and the state and not subject to the conflicts and inequities found in these sectors. But, of course, it is deeply embedded in them and probably reflects those same conflicts and inequities. Again, Skocpol has asserted: "Organized civil society in the United States has never flourished apart from active government and inclusive democratic politics.... If we want to repair civil society, we must first and foremost revitalize political democracy."[57] Putnam has many critics who have made this same point,[58] and he himself has to a large extent conceded it.[59]

Social Cohesion

The concepts of social capital and social cohesion have been embraced in Canada, but the emphasis here is dramatically different from that in the United States. In Canada there has been an emphasis on social equality and the role of government and much less on the role of the voluntary sector. As the debate emerged in the mid-1990s, one of the most quoted definitions of social cohesion was that offered by Judith Maxwell, president of the Canadian Policy Research Network, who identified three major elements: "Social cohesion involves building shared values and communities of interpretation, reducing disparities in wealth and income, and generally enabling people to have a sense that they are engaged in a common enterprise, facing shared challenges, and that they are members of the same community."[60]

Concerned about the long-term consequences of downsizing and decentralizing, when the Liberals formed a government in 1993 they appointed a Cabinet Committee of Deputy Ministers to identify "pressure points that are likely to arise in Canadian society by the year 2005 as a result of economic, demographic and social trends" and directed it to focus on four areas – growth, human development, social cohesion, and global challenges and opportunities. In September 1996, as part of the project, Canadian Heritage published a paper that accepted Maxwell's three elements of social cohesion.[61] The paper makes almost no mention of the role of the voluntary sector in promoting social cohesion, except to note: "The voluntary or 'third sector' is frequently cited as an alternative mechanism to foster a sense of community and social cohesion in Canada. Unfortunately, this sector may increasingly lack the human and financial resources to deal with the range of complex social issues likely to come its way."[62] In ongoing revisions of this and related papers, the department eventually settled on a definition of social cohesion as "the ongoing process of developing a community of shared values, shared challenges and equal opportunity within Canada, based on a sense of trust, hope and reciprocity among all Canadians."[63] There is no reference to equality, social justice, or diversity in the definition; however, the objective was to continue to study the three interconnected elements that make up social cohesion as identified by Judith Maxwell.

The Policy Research Committee produced an interim report in October 1996, in which it identified six factors as potentially undermining Canada's capacity for social cohesion: polarization and exclusion (the report noted the growing inequality of earnings); rural–urban cleavage; loss of social capital (the breakdown of networks and trust that enable communities to work together); public–élite disconnection (the paper noted the normative rupture between average citizens and the élite in their core values – while the general public tends to be concerned about idealism and notions of security and moral community, the élites tend to look at the economy and competitiveness); cultural diversity; and the diffusion of new information and communications technologies.[64] The committee published a research update in February 1999.[65] Among the key findings in the chapter on social cohesion it mentioned that "'civil society' is becoming less civil and uncertainty about the future, the danger of economic polarization and declining confidence in government [are] causing widespread anxiety among Canadians." However, there was no explicit recognition of the importance of voluntary organizations, let alone of a key role for them in generating social cohesion.

Alone among Canadian think tanks, the Canadian Policy Research Network has undertaken a major research project on social cohesion. Jane Jenson has summarized and categorized much of its research and related Canadian studies.[66] From the numerous definitions of social cohesion she extracts five shared elements: belonging, inclusion, participation, recognition, and legitimacy. However, after reviewing each of these elements, she concludes her paper on a note of concern "about too enthusiastic an embrace of an agenda that fails to acknowledge continuing claims for social justice and diverse values, particularly in a multinational and modern country such as Canada."[67]

Most recently, the Senate's Standing Committee on Social Affairs, Science and Technology, after a year-long study and after hearing from academics, business and union leaders, and people from the voluntary sector, released its final report, "On Social Cohesion,"[68] in June 1999. One of its key messages was that "Social Cohesion is about shared values, but it is also about distributional issues. Building social cohesion in the new global era will require that we find ways to provide a more reasonable distribution of the benefits generated by trade liberalization and technological change. By doing this we will renew a long-standing Canadian commitment to social justice and sharing."[69] In a section on the role of the voluntary sector, the committee encouraged governments to enter into partnerships with voluntary organizations, particularly at the community level. However, it concluded, "Voluntary organizations ... offer individuals opportunities to express their own personal hopes and dreams for themselves, for their neighbors and their communities. *But it is only through democratic institutions that societies and nations can express their hopes and dreams.*"[70]

One's perspective undoubtedly determines what one reads into these various Canadian reports on fostering social cohesion. However, they appear to place little emphasis on the need to foster social capital through membership in voluntary organizations. Instead, they stress the traditional goals of the welfare state: reinvigorating democratic institutions to ensure equal participation and to reduce scepticism and cynicism about politics; the fundamental need for a job and a degree of economic security; universal access to those services essential to human development, such as education and health; protection of the vulnerable; reducing the social distance between citizens so that social divisions and feelings of relative deprivation do not block mutually beneficial collective action; restructuring political institutions to reflect morally correct action; respect for diversity; and fair sharing of the risks of living in an industrial society. Voluntary organizations, and the "social capital" that might result from membership in them, cannot replace the state and public policies in the pursuit of these goals.

DOWNSIZING: CAN THE VOLUNTARY SECTOR FILL THE GAP?

Introduction

Neo-conservative governments intent on cutting spending on social services have given many justifications for doing so, including the need to reduce deficits and debt, to stimulate productivity, to reduce dependence on government, and to curtail bureaucratic waste. In response to the argument that these cuts will leave many vulnerable people without support, they often reply, or imply, that the voluntary sector will fill in to compensate for the services reduced by budget cuts. The notion that private philanthropy can substitute for government spending is a central pillar of neo-conservative thought.[71] The informal sector of voluntary organizations and family may reduce the need for "coercive" taxes, ease the "deadening" hand of bureaucracy, promote "self-reliance," and encourage "local solutions" to public problems. Moreover, neo-conservatives argue that government poses a threat to the voluntary sector by discouraging voluntarism and reducing the incentive to contribute to charities. None of these, and their many other arguments for "downloading" government services on the voluntary sector, are correct. Indeed, of all the arguments they make for reducing taxes and government spending, this is surely the most fatuous. The arguments for relying more on the voluntary sector and less on government are conceptually flawed, morally reprehensible, and devoid of empirical support. Moreover, downloading will weaken and distort the voluntary sector.

Conceptual Flaws

Downloading services to the voluntary sector will not save money. Assuming that the services are still being provided, someone will have to continue to pay for them. The cost of the services will simply be shifted from taxpayers to those who make charitable donations. Since most of these services provide public benefits, relying on the voluntary sector instead of government means that those who do not donate will be able to "free ride" on the contributions of others. Of course, some services downloaded by government such as care of children, the elderly, and convalescents might be undertaken for free by family members. But, again, that does not mean that these services are not being paid for. Instead of their costs being spread equitably, through the tax system, across the entire population that benefits from their delivery, they are imposed on women, by and large, who now must provide the services unpaid in their own homes.[72]

Another example of conceptual confusion is that neo-conservatives often express concern that government programs are too generous, that they provide a disincentive for the poor to get jobs, that they are not given with enough "strings" attached, or that they are too impersonal. However, these types of arguments relate to the design of the programs, not to the matter of who is signing the cheque. If the government wishes to reduce benefits, make social assistance payments conditional on some aspect of the recipient's character, or have them accompanied with a sermon, it could easily legislate these requirements. Downsizing in favour of the voluntary sector to achieve these objectives is dishonest.

The Morality of Downloading

Downsizing government services in the hope that the voluntary sector will fill the gap is morally reprehensible on several grounds. The development of the welfare state was premised on a theory of citizenship under which everyone, as a member in a common enterprise, had civil, political, and social rights that would ensure full membership in the life of the society. Citizenship necessarily also implied responsibilities and moral obligations. Citizens, acting through governments, were seen as having a responsibility to provide a decent level of services such as health, education, and welfare for everyone, regardless of ability to pay. This obligation for the collective provision of services was not a matter of beneficence but constituted recognition of the fact that humans are intrinsically social beings, completely dependent on each other to be fully human agents. The neo-conservative attempt to download social services is above all an attack on the idea that the most basic human needs give rise to rights. It is a repudiation of the notion of social rights and a return to what Michael Ignatieff has termed "the enslavement of gift relations."[73]

In addition to ensuring the rights of citizenship to everyone, government provision of services essential for human development and the attainment of social equality rested on a number of strong moral judgments: the need to prevent exploitation, to ensure the mutuality of interdependence between individuals, to compensate for the inevitable harm caused to some by the operation of the market economy from which the great majority of citizens benefit, to make welfare judgments following collective deliberation, and to foster a sense of community and social cohesion. All these moral judgments are compromised if individuals receive services essential for human development not as a matter of right but as a matter of charity.

There is an ongoing debate about the extent to which philanthropy is an expression of social control exercised by dominant groups. Whether or not such an emphasis reflects the motives of those who would downsize government social services, it is troubling that many of the charities that do fill in for reduced public services will be churches or affiliated with churches. Faith-based social services appear to be all the rage and are consistent with the social conservative view that personal transformation will rescue most people from social pathology. However, it is fundamentally inconsistent with a long-standing understanding in liberal democracies that receipt of aid should not be contingent on acceptance of religious guidance.

One of the most fundamental axioms of social justice is that people in similar circumstances should be treated alike. Hence, welfare states took great care in developing entitlement programs to ensure generalized rules of administration, equal enforcement, and procedural due process for aggrieved recipients. By contrast, charitable organizations, at their best, deal with their clients as unique individuals, respond to their particular needs, and often ignore guidelines to ensure that these needs, as they see them, are met. While all of this is laudable, in the dispensation of entitlements it is morally unacceptable. In order to avoid arbitrariness and invidious comparisons, social services should be delivered on the basis of universally based and enforced standards of eligibility; otherwise the givers are empowered, but not the recipients.

A final moral problem with such downloading is that it suggests that there is nothing terribly wrong with the organization of the economy and society. It suggests that problems such as hungry children, or the need for home care for seriously ill or disabled people, can be adequately addressed through individual appeals and acts of charity, as opposed to comprehensive public policies. Charity cannot do anything to change the conditions that, for example, place so many vulnerable children at risk. The message of charitable appeals is to be generous – as if generosity is an appropriate and complete response to poverty – but do not "rock the boat." Help hungry children, but do not address poverty. Most charities do not look for ways of changing, and are not able to change, the underlying forces that perpetuate the injustices that they confront. Indeed, they are not allowed to do so under the current law, for that would offend the prohibition on political activities. Charities deal with the symptoms of social problems, not the problems themselves. This is, of course, the social democrats', or even the welfare liberals', well-rehearsed complaint about the voluntary sector – that it legitimates the basic structure and the distribution of power in our economy and diverts attention away from more fundamental responses to social problems.[74]

The Practicality of Downloading

Aside from the morality of downloading, as a practical matter the voluntary sector is incapable of dealing with the problems created by government downsizing. Most voluntary organizations are active only in one geographical area, and have small budgets, few assets, few paid employees, and even fewer professionals on staff. Organizations that serve the poor are especially vulnerable during government retrenchment. It is very difficult for them to attract general private support for their programs. Private donations are much more likely to support "amenity charities," such as the arts, culture, and health. In one of the most careful analyses of the effects of downloading, Michael Hall and Paul Reed conclude: "As our governments attempt to untie and reweave the social safety net it is an easy temptation to presume that there is a second safety net underneath – the non-profit sector – with the capacity to hold a good part of what the first one cannot. Looked at carefully, that second safety net is simply too small and too vulnerable to be counted on to hold an additional load of helping, caring and supporting services."[75]

One irony of downsizing is that most of the funds for voluntary organizations in Canada come from government transfers. In recent years, government money has constituted about 60 per cent of this funding, private-sector giving only slightly more than 10 per cent, and product sales and membership fees the rest.[76] Given the voluntary sector's heavy reliance on government transfers, even modest cuts in such funding would require an enormous increase in charitable giving to compensate. A recent report by the United Way of Greater Toronto calculated that a 1 per cent cut in government funding to non-profits could be compensated for only by a 50 per cent increase in corporate philanthropy.[77] Since many corporations have in recent years reduced their charitable contributions and are increasingly regarding their contributions as part of their marketing strategy, most social services report that corporate donations have declined substantially.

A recent major survey of community-based social service agencies in Metropolitan Toronto revealed that, as a consequence of reduced government funding, large numbers of social services had to disband or reduce programs.[78] Of the 504 agencies that responded to the survey, 54 had to close outright because of funding cuts, and over 300 programs were cancelled. Over a third of the agencies reported reductions in full-time members of staff; over one-quarter, reductions in part-timers. The 293 agencies that provided budget information for 1995 and 1996 reported losing $11 million from government sources while raising $8 million less through fund-raising efforts. The authors of the report concluded that their survey results revealed "a system in turmoil."

Crowding Out

In justifying downsizing by governments, neo-conservatives have argued that the welfare state has suppressed charity and the voluntary sector and that, once the boundaries of the state are rolled back, the voluntary sector will once again emerge to provide a helping hand to vulnerable people and families. That is, the government and the voluntary sectors are substitutes for one another, there is a finite amount of work to be done through collective action, and if the state does it, the voluntary sector will shrink. Thus, the argument runs, if the state retreats, the voluntary sector will rush to fill the void – a good thing, since it will provide these public services more efficiently, less coercively, and more responsively. But the neo-conservatives have it backwards. The weight of the evidence is that public generosity aids and encourages private generosity. As government withers, so too will the voluntary sector.

The theory of human behaviour underlying the argument that increased government expenditures on social services will crowd out donations to related services – in the extreme cases, on a one-for-one basis, making government expenditures on social services useless – is a straightforward application of the economist's model of the individual as a maximizer of rational utility. Individuals donating to a particular social service obviously derive satisfaction from spending on themselves and from spending on the beneficiaries of the social service. On the assumption that it is the total provision of services to the beneficiary that matters to the donor, not the source of the funds, if government spending on the service increases, the donor will give less.

This theory has a number of obvious weaknesses. First, it assumes that donors do not receive any private benefit from giving, aside from the satisfaction of knowing that the recipient has been assisted. In fact, many donors probably receive benefits in the form of higher social status, relief of guilt, or a "warm glow," or they may give simply because they are being responsive to a fund-raising appeal. Second, it assumes that channels for giving and the means for delivering social services are readily available. In fact, as a practical matter, the government must often provide the social and physical infrastructure necessary for the delivery of social services so that private donations can be put to use by voluntary organizations.[79] Third, like most economic theorizing, the theory which suggests that government spending crowds out private giving assumes that an individual's preference for donating is given and is unaffected by external factors such as government actions. In fact, the government's actions may powerfully influence donors' attitudes. If the government through its spending acknowledges particular individuals and activities, it might encourage people to treat them seriously; if it reduces spending on certain individuals and activities, donors might take that as an indication that those subjects are less important and less in need of support.[80] Government funding to a particular organization might also signal to potential donors that its services are needed, are of a high quality, and are being monitored.[81]

These three theoretical reasons suggesting that public spending, instead of "crowding out" private donations, probably "crowds in" such donations receive support from the overwhelming weight of historical, cross-national, and empirical evidence. Those who argue that government spending displaces voluntary efforts appear to assume mistakenly that there was a golden age of voluntary-sector purity, in which that sector was the dominant form of social organization, and that it was gradually corrupted and crowded out with the rise of the welfare state. This is little more than myth. Far from having a competitive relationship with the government, the voluntary sector as we know it in the modern era has always relied heavily on government assistance and experienced its greatest growth as the welfare state expanded.

In the United States, Lester Salamon has shown that co-operation between the voluntary sector and government has always been the case and that "[o]ne of the great ironies of modern American life is that fact that the set of social institutions that most vividly embodies the distinctive American penchant for private solutions to public problems has experienced its most rapid growth during precisely the period of most rapid expansion of the state."[82] This same pattern is common in all welfare states, including Canada. The state has always been inextricably linked to the voluntary sector in Canada, funding and attempting to rationalize its efforts.[83] Further, Shirley Tillotson has shown that during the 1930s, 1940s, and 1950s, when Canadians were paying increased proportions of their earnings to taxation to support the growth of the welfare state, the federated charities (such as United Way) also expanded significantly.[84] She argues that "the willingness to give is not simply the result of a zero–sum calculation about disposable dollars, where more dollar to the taxman means fewer to charities."[85] She also contends that "charitable giving helped prepare the way in public culture for income tax paying as a feature of citizenship in the welfare state."[86]

Contemporary studies have also revealed a strong correlation between government spending and charitable giving. For example, a U.S. study found that communities less generous in their state and local public-sector assistance for the poor are also less generous in their charitable giving.[87] Across countries, generally, there is not an inverse relationship between government social spending and the size of an economy's non-profit sector. For example, social spending in Japan is extremely low by international standards, but that country also has a relatively small non-profit sector. By contrast, Sweden, which is a very well-developed welfare state, also has an extensive and well-developed network of voluntary organizations.[88]

As well, econometric evidence suggests that government spending does not "crowd out" private charitable donations. In a comprehensive survey of the studies to 1991, Richard Steinberg concluded that crowding out of donations is relatively small – usually between ½ cent and 35 cents per dollar of government spending.[89] Subsequent studies have confirmed these results – donations replace only a small fraction of government cutbacks.[90]

Does government spending reduce the number of volunteers or the amount of time they are willing to give? Again, not surprisingly, since government spending often has to provide the social infrastructure to make the opportunities for volunteering meaningful, the studies suggest that government spending does not drive out volunteers.[91] A Canadian study by Kathleen Day and Rose Anne Devlin found that the level of government spending had no effect on the number of hours donated but did affect the decision to volunteer.[92] However, the direction of the effect depended on the services cut. Spending cuts on economic or protection activities resulted in fewer volunteers; cuts on social services and education increased their numbers. But whether volunteering and government spending are mutual complements or substitutes, the studies show that volunteering cannot come close to compensating for decreases in government spending.

Finally, there have been suggestions that the government could expand the size and influence of the voluntary sector, and therefore assist it in dealing with the problems of downsizing, by increasing the tax credit for charitable contributions. Such a policy is contradictory and unsound: increasing the tax credit expands government spending, will do little to assist those sectors hit hardest by cutbacks – social services – and, as I have argued elsewhere,[93] would result in a misallocation of government funds.

Downsizing is not only unlikely to result in the mobilization of the voluntary sector but will also, to the extent that charitable organizations are able to continue delivering services, force them to become more commercialized, charging fees for services and selling products to generate revenues, and generally to mimic the organizational structures of for-profit firms. As the voluntary sector is required to become more competitive and entrepreneurial, its organizations become less institutions for the pursuit of collective goals and more integrated into the private, market economy – "merchants of care."[94] For-profit firms then begin to compete with them in the delivery of social services, and eventually the existence of the voluntary sector itself is at risk, even though there is some evidence that non-profit firms deliver higher-quality social services than for-profit firms.[95] Also, as social services become increasingly commercialized, fund-raising become more difficult, and access to social services for the most disadvantaged is jeopardized.[96]

CONTRACTING WITH VOLUNTARY ORGANIZATIONS TO DELIVER SOCIAL SERVICES

Instead of simply downsizing and hoping that the voluntary sector will step in and provide comparable services, governments might contract with voluntary organizations to provide social services previously provided by government bureaucrats. Although contracting out social services to voluntary bodies has a long history in Canadian public administration, over the past two decades it has increased dramatically,[97] as it has in most industrialized countries, giving rise to what is frequently referred to as a "contract culture" in the voluntary sector.[98]

The passion of governments for contracting out social services has appeared justified, in large part, by the 30-year-old attacks on public bureaucracies. In the early part of this century, bureaucratic organization was championed for its rationality, technical expertise, impartiality, uniformity, and accountability. Even before the 1960s and later the all-out neo-conservative attack on the welfare state, however, organization theorists were questioning the effectiveness of bureaucracy as a form of organization. They accused it of being inflexible, impersonal, subject to empire-building and self-perpetuation, resistant to change, shrouded in secrecy, and anti-democratic.[99] During the past 30 years the assault has intensified, drawing heavily on public-choice theory, which teaches that bureaucrats are primarily motivated by their private interests in pay, status, and personal advancement, and by principal–agent analysis, which teaches that often costs such as monitoring employees' shirking justifies moving transactions out of a firm or bureaucracy and into the marketplace. Property-rights analysis suggests that ownership generally provides better incentives for efficiency than any other form of relationship, and other varieties of the institutional economics of firms and bureaucracies purport to show that usually markets are a much more effective form of social organization than hierarchies and bureaucracies.[100] As a result of these various analyses there has been enormous pressure to "fix" the public service.[101]

The various approaches to reform that followed from this literature are often referred to collectively as the new public management reform movement or the movement to reinvent government. Whatever government services can be privatized or contracted out should be, and delivery of the remaining services should be run much like a private business. Government should "enable" or " steer," but not "provide" or "row." It should retain its core function of setting policy, while in many (or most) cases leaving delivery to outside organizations. This approach has also become known as the purchaser–provider split in the new public administration literature.[102] In their international best seller *Reinventing Government,* David Osborne and Ted Gaebler illustrate 36 ways in which governments can arrange private delivery of services.[103] The main options have been categorized as contracting out, management contracts, franchising, licensing, and individual contracting.[104] Contracting out has become one of the most popular methods:[105] the government hires or subsidizes a private firm to provide the needed service. Clearly, there is a continuum of relationships possible between governments and their suppliers, from detailed contract to partnership arrangement.[106] Indeed, there are more permutations of arrangements than terms to describe them.

In contracting out, the government has the choice of dealing with either a for-profit firm or a voluntary organization.[107] If there is competition among providers, if the terms of the contract can be clearly specified, if compliance with the terms is easily monitored, and if the effectiveness of the service delivery can be easily determined, then contracting with for-profit firms is alleged to ensure greater efficiency. However, if competitive tendering is problematic because of natural monopoly conditions or if the service to be delivered is difficult to define and measure and it is difficult to determine whether the terms of the contract are being met, then there might be advantages to contracting with non-profit firms. Managers of non-profit firms have less incentive than those of for-profit firms to engage in sharp practices or to cheat, since the profits of the firm cannot be distributed. Also, it may be the case that non-profits attract as managers and employees people who are less preoccupied with pecuniary gains for themselves and more interested in delivering effective public services. Because of their increased trustworthiness, working with non-profits in these situations will afford some assurance that the subsidy will be spent on the intended purpose. Thus the issues of asymmetric information and trustworthiness, which economists have hypothesized might account for the presence of non-profits in certain markets such as social services, affect the choice of non-profit organizations, as the result of the behaviour not of consumers but of governments. Of course, because non-profit managers have less incentive to make profits, they also have less incentive to operate efficiently.

But, although it is possible to theorize why non-profits might be preferable to for-profit firms for delivering social services, it is less easy to see why they should be preferred to government departments. In areas where the government can generate competition by contracting out and where standardized services or products are being produced, there may be efficiency gains to contracting out. But where there is a need to produce human services of high quality on a sustained basis, and where there is no opportunity for competition, in theory there would appear to be little reason to suppose that the voluntary sector could deliver higher-quality services more cheaply than the public sector. While there might be some short-run gains, largely because of what might be called the "shake-up factor," over the long haul a voluntary organization linked to the government in a long-term contractual relationship is likely to be subject to the same forces as the bureaucratized public sector. There is surprisingly little evidence that the non-profit organizational form is a more efficient or effective mechanism for service delivery than government departments. Although the virtues attributed to non-profit organizations – inventiveness, flexibility, and responsiveness – have some reasonableness for a partially volunteer, partially donation-financed organization, and possibly in the context of competing mutual non-profits, they are less compelling for a professional organization that exists solely to supply services under contract to the government.

Although the rhetoric of alternative service delivery often emphasizes efficiency, responsiveness, and flexibility, a cynic might be forgiven for suspecting that there are other reasons why contracting with voluntary organizations has become popular with neo-conservative governments. First, they allow public services to be delivered by younger,[108] lower-paid, non-unionized, flexible workers[109] and volunteers;[110] second, non-profits can insist on moral, or at least impose more flexible, standards on those whom they help, ostensibly without infringing upon their freedom; and third, reducing the civil-service payroll gives the appearance of downsizing government.[111] But, of course, savings that the government can realize by contracting with voluntary organizations are the result not just of contracting out; in theory governments could achieve the same savings if they had more flexibility in establishing wages and terms of work. Basically, governments are thereby able to by-pass the civil-service rules, such as hiring requirements, job definitions, and pay scales, which they either imposed on themselves or negotiated with their employees. Little wonder that public employees' unions are suspicious of arguments for contracting out. However, aside from probably not avoiding the purported disadvantages of bureaucratic delivery of services and probably saving money only by evading civil service rules, contracting out poses a number of dangers to both government and to the voluntary sector.[112]

There are problems for government with contracting out – at least five, in my view. First, social services do not lend themselves particularly well to it. The conditions that must be satisfied for it to work efficiently are widely agreed upon. As summarized by Michael Trebilcock, the market provision of a firm's inputs, or the contracting out of government services, will be most effective under four conditions – "when needs can be easily specified and are relatively constant; when compliance with contractual terms is easily monitored; when negotiation of contracts is relatively inexpensive; and when there are highly differentiated inputs with few economies of scale and scope but large returns to specialization."[113] The provision of social services meets none of these criteria. As Purchase and Hirshhorn note, "[S]ocial service goals lack precise definition, results are difficult to measure, and often there is only one supplier immediately in a position to satisfy the government's requirements."[114] Of course the difficulty of specifying objectives and measuring performance is the justification for contracting with non-profit organizations instead of with for-profits firms. However, even if non-profits are generally more trustworthy than for-profits, the general absence of well-defined performance criteria means that the government can never be sure that it is getting what it actually wants.

Second, contracting out may negate the principles of universality and uniform standards and the perception of social services as entitlements. Contracting with non-profit organizations is not logically incompatible with broadening entitlements, to be sure. Yet services received from such organizations, as opposed to government employees, are less likely to be perceived as entitlements.

Third, on a related point, contracting out is likely to weaken the claim for equity and due process in the delivery of social services. In the distribution of social benefits, government has traditionally been overwhelmingly driven by concerns of equity. Public officials must legitimize the use of public resources that will help some and not others. The remedies for citizens who feel that they were not treated equitably are probably less extensive against a voluntary organization than they would be against a government employee. To be sure, voluntary organizations can be contractually bound to disburse benefits by clear and straightforward rules and to ensure that all beneficiaries are informed of their rights. However, since one of the purported advantages of voluntary organizations is that they can fashion their services to be responsive to individual "clients," there is a danger that equity and the safeguards provided by procedures of due process may be weakened if the service is not provided by a government employee.

Fourth, democratic governance requires that governments be accountable for the implementation of public policy, particularly authoritative decisions affecting vulnerable people. Both government accountability to citizens and cabinet accountability to the legislative body diminish when private organizations deliver social services. When public servants deliver services, the lines of responsibility are clear. When social services are contracted out, the role of government policy and the areas of government responsibility are obscured. Although the government might assume responsibility for the actions of the voluntary organizations with which it contracts, in fact, particularly with social service contracts, auditing and monitoring of programs are often rudimentary.

Fifth, and perhaps more worrisome, in combination with the increasing use of a broad range of alternative delivery mechanisms, contracting out may reduce the institutional capability of government – its ability to set policy, oversee and control providers, co-ordinate activities, and maintain an institutional memory – perhaps to the point where democratic governance will be threatened, through the "hollowing out" of the state. The long-term implications of this process are not yet well understood, but potentially they could deprive the state not only of its institutional capability but also of its legitimacy.[115]

The litany of dangers that the so-called contract culture poses to voluntary organizations is also well known and reasonably well documented. I would suggest at least six. First, government contracts divert the resources of voluntary organizations from delivering services to competing for, negotiating, administering and monitoring contracts. Second, formation of their operations may reduce their innovativeness, flexibility, and responsiveness to the community. In order to compete for government contracts, organizations might need more professionals, a larger scale of operations, and greater administrative capacity.

Third, contracting with government may require a significant change in governance of voluntary organizations. Boards of directors may require members who can help with the politics of obtaining contracts, and administrators may need more powers. Moreover, administrators' interests are likely to become linked to government policy and funding instead of to the communities being served.

Fourth, voluntary organizations will have less potential to engage in advocacy work that identifies and attempts to redress deficiencies and inequities in government programs. Reduced campaigning for changes in public policy and less lobbying may be explicit conditions of receiving government contracts or a form of self-censorship, as the organization positions itself politically to compete for contracts. Also, as a practical matter, as they administer the contract, senior members of staff are likely to have less time for advocacy.

Fifth, to the extent that competing for and administering government grants detract from private fund-raising and looking for other potential resources, the organization will become more financially insecure.

Finally, and somewhat ironically, and in part the result of the collective effects of contracting, voluntary organizations will lose the characteristics that make them a unique and valuable alternative form of social organization – flexible, innovative, cost-effective, participatory, and advocates for their clients. Contracting out might become not the privatization of government services but the "statization" of the voluntary sector. Large voluntary organizations receiving government contracts begin to act and look like government departments; indeed, they often hire former public servants as executive directors and employees. In a way, then, contracting out may in fact have facilitated an expansion of government activities by making its growth less politically visible.

This transformation of the voluntary sector, and the consequent enlargement of government, have not been lost on neo-conservatives. For example, Joe Laconte, deputy editor of the Heritage Foundation's bi-monthly magazine, *Policy Review*, which is dedicated to reviving civil society and dismantling the welfare state, has noted the phenomenon,[116] as has the right-wing British think tank, the Institute of Economic Affairs.[117] Sonia Arrison, program officer at the Donner Canadian Foundation, has urged charities not to accept grants or contracts from government, because by doing so they lose their "independence."[118]

I draw just the opposite lesson from the experience. Instead of distancing themselves from government by refusing to accept contracts, voluntary organizations that take on such contracts should become *part* of government. When government contracts with voluntary organizations, those bodies often become, in effect, agents of government; therefore, in law, they should become exactly that. That is, as a basic conceptual matter, it is more useful to think about government's delegating functions to non-profit organizations through contracting as an issue in public administration. Undoubtedly, there are circumstances where it makes sense for the government to deliver services through semi-autonomous agencies. However, the organization that it creates or co-opts usually has little in common with other groups in the voluntary sector. By accepting such contracts, the non-profits simply become agencies of government. When public funds play so vital a role in a private agency's budgets, it is disingenuous to think that the non-profit sector would not be in danger of losing its separate identity. Most non-profits today that accept large contracts from government expect to conform their operations to public purposes and priorities and do come under the partial control of public officials. Indeed, some are founded expressly to act as vehicles to carry out public purposes. They should be treated as government agencies in every respect: accountable to a minister, subject to the same pay scales and other labour practices as government employees, and accountable to government for their revenues and expenditures.

The obvious response to this suggestion is that then we are back where we started – more government bureaucracy. The whole point of delegating the delivery of public services to non-profits was to avoid the "down-sides" of bureaucracy – rigidity, goal displacement, empire-building, resistance to change, unresponsiveness, and impersonal and non-participatory operations. However, my arguments are, first, that large voluntary organizations locked into long-term contracts with the government *are* bureaucracies, and, second, the case against bureaucracy in the delivery of social services has yet to be made.

I dealt with the first point above, and the second calls for a whole new set of arguments. I will note here only that over the past 30 years there have been countless attempts to reform the public services, and just classifying the various theories has become a difficult conceptual challenge. Generally the reform programs fall into one of four camps: privatize and marketize government services, increase democratic participation in the delivery of public services, make government administration more flexible, or deregulate the internal management of government.[119]

This is not the place to defend bureaucracy,[120] but it does seem to me that government, by contracting with non-profits for the delivery of social services, is sacrificing the virtues of the old bureaucratic model – accountability, service to the public as a whole, reliability, probity, cohesion, continuity, and provision to recipients of a sense of entitlement and due process of law – while not gaining the virtues traditionally attributed to voluntary organizations. It does not follow that decentralization and experiments with alternative service delivery have no place in the social services, including neighbourhood services and other forms of innovation, but government employees should carry them out and within the traditional paradigm of government administration. The government's increasing dependence on the private sector, whether for-profit or non-profit firms, raises serious questions about the uniform and equitable delivery of social services, the perception of social services as entitlements, the capacity of the government to oversee and co-ordinate activity and develop responsive public policies, the accountability of the executive, and ultimately the legitimacy of government.

CONCLUSION: LOCATING VOLUNTARY ORGANIZATIONS AS A FORM OF SOCIAL ORGANIZATION

The central thesis of this chapter is that the role of the voluntary sector is to complement government, not to act as a substitute for it. Instead of summarizing the arguments in support of this thesis, which I did at the outset, I simply offer four points about voluntary organizations as a form of social organization that will reinforce those arguments. As the title of this volume implies, in many contexts it is useful to imagine that the voluntary sector is located between the government and markets; however, the relationship between these forms of social organization is more complicated.

First, prior to the 1980s, it was common to divide the economy into just two sectors, markets and government. The voluntary sector was considered too insignificant to require a theory of why it would be used as a form of social organization to allocate resources instead of markets or government. Despite rapid growth in the voluntary sector over the past two decades, its analysis still attracts only a small group of scholars. Standard political economy and economic texts continue to divide the economy into markets and government activities. Indeed, some commentators consider the notion of a voluntary sector as an idea promoted largely by neo-conservatives anxious to convince citizens that there is another sector in the economy that can largely replace the government in the provision of public goods. A small number of economists have attempted to provide a normative justification for the voluntary sector based on the concept of economic efficiency or an excess and differentiated demand for public service on the part of citizens not represented by the median voter, but their efforts have been unconvincing.[121]

Second, although it is helpful in many contexts to think of each form of social organization as having some fixed and unique attributes, and as being relatively autonomous vis-à-vis each other, they are all products of government action. Although economists are fond of referring to a self-regulating, free, and neutral private marketplace, there is, of course, no such thing. Marketplace transactions are shaped and determined by countless detailed and complex rules of contract and property law that are coercive and have decisive and pervasive distributional consequences. In this respect, the background rules for the market in important respects do not differ from any other form of government regulation, including taxation.[122] One of the central insights of feminist legal scholarship has been that even family relations, which were traditionally regarded as private and personal, reflect broader power relations in society, which are in turn determined by laws and government action or inaction and that have been responsible for women's oppression and subordination.[123]

In the same way, voluntary organizations do not arise solely as the result of a spontaneous ordering process reflecting some deep-seated needs of human nature. Almost every aspect of the voluntary sector is defined and shaped by government policy, most obviously through funding arrangements, tax treatment, and the regulation of governance structures, and more subtly through the tasks undertaken by government. The point is that while it often promotes clear thinking to divide forms of social organization into various categories, these are only categories of social constructs whose boundaries are profoundly influenced by government action.

Third, even treating the voluntary sector as embodying forms of organization significantly different from those in the marketplace and government – because all three sectors have a large variety of organizational forms that appear to have little in common – no matter how we classify the forms of social organization, there will always be a continuum between them, and any lines distinguishing them will be somewhat arbitrary. For example, the government itself is a multi-faceted entity, comprising a bewildering array of central departments, regional offices, non-departmental public bodies, numerous quasi-autonomous local entities, and so on. Particularly with the massive wave of bureaucratic reorganization ushered in by adherents of the new public management, which emphasizes delegation, disaggregation, and contracting out, it is difficult to know where government ends and the private sector begins.[124] The line drawn between sectors will depend on the particular context and purpose of classifying the forms of social organization; some classifications may promote clarity of thought in some contexts, but not others. However, in almost any context, non-profit organizations that depend on public contracts to such an extent that they are largely vehicles for the delivery of government services have more in common with organizations in the government than with those in the voluntary sector.

Finally, the voluntary sector consists of organizations many of which have almost nothing in common with each other. Although there are many ways of classifying them, commonly we do so by reference to the three types of societal functions that they perform:[125] socialization (voluntary bodies, usually studied by sociologists), service delivery (non-profit, usually studied by economists), and representation (intermediary, usually studied by political scientists). If my analysis of the role of the voluntary sector in a modern welfare state is correct, then arguably the most important organizations in the sector are those performing a representation function: providing information so that citizens can effectively participate in the policy process; representing the public interest and minority viewpoints; and overseeing, monitoring, and evaluating government and other powerful institutions in society. Yet in recent years, because the neo-conservative agenda is shaping the voluntary sector, more attention has focused on civic-engagement organizations, and the contract funding provided to service delivery organizations has increased, while representational groups have had their funding cut dramatically and their credibility diminished by the label "special interest" groups.[126]

NOTES

1 The influence of neo-conservative ideology on public policy affecting the voluntary sector has been discussed by numerous authors. See generally P.L. Browne, *Love in a Cold World: The Voluntary Sector in an Age of Cuts* (Ottawa: Canadian Centre for Policy Alternatives, 1996); J. Debart, *Public Funds, Private Provision: The Role of the Voluntary Sector* (Vancouver: University of British Columbia Press, 1993); J. Jenson and S.D. Phillips, "Regime Shift: New Citizenship Practices in Canada," *International Journal of Canadian Studies* 14 (1996), 111–36.

2 I use the term "neo-conservatism" here to refer not to a specific right-wing political philosophy but rather, compendiously, to a broad range of ideas, practices, and approaches – most notably, a normative preference for a small government and reliance on market mechanisms for allocating resources – expounded by those on the political right.

3 Commission on Private Philanthropy and Public Needs, *Giving in America: Toward a Stronger Voluntary Sector* (Washington, dc: Commission, 1975).

4 Ibid., 1.

5 See, for example, J. Estelle, ed., *The Nonprofit Sector in International Perspective: Studies in Comparative Culture and Policy* (New York: Oxford University Press, 1989); S. Rose-Ackerman, ed., *The Economics of Nonprofit Institutions: Studies in Structure and Policy* (New York: Oxford University Press, 1986); and W.W. Powell, ed., *The Nonprofit Sector: A Research Handbook* (New Haven, Conn.: Yale University Press, 1987).

6 See P.D. Hall, "The Dilemmas of Research on Philanthropy," in J. Van Til and Associates, *Critical Issues in American Philanthropy: Strengthening Theory and Practice* (San Francisco: Jossey-Bass Publishers, 1990), 242. On the historical development of the academic study of U.S. philanthropy, see also S.N. Katz, "Where Did the Serious Study of Philanthropy Come from, Anyway?" *Nonprofit and Voluntary Sector Quarterly* 28 (1999), 74.

7 The project will result in over a dozen published books detailing the research findings. The first book apeared in 1996 and describes the project in detail. L.M. Salamon and H.K. Anheier, *The Emerging Nonprofit Sector: An Overview* (Manchester: Manchester University Press, 1996). Since then several other volumes have been published.

8 The Association for Research on Non-Profit Organizations and Voluntary Action publishes the *Nonprofit and Voluntary Sector Quarterly*. This journal began publication in 1972 under the title *Journal of Voluntary Action Research*. The change in its name in 1989 reflected the increasing acceptance of the area of study as embracing a sector of the economy. The International Society for Third Sector Research publishes *Voluntas: International Journal of Voluntary and Non-Profit Organisations*. It began publication in 1990 and reflected the growing international interest in the study of the sector.

9 See generally Katz, "Where?"

10 Powell, *The Nonprofit Sector*.

11 B. Karl, "Philanthropic Institutions," *Science* (22 May 1987), 984.

12 Many of these comments are referred to in Hall, "Dilemmas."

13 A. Cylmer, "Filter Aid to Poor through Churches," *New York Times*, 23 July 1999; T.M. Neal, "Bush Outlines Charity-Based Social Services," *Washington Post*, 23 July 1999.

14 For a review of these reports, see Ontario Law Reform Commission, (OLRC), *Report on the Law of Charities*, vol. 1 (Toronto: Law Reform Commission, 1996), 36–50.

15 D.C. Wilson, "The Voluntary Sector in the 1990s and Beyond," in S.K.E. Saxon-Harrold and J. Kendall, eds., *Researching the Voluntary Sector*, 2nd ed. (London: Charities Aid Foundation, 1994), 72. On the growth of Britain's voluntary sector generally, see J. Kendall and M. Knapp, *The Voluntary Sector in the UK* (Manchester: Manchester University Press, 1996).

16 Commission on the Future of the Voluntary Sector, *Meeting the Challenge: Voluntary Action into the 21st Century* (London: NCVO Publications, 1996).

17 *Compact: Getting it Right Together – Compact on Relations between Government and the Voluntary and Community Sector in England*, presented to Parliament by the Secretary of State for the Home Department (London, Nov. 1998).

18 For a review of these reports, see *OLRC, Report*, 21–36.

19 *Royal Commission on the Economic Union and Development Prospects for Canada, Report*, vol. 2 (Ottawa: Minister of Supply and Services, 1985), 826.

20 Ibid., 807.

21 See G. Paquet and R. Shepherd in "The Program Review Process: A Deconstruction," in G. Swimmer, ed., *How Ottawa Spends 1996–1997: Life Under the Knife* (Ottawa: Carleton University Press, 1996), 39–72.

22 On 15 June 1999, the Privy Council Office released a series of press releases announcing the status of these initiatives. See Government of Canada, Privy Council Office, "Federal Government and Voluntary Sector Seek New Strategic Relationship," June 15, 1999; "The 'Joint Table' Process," 15 June 1999; "Joint Work: Federal Government and Voluntary Sector," 15 June 1999; and "The Voluntary Sector: Society's Vital Third Pillar" 15 June 1999.

23 Advisory Board on the Voluntary Sector, *Sustaining a Civic Society: Voluntary Action in Ontario* (Toronto: Queen's Printer for Ontario, 1997), ii.

24 For leading Canadian texts, see R.B. Blake, P.E. Bryden, and J.F. Strain, eds., *The Welfare State in Canada: Past, Present and Future* (Concord, Ont.: Irwin Publishing, 1997); S. McBride and J. Shields, *Dismantling a Nation: Canada and the New World Order* (Halifax: Fernwood, 1993); and G. Teeple, *Globalization and the Decline of Social Reform* (Toronto: Garamond Press, 1995).

25 There is an enormous amount of historical, sociological, and political science literature on the comparative development of welfare states, and there have been attempts to categorize them into three or four qualitatively different types of states. However, none of these theories and studies examines the role of voluntary organizations. The theoretical frameworks used in explaining development of the welfare state excluded any role for the voluntary sector. See S. Kuhnle and P. Selle, eds., *Government and Voluntary Organizations: A Relational Perspective* (Aldershot: Avebury, 1992), chap. 1; and B. Gidron, R. Kramer, and L. Salamon, eds., *Government and the Third Sector: Emerging Relationships in Welfare States* (San Francisco: Jossey-Bass, 1992).

26 For some of the philosophical ideas about justice and desert noted here, see Kymlicka, chapter 4 in this volume.

27 See, for example, M.J. Trebilcock, *The Prospects for Reinventing Government* (Toronto: C.D. Howe Institute, 1994), 31–2 (suggesting that in a 1982 publication, in which he and his co-authors had predicted that widespread privatization would not take place because the "iron triangle of special interest groups, politicians and bureaucrats (or regulators) ... was impervious to change," they had "underestimated the power of ideas in the political system").

28 See N. Chandhoke, *State and Civil Society: Explorations in Political Theory* (Thousand Oakes, Calif.: Sage Publications, 1995); J.L. Cohen and

A. Arato, *Civil Society and Political Theory* (Cambridge, Mass.: MIT Press, 1993); J. Ehrenberg, *Civil Society: The Critical History of an Idea* (New York: New York University Press, 1999); J.A. Hall, ed., *Civil Society: Theory, History, Comparison Policy* (Cambridge, Mass.: MIT Press, 1995); and J. Keane, ed., *Civil Society and the State* (New York: Verso, 1988).

29 Dissidents hailed civil society as democratic sites of self-organization and major obstacles to the expansion of the communist state. See Ehrenberg, *Civil Society*, chap. 7.

30 A. Portes, "Social Capital: Its Origins and Applications in Modern Sociology," *Annual Review of Sociology* 24 (1998), 24. On the various usages of the terms "social capital" and "social cohesion," see generally J. Jenson, "Mapping Social Cohesion: The State of Canadian Research," CPRN Discussion Paper No. F 03 (Ottawa: Canadian Policy Research Networks, 1998).

31 R.D. Putnam, *Making Democracy Work: Civic Traditions in Modern Italy* (Princeton, NJ: Princeton University Press, 1993), 167. Or, as slightly reworded, "features of social life – networks, norms, and trust – that enable participants to act together more effectively to pursue their shared objectives." R.D. Putnam, "The Strange Disappearance of Civic America," *American Prospect* 24 (1996), 34.

32 Government of Canada, Policy Research, "Social Cohesion Network," http://policyresearch.schoolnet.ca/networks/cohsoc/sociales-e.htm (viewed in August 1999).

33 See, for example, W.J. Bennett, *The Book of Virtues* (New York: Simon and Schuster, 1993); A. Etzioni, *The Spirit of Community: The Reinvention of American Society* (New York: Touchstone, 1993); D. Frum, *What's Right* (New York: Basic Books, 1996); W.D. Gairdner, *The War against the Family* (Toronto: Stoddart, 1992); G. Himmelfarb, *The Demoralization of Society: From Victorian Virtues to Modern Values* (New York: Vintage, 1994); and E. Shils, "The Virtue of Civil Society," *Government and Opposition* 26 (1990), 3.

34 G. Himmelfarb, "Beyond Social Policy: Re-Moralizing America," *Wall Street Journal*, 7 Feb. 1995.

35 F. Fukuyama, *The Great Disruption: Human Nature and the Reconstitution of Social Order* (New York: Free Press, 1999).

36 Although it is hard to oppose calls for more virtuous behaviour, there are a number of problems with attempts to deal with social issues by sermons or increased support for voluntary organizations. First, civility by itself would not appear to be a major virtue; certainly the friendly co-operation that appears to characterize voluntary organizations does not rank with courage or honesty. Second, a moral diagnosis of social disintegration may divide citizens into two groups: righteous citizens and malevolent others. Then, instead of searching for underlying causes and overarching solutions to social problems, diagnosticians may search for

"depraved people" who threaten the public good, such as "squeegee kids," and for ways to deal with "them." Third, even if it made sense to try to target immoral behaviour, why concentrate on single mothers, drug users, and street people, as most of these social commentators do. Why not concentrate on the immoral behaviour of corporate executives, for example, and their lack of loyalty to workers, indifference to communities, and lack of felt obligation vis-à-vis those made vulnerable by their actions.

37 See R. Dahrendorf, "The Third Way and Liberty: An Authoritarian Streak in Europe's New Center," *Foreign Affairs* 78 No. 5 (1999), 13.

38 In a recent article, Larry Diamond enumerated the democratic functions of civic organizations from a pluralist perspective: "containing the power of democratic government[s], checking their potential abuses and violations of the law, and subjecting them to political scrutiny"; supplementing "the role of political parties in stimulating political participation, increasing political efficacy and skill of democratic citizens"; developing "democratic attributes, such as tolerance, moderation, a willingness to compromise, and a respect for opposing viewpoints"; "creating channels other than political parties for the articulation, aggregation, and representation of interests"; generating "a wide range of interests that may cross-cut, and so mitigate, the principle polarities of political conflict"; "recruiting and training new political leaders"; and disseminating information, "thus aiding citizens in the collective pursuit and defense of their interests." L. Diamond, "Rethinking Civil Society: Toward Democratic Consolidation," *Journal of Democracy* 5 (1994), 7–10.

39 See P. Bourdieu, "The Forms of Capital," in J.G. Richardson, ed., *Handbook of Theory and Research for the Sociology of Education* (New York: Greenwood, 1983), 241–60, and J. Coleman, *Foundations of Social Theory* (Cambridge, Mass.: Harvard University Press, 1990), chap. 12. For the development of the concept, see Portes, "Social Capital."

40 Putnam, *Making Democracy Work.*

41 Ibid., 6.

42 R.D. Putnam, "The Prosperous Community: Social Capital and Public Life," *American Prospect* 13 (1993), 35.

43 R.D. Putnam, "Bowling Alone: America's Declining Social Capital," *Journal of Democracy* 6 (1995), 65.

44 Putnam, "Strange Disappearance."

45 See M.W. Foley and B. Edwards, "Beyond Tocqueville: Civil Society and Social Capital in Comparative Perspective," *American Behavioral Scientist* 42 (1998), 5 (introducing the second of a two-part series on the debate on civil society and social capital); P. Hall, "Social Capital in Britain," *British Journal of Politics* 29 (1999), 417; M. Levi, "Introduction," *Politics and Society* 24 (1996), 5 (introducing a symposium on Putnam's work);

and S. Tarrow, "Making Social Sciences Work across Space and Time: A Critical Reflection on Robert Putnam's *Making Democracy Work*," *American Political Science Review* 90 (1996), 389.

46 J. Rifkin, *The End of Work: The Decline of the Global Labor Force and the Dawn of the Post-Market Era* (New York: Putnam's Sons, 1995).

47 Ibid., 238.

48 F. Fukuyama, *Trust: The Social Virtues and the Creation of Prosperity* (New York: Free Press, 1995).

49 OECD, *Societal Cohesion and the Globalising Economy: What Does the Future Hold?* (Paris: OECD, 1997).

50 Ibid., 3. As another illustration of the worldwide interest in social capital and cohesion, in the preface to a recent report of the Bertelsmann Foundation to the Club of Rome, Werner Weidenfeld acknowledged: "In the new world political era, the cultural resources that lead to social cohesion and the limits of that cohesion in our societies are of the utmost importance. It will be the primary task for societies to promote social cohesion as the basic source of economic development and ecological sensibility. The cultural foundations of society deserve our full attention as the basis of sustainable development": P.L. Berger, ed., *The Limits of Social Cohesion: Conflict and Mediation in Pluralist Societies* (Boulder, Col.: Westview Press, 1998), x.

51 Council on Civil Society, *A Call to Civil Society: Why Democracy Needs Moral Truths* (New York: Institute for American Values (1998).

52 National Commission on Civic Renewal, *A Nation of Spectators: How Civic Disengagement Weakens America and What We Can Do about It* (College Park, Md.: University of Maryland, 1998).

53 See M. Schudson, "What If Civic Life Didn't Die," *American Prospect* 25 (1996), 17: J. Hall and C. Lindholm, *Is America Breaking Apart* (Princeton, NJ: Princeton University Press, 1999).

54 See K. Pollitt, "Subject to Debate: For Whom the Ball Rolls," *Nation*, 15 April 1996. With respect to Putnam's bowling club example, she observes, "Putnam treats these as if they arose merely from the appetite of individuals for fellowship and tenpins. But in fact they came out of specific forms of working-class and lower-middle-class life: stable blue-collar or office employment (businesses and unions often started and sponsored teams) that fostered group solidarity, a marital ethos and permitted husbands plenty of boys' nights out, and a lack of cultural and entertainment alternatives. It would be amazing if league bowling survived the passing of the way of life that brought it into being, nor am I so sure we need mourn it."

55 See A. Portes and P. Landolt, "The Downside of Social Capital," *American Prospect* 26 (1996), 18.

56 T. Skocpol, "Unraveling from Above," *American Prospect* 25 (1996), 20.

57 Ibid.

58 See, for example, a description of the importance of political institutions (including political parties) in generating northern Italy's social capital: Tarrow, "Making."

59 He recently wrote: "For good historical reasons, progressives should resist the view, now being articulated by some simple-minded reactionaries, that government can be replaced by 'civil society'. As I wrote in this journal three years ago (rather plainly, I thought, and in italics, no less): 'Social capital is not a substitute for effective public policy but rather a prerequisite for it and, in part, a consequence of it": R.D. Putnam, "Robert Putnam Responds," *American Prospect* 26 (1996), 28.

For a somewhat similar debate in Canada see E. Shragge, "Civil Society: Civility or Resistance?" *Canadian Review of Social Policy* 41 (1998), 60. In critiquing a paper on civil society by Sherri Torjman of Ottawa's Caledon Institute of Social Policy, Shragge argues that the shift from the state to civil society is an integral part of the attempt by those with economic power to reject collective provision and consolidate their power so that "the promotion of community (civil society) as part of the consensus of redefining 'caring' will act to demobilize the oppositional role of community organizations." See also S. Torjman, "Response to Comment on *Civil Society: Reclaiming our Humanity*," *Canadian Review of Social Policy* 41 (1998), 61, 62, responding that the interest of "Civil Society: Reclaiming our Humanity" was simply "to find resources to help fight poverty" and that, like all Caledon Institute publications, its recommendations rested on "the crucial (and perhaps more important than ever) role of government in promoting economic and social well-being. The paper does not propose or even suggest – implicitly or explicitly – the devolution of government programs to the voluntary sector.".

60 Quoted in Jenson, *Mapping*, 3.

61 "Canadian Heritage, Canadian Identity, Culture and Values: Building a Cohesive Society," challenge paper prepared for the ADMs' Policy Research Committee, (Ottawa, 13 Sept. 1996).

62 Ibid., 16.

63 See Canadian Heritage, Strategic Research and Analysis Directorate, *Canadian Identity, Culture and Values: Building a Cohesive Society: The Social Cohesion Research Program for the Department of Canadian Heritage*, (Ottawa, 15 July 1997).

64 Policy Research Committee, *Report on Growth, Human Development and Social Cohesion: Overview – Pressure Points in the Medium Term*, (Ottawa, Oct. 1996), 35–41.

65 Policy Research Committee, *Sustaining Growth, Human Development, and Social Cohesion in a Global World: A Research Update Prepared by the Policy Research Initiative* (Ottawa, Feb. 1999).

66 Jenson, *Mapping*.
67 Ibid., 38.
68 Canada, Standing Senate Committee on Social Affairs, Science and Technology, *Final Report: On Social Cohesion*, June 1999.
69 Ibid., "Introduction," 7.
70 Ibid., 3.
71 See N. Glazer, *The Limits of Social Policy* (Cambridge, Mass.: Harvard University Press, 1989; C. Murray, *In Pursuit of Happiness and Good Government* (New York: Simon & Schuster, 1988); D.G. Green, *Reinventing Civil Society: The Rediscovery of Welfare without Politics* (London: IEA, 1993); T.R. Machan, *Generosity: Virtue in Civil Society* (Washington, DC: Cato Institute, 1998); and M.N. Olasky, *The Tragedy of American Compassion* (Washington, DC: Regnery Gateway, 1992).
72 See C. Pateman, "The Patriarchal Welfare State," in A. Gutman, ed., *Democracy and the Welfare State* (Princeton, NJ: Princeton University Press, 1988) 231: "It is not surprising that the attack on public spending in the welfare state by Thatcher and Reagan governments goes hand-in-hand with praise for loving care within families, that is, with an attempt to obtain even more unpaid welfare from (house)wives."
73 M. Ignatieff, *The Needs of Strangers* (New York: Viking, 1985), 18: "The bureaucratized transfer of income among strangers has freed each of us from the enslavement of gift relations."
74 See J. Poppendieck, *Sweet Charity? Emergency Food and the End of Entitlement* (New York: Viking, 1998), who speculates that emergency food banks may be contributing to the problems that they were meant to solve by deterring recipients from exercising their rights to entitlements, assuring neo-conservative legislators that no one will starve if they continue to download social services, acting as a moral safety value, and distracting and absorbing the time of advocates for more fundamental change. See also S. Flounders, "Her Holy Message: 'Poverty is Beautiful': Behind the Ruling-Class Rush to Make Mother Teresa a Saint," *Canadian Dimension* (Nov.–Dec. 1997), 16. In explaining why so few poor mourners turned out to Mother Teresa's funeral, Flounders notes, "While the rich and powerful move to canonize Mother Theresa as a saint, the 'poorest of the poor' are far more likely to look for leadership that seeks to end poverty, not to bless it."
75 M.H. Hall and P.B. Reed, "Shifting the Burden: How Much Can Government Download to the Non-profit Sector?" *Canadian Public Administration* 41 (1998), 1.
76 K.M. Day and R.A. Devlin, *The Canadian Nonprofit Sector*, Working Paper No. CPRN02 (Ottawa: Canadian Policy Research Networks, 1997), 16.
77 United Way of Greater Toronto, *Metro Toronto: A Community at Risk* (Toronto: United Way of Greater Toronto, 1997), 66.

78 Municipality of Metropolitan Toronto, Social Planning Council of Metropolitan Toronto, *Profile of a Changing World: 1996 Community Agency Survey* (Toronto, 1997); figures and quotations below appear on 19, 24, 36, and 61.

79 A survey of social agencies in Metropolitan Toronto found that government cutbacks in funding resulted in a significant drop in volunteers because agencies have "less capacity to recruit, train, coordinate and supervise volunteers due to diminished staff capacity." Ibid., 28.

80 For a discussion and evidence of the government's "demonstration effect," see P.R. Jones, J.G. Cullis, and A. Lewis, "Public versus Private Provision of Altruism: Can Fiscal Policy Make Individuals 'Better' People?" *Kyklos* 51 (1998), 3.

81 See S. Rose-Ackerman, "Do Government Grants to Charity Reduce Private Donations?" in M.J. White, ed., *Nonprofit Firms in a Three Sector Economy* (Washington, DC: Urban Institute, 1981), 95.

82 L.M. Salamon, *Partners in Public Service: Government–Nonprofit Relations in the Modern Welfare State* (Baltimore, Md.: Johns Hopkins University Press, 1995), 1. See also F.M. Loewenberg, "Ideology or Pragmatism? Further Reflections on Voluntary and Public Sector Relations in the Nineteenth Century," *Nonprofit and Voluntary Sector Quarterly* 21 (1992), 119.

83 Valverde, "Mixed."

84 S. Tillotson, "A New Taxpayer for a New State: Charitable Fundraising and the Origins of the Welfare State," in R.B. Blake, P.E. Bryden, and F.F. Strain, *The Welfare State in Canada: Past, Present and Future* (Toronto: Irwin Publishing, 1997), 138. She suggests that increased federated, or collective fund-raising and higher taxes were both responses to similar concerns – cost-effective collection, accounting controls, use of 'ability to pay' measures, and the need to increase the number of individuals from whom funds were collected.

85 Ibid., 152–3.

86 Ibid., 141–2.

87 J. Wolpert, *Patterns of Generosity in American: Who's Holding the Safety Net?* (New York: Twentieth Century Fund, 1993).

88 T. Lundstrom and F. Wykstrom, *The Nonprofit Sector in Sweden* (Manchester: Manchester University Press, 1997).

89 R. Steinberg, "Does Government Spending Crowd out Donations? Interpreting the Evidence," *Annals of Public and Cooperative Economics* 62 (1991), 591.

90 J. Andreoni, "An Experimental Test of the Public Goods Crowding-out Hypothesis," *American Economic Review* 83 (1993), 1317: E. Becker and C.M. Lindsay, "Does the Government Free Ride?" *Journal of Law and Economics* 37 (1994), 277; J. Khanna, J. Posnett, and T. Sandler, "Charity Donations in the UK: New Evidence Based on Panel Data," *Journal of*

Public Economics 56 (1995), 257; B.R. Kingma and R. McClelland, "Public Radio Stations Are Really, Really Not Public Goods: Charitable Contributions and Impure Altruism," *Annals of Public and Cooperative Economics* 66 (1995), 65. For a review of the studies, see B.R. Kingma, "Public Good Theories of the Non-Profit Sector: Weisbrod Revisited," *Voluntas* 8 (1997), 135.

91 P. Menchik and B. Weisbrod, "Volunteer Labor Supply," *Journal of Public Economics* 32 (1987), 159; and J. Schiff, *Charitable Giving and Government Policy: An Economic Analysis* (Westport, Conn.: Greenwood Press, 1990).

92 K.M. Day and R.A. Devlin, "Volunteerism and Crowding Out: Canadian Econometric Evidence," *Canadian Journal of Economics* 29 (1996), 37.

93 See my chapter 14 in this volume.

94 Social Planning Council of Metropolitan Toronto, *Merchants of Care? The Non-Profit Sector in a Competitive Social Services Marketplace* (Toronto: Council, 1997).

95 For a review of the empirical work, see S. Rose-Ackerman, "Altruism, Ideological Entrepreneurs and the Non-Profit Firm," *Voluntas* 8 (1997), 120; Social Planning Council of Metropolitan Toronto, *Merchants of Care?*

96 The increasing commercialization of the non-profit sector as the result of downsizing and its consequences has been widely noted. For evidence of growing commercialization of non-profits in the United States as a result of downloading and the displacement of their social mission goals in the drive for additional revenue, see Salamon, *Partners in Public Service,* chap. 14, and B.A. Weisbrod, ed., *To Profit or Not to Profit: The Commercial Transformation of the Nonprofit Sector* (New York: Cambridge University Press, 1998). For a comprehensive examination of the issues relating to the commercialization of voluntary organizations, see B. Zimmerman and R. Dart, *Charities: Doing Commercial Ventures: Societal and Organizational Implications* (Ottawa: Canadian Policy Research Networks, 1998).

97 See R. Chappell, *Social Welfare in Canadian Society* (Toronto: ITP Nelson, 1996), chap. 7; R.M. Jaco, "Social Services and Human Service Organizations," in J.C. Turner and F.J. Turner, eds., *Canadian Social Welfare,* 3rd ed. (Scarborough: Allyn & Bacon, 1995), chap. 21; and A. Armitage, *Social Welfare in Canada Revisited,* 3rd ed. (Toronto: Oxford University Press, 1996), chap. 6.

98 The critical literature on governments' contracting with voluntary organizations is voluminous. For Canada, see Browne, *Love*; J. Rekart, *Public Funds, Private Provision: The Role of the Voluntary Sector* (Vancouver: UBC Press, 1993); and J. Shields and B.M. Evans, *Shrinking the State: Globalization and Public Administration "Reform"* (Halifax: Fernwood Publishing, 1998). For the United States, see S.R. Smith and M. Lipsky, *Nonprofits for Hire: The Welfare State in the Age of Contracting* (Cambridge, Mass.: Harvard University Press, 1993); G. Nowland-Foreman, "Purchase-of-Service Con

tracting, Voluntary Organizations, and Civil Society," *American Behavioral Scientist* 42 (1998), 108: and J. Wolch, *The Shadow State: Government and the Voluntary Sector in Transition* (New York: Foundation Center, 1990). For the United Kingdom, see N. Johnson, *The Welfare State in Transition: The Theory and Practice of Welfare Pluralism* (Amherst: University of Massachusetts Press, 1987), and Perri 6 and J. Kendall, eds., *The Contract Culture in Public Services: Studies from Britain, Europe and the U.S.A.* (Aldershot: Arena, 1997).

99 See A.J. Mills and T. Simmons, *Reading Organizational Theory: A Critical Approach to the Study of Organizational Behaviour and Structure* (Toronto: Garamond Press, 1999), 54–61; and A. Dunsire, "Then and Now: Public Administration, 1953–1999," *Political Studies* 47 (1999), 360.

100 For brief summaries of this literature, see G.B. Doern, *The Road to Better Public Services: Progress and Constraints in Five Canadian Federal Agencies* (Montreal: Institute for Research on Public Policy, 1994), 23–7; and Trebilcock, *Prospects*, 7–14. For a more detailed review, see A.R. Khursheed and T.E. Borcherding, "Organizing Government Supply: The Role of Bureaucracy," in F. Thompson and M.T. Green, ed., *Handbook of Public Finance* (New York: Marcel Dekker, 1998), chap. 2.

101 Although the pressure to contract out government functions to voluntary organizations came largely from the right and consisted of the same pressures that were pushing more generally for the privatization of public service, it also came from the left, at least in the late 1970s and early 1980s, before the left was placed on full alert just defending the welfare state. The left assumed that contracting out might lead to greater decentralization of government and increased citizens' participation. See, for example, J. Keane, *Public Life and Late Capitalism: Toward a Socialist Theory of Democracy* (Cambridge: Cambridge University Press, 1984), 2: "the radical reform of late capitalist societies depends crucially upon the weakening of the power of corporate and state bureaucracies through the establishment and strengthening of spheres of autonomous public life."

102 See E. Davis, *Public Spending* (London: Penguin Books, 1998), chap. 9.

103 D. Osborne and T. Baebler, *Reinventing Government* (New York: Plume, 1993).

104 These various organizational options for the private provision of public goods, and the incentive properties and other considerations that might influence the selection of one over the other, are summarized in Trebilcock, *Prospects*, 14–33.

105 See, generally, K. Ascher, *The Politics of Privatization: Contracting out Public Services* (New York: St Martin's Press, 1987), and I. Harden, *The Contracting State* (Buckingham: Open University Press, 1992). New Zealand has adopted this new model of public administration most

thoroughly. In New Zealand almost the whole public service is governed by contractual arrangements between government and service providers, including individual service providers such as policy advisers and even heads of departments: see J. Boston, *The State under Contract* (Wellington: Bridget Williams Books, 1995), and M.J. Ormsby, "The Provider/Purchaser Split: A Report from New Zealand," *Governance* 11 (1998), 357. See also J. Alford and D. O'Neill, eds., *The Contract State: Public Management and the Kennett Government* (Geelong: Centre for Applied Social Research, Deakin University, 1994), describing the extensive contracting out by the Kennett government in Victoria, Australia, in the early 1990s, following the New Zealand model.

106 Unlike purchase-of-service contracts, under partnership arrangements the parties normally share decision-making authority. On partnerships generally, see K. Kernaghan, "Partnership and Public Administration: Conceptual and Practical Considerations," *Canadian Public Administration* 36 (1993), 61; S. Phillips, "Fuzzy Boundaries: Rethinking Relationships between Governments and NGOs," *Policy Options* 15 (1994), 13; A. Rodal and N. Mulder, "Partnerships, Devolution and Power-Sharing: Issues and Implications for Management," *Optimum* 24 (1993), 3; and F.L. Seidle, *Rethinking the Delivery of Public Services to Citizens* (Montreal: Institute for Research on Public Policy, 1995), chap. 7.

107 On relevant factors in choosing between for-profit and non-profit firms for service delivery in the context of social services, see P. de L. Panet and M.J. Trebilcock, "Contracting-out Social Services," 1 *Canadian Public Administration,* 41 (1998), 21, 23–9.

108 Many governments will have an ageing workforce with a higher average salary than a new voluntary organization, operating with relatively young and inexperienced workers.

109 Only 10 per cent of charities have unionized staff; 24 per cent offer no benefits to their employees; and only 7 per cent pay clerical and support staff more than the average industrial wage: Browne, *Love,* 23–8.

110 Theoretically, the government could make more use of volunteers. Indeed, their use is extremely common, and their work invaluable, in public schools. See J.L. Brudnoy, *Fostering Volunteer Programs in the Public Sector: Planning, Initiating, and Managing Voluntary Activities* (San Francisco: Jossey-Bass, 1990).

111 Public criticism of government growth tends to focus on taxes, expenditures, and, as a measure of growth, the number of government employees. By giving the appearance of a reduction in the size of the civil service, the rise of the non-profit organization owes more, some commentators have suggested, to political optics than to superior organizational efficiency. Moreover, in their study of contracting out in the

United States, Steven Smith and Michael Lipsky conclude that privatization involving transfer of activities formerly carried out by governments to voluntary organizations have had the ironic effect of facilitating an expansion of government activities by making this growth less politically visible. Smith and Lipsky, *Nonprofits.*

112 These arguments are drawn largely from the works cited above in note 98.

113 Trebilcock, *Prospects*, 13.

114 B. Purchase and R. Hirshhorn, *Searching for Good Governance: Government and Competitiveness Project – Final Report* (Kingston: School of Policy Studies, Queen's University, 1994), 106.

115 See L.A. Blanchard, C.C. Hinnant, and W. Wong, "Market-Based Reforms in Government: Toward a Social Subcontract," *Administration and Society* 30 (1998), 483; B.H. Milward, K.G. Provan, and B. Else, "What Does the Hollow State Look Like?" in B. Bozeman, ed., *Public Management: The State of the Art* (San Francisco: Jossey Bass, 1993) 309–22; and R.A.W. Rhodes, "The Hollowing Out of the State: The Changing Nature of the Public Service in Britain," *Political Quarterly* 65 (1994), 138.

116 J. Laconte, *Seducing the Samaritan: How Government Contracts Are Reshaping Social Services* (Boston, Mass.: Pioneer Institute for Public Policy Research, 1997). See also K. Dennis, "Charities on the Dole," *Policy Review: The Journal of American Citizenship* 76 (1996), 5: "Although charities are supposed to offer an alternative to government provision of social welfare, they have become so dependent upon and aligned with government that they no longer represent a way out of the welfare state.... Before we can rely on charities to help us dismantle government, they must wean themselves off the dole."

117 R. Whelan, ed., *Involuntary Action: How Voluntary Is the Voluntary Sector?* (London: Institute of Economic Afairs, 1999).

118 S. Arrison, "Are Non-profits Selling Their Souls to Government?" *National Post,* (Toronto), 30 Dec. 1998. Presumably she had no objection if they sell their souls to the Donner Foundation by accepting its grants.

119 For a classification and a description of various models of reform, see G. Albo, "Democratic Citizenship and the Future of Public Management," in G. Albo, D. Langille, and L. Panitch, eds., *A Different Kind of State? Popular Power and Democratic Administration* (Toronto: Oxford University Press, 1993), chap. 2; H.W. Arthurs, "'Mechanical Arts and Merchandise': Canadian Public Administration in the New Economy," *McGill Law Journal* 42 (1997), 29; C. Hood, *The Art of the State: Culture, Rhetoric, and Public Management* (Oxford: Clarendon Press, 1998); and B.G. Peters, *The Future of Governing: Four Emerging Models* (Lawrence,

Kan: University Press of Kansas, 1996). In Canada there has been an enormous interest in improving the delivery of public services over the past three decades. In 1993 the Institute for Research on Public Policy (IRPP) began a project on "Rethinking Government," and publications that resulted from this project review much of the research and attempts at reform. See F.L. Seidle, ed., *Rethinking Government: Reform or Reinvention?* (Montreal: IRPP, 1993); G.B. Doern, *The Road to Better Public Services: Progress and Constraints in Five Canadian Federal Agencies* (Montreal: IRPP, 1993); P. Aucoin, *The New Public Management: Canada in Comparative Perspective* (Montreal: IRPP, 1995); and F.L. Seidle, *Rethinking the Delivery of Public Services to Citizens* (Montreal: IRPP, 1995). The School of Policy Studies at Queen's University also undertook a major project on government and competitiveness in the early 1990s. The final report is B. Purchase and R. Hirshhorn, *Searching for Good Governance* (Kingston: School of Policy Studies, Queen's University, 1994).

120 See C.T. Goodsell, *The Case for Bureaucracy: A Public Administration Polemic*, 3rd ed. (Chatham, NJ: Chatham House Publishers, 1994).

121 For a sophisticated effort to test empirically various theories of the voluntary sector using cross-national data, see L.M. Salamon and H.K. Anheier, "Social Origins of Civil Society: Explaining the Nonprofit Sector Cross-Nationally," *Voluntas* 9 (1998), 213, 215. They conclude that "the data seem to suggest that many of the prevailing nonprofit theories, though useful as heuristic devices, are too sweeping and one-dimensional, or have too restrictive 'boundary conditions,' to account adequately for the tremendous complexity of cross-national experience in this field. Instead, we suggest the usefulness of what we term the 'social origins' approach, which explicitly acknowledges what one author has termed the nonprofit sector's 'embeddedness' in broader social, political, and economic realities."

122 There is a vast literature in institutional economics and in critical legal studies making this point. Much of the literature is referred to and discussed in B.H. Fried, *The Progressive Assault on Laissez Faire: Robert Hale and the First Law and Economics Movement* (Cambridge, Mass.: Harvard University Press, 1998).

123 For a recent, excellent collection of essays, see S.B. Boyd, ed., *Challenging the Public/Private Divide: Feminism, Law and Public Policy* (Toronto: University of Toronto Press, 1997).

124 See M. Rein, "The Social Structure of Institutions: Neither Public nor Private," in S.B. Kamerman and A.J. Kahn, eds., *Privatization and the Welfare State* (Princeton, NJ: Princeton University Press, 1989), 49–72. For a recent attempt to categorize quasi-government organizations, see C. Greve, M. Flinders, and S. Van Thiel, "Quangos – What's in a Name?

Defining Quangos from a Comparative Perspective," *Governance: An International Journal of Policy and Administration* 12 (1999), 129 (quangos are quasi-autonomous, non-governmental organizations).

125 See J.T. Scott, "Defining the Nonprofit Sector," in R. Hirshhorn, ed., *The Emerging Sector: In Search of a Framework*, Study CPRN No. 01 (Ottawa: Canadian Policy Research Network, 1997), 44. For related categories, see J.M. Ferris, "The Role of the Nonprofit Sector in a Self-Governing Society: A View from the United States," *Voluntas* 9 (1998), 137.

126 See Jenson and Phillips, "Regime Shift," and L.A. Pal, "Civic Re-Alignment: NGOs and the Contemporary Welfare State," in R.B. Blake, P.E. Bryden, and J.F. Strain, *The Welfare State in Canada: Past, Present and Future* (Concord, Ont.: Irwin Publishing, 1997), 88–104.

PART TWO

The Legal Meaning of Charity

7 The Federal Court of Appeal and the Legal Meaning of Charity: Review and Critique

JIM PHILLIPS

The Federal Court of Appeal is Canada's "charities court." Its jurisdiction, conferred in the early 1970s, is to hear appeals from refusals by the Canada Customs and Revenue Agency (CCRA) to register an organization as charitable or to remove its registration,[1] and the majority of litigation over the meaning of "charitable purposes" in Canada today arises in the context of taxation. The Court's decisions shape the way in which the CCRA administers the registration process.[2] Two features of its work are immediately apparent: first, it has rendered remarkably few decisions on the legal meaning of "charity" – just seventeen – and second, most – fourteen – have been victories for the agency, not the applicant.[3] The first of these observations is not the subject of this paper, although it seems likely that it is related to the second: clearly applicants rejected by the CCRA have little incentive to appeal.[4]

My interest here is with the second observation. Rightly or wrongly, the Court has been unwilling to expand the meaning of charity. This chapter shows that that is indeed the case and, more important, asks why that has happened, what is it about the Court's approach that has brought about these results? It concentrates on how the Court has adjudicated claims that an organization's purposes can be said to be charitable under the "fourth head" of the common law categorization of charity – "other purposes beneficial to the community."[5] This head of charity has attracted much more attention in the Court than any other[6] – not surprising, given that one would expect novel claims for purposes not previously considered charitable to be adjudicated under this most open-ended of the four principal categories. These cases permit us to see how the Court deals with novel claims, how it goes about deciding what it considers appropriately charitable today.

This is not a "policy" paper, concerned primarily with what kinds of purposes should be charitable, and why. It is largely a technical analysis of the ways in which the Court has dealt with the claims that it has adjudicated. It identifies three major themes in the Court's jurisprudence that I think account for the pattern of results. Although I believe that it is useful to isolate these themes, they are none the less related, and many of the cases contain two or more of them. In the second section, I argue that the Court has relied extensively on a categorical approach to the meaning of charity derived from English law and given too much weight to English categories and precedents. That approach has led it to deny charitability to purposes not obviously within the established categories. In the third section, I examine the way in which the Court has interpreted and used the Income Tax Act's reference to the need for charitable organizations to pursue "charitable activities." I argue that the Court has been inconsistent in how it has distinguished between charitable "activities" and charitable "purposes" and, more important, that in practice it has given too much weight to an organization's "activities" as opposed to the broader issue of charitable "purposes." The more one concentrates on isolated "activities," the easier it is to decide that they are not charitable according to the decided cases.

These two sections thus analyse technical aspects of the Court's jurisprudence – its interpretive canons. In the fourth section I look at the principal concrete result of those canons – that the Court has very rarely sought to characterize the purposes of an organization in a purposive, modern light – that is, in ways that fit both what the organization is actually trying to do and the contemporary issue(s) to which it is responding. As a result it has too frequently not seriously considered whether the purpose should be considered charitable. I do not suggest that the answer would necessarily be affirmative, but the question ought more often to be asked. In most cases it is *not* asked, the Court not considering a purpose to be charitable unless prior jurisprudence has already established it to be so. The conclusion that a purpose has not previously been considered charitable tends to substitute for reasoning about what *should* be charitable. As I noted above, this chapter is principally a descriptive analysis of the Court's methods – its interpretive canons and analytical processes. As part of the critique developed in the fifth section I also take one example from the cases and suggest a better way of considering whether an organization's purposes might be – indeed should be – considered charitable. It is not my intention to offer a general theory of the meaning of charity here,[7] although I do offer both a justification for greater innovation by the Court and some suggestions about guidelines for putting that innovation into practice. The final section of the chapter briefly considers the prospects for legislative change to the definition of charity, arguing that it is unlikely.

Before turning to my substantive analysis, I would note three caveats. The first concerns other aspects of the Court's jurisprudence. Many cases involve discussions of the second category of charity – the advancement of education – and/or the political-purposes doctrine.[8] I have chosen not to discuss these here, for two reasons. First, for education, the claim under this head has, with one exception, always appeared in cases where the Court has also considered the fourth head and, to the extent that there is an argument for charitability in those cases, I believe that it must be as a purpose beneficial to the community, not as education.[9] Generally in cases where the education argument is advanced, it is claimed that the organization provides "education to the public at large" by publishing material about a particular issue. While education should not be narrowly construed, permitting such claims would make it much too broad. This is the position that the Court has consistently taken, and I believe it correct. Indeed while the Court has other critics, none appears to want to argue with it on this point.[10] Providing material to the public on an issue may be a way of carrying out a charitable purpose, but only if the claim to charitability includes something more than the mere supplying of information. The Supreme Court of Canada's recent decision in the *Vancouver Society* case has somewhat refined the Court's approach to the meaning of education, although the Court has not endorsed the idea that "educating the public" counts. That case is discussed elsewhere in this volume.[11]

The political-purposes doctrine is much more controversial, but I do not discuss it here. It is the subject of another chapter in this collection,[12] and it is in any event too large and important a topic to be dealt with as one part of an analysis of the Federal Court of Appeal's jurisprudence. I do, however, discuss most of the cases in which the Court has invoked the doctrine, for many of them also involve the fourth head of charity.

My second caveat is one that I have already implied. This chapter assumes that the essential structure of the current regime regulating "charity" in the Income Tax Act will remain. That is, there will be a continuing need for the Court to define "charity" because the act will almost certainly retain the existing distinctions in fiscal privileges between those organizations that qualify as "charitable" and those that do not, and Parliament will probably not amend it to include a broader definition of what is charitable. Of course the government could choose to harmonize the tax treatment of all non-profit organizations, or at least of all those that do not exist strictly to provide benefits for members.[13] If it did so, there would obviously be no definition of "charity" required for tax purposes, although there would still be a need to continue to define the term in the law governing purpose trusts. Alternatively, the government could choose to define charity by statute or by an ongoing regulation-making process. Its doing so would substantially narrow the Court's operations but not eliminate all litigation, even if it gave jurisdiction to another body.[14] Again, if this route were chosen, this chapter would become otiose. Without commenting on the merits of the kinds of statutory interventions that some have advocated, I assume that no significant changes will occur and that the courts will retain responsibility for interpreting the meaning of "charitable" on a case-by-case basis.

Third, this chapter does not contain an analysis of the Supreme Court of Canada's recent and very important decision on interpreting charity under the Income Tax Act, which is discussed extensively elsewhere in this volume.[15] But the Supreme Court approved of much of the Federal Court of Appeal's approach discussed here. As a result, understanding the Court's jurisprudence is crucial for those interested in the meaning of charity in this country.

THE *NATIVE COMMUNICATIONS* CASE: A FALSE DAWN

Although I have generally eschewed a case-by-case approach to the Court's jurisprudence, I begin with an extended discussion of the 1986 decision in *Native Communications Society v. Minister of National Revenue*.[16] This is the first case in which the Court had to address the meaning of the fourth head of charity and is still cited as the leading case. More important, it highlights all three of the themes that I will deal with in subsequent sections. This is not to suggest that it is a typical case. Indeed it is something of a paradox: it insists on a nearly four-hundred-year-old English statute as the guide to defining charity while in effect largely denying that statute's relevance in Canada today. After examining the case in some detail, I seek to show that subsequent cases have retained the explicit adherence to that statute while abandoning the implicit message that in practice the statute does, and should, mean little.

The appellant organization in *Native Communications* was established to do essentially three things for the Aboriginal communities in British Columbia: it published a bi-weekly newspaper, *Kahtou*; it offered training for Native people in communication technology; and it intended to move into radio and television, producing programs and providing training in their production. It did all of this with a concentration on Native people and their issues. The newspaper stories, for example, consisted of news items of relevance and reports of Native cultural events, encouraged use of native languages, and publicized traditional crafts, music, stories, and so on. The planned radio and television programs would do the same kinds of things. The purpose of these activities was to "procure and deliver information on subjects facing native people of British Columbia," to "promote ... the image of native people in the national scene and to create incentives for development of mutual understanding," and to "communicate with and to broaden social interactions among other native groups from various parts of the world."[17]

The correspondence between the society and the department reveals that their discussions revolved principally around whether the former's purposes could be said to be educational. This issue was discussed, albeit very sparingly, in Mr Justice Stone's judgment (for a unanimous court), which held, correctly I think, that that was not the real issue. Stone concentrated largely on whether the society qualified as charitable under the rubric of "other purposes beneficial to the community." We can divide into three parts his finding that it did.

First, he began by laying out the principles, and the sources from which they were derived, for determining what was charitable as a "purpose beneficial to the community." Citing only English cases, he identified two basic "propositions," only one of which need concern us here – that "the purpose must be beneficial to the community in a way which the law regards as charitable by coming within the 'spirit and intendment' of the *Statute of Elizabeth*, if not within its letter."[18]

Thus the Court quickly, and without canvassing alternatives, decided that the principal source of the Canadian law of charity under the Income Tax Act was English law, in which the courts have long held that to be charitable a purpose must either be mentioned in the preamble to the Statute of Charitable Uses[19] of 1601 (usually referred to as the Statute of Elizabeth) or be analogous to a purpose mentioned, or analogous to an analogous purpose – what is usually referred to as being "within the spirit and intendment" of the preamble. Whether or not the English courts and charity commissioners adhere in substance to the test of "spirit and intendment" is debatable,[20] but there is no doubt that the test has not been disavowed in England and that the courts there still cite it as the origin of the meaning of charity.[21] Many Canadian courts have also cited the preamble over the years, although the Ontario courts have now disavowed it.[22] The most recent decision by the Supreme Court of Canada refers principally to the *Pemsel* categorization, not the preamble, although *Pemsel* is often said to incorporate it.[23] The Court, faced with interpreting "charitable" in a statute that does not define the word, chose to follow the traditional English categorization.

Justice Stone, however, went on to apparently qualify his reliance on the preamble – and this is the second significant part of the judgment. He did so by quoting from two English cases. From *Temperley v. Attorney-General*[24] he drew out the statement that "[the] preamble set out what were then regarded as purposes which should be treated as charitable in law. It is obvious that as time passed and conditions changed common opinion as to what was properly covered by the word charitable also changed." And from *Scottish Burial Reform and Cremation Society Ltd v. Glasgow City Corporation*[25] he cited two speeches. From Lord Wilberforce he took the notion that the requirement for a purpose to come within "the spirit and intendment" of the preamble "does not mean quite what it says," for "it is now accepted that what must be regarded is not the wording of the preamble itself, but the effect of decisions given by the courts as to its scope, decisions which have endeavoured to keep the law as to charities moving according as new social needs arise or old ones become obsolete or satisfied." And from Lord Upjohn he quoted the statement that the "so-called fourth class" was "incapable of further definition and can today hardly be regarded as more than a portmanteau to receive those objects which enlightened opinion would regard as qualifying."

The quotations chosen appear to suggest that the Court chose a reasonably innovative approach – albeit not so innovative as to ditch entirely reference to the Statute of Elizabeth or to adopt the most radical position advanced by the English judiciary – the so-called Russell test, which generally assumes charitability if the purpose is shown to be of sufficient public benefit.[26] The third part of Justice Stone's judgment analyses whether the purposes pursued by the society were indeed charitable within the "spirit and intendment" of the preamble. Here he asserted that Canadian context was crucial. Specifically, he argued that the Court could not decide the case "without taking into account the special legal position" of Native peoples, including the constitution's special mention of Aboriginal rights and the state's "large role in the lives of the Indian people."

This meant that a departure from previous cases was necessary; indeed it would be a "mistake" to decide the case "on the basis of how this purpose or that may or may not have been seen by the Courts in the decided cases as being charitable or not." These facts rendered particularly unhelpful the English jurisprudence, for "none" of those cases "are concerned with activities directed toward aboriginal people." Thus if "the law of charity is a moving subject," the court's "duty" is "to see whether in the circumstances ... the appellant's purposes at this point in time fall within [the] ... fourth head of charities."

He found that they did so, and the key to his doing so was his characterization of the society's purposes. It published a newspaper, and proposed development of other media products, not merely to convey news, but with a much broader function: "[T]hrough them ... Indian[s] ... are made aware of activities of a cultural nature going on elsewhere in the wider Indian community and of attempts being made to foster language and culture ... All of this may well instill a degree of pride of ancestry ... , deepen an appreciation of Indian culture and language and thereby promote a measure of cohesion among the Indian people of British Columbia that might otherwise be missing." In short, Justice Stone saw this as a case not about the "activities" of publishing a newspaper or producing other media programs, but rather about the underlying purposes. The case contains no explicit discussion of the distinction between an organization's specific "activities" and its overall "purposes"; but implicitly it rejected any concentration on activities, for the organization's underlying purpose – promotion of "a measure of cohesion among the Indian people" – was what the Court stressed.[27]

Having so characterized the purpose, Justice Stone returned to the contemporary Canadian context. He noted that the state played a significant role in "protecting and assisting the Indian people" and that Aboriginal peoples were "a people set apart for particular assistance and protection in many aspects of their lives." This was a "circumstance" that "cannot be disregarded in deciding whether the purposes of the appellant fall inside or outside the fourth category of charities."[28] And from all of this the Court shortly concluded that the purposes were charitable, although the form of its conclusion certainly has an odd ring to it – "the appellant's purposes are beneficial to the Indian community of British Columbia within the spirit and intendment of the preamble to the *Statute of Elizabeth* and, therefore, they are good charitable purposes."[29]

While the notions that Aboriginal people are objects of charity and the Aboriginal cause is a charitable one will strike many as inappropriate today, neither of these points is important for my purposes. What is important is that the Court, although it ultimately and rather formalistically linked the purpose of promoting the well-being of Aboriginal people back to the preamble, chose both to express some scepticism about the real usefulness of that document and to consider the Canadian context. It judged English authority irrelevant (because there was none), and the only precedent that it discussed extensively was an Australian case, *Re Matthew*[30] which had found a trust "for the benefit of the Australian aborigines" to be charitable under the fourth head for much the same reasons given in *Native Communications* – a community in need of assistance that had a special relationship with the state.[31]

ADHERENCE TO THE STATUTE OF ELIZABETH

Contemporaries saw *Native Communications* as path-breaking – "a major step towards modernizing the judicial process of determining what are charitable purposes" and "plac[ing] the common law definition of charity within a twentieth century Canadian context."[32] Some expressed regret that the Court did not simply abandon the preamble, on the ground that there was really no connection between the Statute of Elizabeth and the purposes at issue in the case. None the less they approved the fact that it "implicitly tempered" the force of that document, and assumed that this was a first step on the road to renouncing "a particularly outdated piece of legislation."[33]

These commentators could not have been more wrong. Far from renouncing the Statute of Elizabeth, the Court has adhered increasingly strictly to it. Long quotations from *Native Communications* appear in many subsequent cases,[34] and the Court has described it as the "leading authority" in Canada.[35] But *Native Communications* managed both to assert the importance of the preamble in theory and to ignore it in practice, and thus its subsequent primacy alone does not tell us that English-derived categories are dominant. We can find more concrete indications of the Court's approach in two cases where the preamble was directly at issue and in the sources of law employed in the generality of cases.

The first of these two cases is *Canada Uni Association*.[36] Here the court was invited, in the absence of any definition of "charitable" in the Income Tax Act, to adopt Ontario's position on the fourth head – namely, that there was no need to refer to the preamble (which one Ontario judge labelled "archaic") because it could use a different, and more "liberal," definition in the province's Charities Accounting Act.[37]

The Court refused to do so, stating that it would decide the case "on the basis of the existing law."[38] While it was constitutionally correct for the Court to believe that it was not bound by a provincial definition when it was interpreting a term in a federal statute,[39] nothing in law precluded it from doing so, yet it reaffirmed the preamble as the source of the law.

Even more revealing is one of just two cases after *Native Communications* in which the purpose was found to be charitable – *Vancouver FreeNet*.[40] The appellant established a freenet, a volunteer-built computer network that provides free access to the internet. By a majority of two to one the Court found that this was a charitable purpose.[41] Justice Hugessen's majority judgment began by suggesting that he was not entirely happy with the fact that in the law of charity "the Courts of necessity are thrown back to an obscure and not always entirely consistent corner of the law of England." Yet he was certainly not prepared to let go of the preamble: "this Court, in deciding whether the appellant falls within the fourth category of charities, is required to determine whether its purposes fall within the spirit and intendment of the *Statute of Elizabeth*."[42]

More significantly, he did not simply say that with access to information increasingly important, and an increasing volume of it available through computers, it served a useful, perhaps even a crucial, social purpose to try to ensure that everybody, even those who could not otherwise afford it, had such access. He probably thought so, and indeed hinted at it,[43] but that was not the only reason why this purpose was charitable. There was in it a conceptual link to the preamble, which "speaks of the repair of bridges, ports, causeways and highways." These were "the essential means of communication" at the time, and while he did not want to "insist unduly" on an analogy to the information highway, "there is absolutely no doubt in my mind that the provision of free access to information and to a means by which citizens can communicate with one another on whatever subject they may please is a type of purpose similar to those which have been held to be charitable; it is within the spirit and intendment of the preamble to the Statute of Elizabeth."[44] Justice DeCary dissented, expressing some reluctance to use such an analogy to the preamble approach; but it is quite unclear what he would put in its place, for he clearly rejected a broad "public benefit" test.[45]

Vancouver FreeNet suggets that the preamble has come to play a much more substantive role than a reading of *Native Communications* would suggest. But in a less obvious way all the other cases since *Native Communications* support it also. Sometimes the Court merely states that if a purpose cannot be linked to the preamble or cases decided pursuant to the *Pemsel* categorization it will not be charitable.[46] At other times it simply recites general statements about the primacy of the preamble, often omitting the qualifying quotations used by Justice Stone in *Native Communications*,[47] but says nothing further of any substance about how charitability is to be decided, while holding that the purpose in issue is not charitable. This leaves one to conclude that the preamble does indeed play a large role. In some recent cases the Court has stressed the following passage from *D'Aguiar v. Guyana Commissioner of Inland Revenue*,[48] a case not cited in *Native Communications*: "[T]he process which the Court must follow ... is now fairly well- established. It must first consider the trend of those decisions which have established certain objects as charitable under [the fourth head], and ask whether, by reasonable extension or analogy, the instant case may be considered in line with these. Secondly, it must examine certain accepted anomalies to see whether they fairly cover the objects under consideration." The meaning is tolerably clear – look to decided cases, with existing categories as the principal guide.

A prime example of this interpretive approach is the recent decision in the *Vancouver Society* case. The society's principal purpose, as stated in its articles of incorporation, was "to provide educational forums, classes, workshops and seminars to immigrant women in order that they may be able to find or obtain employment or self employment."[49] It argued that in assisting its specified targets to find employment it was undertaking a purpose not unlike that of advancing Native well-being found to be charitable in *Native Communications*. It also asked for special consideration for purposes designed to assist groups specifically protected by the equality guarantees in section 15 of the Charter of Rights. Despite the apparent conceptual similarity between the issues in *Vancouver Society* and those in *Native Communications*, the contrast in the Court's approach could hardly be greater. The judgment in *Vancouver Society* was given orally at the end of the hearing, and – apart from the summary of the facts and a reproduction of part of the refusal letter from the CCRA – was extremely short – about a page. That alone suggests that the judges gave little consideration to whether the society's purposes ought to be considered charitable, even if one were to answer in the negative. (Unfortunately this is not the only case in which the Court has very cursorily dismissed a claim).[50]

An examination of the little that the Court did say confirms this. It first stated that the issue was whether the society's purposes "come within the conceptual ambit of the well-established divisions of charity," citing *Pemsel* and *Native Communications*. It then found the arguments advanced "not persuasive" because "the focus when deciding whether or not to grant charitable status is ... on the answer to the question 'do the proposed purposes and activities constitute charitable activities within the ambit of the law of charities?'" But it gives no indication of how one is to answer that question – only an assertion that registration of the society would "open ... the door to purposes beyond the legal definition of 'charity.'"[51] It does not state why and how it would so, and the absence of any such analysis is highly revealing. What is charitable is what is charitable – that is, what has previously been decided to be charitable.

Variants of this approach appear in many cases. In *Positive Action* the Court said that "to be charitable, a purpose or activity must be so in a way that the law regards as charitable. There are, no doubt, many purposes and activities that are beneficial to the community in a loose or popular sense though not in the legal sense."[52] And in *Stop the Violence,* it stated that "it is not enough that the activities in question be laudable and worthwhile ... they must also be beneficial to the community in a way which the law regards as charitable."[53] But in each case it said nothing more about how it was to decide that question, leaving the reader to conclude that "charitable" means "charitable according to the decided cases flowing from the preamble."

Recently we have heard indications that some of the Court's judges are less than happy with this state of affairs – a point on which I elaborate below. But it is odd to hear lamentations that the Court is somehow confined to a peculiar corner of the past, for this is a corner into which it has painted itself. The judicial role is a circumscribed one, but the law of charity is not a strait-jacket, as *Native Communications* demonstrated. The Court might not feel able to disavow the preamble, but it has clearly chosen to do more than not disavow it; it has given life and meaning to the need to adhere rigidly to the past. The preamble matters.

CHARITABLE PURPOSES AND CHARITABLE ACTIVITIES

The second feature of the Court's jurisprudence which has made it less than accommodating to novel claims is its tendency to concentrate on an organization's "activities" rather than on its overall purposes. As it did in my first section, *Native Communications* provides a reference point and a contrast to what comes later in this chapter. In that case the Court looked to the overall purposes of the organization, not to its particular activities.[54] In subsequent cases it has been inconsistent in its approach.

In fact the activities issue has two facets. First, when the Court considers a novel claim, it sometimes, as in *Native Communications*, looks at an organization's general purposes, but it sometimes considers only its activities. The latter approach makes it easy for the Court to find that the "activities" in question are not charitable according to existing categories – a link to the previous section of this chapter. It is this issue of characterization that concerns me in this section. Second, the law of charitable trusts, on which the Court generally bases its jurisprudence, asks whether a purpose is charitable overall, not whether any activity is charitable in itself. It then considers whether any non-charitable activities are merely ancillary – a means to an end.[55] This "ancillary purposes doctrine" acknowledges that officers of charitable organizations of necessity carry out all kinds of activities that are not directly in pursuit of charitable purposes, but which help achieve those ends.

The ancillary purposes doctrine gets very little play in the Court's jurisprudence, for reasons that I shortly explain. What the Court has done with it, however, provides the background of, and explanation for, the Court's approach to characterization based on activities. I therefore begin with the ancillary purposes doctrine, and specifically with the Court's judgment in a political purposes case – *Scarborough Community Legal Services v. The Queen*.[56] Justice Marceau's judgment for the Court[57] held that a community legal aid clinic could not be registered as charitable because, although the purpose of providing legal aid was charitable, the clinic had engaged in some political activities. When observers suggested that such activities were merely ancillary – a means to the end of the overall charitable purpose – he acknowledged that the means–end distinction was a valid part of the law of charitable trusts but asserted that it was unavailable under the Income Tax Act.

The problem, according to Justice Marceau, had its roots in the act's definition of "charitable organization" – "an organization ... all the resources of which are devoted to charitable activities carried on by the organization itself." This was to be contrasted with the definition of "charitable foundation" – "a corporation or trust constituted and operated exclusively for charitable purposes."[58] Justice Marceau held that the different definitions meant, first, that all of a charitable organization's activities had to be charitable in themselves and that, second and concomitantly, one could not argue that some activities were merely the non-charitable means to pursuing charitable ends. Thus the particular political activities in that case entirely precluded any possibility of registration.[59]

Scarborough is the only decision of the Court that contains any discussion of ancillary purposes in the context of charitable organizations,[60] and we must therefore conclude that the Court finds it inapplicable, presumably for the reasons given. I move shortly to the ways in which this general approach has affected the Court's decision-making. First, however, I explain why the *Scarborough* decision is wrong – for at least two reasons.[61]

First, the different wording of the statutory definitions does not mandate that only an organization's "activities" be considered. The current taxonomy of "organizations" and "foundations," and the activities–purposes distinction, both date from 1977, when Parliament established a distinction between operating charities (charitable organizations) and foundations,[62] although it had previously defined charitable organizations with reference to activities and charitable trusts with reference to purposes. The definition of a charitable organization as one that devotes its resources to charitable activities goes back to the 1950 version of the Income Tax Act,[63] but there is no evidence of any intention to require that each and every activity of an organization be separately devoted to charitable ends. Rather, the intention was to ensure that such bodies not pursue non-charitable purposes. This is the common law test, and the statute's drafters simply intended to omit from tax privileges organizations that were only partly pursuing charitable ends. "Trusts" and "foundations" have at different times been defined in terms of "charitable purposes" because they are essentially funding agencies, not "operating charities," and it would therefore be difficult to describe them primarily by their "activities." Indeed, they have consistently been required to devote their disbursement quota either to "charitable activities" or to donations to operating charities.[64] Thus there is no evidence that the terms in the act represent a desire by the drafters either to make the means–ends distinction unavailable or to insist that the Court look at each and every activity to decide charitability.[65]

Second, and more important, the notion that one can concentrate solely on activities makes little sense. As Cullity has argued, such an approach is "meaningless" because "it is impossible to characterise activities in the abstract," for one cannot "characterise as charitable or non-charitable the means of accomplishing charitable objects without reference to those objects."[66] Indeed, if the test were applied literally, very few, if any, organizations would be able to qualify for charitable status. Officers of charitable bodies engage in a host of "activities" that are on their face non-charitable – from political lobbying, through raising funds, to operating an office – and a literal application would prevent most organizations from being registered. The Supreme Court has now reaffirmed the necessity of an ancillary purposes doctrine in the law of charities.[67]

This point brings me, finally, to the principal issue with which I am concerned in this section – the Court's use of "activities" in deciding whether an organization is charitable. Here we find inconsistency both in theory and in practice. In doctrine, only Justice Marceau seems prepared to assert the logical corollary of the judgment in *Scarborough* – namely, that particular activities are all that matters. In *Toronto Volgograd* he made this position explicit, arguing that "to be assigned validly and usefully to one of the four headings of the classification [of charitable purposes], activities must necessarily ... be considered with respect to their immediate result and effect, not their possible eventual consequence." That is, "the activity will draw its charitable quality from what it itself accomplishes not from what may eventually flow from it or be somehow indirectly achieved by it," and each and every activity must "have the immediate effect of relieving poverty, advancing education or religion or, possibly, realizing something beneficial to the community as a whole."[68]

Other judges of the Court have rejected this idea. In *Toronto Volgograd*, Justice Stone argued that the Court should "look at both purposes and activities" and thought this view "the traditional English" one employed by the Court of Chancery in its supervision of charitable trusts.[69] And Justice Mahoney was more forceful. He pointed out that the "Marceau approach" was inconsistent with other decisions, and with particular reference to *Native Communications* he said:[70] "The 'activities' ... were the collection and dissemination of information of interest and concern to the native peoples of British Columbia.... It seems to me that, divorced from purposes which would only indirectly be achieved, [the] organization could [not] have met the test proposed.... [T]he real charitable purpose did not lie in making available information and vehicles for its exchange but in the expectation of their advantageous use by native peoples; achievement of the charitable purpose was inherently an indirect result of the organization's activities." It is indeed remarkable that the Court could treat *Native Communications* and *Scarborough* so differently, for it decided them just one year apart. Without otherwise referring to the doctrine, it has in practice gone on to treat other cases inconsistently when dealing with the threshold question of charitability, looking sometimes at "activities" and sometimes at "purposes."

The Court has concentrated on the overall purposes of an organization in four cases, including the three that went against the department. One, of course, is *Native Communications*. A second is *Everywoman's*, in which Justice DeCary said that he saw no reason "not to apply to the 'activities' of an organization the principles established with respect to the 'purposes' of an organization unless, of course, the context prevents us from so doing."[71] He then went on to find – not surprising, given the support in past cases for the proposition – that the purpose of providing health care was charitable.

Purposes also seem to have triumphed over activities in *Vancouver FreeNet*. My statement here is an inference, for Justice Hugessen's majority judgment does not mention the purposes–activities distinction. But consider the manner in which he deals with an argument that provision of free access to the internet was not charitable because the applicant could not control what that free access was to be used for. This argument "misses the mark," for it was the purpose of providing access that mattered, not the fact that individuals with access could then use it for private or commercial, or for that matter criminal, activities.[72] It was this fact – the breadth of possible non-charitable activities by users of the internet – that largely led Justice DeCary to dissent in *Vancouver FreeNet*.

However, in other cases its concentration (sometimes more implicit than explicit) on activities has been a crucial part of the Court's unwillingness to consider novel claims to charitability. Perhaps the best example of explicit use is *NDG Neighbourhood Association*. The applicant society was a community organization that sought, among other things, to let residents know about community services, put on adult education programs, and organize about issues that affected the community, such as street safety, conversion of rental housing to condominiums, and public transportation. The Court found many reasons to deny it charitable status, including the fact that it did not devote all of its resources to "charitable activities." While it did help the poor in various ways, its ambit was broader than that – there was an "ambivalence ... as to its real goal."[73] Some things that it did involved "relief of poverty," while others did not and fell outside the categories of charity. In fact there was no ambivalence on the part of the association, only an ambivalence on the part of the Court about doing more than saying that some activities were outside the existing legal ambit of charity – or, more important, an ambivalence about looking at the overall purposes of the organization and asking if they were charitable.

In *Stop the Violence* – perhaps the Court's most cursory judgment – use of the activities test is more implicit. (It is perhaps difficult to be too explicit in a one-page judgment). The organization's clearly stated goal was to provide young people with material dissuading them from violence, drug use, and crime. Its clearly stated methods were the production of CDs, tapes, and booklets and their distribution free of charge to youth organizations. Yet the Court ruled that the organization's "activities" were not "clearly focused on charitable objects."[74] It did not state which "activities" lacked such focus, but it required that each "activity" pursue a charitable end rather than looking at the body's overall purpose. This case shows the link between an activities test and the characterization of purposes discussed in the following section. The Court by-passed characterization through a technique it has used increasingly in recent years – stating that the applicant had not sufficiently defined what it would do. It held that while the applicant's purposes were "laudable," they were too "broad and loosely defined" to satisfy "the test in law that the stated purpose of the organization be sufficiently specific to enable the Minister to be satisfied that the organization will be engaged in and will direct all of its resources to charitable activities." In fact both the overall purpose and the methods were quite clear; such language about "vagueness" can mean only that the applicant's "activities" included at least some not already acknowledged as charitable.

It would not be profitable to multiply examples.[75] Whatever some of the Court's judges may have said about looking at purposes as well as activities, activities hold centre stage. This approach has significantly influenced adjudication of novel claims on more than one occasion. The combination of isolating activities and adhering to the categories in the Statute of Elizabeth has been a potent one for denying charitability; given that the Supreme Court has now placed much greater emphasis on purposes rather than activities, it is likely to be much less so in the future.[76]

CONTEMPORARY CONTEXT AND MODERNISING THE DEFINITION OF CHARITY

The third, related theme in the Court's cases on the fourth head is its minimal appreciation of contemporary Canadian context. In *Native Communications* its paying attention to the fact that the case involved Native peoples was crucial to its finding the appellant's purposes charitable. In subsequent cases it appears to have lost this sensitivity. Although it likes to say that charity is a "moving subject"[77] or to assert that it is "willing to recognize any relevant change in societal conditions,"[78] there is little evidence in practice that either is the case. There is some recognition of new conditions in *Everywoman's*, where it found that provision of "health care," broadly defined, was a more suitable way to characterize the purpose at issue than "care of the sick."[79] But generally the decisions are notable for their lack of attention to changing social conditions. Indeed the Court has often ignored the question by characterizing the issues before it as relating to "charitable activities," the problem discussed in the previous section; if the underlying purpose is not exposed, there is no need to assess it against contemporary needs.

Plenty of cases illustrate this point, although one cannot say much about them, precisely because the point is a negative one, concerning what the Court does *not* say. In *Canada Uni* the Court did not consider at all whether "the promotion of multiculturalism and the bilingual character of Canada" constituted a charitable purpose under the fourth head." In *Stop the Violence*, another very cursory judgment, the Court did not ask whether persuading young people in the ways hoped for could in itself be a charitable purpose. I am suggesting not that it should necessarily have decided all, or indeed any, of these cases differently, only that it should have asked the question.

In only one case among the Court's judgments since *Native Communications* does it undertake any sustained attempt to look to broader social questions. In *NDG Neighbourhood Association* Justice McGuigan referred to the possibility that "in the light of" *Native Communications* "there may well be an argument to be made that an organisation similarly dedicated to the interests of the urban disadvantaged ... should qualify as a charity." But because access was not limited to the poor, he decided that "on its facts, this is not such a case."[80] This conclusion, which seems to depart from precedent in suggesting that only the poor can benefit from charity, ignores the fact that the association operated only in a poor urban neighbourhood and could also be seen as a "community-building" enterprise, not simply as a group helping the poor. And here it is useful to return briefly to the *Vancouver FreeNet* case. The organization provided a crucial service to the community, particularly to those members not able to afford internet access in their homes, and hence its purposes could well have been considered charitable. But to find it so on the basis of conceptual similarity to the repair of bridges and causeways in the preamble is to risk ridicule. There are clearly good reasons for thinking the decision correct; there are equally good reasons for deprecating the route taken to get to it.

There is little point in my reviewing all the cases to make the same point repeatedly, but I want to consider one of them, *Vancouver Society*, largely because it seems the most egregious example of the Court's failing to look seriously at whether purposes are charitable.[81] The Court did not consider at all whether the integration of immigrant and visible-minority women into the economy should be a charitable purpose in and of itself. The successful argument in *Native Communications* was that advancement of ancestral pride and development of community cohesion for Native peoples was a charitable purpose, given Canada's history and constitution and Native communities' difficulties. A parallel argument in *Vancouver Society* would also look at facts peculiar to Canada in the 1990s and ask whether they make a difference, whether they render irrelevant the absence of prior cases finding the purposes charitable.

First, one would ask what the purposes of the organization are. That would be an easy question to answer – the full and effective participation of immigrant and visible-minority women in the economy. That would bring greater economic self-sufficiency and increases self- and community respect – parallel to the society's purposes in *Native Communications.* Second, one would ask if there were no decided cases finding this charitable because it was not a concern historically, especially in England, rather than its being a product of principled exclusion. Third, one would ask if there were features particular to Canada today that made these purposes of special concern and importance. Obviously such a group does not have the same kind of unique relationship with the state that Aboriginal people do, but then nobody else does, and if that is the test *Native Communications* is a case not illustrative of a principled approach but one about Native people.

Assuming that the case is more than that, three related facts would place the claim in contemporary social context. First, Canada is a heterogeneous society, increasingly made up of people who have arrived relatively recently; second, many immigrants face barriers to effective participation such as lack of familiarity with official languages and their new society; and third, both immigrant and visible-minority women often face social barriers in the form of race and gender discrimination. And while this group does not have the same special status as Aboriginal peoples, constitutional provisions such as the equality rights in the Charter of Rights would presumably suggest that the state has given priority to efforts to ameliorate the effects of discrimination. The Court dismissed a similar argument by simply stating that "[p]roviding a benefit to those who are in a position to invoke Charter rights will not in itself result in an activity falling within the fourth head."[82]

No doubt I could say more along these lines, including the fact that many recognized charitable purposes could, like the ones at issue here, be broadly characterized as involving "social welfare." My point is simply that the Court could have decided the case differently, or at the very least have discussed it differently, simply through a principled application of its own prior judgment, through giving teeth to the interpretive approach offered in *Native Communications.* Alternatively, one might adopt the conceptual approach to the meaning of charity proposed by the OLRC and thereby add "work" to the list of universal human goods that charity provides.[83]

As I stated at the outset, my purpose here is not to propose a new way of defining charity. But it is difficult to avoid that temptation when assessing the existing definition – or its lack. One need not go further than a principled application of *Native Communications.* Instead, the Court has not followed the substance of that case, and has tended to argue that it should be confined to the facts. We have seen this point argued in *Vancouver Society,* and it has been repeated elsewhere. For example, in *Canada Uni* the Court shortly and simply stated that no analogy existed between the *Native Communications* case and promotion of national unity through, among other activities, enhancing Canadians' "appreciation and tolerance of linguistic and cultural differences." *Native Communications* was about "native persons who hold a special position in Canadian society."[84] The Court itself has admitted that the fourth head of charity "has been interpreted cautiously, if not narrowly."[85] I would go further and say that the Court has effectively abdicated any role as modernizer of the law; it has decided to add very few, or no, new charitable purposes. It has all but ignored the idea of paying attention to the specifics of Canadian society. Not all of the judges of the Court would agree with my characterization of its work,[86] but the results tell their own story.

AMENDING THE MEANING OF CHARITY: COURTS OR PARLIAMENT?

The Court has offered two implicit justifications for its approach over the years. First, it has complained that the Income Tax Act gives little guidance on the meaning of charity and has suggested that Parliament should legislate in the area. In *Positive Action* the Court noted that the act gave "little or no assistance" in defining charity.[87] It did not often raise this issue before 1996, being content, as we have seen, in the line of cases starting with *Native Communications,* to follow English law and its ultimate reliance on the preamble to the Statute of Elizabeth. In that year, however, both the majority judgment of Justice Hugessen and the dissent of Justice DeCary in *Vancouver FreeNet* adverted to the problems caused by the lack of a statutory definition. I quoted above Hugessen's apparent lament about the need to rely on the preamble; he went on to say that "given the circumstances of life on the eve of the third millennium," he thought this "an area where some creative legislative intervention would not be out of order."[88] The most recent manifestation of this concern about past precedents appears in the judgment of Justice Strayer in *Human Life International*. After noting that it was "commonly said" that the fourth head of charity "can be given more precision by reference to a 1601 English statute" (omitting to mention that it was most commonly said by his own court), he suggested that "one may well question its [the preamble's] relevance to Canadian society four centuries later" and asserted that "this area of the law requires better definition by Parliament which is the body in the best position to determine what kinds of activity should be ... charitable."[89]

A second concern ever-present in the cases is that the Court should exercise its jurisdiction conservatively because it is deciding tax policy. It has called the tax exemption and the donation deduction "exceptional privileges"[90] and said that charities have "very special status."[91] Implicitly, therefore, the Court is saying that it is one thing to take a liberal view of the meaning of charity for purposes of trust law, another to do so for tax law – an argument that others have made more explicitly.[92]

Both these arguments have some merit, especially the latter. But while the Income Tax Act does not define charity, that fact does not preclude innovation. The history of the development of the law of charity shows courts willing and able to extend it, and the choice to freeze it now is one that the Court has made. Not deciding is deciding; it is not a neutral position. *Native Communications* makes the point again, for there the Court, for all it felt the need to refer to the preamble, manipulated the law in a purposive way. Its failure to do so since is as much a choice as was its willingness to do so then, and neither choice was driven by the provisions, or lack thereof, of the Income Tax Act. Moreover, it is unlikely that there will be wholesale statutory change[93] and even more unlikely that any statutory definition would obviate the need for judicial interpretation. While a detailed definition might solve many problems, anything short of an exclusive and extremely long list would still leave many issues up in the air.[94] All significant statutes produce much litigation over the meaning of terms, and thus the attempt to move the problem to Parliament is unlikely to produce a lasting solution. Indeed, there is some reason to worry that a statutory definition could be confining, could make it more difficult thereafter to add new purposes.

Perhaps most important, failing to change the law of charity judicially risks making it the subject of some ridicule. Some years ago Britain's Charity Law Reform Committee put out a leaflet that asked people which of a series of organizations they thought charitable and which not. Present on the list, but not charitable, were Amnesty International, the United Nations Association, the Disablement

Income Group, the Campaign Against Racial Discrimination, the National Council for Civil Liberties, and the Defence and Aid Fund (South Africa). Also included, as registered charities, were Eton College, the British Goat Society, the Reading Temperance Society, and the British Society of Dowsers. The point of this exercise was obvious – to demonstrate the substantial gap between the public perception of what should be charitable and its legal definition.[95] Readers of the Federal Court of Appeal's cases on the legal meaning of charity might share some of the confusion of those surveyed in Britain. They would discover that the promotion of multiculturalism and national unity, the integration into Canadian society and the economy of immigrant and visible-minority women, and the promotion of good relations between peoples of different countries are, among other purposes, not charitable. But they would also learn that an organization devoted principally to model railroading, albeit also and to a lesser extent to historical research and preservation, passed the threshold test of charitability.[96] Strange perhaps is the law that manages to prefer model railroading to things such as improving international relations.

This last point also seems to me to be an answer to the argument about taxation. On the whole the idea that tax privileges should be carefully tailored to social needs has much to commend it. Indeed, the Income Tax Act already does so by distinguishing between the tax privileges accorded to non-profit organizations (exemption from taxation on income) and those given to charitable organizations (income-tax exemption plus deductibility of donations). But concerns about appropriate tailoring do not disappear under a policy of refusing to expand the list of charitable purposes simply because certain purposes are new and not previously recognized by the law to be charitable. The status quo would make sense only if there were some coherence in the current list of charitable purposes,[97] some clear sense that "charity" as legally defined is different from purposes that do not qualify. But there is, I believe, general acceptance that it is difficult to find much coherence in the current list. More than a century of judicial decisions has resulted in a list of charitable purposes that includes ends as diverse as relieving the poor, supporting "élite" forms of art such as opera, assisting the sick, and providing scholarships at private schools.

Thus if there is no underlying principle uniting what purposes are charitable and distinguishing them from non-charitable purposes, there seems no principled reason to adopt a restrictive approach to new claims. There seems much more reason, as a matter of tax policy, to rationalize the definition and to add new purposes while excluding some traditionally considered charitable. Courts cannot do this, but if innovation by them led to undue expansion of the tax subsidy, government could respond precisely through such a rationalization.[98] Or it might conclude that an expanded charitable sector is still good value for money, that it is worth the increased tax expenditure. Neither of these two responses seems intuitively to be worse than the status quo, and, depending on one's views, one or the other would be much preferable to it.

CONCLUSION

I began this chapter with the observation that most charitability cases before the Court are lost by the applicant. I have tried to show why the Court's approach to the threshold question of what constitutes charity has brought about this situation. Its failure to expand the definition of charity is the result of three, often related doctrinal principles and interpretive approaches. In many cases involving the fourth head of charity, the Court has chosen in effect to define charity according to the tenets of traditional English law and, as a result, to eschew any inquiry into whether the actual purpose of the organization ought to be considered charitable in current day Canada. It has often been aided in this by its willingness to invoke the "activities" part of the act's definition of charitable organization, which has allowed it to analyse what an organization does, hold selected activities up to the light, and almost invariably declare some of them to be non-charitable. While the themes elucidated are related, it is probably the third that has been of most significance. In the one case where the Court was truly sceptical of the use of English authority – *Native Communications* – it was able to avoid looking piece by piece at the body's activities and, more positively, to characterize the purpose functionally and in light of specific contemporary Canadian conditions. The law of charity under this country's Income Tax Act might have been very different had the Court, in the last decade or so, followed *Native Communications* in substance, not just in form.

NOTES

I am grateful to Abraham Drassinower, John Gregory, and Russell Sacks for comments on a previous version.

1 The appeal provision is now Income Tax Act, RSC 1985, c. 1 (5th Supp.), s. 172 (3). It was originally enacted in 1971: SC 1970–71–72, c. 63, s. 172 (3), although there were minor amendments in SC 1974–75–76, c. 26, s. 108 (1), and SC 1977–78, c. 1, s. 79.

2 For this, see Sossin, chapter 12 in this volume.

3 The total of seventeen cases noted above includes three deregistration cases and fourteen appeals from a refusal to register. There have been many more appeals filed than this, but the vast majority are abandoned: see ibid. All three deregistration cases were decided in favour of the department, which also won eleven of the fourteen other appeals. When I say that a case is about "the legal meaning of charity" I mean that it concerns whether an organization pursues charitable purposes. I do not deal here, therefore, with other "charity" cases that have come before the Court and which concern other aspects of the administration of the charitable designation by Revenue Canada/CCRA, such as procedural issues in the deregistration process, the bar on carrying on unrelated businesses, and the requirement that an organization not exist to provide benefits to its members: see *Renaissance International v. Minister of National Revenue*, [1983] 1 FC 860 (CA); *Alberta Institute on Mental Retardation v. The Queen*, [1987] 2 CTC 70 (FCA); and *National Model Railroad Association v. Minister of National Revenue*, [1989] 1 CTC 300 (FCA).

4 There are, of course, other reasons for the paucity of appeals, including the expense of having to appeal to the Federal Court of Appeal rather than a lower court and the time that such appeals take. One suspects that these reasons limit litigation of the CCRA's decisions, as only one case was actually appealed before the mid-1980s (*Renaissance International*), and the series of decisions that might have discouraged appeals began only in the late 1980s. Requiring an appeal directly to the Federal Court is, as one judge of the Court recently noted, rather "peculiar": *Human Life International of Canada v. Minister of National Revenue*, [1998] 3 FC 202 at 208 (CA), Strayer JA. For a critique of the appeal process see A. Drache, *Canadian Taxation of Charities and Donations* (Toronto, 1994), chap. 6, and for proposed changes to this process, see Sossin, chapter 12 in this volume.

5 As is well known to charity lawyers, since the House of Lords' decision of 1891 in *Commissioners for the Special Purposes of the Income Tax v. Pemsel* [1891] AC 531 (HL), "charity" in common law jurisdictions has been divided into four categories: relief of poverty, advancement of education, advancement of religion, and "other purposes beneficial to the community." The Supreme Court of Canada has accepted the House of Lords' categorization: see *Guaranty Trust Company of Canada v. Minister of National Revenue*, [1967] SCR 133, and *Vancouver Society of Immigrant and Visible Minority Women v. Minister of National Revenue*, [1999] 1 SCR 10.

6 Twelve of the cases, to a greater or lesser degree, have concerned the fourth head, although one of them, *Polish Canadian Television Production Society v. Minister of National Revenue*, [1987] 1 CTC 319 (FCA) is not considered here, since it consists solely of one short paragraph stating that

the minister had not erred in refusing registration. Religion is not the category in any case, and relief of poverty gets mentioned only twice, in *NDG Neighbourhood Association v. Minister of National Revenue,* [1988] 2 CTC 14 (FCA) and *Briarpatch Inc. v. The Queen,* [1996] 2 CTC 94 (FCA), and on the latter occasion the appellant apparently did not rely on that category in its oral argument (see at 97). The advancement of education appears in a good number of cases, but, for reasons that appear immediately below, I have chosen not to deal with that category.

7 See here Moran, chapter 8 in this volume, and Ontario Law Reform Commission (OLRC), *Report on the Law of Charities,* 2 vols. (Toronto, 1996), 1: chap. 6.

8 There is some discussion of education in five of the cases and an extended treatment of the issue in five others. The political purposes doctrine is a central issue in seven cases and is discussed briefly in two others.

9 Anglo-Canadian courts have consistently rejected the suggestion that "the advancement of education" can include the publication of news and other similar items as a means of "educating the public." The Court has frequently relied on the definition of education contained in *Incorporated Council of Law Reporting for England and Wales v. Attorney-General,* [1972] 1 Ch. 73 (CA), which stated that education was the "improvement of a useful branch of human knowledge and its public dissemination" (at 102). See especially *Positive Action against Pornography v. The Queen,* [1988] 1 CTC 232 at 237 (FCA), where Justice Stone stated that the society's purposes were simply "the presentation to the public of selected items of information and opinion on the subject of pornography. That, in my view, cannot be regarded as educational in the sense understood by this branch of the law." The only case in which education alone has been the issue is *Interfaith Development Education Association v. Minister of National Revenue,* [1997] 97 DTC 6096 (FCA).

10 Other recent critiques of the Court's work, none as detailed as this chapter, include A. Drache, "Charities, Public Benefit, and the Canadian Income Tax System: A Proposal for Reform," unpublished ms., 1999; Panel on Accountability and Governance in the Voluntary Sector, *Building on Strength: Improving Governance and Accountability in the Voluntary Sector* (1999), 51–5; Drache, *Canadian Taxation,* 1-20–1-23.

11 *Vancouver Society.* For a detailed analysis see Moran and Phillips, chapter 11 in this volume.

12 See Drassinower, chapter 9 in this volume.

13 This is effectively the approach advocated in Drache, "Charities." Drache argues for replacing "charitable" in the act with "public benefit organization," which would include "a charity" and which is defined as "an organization (other than a mutual benefit organization) substantially all the

resources of which are devoted to public benefit activities." The last term is defined as "actions designed to promote activities or provide services which are intended to improve the quality of life of the community or of a group within the community."

14 The most recent arguments for a statutory definition appear in Panel, *Building on Strength*, especially 55, and Sossin, chapter 12 in this volume. The issue of whether a statutory definition would be useful is discussed below. The federal joint tables' report advocates transferring both initial registration decisions and appeals to a quasi-judicial commission: see *Report of the Joint Tables: Working Together – A Government of Canada/Voluntary Sector Joint Initiative* (Ottawa, 1999), 54–7.

15 This is, of course, the *Vancouver Society* case; see Moran and Phillips, chapter 11 in this volume.

16 (1986), 23 ETR 210 (FCA).

17 *Native Communications*, 213–4.

18 Ibid., 219.

19 (1601) 43 Eliz. 1, c. 4.

20 See S. Bright, "Charity and Trusts for the Public Benefit: Time for a Re-think," *Conveyancer* 53 (1989): 28; OLRC, *Report*, 1: 167ff; B. Bromley, "Contemporary Philanthropy: Is the Legal Concept of 'Charity' Any Longer Adequate?" in D. Waters, ed., *Equity, Fiduciaries and Trusts* (Toronto, 1993); and E. Zweibel, "A Truly Canadian Definition of Charity and a Lesson in Drafting Charitable Purposes," *Philanthropist* 7, no. 1 (1987), 4.

21 For a recent example see *Inland Revenue Commissioners v. Oldham Training and Enterprise Council*, [1996] BTC 539 (Ch.D.).

22 See the discussion below.

23 See *Vancouver Society*. See also *Guaranty Trust*, 141: "This [*Pemsel*] definition has received general acceptance in this country." For a discussion of the links between the *Pemsel* test and the "spirit and intendment" approach see OLRC, *Report*, 1: 171–2.

24 [1949] Ch. 529 at 537 (CA).

25 [1968] AC 138 at 150 and 154 (HL).

26 The test is from the judgment of Justice Russell in the *Law Reporting* case, 87–9. It was disavowed in *Inland Revenue Commissioners v. McMullen*, [1979] 1 WLR 130 (CA), and in *Re South Place Ethical Society*, [1980] 1 WLR 1565 (Ch.). It has also been rejected by the charity commissioners: see Bromley, "Contemporary Philanthropy," 89. For a discussion of the test see Bromley, "Contemporary Philanthropy," 86–93, and OLRC, *Report*, 1: 171–2. One author argues that Justice Stone did in effect employ the Russell test, but I believe that interpretation goes too far: see Zweibel, "A Truly Canadian Definition of Charity," 7.

27 *Native Communications*, 221–2.

28 Ibid., 223. Here Justice Stone cited various provisions of the Indian Act (then RSC 1970, c. I-6), and the then-recent case of *Guerin v. The Queen* (1984), 13 DLR (4th) 321 (SCC), which first established the existence of a fiduciary relationship between the Crown and aboriginal peoples.

29 *Native Communications*, 223.

30 [1951] VLR 226 (SC).

31 In *Re Matthew*, the court also said that Aborigines were "a class of persons analogous to those which the statutory preamble enumerates"; specifically they were "analogous to those mentioned in the statute as 'the aged, impotent and poor people ... people decayed.'"

32 Zweibel, "A Truly Canadian Definition of Charity," 4. Ironically, in view of what has followed, Zweibel also suggested (7) that the approach in *Native Communications* could well result in such purposes as the promotion of multiculturalism being held to be charitable: "a non-profit organization concerned with preserving ethnic or national cultural traditions may find a more receptive hearing in Canada than in England." This is not the case; for Revenue Canada's position see Drache, *Canadian Taxation*, 1-41 – 1-43.

33 D. Spiro, "Case Comment," *Canadian Tax Journal* 34 (1986), 856.

34 See *Positive Action*, 79–80 and 81; *Everywoman's Health Centre Society (1988) v. Minister of National Revenue*, [1991] 2 CTC 320 at 324–5 (FCA); *NDG Neighbourhood Association*, 15–17; *Toronto Volgograd Committee v. Minister of National Revenue* (1988), 29 ETR 159 at 168–9 (FCA); and *Vancouver Regional FreeNet Association v. Minister of National Revenue*, [1996] 3 CTC 102 at 106–8 (FCA).

35 *Vancouver FreeNet*, 106. See also its description as the "fundamental approach" of the Court in *NDG Neighbourhood Association*, 15. See also the statement of Justice Muldoon of the Court's trial division in a charities-related case, albeit one that does not deal with the legal meaning of charitable purposes: "The *Income Tax Act* provides no comprehensive definition of charity and so the Minister and taxpayers alike must look to the common law of England ... in order to appreciate the legal meaning of the concept": *J. Reed v. Canada*, [1989] 2 CTC 192 at 195 (FC–TD); affd. [1989] 2 CRR (2d) 192 (FCA).

36 *Canada Uni Association v. Minister of National Revenue*, [1993] 1 CTC 46 (FCA).

37 RSO 1990, c. C-10. This was the interpretation given to the act in *Re Laidlaw Foundation* (1984), 48 OR (2d) 549 (Div. Ct), and affirmed by the Court of Appeal in *Re Levy Estate* (1989), 58 DLR (4th) 375 (Ont. CA). The quotation is from the judgment of Justice Blair in the latter case, at 383. For an excellent account of the history of the Ontario statutory provision and an explanation of how it has come to be seen as more "liberal" see A. Oosterhoff and E. Gillese, *Text, Commentary and Cases on Trusts*, 5th ed. (Toronto: Carswell, 1998), 854–5.

38 *Canada Uni*, 47.

39 In *The Queen in Right of British Columbia v. Henfry Samson Belair Ltd.* (1989), 59 DLR (4th) 726 (SCC), the Supreme Court of Canada had to decide whether the term "property held by the bankrupt in trust for any other person" in the federal Bankruptcy Act included money held on trust by virtue of provincial legislation deeming a trust for the benefit of the provincial government. While the court's judgment concentrates on the definition of the word "trust" in the statute, the thrust of its decision is that a province cannot legislate to determine the meaning of a term in a federal statute. If provincial legislation cannot do this, it is difficult to think that a provincial court's decision could achieve the same ends.

40 *Vancouver FreeNet.* The other case is *Everywoman's*, which cannot be seen as an exception to the general picture painted here, because the Court simply followed a long line of well-settled authority that the provision of health care was a charitable purpose.

41 Justice DeCary dissented, principally on the ground, discussed below, that the society's activities were too broadly defined.

42 *Vancouver FreeNet*, 104 and 110.

43 "Information," he asserted, was "the currency of modern life," and "the free exchange of information amongst members of society has long been recognized as a public good" and, indeed, as "essential to the maintenance of democracy": ibid., 110.

44 Ibid., 110–1.

45 Ibid., 117–8.

46 See the statement that the "*locus classicus* at common law" of the meaning of charity is the *Pemsel* case and the conclusion that the appellant's purposes were not "within the spirit and intendment of the Statute of Elizabeth": *NDG Neighbourhood Association*, 15 and 18. See also: "the well-established categories of charitable activities ... [were] laid down ... in *Pemsel*" and "[w]hat constitutes a charitable benefit to the community must be determined in light of the preamble": *Briarpatch*, 96 and 97.

47 See *Toronto Volgograd*, 168–9; *Vancouver Society of Immigrant and Visible Minority Women* v. *Minister of National Revenue*, [1996] 2 CTC 88 at 90 (FCA); *Positive Action*, 79–80.

48 [1970] TR 31 (PC); quotation at 33. This passage first appeared in 1988 in *NDG Neighbourhood Association*, 15. It has since appeared, in quotation or paraphrase, in *Briarpatch*, 98. The case, but not this passage, was used in *Vancouver Society*, 92.

49 *Vancouver Society*, 89.

50 See also *Canada Uni* – two substantive paragraphs; *STV Stop the Violence v. The Queen*, [1997] 2 CTC 10 (FCA) – facts and judgment together comprise just one page; and *Polish Canadian Television* – one short paragraph in total.

51 *Vancouver Society*, 90, 91, and 92.
52 Ibid., 81.
53 *Stop the Violence*, 11.
54 For a detailed discussion of the ways in which the Court ignored particular activities in favour of general purposes in *Native Communications*, see Zweibel, "A Truly Canadian Definition of Charity," 7–10.
55 See *Re Koeppler's Will Trusts*, [1986] Ch. 423 (CA); *Ontario (Public Trustee) v. Toronto Humane Society* (1987), 40 DLR (4th) 111 (Ont. HC). See generally M. Cullity, "The Myth of Charitable Activities," *Estates and Trusts Journal* 10 (1990–1), 7.
56 (1985), 17 DLR (4th) 308 (FCA).
57 The Court dealt both with the charitability issue and with a procedural point. Three judgments were written, with that of Justice Heald dealing only with the procedural issue and resolving it in such a way that he did not address the merits of the case. Justices Marceau and Urie handled the procedural issue differently, and the latter concurred with Marceau on the substantive question. For a discussion of the procedural question see Sossin, chapter 12 in this volume.
58 The definitions are contained in s. 149.1 (1) (a) and (b) of the Income Tax Act.
59 The Income Tax Act was amended shortly after the *Scarborough* case to include a form of the ancillary purposes doctrine for "political activities" in what is now s. 149.1 (6.1) and (6.2): SC 1986, c. 6, s. 85 (2). The section deals only with political activities, not any other non-charitable activities.
60 In *Alberta Institute*, the Court, without any discussion, found the doctrine applicable to charitable foundations, presumably because of the "purposes" reference in the definition of "foundation."
61 It may also be wrong in a third sense, that it runs counter to what was then the leading Supreme Court of Canada decision on the ancillary purposes doctrine, the *Guaranty Trust* case. In that case the Court applied the doctrine when dealing with a provision of the since-repealed Estate Tax Act, which removed from the taxable value of estates any property given to "any organization in Canada that ... was ... constituted exclusively for charitable purposes, all or substantially all of the resources of which ... were devoted to charitable activities." The wording is different from the current Income Tax Act provision, referring to both "purposes" and "activities" in different places, and thus it is unclear whether Justice Marceau's approach is at odds with the use of the doctrine there. But two things are clear. First, the Court used the doctrine to decide whether the organization was constituted for charitable purposes, without reference to the requirement, very similar to the Income Tax Act's current provision, that "all or substantially all" of

the resources be devoted to charitable "activities." Second, Justice Marceau stated, incorrectly, in *Toronto Volgograd* (and implied much the same thing in *Scarborough*), that "the *Guaranty Trust Company* case was ... concerned with the validity of a trust" and was therefore not authority for adopting a liberal use of the means–ends distinction in tax law (at 181).

62 SC 1976–77, c. 4.

63 Income Tax Act, RSC 1950, c. 40. The definitions laid out in the 1950 revision remained substantially unchanged until 1977.

64 See F. Woodman, "The Tax Treatment of Charities and Charitable Donations since the Carter Commission: Past Reforms and Present Problems," *Osgoode Hall Law Journal* 26 (1988), 547–51.

65 Woodman argues to the same effect that "[o]n a fair and liberal interpretation of the provisions, it is arguable that resources devoted to ancillary and incidental ... activities are in fact resources devoted to the charity's activities or purposes": ibid., 560.

66 Cullity, "The Myth of Charitable Activities," 7 and 12.

67 See Moran and Phillips, chapter 11 in this volume.

68 *Toronto Volgograd*, 182.

69 Ibid., 170.

70 Ibid., 178. The other case that he cited as inconsistent was *Alberta Institute*, which involved a foundation. Thus he seems to have seen no difference in the approaches to be taken to foundations and to organizations.

71 *Everywoman's*, 326. The statement about context is footnoted with a citation of *Scarborough* and *Toronto Volgograd*, although it is unclear what distinguished "the case at bar" from those other decisions. Later in the same judgment Justice Decary stated that in *Scarborough* the "essential part" of the clinic's activities was "devoted to influence the policy-making process" (at 329, note 2), a gross exaggeration but perhaps one required by his disagreement with the decision and his unwillingness to follow it.

72 *Vancouver FreeNet*, 111.

73 *NDG Neighbourhood Association*, 18.

74 *Stop the Violence*, 11.

75 In *Vancouver Society*, the Court referred initially to "purposes and activities," but its substantive analysis referred only to "activities." *Briarpatch* also provides an example of the implicit use of the activities-only analysis. At issue was whether the publishing of a magazine that concerned itself mostly with poverty was charitable under the fourth head. Because "the topics canvassed ... are not restricted to matters that are of direct relevance to Canada's poor" the argument failed (at 99). While the Court said nothing about the distinction between purposes and activities, it was surely at least arguable that a magazine ought to be able, or perhaps

needs to, publish general interest articles as well as its more focused ones. To be fair, it appears from the case report that the appellant did not make this argument.

76 See Moran and Phillips, chapter 11 in this volume.

77 See *Briarpatch*, 98; *Vancouver Society*, 90; and *Vancouver FreeNet*, 117 (DeCary's dissent).

78 See *Positive Action*, 81; *Toronto Volgograd*, 171.

79 *Everywoman's*, 327.

80 *NDG Neighbourhood Association*, 17.

81 The Supreme Court of Canada, while it decided against the applicant, did provide a close analysis of the issue. For a review see Moran and Phillips, chapter 11 in this volume.

82 *Native Communications*, 91.

83 The OLRC's Report suggests the judicial adoption of a working definition of "charity" as altruism. It defines altruism as "doing good for others" and then defines "doing good," the issue of what purposes are charitable, as the provision of the means to pursue "basic human goods." These basic human goods, derived from the natural law philosopher John Finnis, are those that are self-evidently desirable – life, knowledge, play, aesthetic experience, friendship, religion, and practical reasonableness. While this list of goods is remarkably congruent with what the law recognizes as charitable, the commission suggests that "work" be added to the list as something that contributes to "human flourishing." The commission's list of human goods is a definition of charity, not a listing of charitable purposes. Charitable purposes are ways of providing these goods: see generally OLRC, *Report*, 1: chap. 6, and, for a summary, J. Phillips, "The Ontario Law Reform Commission and the Legal Meaning of Charity," *Philanthropist* 14, no. 2 (1997), 45. Without any such philosophical prompting, the English courts have extended charity to the provision of work: see *Oldham Training and Enterprise Council.*

84 *Canada Uni*, 48; see comments to the same effect in *Briarpatch*, 100.

85 *Briarpatch*, 97. See also Justice Decary's comment in his *Vancouver FreeNet* dissent (at 117) that the "gradual extension" of the fourth head "has been allowed in only the most meritorious of circumstances."

86 Justice Strayer has recently suggested the opposite – that the Court of which he is now a member "has ... been obliged to develop principles appropriate for Canada," principles to which the Court should give "primary consideration": *Human Life International*, 214. He may have been setting up an opportunity for later innovation, but his statement, I would argue, is not a very accurate summary of what has gone before.

87 *Positive Action*, 79.

88 *Vancouver FreeNet*, 104.
89 *Human Life International*, 214 and 221.
90 *Everywoman's*, 324. See also Justice DeCary's reference to the "privilege" of charitable registration in his dissent in *Vancouver FreeNet*, 116.
91 *Scarborough*, 318, per Marceau JA. This is the first substantive case on the meaning of charity decided by the Court and has not been discussed to this point because it involved the political purposes doctrine. The "special status" point was also made in *Toronto Volgograd*, 171. See also *Stop the Violence*, 11, where the Court referred to the fact that "the benefits attaching to charitable status are significant," and *Human Life International*, 214, where Justice Strayer referred to the "advantages" of tax exemption and credits for donation.
92 See, among others, Lord Cross's comments in *Dingle v. Turner*, [1972] AC 601 at 624–5 (HL); N. Brooks, "Charities: The Legal Framework," unpublished paper, Secretary of State, 1983; and Bromley, "Contemporary Philanthropy," 96.
93 There were a considerable number of proposals for a statutory definition in the 1970s and early 1980s, but none came to fruition: see Drache, "Charities," 37–41.
94 As Woodman argues, "it is not at all certain that the 'hard cases' would be any easier to determine under detailed legislation than under the common law": Woodman, "Tax Treatment," 571. The OLRC has recommended against a statutory definition, arguing that "the assessment of whether an act is charitable is a very context-specific question" and that therefore "very little is to be gained ... in attempting to define charity in any but the most general terms." While the commission believes that we can do better than the *Pemsel* categorization, "significantly more specificity may well be impossible": OLRC, *Report*, 1: 154. For a different view see, among others, I. Morrison, "Redefining 'Charities' in the *Income Tax Act*," *Philanthropist* 3, no. 3 (1982), 10; *Building on Strength*; and Sossin, chapter 12 in this volume.
95 Bright, "Charity," 33.
96 *National Model Railroad Association.* I do not discuss the case here because the Court agreed without comment that the association qualified as an organization which pursued charitable purposes – under both " advancement of education" and "other purposes beneficial to the community." The Court refused it registration because it was organized principally to provide benefits to its members rather than to the public.
97 The OLRC has recently argued that there is some coherence to the list, but its view is, I believe, a minority one: see OLRC, *Report*, 1: chaps. 6 and 7. The majority judgment in the Supreme Court of Canada's recent decision in *Vancouver Society* suggests lack of coherence. Although the dissent of Justice Gonthier argues for some underlying principles, those enunci-

ated are concerned more with process (providing a benefit to strangers without personal benefit to the donor) than with the substance of which purposes are charitable: see Moran and Phillips, chapter 11 in this volume.

98 One commentator has argued that this is, in his view lamentably, exactly what government would do if it heeded the calls for a statutory definition of charity: see B. Bromley, "Answering the Broadbent Question: The Case for a Common Law Definition of Charity," paper presented to the Canadian Association of Gift Planners Conference, April 1999.

8 Rethinking Public Benefit: The Definition of Charity in the Era of the Charter

MAYO MORAN

The definition of charity has long been the subject of considerable controversy. The questions are fundamental and involve such issues as why we privilege charitable trusts, what we hope to achieve thereby, and the relationship of those trusts to the prevailing social and legal order. The standard definition of charity was formed in the world of Elizabeth I, far removed socially, politically, and constitutionally from our own. And over the last few centuries the definition has largely been elaborated in England, which does not as yet have a written constitution with entrenched rights.

But the meaning of charity varies with its social and legal context. Indeed, trust law itself recognizes the importance of evolution in its repeated insistence that charity of necessity responds to changes in context.[1] Yet in Canada, the definition has failed to respond to profound political and constitutional changes, in particular the 1982 advent of the Charter of Rights and Freedoms. Even the recent *Report on the Law of Charities* by the Ontario Law Reform Commission (OLRC),[2] though thoughtful on most matters concerning the definition of charity, does not sufficiently attend to the implications of the constitution. None the less, the OLRC's report provides a very useful working definition of charity – the altruistic provision to others of "the means of pursuing a common or universal good."[3] The goods associated with charity encompass the basic forms of human flourishing, including life, knowledge, religion, aesthetic experience, and friendship.[4] Thinking through the report's understanding of charity in the light of profound constitutional and other changes reveals how the confines of charity must adjust to new conditions in the society in which it operates and from which the meaning of what it is to do good must certainly spring.

THE CHARTER AND CHARITY

Charity and the Income Tax Act

The relationship between the Charter and the definition of charity is not straightforward. The definition has been elaborated through the common law. However, in general the Charter applies only to state action, not strictly speaking to judicial decisions.[5] The Charter, however, has considerable significance for the meaning of charity. A finding that an organization is charitable bestows considerable taxation benefits on it. Thus, the relevance of the Charter for the definition of charity is examined primarily from the perspective of conferral of charitable tax status.

The provisions of the Income Tax Act[6] that deal with taxation of charities also establish a comprehensive regime that regulates and supervises charities, provides for deductibility of charitable donations, and creates tax-exempt status for charitable organizations.[7] These benefits give a registered charity considerable public resources in the form of tax expenditures or forgone revenue.[8] The minister of revenue's authority to assess registration as a charitable organization is delegated to the director of the Charities Division.[9]

Registration depends most centrally on an organization's ability to establish that it is a charity, but the Income Tax Act does not define "charity." The Canadian Customs and Revenue Agency (CCRA) makes it clear that in its determinations of registered status, it relies on a relatively uncomplicated reading of the common law definition of charity – in particular, the *Pemsel* test.[10] The CCRA's interpretation also adopts other aspects of the common law, including the disqualification of political activities as charitable.[11] Although this narrow approach has frequently been criticized, the Federal Court of Appeal has generally upheld it.[12] Thus the common law definition of charity established in the Statute of Elizabeth of 1601 largely determines which organizations should receive the considerable public resources associated with being registered charities.

The Definition of Charity and the Charter

Even though the definition of charity employed under the Income Tax Act is a matter of common law and the Charter does not apply to the common law,[13] *Dolphin Delivery* makes it clear that where the common law is incorporated into a statutory regime, the Charter applies.[14] Thus, to the extent that the definition of charity now has a statutory basis in the Income Tax Act, its underpinnings in the common law cannot operate to preclude the operation of the Charter.

The director of the Charities Division exercises discretion in accordance with the common law definition of charity, but that discretion would not be broad enough to encompass a definition that would violate the Charter. This is because the minister cannot delegate any power that he or she does not possess, and the minister cannot violate the Charter. Thus the definition of charity in the legislative scheme under the Income Tax Act must be subject to Charter scrutiny.

Similarly, it is no objection to the application of the Charter that the legislative scheme involves the distribution of benefits. The Supreme Court of Canada has repeatedly affirmed that that fact does not relieve the government from the responsibility of complying with the Charter. So, for instance, in *Schacter v. The Queen*, the Supreme Court found that the limitation of child care benefits to natural parents under the Unemployment Insurance Act violated section 15 of the Charter because it discriminated against adoptive parents with respect to parental leave.[15] And in *Tétreault-Gadoury v. Canada*,[16] the Supreme Court found that the restriction of benefits under the Unemployment Insurance Act to persons under the age of 65 violated section 15 of the Charter and was not justifiable under section 1. In *Eldridge*, it found that the exclusion of sign-language interpretation from funding under the Medical Protection Act in British Columbia violated section 15. Further, the Supreme Court has now authoritatively rejected on a number of occasions suggestions that the Charter did not apply to fiscal legislation, particularly to the Income Tax Act. Indeed, cases such as *Symes* and *Thibaudeau* make it clear that the Charter does apply to the Income Tax Act, even where the benefit is a deduction, rather than the conferral of preferential tax status. Further, in *Symes* the Supreme Court found that Charter scrutiny also applied to the exercise of administrative discretion by CCRA officials.[17]

Therefore, it is clear that the definition of charity under the Income Tax Act must be consistent with the Charter. As well, even apart from the question of direct application, the common law must itself develop in accordance with Charter principles.[18] While recourse to this weaker principle may be significant for the definition of charity outside taxation, and may therefore bolster the relevance of the Charter for the general definition of charity, the stronger principle of direct Charter application will have more general salience and is the focus of this chapter.[19]

THE IMPLICATIONS OF THE CHARTER

If the Charter does necessarily apply to the definition of charity, what follows from that conclusion? The subject has received very little attention. As I noted above, ministry officials continue to rely on a rather rigid version of the traditional common law test, and this continues to be in large part approved by the Federal Court of Appeal. And this tradition of inattentiveness seems to have continued in the Supreme Court of Canada's recent decision in the *Vancouver Society* case.[20] That case presented the Supreme Court with its first opportunity in over 25 years to consider the definition of charity. Unfortunately, neither the majority nor the dissent discussed the relationship between the Charter and the definition of charity. While the majority and the dissent differed on the import of the common law definition, they agreed that the dispute required no significant consideration of the relationship between the definition of charity and the Charter.[21] The Supreme Court's power of review in matters of charity makes this omission unfortunate. Courts are quite naturally hesitant to embark on issues that they need not resolve to decide a particular dispute. The Income Tax Act, however, leaves to the common law courts the task of defining a term – "charity" – that is critical to the distribution of significant benefits under a legislative scheme. Indeed, the fact that the courts so rarely exercise their power of definition only strengthens the argument for a more expansive judicial role. One would think that some further comment would have been desirable to provide guidance to the ministry's officials.

So while *Vancouver Society* is important, it provokes more questions than it answers. Issues surrounding the relationship between the Charter and charity extend beyond those raised in that case. Thus it is worth considering the Charter's influence on the definition more broadly and, in that context, how that influence could have been understood in *Vancouver Society*.

There are at least two ways in which the Charter may influence the definition of charity. First, and perhaps least controversial, attentiveness to Charter values may limit the kinds of purposes that may be considered charitable under the traditional classifications of the Statute of Elizabeth – the 'restrictive' effect of the Charter. Second, the Charter's effect may be expansive, for certain kinds of activities precluded under the traditional common law definition may be classified as charities because of the Charter. I consider these two effects in turn.

The Restrictive Effect of the Charter

One of the most obvious implications of applying Charter scrutiny to the definition of charity is that it will require invalidation as charitable of certain kinds of trusts that may notionally come within the *Pemsel* test but offend the Charter. Thus the CCRA, when it makes determinations about what kinds of organizations count as charitable, cannot register any organization that offends basic principles of the Charter. To take a straightforward example, any body that discriminates within the meaning of section 15 of the Charter should not be eligible; otherwise the government would effectively be supporting discrimination through the provision of tax benefits.

The infamous Leonard Foundation and the related litigation in *Canada Trust* serve both as an example and as an illustration of the utility of thinking more thoroughly about the impact of constitutional norms on the doctrines of trust law.[22] In 1923, Colonel Leonard established a trust to provide scholarships. The trust was explicitly discriminatory. In the recitals, the settlor constantly reiterated his belief in the superiority of the white race and of non-Catholic Christians. The trust restricted management to non-Catholic "Christians of the White Race" and limited eligibility for scholarships to British subjects "of the White Race and of the Christian religion in its Protestant form." The trust had been long been controversial. Eventually, universities began to refuse to process its award payments. Finally in 1986 the chair of the Ontario Human Rights Commission advised the foundation that its terms were contrary to public policy and requested that it change those terms. The foundation took the position that it was administering a private trust whose provisions did not offend the Human Rights Code, 1981. The commission then filed a formal complaint, alleging that the terms of the trust violated the code, following which the trustee sought the advice and direction of the court pursuant to the Trustee Act.

In the first instance, Justice McKeown held that the trust did not fall within the terms of section 1 of the code, since it was not a service or facility. But even if section 1 did apply, he found that the foundation would be protected by sections 13 and 17, which exempt certain special programs and special-interest organizations. There were, he noted, many scholarships in Ontario that restricted benefits to students on the basis of "race, ethnic origin, sex, creed, and so on."[23] Further, he found that the terms of the trust did not violate other public policy, since there was not "incontestable harm" to the Ontario public. He thus upheld the trust as valid.

The Ontario Court of Appeal unanimously overturned Justice McKeown's decision. Justice Robins, with Justice Osler (*ad hoc*) concurring, held that the trust, because it was premised on notions of racism and religious superiority, contravened public policy. They applied the *cy-pres* doctrine and thus eliminated the discriminatory recitals and restrictions. Justice Tarnopolsky (concurring in the result) agreed that the trust violated public policy. However, he addressed the issue of how one ought to give content to "public policy" and thus considered more carefully the relationship between public law norms and the meaning of charity. And while he agreed that public policy could be invoked only in extremely clear cases, he found that racial harmony, tolerance, and equality are "clearly and unquestionably part of the public policy of modern-day Ontario."[24]

A review of the sources on which Justice Tarnopolsky relied to reach that conclusion reveals the extent to which norms of public law do influence – as they properly should – the validity of a charitable trust. Thus, for instance, he found a statutory basis for the public policy against discrimination not only in the Human Rights Code but also in various other statutes and government policies.[25] Public policy, he suggests, is "gleaned from a variety of sources, including provincial and federal statutes, official declarations of government policy and the Constitution."[26] He makes particular note of sections 15 and 28 of the Charter and of the instruments of international law that address discrimination.[27] Indeed, by drawing on public law norms such as those found in the Charter, he provides a principled basis for such findings of invalidity and thus limits their scope to contravention of our most fundamental legal norms.

In this way, *Canada Trust* reveals that the "trusts" question of public benefit requires some reference to constitutional norms, because courts cannot interpret the public benefit requirement of a charitable purpose trust so as to contravene the Charter. And since a trust cannot be valid unless it is for public benefit, it must, at a minimum, be consistent with our most basic legal norms. Although Justice Tarnopolsky and the rest of the Court of Appeal in *Canada Trust* deploy the available tools of trust law and thus use the language of public policy, it is more sound to identify the underlying issue in terms of the intimate – though rarely attended to – relationship between the public benefit requirement of trust law and the constitution. So put, it hardly seems controversial: how could a trust that contravened basic legal norms offer the kind of public benefit that trust law requires as a criterion of validity? And this "public nature" of charitable trusts – which justifies their support – also attracts the requirement that they conform to the public policy against discrimination.[28] Simply put, a trust that violates fundamental legal principles cannot possibly be for public benefit.

Focusing on the salience of broader constitutional guarantees in *Canada Trust* is also helpful for a number of other reasons. Because consideration of underlying constitutional norms provides a more solid foundation for such holdings than public policy, it should be easier not only to defend but also to identify the nature and the limits of the analysis. Thus attention to just how constitutional norms affect assessments of public benefit actually helps address worries about the scope of public policy rules against discriminatory trusts. But the charitable trust is neither a purely private nor a purely public institution; instead it is a hybrid of public and private relationships and must be assessed as such. For this reason, while the equality jurisprudence under human rights codes and under the Charter will be relevant, that relevance must be understood in the light of the unique nature of the charitable trust.

Human rights norms alone, for instance, contain too limited a conception of equality. The restrictions and exceptions found in the Human Rights Code, 1981,[29] reflect the fact that an unlimited rule of non-discrimination would undermine the legitimate interests of communities and organizations to define their own interests and memberships. Indeed, many activities that are generally considered "good" – religion here seems paradigmatic, but so do ethnic or cultural organizations – restrict their membership in ways that seem legitimate.[30] The code's limitations also recognize that private actors are generally entitled to determine things for themselves, including their use of their property and resources and their personal and communal associations. If they are unfair or inegalitarian in these matters, they may be subject to criticism or moral censure, but not legal censure. For these reasons then, human rights norms restrict their application to the kind of exclusionary behaviour that has public significance – such as provision of a facility, good or service.[31]

The *Report on the Law of Charities* by the Ontario Law Reform Commission (OLRC) speaks, if somewhat obliquely, to the unique public–private nature of the charitable trust when it distinguishes between "public" "in the sense of common" and in the sense of "governmental or 'of the state.'"[32] The report clearly prefers the former understanding in assessing the validity of a charitable trust. But the requirement of "publicness" in charitable trusts must also acknowledge the state's extensive involvement with charitable trusts. The very fact that the state sanctions and supports charitable trusts precludes understanding publicness exclusively in terms of a purely "civil society" notion like whether the provision of the good is common.

But if human rights norms are therefore not straightforwardly applicable, neither are constitutional norms. The public stature and support that charities receive does mandate a different assessment of validity because of the political and constitutional significance of such support. None the less, it is too strong to say that charity thereby becomes a thoroughly public institution. That conclusion would ignore the important fact that the state has not chosen to accomplish the particular purposes on its own. Indeed, the state presumably sees some significant benefit in leaving certain kinds of public purposes to be selected by private actors with its help and support.[33] So while the state supports and condones this kind of private action, charity is not simply an arm of the state, any more than it is purely private altruism. It is in the light of this complex relationship between the state and the charity that assessments of validity and determinations of what counts as discrimination must take place.

It seems easy enough to assess the validity of a charitable gift in the extreme cases. As we saw above, there are good reasons to hold that a trust that is overtly discriminatory, such as the Leonard Foundation, will be invalid because it cannot satisfy the public benefit requirement of trust law. Similarly *Canada Trust* also makes it clear that restrictive trusts designed to benefit the disadvantaged will be valid. Thus Justice Tarnopolsky points out that "a charitable trust established to promote the education of women, aboriginal people, the physically or mentally handicapped, or other historically disadvantaged groups" will not be void as against public policy.[34] He points out that section 13 of the code has an exception for distinctions designed to assist the disadvantaged. He also points to the meaning of discrimination under the Charter's guarantee of equality in section 15. Similarly, the OLRC's report notes that gifts favouring a disadvantaged race, for instance, will generally be valid, since they are invariably motivated by "a desire to redress a disadvantage."[35] In the language of section 15, one would say that such restrictions are not discriminatory because they redress or ameliorate, rather than exacerbate or perpetuate, social and historical disadvantage.[36]

However, Tarnopolsky's ruling has been interpreted to mean that any trust that makes distinctions on suspect grounds will be discriminatory unless it is designed to ameliorate the condition of the disadvantaged. Thus, the OLRC's report suggests that his rule would invalidate, for example, a scholarship for English Canadians to learn French, or for Presbyterians at a teacher's college, or a gift to support a Welsh community centre. The report's solution to the potential difficulties with such trusts is to make their validity turn on the motive of the donor. Thus, the report concludes that "although they are discriminatory on suspect grounds," such trusts ought to be valid, "since there is no malevolent motive."[37] But if everything except amelioration of disadvantage captures much more than discrimination, it is equally true that that motive captures much less. Recourse to the donor's motives cannot provide the robust assessment needed to account for why we treat a particular trust not as simply an acceptable exercise of private power but rather as worthy of public support and stature.[38] But how should we approach the problem when the settlor does not express any overt discrimination, but simply shows "favouritism"?

Interpreting analysis of section 15 equality in the light of the complex public–private nature of the charitable trust helps to provide a more satisfying account of when such trusts will and will not be valid, and it does so without minimizing their public significance. Under section 15 it is essential to distinguish between discrimination and a mere distinction or difference in treatment; hence the oft-stated rule that "not all legislative distinctions constitute discrimination contrary to s. 15."[39] So finding a distinction only triggers but does not answer the discrimination inquiry. As Justice Tarnopolsky's analysis suggests, it is necessary to go on to examine the context, purpose, and effect of such a distinction. The analysis proceeds by determining whether the distinction is made on the basis of an enumerated or analogous ground.[40] But it is still necessary to determine whether the impugned distinction has a discriminatory impact, because, for instance, it exacerbates or perpetuates historical and social disadvantage on the basis of enumerated or analogous grounds.[41] Importantly, the absence of an intention to discriminate is irrelevant.[42]

On the critical question of whether a distinction or restriction has a discriminatory impact, it is necessary to be attentive to just how the state is implicated in charitable trusts. This is because the legitimacy of some preferences may depend on who is expressing them. As I noted above, in particular instances the state may have good reasons to leave a matter to private choice. Thus we agree that choices about support for religions should be determined by individuals, even if some of that support actually comes from the public. In fact, state support of individually selected distinctions on religious grounds will rarely be problematic because we conceive of religion as the proper domain of individual choice. And this understanding finds constitutional expression in the fact that the guarantee of fundamental freedoms in section 2 of the Charter gives prominence to "freedom of conscience and religion."[43] The state's support of religions through the mechanism of charitable registration can be seen as a means of enhancing the individual's ability to exercise his or her constitutional rights. Thus, if we think that religions should be supported at all, then we will not be suspicious about state support of individually selected gifts that restrict benefits on religious grounds.[44] This suggests that state support of trusts that distinguish on religious grounds will be very unlikely to exacerbate or perpetuate a historical disadvantage. Thus the scholarship in favour of Presbyterians at a teacher's college will be valid as a charitable trust because while there is a distinction on religious grounds its impact is not discriminatory. We may, however, take a different view of religious restrictions designed and enforced by the state because we do not think that the state should be making religious decisions.

The other gifts mentioned in the OLRC's report would similarly be valid under this understanding of discrimination. And determination of which of these categories any particular restriction falls into will also require the kind of contextual assessment of the impact of the restriction noted above. In this inquiry, public law norms drawn from human rights and Charter analysis will be invaluable, although of course they must be adapted to the particular nature of the charitable trust. The question will ultimately turn on the nature and the meaning of having the state endorse the kind of distinction that is at issue. In fact, looking to constitutional norms would actually provide a justification for the state's role in, for example, enabling individuals to learn both official languages.[45] Similarly, state support for a gift for a Welsh community centre may also find constitutional support in section 27 of the Charter, which requires interpretation in "a manner consistent with the preservation and enhancement of the multi-cultural heritage of Canadians." Once again this suggests that state support of these kinds of privately chosen ends actually enhances – rather than undermines – the ability of individuals to enjoy their constitutional rights.

Thus attending to the full significance of constitutional norms for restrictive trusts helps in the assessment of when such restrictions involve the kind of discrimination that renders a trust invalid. The equality inquiry of section 15 seems especially apt for capturing the public significance of a particular distinction – a significance that gets lost if the exclusive focus is on the motive of the donor or on the limits of private discrimination. This suggests that a troubling restriction in a charitable trust will inevitably require an analysis of the meaning of state involvment in that trust. This in turn will necessitate a contextual assessment of the constitutional significance of the particular restriction in the light of the complex public–private nature of the charitable trust.

The Expansive Effect of the Charter

In this way, then, the impact of the Charter and other norms of public law on the definition of charity will limit the purposes that can properly qualify as charitable. But while equality may rule out certain kinds of purposes, it will also make other purposes eligible. Thus, for example, trusts that seek enforcement of constitutional rights, either through provisions of services or through advocacy and litigation, should be considered charitable. Here, attending to the significance of constitutional norms will limit the operation of the political purposes doctrine because a constitutional regime of necessity positively values changes to the law that enhance conformity with constitutional norms. A second, and perhaps more controversial, effect of constitutional norms on the definition of charity goes to the consideration of what kinds of advocacy and public education programs will be eligible to count as charities. In addressing these kinds of issues, the centrality of democracy and of the attendant democratic goods must be considered in articulating the range of charitable purposes.

Enforcement of Constitutional Rights as a Charitable Purpose

Consideration of the relationship between the Charter and the meaning of charity raises questions about the legitimacy of restrictions associated with the standard definition of charity relied on by the CCRA and generally upheld by the Federal Court of Appeal. Trusts that assist groups that may be considered disadvantaged under the Charter are of particular significance here. First, can efforts to eradicate the kind of disadvantage addressed by section 15 properly be understood as a charitable purpose? Second, to what extent are groups devoted to overturning unconstitutional laws – in essence, to dismantling the legal structures of disadvantage – pursuing charitable purposes? Whatever authority there appears for the contrary position, if we take the definition of charity seriously in the light of our constitutional regime, it appears that such purposes should in fact be treated as charitable.

Ameliorating Conditions of Disadvantage. Let us first take the easier case of a purpose devoted to ameliorating the position or effects of disadvantage within the meaning of section 15. The Supreme Court of Canada case of *Vancouver Society of Immigrant and Visible Minority Women* can be understood as an example. As I noted above, the Supreme Court did not find it necessary or desirable to address the Charter arguments presented in that case. None the less, a simplified version of the facts that focuses on the predominant purpose of the society – and thus avoids the ambiguities that troubled the majority of the Court – shows how such an analysis might proceed.

The society's stated predominant purpose is to "facilitate immigrant and visible minority women in achieving economic and social independence and their full potential in Canadian society"[46] – in effect, to assist individuals "doubly disadvantaged" within the meaning of section 15 of the Charter. The people served are women and on that ground fall within both sections 15 and 28. They are also either immigrants or members of a visible minority and on those bases entitled to Charter protection.[47] Further, many of the women who benefit will also suffer other forms of disadvantage, such as those based on linguistic incapacities and poor economic status. Among the materials that the society provided to Revenue Canada was *A Study of Immigrant Women in Vancouver*,[48] which found immigrant women underemployed, supporting large families, and earning low family incomes. Assistance with finding employment would be the most effective way of remedying their disadvantage. The society directs its primary activities to redressing this disadvantage by providing "educational forums, classes, workshops and seminars to immigrant women in order that they may be able to find employment."[49]

Setting aside any particular complexities that may arise on the facts of that case, it seems difficult to see how this kind of purpose could fail to qualify as charitable even under a fairly standard interpretation of the traditional definition of charity. Relief of poverty and other forms of privation is undeniably one of the core purposes of charity. Thus, as Waters notes, the relief of poverty is so close to the relief of distress and suffering – all of which are traced back to the preamble – that both types of gifts have typically been brought within the relief of poverty or simply classified as clearly charitable under no specified head.[50] Similarly, the OLRC's report notes, "Aiding the emotionally, physically, mentally, and spiritually distressed" is typically included in relief of poverty and also in other purposes beneficial to the community, under the fourth head of charity.[51]

Thus, for instance, hospitals and medical services are typically treated as charitable,[52] as are gifts to the elderly,[53] or to those who experience other forms of need,[54] even where there is no necessary element of poverty. In *Re Forgan Estate*, Justice Riley found charitable a gift for the establishment of a home for the care of children of others, orphans, wards of the province, or children whose parents are unable to take care of them. Despite the difficulty of classifying the purpose, he upheld the gift on the following grounds: "for the relief of poverty in general, for the relief of suffering and distress of children, a gift to the destitute, and, in part, a gift to help accomplish governmental purposes, all of which, alone or together, have been held charitable."[55]

Inclusion of such services, however classified, is not only justifiable but indeed central to the meaning of charity. As Waters notes, the theme behind these objects is concern with those in a position of "privation or want," and on this basis he suggests that a number of cases can be understood not as relieving the specific needs of the poor but rather as relieving "distress and suffering."[56] Here thinking of charity as the provision to others of the material, social, or emotional means to pursue basic human goods, so that they may flourish, seems compelling as a deeper account of why we consider such purposes charitable.[57] So long as individuals lack fundamental material, social, and other amenities, they will not be in a position to flourish. Thus such purposes are charitable because they enable individuals to live a good life.

In this light, let us consider the primary purpose of the Vancouver Immigrant Women's Society. The study relied on by the society describes the privation suffered by local immigrant women and shows how they are deprived of the means of flourishing. Often their distress takes a non-economic form. But even where it does not, their inability to pursue work and their resultant social isolation and dependence seem to be the kind of want or distress that charity is devoted to relieving. Indeed, the OLRC's report adds work to John Finnis's list of basic human goods.[58] In addition, building on the insight of Justice Riley in *Re Forgan*, to the extent that the society helps to accomplish a governmental purpose – here employment and integration of immigrants into society and perhaps the eradication of disadvantage – the provision of educational assistance to enable disadvantaged individuals to realize their employment opportunities should be uncontroversially charitable. In fact, the dissent in *Vancouver Society* characterizes assisting in the settlement and integration of immigrants as itself a charitable purpose under the ordinary common law understanding of charity.[59]

In addition, the primary beneficiaries of the society's activities are individuals selected out for constitutional notice under section 15 of the Charter. How is it possible to hold that relieving emotional, physical, and mental distress counts among the primary purposes of charity and yet to refuse to treat as charitable an organization devoted to alleviating the isolation, disadvantage, and prejudice suffered by individuals identified under section 15 of our Charter as deserving of special concern because of their marginalization? What meaning can we give to providing the means of human flourishing if we rule out remedying discrimination, isolation, and social and economic disadvantage?

In *Native Communications*, the Federal Court of Appeal found that in order to determine whether a purpose was charitable, one had to examine the relevant social conditions.[60] And in doing so, it considered the constitutional status of Aboriginal people and their consequent relationship with the federal government.[61] While the Federal

Court of Appeal in *Vancouver Society* may have been technically correct in pointing out that the position of immigrant and visible minority women was not constitutionally identical to that of Aboriginal peoples, it seems to have missed the more fundamental point. In *Native Communications* the Court emphasizes that constitutional arrangements must inform assessment of whether the position of Aboriginal peoples and their relationship to the federal government made the purpose of assisting them charitable. If this is the correct way to construe charitable purposes in a constitutional regime, the entire legal and constitutional framework need not be identical in both cases. Instead, the method should be applied to the situation of immigrant and visible-minority women with appropriate attention to any relevant differences in the legal and constitutional, as well as the factual, framework. Considering the primary purpose of the Vancouver Society in the light of this method suggests that the society's primary beneficiaries are analogous to the needy groups identified by the preamble. In this light, it is worth recalling that section 15 serves at least in part as a directive to government to remedy and prevent discrimination against groups suffering social, political, or legal disadvantage.[62]

So assessing the primary purpose of the Vancouver Society against the backdrop of *Native Communications* provides some valuable lessons. The enumeration of the various attributes of the beneficiaries under section 15 of the Charter identifies them as a group deserving of special concern. As Justice Stone noted in *Native Communications*, a constitutional directive is one way to give content to the "new social needs" that Lord Wilberforce discussed in *Scottish Burial Reform*.[63] Looking to section 15 for at least some of the proper objects of charity seems not only desirable but the most legally and politically justifiable way for the court to ensure that the meaning of charity evolves in a principled way. Further, the "broad and remedial purpose" of section 15 also mandates particular governmental attentiveness to the conditions of the disadvantaged partly to counteract the state's historic indifference or even hostility towards their condition. Again, although the constitutional specifics and the relationship to the state differ from that in *Native Communications*, attentiveness to the constitutional requirements of the relationship between the beneficiaries and the government may yield similar conclusions.

In the face of this, it is troubling that the CCRA has to date received little guidance about how to administer benefits in the light of the directive of section 15. Reflecting on the core purposes of charity, even as articulated by the Statute of Elizabeth, makes it difficult to understand how the same court that found charitable the provision of free access to the internet can shortly thereafter find non-charitable the provision of education designed to achieve employment for a group constitutionally recognized as disadvantaged. It is yet more unfortunate that the Supreme Court placed so much emphasis on the traditional definition of charity when it had the rare opportunity to provide the CCRA with some guidance about how to administer the charitable regime in the light of the Charter. In any event, as has long been recognized, any principled understanding of charity must take account of changing social conditions, which must surely include the needs of those singled out by the constitution as objects of special attentiveness and concern.

The Political Process, Enforcement of the Constitution, and the Objects of Charity. If *Vancouver Society* serves as an illustration of an "easy" case of account being taken of the Charter in giving content to the meaning of charity, the more challenging examples are found in the interactions between the meaning of charity, the constitution, and the political purposes doctrine. The orthodox position of the law of charity is that no purpose that involves advocating changes to the law can be charitable under the "political purposes" doctrine.[64] This doctrine is often interpreted more broadly to encompass any activity that puts pressure on governments or that takes a position on a controversial public issue, whether in favour of the existing law or not.[65] However, the doctrine – and the consideration of public benefit that it addresses – emerged in England under a system of parliamentary supremacy. The pre-eminence of constitutional norms in the Canadian legal order suggests that it is no longer possible for Canada to hold to a political purposes doctrine that comports more with legislative supremacy than with a system based on constitutionally entrenched rights. Instead the doctrine must be responsive to the possibility that changes to the positive law may actually further constitutional values.

How might the meaning of charity and the political purposes doctrine intersect with basic constitutional rights? The OLRC's report summarizes the "real" definition of charity as consisting of the altruistic provision to others of "the means of pursuing a common or universal good."[66] The report suggests that this idea helps to explain the categorical distinction between charitable objects and political purposes. In a liberal democracy, politics is society's collaborative process of agreeing on some particular determination of the good. To engage is politics is to play a part in this process, but only the process of lawmaking itself can resolve the debate on what constitutes the good on any particular issue. So while any particular political position runs the risk of being rejected as wrong, law by contrast represents a society's "settled convictions as to what purposes, acts, or provisions ... are determinations of the good."[67] Indeed, a *just* law is "by definition ... a determination of the good."[68] Charitable ends provide goods to others, while politics engages the conceptually prior question of what the good consists in on any given question.[69] So politics cannot provide "goods" in the charitable sense, since its task is to sort out what the good is. Only once the law-making process determines the "good" is it possible to identify – and thus provide altruistically – those goods to others. So, at least where there is any controversy, law serves as the touchstone for the good and thus for the meaning of charity.

However, in the light of the impact of entrenched constitutional rights, this understanding of the relationship between social goods, charity, and law becomes problematic. To begin with, the OLRC's report limits the justification of the charity–politics divide to "just" laws. The significance of this caveat, and its interaction with constitutional norms, reveal at least one limitation to the political purposes doctrine: it must account for the "good" of striking down unconstitutional laws. The significance of political debate to determination of the good and thus to the charitable project, and the salience of democratic rights in our constitutional order, suggest that there may well be some "meta-level" goods provided by the political process that any model of charity in a liberal-democratic society must recognize.

Charity and Challenging Unconstitutional Laws. As I noted above, the Charter may require us to rethink charity in the light of the importance of alleviating the forms of disadvantage outlined in section 15. But this may require challenging the legal structures that make disadvantage possible. We can easily identify a number of organizations whose aim is to secure constitutional rights, often through litigation, including the Canadian Civil Liberties Association (CCLA), the Legal Education and Action Fund (LEAF), and organizations for the disabled such as the Disabled Women's Network (DAWN) and the Council of Canadians with Disabilities. Let us simply assume an organization whose activities easily satisfy the "practical utility" requirement and that devotes most of its resources to attempting to change the positive law to bring it into conformity with the constitution. Presumably any one of the above organizations, and a substantial number of others, would satisfy these conditions. Should they be treated as charities or be rejected on the basis of their political purposes?

The OLRC's report takes the position that an organization that is, for example, founded to promote compliance with the Charter cannot be classified as a charity primarily because it is political. What makes these activities political, according to the report, is their desire to persuade fellow citizens to take a certain view on certain issues. This standard applies, according to the report, even where the purpose is "to benefit others through the removal of legal or social obstacles to the full recognition of their human dignity."[70] This is because "reasonable people may disagree that the particular awareness aimed at is valid or that the particular provision of law challenged is the cause of the particular injustice identified, or that the particular project chosen is the proper one under the circumstances."

Yet the report itself is unwilling to commit itself to the full implications of such a position. Thus, for instance, despite its insistence about organizations sucy as LEAF, elsewhere the document adopts what seems to be a contrary position. So it draws the line at decisions such as *McGovern*, which refused to grant charitable status to Amnesty International, and *Lewis v. Doerle*,[71] where the court upheld as charitable a devise whose purpose was to enable African–Americans fully to enjoy their civil rights.[72] Despite the political purposes doctrine, the report argues that such purposes are properly treated as charitable. Similarly, the report states that only where a political effort is "aimed at overturning an unjust law" will it be essentially altruistic and therefore charitable. The apparent rationale seems to be that in a limited group of cases the overtly political objective is of unquestionable validity – these are objectives about which reasonable people could not disagree. But let us juxtapose this conclusion with the earlier insistence that groups dedicated to securing compliance with the Charter cannot be charitable.

The report – correctly, I believe – admits that some attempts to change or enforce the law are of such undoubted value that regardless of the political purposes doctrine they must be counted charitable. To conclude otherwise would risk a troubling irony: a trust to ensure that other human beings enjoy the most basic civil and political rights, including the right to count as fully human, would not be charitable, while publication of law reports and provision of free access to the internet would be. Indeed, treating as charitable a trust to ensure that other human beings enjoy basic civil and political rights, such as the right not to be tortured and the right to vote and to enter public places freely, is among other things consistent with the report's definition of charity as providing others with the means to ensure human flourishing and enjoyment of the goods. But how, given this position, is it then possible to conclude that organizations devoted to ensuring compliance with the Charter and individual enjoyment of Charter rights are not charitable?

The OLRC's report invokes the idea that even a political purpose will count as charitable when its validity is undoubted. But if this is the correct way to understand the scope of the political purposes doctrine, it has implications for a constitutional democracy. A "political" purpose must count as charitable because of its unquestionable validity at least when it is designed to ensure conformity with basic constitutional rights and freedoms, which serve as a guide against which to measure the justice or injustice of particular positive laws. The report suggests that one reason why politically-motivated organizations do not count as charitable is that their objectives are open to public doubt[73] – reasonable people could disagree on the validity of the objects.

But is the validity of securing compliance with the Charter and of ensuring that all citizens enjoy the basic rights and freedoms set out in the Charter open to doubt? Or one about which reasonable people disagree? Now actual people may disagree about the validity of these objectives because they do not support one or more of the basic norms of the constitution. But we cannot measure the validity of an objective by asking if there is any disagreement about it. On such a test, it is extremely unlikely that the trusts in *Lewis* and in *McGovern*, or indeed the trust in favour of the abolition of slavery in *Jackson v. Phillips*, would count as charitable despite the report's conclusions to the contrary.

Phrasing the test in terms of whether "reasonable" people would accede to the validity of the purpose suggests how such inquiries might be addressed. Rawls's notion of public reason, with its emphasis on the fundamental idea of what would be agreed to by citizens conceived of as free and equal, seems useful here in thinking about what kinds of purposes are good in the charitable sense. The emphasis that public reason places on the freedom and equality of all seems to explain why we would treat as charitable the political trusts that the report identifies as acceptable. And in Canada at least, the Charter and its enshrinement of the equal moral worth of all citizens would generally satisfy the fundamental requirements of public reason. In such a situation, surely reasonable people – that is, citizens conceived of as free and equal – would find the enforcement of the fundamental rights and freedoms entrenched in the constitution a purpose of unquestionable validity. The trusts in *McGovern* and in *Lewis*, for instance, are on this ground clearly valid, since they further the fundamental idea of equal human freedom and dignity. And this is consistent with the "real" definition of charity in the report. What among the basic human goods could be more fundamental than the right not to be tortured for one's opinions or the right to be treated as a free and equal member of society?

But this seems to lead inexorably to the conclusion that trusts designed to secure compliance with constitutional norms must similarly be classified as charitable. Thus, I consider the purposes of a group such as the Disabled Women's Network, which seeks to ensure conformity with section 15's guarantee against discrimination on the ground of disability: is this objective of dubious validity, or could reasonable people disagree about whether the disabled should enjoy guarantees of legal equality? It seems unlikely. Similarly, if we consider the case of LEAF, is there room for reasonable disagreement on the validity of promoting the enforcement of the human and civil rights contained in section 15's anti-discrimination guarantee? Now the exact contours of the enforcement of particular rights will undoubtedly be controversial – as they no doubt were also in *Lewis* and in *McGovern.* But perhaps the most principled way to approach this question is to look to practical utility. There may be a point at which a group that never succeeds in having its understanding of the meaning of particular rights recognized – by courts, for example, – will be found to lack the practical utility necessary for a finding of charity. But as long as such organizations manage to establish the validity of their understandings of constitutional rights by at least sometimes persuading decision-makers, then by ensuring compliance with the most basic legal norms they surely are providing a good of undisputed validity. On the basis of such a test, it would be difficult to conclude that the CCLA, LEAF, or groups for the disabled community, for instance, would fail to count as charities.

The OLRC's report suggests approaching the question of public benefit by asking whether a project "advances a common good."[74] But any defensible understanding of public good surely must include activities designed to ensure that the particular rules of the legal system are consistent with constitutional norms. There is a strong argument that the best way to ensure such compliance is through providing state support to organizations whose members may be most affected by the failure of law to comport with constitutional norms. Granting decision-making power to determine the relative seriousness of constitutional problems to individuals and social groups and then providing public support for those decisions may actually be the most effective (and cost-efficient) way to ensure a democratic and responsive constitutional regime. Since compliance with basic constitutional norms is a good of crucial importance to all citizens, it undoubtedly warrants public support. While we hope that much of this will occur at the legislative level, challenges through the process of constitutional litigation are also necessary. And although allocating public resources to such litigation can therefore be justified, it would be problematic to give the state too much decision-making power about the allocation of such funding. There are also good reasons not to leave all the power to pursue such challenges in the hands of private individuals, for such a process would most certainly fail to correct the constitutional problems that most affect those without resources. And this would be troubling both as a matter of constitutional law and as a matter of democracy.

For this reason, it seems clear that a truly democratic constitutional regime would need to provide some significant amount of public funding for constitutional challenges. This is another instance where the benefit that undeniably accrues to all citizens in a system with rigorous enforcement of constitutional norms seems most likely to be secured through the charitable mechanism, which provides public support for private initiatives that seek the common good. Although this argument may not alone be enough to make a purpose count as charitable, it is a strong reason to support a finding of charity that is plausible on other grounds.

Thus closer examination suggests that, at least in a constitutional regime with entrenched rights and freedoms, it is not possible to hold to the strong version of the political purposes doctrine. Instead, the law of charity must recognize a public benefit of unquestionable validity in rigorous enforcement of constitutional norms. The centrality of constitutional litigation to this goal means that organizations that seek enforcement of constitutional laws cannot be disqualified as charitable simply because they seek changes to particular laws. Instead, the good of the end that they seek must be measured against the yardstick of the constitution. And by this standard, groups such as the CCLA, DAWN, and LEAF properly count as charitable.

Public Education, Democracy, and the Meaning of Charity. In addition to ensuring effective enforcement of constitutional guarantees, how else must the values of democracy influence the meaning of charity? It may be that certain kinds of advocacy that invoke Charter values can actually be understood as part of the pursuit of education or as some combination of education and public benefit. Groups designed to raise public awareness about the unfair or discriminatory treatment of other human beings may serve as relevant examples here. The traditional understanding of trust law has typically viewed with suspicion "education," which encourages individuals to reflect on critically, question, and perhaps even challenge the status quo. Criticism of the status quo, or even support for a legal status quo that is somehow controversial, has typically removed a purpose from the category of knowledge or advancing human understanding and located it instead in the category of propaganda, which is inherently suspect. However, at least where such public education is designed to achieve compliance with constitutional or other related norms,[75] conflict or tension with social practices or positive laws should not disqualify it. Indeed, reading the traditional definition of charity in the light of the centrality of democracy makes this approach difficult to refute.

The Federal Court of Appeal's 1988 decision in *Positive Action Against Pornography v. M.N.R.* [76] is helpful here, because it involves the distinction between education and propaganda and has complicated connections with Charter values. In *Positive Action* the objective of the organization – about which it was arguably not very forthcoming – concerned raising public awareness about the violence and degradation that it saw as inherent in pornography. The organization was also involved in some activity that the court considered political "in the broad sense of the term."[77] Ironically, it was not clear that *McGovern* supported the characterization of the organization as political. This was because the organization primarily supported the legal status quo through vigorous enforcement of the existing law and the prevailing judicial interpretations of it in cases such as *R. v. Red Hot Video.*[78] Now finding that an organization supports the legal status quo ordinarily facilitates finding a charitable purpose. But while Justice Stone does admit that the only "anti-legislation" point of view that the organization expressed was its counselling against legislative reform, he goes on to insinuate its "political" or "propagandistic" nature by pointing to its bias – its absence of neutrality on the question of pornography – commenting that its material seems, if anything, "weighted very much in favour of greater state control."[79] And ultimately its lack of neutrality leads him to conclude that it cannot qualify as a charity.

But let us consider how *Positive Action*'s claim to charitable status may actually have raised significant Charter values downplayed or ignored by the Court. The organization argued, first, that it ought to be seen as providing a public benefit because pornography was an important issue and the public "stands to benefit from the freest and fullest possible public analysis, examination, discussion and review of the issues presented and options available." Since the organization's activities facilitate informed discussion and debate, it argued that it should be seen as charitable. Second, it claimed that its purposes were of public benefit because they were consistent with the widely accepted view that material condoning degrading and violent depictions of women and children was pornographic in the sense needed to justify regulation by the criminal law. Although neither of these arguments was explicitly put in terms of Charter values, they actually do raise serious and interrelated constitutional concerns.

The first argument focuses on the good of providing information to the public on an important issue of public debate. Arguably in its decision the Court ignores major considerations of public benefit. The organization's emphasis on informed public debate implicitly raises fundamental Charter values related to democracy, freedom of expression, and equality. Justice Stone seems to dispose of these questions by pointing to the organization's lack of "neutrality." Is this an adequate response? Public debate about the issue was – and continues to be – the focus of considerable legislative concern, as well as the subject of some very important judicial opinions and significant public controversy.[80]

In fact, it seems difficult to deny the centrality of informed public debate about major issues, particularly in a democratic society. The vitality of democracy depends on a citizenry capable of making informed and autonomous decisions. In *Political Liberalism* Rawls summarizes the good of participation in political life.[81] He notes that citizens realize these goods not only collectively but also individually and personally. Thus, as Rawls describes it, "the good involved in the exercise of the moral powers and in the public recognition of persons' status as citizens belongs to the political good of a well-ordered society."[82] This principle finds constitutional expression in the democratic rights contained in the Charter and in their significance to our political order more generally.[83]

But this good cannot be realized without ongoing education and information from a variety of sources, which suggests that the definition of charity ought to yield the conclusion that providing others with the means to participate fully in public life counts as a good in the charitable sense. If participation in public life is a good – which democracy must, I would think, count it to be – then providing the means of such participation to others should be the kind of purpose that would count as charitable, if that provision is made altruistically. So the basic human goods on which the definition of charity draws must include the goods – both collective and individual – of democracy. This in turn argues for the classification of the provision of at least certain kinds of public education and advocacy as charitable.

Now we should not be surprised that the traditional classifications of charity provide little recognition of the goods of democracy. After all, the realm in which the Statute of Elizabeth, 1601, was enacted was hardly a democracy and certainly did not value popular participation in public life. But, as noted in *Native Communications* and elsewhere, the meaning of charity cannot be fixed with reference to the idiosyncrasies and perhaps even failings of a particular historical moment. Society has changed dramatically since the reign of Elizabeth I, perhaps in no respect so fundamentally as in the rise of democratic government. And if we fail to take account of the profound effect of that change on the meaning of public benefit – of what it is to do good for others – our definition of charity will remain inadequate both to our time and to our constitutional order.

Taking democracy seriously may sound controversial in the context of *Positive Action*. But even though the Federal Court of Appeal did not pay attention to the democratic argument in *Positive Action*, in *Vancouver Freenet* it did recognize that democracy informed the meaning of charity. There, Justice Hugessen (with Justice Pratt concurring) found that provision of free access to the internet was a charitable activity, regardless of how that such access was used. The fact that such access fostered democracy helped to justify this conclusion: "Information is the currency of modern life. This has been properly called the information age. The free exchange of information amongst members of society has long been recognized as a public good. It is indeed essential to the maintenance of democracy, and modern experience demonstrates more and more frequently that it more than any force of arms, has the power to destroy authoritarianism. The recognition of freedom of speech as a core value in society is but one aspect of the importance of freedom of information."[84] Thus, Justice Hugessen finds that there is "absolutely no doubt ... that the provision of free access to information and to a means by which citizens can communicate with each other" is a charitable purpose within "the spirit and intendment of the preamble to the Statute of Elizabeth."[85] Thus, here at least, the court seems to view goods provided by charity in the light of the fundamental importance of democracy.

But even if we grant that charity should recognize as beneficial certain goods associated with the democratic process, there remain difficulties with treating an organization such as Positive Action as charitable. To begin with – and this may be one way to understand Justice Stone's objection in *Positive Action* – it may be argued that because the organization and its materials were not neutral regarding pornography, they did not in fact provide to others the means of meaningful participation in public debate. However, this objection seems untenable as a way of understanding what enhances such meaningful participation. Certainly it does seem necessary to impose some quality controls on what actually achieves the good sought (here, meaningful participation). But it is surely wrong simply to dismiss any material that adopts a position as at odds with meaningful public debate.

Given the centrality of the "marketplace of ideas" to both our political and our legal systems, it seems particularly problematic to reject any viewpoint as inimical to the search for truth. In fact, one might argue exactly the contrary: that meaningful debate will occur only when all principled viewpoints are put forward by articulate advocates so that citizens can assess all reasonable positions. Now, words such as "principled" and "reasonable" are doing a lot of work here. But that fact alone is not, I would suggest, problematic. Looking to the facts of *Positive Action* here and to how they implicate other Charter values besides democratic ones may help flesh out such terms. At least one version of the second argument made by Positive Action actually complements the first (perhaps unwittingly) and reveals why its materials may be of public benefit.

Thus one could argue that the viewpoint undoubtedly contained in the material should not have disqualified it as a meaningful contribution to public debate. In fact, considering this possibility encourages us to identify superior alternatives to "neutrality" in the assessment of contributions to public debate? While "quality controls" are useful, it is difficult to see why neutrality should determine what counts as a meaningful contribution. I have used the terms "principled" and "reasonable" to refer to the kinds of positions that might instead be considered to meaningfully contribute to public debate. How ought those terms to be understood?

Positive Action provides a useful example here. The materials and arguments of the organization make reference – as do such cases as *R. v. Red Hot Video*[86] and *R. v. Wagner*[87] itself – to the other constitutional values that it is asserting in this debate. Its basic position was validated in the Supreme Court of Canada's 1992 decision in *Butler*, which upheld the Criminal Code's prohibition of obscenity, defined as any publication that has as a dominant characteristic "the undue exploitation of sex, or of sex and ... crime, horror, cruelty and violence."[88] The Court found that while the material did offend section 2(b) of the Charter, it was justifiable under section 1. Justice Sopinka held that the exploitation of sex was "undue," and therefore obscene, when it treated women (and sometimes men) in a degrading or dehumanizing manner by placing them in "positions of submission, servile submission, or humiliation."[89] *Butler* focuses on how certain pornographic depictions of women damage equality interests protected under the Charter. Thus Justice Sopinka notes that such materials potentially victimize women and inhibit development of more egalitarian attitudes towards and treatment of women.[90] On this basis he finds that the criminal sanction of materials is justified because the sanction prevents the harm to constitutionally protected equality interests that would be occasioned by the materials.

The fact that Positive Action's point of view sought to underscore how certain pornographic depictions damage women's constitutionally protected equality interests should have been sufficient to settle the question of whether its contribution to public debate was meaningful. However, Justice Stone sidestepped this important question by focusing on neutrality. But *Positive Action* suggests that materials need not be neutral to serve a powerful educative function in a democracy. The fact that the organization's position rests on constitutional values should have made it easy to determine that its viewpoint was a meaningful contribution to public debate and was therefore within the rubric of charity. And since the public benefit here is based on the democratic good of meaningful participation in debate on important public issues, an organization need not be "correct" so long as it has a principled and reasonable position that ought to be articulated powerfully in any public debate. In fact, had Justice Stone addressed that question squarely, it is difficult to believe that he could have denied that Positive Action made a meaningful contribution to the debate on pornography. Treating charity as informed by the constitutional value of democracy would not necessarily confine its scope to those positions that assert constitutional values in major public debates.[91] But it does seem that a position that addresses the impact of public choices on constitutional values ought, on the face of it, to be considered the kind of meaningful contribution to public debate that justifies classification as a charity.

So if we take the definition of charity found in the OLRC's report seriously, we should find at least some kinds of public education activities charitable, on the basis that they are providing the good of meaningful public debate altruistically to others. However, this does not mean that every public education group ought to be funded under the rubric of charity. An example of what kinds of purposes will not quality as charitable concerns organizations that actually seek to undermine constitutional values. Let us imagine a group – called, for example, "White Canada," – which took the position that Canada's immigration policies should be designed to ensure that Canada remains a predominantly "white" country,[92] and let us simply assume that its materials were of a sufficiently high quality that it could not be disqualified on other grounds.[93] Should such an organization be registered as a charity on the ground that it is making the good of meaningful public debate available to all? Recall that in the discussion of *Positive Action* we assessed whether an organization provided that good not in terms of its neutrality, but rather in terms of whether it took a principled and reasonable position. And "principled" and "reasonable" take their meaning at least in part from the values of the constitution. How ought a group such as White Canada to fare under such an approach to charity?

If constitutional values serve as a baseline for what can be considered to be meaningful participation in public debate, then it seems that while we perhaps ought to tolerate White Canada in the interests of freedom of expression, we cannot treat its values as the kind of contribution to public debate that should be fostered as one of the goods of charity. In a robust democracy we cannot use the yardstick of neutrality to determine what kind of advocacy or public education facilitate meaningful exercise of democratic citizenship rights. Yet, even a democracy requires some way of distinguishing the kinds of contributions that it should foster from those that it may merely have to tolerate.

In an essentially just constitutional order, the most principled and defensible way of drawing this kind of line is by reference to the values of the constitution itself. Thus we should encourage and support – as a vital part of any functioning democracy – public education that seeks to further constitutional values. So, in the case of a group such as Positive Action, or a group that works on behalf of those with disabilities, or the CCLA, we can count their participation in public debate as meaningful, since their positions assert constitutional values such as equality and freedom of expression. In contrast, a group such as White Canada actually invokes values such as racial segregation and the notion of a race-based state that are fundamentally at odds with constitutional values, including equality and multiculturalism, and with the principle of equal human dignity that the Supreme Court has repeatedly affirmed is at the heart of the Charter and of our constitutional order more generally. Rather than invoking and supporting constitutional values, such an organization actually seeks to subvert such values and perhaps ultimately alter them. Thus it does not provide the kind of meaningful contribution to public debate that counts as a public good.

Now one could object that even a group such as White Canada does encourage constitutional values, because freedom of expression is a constitutional value – indeed, it underscores the centrality of democracy. However, while such a body may use the guarantee of freedom of expression, its purpose is not actually to further that guarantee but rather to restrict its availability – and that of other constitutional guarantees – to those who are white. Rather than taking a position that emphasizes, for instance, the value of freedom of expression to all citizens, White Canada instead asserts its own use of freedom of expression. The OLRC report's definition is relevant here, for even assuming that such a group is asserting freedom of expression, it is not doing so altruistically, since it actually seeks to undermine others' entitlements to fundamental constitutional rights.[94]

Further, White Canada's position on the constitution more generally is also of fundamental relevance to the assessment of public benefit. While groups such as the CCLA, LEAF, and advocacy groups for the disabled may disagree about how best to reconcile various constitutional rights, they nonetheless support the values of the constitutional order and affirm the principle of equal human dignity as the touchstone of the entire constitutional regime. In contrast, to the extent that an organization such as White Canada affirms any constitutional values, it does so only selectively, in the hope of subverting the Charter's fundamental principle of equal human dignity.[95] For this reason, such a group does not provide the kind of meaningful contribution to public debate that qualifies it as a charity.

Looking at the meaning of charity in the light of the argument from democracy therefore suggests that some public education activities must count as charitable. Assuming that the activities of the organization had the kind of practical utility necessary, it is plausible on this ground to claim that *Positive Action* was wrongly decided. And this seems to be an attractive and politically sensitive way to approach the state's positive role in public education and democratic debate. While funding privately selected public goods through the tax system will continue to be plagued by problems of democratic justification, it seems arguable that the way in which this system is currently administered actually exacerbates those difficulties. Thus, for instance, when one combines the implications of *Positive Action* with the fact that gifts to education are rarely disqualified on any grounds – including failures of "neutrality" – when they are made to established institutions,[96] it seems that certain kinds of grassroots, critical public education efforts are likely to be disqualified as charities, while their more complacent counterparts are not. This fact alone provides a sufficiently persuasive reason to be more attentive to the goods of democracy in assessing whether an organization's contribution to public debate is sufficiently meaningful to be treated as the kind of public benefit considered uncontroversial when it is generated by an established educational institution.

In the case of the democratic goods secured by public education of various sorts, there are also other reasons to develop mechanisms to register and support publicly the expression of private concerns. Although the concerns associated with too much state-directed decision-making are different here than in the case of religion, they are at least as pressing. It is perhaps too obvious even to note the dangers of an inherently self-interested state and bureaucracy making funding decisions about what public information and education would most further meaningful public debate. The impetus to self-protection would seem to be almost too much for even a fair government to resist. For these reasons then, it seems critical to have a mechanism that ensures meaningful debate on major issues and that secures state support of that good, without having the state itself directly make the decisions.

Viewed in this light, not only do certain public education programs provide the kind of public benefit that any properly functioning democracy must count as the sort of good that is the proper subject of charity, but this allocation of decision-making may itself have a democratic justification. There are remaining questions, of course, about how far such decisions should be left – at least without considerable additional guidance – to CCRA officials, but such questions plague determinations about what is charitable more generally. If we worry about how officials would interpret the meaning of initiatives in public education, then we should be at least as concerned about what is currently happening (and what is not) under the cloak of the Statute of Elizabeth.

CONCLUSION

According to received wisdom, charity is a moving subject that cannot be authoritatively defined by the idiosyncrasies of any particular historical or social moment. There is undoubtedly an overarching meaning to charity, but that meaning becomes concrete only in a given social and legal context. In all of this, the OLRC's report seems not only correct but surprisingly subtle. But there is one curious oversight there, and it concerns the implications of constitutional rights and freedoms for the assessment of charitable purposes. If we are to take seriously the definition of charity as the altruistic provision to others of the goods that enable human flourishing, then the impact of such constitutionally entrenched rights and freedoms must be profound. As we saw above, the impact can be felt, more or less controversially, in several corners of the law of charity at least.

Perhaps least controversially, looking to constitutionally protected rights provides us with a more satisfying basis for the disqualification of discriminatory trusts and enables us better to identify the scope of this rule. But constitutional norms also force expansion of the traditional common law definition in a number of ways. At a minimum, assessment of what forms of suffering fall within the ambit of charity must attend to constitutional directives to pay particular attention to certain groups whose interests we have systematically ignored. So when purposes are designed to alleviate the disadvantage experienced by groups protected under section 15 of the Charter, for instance, those purposes must – all other things being equal – count as charitable.

The expansive effect of constitutional norms on the definition of charity also takes other forms. In a regime where the validity of any particular law depends ultimately on its compliance with constitutional norms, reasonable and principled efforts to ensure compliance with and rigorous enforcement of those norms must be counted as a good. The least controversial meaning of "just law" in a properly structured constitutional regime perforce looks to the constitution itself. Thus the purpose of securing compliance with constitutional norms must be charitable. Further charity must attend to the goods of democracy, particularly given their constitutional expression. This means that groups that offer the kind of education that enables meaningful participation in public debate do provide a charitable "good," since undeniably such participation is an important form of human flourishing. The notion of what constitutes meaningful public education in turn also looks to constitutional norms, perhaps in this way affirming the centrality of Rawls's idea of public reason, with its emphasis on individuals conceived of as free and equal.

Thus, looking to the definition of charity as doing good for others altruistically enables us to identify a number of areas where the effect of constitutional norms actually requires some substantial rethinking of traditional doctrines of the law of charity. This should not be cause for alarm or regret. After all, as Lord Wilberforce noted, charity is a complex and moving subject. And if its meaning is to shift or change in substantial ways, what better guidelines could be found than those in the constitution? Indeed, why would we even pause to consider what should carry more weight – our constitution or a statute passed almost four hundred years ago? The question, of course, derives its force from the profound effect of history on the charitable trust. Sir Isaiah Berlin, commenting on Hegel, noted the pattern of "great liberating ideas" inevitably turning into "suffocating straitjackets."[97] With the constitution as our guide, perhaps the time for at least a modest liberation has come.

NOTES

1 See, for instance, *Scottish Burial Reform* v. *Glasgow Corp.*, [1968] AC 138 at 154 (per Lord Wilberforce), *Native Communications Society v. Minister of National Revenue* (1986), 23 ETR 210 (FCA); *Vancouver Regional Freenet Association v. Minister of National Revenue* (1996) 137 DLR (4th) 206 (Fed. CA); *Re Laidlaw Foundation* (1984), 48 OR (2d) 549 (Div. Ct).
2 Ontario Law Reform Commission (OLRC), *Report on the Law of Charities* (Toronto: Publications Ontario, 1996).
3 Ibid.,152.
4 Ibid., 148, discussing John Finnis.
5 *RWDSU v. Dolphin Delivery*, [1986] 2 SCR 573.
6 RSC 1985, c. 1 (5th Supp.). This feature of charities is discussed in OLRC, *Report*, 249.
7 The provisions that deal with the deductibility of charitable donations are contained in s. 110.1, as am. by SC 1994, c. 7 s. 79; Sch. VIII, s. 46 (1) (deduction for corporations) and s. 118.1, as am. by SC 1994, c. 7, Sch. II, s. 88; Sch. VIII, s. 53(1); 1995, c. 3, s. 34(1); c. 38, s. 3 (tax credit for individual taxpayers). Tax-exempt status is addressed in s. 149.1(4).
8 Thus, for instance, in 1993, 5.5 million taxpayers made gifts to charities estimated at $3.5 billion. Richard Domingue estimates that in that same year, $8.2 billion was donated by individuals and $1.2 billion by corporations: "The Charities Industry and Its Tax Treatment," Background Paper, Research Branch, Library of Parliament, 1995, 1.
9 Income Tax Regulations, Can. Reg., c. 945, s. 900(8).
10 See, for instance, Form T4063, Registering a Charity for Income Tax Purposes.
11 Ibid.
12 This trend is noted by Phillips, chapter 7 in this volume. Phillips reviews the record of the Federal Court of Appeal in the exercise of its jurisdiction to hear appeals from refusals of the CCRA to register an organization as charitable or from decisions to remove the registration of an organization. He notes that of the mere sixteen cases that arise out of the exercise of this jurisdiction, thirteen have been victories for the Department, not for the applicant. For some recent examples, see *Briarpatch Inc. v. The Queen*, (1996), 96 DTC 6294 (Fed. CA) (magazine for poor not charitable); *Vancouver Society of Immigrant and Visible Minority Women v. Minister of National Revenue* (1996), 195 NR 235 (society designed to ameliorate conditions of immigrant and visible-minority women not charitable).
13 See, for example, *Dolphin Delivery*.
14 Ibid., 599, per McIntyre, J.
15 [1992] 2 SCR 679.

16 [1991] 2 SCR 22.

17 Thus, for instance, in *Symes* the Supreme Court found that the interpretation of business expenses adopted by Revenue Canada officials had to be consistent with section 15 of the Charter.

18 *Dolphin Delivery*, 603; *Dagenais* v. *CBC*, [1994] 3 SCR 835 at 878; *Hill v. Church of Scientology*, [1995] 2 SCR 1130.

19 Interesting questions potentially arise here, including problems about the extent to which the courts could continue to rely on a common law definition of charity abandoned by the ministry as violating the Charter. Presumably, the potential for such conflict would strain the *Dolphin Delivery* rule that the Charter does not apply directly to the common law.

20 [1999] 1 SCR 10, hereafter *Vancouver Society (SCC)*.

21 See *Vancouver Society (SCC)* per Gonthier, J., 90, and per Iacobucci, J., 139–40. Unlike Justice Gonthier, who does not consider it necessary even to consider the relevance of the Charter, Justice Iacobucci does seem to agree that the Charter notionally applies in at least some way. However, he inteprets registration requirements as "guidelines of uniform application," the application of which does not constitute discrimination under section 15. For a more detailed discussion of this case, see Moran and Phillips, chapter 11 in this volume.

22 *Canada Trust Co. v. Ontario Human Rights Commission* (1990), 74 OR (2d) 481 (CA).

23 Ibid., 492.

24 Ibid., 511.

25 Thus, for instance, he refers to the *Conveyancing and Law of Property Act*, RSO 1980, c. 90, s. 13; *Ministry of Citizenship and Culture Act, 1982*, SO 1982, c. 6 s. 4; *Insurance Act*, RSO 1980, c. 218, s. 117, and *Labour Relations Act*, RSO 1980, c. 228, s. 13. He also refers to *Ontario Policy on Race Relations* and the premier's introduction to it: *Hansard*, 33rd Parl., 2nd Sess. 28 May, 1986, 937.

26 *Canada Trust*, 512–3.

27 Ibid., 512–3, citing the International Convention on the Elimination of All Forms of Racial Discriminator (1965), (UN)GA Res. 2106 A (XX), and the International Convention on the Elimination of All Forms of Discrimination against Women (1979), GA Res. 34/180, as well as articles 2, 3, 25, and 26 of the International Covenant on Civil and Political Rights (1966), GA Res. 2200 A (XXI). He further notes that all three instruments were ratified by Canada with the unanimous consent of the provinces.

28 *Canada Trust*, 515.

29 Thus, for instance, the code limits the right to equal treatment and non-discrimination to "services, goods, and facilities." There is also an exception, even to this limited right of non-discrimination, where "member-

ship or participation in a religious, philanthropic, educational, fraternal or social institution or organization that is primarily engaged in serving the interests of persons identified by a prohibited ground of discrimination is restricted to persons who are similarly identified."

30 *Canada Trust,* 92. Indeed, Justice McKeown applies this reasoning to the Leonard Foundation and finds that even if the code applies, the foundation is exempt from the non-discrimination principle because it is an institution engaged primarily in serving the "interests of persons identified by ... race, ancestry, colour, ethnic origin and creed" and because participation in that institution is limited on those grounds. Although the Court of Appeal rejects his finding that the trust is valid, none of its members takes issue with his conclusion on the code.

31 I am not here attempting to pass any judgment on the wisdom of this approach to the regulation of private conduct. My point is simply that the restricted definition of discrimination, though perhaps understandable in the context of regulating private conduct, is not similarly appropriate for assessing whether a bequest can be considered charitable.

32 OLRC, *Report,* 218.

33 There are important questions here I am leaving unanswered. What of the basis for this kind of mechanism of private choice and public support? Whose interests might thereby be favoured? For instance, Linda McQuaig notes how our current system results in a disproportionate benefit to "established cultural and educational institutions" and how little benefit goes to "anything directly helping the poor": *Behind Closed Doors* (Markham, Ont.: Penguin Books, 1987) 57, cited in OLRC, *Report,* 146.

34 *Canada Trust,* 514.

35 OLRC, *Report,* 218. In contrast to Justice Tarnopolsky's approach, the report speaks of the motivation of the gift and thus seems even here to address validity through assessment of motive.

36 See, for instance, *R. v. Turpin,* [1989] 1 SCR 1296. Although, as I noted above, the Supreme Court in *Vancouver Society* refuses to address the relevance of the Charter, Justice Gonthier invokes a normative notion of discrimination recognizable from the public law context to find that the society did not impermissably limit its class of beneficiaries. He notes that "there is at least some authority in support of the view that an organization seeking to aid a disadvantaged group may draw distinctions on the basis of certain personal characteristics": *Vancouver Society (SCC),* 79–81, citing *Canada Trust.*

37 OLRC, *Report,* 218.

38 This comports with a basic principle of the law of charitable trusts which holds that in questions of public benefit, the motives and beliefs of the donor cannot be determinative. See, for example, *Re Pinion,* [1965] Ch. 85. Even a trust structured such as the one in *Canada Trust* could,

without the discriminatory recitals, be construed as "mere chauvinism or favouritism." Elsewhere in the OLRC's report, the term "chauvinism" refers to an illegitimate preference for one's own views, in its discussion of religion: OLRC, *Report*, 194–5.

39 *Andrews*, 168–9 (McIntyre, J.).

40 Ibid., 165 and 168 (McIntyre, J.); *Turpin*, 1326 (Wilson, J.).

41 *Turpin*; *Egan v. Canada*, [1995] 2 SCR 513.

42 See, for instance, *Andrews* and *Egan*.

43 *Charter*, section 2(a).

44 The caveat that I would add here is applicable to all of the questions related to allocating support through the tax system via charitable donations. This method will inevitably grant disproportionate control of public expenditures to those who have sufficient financial resources to make charitable contributions. Thus, to take the example of religion, we might imagine that a widely supported faith whose adherents were primarily poor immigrants would not receive the public support that, for example, the Anglican church receives.Thus, measuring private choice through a mechanism such as charitable deductions carries with it the inevitable hazard of overvaluing the choices of the wealthy and undervaluing those of the poor. To the extent that the justification for funding certain kinds of organizations through publicly supported private donations is found in its relation to individual choice in that domain, the "justification" may actually fail to justify the practice as expressed in the tax system. Indeed, the way in which this system skews the recognition of choices and interests may itself raise constitutional issues.

45 Thus see, for example, sections 16–23 of the Charter, which enshrine English and French as the official languages of Canada and guarantee equality of status between them.

46 Society's Supreme Court Factum, 22–3.

47 Citizenship was found an analogous ground in *Andrews*. Further, race and colour are enumerated grounds under section 15, as are national or ethnic origin.

48 Society's Supreme Court Factum, 115–16.

49 Ibid., 115–6.

50 D. Waters, *The Law of Trusts*, 2nd ed. (Toronto: Carswell, 1984), 552.

51 OLRC, *Report*, 186.

52 *Re Resch's Wills Trusts; Le Cras v. Perpetual Trustee Co.*, [1969] 1 AC 514; *Everywoman's Health Centre (1988) v. Minister of National Revenue*, [1991] 2 CTC 320 (FCA).

53 *Marie F. Ganong Old Folks Home v. Minister of Municipal Affairs (NB)* (1981), 37 N.B.R. 225 (CA) (poverty not necessary to support charitable status of gifts to the aged). But see, contra, *Marville Manor* v. *Regional Assessment Commissioner*, [1995] OJ No. 4064 (Gen. Div.).

54 *Big Sisters of Kitchener–Waterloo & Area* v. *Waterloo Regional Assessment Commissioner*, [1996] OJ No. 388 (QL) (Big Sisters charitable under first head); *Family Service Association of Metropolitan Toronto v. Regional Assessment Commissioner* (1995), 23 OR (3d) 382 (Gen. Div.) (family service association charitable), to cite but a few such examples.

55 (1961) 34 WWR 485 (Alta QB) at 499.

56 Waters, *The Law of Trusts*, 584.

57 OLRC, *Report*, 149.

58 Ibid., 148.

59 *Vancouver Society (SCC)*, 67–79 (Gonthier, J.). This conclusion forms one of the central differences between the majority and the dissent. For a more detailed discussion, see Moran and Phillips, chapter 11 in this volume.

60 *Native Communications*, 220–1, citing *In Re Strakosch*, [1949] Ch. 529 (CA) at 537, and Lord Wilberforce in *Scottish Burial Reform*, 154.

61 *Native Communications*, 221–3.

62 *Turpin*, 1333. See also *Haig v. Canada*, [1993] 2 SCR 995 at 1043–4 (L'Heureux-Dubé, J.).

63 *Scottish Burial Reform*, 220–1, relying on *Re Mathew*, [1951] VLR 226 (Aust.), which involved deciding whether Australian Aborigines were analogous to the groups mentioned in the preamble. Note the methodological similarity between these cases and the assessment of whether a group is an "analogous ground" under the Charter: *Andrews*. Given the similarity of the underlying concerns of need and disadvantage, it is somewhat surprising that the Federal Court should seem so hostile to taking account of the most basic constitutional norms in assessing what social conditions are deserving of the appellation "charity." I cannot help but wonder whether it feels some suspicion that there is something "political" and hence non-charitable about the purposes of section 15 – although, of course, section 15 is formally legal.

64 See, for instance, *National Anti-Vivisection Soc. v. IRC*, [1948] AC 31 (HL); *McGovern v. AG.*, [1982] Ch. 321.

65 *McGovern*; *Positive Action against Pornography v. The Queen*, [1988] 1 CTC 232.

66 OLRC, *Report*, 152.

67 Ibid., 153.

68 Ibid., 153.

69 Thus, "the debate about the content of the good and a determination of the good itself are two different things": ibid., 153.

70 Ibid., 210.

71 (1898), 25 OAR 206 (CA).

72 OLRC, *Report*, 221, discussing *Lewis*.

73 Ibid., 221.

74 Ibid., 75.

75 I am thinking here, for example, about the advocacy engaged in by groups designed to eradicate child labour or practices such as torture or the death penalty. As noted in *McGovern*, while some of this activity takes the form of attempting to change various laws, much of it also involves broader public education. This is also true of many environmental groups, which seek simultaneously public awareness, education, and legal change. Sometimes these groups invoke constitutional norms, but they may also invoke international law or international or regional human rights norms.

76 [1988] 2 FC 340 (FCA).

77 *Positive Action*, 352.

78 (1985), 18 CCC (3d) 1 (BCCA).

79 *Red Hot Video*, 351–2.

80 See, for instance, *R. v. Butler*, [1992] 1 SCR 452; *Little Sister Book and Art Emporium v. Canada* (1996), 131 DLR (4th) 486 (BCSC); *Ontario (AG) v. Langer* (1995), 123 DLR (4th) 289 (Ont. GD) to cite examples.

81 J. Rawls, *Political Liberalism* (New York: Columbia University Press, 1996).

82 Ibid., 203. This valuable political good does not seem to play a role – or at least certainly not a significant one – in the OLRC's report, despite the document's emphasis on the democratic process. The report seems to depict the process primarily in consequentialist terms, in the relationship between charity and politics. However, any list of the basic human goods must take account of the social and political goods of self-determination provided by a well-functioning democracy. The closest that the report's list seems to get to this value is perhaps in the good of practical reasonableness, but even there it focuses on the personal dimensions and thus misses the values expressed in the social and political spheres: OLRC, *Report*, 148–9, discussing J. Finnis, *Natural Law and Natural Rights* (Oxford: Clarendon Press, 1980), chap. 4. Thus the report may be correct in noting the congruity between Finnis's list of goods and those identified by the law of charity, but, as Rawls's works suggests, both the law of charity and Finnis's classification may here be underinclusive.

83 See, for instance, section 1 (any limitation must be justified according to the fundamental principles of a free and *democratic* society); section 2 (fundamental freedoms, including conscience, thought, expression, press, assembly, and association); and sections 3–5 (democratic rights). See also *Reference re Secession of Quebec*, [1998] 2 SCR 217, which emphasizes the centrality of democracy in the Canadian constitutional order.

84 *Vancouver Freenet*, 892 (per Hugessen, JA).

85 Ibid., 892.

86 *Red Hot Video.*

87 (1985), 36 Alta. LR (2d) 301, affd. 69 AR 78.

88 RSC 1985, c. C–46, s. 163(8).

89 *Butler*, 479.

90 Ibid., 479.

91 So, for instance, while organizations that advocate preservation of the environment may not be asserting constitutional values in any straightforward way, it may be possible to find that their contributions to certain public debates are sufficiently important and principled to be meaningful.

92 There are, of course, serious definitional and other issues surrounding the use of such terms as "white." For the moment I am putting them aside to focus on the issue of discriminatory advocacy on public questions.

93 This is why I am focusing on a group designed to address immigration issues as well. It seems quite possible that an organization that is more generally racist – an organization such as the Ku Klux Klan, dedicated to maintaining and enforcing by violent means the privileges of white power – could be denied charitable status because the "colour" of power is not seen as an issue of public importance, at least not in the sense that it is "up for debate" that power should have a colour.

It is, of course, a different matter to say that power should not have a colour but that it does and that we had therefore better attend to that fact in order to make good on the basic constitutional guarantees of equal citizenship and non-discrimination. Of course, it is possible that a racist organization could recast its position – as authors such as Hernnstein and Rushton arguably do – by arguing that our society has made good on our promises and that it is only the inherent shortcomings of "non-whites" that can account for their social, economic, and political disadvantage. It is this position that I mean to address in the text.

94 The jurisprudence of the Supreme Court in cases such as *Keegstra* will be of obvious relevance to this inquiry.

95 It is important to distinguish between any incidental "benefits" that may arise from airing of an abhorrent opinion and a substantive position in favour of freedom of expression. So it is unlikely that the information supplied by White Canada contributes to public debate in a meaningful way – that is, in a way that furthers constitutional values – since it seeks to make the skin colour of those seeking to enter Canada a central issue in the debate. Thus, it cannot be said that the actual education that it provides facilitates meaningful public debate. None the less, such a group may provoke debate, not on the substantive issues that it addresses but rather on what views we may have to tolerate in the interests of democracy. But it is neither its purpose nor its substantive information that prompts this kind of self-examination. It is rather the very existence of such groups within an egalitarian and democratic polity that challenges the commitment to – and form of – democracy. But a racist militia that

advocates violent overthrow of the constitutional regime fundamentally challenges our constitutional commitment but cannot, simply on that ground, be understood to provide a "public good." Thus, if the "education" actually seeks to subvert constitutional values, then it cannot be the kind of public good that qualifies as charitable, even if a by-product of the organizations activities stimulates public debate about the limits of democracy. No public benefit accrues from funding the actual programs of the group. Any assessment of the "democratic" goods that spring from such activities is unlikely to conclude that such activities contribute to the health of a democracy.

96 Thus, for instance, Waters notes that even institutes that promote law reform are not challenged as uncharitable so long as they exist within the walls of a university: *The Law of Trusts*, 588. Institutional considerations are perhaps too heavily relied on as proxies for both quality control and neutrality. Their overuse may explain why a clearly non-neutral body such as the Fraser Institute has charitable status, while Positive Action was rejected as non-neutral. Clearly neutrality alone cannot explain this difference in treatment. However, serious dangers attend the use of institutional structures as such proxies. Established institutions – perhaps especially well-funded ones – systematically overrepresent certain kinds of interests and underrepresent others. The use of such proxies will therefore skew the democratic debate in favour of thc status quo and will fail properly to register the concerns of the marginalized and disadvantaged who, by definition, are less likely to have their interests well-represented in such institutions. The use of such proxies therefore should raise serious concerns on democratic grounds.

97 "Does Political Theory Still Exist?" in P. Laslett and W.G. Runciman, eds., *Philosophy, Politics and Society 1*, 2nd ed. (London, 1962), 19.

9 The Doctrine of Political Purposes in the Law of Charities: A Conceptual Analysis

ABRAHAM DRASSINOWER

The doctrine of political purposes in the Canadian law of charities provides that political purposes cannot attain charitable status. The stated rationale for the doctrine is that courts have no means of judging whether a political purpose is for the public benefit, with the result that courts are unable to determine whether a gift to implement the purpose is a charitable gift.[1] This chapter presents a conceptual analysis of that rationale. Its orientation is conceptual in the sense that it approaches the doctrine of political purposes from the internal point of view of the doctrine's own presuppositions.

The doctrine rests on two related presuppositions. One is that a coherent distinction between political purposes and charitable purposes, between politics and charity, can be drawn. The other is that a non-political determination of the public benefit is possible.

This chapter attempts to develop two related propositions. One is that a non-political determination of the public benefit is possible only on the basis of a conception of a natural law – comprised of the minimal conditions of human dignity – to which positive laws must aspire to conform. The other is that the doctrine of political purposes can sustain its own coherence only if it lays claim to a standard that, at the very least implicitly, both invokes and evokes the minimal conditions of human dignity.

Thus I am here concerned less with the ways in which the doctrine has been applied than with the logical conditions of its very possibility. My central thesis is that, as a matter of coherence, the justification of the doctrine necessarily involves an appeal to the minimal conditions of human dignity. The central implication of this thesis is that the doctrine cannot be invoked to deny charitable status to trusts seeking the attainment of those conditions.

I first locate the doctrine of political purposes in the general terrain of the law of charities. I then describe a line of criticism that views the doctrine as incoherent. I respond by analysing the role of the minimal conditions of human dignity in the justification of the doctrine. I conclude with some remarks about the doctrinal adjustments entailed in such a justification and the difficulties that it would encounter.

I

In the law of trusts, the "beneficiary principle" means that a trust, in order to be valid, must benefit a person. "There must be somebody in whose favour the Court can decree performance."[2] A trust to benefit a purpose, as distinct from a person, is therefore invalid.[3] The absence of a beneficiary amounts to the invalidity of the trust.

Yet within the law of trusts, the law of charities carves out a terrain that suspends the operation of the beneficiary principle: "this doctrine does not hold good with regard to trusts for charity."[4] The law of charities upholds the validity of purpose trusts provided both that the purposes in question fall within legally recognized categories of 'charity' and that the purposes in question are for the benefit of the public.[5]

Generally speaking, the legally recognized categories of charity remain those formulated by Lord MacNaghten in *The Commissioners for Special Purposes of the Income Tax v. Pemsel*:[6] "'Charity' in its legal sense comprises four principal divisions: trusts for the relief of poverty; trusts for the advancement of education; trusts for the advancement of religion; and trusts for other purposes beneficial to the community, not falling under any of the preceding heads."[7] The legal and the popular meanings of "charity" are not the same. Regardless of whether it may be viewed as "charitable" in some extra-legal sense, a purpose, to be charitable at law, must fall within one of the above four heads.[8]

In addition to being charitable, the purpose in question must be of "public benefit." The requirement is stated by Lord Simonds in *Oppenheim*:[9] "It is a clearly established principle of the law of charity that a trust is not charitable unless it is directed to the public benefit. This is sometimes stated in the proposition that it must benefit the community or a section of the community. Negatively it is said that a trust is not charitable if it confers only private benefits."[10]

Thus "a trust established by a father for the education of his son is not a charity."[11] The trust falls within the "advancement of education" but it fails as a charitable trust because it lacks the element of public benefit. Similarly, a trust for holding masses in a monastery falls within the "advancement of religion" but lacks the element of public benefit.[12]

Thus not every purpose falling within the legally recognized categories of charity is necessarily a charitable purpose; the purpose must also be of public benefit. But while a charitable purpose is necessarily a purpose that is of public benefit, not every purpose capable of sustaining a finding that it is of public benefit is necessarily charitable. The purpose must also fall within the legally recognized categories of charity. Thus, for example, even on the assumption that it is of public benefit, a trust – as in *Re Astor* – for the "improvement of journalism" is not a charitable trust.[13]

In *Bowman*, Lord Parker of Waddington captures succinctly the requirements of "charity" and "public benefit" vis-à-vis the operation of the beneficiary principle: "A trust to be valid must be for the benefit of individuals, which this is certainly not, or must be in that class of gifts for the benefit of the public which the courts in this country recognise as charitable in the legal as opposed to the popular sense of that term."[14] A trust can avoid the operation of the beneficiary principle only where it satisfies the requirements of charity and public benefit.

Like the "charity" and "public benefit" requirements, the doctrine of political purposes restricts entry into the privileged terrain wherein the law of charities suspends the operation of the beneficiary principle. It further limits the scope of purposes that attract that suspension. It refuses validity to trusts for political purposes. "Political" purposes are not "charitable."

Lord Parker's formulation of the doctrine, and of the rationale for it, remains the most widely cited:

> The abolition of religious tests, the disestablishment of the Church, the secularisation of education, the alteration of the law touching religion or marriage, or the observation of the Sabbath, are purely political objects. Equity has always refused to recognise such objects as charitable. It is true that a gift to an association formed for their attainment may, if the association be unincorporated, be upheld as an absolute gift to its members, or if the association be incorporated as an absolute gift to the corporate body; but *a trust for the attainment of political objects has always been held invalid, not because it is illegal, for everyone is at liberty to advocate or promote by any lawful means a change in the law, but because the court has no means of judging whether a proposed change in the law will or will not be for the public benefit, and, therefore, cannot say that a gift to secure the change is a charitable gift.*[15]

Once a given purpose is deemed "political," it can no longer attract the privileges attendant on charitable purposes. Thus Lord Parker says that a gift for political purposes can be valid as an absolute gift but not as a trust. It must fail as a trust because it would amount to a purpose trust unable to make out the legal requirements of charitable status. The application of the doctrine reinstates, or rather refuses the suspension of, the operation of the beneficiary principle.[16]

II

The line of criticism of the doctrine of political purposes that I want to explore is that the doctrine must founder on the ultimate arbitrariness of any distinction between politics and charity. The central proposition of this criticism is that the doctrine is incoherent because it rests on an untenable distinction between political and non-political determinations of the public benefit – between political and charitable purposes.

In his seminal "Charitable Causes, Political Causes and Involvement," L.A. Sheridan observes:

> Lord Parker of Waddington, quoted with approval by two law lords in the *National Anti-Vivisection* Case, said: ' ... the court has no means of judging whether a proposed change in the law will or will not be for the public benefit ... ' That is true pathos. It is also a strain on credulity. There are few people better qualified than judges to assess whether a change in the law would be for the public benefit. Change of the law so as to prohibit vivisection is not a charitable object because vivisection was proved in court to be for the public benefit. Change of the law so as to reduce cruelty to animals is a charitable object because reduction of cruelty to animals was proved in court to be for the public benefit. In cases where the judge cannot make up his mind whether a change would be for the public benefit or not, he ought to hold the achievement of that change not to be a charitable purpose, for no purpose is charitable unless it is proved to be for the public benefit. But that need not govern, and does not in reality govern, cases where the judge can make up his mind on the issue of public benefit.[17]

For Sheridan, the posited difference between politics and charity is "a strain on credulity" because there is nothing specific or distinct about political purposes as such. If a court can determine whether any purpose is of public benefit, then a court can decide whether a political purpose is of public benefit. Political purposes may – more often than other purposes – present evidentiary difficulties preventing judges from making the required determination. Or political purposes may – more often than other purposes – involve issues in regard to which judges find themselves unable to make up their minds. But if such is indeed the case, then judges ought to say just that – that the requirement of public benefit has not been met, that public benefit has not been proved in court. There is no need to come up with an independent requirement that, in order to be charitable, a purpose must be non-political. There is no need to formulate an independent doctrine of political purposes. Rather, the problem of political purposes is but an aspect of the problem of public benefit. As Sheridan himself puts it, "This analysis is based on the theory that the question of whether a purpose fails to qualify as a charity because it is political is *simply one facet of whether it is a purpose which advances the public benefit* in a way that is within the spirit and intendment of the Statute of Elizabeth I."[18]

More recently, in "The Political Purposes Doctrine in Canadian Charities Law," Paul Michell writes along similar lines: "The rationale he [Lord Parker] advanced to support it – that the Court has no means of judging whether a proposed change in the law will or will not be for the public benefit – is inconsistent with courts' general assertion of their ability, indeed of their duty, to assess public benefit in the law of charities."[19] Like Sheridan's, Michell's criticism presupposes that political purposes are devoid of any specificity that renders judges genuinely unable to determine whether such purposes are of public benefit. It is only on the basis of some such presupposition that Michell can state that a court's refusal to determine whether a political purpose is of public benefit is inconsistent with that court's duty to make determinations of public benefit in accordance with the law of charities. If judges are able to make determinations of public benefit in respect of non-political purposes, then it follows that they must also be able to do so for political purposes. Their ability in regard to the one necessarily entails their ability vis-à-vis the other. Thus whereas the doctrine of political purposes asserts a distinction between political and non-political purposes, Michell – like Sheridan – denies such a distinction.

Sheridan and Michell may well be correct that, as a matter of bare capacity, the ability to decide public benefit in regard to non-political purposes must necessarily entail the ability to do the same for political purposes. But – to anticipate the viewpoint I develop below – the coherence or lack thereof of the doctrine has nothing to do with that proposition. In fact, to suggest that the proposition amounts to a criticism of the doctrine rests on a particular interpretation of that doctrine – namely, that the doctrine is about a judicial inability, as a matter of bare capacity, to make public benefit determinations in regard to political purposes. Yet the distinction between charity and politics implicit in the doctrine is not one between cases in which judges are able and cases in which they are unable to make such determinations. This line of criticism assumes that the kind of difficulty of which judges speak when they say that they have "no means of judging" whether a political purpose is of public benefit is a difficulty pertinent to the assessment of data – a difficulty present at an evidentiary level. But the difficulty pertains rather to their institutional role. Judges are saying not that they are unable to make such a decision but that it is not their place, as judges, to do so. What Sheridan and Michell criticize, therefore, is not the doctrine itself, but only their own view of it.

In *An Introduction to the Law of Trusts*, Simon Gardner presents a more accurate assessment of the problem:

> There is also the special rule that a trust cannot be charitable if its purpose is political. At one time the reason was said to be that judges could not tell whether such a trust's aim was beneficial to the public. If this was intended to mean that judges were incapable of making such decisions, it was implausible: they are not less capable than anyone else. Moreover, a purpose which the judges thus refuse to consider as beneficial in a political trust may be exactly the same as one which they actually accept as non-political in a non-political trust. For example, a trust to oppose the abolition of private education would not be charitable, since it is political; while a trust to found a (non-profit-distributing) private school would, as advancing education. The latter assumes that private education is beneficial to society; which is the very question which, in the former, the judges say they cannot decide. The difference is simply that the presence of an explicitly political element makes it more awkward than ever for the judges to take on the question: so they refuse to become involved at all. *The point, then, is not that judges cannot decide whether such purposes are beneficial, but that they should not: the impediment is constitutional, rather than intellectual.* Indeed, this is the explanation nowadays given by the judges themselves: as a matter of not usurping the function of the legislature or executive, or embarrassing the government in its dealings with other governments, or becoming involved in party politics.[20]

Thus Gardner grasps the doctrine as a matter not of intellectual capacities but of institutional roles.

But even in Gardner's own view, the distinction between charity and politics does not emerge as forcefully as it might have. This is because Gardner does not himself regard his distinction between the "intellectual" and the "constitutional" in an altogether serious light. When judges invoke that distinction, they presuppose a distinction between purposes in respect of which they can legitimately make public benefit determinations and purposes in respect of which they cannot – that is, between "charity" and "politics." For Gardner, however, all determinations of the public benefit are political. The only operative distinction is between "explicitly" and "implicitly" political determinations. The difference for him "is simply that the presence of an explicitly political element [in the latter] makes it more awkward than ever for the judges to take on the question: so they refuse to become involved at all."[21] The doctrine protects judges from the awkwardness of deciding explicitly political matters. It does not, however, genuinely or substantively distinguish arenas of action and judgment characteristic of political and non-political determinations of the public benefit respectively or of politics and charity. The difference between charity and politics, between charitable and political trusts, is merely between trusts in respect of which judges can avoid the appearance of making political determinations and trusts in respect of which they cannot. It is almost as if judges refuse to enter into politics only where and only when they cannot get away with it.

Gardner's position implies that all purposes are in the end political. The question of whether a given purpose is of public benefit requires reference to value-judgments, which are inherently political:

> Presumably, if they [courts and charity commissioners] had to, they could produce some sort of answer (albeit an incompetent one) about the relevant social costs and gains, but the business of putting comparable valuations on so many disparate possibilities, so as to establish the net balance of social advantage, would take them outside their province, and into that of the executive and legislature. Say we know that the cost of recognizing a particular trust to build a church as charitable would be the loss of one quarter of a new submarine (though in reality even this would be an impossibly simple equation): the question that then arises is whether the one or the other is the more desirable to society. The only way that we have of answering questions like this is through the electoral process. No doubt, in their personal capacity, the judges might have opinions on the subject, but our constitution does not leave it to them.[22]

Thus there neither is nor can be an arena within which the judiciary may legitimately make specifically legal, non-political determinations in respect of the public benefit. To make such a determination is rather to make a political determination. As Gardner puts it, "it is improper to expect the judges and Charity Commissioners to assess putative charities by undertaking a cost–benefit calculus from first principles themselves. Nevertheless, the law does leave the decision whether a trust qualifies as charitable with them. So how do they deal with the matter?"[23]

Gardner's answer reflects his view that all determinations in respect of the public benefit are "political" and therefore not for the judiciary: "The solution has been to insist that whether a trust is charitable or not is to a very large extent decided by rules of law, rather than by the assessment of its merits from first principles in the individual case. So the kinds of objects which are regarded as sufficiently beneficial to be worth the costs involved are defined by a rigid-looking set of rules (mostly developed by the courts themselves, through the system of precedent). The task of the judges or Charity Commissioners in individual cases is to match this definition against the objects of the particular trust in front of them so as to declare it charitable or otherwise, without having to go back to first principles."[24]

Gardner implies his answer in the very way in which he raises the question. He does not look for the fundamental conditions, if any, for the possibility of a non-political determination of the public benefit. Rather, he asks how judges can deal with an "improper" situation that contradicts their own position as judges. He answers, unsurprisingly, that judges hide behind rules of law, which permit them to make determinations that appear "merely" legal.

This point of view makes the entire jurisprudence of charity a kind of sleight of hand. Charity law is understandable only as an anomaly, as something that, strictly speaking, ought not to be there in the first place. It is a "dealing" with an impossible situation, a minimizing of an awkwardness that is scarcely relieved or hidden by outdated rules of law and rigid precedents. "We can see this phenomenon," Gardner writes,

> in *National Anti-Vivisection v. IRC* and *Gilmour v. Coats* ... . In both, ... being able to invoke a rule ultimately saved the judges from the awkwardness of having to rest their decision on a contentious value-judgment. In *National Anti-Vivisection Society* v. *IRC*, the rule in question – that disallowing political purposes – was adventitious in its applicability, but certainly convenient. In *Gilmour* v. *Coats*, the rule was directly concerned with the question in hand: whether a trust for a cloistered order is charitable. And significantly, the leading judgment contains a prominent appreciation of the role of rules in decisions about charitable status – even if they appear irrational. *The point is that questioning their rationality involves returning to the underlying merits: and that is the very thing that needs to be avoided.*[25]

Thus, in the end, and despite of his fundamental distinction between "intellectual" and "constitutional" impediments, Gardner's view of the political purposes doctrine is of the same kind as that of Sheridan and Michell. There is no basic difference – such as that claimed by judges – between charity and politics. Gardner renders the distinction as one between implicitly and explicitly political purposes. The doctrine distinguishes not between charity and politics – since charity is itself a political category – but between more or less inconspicuous or subtle and more or less obvious or crass politics.

III

I want to begin my response to the line of criticism sketched above by observing that trusts for political purposes are *sui generis*. They are refused charitable status neither because they do not fall within the legally recognized categories of "charity" nor because they are not of "public benefit." For example, a trust to eliminate poverty by way of the abolition of private property in the means of production is not a charitable trust. It is true, of course, that the alleviation of poverty is a legally recognized category of charity. It may even be true – or at least let us assume it to be true for the purposes of this example – that the abolition of private property in the means of production is of public benefit. None the less, the trust fails as a charitable trust. Its failure is a matter neither of "charity," nor of "public benefit," but of "politics." Political trusts are invalid because they are political. They are *sui generis* in the sense that the grounds of their invalidity cannot be referred to a failure to meet the requirements either of "charity" or of "public benefit."

The doctrine of political purposes is an independent doctrine. It expresses a third requirement constitutive of charitable status. This emerges clearly in *Anti-Vivisection*. In that case, Lord Wright, having found that the trust at issue failed for lack of public benefit, added: "But there is *another* and *essentially different* ground on which in my opinion it must fail; that is, because its object is to secure legislation to give legal effect to it. It is, in my opinion, a political purpose within the meaning of Lord Parker's pronouncement in *Bowman* v. *Secular Society*."[26] The requirement that a charitable trust be *non*-political is "essentially different" from the requirement that it be of public benefit. A trust that fails for being political is not by that token alone a trust that fails for lack of public benefit. The "non-political" requirement is not an aspect of the public-benefit requirement. It is rather a third requirement in its own right, independent from and additional to the requirements of "charity" and of "public benefit." The doctrine of political purposes is as autonomously constitutive of the legal meaning of charity as are the *Pemsel* categories and the requirement of public benefit.[27] Once ascertained, this autonomy of the doctrine allows us to make three observations.

First, the assertion that the court "has no means of judging" whether a political purpose is of public benefit is not a statement about lack of evidence required to make such determination. It is not as if the court, if it had the requisite evidence, would make a determination in respect of whether a given political purpose is of public benefit. On the contrary, even where the court does have the requisite evidence and could make an informed determination, it would still refuse either to make that determination or to use it in order to grant charitable status. The doctrine of political purposes would bar it from so doing.

Thus, in *Anti-Vivisection*, the court did, on the basis of the evidentiary record before it, determine that the purpose was not of public benefit. But, once again, this determination did not decide whether the purpose failed for being political. Had the court in *Anti-Vivisection* found on the basis of the evidentiary record before it that the purpose in question was indeed of public benefit, it would have still had to fail the trust on the essentially different ground of its being a political purpose trust.

The autonomy of the doctrine means that it is in principle possible for a court to determine that a given purpose is of public benefit yet fail that very purpose on the grounds that it is political. The point is that courts are unwilling to make public benefit determinations in regard to any political purpose. In *McGovern*, Justice Slade formulates the matter as follows: "From the passages from the speeches of Lord Parker [in *Bowman*], Lord Wright and Lord Simonds [in *Anti-Vivisection*] which I have read I extract the principle that the court will not regard as charitable a trust of which a main object is to procure an alteration of the law of the United Kingdom for one or both of two reasons: first, the court will ordinarily have no sufficient means of judging as a matter of *evidence* whether the proposed change will or will not be for the public benefit. Secondly, even if the evidence suffices to enable it to form a prima facie opinion that a change in the law is desirable, it must still decide the case on the *principle* that the law is right as it stands, since to do otherwise would usurp the function of the legislature."[28]

In *McGovern*, Justice Slade failed, as political, a purpose that "many will regard as of great value to humanity."[29] The purpose was – paraphrasing the headnote to *McGovern* – to secure the release of prisoners of conscience and procure the abolition of torture or inhuman or degrading treatment or punishment. This purpose was to be achieved by pursuit of changes in foreign legislation and reversals of administrative decisions of foreign governments. It is true that Justice Slade does not quite make the finding that the purpose in question *is* of great value to humanity. Still, his point is quite clearly that, even if he had, he would have still failed the trust for being political.

The doctrine addresses not the court's ability but the court's willingness to make determinations of public benefit in respect of political purposes. It addresses not evidentiary but normative concerns pertinent to the proper bounds not of the court's competence but of its jurisdiction. The point is that the court *as court* – or as matter of principle, or on penalty of usurping the function of the legislature – ought not to make determinations of public benefit in respect of political purposes.

Second, where a court does indeed make assessments of public benefit, it does not regard these as political determinations. What is public is not by that token alone political. It may be charitable rather than political. The distinction between politics and charity is simultaneously a distinction between politics and publicness. The doctrine of political purposes is in effect a refusal to reduce the public to the political. It represents an effort to differentiate the political from the public.

From the point of view implicit in the doctrine, political life is a particular aspect of public life. The political neither comprehends nor coincides with the public. On the contrary, the public contains the political. The public is wider in scope than the political. The category of the public is of a higher order of abstraction than that of the political. Both politics *and* charity fall within the scope of the public. The doctrine in fact traverses the public so as to bifurcate it into the terrains of politics and of charity.

Third, the doctrine of political purposes demarcates a terrain – that of charity – that is simultaneously public *and* non-political. It is only by dividing the public into politics and charity that a charitable trust can be said to be public but not political. To formulate a legal definition of charity is necessarily to insist that there are non-political aspects of public life. The distinction between politics and publicness is thus a condition for the very possibility of the legal concept of charity. Far from being a merely evidentiary aspect of the public-benefit requirement of charitable status, the doctrine of political purposes is rather both a reminder and an insistence that, as a matter of coherence, the law of charities stands or falls with the proposition that there is such a thing as a non-political determination of the public benefit.

IV

The concepts of "non-political" and of "political" in the doctrine of political purposes may be said to reflect a distinction between changes *in* society and changes *of* society. For example, whereas a purpose identified as the *relief* of the suffering of the poor in a given society is a *charitable* purpose, a purpose identified as the abolition of poverty by way of the transformation of the very structures that produce poverty is a *political* purpose. "Charity" seeks changes *in* society. "Politics" seeks changes *of* society. From this point of view, the doctrine is intelligible as a refusal to grant charitable status to purposes aimed at the alteration of fundamental social structures. The proposition that a court has no means of judging whether a political purpose is or is not for the public benefit is but a way of saying that a court will refuse to enter into what it views as a specifically political mode of argument – a mode of argument not about what *is* but about what *ought to be.*

The question of whether a given change *in* society is for the public benefit is a matter internal to that society itself. The proposed change may or may not be beneficial to the public, and the determination as to whether it is or is not is an exercise that does not require an appeal to standards that do not form part of the society's own structure. But, by contrast, the question of whether a proposed change *of* society is for the public benefit is not a question exclusively internal to that society itself. Of course, members of that society can pose the question from within that society. But, albeit from within it, they will be asking a different kind of question. This is because the determination of whether a proposed change *of* society is or is not for the public benefit requires an appeal to standards that do not form part of the society's own structure. The question posed after all deals with whether that structure ought to be changed – or about whether a change in that structure is of public benefit. Its determination requires a move from an intra- to an extra-societal standpoint – from a mode of argument about whether certain standards are met to one about what those standards ought to be. It is this move that the doctrine of political purposes opposes. The distinction between charitable and political purposes is thus between evaluation of public benefit via intra-societal standards (charity) and evaluation of public benefit via extra-societal standards (politics).

The proposition that a distinction between changes *in* and *of* society is at the heart of the doctrine of political purposes can be illustrated and supported by a brief comparative analysis of *McGovern* and *Everywoman's Health Centre Society (1988) v. Minister of National Revenue.*[30] Whereas in *McGovern* an uncontroversial purpose – the abolition of torture or inhuman or degrading treatment or punishment – is deemed political, in *Everywoman's* a controversial purpose – the operation of a free-standing abortion clinic – is found charitable. The juxtaposition of these two cases suggests that a purpose is "political" not so much because it is controversial but rather because it requires extra-societal standards for its evaluation in respect of public benefit.[31]

Justice Slade concludes his decision in *McGovern*:

In eloquent passages at the end of their addresses, Mr. Knox and Mr. Hoffman made reference to the classic problem facing Antigone, who believed that there are certain laws of men which a higher law may require them to disregard. Mr. Hoffman, by reference to the various international conventions to which this country has been a party, submitted that it is committed to the elimination of unjust laws and actions wherever these may exist or occur throughout the world.

Indisputably, laws do exist both in this country and in many foreign countries which many reasonable persons consider unjust. No less indisputably, laws themselves will from time to time be administered by governmental authorities in a manner which many reasonable persons consider unjust, inhuman or degrading. Amnesty International, in striving to remedy what it considers to be such injustices, is performing a function which many will regard as being of great value to humanity. Fortunately, the laws of this country place very few restrictions on the rights of philanthropic organisations such as this, or of individuals, to strive for the remedy of what they regard as instances of injustice, whether occurring here or abroad. However, for reasons which I think adequately appear from Lord Parker of Waddington's pronouncement in *Bowman's case* [1917] A.C. 406, the elimination of injustice has not as such ever been held to be a trust purpose which qualifies for the privileges afforded to charities by English law. I cannot hold it to be a charitable purpose now.[32]

The decision rests on the proposition that as a matter of principle – or on penalty of usurping the function of the legislature – the court has no means of judging the public benefit or lack thereof in respect of matters that require an appeal to standards external to the legal order within which it operates. It is this refusal to enter a specifically political mode of argument, or to adopt an extra-societal standpoint, that Justice Slade voices by way of his concluding reference to Antigone's legendary rebellion against the established order in the name of a higher law. His is a self-conscious refusal to enter into deliberations about this higher law. As a matter of principle, Justice Slade – as court – will not formulate the public benefit from the point of view of such higher law, and this is true even if we were to assume that he – as a man – himself thinks of this higher law as just and the laws it condemns as unjust.

It is true, of course, that Justice Slade formulates the concluding passages of his decision very carefully. At no point does he expressly say that the laws in question are in fact unjust. He tells us *not* that the laws that Amnesty International seeks to alter *are* unjust but rather that "many reasonable persons *consider* [them] unjust."[33] Similarly, he refrains from stating unequivocally that Amnesty International (AI) strives to remedy injustices and that, in so doing, it is performing a function of inestimable value. Rather, he writes carefully that "Amnesty International, in striving to remedy what it *considers* to be such injustices, is performing a function which *many will regard* as being of great value to humanity."[34]

Justice Slade's cautious formulations may raise some doubt as to whether the beliefs of "many reasonable persons" are sufficient evidence "for the court to form a prima facie opinion that a change in the law is desirable."[35] None the less, even on the abundantly safe assumption that the purposes to which AI devotes itself are thoroughly unquestionable in his own mind, his formulation of political purposes would still hold against its charitable status. As he puts it, "the elimination of injustice has not as such ever been held to be a trust purpose which qualifies for the privileges afforded to charities by English law."[36] Thus the case must be decided on the "*principle* that the law is right as it stands."[37] Justice Slade's point is that, where it requires a change in the law, not even the most uncontroversial of purposes can survive the application of the doctrine of political purposes in the law of charities.

In *Everywoman's*, in contrast, a controversial purpose – a purpose certainly more controversial than the abolition of inhuman and degrading treatment and punishment – none the less survives the application of the doctrine. *Everywoman's* involved the charitable status of a free-standing abortion clinic. The minister of national revenue stated that "there can be no benefit for the public, and therefore no charity, where, all other conditions being fulfilled, the object of the charity is controversial."[38] In granting the clinic's charitable status, Justice Decary held that the mere fact that an object is controversial does not thereby deprive it of charitable status:

With respect to the argument that there can be no charity at law absent public consensus, counsel for the respondent was unable to direct the Court

> to any supporting authority. Counsel was indeed at a loss to define what she meant by 'public consensus,' what would be the degree of consensus required and how the courts would measure that degree. To define 'charity' through public consensus would be a most imprudent thing to do. Charity and public opinion do not always go hand in hand; some forms of charity will often precede public opinion, while others will often offend it. Courts are not well equipped to assess public consensus, which is a fragile and volatile concept. The determination of the charitable character of an activity should not become a battle between pollsters. *Courts are asked to decide whether there is an advantage for the public, not whether the public agrees that there is such an advantage.*[39]

And more explicitly in respect of the doctrine of political purposes, Justice Decary stated: "In the case at bar, according to the evidence before the Court, the 'trust' is for dispensation of health care to women who want or need an abortion; it is not a 'trust' for alteration of the law with respect to abortion, nor is it a 'trust' for the political purpose of promoting the 'pro-choice' view. *The controversy that surrounds abortion should not deter us from seeking the true purpose of the clinic, which is to benefit women receiving a legally recognized health care service in a legally constituted clinic.* The record before us does not contain even the slightest hint that the Society engages or intends to engage in political activities and, as I have already noted, the respondent does not allege political purpose."[40] The holding supports the inference that, had the trust in question been for alteration of the law on abortion, or for the purpose of promoting the pro-choice point of view, then Justice Decary would have denied the clinic charitable status. In other words, the holding is not in favour of a worthwhile social goal such as the availability of abortion to women who need it. It is rather an affirmation of the charitable status of the purpose in question, "which is to benefit women receiving a *legally* recognized health care service in a *legally* constituted clinic."[41]

Justice Decary's point is not that the availability of abortion is *per se* a socially desirable goal. That might or might not be the case. His point is that the controversy surrounding a legally recognized health care service such as abortion is not sufficient to deprive the provision of that service of charitable status. His holding is not that the provision of abortion is charitable because abortion is a socially desirable goal. His point is that, notwithstanding the attendant controversy, it is charitable because it is a legally recognized health service.

Justice Decary states that "courts are asked to decide whether there is an advantage for the public, not whether the public agrees that there is such an advantage."[42] This statement does not imply that the public benefit of a given purpose can be determined by reference to standards external to the society in which the purpose is sought, but means only that the intra-societal standards that orient the determination of whether a given purpose is of public benefit are not to be found in "public consensus." Justice Decary's distinction between the question of whether there is an advantage to the public and that of whether the public thinks that there is advantage does not suggest a movement from an intra-societal to an extra-societal standpoint of judgment. At issue is nothing more than a claim about where one looks, within any given society, in order to find the pertinent intra-societal standards. "Public consensus" is not where one finds that standpoint.

Thus, in *Everywoman's*, Justice Decary looks to patterns of public spending, not to public consensus, to determine whether there is an advantage for the public: "the fact that physicians performing abortions in these clinics are paid with provincial funds spent in accordance with federal legislation, would tend to confirm that the performance of abortions at these clinics does not offend any public policy. Public funds, in my view, are presumed to be spent in accordance with public policy and absent any challenge to the validity of that public spending I am not ready to assume that public funds are not spent for the public good."[43] It is true that Justice Decary is willing to go against public consensus – or at least to dismiss its relevance – in his determination of the public benefit. But his standpoint does not thereby become extra-societal. He states that the public does not always know what the public benefit is. But this is a far cry from saying that a trust for the alteration of law or for political purposes is or can be a valid charitable trust. Were abortion illegal, then a trust to change that law would itself be a political trust devoid of charitable status. In fact, Justice Decary's holding is perfectly compatible with the proposition that a trust to promote the pro-choice point of view, even in a society where the provision of abortion is legally recognized as a health care matter, could still be itself viewed as a political trust.

From this point of view, *Everywoman's* does not deny but rather confirms the doctrine of political purposes as formulated in *McGovern*. There is little in *Everywoman's* that supports the proposition that trusts for the alteration of laws, whether just or unjust, are charitable in nature. For while *Everywoman's* widens the field of the charitable by refusing to constrain it to public consensus, it does not suggest that the alteration of law is a charitable purpose. Justice Decary avoids going as far as the proposition that courts, when confronted with a trust for the alteration of law, should ask whether the law in question is patently unjust.

Thus *Everywoman's* does not challenge the proposition at the heart of *McGovern* – namely, that the court must decide on the principle that the law is right as it stands. Both cases exhibit a self-conscious refusal to enter into determinations of the public benefit at the level of a political mode of argument, focused not on whether the standards of a given social formation are met but on what those standards ought to be. Both cases show that the doctrine proceeds along the lines of the distinction between changes *in* society and changes *of* society.

V

Thus the proposition that a non-political determination of the public benefit is possible admits formulation in terms of a distinction between changes in society and changes of society. The doctrine of political purposes views a purpose as charitable where the determination of the public benefit of that purpose can take place by reference to intra-societal standards; and it views a purpose as political where determination of its public benefit necessitates reference to extra-societal standards.

But this distinction, while useful as far as it goes, does not establish the conditions for the possibility of a non-political determination of the public benefit. The problem is that the proposition that intra-societal determinations of public benefit are non-political is only partially true. They are non-political in the sense that they take place within a more-or-less established or settled horizon of fundamental standards, principles, or co-ordinates. Yet they are highly political in the sense that the horizon that orients them is itself a political fact.The appearance of this horizon as a settled non-political set of co-ordinates is nothing more than an indication of the depth of the political victory that this very horizon embodies. From this point of view, there is no such thing as a non-political determination of the public benefit. Intra-societal standards are after all political. They are not non-political merely by virtue of their being intra-societal. À la Gardner, the distinction between charity and politics is itself political.

The central implication of this viewpoint is that the court's principled refusal to enter into a specifically political mode of argument turns out to be devoid of a principled basis. For the principle that, for fear of usurping the function of the legislature, the court should decide matters on the basis that the law is right as it stands, turns out to be little more than a functional necessity constitutive of a particular view of a legitimate legal and political system. Therefore it is itself a political principle. In the absence of justification, the courts' "principled" deference to the legislature even in the face of patently unjust laws is little more than politics masquerading as law. One can hardly justify the distinction between charity and politics by way of an appeal to a particular politics.

The sense that the political purposes doctrine is incoherent is thus explained by the circularity that besets its rationale as currently formulated. The sense of incoherence stems from the fact that while the political purposes doctrine seeks to present itself as a principled refusal to enter into the political arena, this refusal is itself reflective of a particular political viewpoint.

The unveiling of this shortcoming, however, does not by any means necessarily amount to a condemnation of the political purposes doctrine. On the contrary, it raises the fruitful question of whether the justificatory lacuna at heart of its rationale as currently formulated can be remedied. In this regard, the very sense of incoherence surrounding the political purposes doctrine already suggests the direction to be followed.

It may well be the case that, as the current formulation of the political purposes doctrine has it, the court must decide on the principle that the law is right as it stands. But this need not mean that the "law" in question is any and all laws – regardless of how unjust – proclaimed by an absolutely sovereign legislature. There is no other way to say it but simply to insist that the idea of "law" cannot be reduced to that of positive law. There is no conceivable idea of "legality" which recognizes no limits, which suggests that "legality" is compatible with tyranny. Law without boundaries is not law at all. It is true, of course, that the contents and nature of the higher law to which Antigone appeals as against the laws of men are not often, if ever at all, above the fray of political contestation. But the point here is not about the particular content of the limits that legality entails. It is rather about the recognition that such limits, whatever their content, do exist.

What rings hollow about Justice Slade's judgment in *McGovern* are not the stoic heroics with which he renounces the claims of fundamental normative intuitions in the name of an institutional duty to defer to the pronouncements of the legislature. What rings hollow, rather, is that however problematic the concept of a higher law may be, however politicized may the determinations of what is wrong and what is right may be, *McGovern* is a case where the limits have been reached, where fundamental normative intuitions ought to find expression. To refuse to voice such intuitions in a case involving a *patently* unjust law[44] is entirely to forgo the possibility of a non- political determination of the public benefit. Such failure deprives the doctrine of political purposes of its very ground. Justice Slade cannot assume, in the name of a distinction between charity and politics, a point of view that, by refusing altogether the operation of non-political normative intuitions, in effect undoes the very distinction that it purportedly vindicates.

The coherence of the doctrine thus calls for an effort to formulate the minimal standards of a natural law that no conceivably civilized community could violate. It goes without saying that even when claimed as minimal standards, the contents of natural law are by no means devoid of controversy. But it also goes without saying that the patently unjust laws at stake in *McGovern* are violations of those minimal standards. These standards are non-political not in the sense that they are above the relentless fray of political contestation, but rather in the sense that any community that routinely violates them neither has nor deserves the prospects of a lasting existence. They are non-political in that they are fundamental minimal presuppositions of any – to borrow Aristotle's phrase – "polis which is *truly so called.*"[45] They are basic minimal presuppositions of politics rather than violence, of contestation rather than war.

The transformation *of* society is a charitable act where that society stands in violation of minimal standards of natural law. This may well be the as-yet-unheeded lesson of Antigone: politics and charity coincide where what is at stake is not so much the improvement of the world as the attainment of minimal conditions of human dignity.[46]

VI

The foregoing entails the following adjustment to the doctrine of political purposes – a trust for the attainment of a political purpose is invalid, *unless it can be shown to seek to remedy a situation that violates the minimal conditions of human dignity.*

This adjustment does not so much modify as complete the doctrine. The adjustment is not externally imposed but rather internally required, as a matter of coherence, by the doctrine itself. The distinction between charity and politics dissolves where even minimal conditions of human dignity are precluded from restricting and defining the legitimate scope of the political. To put it otherwise, the distinction between non-political and political determinations of the public benefit dissolves where even the most fundamental of normative intuitions responsive to the minimal conditions of human dignity are disowned in the name of an absolutely sovereign legislature. Deference to an absolutely sovereign legislature even in the face of violations of the minimal conditions of human dignity contradicts the assertion, central to the doctrine of political purposes, that a non-political dimension of public life can be meaningfully demarcated. The proposition that a court has no means of judging whether the attainment of the minimal conditions of human dignity is of public benefit is at odds with a doctrine that, in asserting a distinction between charity and politics, cannot help but both restrict and define the legitimate scope not only of charity but also of politics. Hence the doctrine cannot sustain its own coherence in the absence of an exception pertinent to the attainment of the minimal conditions of human dignity.

At stake in the doctrine is a definition not only of charity but also of politics. To suggest that the political is what the legislature happens to take as the object of its attention at any given time is to propose that the distinction between charity and politics is itself political. Hence the doctrine cannot afford to leave the demarcation of the scope of the political to the legislature any more than it can afford to vitiate the very possibility of a coherent distinction between charity and politics. On penalty of precluding the possibility of a genuinely non-political aspect of public life, the doctrine cannot leave the definition of politics to politics itself. For to do so is to suggest that the terrain of the non-political is but a contingent concession that politics may undo at will.

In this regard, for the doctrine, the minimal conditions of human dignity delineate – in as innocuous a manner as possible – the minimal features of the non-political. If the minimal conditions of human dignity cannot provide boundaries for the legitimate scope of politics, then nothing can. Politics would in that case be devoid of limits. But if anything is indeed non-political in the sense of amounting to a limit imposed on the legitimate scope of politics, then so are the minimal conditions of human dignity. This does not mean that politics cannot, as a matter of fact, venture beyond its legitimate scope, in violation – as in the case of the patently unjust laws cited in *McGovern* – of the minimal conditions of human dignity. However, when politics does overflow its legitimate boundaries, the doctrine of political purposes cannot, unless it would concede the very distinction between non-political and political on which it rests, render non-charitable the purpose of (re-)attaining the minimal conditions of human dignity on the grounds of its being political.

The insertion of an exception for "minimal conditions of human dignity" into the doctrine does not so much modify the doctrine as clarify the meaning of "politics" that it presupposes. Once it is clearly ascertained that the doctrine cannot leave the meaning of "politics" to politics itself, then a distinction arises between politics as a matter of fact – comprising what the political sovereign happens to have as the object of its attention at any given time, including violations of the minimal conditions of human dignity – and politics proper, comprising what the sovereign may have as the legitimate object of its attention at any given time. Where the sovereign overflows its legitimate boundaries, its acts are political as a matter of fact but not properly political. From this point of view, the (re-)attainment of the minimal conditions of human dignity is a political purpose only descriptively, not normatively. But since the doctrine presupposes a normative definition of "politics," it cannot be invoked in order to deprive that purpose of charitable status.[47]

The exception for "minimal conditions of human dignity" is a clarification and not a modification because it acknowledges that the doctrine must operate on the basis of a normative definition of the political. It is not so much an exception as an adequate formulation of an aspect of what "politics" must mean under the doctrine. The minimal conditions of human dignity are the minimal conditions of any politics truly or properly so-called. No normative view of the political can afford to disown them.

The court's principled deference to the legislature – i.e., the view that the court must work on the principle that the law is right as it stands – must itself be justified. The institutional differentiation of courts and legislature is but an aspect of the rule of law. Whatever form its justification ultimately assumes, it cannot avoid attentiveness to the minimal conditions of human dignity. For such avoidance would render the rule of law consistent with the violation of the very standards that, minimally, it is intended to protect.

McGovern is wrongly decided precisely because it invokes the rule of law as an injunction to defer to conditions that patently violate it. The point is not that the court ought to take an activist stance towards the legislature. The point is only that the court cannot, by way of the doctrine of political purposes, consistently invoke the rule of law in order to deny charitable status to a trust seeking to remedy its violation.

VII

The foregoing has sought to establish that the doctrine of political purposes must, as a matter of coherence, incorporate a normative concept such as that of the minimal conditions of human dignity. What about the specific content of that concept? If we grant that courts cannot deny charitable status to efforts to remedy violations of the minimal conditions of human dignity by citing the doctrine of political purposes, how do they identify those violations? What is the specific content of those minimal conditions?

The answer may well be a matter of fact. It pertains to the application, rather than the formulation, of appropriate principles. One might say that the question engages matters of judgment rather than of theory. Nevertheless, we can gain a great deal – and perhaps not only at the level of coherence – by posing the question in the concreteness of the circumstances surrounding any given case. By way of conclusion, I want to illustrate that proposition through a brief comment on *Jackson v. Phillips*.[48]

Jackson involved three bequests: first, "the preparation and circulation of books, newspapers, the delivery of speeches, lectures, and other such means, as ... will create a public sentiment that will put an end to negro slavery in this country"; second, "the benefit of fugitive slaves who may escape from the slaveholding states of this infamous Union from time to time"; and third, "to secure the passage of laws granting women, whether married or unmarried, the right to vote; to hold office; to hold, manage, and devise property; and all other civil rights enjoyed by men."[49]

Justice Gray held that the first two bequests, but not the third, are charitable. As regards the first bequest, he held:

> The authorities already cited show that the peaceable redemption or manumission of slaves in any manner not prohibited by law is a charitable object. It falls indeed within the spirit, and almost within the letter, of many clauses in the Statute of Elizabeth. It would be an anomaly in a system of law, which recognized as charitable uses the relief of the poor, the education and preferment of orphans, marriages of poor maids, the assistance of young tradesmen, handicraftsmen and persons decayed, the relief of prisoners and the redemption of captives, to exclude the deliverance of an indefinite number of human beings from a condition in which they were so poor as not even to own themselves, in which their children could not be educated, in which marriages had no sanction of law or security of duration, in which all their earnings belonged to another, and they were subject, against the law of nature, and without any crime of their own, to such an arbitrary dominion as the modern usages of nations will not countenance over captives taken from the most barbarous enemy.[50]

As regards the second bequest, Justice Gray held: "A bequest for the benefit of fugitive slaves is not necessarily unlawful. ... To supply sick or destitute fugitive slaves with food and clothing, medicine and shelter, or to extinguish by purchase the claims of those asserting a right to their service and labor, would in no wise have tended to impair the claim of the latter or the operation of the Constitution and laws of the United States; and would clearly have been within the terms of this bequest."[51]

Yet Justice Gray denied charitable status to the third bequest, on grounds that resemble the doctrine of political purposes: "This bequest differs from the others in aiming directly and exclusively to change the laws; and its object cannot be accomplished without changing the Constitution also. Whether such an alteration of the existing laws and frame of government would be wise and desirable is a question upon which we cannot, sitting in a judicial capacity, properly express any opinion. Our duty is limited to expounding the laws as they stand. And those laws do not recognize the purpose of overthrowing or changing them, in whole or in part, as a charitable use. This bequest, therefore, not being for a charitable purpose, nor for the benefit of any particular persons, and being unrestricted in point of time, is inoperative and void."[52]

I have argued that the doctrine of political purposes, because its justification involves an appeal to the minimal conditions of human dignity, cannot be invoked to deny charitable status to trusts seeking the attainment of those conditions. In *Jackson*, the question is whether the alteration of laws denying women civil and political rights enjoyed by men amounts to an attainment of the minimal conditions of human dignity. To be sure, there is no guarantee that, had Justice Gray posed that question explicitly, he would have answered it affirmatively. But its very posing would have at the very least opened that possibility – rescued it from the untenable assumption that, merely because the laws are what they are, it is not charitable to seek to change them.

NOTES

I would like to thank Jim Phillips for his helpful comments on earlier versions of this chapter. Thanks also to Nick Devlin, Jeremy Freiberg, Alkis Kontos, Mia London, and Jill Manny for their comments. The responsibility is all mine.

1 *Bowman and Others* v. *Secular Society*, [1916-17] 1 All ER at 18.

2 *Morice v. The Bishop of Durham* (1804), 32 ER 656 at 658. See also *Re Astor's Settlement Trusts*, [1952] 1 All ER 1067. The beneficiary principle permeates the following "familiar definition" of a trust: "A trust is an equitable obligation binding a person (who is called a trustee) to deal with property over which he has control (which is called the trust property), for the benefit of persons (who are called the beneficiaries or *cestuis que trust*), of whom he may himself be one, and anyone of whom may enforce the obligation." Cited from *Underhill's Law of Trusts and Trustees* in D.W.M. Waters, *Law of Trusts in Canada*, 2nd ed. (Toronto: Carswell 1984), 5.

3 Thus, for example, in *Re Astor* a trust for the "improvement of journalism" is found invalid.
4 *Morice*, at 658.
5 See, for example, *Morice* and *Oppenheim* v. *Tobacco Securities Trust Co. Ltd. And Others*, [1951] AC 297. Keeton and Sheridan's well-regarded definition of a trust incorporates the possibility that a trust may benefit an "object permitted by law": "A trust is the relationship which arises wherever a person (called the trustee) is compelled in equity to hold property, whether real or personal, and whether by legal or equitable title, for the benefit of some persons (of whom he may be one and who are termed beneficiaries) or for some object permitted by law, in such a way that the real benefit of the property accrues, not to the trustees, but to the beneficiaries or other objects of the trust." See L.A. Sheridan, *Keeton and Sheridan's The Law of Trusts*, 12th ed. (Chichester: Barry Rose, 1993), 3.
6 [1891] AC 531 (HL).
7 At 583. Lord MacNaghten did not fail to mention the Charitable Uses Act, 1601, 43 Eliz. 1, c. 4, known as the Statute of Elizabeth, whose preamble contained a listing of charitable purposes, which was rendered in modern English by Justice Slade in *McGovern and Others v. Attorney General and Another*, [1981] 3 All ER 493 (Ch.D.) at 502–3: "The relief of aged, impotent and poor people; the maintenance of sick and maimed soldiers and mariners, schools of learning, free schools, and scholars in universities; the repair of bridges, ports, havens, causeways, churches, seabanks, and highways; the education and preferment of orphans; the relief, stock, or maintenance of houses of correction; marriage of poor maids; supportation, aid, and help of young tradesmen, handicraftsmen, and persons decayed; the relief or redemption of prisoners or captives; and the aid or ease of any poor inhabitants concerning payments of fifteens, setting out of soldiers, and other taxes."
8 The Supreme Court of Canada adopted the *Pemsel* categories in *Guaranty Trust Company of Canada v. Minister of National Revenue*, [1967] SCR 133. Debate abounds regarding the appropriateness of the *Pemsel* categories, as well as that of the preamble of the Statute of Elizabeth. In *Re Laidlaw Foundation* (1984), 48 OR (2d) 549 (Div. Ct), Justice Southey, favouring "a more liberal definition of charity," (at 586) stated: "... I think it is highly artificial and of no real value in deciding whether an object is charitable for courts in Ontario today to pay lip-service to the preamble of a statute passed in the reign of Elizabeth I" (at 582). See also *Incorporated Council of Law Reporting for England and Wales v. Attorney General*, [1972] Ch. 73. For discussion of the issues involved, see Phillips, chapter 7 in this volume; Moran, chapter 8 in this volume; Ontario Law Reform Commission (OLRC), *Report on the Law of Charities*, 2 vols. (Toronto 1996),

1: chaps. 6, 7 and 8; and E.B. Bromley, "Contemporary Philanthropy: Is the Legal Concept of 'Charity' Any Longer Adequate?" in D.W.M. Waters, ed., *Equity, Fiduciaries and Trusts 1993* (Scarborough, Ont.: Carswell 1993), 59–98. The Supreme Court of Canada's most recent case dealing with the definition of charity – *Vancouver Society of Immigrant and Visible Minority Women v. Minister of National Revenue,* [1999] 1 SCR 10 – retains the traditional framework.

9 See also *National Anti-Vivisection Society v. Inland Revenue Commissioners,* [1947] 2 All ER 217 (HL); *Gilmour v. Coats,* [1949] AC 426 (HL); *Re Scarisbrick,* [1951] Ch. 623 (CA).

10 *Oppenheim,* 305.

11 Ibid., 306.

12 See *Gilmour.* At 454–5, Lord Reid states: "The question for decision is whether or not the purposes of that community are charitable in the legal sense of that word. It is admitted, and properly admitted, by the appellant that it is not enough to make this gift charitable in the legal sense that it is a gift for religious purposes: the appellant can only succeed by showing that the gift involves a benefit to the public."

13 In *Anti-Vivisection,* Lord Wright writes at 220: "It is not necessary at this time of day to observe that not every object which is beneficial to the community can be regarded as charitable. The legal significance is narrower than the popular. ... Even if the object were in some sense beneficial to the community, it would still be necessary to discover that it fell within the spirit and intendment of the instances given in the Statute of Elizabeth. Healthy and manly sports are certainly in fact beneficial to the public, but apart from special concomitants are not generally entitled to qualify as charitable objects." Thus it is a commonplace of the law of charities that a purpose must benefit the public in a way that is "within the spirit and intendment" of the Statute of Elizabeth.

14 *Bowman,* 18.

15 Ibid., 18 (emphasis added).

16 In *McGovern,* at 509, Justice Slade states that trusts for political purposes include "(inter alia) trusts of which a direct and principal purpose is either – (i) to further the interests of a particular political party, or (ii) to procure changes in the laws of this country, or (iii) to procure changes in the laws of a foreign country, or (iv) to procure a reversal of government policy or of particular decisions of governmental authorities in this country, or (v) to procure a reversal of government policy or of particular decisions of governmental authorities in a foreign country."

Recently, in *Human Life International of Canada v. Minster of National Revenue,* [1998] 3 FC 202, leave to appeal dismissed, 21 Jan. 1999, *Supreme Court Bulletin,* 1999, 102, the Federal Court of Appeal included "advocacy of opinions on various important social issues" as a political purpose. Justice Strayer stated: "The same [*Bowman*] rationale leads me to conclude that this kind of advocacy of opinions on various important social issues can never be determined by a court to be for a purpose beneficial to the community. Courts should not be called upon to make such decisions as it involves granting or denying legitimacy to what are essentially political views: namely, what are the proper forms of conduct, though not mandated by present law, to be urged on other members of the community?"

17 L.A. Sheridan, "Charitable Causes, Political Causes and Involvement," *Philanthropist* 2, no. 4 (1980), 12.

18 Ibid., 16 (emphasis added).

19 P. Michell, "The Political Purposes Doctrine in Canadian Charities Law," *Philanthropist* 12 (1995), 6.

20 S. Gardner, *An Introduction to the Law of Trusts* (Oxford: Clarendon Press, 1990), 107–8 (emphasis added).

21 Gardner, *Law of Trusts,* 108.

22 Ibid., 102.

23 Ibid., 105.

24 Ibid., 105.

25 Ibid., 105–6 (emphasis added).

26 *Anti-Vivisection,* 224 (emphases added). The judgments in *Anti-Vivisection,* including Lord Porter's dissent, clearly distinguish between the public benefit and the non-political requirements. They posit that the question of whether a given purpose is of public benefit is distinct from the question of whether that purpose is political.

Lord Porter writes (at 226): "The difficulties of the present case arise firstly in determining what is of benefit to the public and who is to determine that question, but a not less difficult, though perhaps less subtle, question is whether the objects of the society are political within the meaning of that word as used by Lord Parker in *Bowman's* case."

Similarly, Lord Normand (at 240), having found that the National Anti-Vivisection Society is an association for political purposes, discusses the "other question" at issue in the case: "This [other] question, which in my opinion only arises on the assumption that the society is held not to be a political body, is in brief whether it is sufficient for it to prove that its purpose is to alleviate or prevent the suffering of animals or whether it must prove that on balance its purpose is beneficial to mankind."

And Lord Simonds (at 232), with whom Viscount Simon concurs (at 218–19) in a brief note to that effect, cites with approval – and with the express intention of elaborating on the meaning of Lord Parker's pronouncement in *Bowman* – a passage from *Tyssen on Charitable Bequests.* Apart from the question of whether it provides a flawless interpretation of the position formulated by Lord Parker in *Bowman,* this passage clearly differentiates the issue of public benefit (i.e., whether the proposed change in the law is desirable) from that of political purpose (i.e., whether it is proper for the court to make the public benefit determination in question): "It is a common practice for a number of individuals amongst us to form an association for promoting some change in the law, and it is worth our while to consider the effect of a gift to such an association. It is clear that such an association is not of a charitable nature. However desirable the change may really be, the law could not stultify itself by holding that it was for the public benefit that the law itself should be changed. Each court in deciding on the validity of a gift must decide on the principle that the law is right as it stands."

27 Thus in her recent text *The Law of Trusts* (Concord: Irwin Law, 1997), 64, E.E. Gillese lists the absence of political purpose as a requirement of a charitable trust.

28 *McGovern*, 506 (emphases added).

29 Ibid., 519.

30 [1992] 2 FC 52 (FCA).

31 For commentary on *McGovern*, see C.J. Forder, "Too Political to be Charitable?" *Conveyancer and Property Lawyer* July–Aug (1984); and R. Nobles, "Politics, Public Benefit and Charity," *Modern Law Review* 45 (1982), 704. For commentary on *Everywoman's*, see J. Phillips, "Case Comment: *Everywoman's Health Centre v. Minister of National Revenue*," *Philanthropist* 11, no. 1 (1992), 3.

32 Ibid., 519.

33 Ibid. (emphasis added).

34 Ibid. (emphasis added).

35 Ibid., 506.

36 Ibid., 519.

37 Ibid., 506 (emphasis added).

38 *Everywoman's*, 67.

39 Ibid., 68 (emphasis added).

40 Ibid., 70 (emphasis added).

41 Ibid. (emphasis added).

42 Ibid., 69.

43 Ibid., 68.

44 This is the position adopted in OLRC, *Report*, 153, 221. For commentary on ibid., see J. Phillips, "The Ontario Law Reform Commission and the Legal Meaning of Charity," *Philanthropist* 14, no. 2 (1997), 45.

45 *The Politics of Aristotle*, trans. and ed. Ernest Barker (Oxford: Oxford University Press, 1958), 119 (emphasis added).

46 The fact that *McGovern* involved an effort to change law and policy in a foreign jurisdiction is not relevant to this aspect of the argument. The minimal conditions of human dignity are not geographically specific.

Because its justification involves an appeal to the minimal conditions of human dignity, the doctrine of political purposes cannot be invoked to deny charitable status to trusts seeking the attainment of those conditions. *McGovern* is wrongly decided because that is exactly what it does.

This view is indebted to but different from that adopted by the OLRC, *Report.* In the view of that document, "the distinction between politics and charity parallels the distinction between politics and law [in a liberal democracy]: the debate about the content of the good and a determination of the good itself are two different things" (153). Hence *McGovern* is a "special case" in that "there is truly no debate" about the validity of its purpose: "advocating and acting lawfully to aid and abet the release of prisoners of conscience and the cessation of torture are obviously valid determinations of the good, even if they involve trying to persuade others and are therefore also political" (at 221).

In my view, the purpose in *McGovern* is best grasped not as an obviously valid determination of the good itself but as a *sine qua non* of any meaningful debate about the content of the good. The release of prisoners of conscience and the cessation of torture are not a necessary conclusion but a presupposition of truly political debate. *McGovern* is a special case not because its purpose is good from the point of view of some external standard but because the doctrine of political purposes itself both posits and presupposes a view of "politics" as necessarily respectful of the minimal conditions of human dignity. This way of framing the matter would make it more difficult to suggest, as does the OLRC, *Report* (210), that seeking "to benefit others through the removal of legal or social obstacles to the full recognition of their human dignity" is not a charitable purpose. For commentary on this aspect of the OLRC's report, see Moran, chapter 8 in this volume.

47 This does not mean that the purpose is necessarily charitable. It means only that the purpose cannot be denied charitable status on the grounds of its being political under the doctrine of political purposes.

48 (1867), 96 Mass. 539.

49 *Jackson,* 541–2.

50 Ibid., 568.

51 Ibid., 569–70.

52 Ibid., 571.

10 Religion, Charity, and the Charter of Rights

JIM PHILLIPS

This chapter examines the relationship between the law of religious charity in Canada and the Charter of Rights.[1] Specifically, it asks whether three doctrines of charities law in the area of religion may violate sections of the Charter. Because the Charter applies only to governments and to legislatures, I pose these questions in the context of the registration of charities under the Income Tax Act.[2] The chapter has two sections. The first looks at two definitional matters – the definition of religion in Canadian charities law and that of "public benefit" in religious charity. This analysis is a prerequisite to the second section, which assesses these definitions against two provisions of the Charter – the guarantee of freedom of religion and conscience in section 2(a) and the equality provision, section 15.

While I am not the first to write on this subject, it is remarkable how little Canadian academic writing or case law exists in the area of religion as charity, and perhaps even more so that there has been so little serious attention paid to the constitutional issues discussed here.[3] This situation will soon change, however, as the issue of definition is presumably currently front and centre in the Canada Customs and Revenue Agency's (CCRA) continuing consideration of the Church of Scientology's application for registration,[4] and the department, and perhaps the courts as well, will have to grapple with the question.

THE DEFINITION OF RELIGION IN CHARITIES LAW

The Meaning of "Religion" in the Advancement of Religion

Because of the dearth of Canadian cases on the meaning of religion I assume in this section that its meaning, for the purposes of charitable registration under the Income Tax Act, is that given to the term by the (largely English) case law. The Income Tax Act, of course, does not define even "charity," let alone religion. But two reasons suggest that English law is the right place to look. First, the Federal Court of Appeal, which ultimately decides the meaning of charity for the purposes of the act, has invariably looked to English law for the meaning of charity generally, including, of course, the fact that "the advancement of religion" is one of the particular categories of charity. The Supreme Court of Canada has recently approved this approach.[5] While neither court has said anything about religion, there is no reason to suppose that either would depart from that guidepost in this area.

Second, the definition employed by the CCRA, laid out in its pamphlet *Registering a Charity for Income Tax Purposes*,[6] effectively reproduces the principal aspects of the English-derived definition: "This category refers to promoting the spiritual teachings of a religious body, and maintaining the doctrines and spiritual observances on which those teachings are based. *There has to be an element of theistic worship, which means the worship of a deity or deities in the spiritual sense. To foster a belief in proper morals or ethics alone is not enough to qualify as a charity under this category.* A religious body is considered charitable when its activities serve religious purposes for the public good. The beliefs and practices cannot be what the courts consider subversive or immoral." The key aspects of this definition, which I elaborate on below, are two-fold: there must be a deity, and religion means something different from the inculcation of "morals" or "ethics."

I turn then to the English and, to a much lesser extent the Canadian, cases on the definition of religion. Most commentators assert that English law on charities is marked by a large measure of "toleration" in this area – that the law of charity has not, at least for some time, preferred one religion to another.[7] Subject to what I say in the next section about the problem of public benefit, this is largely true. All varieties of Christianity have been held to qualify as charitable within the category of the advancement of religion, including sects very much on the fringe of the faith,[8] as have all the world's other major religions. There is some older authority to the effect that the religion must be monotheistic,[9] although a leading text argues that the law no longer draws a distinction between monotheism and polytheism and the charity commissioners have recently confirmed this.[10] Only religions that are in some way harmful to the public interest or clearly "bogus" would now be excluded.

English law, however, has drawn two clear lines to demarcate the meaning of "religion." It has held both that a "religion" requires the presence of a god and worship of that god and that religion is fundamentally different from what might be termed "ethical systems of belief." The first point can be traced back to *Bowman v. Secular Society*,[11] in which the House of Lords said that religion must include some form of deism. This view was upheld in the more recent case of *Regina v. Registrar-General, Ex Parte Segerdal.*[12] Although this was not a charities case, it was closely related, for the Church of Scientology wanted one of its English properties to be registered as a place of religious worship under the Places of Worship Registration Act. All three judges of the Court of Appeal held that Scientology was not operating a place of religious worship. Although there were gatherings of people and services according to the creed of Scientology were held, a "place of meeting for religious worship" was one "where people come together as a congregation or assembly to do reverence to God." The court stated that it need not be the Christian God – it may be another, or "an unknown God." But "it must be reverence to a deity." Scientology did not qualify, for it was "more a philosophy of the existence of man or of life, rather than a religion," for "religious worship means reverence or veneration of God or of a Supreme Being."[13]

There are other cases to the same effect.[14] The leading modern case, which stands both for the proposition that a god is required and for the distinction between "religion" and "ethics," is *Re South Place Ethical Society.*[15] At issue was an organization whose stated objects were "the study and dissemination of ethical principles, and the cultivation of a rational religious sentiment." The organization was committed to "the discovery of truth through intellect," not a supernatural being, although its members were agnostics, not atheists. The court held that not only did there need to be a God, but that religion included the notion of worship of that God: "two of the essential attributes of a religion are faith and worship; faith in a god and worship of that god." Thus even if it was possible to substitute something else for belief in the supernatural, it was hardly likely that that something else would be worshipped. Justice Dillon stated: "Religion, as I see it, is concerned with man's relation with God, and ethics are concerned with man's relation with man. The two are not the same, and are not made the same by sincere inquiry into the question: what is God? If reason leads people not to accept Christianity or any known religion, but they do believe in the excellence of qualities, such as truth, beauty and love, ... their beliefs may be to them the equivalent of a religion, but viewed objectively they are not religion." The court did, however, find the organization to be charitable, on the grounds that it advanced education and was beneficial to society in general.[16]

The only exception to the need for a god appears to be Buddhism. Perhaps to avoid debates about whether Buddhists do recognize a god, or more likely because it would be invidious to exclude one of the world's major religions, the charity commissioners have accepted Buddhism as qualifying, and in *R. v. Registrar-General*, discussed above, Lord Denning would have made an exception for a Buddhist temple as being a place of worship, whether or not Buddhists could be said to believe in god. The charity commissioners have recently held that religion necessarily requires belief in a "supreme being" and worship of that supreme being, although they have also said that that does not mean a "god" in the Western sense of the term.[17]

Not all common law jurisdictions have taken the same approach. American law is somewhat confusing, because of the constitutional protection of religion and because the term has been defined in a variety of contexts. But overall the definition used for the purposes of the Internal Revenue Code is broader, especially given the fact that Scientology is considered a religion, which it is not in Britain.[18] More centrally to the common law definition, the courts in both Australia and New Zealand have not insisted on the need for faith in, and worship of, a God, although they have (probably) defined religion as distinct from humanism.[19] There is no evidence, however, that Canadian law has departed from the English standard. Canadian courts, though like their English counterparts upholding a variety of forms of religion as charitable,[20] have said very little indeed about the meaning of religion in charities law. There is a hint in *Re O'Brien*[21] that religion entails the worship of a god, although the court was considering there the meaning of bequests "to each and every church in the Town and County of Yarmouth." Chief Justice Ilsley of Nova Scotia held that the testator meant "a congregation ... associated together for the worship of God". In the more recent case of *Re Russell*[22] the issue was whether a bequest to the Edmonton Lodge of the Theosophical Society created a charitable trust. Justice Stevenson simply followed the English case of *Berry v. St Marylebone Borough Council*[23] in holding that theosophy was not a religion. He did not say why it was not: the entirety of the judgment on this point states that "[t]he evidence before me shows that the society, and theosophy, is not a religion." We are left to assume that he adopted the reasons in *Berry* – namely, that theosophy did not involve worship of a god and was "the teaching of a doctrine ... of a philosophical or metaphysical conception."[24]

The Canadian jurisprudence on the meaning of religion in charity law is therefore scanty and tells us very little. But if we can discern anything, it is that, as in English law, "religion" for these purposes requires a god and worship of that god and that religion is different from other forms of ethical belief. Religion has been defined as involving faith and worship in non-charities cases also.[25] The Ontario Law Reform Commission has recently approved this notion. Following a review of much of the case law canvassed here, it suggests an "outline" of a definition, as follows: "the worship and knowledge of God, the pastoral and missionary propagation of an established theology, and observances and practices."[26] Finally, as we saw above, the CCRA clearly bases its practice on the dominant themes enunciated in the English cases – the need for a god and worship of that God, and a distinction between religion and ethics. The only exception seems to that, again as in England, Buddhism is accepted, whether or not one can say that Buddhists believe in a God.[27]

Public Benefit and Religion

Having established that existing case law, and the CCRA's practice, suggest some limitations on what constitutes "religion" in the law of charities, I turn now to consider which religious practices do not qualify as charitable on the grounds that they do not provide a public benefit. Here again I rely largely on English cases, given the paucity of Canadian ones. Although Canadian law is probably different from English in one major respect, the general question of whether some practices do not provide a public benefit remains a live issue, certainly in the content of the Income Tax Act.

There is not space here for a general discussion of public benefit and religion. But before I examine the problem at issue here, I note that the courts have been shy about articulating why it is that religion *per se* provides a public benefit. Most cases deal with whether some particular purpose *advances* religion; thus there is ample case law on what one might call the infrastructure of religion.[28] I am not myself religious: I was raised in the Church of England and later became an atheist, and neither designation makes a person religious! But I do understand that infrastructure is hardly the essence of religion; that must be located in beliefs and practices. One would therefore assume that if the law of charity accepts the utility of religion it would do so on the basis that all religious beliefs and practices have public benefit. And that must be an assumption – a matter not to be proved but, if I may be excused the expression, to be taken on faith. As the Ontario Law Reform Commission (OLRC), which strongly supports the inclusion of religion in the lists of charity as a universal human good, has succinctly noted, "depending on how one values the good of religion, few or none of the benefits of a gift for the advancement of religion will have practical utility."[29] Donovan Waters has made the same point, noting that "there is essentially nothing in religion which can be proved objectively in court to promote the observable well-being of persons or to be for the observable benefit of the public."[30]

Despite the apparent logic of the notion that all purely religious practices should be treated equally, it is not the case that the law of charities, at least the English version, accepts all religious observances and practices as providing a public benefit and therefore charitable. The leading English case, *Gilmour v. Coats*,[31] says otherwise. At issue was a gift to a Roman Catholic priory of Carmelites – contemplative nuns who did nothing outside the priory but lived a cloistered life of prayer and devotion. The House of Lords held that the gift was not charitable because it lacked any element of public benefit. The religious services held at the priory were not open to the public, and the nuns provided no other "services" to the community. There was no "infrastructure" aspect to provide public benefit, and the court held that the purpose was therefore not charitable. Along the way it rejected an argument that it should accept Catholic views on the value of intercessory prayer and that that would provide sufficient public benefit. Lord Reid held that while the law treated all religions alike, it could show "no preference ... to any church" and must "remain neutral." He stated: "The law of England has always shown favour to gifts for religious purposes. It does not now in this matter prefer one religion to another. It assumes that it is good for man to have and to practise a religion but where a particular belief is accepted by one religion and rejected by another the law can neither accept nor reject it. The law must accept the position that it is right that different religions should each be supported irrespective of whether or not all its beliefs are true. A religion can be regarded as beneficial without it being necessary to assume that all its beliefs are true, and a religious service can be regarded as beneficial to all those who attend it without it being necessary to determine the spiritual efficacy of that service or to accept any particular belief about it."

Thus the court found that while all religions qualified as charitable for the purposes of the "advancement of religion," not all religious purposes provided a public benefit. Whether a purpose did so was for the court to decide on the evidence before it, and it could not simply accept the Catholic church's view that intercessory prayer was beneficial. Nor could it accept an alternative argument – that the convent provided a public benefit in the form of edification to those outside. While edification may in some cases constitute public benefit, "there must be some limit to the kind of indirect instruction or edification which will constitute a public benefit," and in this case "the public benefit is too remote."

The essential message from *Gilmour v. Coats* is that while providing the infrastructure of religion is charitable, and while holding religious services in public provides a public benefit which makes them charitable also, religious practices carried out "privately" do not count in the law of charity, for there is no way to establish that they provide a public benefit. The case is often cited as settling the issue of whether or not public benefit is assumed for religion. But whatever it resolved doctrinally, the decision is obviously open to much criticism.[32] There are two major problems with the reasoning, one of logic and the other of practical common sense. First, logically, the judgment in *Gilmour* is entirely self-contradictory. How can charities law assert that public benefit from religion is a thing to be proved rather than assumed and that not all religious purposes are charitable, and then concede that such matters are beyond legal proof and steadfastly ignore the issue of benefit in the vast majority of cases?

The second problem is equally obvious. By accepting without question the pubic benefit from, and thus the charitability of, a host of "infrastructural" projects, while at the same time saying that there will be occasions when the public benefit of prayer or other ritual will be questioned, the law prefers means to ends, trappings to essentials. It is charitable to build churches, to support missionaries, or to publish religious works, and none of this requires that the law accept a single tenet of the beliefs underlying the activity. Yet those beliefs are what motivate the activity, and thus the law supports the cosmetic apparatus of religion and not its essential purpose. The OLRC's views are surely right: "if one accepts that the advancement of religion is charitable per se, as Lord Reid ... seems to, then one does not value religion mainly as a means to some other good or for its by-products."[33]

No matter how wrong the *Gilmour* decision seems to be, however, it lives on in English law. Two recent cases have applied it. In one the charitability of masses for the souls of the dead was at issue, and the court decided that they were acceptable, because they were held in public and because the money paid for the mass helped to support the clergy who officiated.[34] Another case concerned a small Protestant sect that met in private houses. The court argued that this fact rendered it non-charitable, although it also held that the religious services were an ancillary purpose to the sect's more public faith-healing work, which was held to be charitable. In addition, the charity commissioners have recently used the fact that Scientology's observances are essentially private as a ground for holding it not to be charitable.[35]

Gilmour v. Coats has never been the subject of judicial consideration in Canada, although there is a line in the Supreme Court of Canada's judgment in *Cameron v. Church of Christ Scientist*, a pre-*Gilmour* case, that seems to be in accord with it.[36] It is unlikely that the Canadian courts would follow it down the road of declaring private masses to be non-charitable, for there is a line of cases accepting them.[37] Some of these cases argue that whatever adherents think advances their religion is good enough to prove public benefit, while others refer to the special position of the Catholic church in Quebec. Donovan Waters has suggested that there is some uncertainty in this area because the court decided the leading case on masses, *Re Hallisy*,[38] on the basis that it was following an earlier English case, *Bourne v. Keane*,[39] which had held gifts for masses to be charitable. In fact *Bourne* merely said that they were legal.[40] However, one much more recent Canadian decision has followed *Hallisy*,[41] and it is difficult to think that a Canadian court today would have a problem with private masses.

This does not mean, however, that Canadian law clearly accepts all forms of religious observance as charitable. The CCRA's definition of religion, quoted above, asserts: "A religious body is considered charitable when its activities serve religious purposes for the public good," and this suggests that the agency, and the courts, would not assume, but would inquire into, public benefit. More important, the CCRA does apply *Gilmour v. Coats* when adjudicating claims for registration, even though it is not required to do so often.[42] We should also note that the agency's definition, laid out above, includes examples of particular purposes which advance religion that are examples of activity "in the world" – "promoting ... spiritual teachings," "maintaining ... doctrines and spiritual observances." And the general definition is followed by examples of "other activities which advance religion" of the same nature – "organizing and providing religious instruction," "performing pastoral and missionary work," and "establishing and maintaining buildings for worship and other religious use."[43]

Given that *Gilmour* is good law in Canada, it is subject to a third criticism in addition to those noted above, which could be considered internal to charities law. What *Gilmour* effectively does is to express a preference for religions that do not include private observance. Its effect is to draw distinctions between religions. The *Gilmour* doctrine may therefore be susceptible to public law challenges that it discriminates between religions. And that is the subject to which I now turn.

THE DEFINITION OF RELIGION AND THE CHARTER OF RIGHTS

State Action

The Charter of Rights applies to governments and legislatures in Canada. While this requirement has been interpreted to mean that it does not apply directly to the common law or equity when either is being used to decide private disputes, and thus not to the law of charitable trusts, the fact that the federal government, in its administration of the charity provisions of the Income Tax Act, uses common law definitions of charity brings those definitions within the scope of section 32 of the Charter.[44] The exemption from taxation of the income of charitable organizations, and their ability to issue receipts for donations, is therefore sufficient "state action" to engage the Charter.

Violations of Sections 2(a) and 15

What follows is an assessment of the kinds of arguments that might be offered for why the issues of definition and public benefit discussed above may create a problem in the context of the Charter. I do not believe that there is enough case law on either section 2(a) or 15 to make definitive statements. But there is enough to suggest that the issues would be taken seriously.

The relationship between the Charter and the law of religious charity involves three distinct, albeit related, inquiries. First, does a definition of religion that requires the presence of a god and worship of that god contravene either or both of the guarantees of freedom of religion and equality? Would the courts find that "religion" for the purposes of the Charter had a wider meaning than religion in charities law and that the failure to adopt that wider meaning represents an invalid distinction in the provision of tax privileges? Second, would the doctrine that excludes private devotion from religion in charities law similarly contravene either section of the Charter? Third, would the preference for "religion" at all over other forms of belief, including overtly non- or anti-religious belief, violate either section? This third inquiry might appear to be not too different from the first – the line between "religious" belief that did not involve a god and non-religious belief might be too fine to worry about – but I wish to keep it separate because it arguably makes charity law's preference for religion an invalid form of "establishment" of religion.

While I consider the effect of both sections 2(a) and 15 here, I concentrate on the former. That is the section that most clearly engages "religion," and some of the definitional questions, particularly the meaning of "religion" in the constitution, are common to both sections. Before one could decide whether there was a violation of the right to equal treatment irrespective of religion, one would need to decide what the meaning of "religion" in section 15 is. There is no requirement that the meaning given to the term in section 2(a) be the one adopted for section 15, but it seems very likely that the courts would want to achieve substantial consistency between the two.

First, let us look at what the Supreme Court of Canada has said about the scope and meaning of section 2(a), which provides: "Everyone has the following fundamental freedoms: (a) freedom of conscience and religion." The Court has considered this right in a number of cases, but the most relevant one remains its first decision on the subject, *R. v. Big M Drug Mart*.[45] In defining "freedom of religion," Chief Justice Dickson's judgment for the Court began by saying that its "essence" is "the right to entertain such religious beliefs as a person chooses, the right to declare religious beliefs openly and without fear of hindrance or reprisal, and the right to manifest belief by worship and practice or by teaching and dissemination." Clearly there is nothing in charities law that interferes with such rights.

However, the Court went on to find that freedom of religion includes more than simply the right to hold religious beliefs and exercise religious practices. It also means "the absence of coercion or constraint," because if a person is pushed one way or another he or she is not choosing freely. And such coercion includes "indirect forms of control which determine or limit alternative courses of conduct." Thus freedom of religion means "both the absence of coercion and constraint, and the right to manifest beliefs and practices"; that is, "no one is forced to act in a way contrary to his beliefs or his conscience." Chief Justice Dickson then applied this principle to the statute at issue, the federal Lord's Day Act: "To the extent that it binds all to a sectarian Christian ideal, the Lord's Day Act works a form of coercion inimical to the spirit of the Charter and the dignity of all non-Christians. In proclaiming the standards of the Christian faith, the Act *creates a climate hostile to, and gives the appearance of discrimination against, non-Christian Canadians.* It takes religious values rooted in Christian morality and, using the force of the State, translates them into a positive law binding on believers and non-believers alike. The theological content of the legislation remains as a subtle and constant reminder to religious minorities within the country of their differences with, and alienation from, the dominant religious culture" (emphasis added). And the chief justice added: "The protection of one religion and the concomitant non-protection of others imports disparate impact destructive of the religious freedom of the collectivity."

The Court therefore made two moves that appear to implicate two of the questions about charities law raised above: public benefit and the definition of religion as requiring deism. First, the Court defined freedom of religion as more than the right to exercise one's religion; it defined it to include the absence of coercion. Second, the Court's notion of what coercion entails is broader than legislation which compels one form of belief; it includes a prohibition of, in the words just quoted, "[t]he protection of one religion and the concomitant non-protection of others." Such government action "imports disparate impact destructive of the religious freedom of the collectivity." Coercion was clearly present in the case of laws on Sunday observance at issue in *Big M Drug Mart.* And while coercion *simpliciter* seems the wrong term to apply to the preference for deistic religions and the effects of discrimination against religious practices that fail the test of public benefit, the wider meaning of coercion – protection of one religion and non-protection of another – seems engaged by charities law.

It is not difficult to argue that financial support that favours some forms of religious belief over others violates the rights of those left out. If, for example, the Income Tax Act were to include in its definition of religion only Christianity, or only Protestantism, then surely we would find this to violate the religious freedom of the excluded adherents. The state sends a clear message to those not preferred – that their religion is less worthy than others. Adopting to the Income Tax Act what Chief Justice Dickson said in the passage above from *Big M Drug Mart,* we can say that charities law "creates a climate hostile to, and gives the appearance of discrimination against," those religions that are excluded. While this is obviously the case in the hypothetical examples used here, the distinctions drawn by the law in its definition of religion and in its understanding of public benefit are different only in degree, not in principle.[46]

Some admittedly limited support for this argument comes from *Adler v. Ontario*,[47] in which it was contended that Ontario's provision of public funding for Catholic schools violated both the freedom of religion and the equality rights of Jewish and Christian fundamentalist parents. The Supreme Court found that it did not. But Justice Iacobucci premised his conclusion for the majority of the Court entirely on the fact that section 93 of the Constitution Act, 1867, mandated the funding of Catholic schools in Ontario, and was itself part of the historical political compromise that brought about Confederation. Section 93 thereby formed a "comprehensive code of denominational school rights," which admittedly gave special status to some and denied it to others. To allow the arguments based on the Charter would be both to expand the scope of the historical compromise in an unacceptable way and to allow one part of the constitution to trump another.

Justice Iacobucci's judgment in *Adler* does not overtly discuss the question of whether, without the existence of section 93, such government action would violate the Charter. Indeed he said that section 93 is "immune from Charter scrutiny."[48] But the judgment seems, if anything, to see it as self-evident that there would otherwise have been a violation. On two occasions Justice Iacobucci quoted a phrase from Justice Wilson's judgment in *Reference Re Bill 30*[49] to the effect that special status for one religion "sit[s] uncomfortably with the concept of equality embodied in the Charter," but he insisted that "it must nonetheless be respected."[50] In addition, he noted at the end of his section on funding of religious schools that it was only the fact of government expenditures on Catholic schools that was protected; other legislation – presumably that which drew distinctions on Charter-protected grounds not covered by section 93 – would invoke scrutiny.[51]

Thus, to the extent that charities law prefers certain religious practices within its own definition of religion by offering a benefit only to them, it discriminates against other practices. It does so, of course, not directly, but through the meaning of "public benefit." But this fact would not matter, for the Court has consistently said, and indeed said in *Big M Drug Mart*, that both the purpose and the effect of legislation should be looked at to see if it contravenes the Charter.[52]

However, if we are also to conclude that the deism requirement is a violation of the *Charter* under section 2(a), there is one more hurdle to overcome. We must also find that the definition of religion in that section is broader than the one in the Income Tax Act. If it was not, charities law would simply be congruent with constitutional law. This, however, should not be a difficult task. There is nothing in the

Charter which suggests that religion means deism. And in *Big M Drug Mart* the Court discussed the purpose behind the provision on freedom of religion. It recognizes "the centrality of individual conscience and the inappropriateness of governmental intervention to compel or to constrain its manifestation." According to Chief Justice Dickson, "[t]he values that underlie our political and philosophic traditions demand that every individual be free to hold and to manifest whatever beliefs and opinions his or her conscience dictates." Religious beliefs are, "in many ways, paradigmatic of conscientiously-held beliefs and manifestations and are therefore protected by the *Charter*.... Whatever else freedom of conscience and religion may mean, it must at the very least mean this: government may not coerce individuals to affirm a specific religious belief or to manifest a specific religious practice for a sectarian purpose."[53] This approach to the purposes underlying the religion clause surely suggests that the Court would not restrict the meaning of religion in the *Charter* to deistic beliefs. The section protects "whatever beliefs and opinions" a person's "conscience dictates"; it does not protect them only when they have their foundation in deism.

Does the preference for "religion" at all over other forms of belief also violate section 2(a)? Obviously if this argument were accepted it would render otiose the preceding discussion; that is, if a distinction between religion and non-religion is unacceptable, then surely so is that between religions, based on deism. We might make two arguments here. The first, and easiest and strongest, is that the special status of religion elevates it over "conscience" in an unacceptable manner. In *Big M Drug Mart* Chief Justice Dickson held, as part of his discussion of the underlying purposes of section 2(a), that "[e]qually protected, and for the same reasons, are expressions and manifestations of religious non-belief and refusals to participate in religious practice."[54] Thus if one accepts all of the arguments made above – that the section is about more then free exercise of beliefs and prohibits compulsion and that state support for religion is a message of preference and a form of compulsion, then the distinction between religion, with or without deism, and non-religion, or "conscience," is as invalid as that between different forms of religion. Indeed, Chief Justice Dickson came close to saying this in *Edwards Books*: "The purpose of s. 2(a) is to ensure that society does not interfere with profoundly personal beliefs that govern one's perceptions of oneself, humankind, nature, *and in some cases,* a higher or different order of being" (emphasis added).[55] A belief in "a higher ... order" is thus only one of the forms of belief protected by the section.

A second, alternative argument, albeit related, is that the preference for religion, especially as it involves government spending, is an invalid form of "establishment." Unlike the American Bill of Rights, the Charter contains no "establishment clause."[56] But there are some hints in the cases that section 2(a) would capture at least some forms of establishment. In *Big M Drug Mart* the Court did essay a somewhat inconclusive discussion of establishment. On the one hand, Chief Justice Dickson noted that "preferential treatment of, or State financial support to, particular religions or religious institutions" constituted perhaps a type of establishment. On the other hand, he conceded that section 29 of the Charter (nothing to derogate from other constitutional rights of denominational schools) and section 93 of the Constitution Act, 1867 (protecting denominational school rights existing at the time of Confederation), might show that there was no anti-establishment principle. He left it that "[t]he acceptability of legislation or governmental action which could be characterised as State aid for religion or religious activities will have to be determined on a case by case basis."[57] Thus state aid might be unacceptable.[58] There is not space here for a full discussion of establishment, which I leave to the constitutional experts. In any event, the issue can be avoided by sticking with the first argument – that the preference for religion over conscience is a form of compulsion clearly excluded by section 2(a), whether or not it is also "establishment."

I have devoted a good deal of space to section 2(a), but it seems likely that at least some of the aspects of charity law discussed here would also involve violations of section 15 of the Charter – equality rights. Section 15 provides: "Every individual is equal before and under the law and has the right to the equal protection and equal benefit of the law without discrimination and, in particular, without discrimination based on race, national or ethnic origin, colour, religion, sex, age or mental or physical disability." An analysis of section 15 would first decide what the relevant comparison groups are and then ask whether there has been unequal treatment.[59] In the case of public benefit, the analysis seems straightforward: religions that charities law itself considers within the definition of religion are treated differently, with private observances not receiving the equal benefit of the law.

In the case of the requirement of deism, one would have to deal with the argument that like is being treated alike: all deistic religions receive charitable status, all non-deistic ones do not. Thus a non-deistic "religion" denied registration is being treated like all other non-deistic religions. The response to this must be that the definition of religion in section 15 is broader than its meaning in charity law, and the arguments for doing so would be the same as those discussed above with reference to section 2(a). As I noted above, while there is nothing in the constitution which requires that the meaning of religion in section 15 be the same as in section 2(a), it seems highly likely that the Court would want to make the definitions consistent and would look to section 2(a) jurisprudence to guide it. If it did, it would find that some religions are indeed treated differently from others.

The distinction between religious and non-religious forms of belief is perhaps less easy to deal with under section 15. It seems unlikely that the Supreme Court would say that "religion" in section 15 means "religion and conscience," for while both terms appear in section 2(a), only one is present in section 15. Thus the law does not provide unequal treatment within an enumerated ground, but unequal treatment between an enumerated and an unenumerated ground. The way forward might be to use the fact that the grounds in section 15 are not exhaustive and include "analogous grounds" to those enumerated.[60] Presumably "conscience" is a closely analogous ground to "religion," especially as both terms appear in section 2(a). If that were accepted it would set up what I think is a unique situation to date with regard to section 15 – a law that prefers one ground in that section to another. One would then argue that there cannot be unequal treatment between grounds. Defenders of the law, of course, would argue either against inclusion of an analogous ground or that when the government prefers an enumerated category to an unenumerated one, whether analogous or not, it does not violate the Charter. Opponents of the current law might be forced to rely on section 2(a) for this part of the challenge.

Section 1

If a violation of either section 2(a) or section 15 were found in each of the ways discussed, it is unlikely that the distinctions drawn by the law of charity would be saved by section 1 of the Charter, which provides that the rights guaranteed are subject "to such reasonable limits prescribed by law as can be demonstrably justified in a free and democratic society." The test laid down by the Supreme Court for analysing section 1 is two-pronged. First, it must be established that "the legislative objective which the limitation is designed to promote must be of sufficient importance to warrant overriding a constitutional right" – it must represent a "pressing and substantial concern." Second, "the means chosen to attain those objectives must be proportional or appropriate" to the ends. This proportionality test has three components: "the limiting measures must be carefully designed, or rationally connected to the objective; they must impair the right as little as possible; and their effects must not so severely trench on individual or group rights that the legislative objective ... is outweighed by the abridgment of rights."[61]

I assume that each of the three violations discussed above has been found and deal in turn with how the courts might engage section 1 in each case. First, in the case of "public benefit," the government would presumably argue, with reference to the first part of this test, that the law of charities assumes that the courts must be satisfied that there is indeed a public benefit to every charitable purpose and that that requirement could function as a valid legislative objective. Even if that were good enough for the first part of the *Oakes* test, however, the government could not hope to prove that "the limiting measure" was "rationally connected to the objective." It might be rationally connected in the abstract, but no proof could be offered, for the simple reason that, as the courts have stated on numerous occasions, including in *Gilmour v. Coats*, there is no way of proving in court the efficacy of any religious belief, whether or not it is carried out in public.

The second violation is the preference for religions that worship a god over those that do not. Here the obvious problem for section 1 is that once it has been decided that the right itself is infringed, it is very difficult to see what the pressing and substantial concern is – other than distinguishing between types of religions, the very objective which infringes the right. One cannot hold out a constitutionally invalid distinction as the objective that permits a limitation of rights under section 1.[62]

The government might try to go further, and offer as an objective the need to distinguish "true" religion from "sham" operations. Assuming that this was sufficient to pass the first stage of the *Oakes* test, there would be all kinds of problems with proportionality. Requiring deism is not a rational connection, for it has nothing to do with whether the religion is genuine or not, and at the same time it impairs rights substantially, for it excludes much more than "sham" religions. While it would not be the job of the court to develop a constitutionally valid definition of religion for purposes of charity law that would deal with the problem, the one offered by the Australian High Court in *Church of the New Faith* would eliminate most, if not all, sham religions.[63] More important, charities law has other internal devices to deal with essentially commercial operations or colourable religions –

most obviously, the political purposes doctrine and the requirement that there not be private benefit.

The third violation – the invalid distinction between religion and other forms of conscience – creates the same difficulty with respect to section 1 as the second. That is, the objective would be to prefer religion – the same thing as the violation. Here the government might try to situate the objective in fiscal policy. It might say that the striking down of the distinction it now uses will leave it without any way of denying special tax status to a large number of applicants. That is, every applicant that has as its principal purpose the propagation of a view about how people should live is entitled to special tax status, with the courts having effectively converted "the advancement of religion" into "the advancement of beliefs and values."

An obvious difficulty with this argument is that "fiscal" concerns justifying limitations on rights have not been received very favourably in previous cases.[64] As important, it would be a mistake to believe that for practical reasons the court should somehow use section 1 to preserve some form of distinction in the administration of tax privileges. The "floodgates" problem is either a red herring or proof of the unacceptability of the distinctions that the law now draws. It seems quite unlikely that large numbers of organizations will be created devoted to new religions or to ethical societies just because it is now possible to do so. Even if some were, the government subsidy is not a direct payment to registered organizations, but a tax credit for donations that they receive. It thus rewards success with a kind of matching grant. To get the tax subsidy the organization would have to persuade people to give to it. And if it did so, then would that not suggest that the current law is indeed invalid, discouraging some people from supporting their preferred form of belief? In short, it is not likely that any great change will occur through a broadening of preferred categories, but if it did, that would be a good thing. And if the government decided that it could not afford to give credits for donations to too many organizations, it could treat all forms of belief equally by supporting none.

Charter Values

To this point I have assumed that we are dealing with the Income Tax Act. But the principles of charities law that I elucidated above and tested against the provisions of the Charter emerged, of course, largely in the context of charitable trusts. If a trust for an apparently religious purpose failed the test of public benefit, or was not considered to come within the definition of religion, it was deemed a non-charitable purpose trust and was therefore void under the general rule that purpose trusts are invalid. While these rules of law, as common law (or, more accurately, equitable doctrines) governing disposition of private property, would not be directly affected by the Charter, they might be indirectly influenced by it. The route to this is the idea, stated first by the Supreme Court in *Dolphin Delivery*, that the common law should be interpreted in a manner consistent with Charter values. In that case the Court, after holding that the Charter does not apply to the common law when it governs a dispute between private parties, went on to say: "I should make it clear ... that this is a distinct issue from the question whether the judiciary ought to apply and develop the principles of the common law in a manner consistent with the fundamental values enshrined in the Constitution. The answer to this question must be in the affirmative."[65]

It is arguable that this doctrine could be invoked so that some or all of what I have said above about the Charter and the Income Tax Act could apply to the law governing which trusts were charitable and which were not. I am straying somewhat from my principal subject here and will not repeat the arguments made above. I simply make two points about their application in this context.

First, the limited indications that we have about the application of "Charter values" suggest that the courts would be reluctant to take on every aspect of the Charter analysis sketched above and apply it to the common law. That would be effectively to achieve by the back door the same result that might be accomplished through the front door in the context of the Income Tax Act. In *Hill* Justice Cory limited the ambit of this doctrine to "incremental revisions to the common law" and urged caution in its use. Charter "rights" were different from Charter "values," and an assessment of the common law in the light of the latter required a flexible balancing of the principles underlying the common law with the values of the Charter.[66]

Second, and related, the likelihood of the doctrine's being employed will perhaps increase as one moves along the continuum of issues discussed above. That is, the argument about Charter values would surely have particular force in dealing with public benefit. This seems a particularly egregious distinction between otherwise "valid" religions, and one that would be hard to justify by opposing religious equality with underlying common law principles, precisely because those underlying principles about public benefit are not coherent and have been much criticized. Conversely, the doctrine would perhaps have least force when dealing with the preference for religion over other forms of ethical belief, for that preference is a deeply embedded part of the law of trusts and represents an expression of charity law's historical preference for religion, and thus amendment should perhaps be achieved by legislative intervention. To use Charter values in this context would not be to "develop" the common law but to change it fundamentally, and in *Hill* Justice Cory said that "far-reaching changes to the common law must be left to the legislature."[67]

The deism requirement perhaps sits somewhere in the middle, more of an "incremental" development than doing away with the public benefit distinction between religions but less of a fundamental reorientation than equating religion and non-religious forms of belief. And here the courts could perhaps draw not just on the Charter value of religious equality but also on judgments of the Australian and New Zealand courts to suggest that there is no longer any reason for the distinction.[68] And there would be concomitantly little principled justification underlying the common law rule. Dealing fully with this issue requires much more space than I have here. But the problem may affect the law of religious charitable trusts in the future.

CONCLUSION

Certain long-standing principles of the Anglo-Canadian law of religious charity are now, at the very least, constitutionally suspect. There are doubtless observers who find in this fact a source of regret, yet a further example of the baneful effects of the "rights culture" that has so dramatically entered into Canadian law in the last two decades. In response to such sentiments, I would make two points.

First, whether one likes it or not, the issues discussed in this chapter represent neither the first nor the last occasion on which "public" law has invaded, or will invade, what has traditionally been seen as a matter of purely "private" law, immune from constitutional or similar considerations. Nearly a decade ago the Ontario Court of Appeal struck down discriminatory provisions in a charitable trust as offensive to public policy, a decision with which few people would take issue, given the content of those provisions.[69] And it is very likely that in the future the Charter will at least form the basis of challenges to other aspects of charities law. For example, it has been argued unsuccessfully that the political purposes doctrine offends the right to freedom of expression,[70] and while that position is unlikely to be accepted by the courts, the CCRA's uneven application of the doctrine may lead to a successful challenge.[71] Another example of the possible reach of the public law is provided by Mayo Moran's chapter (8) in this volume, which argues that a modernization of the Canadian definition of charity must take account of Charter values. In short, it is unlikely that the tide of public law's intrusion into charities law will slow.

Second, I see no reason to treat the "advancement of religion" with any great tenderness. If a constitutional challenge effectively collapses "religion" into "belief systems," and the state then removes religion *per se* from the catalogue of favoured purposes,[72] neither the law nor the policy on charities would be much the worse off. In law, religion has always been something of an anomaly. As I noted above in relation to *Gilmour v. Coats*, the courts have never effectively articulated why it is that religion is favoured; they have simply accepted it on the basis of precedent. Nor have they resolved the inconsistency of saying that public benefit is required for charitability while asserting that the public benefit from religion cannot be proved. Indeed, some see religion as the quintessential example of an area in which the benefit is private. People hold sincere beliefs about the world, and religious organizations allow them to affirm, practise, and propagate those beliefs. That is certainly a good thing, but it is no more the provision of a public benefit than many other ways in which individuals spend their time or find meaning in their life. In a secular age, there seems little justification for the state to assist the expression of that preference.[73] Such a reform would not, of course, remove from charitable status those activities, of which there are many, carried out by religious groups and that otherwise qualify.[74] Indeed, because we are hearing increasing demands for expansion of the definition of charity, we may need to face the fact that expansion alone is not the best policy. We may need to rationalize the definition – expand it in some areas and contract it in others – to ensure that the state's not-unlimited subsidy for charitable activity is put to the most effective use.

NOTES

I thank my colleagues Dick Risk and Carol Rogerson for discussions of the constitutional aspects of this chapter. I also thank Stephanie Marrie for research assistance.

1 Canadian Charter of Rights of Freedoms, Part I of Constitution Act, 1982.
2 RSC 1985, c. 1 (5th Supp.).
3 A very useful article that covers some of the issues dealt with here is T. Marriott, "The Possible Impact of the Charter on the Law of Religious Charitable Trusts," *Philanthropist* 7, no. 4 (1988), 4. Some of the issues

discussed here are also considered in Ontario Law Reform Commission (OLRC), *Report on the Law of Charities* (Toronto, 1996), passim. Canadian texts of the law of trusts cover religion: see D. Waters, *The Law of Trusts in Canada,* 2nd ed. (Toronto, 1984), chap. 14; A. Oosterhoff and E. Gillese, *Text, Commentary and Cases on Trusts,* 5th ed. (Toronto, 1998), chap. 14; J. Phillips, "Purpose Trusts," in M. Gillen and F. Woodman, eds., *Cases and Materials on the Law of Trusts* (Toronto, 1999). The only other Canadian article on religion is a short piece by D. Waters, "The Advancement of Religion: A Form of Charity," *Philanthropist* 1, no. 2 (1973), 7. The only text devoted to religion and law in Canada – M. Ogilvie, *Religious Institutions and the Law in Canada* (Toronto, 1996) – has only one paragraph (201–2) on definition in this context.

The courts have dealt even less with the problem. There has been no reported case on the meaning of religion in charities law since *Re Tufford* (1984), 6 DLR (4th) 534 (Ont. CA) – a bequest for the maintenance of a cemetery was ruled a valid charitable trust. There are, of course, recent and important cases implicating religious charities – *Re Christian Brothers of Ireland in Canada* (2000), 47 OR (3d) 674 CA – and limiting settlors' abilities to make distinctions on, among other things, religious grounds – *Re Canada Trust and Ontario Human Rights Commission* (1990), 69 DLR (4th) 321 (Ont. CA). But these cases do not deal with the issue of definition.

4 See the discussion in Sossin, chapter 12 in this volume.

5 For the Federal Court of Appeal's general approach, see *Native Communications Society v. Minister of National Revenue* (1986), 23 ETR 210 (FCA), and Phillips, chapter 7 in this volume. The Supreme Court of Canada adopted the four-fold English categorization of charity in *Guaranty Trust Co. v. Minister of National Revenue* [1967] SCR 133 and confirmed its applicability in *Vancouver Society of Immigrant and Visible Minority Women v. Minister of National Revenue,* [1999] 1 SCR 10.

6 This is the current publication that accompanies form T2050, Application for Income Tax Registration for ... Canadian Charities. For a more extended treatment of the CCRA's position, see an unpublished paper by Carl Juneau, assistant director, Charities Division, "Is Religion Passé as a Charity?," delivered to the Church and the Law Seminar, Bramalea, Ont., Feb. 2000.

7 "As between different religions, the law stands neutral, but it assumes that any religion is at least likely to be better than none": *Neville Estates v. Madden,* [1962] Ch. 832 at 853. The following brief summary of the tolerant approach of English law is derived from, among other sources, G. Keeton and L.A. Sheridan, *The Modern Law of Charities,* 4th ed. (Chichester, 1992), 64–5; Waters, *The Law of Trusts,* 569-71; *OLRC Report,* 1: 191–4.

8 See *Thornton v. Howe* (1862), 54 ER 1042, where the court upheld a trust for the propagation of the works of Joanna Southcote, who believed that she was pregnant by the Holy Ghost and would give birth to a New Messiah. See also *Re Watson*, [1973] 1 WLR 1472 (Ch).

9 *Bowman v. Secular Society*, [1917] AC 406 at 449 (HL).

10 J. Warburton, *Tudor on Charities*, 8th ed. (London, 1995), 63. See also Keeton and Sheridan, *The Modern Law of Charities*, 65. Charity Commission, *Decision of the Commissioners: Application by the Church of Scientology (England and Wales) for Registration as a Charity* (1999).

11 *Bowman*, 449.

12 [1970] 2 QB 697 (CA).

13 *Registrar-General*, 707, per Lord Denning MR. Both Justice Wynn and Justice Buckley wrote concurring judgments, the latter stating that worship was essential for registration under the statute and that "[w]orship ... must have some at least of the following characteristics: submission to the object worshipped, veneration of that object, praise, thanksgiving, prayer and intercession" (709).

14 See, for example, *Keren Kayemeth Le Jisroel Ltd. v. Inland Revenue Commissioners*, [1931] 2 KB 465, in which the court stressed the need for worship and ritual: religion was "spiritual teaching in a wide sense" supported by "observances that serve to promote and manifest it" (477). See to similar effect *The Oxford Group v. Inland Revenue Commissioners*, [1949] 2 All ER 537 (Ch. D.).

15 [1980] 1 wlr 1565 (Ch.); quotations at 1571 and 1572.

16 See, to similar effect, the earlier case of *United Grand Lodge of Ancient Free and Accepted Masons of England and Wales v. Holborn Borough Council*, [1957] 1 WLR 1080 (CA), in which the Masons were held not to constitute a religion, even though they promoted ethical standards of behaviour. See also *Berry v. St Marylebone Borough Council*, [1958] 1 Ch. 406 (CA), where the Court held that theosophy was not a religion. It said, at 418: "the teaching of the Fatherhood of God and the recognition of the corresponding Brotherhood of Humanity, without distinction of creed, appears to us to be at best the teaching of a doctrine, which is of a philosophical or metaphysical conception, rather than the advancement of religion. If the society is concerned in the advancement of religion it may well be asked, 'What religion does the society advance and how does it advance it?' We can find no satisfactory answer to this question."

17 *Registrar-General*, 707. Charity Commission, *Decision ... Scientology.*

18 The American cases on the meaning of religion are comprehensively reviewed in Note, "Toward a Constitutional Definition of Religion," *Harvard Law Review* 91 (1978), 1056. For ethical societies and religious charity, see especially *Washington Ethical Society v. District of Columbia*, 249

F.2d 127 (1957). The Scientology story is complicated by issues of personal inurement and illegal behaviour, the latter leading the U.S. Supreme Court to uphold the decision by the Internal Revenue Service (IRS) that sums paid to the church could not be deducted as charitable contributions: *Hernandez v. Commissioner*, 490 U.S. 680 (1989). However the IRS has more recently agreed that the organization is entitled to tax-exempt status and that contributors can have the deduction: see A. Eaton, "Can the I.R.S. Overrule the Supreme Court?" *Emory Law Journal* 45 (1996), 987.

19 The leading Australian case is *Church of the New Faith v. Commissioner for Pay-Roll Tax (Victoria)* (1983), 49 ALR 65 (HC). Three judgments were written, and while they represent different degrees of liberality, all adopt a wider definition than the English one. That of Justices Mason and Brennan, for example, is the least liberal but still eschews a deism requirement for a belief in the "supernatural." It sets up a two-fold test: "first, belief in a supernatural Being, Thing or Principle; and second, the acceptance of canons of conduct in order to give effect to that belief" (74). For New Zealand, see *Centrepoint Community Growth Trust v. Commissioner of Inland Revenue*, [1985] 1 NZLR 673 (HC).

20 The cases are reviewed in Marriot, 18–9.

21 (1958), 15 DLR (2d) 484 (NSSC–TD); quotation at 493.

22 (1977), 1 ETR 285 (Alta. SCTD); quotation at 304.

23 *Berry*.

24 Ibid., 418.

25 Religion was defined as "involv[ing] matters of faith and worship" in *Walter et al v. Attorney-General of Alberta* (1969), 3 DLR (3d) 1 at 9 (SCC), per Martland, J.

26 OLRC, *Report*, 1: 195.

27 This summary of the CCRA's approach was confirmed in conversation with Carl Juneau, assistant director, Charities Division. For a more extended treatment see Juneau, "Is Religion Passé?" Juneau notes that the CCRA has registered such organizations as the Khalsa Diwan Society, the Hindu Society of Manitoba, the Zorastrian Society of Ontario, and the Spiritualist Church of Divine Guidance. It did not, however, register the Edmonton Grove of the Church of Reformed Druids or the Mouvement raelien canadien; the latter was apparently rejected because it did not have a belief in god (9–11).

28 "Infrastructure" is the term employed by the OLRC, *Report*, 1: 200. The cases establish that the category includes activities such as establishment and repair of churches, burial plots, and so on; support and training of ministers; missionary activity; and publication of religious works. See generally Oosterhoff and Gillese, *Cases on Trusts*, 823, and Waters, *The Law of Trusts*, 571ff.

29 OLRC, *Report*, 1: 197.
30 Waters, *The Law of Trusts*, 569.
31 [1949] AC 426 (HL); quotations at 457, 458–9, and 461.
32 For a sampling of those criticisms, see Waters, "Advancement," 11, and M. Blakeney, "Sequestered Piety and Charity: A Comparative Analysis," *Journal of Legal History* 2 (1981), 207.
33 OLRC, *Report*, 1: 200.
34 *Hetherington*, [1989] 2 WLR 1094 (Ch.).
35 *Funnell v. Stewart*, [1996] 1 WLR 288. See also *Re Warre's Will Trusts*, [1953] 1 WLR 725 (Ch.), in which a trust for the provision and upkeep of a diocesan retreat house was invalidated on the *Gilmour* principle. Charity Commission, *Decision ... Scientology*.
36 At one stage Chief Justice Fitzpatrick said that "private devotion or edification," while religious activity, was not necessarily charitable: (1918), 57 SCR 298 at 307.
37 Some of these are discussed in Waters, *The Law of Trusts*, 578.
38 [1932] 4 DLR 516 (Ont. CA).
39 [1919] AC 815 (HL).
40 Waters, *The Law of Trusts*, 578.
41 See *Re Sansom* (1967), 59 DLR (2d) 132 (NSSC–TD).
42 Conversation with Carl Juneau.
43 *Application for Income Tax Registration.*
44 In *R.W.D.S.U. v. Dolphin Delivery* (1987), 33 DLR (4th) 174 (SCC), the Supreme Court held that the Charter did not apply to the common law as enforced by the courts in disputes between private parties. However, while "[a]ction by the executive or administrative branches of government will generally depend on legislation," such action "will also be unconstitutional to the extent that it relies for authority or justification on a rule of the common law which constitutes or creates an infringement of a *Charter* right or freedom": per McIntyre, J., at 195. For a fuller discussion, see Moran, chapter 8 in this volume.
45 (1985), 18 DLR (4th) 321 (SCC); quotations at 353 and 354.
46 It may also be possible to draw on another section 2(a) case decided by the Supreme Court, *Edwards Books and Art Ltd. v. The Queen* (1986), 35 DLR (4th) 1 (SCC). As in *Big M Drug Mart*, Sunday closing legislation was at issue, this time an Ontario statute. Four judgments were written, the principal one on the meaning of religion being that of Chief Justice Dickson. His judgment contains a useful discussion of the fact that the legislation made it more expensive for retailers and consumers to observe a day of rest other than Sunday. There was an exemption for small stores from the legislation if they had closed the previous Saturday, and the exemption, it was argued, provided an "indirect" form of coercion, because it was more expensive to close on a day other than Sunday. In the

course of discussing this point, the chief justice said that indirect burdens were as relevant as direct ones, although not every state-imposed cost on carrying out religious practices would offend the Charter. But as an example of the kind of things exempted as "trivial or insubstantial," he cited a sales tax that applied to objects used in religious worship as well as to all other goods. An argument therefore could be made that in addition to saying that charity law offers benefits to some practices and some religions and not others, it makes the non-favoured ones more difficult to practise by imposing a financial burden – lack of an ability to issue deduction receipts. However, this argument cannot automatically be applied here, because Chief Justice Dickson's real concern about cost was the competitive disadvantage suffered by Saturday-observing retailers, and it is difficult to talk about any similar "competitive disadvantage" in religion.

47 [1996] SCR 609; quotations at 639.

48 *Adler*. This reference is to section 29 of the Charter, which specifically protects denominational school rights from Charter review.

49 [1987] 1 SCR 1148. This case dealt with the constitutionality of Ontario's extension of public funding to Catholic secondary schools.

50 *Adler*, 642; the quotation from *Reference Re Bill 30* appears on 642 and 644 of *Adler*.

51 Ibid., 649.

52 *Big M Drug Mart*, 349–52.

53 Ibid., 361–2.

54 Ibid., 361.

55 *Edwards Books*, 34.

56 Article 1 of the U.S. Bill of Rights states that "Congress shall make no law respecting an establishment of religion, or prohibiting the free exercise thereof."

57 *Big M Drug Mart*, 357.

58 The Court has said that the establishment of a state church would clearly contravene section 2(a), although it made the statement by way of a hypothetical example: see *AG Quebec v. Quebec Protestant School Boards* (1984), 10 DLR (4th) 321 at 338 (SCC). In addition, of course, the Court has also hinted that preferential treatment in funding of denominational schools would be unacceptable if not required by another section of the constitution: see discussion of *Adler*.

59 What follows is a necessarily very brief analysis of section 15. A very useful introduction to section 15 jurisprudence appears in P. Macklem et al., *Canadian Constitutional Law*, 2nd ed. (Toronto: Emond Montgomery, 1997), chap. 25. The fact that section 15 talks about "every individual" would not create an application problem, given that "charities" are the bodies registered by the CCRA, for it is individual taxpayers who receive the benefit of the tax credit for donations.

60 *Law Society of British Columbia* v. *Andrews* (1989), 56 DLR (4th) 1 (SCC) (citizenship); *Egan v. Canada* (1995), 124 DLR (4th) 609 (SCC) (sexual orientation).

61 The test is derived from *R. v. Oakes,* (1986), 26 DLR (4th) 200 (SCC).

62 "[L]egislation cannot be regarded as embodying legitimate limits within the meaning of s. 1 where the legislative purpose is precisely the purpose at which the *Charter* is aimed": *Big M Drug Mart,* 374, per Wilson, J.

63 *Church of the New Faith.*

64 See, for example, *Singh v. Minister of Employment and Immigration* (1985), 17 DLR (4th) 422 (SCC).

65 *Dolphin Delivery,* 198. This interpretive canon has been used in a variety of contexts: see, among others, *Canadian Broadcasting Corp. v. Dagenais,* [1994] 3 SCR 835; *Hill v. Church of Scientology* (1995), 126 DLR (4th) 129 (SCC); *R. v. Salituro,* [1991] 3 SCR 654; *M. (A.) v. Ryan,* [1997] 1 SCR 157.

66 *Hill,* 156–7.

67 Ibid., 157. See similar caution about leaving certain matters to the legislature in other cases where the "Charter values" argument has been discussed: *Salituro* and *Ryan,* 172, where the Supreme Court stated that "the basic structure of the common law ... must remain intact, even if particular rules ... must be modified."

68 *Church of the New Faith* and *Centrepoint Community Growth Trust.*

69 See *Re Canada Trust Company.* For an extended discussion see J. Phillips, "Anti-Discrimination, Freedom of Property Disposition, and the Public Policy of Charitable Educational Trusts: A Comment on *Re Canada Trust Company and Ontario Human Rights Commission,*" *Philanthropist* 9, no. 3 (1990), 3, and B. Ziff, *Unforeseen Legacies: Reuben Wells Leonard and the Leonard Foundation Trust* (Toronto, 2000).

70 See especially *Human Life International of Canada v. Minister of National Revenue,* [1998] 3 FC 202 (CA). For an argument to the same effect as that advanced in *Human Life International,* see E. Hyland, "Charities and Political Activity: Reconsidering Traditional Limitations and Prohibitions," University of Toronto Faculty of Law, Centre for the Study of State and Market, Working Paper No. 50, 1998, 21ff.

71 For the problem of inconsistent application, see J. Phillips, "Case Comment: *Human Life International of Canada v. Minister of National Revenue,*" *Philanthropist* 4, no 4 (1999).

72 By "religion *per se*" I refer, of course, to the pure advancement of religion, not to those activities carried out by religions or religiously inspired groups that would otherwise be charitable.

73 There is an interesting irony here concerning the Church of Scientology, whose application for registration as a religious organization is being considered by the CCRA. One of the many issues raised about Scientology by the U.S. Internal Revenue Service (IRS) was whether the money paid

by adherents for "auditing" could be treated as a charitable contribution; the IRS argued that this was simply the purchase of a service. Why is a charitable contribution to church funds by a member any different? It is less direct, for one does not pay for church services on a "tariff," but the principle is not very different.

74 For a useful study of this phenomenon, see F. Handy and R.A. Cnaan, "Religious Non-Profits: Social-Service Provision by Congregations in Ontario," in K. Banting, ed., *The Non-Profit Sector in Canada – Roles and Relationships* (Kingston and Montreal, 2000).

11 Charity and the Income Tax Act: The Supreme Court Speaks

MAYO MORAN AND JIM PHILLIPS

In February 1999 the Supreme Court of Canada handed down its judgment in *Vancouver Society of Immigrant and Visible Minority Women v. Minister of National Revenue*.[1] This was the first occasion on which the Court had dealt with a case in charities law for more than thirty years,[2] and the first time that the Court has ever essayed a general discussion of the meaning of "charity" in Canadian law. It released the judgment after the chapters in this part were completed, but we could obviously not ignore it. It did not seem sensible to disperse commentary about it through the book. Hence we decided to devote a separate commentary to it. This chapter reviews in some detail what the Court had to say both about the general method of deciding the meaning of "charity" and its approach to two of the categories – advancement of education and "other purposes beneficial to the community" – and, where appropriate, it relates what the Court said to those aspects of the law of charity discussed in chapters 7–10. Before we embark on those tasks, we review the context and procedural history of the case.

The Vancouver Society of Immigrant and Visible Minority Women was incorporated in 1985.[3] The Canada Customs and Revenue Agency (CCRA) refused it registration as a charity in 1992, and it made another application commencing in 1993.[4] It made changes to the purposes stated in its constitution between the two applications and during the processing of the second. Those purposes, at the time that the CCRA gave the decision appealed from, read as follows:

a. to provide educational forums, classes, workshops and seminars to immigrant women in order that they may be able to find or obtain employment or self employment;
b. to carry on political activities provided such activities are incidental and ancillary to the above purposes and provided such activities do not include direct or indirect support of, or opposition to, any political party or candidate for public office; and
c. to raise funds in order to carry out the above purposes by means of solicitations of funds from governments, corporations and individuals.
d. [Deleted]
e. To provide services and to do all such things that are incidental or conducive to the attainment of the above stated objects, including the seeking of funds from governments and/or other sources for the implementation of the aforementioned objectives.

The society also submitted a "Statement of Activities" which indicated that it provided "services and workshops" through which it delivered, among other things, "career and vocational counselling" as well as "information and assistance in résumé writing, interview skills, and dealing with Canadian employers." In a telephone conversation with the CCRA it revealed that its membership was comprised of "[a]bout 300 members from all walks of life seeking employment opportunities and general support for integration into Canadian life." That conversation also revealed that the society maintained a "job skills directory" and a listing of some 600 immigrants and their qualifications and that it acted as a kind of employment bureau, receiving job advertisements and distributing them to individuals in the directory who seemed qualified.

The CCRA denied the Society registration on various grounds: it did not qualify as educational or as pursuing any other charitable purposes; some of its purposes were political; and various of its activities – especially "networking, referral services, liaising for accreditation of credentials, soliciting job opportunities and maintaining a job skills directory" – were "not charitable activities."[5] The Federal Court of Appeal dismissed the Society's appeal in a very short judgment.[6] It rejected the argument that the society's purposes qualified as educational, stating that "the activities of the Society described ... are not sufficiently structured and articulated as to respond to the requirements set out by the jurisprudence." It also held that the purposes did not qualify under the fourth head of charity, refusing in particular to accept an analogy between immigrant and visible minority women and Aboriginal peoples. That is, it refused to draw a parallel with *Native Communications Society of British Columbia v. Minister of National Revenue*,[7] stating:

> we are of the view that the comparison with aboriginal people simply does not withstand scrutiny: aboriginal people have a distinct constitutional status ..., being referred to in section 91(24) of the *Constitution Act*, 1867 and section 35 of the *Constitution Act*, 1982. The *Charter* arguments advanced at the hearing before us are not persuasive. It may well be that charitable organizations in assisting those in need will generally deal with persons specifically protected by the equality provisions of the *Charter*, but the focus when deciding whether or not to grant charitable status is not so much, to start with, on the answer to the question 'who are those who are most likely to benefit?' as on the answer to the question 'do the proposed purposes and activities constitute charitable activities within the ambit of the law of charities?' Providing a benefit to those who are in a position to invoke *Charter* rights will not in itself result in an activity falling within the fourth head.[8]

Finally, the court argued that its "basic difficulty" with the application was that the society's "purposes and activities are so indefinite and vague as to prevent the Minister, and this Court, from determining with some degree of certainty what the activities are, who are the true beneficiaries of the activities and whether these beneficiaries are persons in need of charity as opposed to merely being in need of help." That is, "[t]he provision of services and workshops to the community, while laudable, is not necessarily charitable at law and activities and objects of general public utility are not always charitable in the legal sense." Thus it had "opened the door to purposes beyond the legal definition of charity."[9]

In the Supreme Court two judgments were written, with the appeal being dismissed 4–3. Justice Iacobucci, for Justices Bastarache, Cory, Major, and himself, found that purpose (a) listed above was charitable, falling within the advancement of education. But the majority also held that the purpose of assisting immigrant women to find employment was not charitable under "other purposes beneficial to the community." This was fatal to the society's appeal, because it pursued purposes and activities other than educational ones; while some of these were ancillary to the educational ends, the Supreme Court majority held that others were not but rather were directed to helping immigrant women find employment. As that was not a charitable purpose, the society was not exclusively charitable and therefore could not be registered. The dissenting judgment of Justice Gonthier, with whom Justices L'Heureux-Dubé and McLachlin concurred, agreed that some of the society's purposes qualified under the education category and also that the purpose of assisting immigrant women find employment was charitable in itself. The dissent also found that all of the society's activities were related to one or the other of its charitable purposes and accordingly that it did meet the exclusively charitable test.

The more detailed analysis of the case that follows has four thematic sections. The first two deal with general interpretive matters. We begin with what the Court had to say about the sources of the law of charity and about the role of the courts in developing that law. The second section looks at the Court's discussion of the distinction between purposes and activities. The third and fourth sections are more particular, examining in turn the two categories of education and "other purposes beneficial to the community." In the first and fourth sections we discuss both the majority and the dissenting judgments, giving more weight to the former; in the middle two we give the dissent little attention, as it is not materially different from the majority judgment of Justice Iacobucci. There were other issues discussed in the case, but we have concentrated on these four, which we regard as the most important.

DETERMINING THE LEGAL MEANING OF CHARITY

Justice Iacobucci's majority judgment begins with a suggestion that the Court might be ready to modify substantially the definition of charity. After noting that Canadian law "continues to make reference to an English statute enacted almost 400 years ago," he suggested that it was "not surprising" that many commentators have called for change. The case before him represented "an opportunity to reconsider the matter"; not only was the Court being asked "to consider, for the first time in more than 25 years, the application of the law as it presently exists," it was also being invited to consider "the interesting questions of whether the time for modernization has come, and if so, what form that modernization might take."[10] The boldness of this opening did not, however, carry through to what followed. The majority judgment held that any "modernisation," by which we assume it meant wholesale reform, had to come from Parliament, not the courts. In addition, in its analysis of the existing law, the Court confirmed in large measure the Federal Court of Appeal's approach of limiting itself largely to existing categories of charitability.[11]

Justice Iacobucci's consideration of how the courts should go about deciding what "charity" means is actually divided into two sections, one at the beginning of his judgment and the other near its end. The former is principally a restatement of the existing methodology, made prior to assessing whether the society was charitable; the latter, a detailed consideration of whether the law ought to be radically altered. There is an obvious overlap between the two, and in this discussion we therefore conflate the two sections.

In the early section, the starting point of his analysis, Justice Iacobucci provides a descriptive account of the development of the Anglo-Canadian law of charity. He does so because, as he notes, the lack of a definition of "charity" in the Income Tax Act forces a reliance on "common law" (strictly speaking, equitable, or trusts) principles. Justice Iacobucci takes us through the standard account, from the preamble to the Statute of Elizabeth,[12] through *Morice v. Bishop of Durham*,[13] to the well-known categorization of charity under four heads in *Commissioners for the Special Purposes of the Income Tax Act v. Pemsel*.[14] He confirmed the *Pemsel* holding that the preamble was not an exhaustive list of charitable purposes but noted that it had "proved to be a rich source of examples."[15]

More important, at this early stage Justice Iacobucci insisted that the method of deciding on charitability by analogy from existing purposes should remain the one for the courts to follow. Whether or not a purpose is charitable, he said, "is discerned by perceiving an analogy with those purposes already found to be charitable at common law."[16] He confirmed this method, which he called the "*Pemsel* approach," at the end of the introductory section: "In the absence of legislative reform providing guidelines, the best way in which to discern the charitable quality of an organization's purposes is to continue to proceed by way of analogy to those purposes already found to be charitable by the common law, and conveniently classified in *Pemsel*, subject always to the general requirement of providing a benefit to the community, and with an eye to society's current social, moral, and economic context."[17]

Next – and inevitably, given what he had said – Justice Iacobucci explicitly rejected any major reforming role for the courts. He did note the well-known problem that the application of the *Pemsel* approach "to the myriad of modern organizations vying to be identified as charitable has often proved a daunting task" and adverted to recent calls for legislative change.[18] And in the section towards the end of the judgment he accepted the suggestion that "the law of charity has been plagued by a lack of coherent principles on which consistent judgment may be founded" and seemed to agree that judicial reasoning in this area was often circular.[19] But he categorically resisted the suggestion that the court could, or should, do anything about these problems.

Justice Iacobucci gave two reasons to justify this reluctance. First, he adverted to general principles governing when the courts, rather than the legislature, should effect substantial change in the law, citing this passage from the Supreme Court's judgment in *R. v. Salituro*: "Judges can and should adapt the common law to reflect the changing social, moral and economic fabric of the country. Judges should not be quick to perpetuate rules whose social foundation has long since disappeared. Nonetheless, there are significant constraints on the power of the judiciary to change the law.... [I]n a constitutional democracy such as ours it is the legislature and not the courts which has the major responsibility for law reform; and as for any changes to the law which may have complex ramifications, however necessary or desirable such changes may be, they should be left to the legislature. The judiciary should confine itself to those incremental changes which are necessary to keep the common law in step with the dynamic and evolving fabric of our society."[20] Justice Iacobucci's short conclusion was that "[t]here are thus limits to the law reform that may be undertaken by the judiciary."[21]

Second, and more important, he was influenced by the fact that this was a tax case. In his introductory analysis he insisted that it was "imperative" to "preserve the distinction" in the Income Tax Act between charitable and non-profit organizations. The definition of the latter in the act includes "a club, society or association that ... was not a charity ... and that was organized and operated exclusively for social welfare."[22] His concern therefore seems to have been that an expansive approach to the meaning of charity would run the very real risk of subsuming within that category most or all of the bodies "organised ... for social welfare." He returned to the taxation context more forcefully much later in the judgment, when considering whether a new approach should be adopted:

> [A] new approach would constitute a radical change to the common law and, consequently, to tax law. In my view, the fact that the ITA [Income Tax Act] does not define 'charitable', leaving it instead to the tests enunciated by the common law, indicates the desire of Parliament to limit the class of charitable organizations to the relatively restrictive categories available under *Pemsel* and the subsequent case law. This can be seen as reflecting the preferred tax policy: given the tremendous tax advantages available to charitable organizations, and the consequent loss of revenue to the public treasury, it is not unreasonable to limit the number of taxpayers who are entitled to this status. For this Court suddenly to adopt a new and more expansive definition of charity, without warning, could have a substantial and serious effect on the taxation system. In my view ... this would be a change better effected by Parliament than by the courts.[23]

The Supreme Court has therefore provided a clear statement that substantial change in this area must come from legislative, not judicial, action. Justice Iacobucci reviewed various proposals for reform of the law that had been put to the Court in argument. Although he approved of the one offered by the Canadian Centre for Philanthropy, calling it a proposal that "respects both the established law of charity and the need for a flexible approach that will permit movement forward," he thought it no more than "potentially a useful guide for the legislator."[24]

Overall, the majority decision will disappoint those who hoped for a more expansive approach, but it will not surprise those who have lost faith in the likelihood of judicial innovation in this area. The Court does seem, not unreasonably, to have been substantially influenced by the fact that it was dealing with a tax case. That context led Justice Iacobucci to two major conclusions. First, the absence of a definition of "charity" in the Income Tax Act meant that the legislature intended the long line of Anglo-Canadian decisions on charities to apply. Second, whatever scope the judiciary may have for deciding that new purposes qualify, it did not extend to altering the law so substantially as to conflate "charity" with something like "social welfare" or "public benefit," precisely because the statute made a distinction between the two.

Despite these conclusions, the majority judgment was hardly uncritical of the current law. In a section headed "A New Approach" it noted that both the appellant and some intervenors had criticized the traditional method and proposed alternatives. As we noted above, it seemed to agree with some of the critiques. It found it "difficult to dispute" the criticism that "the law of charity has been plagued by a lack of coherent principles on which consistent judgment may be founded." And it thought that while the task of the courts was to keep the law of charity as a "moving subject." it conceded that in that process "very little assistance is provided by such standards as 'in a way which the law regards as charitable' and 'within the spirit and intendment of the Statute of Elizabeth.'" This was because such phrases represented "circular reasoning" and instituted "retrospective bias."[25] But, as we have noted, the court's principal response was that Parliament should reform the law.

Although this comment is principally a review of what the Court said, we would offer two general observations. First, Justice Iacobucci continually displays deference to the legislature. This deference manifests itself, for example, in the determination to preserve the distinction between "social welfare" and "charitable" organizations, which latter must provide a "public benefit." Thus the Court places what we consider unacceptable weight on precedent in distinguishing between "social welfare" and "public benefit," which are otherwise near-identical concepts. However, given that the legislature has clearly left the definition of charity to the courts, it is not clear that history should carry such weight. Legislative intention could as easily, if not more easily, support a much more dynamic approach. One can argue that the legislature has decided that the courts are the institution best suited to ensuring that the definition of charity keeps pace with a changing society. In this account it would be more respectful of legislative intention for the Court to have taken a principled rather than a precedential approach, leaving it to the legislature to put the brakes on if it decided that the Court had gone too far. The deferential posture also arguably fails to account for the significance of judicial pronouncements where the legislature has left it to the courts to provide the guidance necessary to ensure proper functioning of the legislative regime.

Second, and related, the deferential impulse is clearly fuelled by concern about the fiscal implications of decisions on taxation. But every decision interpreting a provision of the Income Tax Act has fiscal implications, and it is not clear why that concern should be so dominant here. Again, Parliament could respond to a decision it does not like by changing the act, as it does in other cases. Overall therefore it seems difficult to understand why the majority was so anxious to preserve a regime that Justice Iacobucci himself admits is "plagued by a lack of coherent principles on which consistent judgment may be founded."[26]

The dissenting judgment of Justice Gonthier takes a subtly, but significantly, different approach. Like Justice Iacobucci he dealt with the question of determining the legal meaning of charity in two sections, one at the beginning and one at the end of his judgment. In the early section, which looked at how courts should deal with novel claims, he did not take exception to the idea that they should analogize from existing case law. But he offered two observations. First, he emphasised that "the *Pemsel* classification is a flexible judicial creation."[27] Second, and more important, he purported to find "underlying principles" within the classification and insisted that courts should look to those principles rather than "become too wedded to outdated conceptions of the existing categories." In fact he thought that there were two "central principles" to the concept of charity in the common law – "(1) voluntariness (or what I shall refer to as altruism, that is, giving to third parties without receiving anything in return other than the pleasure of giving); and (2) public welfare or benefit in an objectively measurable sense." These principles, he insisted, both "underlie the existing categories of charitable purposes" and "should be the touchstones guiding their further development."[28]

This brief statement represents, to our knowledge, the first judicial statement in the Anglo-Canadian jurisprudence that seeks to find a core of principle in the legal meaning of "charity," to define the term conceptually. The definition is not particularly felicitous, given the vagueness of the term "third parties" and the fact that tax law actually gives plenty to the donor in return, yet the search for concepts is laudable. And Justice Gonthier carried the notion into his next section on the test for charitability. While most of this section recites and approves of the well-worn analogy and "spirit and intendment" approach[29] and insists that the test should not be "public benefit" but "public benefit in a way the law recognises as charitable," he argued that the principles that he had delineated should guide future development:

> The best approach, in my view, is one which marries adherence to principle with respect for the existing categories as established by the *Pemsel* scheme. ... It would be unwise to jettison the vast historical inheritance associated with judicial development of the law of charity, although I do think it appropriate to ensure that the existing common law accords with certain identifiable principles which should guide the development of this area of law as a whole. ... Our perceptions as to what should and should not be included ... have changed over the centuries, as they will continue to do. New social needs arise, and old social problems decline in importance. Consequently, it would be a mistake to make a fetish of the purposes enumerated in the preamble. Rather, the Court should adhere to the principles of altruism and public benefit, to which I adverted above, in order to identify new charitable purposes and to ensure that existing ones continue to serve the public good. The law should reflect the realization that although the particular purposes seen as worthy of pursuit change over time, the principles of which they are instantiations endure. Thus, in determining whether a particular purpose is charitable, the courts must look to both broad principles – altruism and public benefit – as well as the existing case law under the *Pemsel* classification. The courts should consider whether the purpose under consideration is analogous to one of the purposes enumerated in the preamble of the Statute of Elizabeth, or build analogy upon analogy. Yet the pursuit of analogy should not lead the courts astray. One's eye must always be upon the broader principles I have identified, which are the Ariadne's thread running through the *Pemsel* categories, and the individual purposes recognized as charitable under them. The courts should not shy away from the recognition of new purposes which respond to pressing social needs.[30]

Justice Gonthier went even further at the end of his judgment, in a section entitled "Should the Common Law Definition of Charity Be

Revised?" Given that, as we see below, he found the society to be pursuing charitable purposes, he did not have to answer that question in this case. But he did essay an answer of sorts, which would give much more scope to the judiciary than Justice Iacobucci was prepared to do. Not only were the courts not "precluded from recognizing new charitable purposes," they were also not prohibited "from revisiting the *Pemsel* classification itself should an appropriate case come before us." The rationale for this bold assertion was that "[t]he task of modernizing the definition of charity has always fallen to the courts," and the legislature is content with that situtation: "There is no indication that Parliament has expressed dissatisfaction with this state of affairs, and it is plain that had Parliament wanted to develop a statutory definition of charity, it could have done so. It has not. This leads me to the conclusion that Parliament continues to favour judicial development of the law of charity."[31]

Although Justice Gonthier saw no need to make such a sweeping change in the case before him, critics of the current approach of the Federal Court of Appeal and the CCRA could hardly wish for a clearer invocation of innovation. Justice Gonthier argued that his approach would still retain the distinction between charitable and non-profit organizations that Justice Iacobucci was so concerned to preserve. But he obviously saw much scope for judicial action, which could include a reduction of the number of purposes categorized as charitable – the likely meaning of his suggestion to "revisit" the *Pemsel* classification. Here his judgment breaks sharply with that of Justice Iacobucci, who throughout assumed that judicial action could lead only to more charitable purposes.

Moreover, Justice Gonthier made passing mention of an argument that the judiciary, in developing the law of charity, should consider "*Charter* values." Again, he said little about this, but he did note that "the *Charter* is the repository of fundamental values which should be taken into account in the development of the common law."[32] He did not go further, even though the question of whether the society's concentration on combating the effects of discrimination helps to make its purposes charitable was raised later. As argued in chapter 8, the *Charter* can be considered relevant to the contemporary meaning of charity.[33] Even though Gonthier understated the role of the Charter, his own decision reveals how much weight he did accord to Charter values in giving content to the meaning of charity. Because of the role of courts in defining charity, and the rarity of judicial pronouncements on the subject, more attention to how the Charter affects the meaning of charity would perhaps have been in order.

PURPOSES OR ACTIVITIES?

A second general issue in charities law that the Court examined was that of whether the test for charitability should focus on the overall purposes of the organization at issue or on its particular activities. In trusts law the answer has long been "purposes," but the wording of the Income Tax Act complicates the issue. Section 149.1(1) defines a "charitable organization" as one "all the resources of which are devoted to charitable activities carried on by the organization itself."[34] As one of us discusses elsewhere in this volume,[35] the act's use of the word "activities" has frequently led the Federal Court of Appeal to concentrate on particular activities and often not even to consider whether an organization is pursuing more broadly defined charitable "purposes."

Justice Iacobucci had no doubt that an activities-only approach was wrong. As he put it: "the character of an activity is at best ambiguous; for example, writing a letter to solicit donations for a dance school might well be considered charitable, but the very same activity might lose its charitable character if the donations were to go to a group disseminating hate literature. In other words, it is really the purpose in furtherance of which an activity is carried out, and not the character of the activity itself, that determines whether or not it is of a charitable nature."[36] As a result, courts "must focus not only on the activities of an organization but also on its purposes." The inclusion of both dimensions means that if an activity clearly furthers charitable objects, the organization would qualify. But even if the activity were not charitable in itself, an organization would still be acceptable, provided that the activity furthered a charitable purpose.[37] Not only is this eminently sensible – indeed, the only workable approach – it is also in line with prior authority.[38] Moreover, it will, we hope, eliminate the double standard of applying an activities test in some cases and a broader purposes test in others.

On a closely related point the Court went further. As part of its discussion of the need for organizations to be exclusively charitable, it confirmed its approval, given over thirty years ago in the *Guaranty Trust* case,[39] of the ancillary purposes doctrine. This doctrine permits charitable organizations to pursue non-charitable purposes that are clearly ancillary to a charitable purpose – a means to an end. This is not quite the same as saying that it is purposes and not activities that must be looked at. To illustrate the distinction we use the example, taken in part from the facts of *Guaranty Trust,* of an alumni organization, whose purposes include supporting an educational institution, hosting an annual golf tournament to raise money for scholarships, and holding an annual dinner to help promote and sustain people's interest in the association. An activities-only test would find the first activity charitable and the second and the third non-charitable. A purposes test would find the second acceptable, as it was designed to help achieve the first purpose, but not the third, whose purpose is to sustain the association – clearly a non-charitable purpose. But a court could hold, as the Supreme Court did in *Guaranty Trust*, that this non-charitable purpose was not really an end in itself, but a means to an end – a way ultimately of supporting the educational institution, providing that that was indeed the association's primary purpose.

In *Vancouver Society* the Court held that "the pursuit of a purpose which would be non-charitable in itself may not disqualify an organization from being considered charitable if it is pursued only as a means of fulfilment of another, charitable, purpose and not as an end in itself." Somewhat confusingly it went on to say that in such a case "the purpose is better construed as an activity in direct furtherance of a charitable purpose."[40] We would suggest that this language not be seen as suggesting that the activities–purposes distinction and the ancillary purposes doctrine are the same. The key phrase here is "construed as"; both non-charitable activities and non-charitable purposes can further charitable purposes, but the former do so more directly than the latter.

The reaffirmation of ancillary purposes is significant, for four reasons. First, it overturns a holding of the Federal Court of Appeal that the doctrine is not available for charitable organizations under the Income Tax Act, which uses the word "activities."[41] Second, it gives charitable organizations two opportunities to argue that things that it does which are not directly in pursuit of charitable objects need not defeat their application for registered status. They can first argue that their activities are not in themselves purposes but are simply activities in pursuit of charitable purposes. If that contention fails, they can then claim that any non-charitable purpose is ancillary. The *Vancouver Society* case itself provides an example. Clause (b) of the society's statement of purposes permitted it to "carry on political activities provided such activities are incidental and ancillary to the above purposes." Justice Iacobucci treated this as a purpose clause, and thus as outside the saving provision in the Income Tax Act for political "activities."[42] But he then held that the clear intention of the document was that the purposes mentioned in clause (b) – and indeed those in clause (c) – were to be carried out in a manner "incidental and ancillary" to purpose (a), which he had found to be charitable – a matter discussed in the next section of this chapter. Third, his holding eliminates the arbitrariness that results from treating non-charitable activities and non-charitable purposes differently. Henceforth little will turn on whether something non-charitable is classified as a purpose or an activity. This seems eminently desirable, particularly in view of the difficulty of drawing the line.

Fourth – and perhaps most important – the Court has effectively placed great emphasis on drafting. Clauses (b) and (c) were ancillary because the society's incorporating document said that they were. The Court stated that "its purposes clause now makes clear that the sole purpose of carrying out political activities and raising funds is to facilitate a valid educational purpose. Thus ... purposes (b) and (c) can be taken as means to the fulfilment of purpose (a), not ends in themselves, and thus do not disqualify the Society from obtaining registration as a charity."[43] This is a clear message to applicants that proper wording of their constitutions may greatly increase their chances of registration.[44]

The obvious danger of this approach is that organizations may present some purposes as ancillary, whether or not they reasonably are.[45] Justice Iacobucci seems to have seen this problem, and his judgment seeks to limit the extent to which drafting facility will influence decisions on registration. First, he insisted that organizations must limit their non-charitable purposes to those that are directly ancillary; clause (e) in this case – "all such things that are incidental or conducive to the attainment of" other purposes – was not truly about ancillary purposes, both because "conducive" means "only that the action leads or contributes to the result, not that it is carried on only in pursuit thereof," and because its content was "exceedingly vague."

Second, and more important, he also took from *Guaranty Trust* the idea that the court must look not only at the purposes of an organization, but also at its actual activities. In *Vancouver Society*, some of the society's activities were neither charitable purposes in themselves nor referrable to any ancillary purpose. Thus they fit under clause (e); hence that clause specifically, and thus the society's constitution generally, "can and do accommodate non-charitable activities."[46] As we noted above, it was for this reason that the society failed the test of being exclusively charitable.

These two qualifications, the second in particular, give some scope to the CCRA and the courts to disqualify organizations if their constitutions are not sufficiently tailored to charitable and ancillary purposes or if their operations show them to have strayed outside the exclusivity boundary. The second limitation will create something of a hurdle for operational charities that apply for first registration, but it will obviously not affect any that do little or nothing operationally before they apply. They now have a greater ability to achieve registration through careful drafting.

THE ADVANCEMENT OF EDUCATION

In this and the following section we move from assessing the Court's general approaches to deciding what is charitable to its consideration of two of the four categories – the advancement of education and "other purposes beneficial to the community." The majority judgment on education begins with the bald statement that "[i]n Canada, 'advancement of education' has been given a fairly restricted meaning." It has, Justice Iacobucci said, "generally been limited to the 'formal training of the mind' or the 'improvement of a useful branch of human knowledge.'"[47] He also cited this passage from the Federal Court of Appeal to demonstrate the relative narrowness of the definition: "[W]hen the word 'education' or 'educational' is used without qualification, it has reference to a fundamental process of learning which is aimed at preparing either for life in general or for a large purpose such as a particular profession or trade, and is in any event without an immediately utilitarian focus."[48]

Given this definition, he concluded, the refusal to find any of the society's purposes charitable was "neither surprising nor incorrect":

> Although purpose (a) does contemplate the provision of 'educational forums, classes, workshops and seminars,' the goal of these programs is clearly 'immediately utilitarian': preparing women 'to find or obtain employment or self-employment.' This does not, in my view, equate to preparation for 'life in general' or for a 'particular profession or trade.' This conclusion is bolstered, I think, by the nature of the activities which the Society viewed as coming within purpose (a). ... [I]t was not unreasonable for Revenue Canada to conclude that there was no systematic instructional structure or format to the supposedly educational activities planned by the Society. Indeed, ... the Society was unable even to show any actual intention to confine its activities to within either the formal training of the mind or the improvement of a useful branch of human knowledge, as those terms have been defined at common law.[49]

However, while Justice Iacobucci thought the Federal Court of Appeal's decision correct according to its own jurisprudence, he held that "the law regarding the educational head of charity should be modified." He disavowed the use of the *Maclean Hunter* test just quoted, given that it did not emanate from a case about charity, and he argued that "the slightly more expansive approach taken by the English courts" was preferable.[50] He stated:

In my view, there is much to be gained by adopting a more inclusive approach to education for the purposes of the law of charity. Indeed, compared to the English approach, the limited Canadian definition of education as the 'formal training of the mind' or the 'improvement of a useful branch of knowledge' seems unduly restrictive. There seems no logical or principled reason why the advancement of education should not be interpreted to include more informal training initiatives, aimed at teaching necessary life skills or providing information toward a practical end, so long as these are truly geared at the training of the mind. ... To limit the notion of 'training of the mind' to structured, systematic instruction or traditional academic subjects reflects an outmoded and under inclusive understanding of education which is of little use in modern Canadian society. ... [T]he purpose of offering certain benefits to charitable organizations is to promote activities which are seen as being of special benefit to the community, or advancing a common good. In the case of education, the good advanced is knowledge or training. Thus, so long as information or training is provided in a structured manner and for a genuinely educational purpose – that is, to advance the knowledge or abilities of the recipients – and not solely to promote a particular point of view or political orientation, it may properly be viewed as falling within the advancement of education.[51]

As support for these views, in addition to English authority, Justice Iacobucci drew on the Ontario Law Reform Commission's *Report on the Law of Charities*, (1996),[52] which argues that "knowledge can take many forms ... theoretical or practical, speculative or technical, scientific or moral" and that "it can be sought in many different ways, and for many different reasons." Thus, according to Justice Iacobucci, "there is no good reason why non-traditional activities such as workshops, seminars, self-study, and the like should not be included alongside traditional, classroom-type instruction in a modern definition of 'education.' Similarly, there is no reason to exclude education aimed at advancing a specific, practical end. In terms of encouraging activities which are of special benefit to the community, which is the ultimate policy reason for offering tax benefits to charitable organizations, there is nothing to be gained, and much to be lost, by arbitrarily denying benefits to organizations devoted to advancing various types of useful knowledge."[53] To the same effect, the majority later asserted that "an informal workshop or seminar on a certain practical topic or skill can be just as informative and educational as a course of classroom instruction in a traditional academic subject."[54]

Applying this approach to the case, Justice Iacobucci held that purpose (a) of the society was charitable under the new, "more expansive" definition of education: "the purpose is to train the minds of immigrant women in certain important life skills, with a specific end in mind: equipping them to find and secure employment in Canada. I find that this is indeed a valid charitable purpose. Moreover, certain activities carried out in furtherance of this purpose, such as the provision of the educational programs contemplated by the purposes clause, are undoubtedly charitable within this expanded definition, whether or not they have the quality of systematic instruction traditionally associated with education in the charitable sense."[55]

Justice Gonthier's judgment in dissent was no different in substance from the majority's, although he did suggest that the "more inclusive" approach taken by Justice Iacobucci was "already latent in the authorities"[56] – a point that we make below. Thus the Court has substantially changed this area of charities law in the context of the Income Tax Act. Over the last decade or so the Federal Court of Appeal has adopted a very narrow meaning of the concept. Although most of its decisions have come in cases where the claimed educational activity was the presentation of information to the public, and thus in cases where the court was concerned more to exclude this from the category than to carefully define "education" in a positive sense,[57] the Federal Court has taken up as its own a definition first used by England's Court of Appeal in *Incorporated Council of Law Reporting for England and Wales v. Attorney-General*:[58] education is "the formal training of the mind" or the "improvement of a useful branch of human knowledge and its public dissemination." And, in consequence, the CCRA has adopted a similarly limited definition.[59] The overturning of this definition in cases of registration under the Income Tax Act does expand the meaning of charity in that context.

The Supreme Court is probably incorrect to have conflated the Federal Court of Appeal's definition with the "Canadian" position.[60] The Canadian law of charities is much more than the sum of the Federal Court's work. It includes provincial decisions given in the context of both trusts and tax law, such as *Re Societa Unita and Town of Gravenhurst.*[61] At issue in that case was a summer camp where children took part in the usual recreational activities but were also taught the Italian language and learned about the history and customs of Italy. It was held to be charitable because it was "learning" designed to produce better citizens by encouraging them to understand their background and themselves.

Moreover, the common law of charities, including its Canadian variant, has long included a much wider variety of purposes within the education category than the majority judgment suggests.[62] It may be that many of these purposes should not be considered educational, that they should be charitable under some other heading,[63] but the law of charities puts them in this box. Even the CCRA, working largely with a definition drawn from the Federal Court of Appeal's cases, includes "providing and maintaining museums and public art galleries" in this category. We stress this point, for there is language in the majority judgment that suggests that the category ought, in some respects, to be narrowed. For example, at one point Justice Iacobucci cautions against education's being "broadened beyond recognition" and seems to insist that it must always include a "teaching or learning component" and thus that "the threshold criterion for an educational activity must be some legitimate, targeted attempt at educating others, whether through formal or informal instruction, training, plans of self-study, or otherwise." He suggests exclusion of some matters previously considered educational, including "providing an opportunity for people to educate themselves," which could be read as removing, for example, the provision of library services.[64] He also suggests that education is not charitable if "provided exclusively to a particular class of individuals, defined only by their creed."[65] Whether or not it ought to be, denominational education is charitable; witness the substantial number of Jewish and Christian fundamentalist private schools registered with the CCRA. In our view the best way to read these kinds of statements is to place them in the context of the Court's desire to respond to the Federal Court of Appeal's narrow approach and in turn to stress the extent to which the latter's judgments have concerned cases where the applicant wishes simply to distribute information, and sometimes political views, to the public at large.

FOURTH HEAD OF CHARITY: OTHER PURPOSES BENEFICIAL TO THE COMMUNITY

Before discussing whether the society could be considered to be pursuing purposes recognized as charitable under the fourth head of *Pemsel*, we need to see why this issue was relevant, given the majority's finding that clause (a) of the purposes was charitable as advancing education. Here we must return to the discussion of ancillary purposes and recall that Justice Iacobucci found that while clauses (b) and (c) were ancillary to (a), (e) was not. It allowed the society to do things broader than the educational activities encompassed by (a). Moreover, and more important, the evidence showed that some of the society's activities were not educational. Thus the society was not constituted or operated exclusively for charitable ends. If, however, some of those activities carried out under clause (e) were in pursuit of some other charitable purpose, they would be charitable also, and the exclusivity standard would be met.

At issue therefore was whether helping immigrant women obtain employment could be considered a charitable purpose in and of itself, under the fourth head of the *Pemsel* categorization. This was the principal issue in the case, and one on which the two judgments diverged substantially. The majority held that it could not be a charitable purpose, the dissenters that it could. We reverse our usual order and look first at the dissent, because the majority judgment on this issue is framed as a response to the dissent.

Justice Gonthier began by asserting that in his view "assisting the settlement of migrants, immigrants, and refugees, and their integration into national life, is a charitable purpose already recognized under the fourth head of *Pemsel*," and in this instance the society's purposes were "subsumed within this subcategory."[66] He supported this contention by reference to a series of Australian, New Zealand, English, and (one) Canadian decisions, all of which had held a variety of immigrant- and refugee-related trusts and other organizations to be charitable.[67] A number of these cases drew an analogy with the resettlement of soldiers returned from war, found by the Judicial Committee of the Privy Council to be a charitable purpose in *Verge v. Somerville*,[68] and Justice Gonthier accepted that analogy and expanded on the point: "Let me pursue the analogy between returned soldiers and immigrants directly. Soldiers return home after a lengthy period of time spent abroad. They may require assistance in integrating back into national life: employment and training opportunities, counselling, support groups, and the like. The same is true with many immigrants. In fact, soldiers may have an easier time of it, as they are unlikely to face language or cultural barriers, and are also likely to have friends and family already in Canada to assist them in the task of reintegration. Nonetheless, the life that the soldier left behind before going abroad may well be gone forever, and he or she may require assistance to making the transition to a new life upon his or her return."[69]

Justice Gonthier also discussed the "discrimination and prejudice" faced by some immigrants. The U.S. Internal Revenue Service had ruled charitable an organization to aid immigrants, in part because they were subject to discrimination,[70] and he stated: "The organization was upheld as pursuing a mixture of purposes, some of which were grounded in the advancement of education head, and some of which were grounded in the elimination of discrimination and prejudice. Yet it cannot be denied that the purpose of the organization itself was to aid immigrants in integrating into national life, and it is that purpose to which I draw the analogy here. I fully agree that not all of the difficulties faced by immigrant women in obtaining employment stem from prejudice and discrimination: but it is undoubted that some of them do. Indeed, the greatest barrier to the integration of immigrant and visible minority women into the workforce is probably not racial or other animus: rather, it is the unintended exclusionary effects of facially neutral practices."[71]

Justice Gonthier concluded by rejecting the majority's position, discussed below, that helping immigrants *per se* could not be a charitable purpose and that one needed some additional element, such as the relief of poor immigrants, to so qualify. "[T]he suggestion that a charitable purpose must be related to the relief of poverty," he stated, "was rejected in Pemsel," and: "[t]he reality is that immigrants may face a number of obstacles to their integration into Canadian society, social, vocational, cultural, linguistic, or economic. It would be futile to focus on one obstacle to the exclusion of the others ... [T]he Society provides assistance, guidance, and learning opportunities. It assists immigrants in developing and acquiring vocational skills, so that they may obtain employment."[72]

Justice Gonthier was thus prepared to find that a broadly defined purpose – assisting immigrants of all kinds to settle in their new home – is charitable. While immigrants may be poor, or may have suffered persecution as refugees, or may suffer discrimination, none of those factors needed to be present:

> The unifying theme to the[se] cases, in my view, is the recognition that immigrants are often in special need of assistance in their efforts to integrate into their new home. Lack of familiarity with the social customs, language, economy, job market, educational system, and other aspects of daily life that existing inhabitants of Canada take for granted may seriously impede the ability of immigrants to this country to make a full contribution to our national life. In addition, immigrants may face discriminatory practices which too often flow from ethnic, language, and cultural differences. An organization, such as the Society, which assists immigrants through this difficult transition is directed, in my view, towards a charitable purpose. Clearly, a direct benefit redounds to the individuals receiving assistance from the Society. Yet the nation as a whole gains from the integration of those individuals into its fabric. That is the public benefit at issue here.[73]

As we saw above, Justice Iacobucci's majority judgment held that the society's purposes were not charitable. He began his consideration of this question by again referring to the test for charitability: that "the purpose must be beneficial to the community 'in a way which the law regards as charitable' by coming within the 'spirit and intendment' of the preamble to the Statute of Elizabeth if not within its letter." Thus the society had to show that helping immigrant and visible minority women obtain work was more than just beneficial "in a loose or popular sense"; it was also "beneficial in a way that the law regards as charitable."[74] He acknowledged that this reasoning was "obviously circular" but then stressed what he had said earlier about the usefulness of analogy, based on "the trend of those decisions which have established certain objects as charitable under this heading."[75]

In the rest of his judgment on this question Justice Iacobucci argued that there was no "trend" of decisions supporting the idea that assisting immigrants in general was charitable. Two points were key to his reasoning. First, one category of immigrants to Canada is the "independent class," persons who come other than to join relatives or as refugees. Potential immigrants for this class are assessed for the extent to which they "will be able to integrate successfully into Canadian society, with particular emphasis placed upon employment skills and opportunities."[76] For Justice Iacobucci the "expectation of successful integration" spoke conclusively against charitability: "I fail to see how providing assistance with integration to independent immigrants is to be considered charitable. ... Of course, many other groups of immigrants may in fact be in special need of such assistance. But in so far as an organization assists all immigrants, I find it difficult to see how such an organization does not run afoul of the exclusive charitability rule, absent either specific legislation or the targeting by the organization of groups with special needs relating to their immigrant status."[77]

It is not entirely clear from this passage what "special needs relating to their immigrant status" are, but that becomes clear from the second point – that the case law used by Justice Gonthier did not support the conclusion that immigrant settlement in general was charitable. *Re Stone*,[78] for example, was not a useful analogy because it dealt with Jewish settlement in Israel and was really about alleviating the problems caused by persecution of Jews. Thus it was not the case that "the analogy embraces the more general case of helping any immigrants to settle in a new land."[79] Another Australian case, *Re Wallace*,[80] similarly dealt with aid to poor immigrants and thus was really about the relief of poverty. Cases about refugee settlement were similarly distinguished. In short, helping migrants who are poor, or persecuted, or have some other "special" problem is a charitable purpose, but immigrants who are simply immigrants are not in the same category.

Justice Iacobucci also looked at another aspect of the society's work – its targeting of "immigrant and visible minority" women. He did not see this as the kind of endeavour that could place it in the category of qualifying immigrant aid organizations. While declining to comment on "whether the elimination of prejudice and discrimination may be recognized as a charitable purpose at common law," he found that the society was not necessarily combating prejudice and discrimination: "The Society is solely aimed at helping immigrant women obtain employment, and it is not clear that all of the difficulties faced by immigrant women in obtaining employment stem from prejudice and discrimination so as to make this an exclusively charitable purpose. For example, making contacts and obtaining information pose difficulties with respect to gaining employment, but these difficulties do not necessarily indicate prejudice and discrimination."[81] In the result, therefore, the society was not charitable under the fourth head, being unable to fit itself into the lists by analogy.

On this issue we think that the majority clearly got it wrong and would make five related points. First, if the Court is saying that immigrants or refugees need to be poor to be "objects of charity" then it is departing from a well-established principle that the charitability of a purpose is not dependent on the economic status of potential recipients. Education can be provided to the rich, because the charitable purpose is advancing education. Religion is advanced whether or not the rich are its beneficiaries. And assisting the young, the elderly, or the sick does not require members of those groups to be indigent.[82] Other examples could be cited; the point is that there seems no reason to suggest that poverty is a prerequisite. An organization devoted to assisting poor immigrants is really one dedicated to the relief of poverty, with immigrants defining the class of beneficiaries rather than the charitable purpose.

Second, the refusal to classify as charitable the integration and assistance of immigrants also runs contrary to an important, albeit only implicit, theme in the definition of charity – charitable purposes frequently fulfil governmental purposes. Commentators and judges have noted the tendency to treat governmental purposes as inherently charitable and have pointed out that in a modern society many of the activities in the preamble are now carried out by public authorities.[83] Viewed in this light, the government's role in helping immigrants integrate should have weighed in favour of classifying the society's purposes as charitable.

Third, the majority's refusal to expand the definition of what is charitable by analogy will encourage the Federal Court of Appeal, as if it needed such encouragement, to interpret analogy very strictly. In effect the Court is saying that the kinds of purposes previously considered charitable will be so in future – and no others. If one cannot move from poor or persecuted immigrants to female visible minority immigrants (let alone to immigrants generally) one cannot get very far through analogy.[84]

Fourth, and closely related, it is unfortunate that the Court so quickly rejected the idea that "discrimination and prejudice" were relevant to this case. As we noted above, the courts help to define charity, and the guidance that they provide to the CCRA shapes officials' decisions.[85] Given the infrequency of judicial pronouncements on the meaning of charity,[86] the Court should have given serious attention to the impact of the Charter and its cognate values on the common law definition. Moreover, since the Charter must affect the distribution of benefits in a legislative scheme such as the Income Tax Act, it is unfortunate that the Court did not take the issue more seriously. As things stand, the Charter's role in determining the meaning of charity for this public law purpose will remain uncertain.

Fifth, and a more speculative point, the majority decision may have narrowed the CCRA's definition of charity under the fourth head. The CCRA did not reject the society's application on the general ground that an organization formed to assist the settlement of immigrants was non-charitable. It stated variously that the society's purposes were not educational, that helping women was not charitable, and that there were political purposes involved. While it is difficult to say what the Federal Court of Appeal thought on the question of whether assisting immigrants was charitable,[87] the department made no comment on it. Indeed, at the conference on which this volume is based, a senior official from the CCRA defended its decision on vagueness grounds, and asserted that it *does* register organizations that assist immigrants. If that is so, it may be that the Supreme Court has now told the department to stop doing so, unless the targeted groups have "special needs." This suggestion is, as we noted above, speculative, and the uncertainty that surrounds it a product of the procedure by which claims are adjudicated and appealed.[88] But it is a possible outcome of the majority judgment, and one much to be regretted.

CONCLUSION

The Supreme Court's ruling in *Vancouver Society* is, and will continue for some time to be, a landmark decision on the meaning of charity. It will doubtless be studied and dissected many times in the years to come. The Court did clarify some methodological questions and help to decide whether an organization should be judged by its purposes or by its activities. The decision is none the less something of a disappointment. Although the Court outlined the need for reform and gestured towards some directions in which such reform might move, it ultimately did little to advance the definition or clarify conceptual questions. Given its determination not to undertake substantial change, it seems likely that the Elizabethan-derived definition of charity and the *Pemsel* method that have been with us for so long will continue to dominate the tax treatment of charity for a considerable time to come.

NOTES

1 [1999] 1 SCR 10. Subsequent page references to the case refer to this report.
2 The last such case was *Guaranty Trust Company v. Minister of National Revenue*, [1967] SCR 133.
3 This account of the background is taken from the Supreme Court judgment, 93–8.
4 The legislative framework governing the registration of charities appears in the Income Tax Act, RSC 1985, c. 1 (5th Supp.), as am. For those provisions, and a review of the CCRA's administration of them, see Sossin, chapter 12 in this volume.
5 Quotation from the CCRA's final refusal letter of 14 October 1994, cited by Gonthier J. at 35.
6 *Vancouver Society of Immigrant and Visible Minority Women v. Minister of National Revenue*, [1996] 2 CTC 88 (FCA).
7 (1986), 23 ETR 210 (FCA). The case is discussed extensively in Phillips, chapter 7 in this volume.
8 *Vancouver Society* (FCA), 91.
9 Ibid., 91–2.
10 *Vancouver Society*, 92.
11 For an analysis of the Federal Court of Appeal's work, see Phillips, chapter 7 in this volume.
12 Statute of Charitable Uses, 43 Eliz. 1, c. 4 (1601).
13 (1805), 10 Ves. Jun. 522, 32 ER 947.
14 [1891] AC 531 (HL).
15 *Vancouver Society*, 104.
16 Ibid., 106.
17 Ibid., 111.
18 Ibid., 106–7. Justice Iacobucci cited only the comments of Justice Strayer in *Human Life International of Canada v. Minister of National Revenue*, [1988] 3 FC 202 at 214 (CA). He might have cited also Panel on Accountability and Governance in the Voluntary Sector, *Building on*

Strength: Improving Governance and Accountability in the Voluntary Sector (1999), and A. Drache, "Charities, Public Benefit, and the Canadian Income Tax System: A Proposal for Reform," unpublished ms., 1998.

19 *Vancouver Society*, 135.

20 [1991] 3 SCR 654 at 670; the quotation appears at p. 107 of Justice Iacobucci's judgment.

21 *Vancouver Society*, 107.

22 Income Tax Act, s. 149 (1)(l).

23 *Vancouver Society*, 134.

24 Justice Iacobucci summarizes the proposal in ibid., 136–7: "the Centre proposes an approach which focuses on whether a given project pursues a good for the benefit of strangers in a way that is practically useful. A three-step inquiry is suggested, as follows: (1) Determine whether the purposes are charitable within the first three heads of *Pemsel*: the relief of poverty, the advancement of religion, or the advancement of education. (2) If not, determine whether a public benefit is offered, by examining whether, (a) the purpose benefits an identifiable group of people, of whatever size, having a common interest; (b) the benefit is physical or spiritual, measurable or intangible, direct or indirect; and (c) the benefit is reasonably recognized and realistically to be provided, as opposed to merely speculative, putative, or hoped-for. If these requirements are met, then a prima facie presumption of charitable purpose is raised. If not, then proceed to determine whether the purpose falls within one of the decided anomalies under the fourth head of Pemsel. (3) Once a prima facie presumption of charity is established, determine whether there are grounds for holding the purpose to be non-charitable by reason of one or more of the following: (a) exceptions previously decided (e.g., political purpose or purpose contrary to public policy); (b) reasons of public policy relating to the nature of the common interest; or (c) a failure to be exclusively charitable because the means or activities undertaken are not primarily concerned with giving actual effect to the stated purpose or, at least, subordinate to the primary concern."

This is a very broad test, very close to a simple public-benefit standard. If Parliament indeed wishes to retain some special meaning for "charity," it seems unlikely that it would opt for such a proposal.

25 Ibid., 135. See Phillips, chapter 7 in this volume, for a more detailed elaboration of many of these criticisms.

26 *Vancouver Society*, 135

27 *Ibid.*, 42.

28 *Ibid.*, 43–4. For the likely origins of the "altruism" idea, and for a similar view that the law implicitly reflects these kinds of values, see Ontario Law Reform Commission (OLRC), *Report on the Law of Charities* (Toronto, 1996), especially chap. 6.

29 See Phillips, chapter 7 in this volume, for a discussion of this as stated by the Federal Court of Appeal.

30 *Vancouver Society*, 50–2.

31 Ibid., 90.

32 Ibid.

33 See Moran, chapter 8 in this volume.

34 Income Tax Act, s. 149.1(l).

35 See Phillips, chapter 7 in this volume.

36 *Vancouver Society*, 108.

37 We have chosen not to discuss Justice Gonthier's judgment on this question, which appears at 52–8. While he formulated matters a little differently from Justice Iacobucci, there is really no substantial divergence between the two on the general approach to activities and purposes. Justice Gonthier's application of the test is briefly discussed below, note 46.

38 See the *Guaranty Trust* case.

39 Ibid.

40 *Vancouver Society*, 111.

41 See *Scarborough Community Legal Services v. The Queen* (1985), 17 DLR. (4th) 308 (FCA). See also, *contra*, *Alberta Institute on Mental Retardation v. Minister of National Revenue*, [1987] 3 FC 286 (CA).

42 The Income Tax Act contains a specific ancillary purposes doctrine for "political activities": see s. 149.1(6.1) and (6.2).

43 *Vancouver Society*, 130–1.

44 For an argument that the Federal Court of Appeal's decision in *Native Communications* prompted a similar development, see E. Zweibel, "A Truly Canadian Definition of Charity and a Lesson in Drafting Charitable Purposes," *Philanthropist* 7, no. 1 (1987), 4. Whether or not Zweibel was right about that case, the subsequent history of the Federal Court's jurisprudence and of the CCRA's practice shows that the particulars of drafting do not play a large role in determining charitability.

45 As well, drafting skills may now matter more: organizations with the resources to engage experienced (and expensive) counsel will fare much better in the registration process than small, perhaps grassroots groups, which cannot do so.

46 *Vancouver Society*, 132. Justice Iacobucci referred at one point to the job skills directory and to support groups for professionals and at another point to "the ... job skills directory ... networking, liaising for accreditation of credentials, soliciting job opportunities, and offering referral services." They were not charitable purposes because they were "directly in furtherance of helping immigrant women to find employment," and this he found not to be a charitable purpose: 132. Justice Gonthier's dissent found these activities to be related to a charitable purpose, but to that of

assisting immigrant women to obtain employment: see 84–9. Thus, as we noted above, the judgments differ materially not on the relationship of activities to purposes but rather on whether helping immigrant women to find work is charitable: for the debate on this, see below.

47 Ibid., 112.

48 The definition originally appeared in *Maclean Hunter Ltd. v. Deputy Minister of National Revenue for Customs and Excise*, [1988] DTC 6096 (FCA), which was not a charities case but rather concerned an excise-tax exemption for "printed books used solely for educational purposes." The definition from *Maclean Hunter* was adopted by Justice Robertson in *Briarpatch Inc. v. The Queen*, [1996] DTC 6294 at 6295 (FCA), which was a charitable registration case.

49 *Vancouver Society*, 113.

50 Ibid., 115. Cited for this more expansive approach were *Inland Revenue Commissioners v. McMullen*, [1981] AC 1 (HL); *Re Hopkins' Will Trusts*, [1964] 3 All ER 46 (Ch. D.), and *Re Koeppler Will Trusts*, [1986] Ch. 423 (CA).

51 *Vancouver Society*, 116–7.

52 OLRC, *Report* deals with education at 202–8.

53 *Vancouver Society*, 117.

54 Ibid., 118.

55 Ibid., 119.

56 Ibid., 64.

57 See, for example, *Positive Action against Pornography v. Minister of National Revenue*, [1988] 1 CTC 232 at 237 (FCA), in which the court, as well as defining education, stated that "the presentation to the public of selected items of information and opinion ... cannot be regarded as educational in the sense understood by this branch of the law." For similar cases, see *Briarpatch*; *Human Life International*; *Interfaith Development Education Association, Burlington v. Minister of National Revenue*, [1997] 97 DTC 5424 (FCA). Justice Gonthier seems to make a similar point about the context of the Federal Court of Appeal's decisions, stating at 65: "When reviewing the authorities which have defined the scope of the concept of 'advancement of education', one must be careful to appreciate the context in which each particular definition has been advanced. So, for example, it has been a recurring theme of the jurisprudence in this area that the advancement of education must be clearly distinguished from the pursuit of political purposes. ... I suspect that the true ground of decision was not that the mode of education selected by the organization in that case was too informal, but rather that the organization was seeking to advance a particular point of view, and gain adherents to it, instead of educating members of the public about a certain subject matter and allowing them to come to their own conclusions."

58 [1972] 1 Ch. 73 (CA).

59 "The courts recognize a purpose or activity as advancing education when it involves significant training or instruction, develops mental faculties, or improves a branch of human knowledge": see "Registering a Charity for Income Tax Purposes," a short publication accompanying Form T2050, Application for Income Tax Registration for ... Canadian Charities.

60 See the following statements: "In Canada, 'advancement of education' has been given a fairly restricted meaning"; the "inclusiveness" of the English approach has not been incorporated into "Canadian law"; "the limited Canadian definition of education as 'the formal training of the mind' or the 'improvement of a useful branch of human knowledge' seems unduly restrictive": 112, 115, and 116. Justice Gonthier also suggested that education "has traditionally been given a relatively restrictive interpretation in Canada": 62.

61 (1977), 16 OR (2d) 785 (HC), affd. (1978), 6 MPLR 172 (Ont. Div. Ct).

62 It includes trusts for libraries, learned societies, and adult learning institutes. Education has also been extended to include what is often termed "aesthetic appreciation," so that trusts for a wide range of artistic and cultural pursuits have been held to be charitable. One can also find authority for the charitability of the production of law reports and the encouragement of chess playing among boys. For all of this see J. Phillips, "Purpose Trusts," in M. Gillen and F. Woodman, eds., *Cases and Materials on Trusts* (Toronto, 2000).

63 The OLRC makes this argument: see *Report.* See also K. Janus, "Artistic Endeavours in Charity Law," *Philanthropist,* 15, No. 1 (1999), 5.

64 *Vancouver Society,* 117–18. Another example given of something that should not be considered educational is that of "a trust to assist the publication of unknown authors" (117). Just such a purpose was held to be charitable in *Re Shapiro* (1979), 107 DLR (3d) 133 (Ont. HC).

65 *Vancouver Society,* 119.

66 Ibid., 68.

67 They were *In re Wallace,* [1908] VLR 636 (SC); *Re Stone* (1970), 91 WN 704 ((NSWSC); *In re Cohen,* [1954] NZLR 1097 (SC); *Re Morrison* (1967), 111 Sol. Jo. 758 (Ch. D.); *Re Fitzgibbon* (1916), 27 WOR 207 (HC). Justice Gonthier also noted a decision of the English charity commissioners, registering an immigrant/refugee organization, the Ethnic Minority Training and Employment Project.

68 [1924] AC 496 (HL).

69 *Vancouver Society,* 70–1.

70 Ibid., 127–8, citing U.S. Revenue Ruling 76–205, in *Internal Revenue Cumulative Bulletin 1976-1.*

71 Ibid., 73–4.

72 Ibid., 75.
73 Ibid., 75–6.
74 Ibid., 120.
75 Ibid., 121, quoting *D'Aguiar v. Guyana Commissioner of Inland Revenue,* [1970] TR 31 at 33 (PC).
76 Ibid., 123.
77 Ibid.
78 *Re Stone.*
79 *Vancouver Society,* 124.
80 *Re Wallace.*
81 *Vancouver Society,* 128–9.
82 For these examples see Phillips, "Purpose Trusts," passim.
83 See, for example, S. Maurice and D. Parker, *Tudor on Charities,* 7th ed. (London, 1984), 90–1, cited in *Vancouver Regional FreeNet Association v. Minister of National Revenue,* [1996] 3 CTC 102 (FCA), 105–6 and 111.
84 One commentator sympathetic to retaining the analogy approach based on the preamble has argued that the Court could have found the society charitable by analogy to "the marriage of poor maids" listed there. He argues: "One begins by establishing the Elizabethan social framework in which marriage was one of the better ways for poor maids to escape from the limited opportunities [they had]. ... Four centuries later society would advocate education rather than marriage ... for women of limited economic means to better their situation. ... In our society the women who need such charitable assistance are not Elizabethan 'spinsters' but immigrant and visible minority women"; see B. Bromley, "Answering the Broadbent Question: The Case for a Common Law Definition of Charity," paper presented to the Canadian Association of Gift Planners Conference, Calgary, 1999, 6. With respect, we think that this is a somewhat strained analogy and that its use reveals the problems with analogy – it is highly manipulable, and the analogy is all too often in the eyes of the beholder.
85 See Sossin, chapter 12 in this volume.
86 See Phillips, chapter 7 in this volume.
87 As we discussed above, the Court rejected the educational claim and the analogy to Native peoples and insisted that the principal problem was the vagueness of the society's objectives. While its decision could be read as saying that assisting immigrants was not charitable, the Court did not say that explicitly. We must assume that if the Court thought the objects clear enough to be so defined, it would not have rested its decision largely on the "indefinite and vague" argument.
88 There is no systematic publication and explanation of Revenue Canada's registration decisions or an appeal process that allows for substantial gathering and adjudication of facts. For a critique of the registration process, see Sossin, chapter 12 in this volume.

PART THREE

Charity and Tax: Policy and Practice

12 Regulating Virtue: A Purposive Approach to the Administration of Charities

LORNE SOSSIN

Charities in Canada are regulated principally by the federal government through the income tax system.[1] The federal government exempts from income taxes organizations that have obtained registration from Revenue Canada as a recognized charity. In addition, registered charitable organizations may issue receipts for donations, making tax benefits available to donors. Much attention, in this volume and others, focuses on the dramatic expansion of the charitable sector. Over 5 million tax-filers now claim in excess of $4 billion in donations each year to the 75,000 registered charities in Canada.[2] In 1990, the auditor general estimated that the value of subsidy in terms of forgone tax revenue per year amounted to approximately $600 million.[3] In 1995, the Department of Finance calculated the annual tax expenditure on charitable donation tax credits to be $940 million, and in 1999, this was estimated to grow to $1.35 billion. Charities depend on this vast federal tax expenditure both to attract donations and to obtain funds that would otherwise be spent on taxes. This represents a substantial public subsidy for private altruism. Notwithstanding the growth of the charitable sector, and the corresponding increase in the public subsidy of that sector, the supervision of charities under the Income Tax Act[4] remains largely a neglected area of study.

We cannot and should not, in my view, divorce the question of how the subsidy to charities is administered from the question of the purpose this subsidy is intended to further. While there seems to be a consensus that charities are subsidized because they do "good works,"[5] beyond this there is little common ground about subsidizing charities in Canada. For some, this subsidy compensates private organizations for providing services and benefits that would otherwise fall to government. For others, it is an inducement to encourage private support for activities of public benefit. Still others would contend that it constitutes a reward for voluntarism and virtue. All of these explanations are reasonable, and the reality may well be a combination of more than one of them.[6] Uncertainty regarding the purpose of the subsidy to charities, I conclude, leaves to those officials charged with administering the subsidy a difficult, if not impossible task.

The departure point for any analysis of state regulation is the trite observation that administration never can be neutral. Discretionary determinations, and the value judgments that they embody, are necessarily a part of administering public programs.[7] Inexorably, government officials either further or inhibit social ends; certain groups obtain benefits at the expense of others. To paraphrase Michael Lipsky, the decisions of such bureaucrats effectively become the public policies they carry out.[8] Without a clear sense of the ends of granting charitable registration, the administration of this process may devolve into an aggregation of subjective and arbitrary determinations, or at least this is how those determinations may seem to those organizations whose interests depend on them.[9]

Neither Parliament nor the courts have provided a practical and principled framework for making such determination. As a result, tax officials must distinguish between those bodies that qualify as charities and those that do not. Tax officials, however, are neither well-equipped nor well-suited to defining the scope of socially desirable activities. This function is inherently political. The absence of such a purposive mandate has prevented the supervision of charities from being conducted in a consistent and coherent fashion, despite Revenue Canada's significant commitment to making the administrative process transparent, responsive, and procedurally fair.

The growing literature appears united in the view that the administrative process needs reform.[10] Revenue Canada has just been reconstituted as the Canada Customs and Revenue Agency (CCRA).[11] Thus the time would appear ripe to re-evaluate the role and function of the tax official in the administration of charities in Canada.

This chapter examines the administration of charities under the Income Tax Act from both a positive and a normative perspective. From a positive perspective, I review the statutory authority, legal obligations, and administrative practices of Revenue Canada/CCRA. From a normative perspective, I explain why I believe it is necessary to determine the ends to which the administration of charities ought to aspire. The analysis has three sections. In the first, I canvass the statutory and common law regime governing the regulation of charities in Canada. In the second, I examine the dynamics of the CCRA's discretion. I explore dilemmas of consistency, coherence, and adaptability stemming from the CCRA's application of vague common law standards. In this section, I also consider the entitlement to fairness at two distinct junctures in the administrative process: registration (the making of the decision to grant or deny charitable registration to an organization) and deregistration (the making of the decision to revoke or annul an organization's charitable registration). Finally, in the third section, I propose a purposive approach to the regulation of charities. I conclude that, under this approach, statutory articulation of the purpose of regulating charities is essential to its effective and efficient administration.

CHARITIES REGULATION AND ADMINISTRATION IN CANADA

History

The history of state regulation of tax benefits for charities is intimately bound up with administrative concerns about fraud and abuse. Indeed, England's Charitable Uses Act, 1601 (the Statute of Elizabeth), which forms the basis of the common law definition of charities, was principally an administrative measure, enacted in response to widespread use of charitable trusts for illegitimate ends.[12] The preamble to this act set out the "good, godly and charitable" uses over which the newly created "commissioners" were to have supervisory jurisdiction (for investigating breaches of trust, misappropriation of charitable funds, and so on).[13]

The Charitable Uses Act, 1601, was not, however, an administrative measure alone. It was part of a concerted response to the widespread increase in the incidence of poverty in England in the 1590s.[14] Providing a benefit to charities, and regulating the scope of its enjoyment, had a distinct purpose – the alleviation not of poverty *per se,* but of the burden that poverty placed on local parishes responsible for the care of the poor.[15] The commissioners administered this act with that goal in mind. For example, they established that the preamble would be interpreted broadly and generously, so that more rather than fewer endowments could be applied to public benefit. They determined that as long as a use benefited the poor, it fell within the equity of the act, even if it had an incidental benefit for the rich (for example, the gravelling of a highway or the maintenance of a public midwife).[16]

The commissioners viewed interpretation of the preamble as a purposive rather than a technical enterprise; their task was to determine which uses fell within the "equity" of the preamble and which did not. This also provided a normative basis for justifying their decision-making as principled and coherent. For example, it made sense to authorize repairs to a church's belltower as charitable, for, at common law, such expenses would otherwise be borne by the parish (thus diverting funds from the relief of poverty). In contrast, the commissioners refused to authorize repairs to private pews in the church, as private (and, generally, wealthy) individuals would otherwise be responsible for that expense. It was clear to the commissioners that the act's purpose was not to identify technical categories of uses (such as religious uses) that would receive public benefit, but to provide the criteria against which to measure all uses (for example the relief of poverty and its expenses for the parish). As I show below, it is this purposive approach to the administration of charities that is missing from the modern equivalent of the commissioners in Canada.

Charities first received tax-exempt status in Britain in the Income Tax Act of 1799.[17] In Canada, federal supervision of charities through the tax system also coincided with the first legislation on income tax, enacted in 1917 as a revenue-raising mechanism to help finance the First World War.[18] This exemption was accompanied by an administrative scheme to prevent its abuse. The War Charities Act, 1917, set up the first registration scheme in Canada to restrict the number of organizations permitted to launch appeals for public donations for war charity purposes (although it exempted churches and the Salvation Army). Registration was denied if the charity was not established in "good faith" for "charitable purposes" or if it was not properly administered. Those organizations that did obtain registration were required to file biennial reports to the federal government covering banking, bookkeeping, and organizational structure. With the end of the war, federal support for, and regulation of, charities ceased.[19] Parliament repealed the registration scheme in 1927.[20] A similar pattern followed the regulation of charities during the Great Depression[21] and the Second World War.[22]

The regulation of charities remained inconsistent and episodic until 1967. As part of a larger overhaul of the income tax, Minister for National Revenue Edgar Benson introduced amendments to the Income Tax Act which required all charitable organizations seeking to issue tax receipts to obtain a registration from the ministry and also obliged them to keep a copy of each tax receipt issued.[23] Once again, the scheme appeared to be a response to fears of widespread fraud and abuse.[24]

The mandate of tax officials has focused narrowly on the prevention of fraud and the enforcement of compliance. However, while this may have been appropriate for an earlier era, the authority vested in tax officials under the Income Tax Act calls for determinations that define the very nature and scope of charitable activity in Canada.

The Legal and Statutory Framework

The unsettled nature and scope of "charitable activities" continues to provide the backdrop for the wide discretion afforded officials in the administration of the Income Tax Act.[25] The act nowhere defines "charity." The departure point for the regulation of charities is sections 149.1(1) and 248(1) of the act, which define "charitable organization" and "registered charity," respectively, as follows:

> 149.1(1) 'charitable organization' means an organization, whether or not incorporated,
> (a) all the resources of which are devoted to charitable activities carried on by the organization itself,
> (b) no part of the income of which is payable or is otherwise available for, the personal benefit of any proprietor, member, shareholder, trustee or settler thereof,
> (c) more than 50% of the directors, trustees, officers or like officials of which deal with each other and with each of the other directors, trustees, officers or like officials at arm's length, and
> (d) where it has been designated as a private foundation or public foundation ... or has applied for registration ... under the definition 'registered charity'... not more than 50% of the capital of which has been contributed or otherwise paid into the organization by one person or members of a group of persons who do not deal with each other at arm's length and, for the purpose of this paragraph, a reference to any person or to members of a group does not include a reference to Her Majesty in right of Canada or a province, a municipality, another registered charity that is not a private foundation, or any club, society or association described in paragraph 149(1)(I).
>
> 248(1) 'registered charity' at any time means
> (a) a charitable organization, private foundation or public foundation, within the meanings assigned by subsection 149.1(1), that is resident in Canada and was either created or established in Canada, or
> (b) a branch, section, parish, congregation or other division or an organization or foundation described in paragraph (a), that is resident in Canada and was either created or established in Canada and that receives donations on its own behalf

that has applied to the Minister in prescribed form for registration and that is at that time registered as a charitable organization, private foundation or public foundation.

Thus the act recognizes three categories of "registered charities" – charitable organizations, public foundations, and private foundations.[26] A charitable organization in this context is usually an organization that engages in charitable activities, while private or public foundations typically fund the charitable activities of other organizations.[27] All these forms of charities must direct their resources and expenditures towards exclusively charitable purposes. Non-profit organizations, in contrast, are exempt from income taxation but may not issue tax receipts for donations, and need not limit their activities to charitable purposes.[28]

Most organizations denied charitable registration typically will qualify as non-profit and thus be able to take advantage of the tax benefits that this status engenders. However, if, in the opinion of the CCRA, an organization would qualify as a charity, it may not register as a non-profit organization. In other words, the CCRA decides whether organizations are charitable or non-profit, not the organizations themselves.[29]

The current scheme of regulating charitable organizations under section 149.1 of the Income Tax Act was enacted pursuant to legislation of 1976. The new scheme "grandparented" charities registered prior to 1977, allowing them to remain registered until such time, if any, as their registration was revoked.[30] However, registration provisions had been more haphazard than is currently the case, and so hundreds of charities remained registered that would not have qualified had they applied after 1976.[31]

The CCRA's key judgment in determining eligibility for registration is whether a body's activities are charitable. In the absence of a statutory definition, the CCRA has turned to the common law, which traces its definition of charitable activities back to the preamble of the Statute of Elizabeth (Charitable Uses Act, 1601).[32] The jurisprudence to which this act gave rise, carefully reviewed in the English case *Commission for Special Purposes of Income Tax v. Pemsel*,[33] identified four areas of charitable activity: relief of poverty, advancement of education, advancement of religion, and other purposes beneficial to the community. Rather than viewing these four spheres as illustrations of acceptable charitable activity, as the House of Lords in *Pemsel* appear to have intended,[34] the Federal Court of Appeal has regarded these as the only acceptable categories,[35] which approach in turn has guided the CCRA's decisions on eligibility for charitable registration.[36]

Even on this basic method, however, there is little judicial consensus. Other courts have concluded that the preamble and *Pemsel's* analysis of its categories are of "no real value" in deciding whether an activity or object is charitable.[37] As for the content of these four categories, Canadian courts agree on little. While the Supreme Court of Canada has acknowledged that the law of charities is a "moving subject," which continues to evolve,[38] its jurisprudence often reflects an inability or unwillingness to appreciate the "contemporary Canadian context."[39]

The Supreme Court's much-anticipated *Vancouver Minority Women* decision reiterated, and to some extent ameliorated, this lack of coherence. The Vancouver Society of Immigrant and Visible Minority Women helps immigrant women to find employment. Revenue Canada rejected its application to be registered as a charity. This rejection was upheld on appeal both to the Federal Court of Appeal and by the Supreme Court of Canada, by a slim 5–4 majority.[40] Both courts found this organization's stated objectives to be vague and outside the common law categories developed to define "charitable activities." Justice Iacobucci, writing for the majority, observed: "[I]t is difficult to dispute that the law of charity has been plagued by a lack of coherent principles on which consistent judgment may be founded. The Statute of Elizabeth was never intended to provide an exhaustive list of charitable purposes, and although the categories enunciated by Lord Macnaghten in Pemsel are to some extent a useful classification of what the common law has decided is charitable, they should not and have not been read strictly by the courts."[41]

It is against this backdrop that the CCRA determines what objects and activities are "charitable" and enforces the restrictions placed on charities' objects and activities. For example, charitable organizations may carry on a "related business" (such as a church bingo, a hospital cafeteria, or a university gift shop) only under certain circumstances[42] and may not engage in "political activities" in order to fulfil their objectives (for example, lobbying government officials, publishing partisan views, picketing and other forms of public demonstration).[43]

CCRA officials must thus adapt the common law on charities to specific applications for registration in order to determine which organizations become or remain charities and which do not. Sometimes, there is Canadian case law directly on the point; in such circumstances, the CCRA merely applies these standards. However, more often, there is no Canadian case law directly relevant. In these circumstances, the CCRA officials must exercise their best judgment as to whether the organization's objects and activities are analogous to existing case law. Not surprisingly, the attempt to adapt imprecise, sometimes archaic jurisprudence to rapidly evolving social and economic structures has led to significant criticism of the CCRA. The aim of this chapter is not to rehearse such criticisms but rather to show that they are inevitable, given the purposive vacuum in which officials exercise their discretion.[44]

THE CHARITIES BUREAUCRACY

Administrative concerns about fraud and abuse were a constant concern of those who designed the tax expenditure for charities, but the administrative process by which organizations obtained and maintained charitable registration rarely received serious scrutiny. The Carter Commission's comprehensive Report on Taxation (1966) said little about the charitable sector, and even less about its administration. However, it did propose an interdepartmental body to supervise charities.[45] As part of the 1967 reform to the administration of charities, the taxation division established a separate bureau of the assessments branch to oversee the new registration system.

Long the victim of federal government cuts and retrenchment in the 1980s and early 1990s, the Charities Division now appears to be expanding dramatically. Following the 1997 federal budget, the number of full-time equivalent employees (FTEs) was to rise from 71 in 1997 to 133 in 1998,[46] and the division's annual budget, from $5,115,050 in 1997 to $8,410,057 in 1998. Between 1987 and 1996, while the number of registered charities escalated from 56,254 to 75,012, the number of FTEs inched upwards from 63.5 to 67.[47]

In this section, I examine the jurisdiction and scope of discretion afforded these officials, as well as the dilemmas that their authority has created.

Jurisdiction

Federal and Provincial governments regulate charities in Canada.[48] Federally, the principal agency for charities is the CCRA, which enforces the laws relating to tax-exempt status and registration of charities as well as the laws relating to deductions from personal and corporate income tax for donations to registered charities.[49] Provincial regulation varies but, for example, in Ontario includes laws governing the creation and conduct of charitable trusts and the licensing of charitable casinos, lotteries, and other fund-raising ventures, including registration of charities by the Office of the Public Trustee. Federal supervision of charities has not changed much since 1917 and focuses on policing the charitable registration process. As one recent study concluded, "the federal jurisdiction [over charities] is exhausted if the tax system is protected from leakages."[50] However, as I show below, because CCRA officials effectively define the scope of charities in Canada, far from just plugging leaks, tax officials keep the charitable ship afloat.

Administrative Discretion and Decision-Making

The key to both the regulation and the support of charities in Canada is the system of registration supervised by the CCRA. In order to access the significant tax benefits of charitable status, an organization must obtain from the CCRA the status of a registered charity. As I noted above, there are approximately 75,000 registered charities in Canada.[51] With the ongoing restructuring of the welfare state, organizations carrying out activities traditionally funded by the public sector have sought status as registered charities to augment diminished state funding.

The Income Tax Act permits a registered charity to carry out its charitable purposes, both inside and outside Canada, in only two ways. First, it may make gifts to other organizations on the list of qualified donees set out in the act. Second, it may carry on its own charitable activities. In contrast to a charity's relatively passive transfer of money or other resources involved in making gifts to qualified donees, its carrying on its own activities implies its active participation in a program or project that directly achieves a charitable purpose.[52]

To qualify for registration as a charity (and the resulting tax advantages), an oganization must meet the following six conditions: it must be created or established in Canada; it must be resident in Canada; its purposes and activities must be charitable; it must carry on its own charitable activities and/or fund certain organizations identified in the act; it must maintain enough books and records in Canada to enable the agency to verify that its funds have been properly spent and that the charity is retaining control and direction over the use of its resources; and it must spend a certain amount on charitable work every year.[53]

The CCRA makes several determinations in deciding whether an organization seeking charitable status has met these conditions. First and most important, does the organization engage in charitable activities? There are two types of appropriate activities: transferring funds to qualified donees identified in the Income Tax Act[54] and a "charitable activity." The CCRA determines which activities qualify as charitable in the light of the applicable or analogous case law. Charities Division examiners, while usually not lawyers, are trained to read and analyse case law. Examiners receive a two-to-three-week orientation session covering the substantive areas of charitable activities. These include "overview of the concept of 'public benefit,' 'advancement of religion,' 'advancement of education,' 'relief of poverty' and 'other purposes which benefit the community.' A seminar conducted in 1994 and 1995 by tax litigators from the Department of Justice covered legal interpretation through such topics as "stare decisis," "ratio decidendi," and "obiter dictum."[55] In materials that employees are required to read, the Charities Division sets out its decision-making "philosophy":

> Charity is an ever-evolving and often 'grey' area of the law. It covers subject matters on which society is divided and on which even the Supreme Court of Canada renders split decisions (e.g. abortion, euthanasia, gay rights). There will always be differences of opinion in these matters. A decision made within the Charities Division at one point in time, given the facts and social climate of that moment, may well be overturned at a later date, due to the evolution of social standards, [*sic*] other principles of the law. Such is the nature of charity ... As an officer in the Charities Division you have an important role to play in ensuring that the decision-making process is transparent. In other words, anyone who reads a file after a decision has been made (whether to grant or deny registration) should be able to easily understand why the decision was made, through documentation which is clear, concise and logical. By adhering to this philosophy, examiners can be confident that they have made the 'right' decision, based on the material presented by the applicant, at a given point in time. This philosophy will become increasingly important as additional information on charities becomes available to the public.[56]

The key to consistency and coherence lies in adherence to precedent. The CCRA must ensure that like cases are treated in a like fashion. For this reason, it summarizes the implications of important case law in "interpretation bulletins" (intended for tax experts such as lawyers and accountants) and "information circulars" (for members of the public without expert training). All these sources are available to the public and thus allow organizations to predict the result of the agency's determinations with some accuracy. I discuss below the "transparency" of its decisions.

Dilemmas of Consistency, Coherence, and Adaptability

Despite these attempts to guide the discretion of tax officials, reliance on analogy and precedent invariably gives rise to decisions that are subjective and likely to appear arbitrary. Three recent examples of organizations applying for registration as charities can illustrate the dilemmas of consistency, coherence, and adaptability caused by reliance on common law definitions of charitable activities.

The first example shows the dilemma of consistency. It involves an Ontario self-help organization that was seeking registration as a charity. The body provides resources and support for medical and social work professionals engaged in running self-help groups. The Charities Division responded to its application for registration with a letter outlining a negative preliminary position. In the letter, the examiner set out the four accepted categories of charitable activity under the common law and indicated that self-help groups lack the necessary element of "altruism" to qualify as a "benefit to the community" under the fourth category and thus concluded that approval was unlikely.

This position puzzled and frustrated the applicant organization for two reasons. First, it did not correspond with its self-perception. All the people involved perceived their efforts as intended to help those in need in return for no material gain. If helping others help themselves was not altruism, they wondered, what was? Second, board members had been in touch with other like organizations around the country and discovered that many, which engaged in substantially similar and in some cases identical activities, had received registration in other parts of Canada, and in the same region at other times.[57] When a board member informed the examiner of the inconsistency of the CCRA's positions, the examiner told her flatly that information regarding the registration process vis-à-vis other organizations was privileged and confidential and that he could not comment on it. The board member concluded that the agency's decision-making was arbitrary and depended mostly on the examiner to which one was assigned. Her informal survey suggested that the only consistent factor in success was tenacity. Those organizations that persevered despite negative letters or rejected applications, who enlisted the support of an MP or municipal councillor, seemed more often than not to receive registration. Problems of consistency arise with particular frequency under the fourth category of charitable activity, because it depends on evolving notions of "benefit to the community," many of which are uncharted in case law.

The second example highlights the problem of coherence. It involves the Church of Scientology's application for registration as a charity.[58] At the time of writing, the decision is pending a comprehensive investigation into the church's activities. The decision will turn on whether the church constitutes a religion and therefore qualifies as a charity. While religious activity is one of the four qualifying spheres, the case law contains no universal definition of a religion. Rather than examining why religions should be entitled to public subsidies, the CCRA's guidelines focus on technical criteria. They state that a religion must have an element of theistic worship, defined as "the worship of a deity or deities in the spiritual sense."[59] Arthur Drache, counsel to the church in its application, raised the case of Buddhist organizations, registered even though Buddhism does not involve the worship of deities. Apparently, the CCRA had determined that Buddhism qualified as an exception to the general rule.[60] Such problems of coherence arise because officials have not been provided with practical and principled guidelines to apply.

The third example shows the dilemma of adaptability. How does the CCRA exercise its discretion in novel cases? This issue arose in the context of non-profit organizations providing free access to the internet. One group in Vancouver sought charitable registration. The CCRA took the position that internet providers, unlike libraries, do not control the content of the material to which they provide access and denied the application.

In *Vancouver Regional FreeNet Assn. v. M.N.R.*,[61] the Federal Court of Appeal considered whether a non-profit organization providing free access to internet qualified as a charity. Given the novelty of the technology, no case law was available. The choice seemed to be whether to analogize the internet to a public library (in which the issue of control over material distributed would be relevant) or to a public highway (in which control would not be relevant). The Court allowed the applicant's appeal. Once again, it used the Statute of Elizabeth as its point of departure. Justice Hugesson, writing for the majority, held that the provision of public access to the modern "information highway" was as much a charitable purpose as was the provision of access by more conventional highways in the time of Queen Elizabeth I. Justice Décary dissented on the basis that the organization did not exercise sufficient control over the uses of the internet to ensure its charitable purpose. He offered the following general observations regarding the dangers of relying purely on analogy in the face of novel claims: "The 'information highway' is a concept that is novel to our era and compares only marginally with the examples raised by the appellant. *The Court should rise above the constraints of analogy and, rather than compare the extrinsic qualities of past charitable purposes with the subject before it, consider the essential charitable nature of the organization on appeal.* Public benefit is an interminably broad concept, which spills over from the pure altruism of community welfare at one end of the spectrum into the realm of collective self-interest at the other. It is the courts' role to decide in each case whether the community values underpinning a certain purpose are overshadowed by what is otherwise its essentially non-charitable character" (emphasis added).[62]

CCRA officials cannot "rise above the constraints of analogy" in this fashion. In the absence of a statutory definition of charitable activity, they have recourse only to the decided case law. While they may have the authority to adapt the law of charities to novel applications, they lack the legitimacy to do so and thus remain dependent on infrequent and sometimes indeterminate judicial pronouncements.

In each of these three examples, the CCRA was called on to apply vague common law standards to specific, complex, and often novel factual circumstances. Because its decisions turn on an appreciation of these factual circumstances, the way in which prospective and charitable organizations are permitted to present their case to it takes on added significance. It is to an analysis of this process that I now turn.

Fairness and the Administrative Process

In its first year of operation in 1967, the Charities Division had received 34,630 applications for registration and approved 31,373 of these. Today, the CCRA receives approximately 5,000 applications annually and approves roughly 3,000.[63] It denies approximately 600 applications[64] and the rest are abandoned or deferred by applicants. The process typically takes between seven and fifteen months. Applicants file Form T2050, accompanied by a certified copy of all constating documents; a statement containing full details of the activities of the applicant; financial statements for the last fiscal year or if they are unavailable, a budget for the first year of operation; names and addresses of all members of the executive; and a statement as to whether the applicant plans to purchase property and, if so, the name of the registered owner of the property. An applicant is not entitled to have any other written or oral submissions considered by the minister in his or her determining whether to grant registration.

Where an organization meets the requirements of the Income Tax Act, the CCRA has no discretion to deny registration to an applicant. This, however, obscures the substantial discretion afforded it in its determining whether or not those requirements have been met. As I indicated above, there is no meaningful legislative direction or guidance as to how its officials should determine what constitutes a charity. Should the applicant receive the benefit of the doubt? Should tax officials take into consideration limitations of resources and expertise which may compromise an organization's application? These are crucial questions and affect the confidence that the CCRA enjoys both within the charitable sector and from the public at large.

Applicants have minimal "due process" rights. The scope of such rights is discussed in *Scarborough Community Legal Services v. The Queen*,[65] In this case, a legal aid clinic had applied for registration. The CCRA denied registration and informed the clinic that it did so because of the clinic's "political activities." The clinic challenged this decision, partly because the agency had failed to comply with the rules of natural justice or procedural fairness in that it reached a decision without giving the clinic prior notice of the case against it and an opportunity to meet that case. The appeal yielded three separate opinions from the Federal Court of Appeal on the issue of procedural fairness. The majority dismissed the clinic's procedural argument. Justice Marceau, writing for himself, held that "the decision to refuse the application in the present case was not made on the basis of information obtained without the interested party's participation; it was made solely on the evidence submitted by the applicant itself."[66] He concluded:

> The function of the Minister in dealing with an application for registration as a 'charity' under the *Income Tax Act* is, in my view, a strictly administrative function, and in spite of the fact that it involves the application of substantive rules and not the implementation of social and economic policy, on the basis of the basic criteria formulated by Mr. Justice Dickson (as he then was) in the leading case of *M.N.R. v. Coopers and Lybrand*, [1979] 1 SCR 495, it does not appear to me to be one subject, in its exercise, to judicial or quasi-judicial process. I am unable to accept the Appellant's suggestion that procedural fairness would call for a hearing of some sort before a contrary decision is reached by the Minister (or his duly authorized representative). Not only do I think that a requirement of that kind would go beyond Parliament's will as reflected in the legislation, I fail to see how such a hearing could better achieve justice and equity. If the decision is wrong because the law was improperly applied to the facts or because improper qualification was attributed to those facts, the appeal will remedy the situation; and if the decision is wrong because of a failure by the applicant to give all the facts or to expose them correctly, there is nothing to prevent him from renewing his application.[67]

Justice Urie reached the same result, but for somewhat different reasons. His analysis of administrative law, and in particular of *Attorney General of Canada v. Inuit Tapirisat of Canada et al.*,[68] led him to conclude that the granting or withholding of registration was a purely policy-based decision. Consequently, he held: "I am unable to find either as a matter of natural justice or of procedural fairness, an obligation on the Minister to invite representations or conduct a hearing before reaching a decision on the application."[69]

Justice Heald dissented and held that the CCRA had failed to comply with its duty of fairness in denying registration. He noted that the distinction between "administrative" and "judicial" decisions had lost favour in recent Supreme Court decisions in administrative law. In particular, Justice Heald relied on his earlier reasons in *Renaissance International v. M.N.R.*,[70] in which the Court had found the agency's revocation of a charitable registration to have violated the duty of fairness. Whereas the majority of the Court distinguished this decision, as it dealt with the more serious act of deregistration, Justice Heald viewed the reasoning of the case as equally applicable to the initial determination of registration. He stated: "I do not contend that the statutory scheme requires a formal hearing before the decision to refuse was made. However, I do think natural justice or the duty to act fairly would require, perhaps, a telephone call or a letter to the appellant advising of the Minister's difficulties or problems with the application, thus giving the appellant the opportunity to, at least, attempt to answer the Minister's objections. This would have resulted in a record reflecting the point of view of both the Minister and the organization concerned. Such a procedure would have given the appellant a reasonable opportunity to answer the allegations made against registration."[71] In the result, the Court dismissed the appeal and denied leave for a further appeal to the Supreme Court of Canada. The CCRA's practice since then appears to be to alert applicants by correspondence to the potential for an adverse disposition.

In addition to the procedural entitlements discussed in *Scarborough Legal Services*, applicants also have a right of appeal directly to the Federal Court of Appeal if registration is not granted.[72] The number of appeals from denials of registration varies sharply from year to year. Between 1987 and 1996, the high was eighteen appeals in 1996, while the low was one in 1993. The average was about eight.[73]

The record for such appeals is usually quite slim, consisting of the application form, the letter of refusal from the minister, and any prior correspondence. As Drache observes, the requirement that a first appeal be made to a "senior" court increases the time and expense of an appeal: "This means that in practical terms, a decision by the Minister not to register a charity is *de facto* final."[74] Not only have there been remarkably few appeals,[75] but the overwhelming majority of appeals taken to the Federal Court of Appeal have been decided in favour of the CCRA.[76] Drache suggests that "this may be a factor in the sometimes seemingly arbitrary decisions made by the Department on the issue of what constitutes a charity."[77] For these reasons,[78] the OLRC's report recommended a right of first appeal to the Tax Court, which, unlike the Federal Court of Appeal, could review findings of fact and law and amount to a trial *de novo* for applicants refused registration.[79]

The charity sector poses unique problems for a system of regulation premised on voluntary reporting and disclosures. Most charities are staffed by volunteers and managed by officers who rotate frequently. The CCRA has accordingly "softened" its enforcement relating to non-compliance with reporting requirements. Indeed, as of July 1990, the auditor general reported that the late-filing penalty imposed under section 162(7) of the act had never been applied and that, had it been, Revenue Canada would have recovered an additional $49 million annually.[80]

The act requires charities to file a return to the CCRA.[81] The return includes schedules and financial statements, which disclose a charity's sources of income and the nature of its disbursements and expenditures.[82] Failing to file this return is grounds for revocation of registration and is the most common cause of deregistration. In 1995–96, for example, 1,639 of 2,555 revocations resulted from failure to file a T3010.[83]

All charities are subject to the same disclosure and reporting requirements, despite the vast disparity in their resources and their ability to comply. The CCRA appears to compensate for this disparity by not rigorously enforcing these requirements, which allows both worthy and potentially unworthy organizations to continue to enjoy public benefits and erodes confidence in the regulation of charities generally. A system of graduated penalties for non-compliance would seem to represent a more effective alternative.[84] Similarly, differential reporting and disclosure requirements – like the current British system – might restore some equity to the system.

Reporting and disclosure help ensure the integrity of the system, but only auditing by the CCRA can ensure compliance.[85] Four recognized sources of information determine which charities are audited: random screening of files using predetermined criteria,[86] internal and external leads, letters of complaint, and press clippings.

Approximately 0.75 per cent of charities are audited regularly.[87] In 1995–96, the last year for which statistics are available, Revenue Canada conducted 576 audits. Only 23 ended in a "clean result" (i.e., the charity was in compliance with requirements).[88] In 331 cases, the department issued an "education letter," indicating some form of problem that could lead to non-compliance but not sufficient to warrant an undertaking or revocation of registration. In another 116 cases, organizations had to undertake to remedy non-compliance. Finally, in 8 cases, registration was revoked. These numbers, if representative, suggest that almost all registered charities are failing, or close to failing, to meet their legal obligations. Problems arguably go deeper than a simple increase in audits could reasonably hope to remedy.

Further, despite random audits, there remains no validation procedure for tax receipts issued by charities. The auditor general's report for 1990 noted this lacuna, as did the OLRC's report.[89]

As I noted above, the only significant enforcement mechanism is revocation of registration. Virtually all observers agree that this provides a sledgehammer where often a chisel would be more useful. There are two types of deregistration – technical and substantive. Technical deregistration result from non-compliance with reporting and filing requirements pursuant to section 168(1) of the act. Remedying the non-compliance, as prescribed in Information Circular 80-10R, usually resolves this sort of problem. In 1995–96, there were approximately 2,550 deregistrations on technical grounds, and approximately 900 of these were voluntary.[90] As for substantive grounds for deregestration, subsection 149.1(2)(a) prohibits a charity from carrying on an unrelated business, 149.1(2)(b) lays down an annual disbursement quota, and 149.1(4.1) prohibits a charity, in concert with another charity, from making a gift to the other charity to delay unduly the expenditure of funds on charitable activities. In 1995–96, there were eight deregistrations based on such "serious breaches of the legislative provisions."[91]

Whether or not the deregistration occurs on technical or substantive grounds, it has the same effect. That organization will be subject to 100 per cent tax on the fair market value of all assets not distributed to other registered charities.[92] This is sometimes referred to as a "penalty tax."

As I indicated above in the discussion of *Scarborough Legal Services*, the Federal Court of Appeal has viewed the act of revoking a registration as more serious than the decision to grant or deny a registration in the first place. As a result, additional duties of procedural fairness accompany deregistration. These duties were discussed in *Renaissance International v. M.N.R.* In *Renaissance*, a charitable organization received the following notification from the CCRA: "You are hereby notified that I propose to revoke the registration of Renaissance International as a result of its failure to comply with the requirements of the Income Tax Act for registration as a charity inasmuch as it has devoted resources to activities that are not charitable activities."[93] While the CCRA followed the notification procedure as set out in the act, it was not in dispute that the appellant had not been made aware either of the allegations made against it or of the intention to revoke its registration.[94] Renaissance appealed the CCRA's decision on two grounds: first, that the decision-maker followed an incorrect procedure in reaching the decision and, second, that the agency had no valid reason for revoking registration.

The Federal Court of Appeal was unanimous in allowing the appeal and setting aside the CCRA's decision. Both Justice Heald., writing for himself, and Justices Cowan and Pratte spoke in general terms of the agency's failure to comply with the requirements of natural justice and procedural fairness.[95] All shared a concern that the record on which the agency based its decision contained no input from the appellant. Reform proposals following *Renaissance* have focused on the requirement that the CCRA adhere to some process capable of producing a record sufficient for an organization to launch an appeal.[96]

Few appeals from deregistrations have reached the Court.[97] An appeal must be filed within 30 days of mailing of the notice to revoke. This is an extremely short time within which to decide to appeal. Additionally, appeals go directly to the Federal Court of Appeal, which does not normally hear testimony but relies instead on the written record, which may or may not reflect the true dimensions of the dispute.

The CCRA also has the authority to "annul" a charity – section 149.1(15) refers to registration that has been "revoked, *annulled* or terminated" (emphasis added). While the act sets out no procedure for "annulment," the agency has taken the position that annulment would apply where the registration of a charity in the first place was in error and should not have occurred.[98] There would also appear to be no statutory right of appeal from an annulment, leading Drache to conclude, based on communications from the CCRA, that the procedure would be used only where all parties consent.[99]

Public Access and Bureaucratic Transparency

In addition to ensuring the rights of applicants and charities to procedural fairness and appeals, the CCRA values openness. It is one of the most "transparent" departments in the federal civil service. It regularly issues interpretation bulletins, information circulars, pamphlets and brochures intended to clarify matters ranging from the definition of a charity to instructions on how to file an annual return.[100]

The Charities Division also has responsibility for ensuring public access to information about charities. As I indicated above, all charities must file an information return, a portion of which the CCRA is authorized to make available to the public. The CCRA also provides a list of all registered charities, which may be downloaded from its website. Finally, the division, to accompany its move to more spacious accommodations in Ottawa, plans for a new charities library for public use.[101]

The most significant and concrete evidence of the CCRA's commitment to transparency, however, has come in the form of a statutory amendment. In 1998, Parliament added section 241(3.2) to the Income Tax Act: "Registered Charities. An official may provide to any person the following taxpayer information relating to a charity that at any time was a registered charity: (a) a copy of the charity's governing documents, including its statement of purpose; (b) any information provided in prescribed form to the Minister by the charity on applying for registration under this Act; (c) the names of the persons who at any time were the charity's directors and the periods during which they were its directors; (d) a copy of the notification of the charity's registration, including any conditions and warnings; and (e) if the registration of the charity has been revoked, a copy of any letter sent by or on behalf of the Minister to the charity relating to the grounds for the revocation."[102]

Transparency, however, comes at a cost. The additional information now required in the annual T3010 lengthened the form from four to thirteen pages for 1998 – a substantial burden for small charities staffed entirely by volunteers. The division, for the first time ever, sent officials across the country to explain the new forms and facilitate compliance.[103]

Despite these efforts, some of the most basic and important information regarding the regulation of charities remains inaccessible to the public. The OLRC's report recommended, for example, that the financial reports of registered charities, currently unavailable to the public, be made available (except information that would identify particular donors) and that for charities with revenues or net assets in excess of $250,000 be required to have their financial disclosures audited.

While the new "transparency" provisions make available to the public "notification" of any charity's registration and, in the case of deregistration, a letter setting out the "grounds for the revocation," members of the public still are not permitted to learn why any particular organization was or was not granted registration. As this is arguably the most significant determination that the CCRA makes in its supervision of charities, this area, in my view, poses the greatest risk of unfairness and therefore has the greatest need for transparency.

Conclusion

It is now well-established that the CCRA owes prospective and current charities a duty of fairness in the administrative process. Clearly, it has gone to considerable lengths to ensure fairness and transparency in its treatment of charitable organizations. However, the very structure of the regulation of charities impairs its ability to meet the most basic tenet of fairness – namely, allowing an affected party to know the case that it has to meet. Because the statute is silent and the case law is ambiguous, the principles and standards that the CCRA will apply in any given case are virtually impossible to know in advance. The result – as the examples of the self-help organization, the Church of Scientology, and the Vancouver FreeNet demonstrate – is that the CCRA's attempts to ensure fairness have been unable to remedy the problems in the areas of consistency, coherence, and adaptability that have come to characterize the supervision of charities in Canada.

A PURPOSIVE APPROACH TO THE REGULATION OF CHARITIES

In earlier examinations of the CCRA's discretion, I have proposed that reforms should focus not on new procedures and rules to limit the tax administrator, but rather on more explicit ways of linking officials' inevitable and important judgments to clearly expressed norms and principles.[104] The foundation of such a reform project is the clearer articulation of those norms and principles through the democratic process.

The current system of charities regulation relies largely on litigation to provide guidance and direction to tax officials. The flaws with this system of regulation are many. Litigation leads to uneven, retrospective, and partial solutions to the many regulatory uncertainties that flow from the Income Tax Act. As Drache has observed, "A great many issues which revolve around what is a charity in the Canadian tax context have not been litigated. Therefore, although Revenue Canada may have views on such diverse issues as day-care centres, ethnic cultural centres or homes for single women vis-à-vis whether they will be registered as charities, no explicit case-law exists. This being the case, even a full understanding of the case law will not guarantee a full understanding of what Revenue Canada considers to be charitable."[105] Litigation also may mean that the ability to obtain legal representation becomes a prerequisite to charitable registration. This imposes an added and often onerous burden on applicants.[106] It also may contribute to the erosion of the CCRA's credibility in the charitable sector.

Additionally, relying on litigation and the common law as a means of developing the law of charity precludes any substantial reconsideration or reform of this area of the law. As the Supreme Court itself acknowledged in *Vancouver Minority Women*, it would be inappropriate for the courts to initiate any substantial change to the law of charities. For the majority, Justice Iacobucci stated, "As I have said, it would not be appropriate for the Court, in the context of this case, to adopt an entirely new definition of charity. If this is to be done, especially for the purposes of the *ITA* [Income Tax Act], the specifics of the desired approach will be for Parliament to decide."[107]

After looking at some proposals for reform from interested groups and academics, Justice Iacobucci returned to this theme: "However, I reiterate that, even though some substantial change in the law of charity would be desirable and welcome at this time, any such change must be left to Parliament. To be sure, the proposed change would amount to much more than merely a clarification of the law; indeed, it would likely result in a major expansion of the range of organizations that can qualify as charitable both under the *ITA* and otherwise. This would go well beyond the type of incremental change to the common law which this Court has been prepared to make."[108]

However, not everyone is enthusiastic about Parliament's heeding the Court's call to legislative reform of the law of charities. The OLRC's report, among other documents, has argued on conceptual grounds against codifying a definition of "charity".[109] The report draws the distinction between the process of determining the content of the "good" (i.e., politics and the legislative process) and that of determining the "good" itself (i.e., law and the judicial process), and it concludes that the meaning of "charity" for the purpose of a system of registration is an example of the latter type of determination. In my view, this distinction is untenable. In the context of charities, the content of charitable activity is inextricably bound up with its value. This is, moreover, appropriate in my view. We do not provide a public benefit to universities as such; rather, we provide a public benefit to universities because they teach students a set of skills and information that is socially valued and viewed as an important public good. Unless those who supervise charities pay attention to the content of an organization's activities, the meaning of charity becomes emptied of meaning and purpose. What then, taxpayers should ask, are we subsidizing?

Contrary to the OLRC's approach, the Voluntary Sector Roundtable, founded by a coalition of major, national non-profit organizations, has recommended that a definition be codified on democratic grounds.[110] The panellists summarized their argument as follows: "The determination of which organizations get the full benefits of the tax system should signal to all Canadians what we most value in civil society when it comes to providing a tax based incentive for giving. This determination and the assignment of privileges and responsibilities associated with it is inherently political, involving trade-offs in values and in expenditures. It therefore should be decided by legislatures, not by the courts."[111]

I reach the same conclusion as the panellists, but for additional reasons. In my view, a statutory definition of charitable activity may be desirable not only from the standpoint of political efficacy but also in order to ensure consistency, coherence, and adaptability in the treatment of charities and prospective charities by the CCRA.

The so-called common law definition of charitable activities has its origins in a statutory instrument – England's Charitable Uses Act, 1601, or the Statute of Elizabeth. Statutes, their administration and the common law are necessarily intertwined. The Statute of Elizabeth arose because lack of clarity in the common law prevented the coherent administration of charitable trusts at a time of urgent pressures on the public purse; our situation is virtually identical today. Passage of the Statute of Elizabeth signalled the beginning rather than the end of the process of clarifying the categories of charity. Its norms and principles had to be interpreted, applied, and adapted to changing legal and factual circumstances. For example, *Pemsel* sought to adapt them to the income tax. By the same token, any attempt to refine and rearticulate them today will invariably give rise to gaps and ambiguities, to which the common law is uniquely well-suited to respond on a case-by-case basis. The goal of codifying the definition of charitable activities should therefore achieve not specificity but purpose. In other words, a definition need not list all the activities that will be accepted as charitable, but rather should provide those who supervise the registration of charities with the ability to understand and apply the distinction between organizations worthy of charitable status and those that are not. This is the crucial function that the common law, to date, has been unable to perform satisfactorily.

To return again to consistency, coherence, and adaptability, the difference between the common law and statutory approaches becomes evident. In explaining its preliminary negative assessment of the self-help organization's application, as we saw above, the CCRA set out the four categories recognized in the common law definition of charity and added that "court have not recognized that self-help activity is charitable" because it lacks the necessary element of "altruism." To the

Church of Scientology, the CCRA's preliminary objections revolved around the absence of worship for a deity. In the Vancouver FreeNet case, the agency puzzled over whether the internet is or is not akin to a library. These three explanations provide the affected organizations with no chance for a meaningful understanding of the distinction between what is and is not a charity.

In denying the Vancouver Society of Immigrant and Visible Minority Women's application for registration, the minister stated: "the courts have not considered women simply by virtue of their gender or racial origin to be in special need of charitable relief. Decisions in common law, upon which the law of charities evolves, originate in the courts; *the Department only administers the law as it now stands*" (emphasis added).[112]

Clear statutory categories would set out the principles underlying acceptable charitable activities; indicate criteria to distinguish charitable from non-charitable activities; and provide examples of acceptable and unacceptable charitable activities. Such a schema would enable tax officials to justify their determinations according to principles and norms reflecting a social and political consensus. Where such justifications were challenged, these criteria would provide a basis on which the courts could refine and clarify legislative intentions. This proposed legislative mechanism could not provide perfect clarity of purpose, but it would replace the purposive vacuum that currently undermines the regulation of charities in Canada.

An example of such an approach is the Income Tax Act's definition of "non-profit organization": "a club, society or association that, in the opinion of the Minister, was not a charity within the meaning assigned by subsection 149.1(1) and that was organized and operated exclusively for social welfare, civic improvement, pleasure or recreation or for any other purpose except profit" (section 149.1[1]). This definition discloses a general principle (i.e., that a non-profit organization must be operated for a purpose other than profit), examples to illustrate the principle (for example, social welfare and civic improvement), and examples of a distinguishable category of organizations (i.e., charities).

In the case of our self-help organization, such a statutory definition of charity would help clarify the scope of altruism. Is altruism about helping others, or does it also include helping others help themselves? Additionally, self-help organizations, among others, could make submissions to the parliamentary drafters of new legislation on why their activities ought to be charitable. A statutory definition of charity would enable the CCRA to approach this and other contexts on a consistent basis.

Similarly, in the case of the Church of Scientology, a statutory definition of charity would probably provide the CCRA with a purposive definition of charity on which to grant or refuse religious organizations registration (and thus avoid distinctions between worship and non-worship of a deity). Finally, in the Vancouver FreeNet case, a statutory definition would probably deal with the internet and other analogous technologies. What we need is a clear, principled, and practical definition, based on wide and comprehensive consultation with the charitable sector, as well as the participation of the federal and provincial administrative bodies charged with supervising charities.

There are many ways in which a purposive approach may alter administrative practices. For example, it would lead to decisions that correspond and are *seen* to correspond to the broader norms underlying the tax expenditure for charities. This can happen only with dissemination of some form of reasons for decision-making in the registration process. Under the recent amendments to the act, the CCRA will make available to the public both notification of registration for any registered charity and any correspondence setting out the grounds for a revocation of registration. Reasons why a particular group was or was not granted registration, however, remain unavailable. The Supreme Court recently has recognized a common law duty to provide written reasons in certain circumstances.[113]

There are clear benefits attaching to the dissemination of reasons. First and foremost, it increases the likelihood of consistency within an administrative agency. As one text on administrative law concludes, "[M]aking a statement of reasons for decisions available to other members of the agency is likely to improve the quality of the subsequent decisions of the agency. Decision makers who are able to consult the reasons for decision in previous cases are likely to interpret their enabling legislation, and to exercise their discretionary powers in a more consistent and informed way. Relating the interpretation of a statute, or the exercise of statutory discretion, in a particular case to the broader framework of agency policies and jurisprudence can help to promote administrative rationality and consistency, and to avoid purposeless "drift."[114]

Concerns about privacy, efficiency, delay, and cost may influence the kind of reasons produced but should not impair the goal of demonstrating a consistent and principled adherence to the norms and rules articulated in a statutory definition of charity.

Finally, a purposive approach should render the government more accountable for the subsidy provided to the charitable sector and more responsive to its needs. It may lead to periodic and independent reviews of the administration of charities; to creation of a charities ombudsman, an office to assist smaller charities in registering and reporting; and to regular reporting of the value of the tax expenditure directed to the charitable sector. Without such an approach, the CCRA will undoubtedly continue to muddle through and improve administrative practices on an incremental and ad hoc basis. However, this is unlikely to satisfy either the charitable sector or the Canadian public in the long run.

CONCLUSION

Charity, in the final analysis, is about the public good. When an organization receives charitable status, this reflects a social consensus that its activities are beneficial to our society. In this sense, the supervision of charities necessarily involves the regulation of virtue. The commissioners assigned to administer the Statute of Elizabeth recognized this duty and had statutory guidance to assist them. The CCRA's officials, by contrast, do not see their task as determining the "equities" of the Income Tax Act, and, whether as a cause or as a result of that fact, the act provides few or no "equities" for them to enforce. Therefore, the first step towards improving the supervision of charities in Canada, in my view, is clarifying the purpose to which the support and regulation of charities aims. This exercise in turn will provide the missing normative basis for the supervision of charities in Canada.

In this chapter, I have concluded that articulating the purpose of the tax benefit for charities through a definition of charitable activities in the Income Tax Act will give rise to more consistent, more coherent, and more flexible exercise of administrative discretion. This situation in turn will lead to enhanced accountability by the government for the vast tax expenditure provided to charities and to more focused judicial decisions interpreting the scope of this tax expenditure. Greater clarity and accountability in the supervision of charities, in my view, will lead to a more vibrant and engaged charitable sector and ultimately to greater public confidence in the regulation of charities in Canada. In short, a clear, purposive mandate makes both the regulation of virtue and the virtues of regulation possible.

NOTES

I would like to thank the participants in the Conference on Charity and Charities Law held at the University of Toronto, 22–23 January 1999, for providing a stimulating and thought-provoking forum in which to develop the ideas contained here. I am especially grateful to Jim Phillips and to Carl Juneau of the CCRA's Charities Division for reading and commenting on an earlier draft.

1 Provinces also have a significant regulatory role in the conduct of charities, especially in providing the legal structures within which charities may operate, in protecting charities against fraud, and in enforcing charitable fiduciary relationships. See Ontario Law Reform Commission, (OLRC), *Report on the Law of Charities* (Toronto: OLRC, 1996), 385–92.

2 These figures are drawn from T1 statistics; see Sharpe, chapter 2 in this volume.

3 *Report of the Auditor General*, 1990 (Ottawa: Supply and Services, 1990), 10.16.

4 Government of Canada, *Tax Expenditures 1999* (Ottawa: Department of Finance, June 1999), 17.

5 See the discussion of the value placed on the charitable sector in OLRC, *Report*, 17.

6 A thorough review of these and other rationales for subsidizing and regulating charities appears in ibid., chap. 9.

7 For a sampling of this literature, see K.C. Davis, *Discretionary Justice: A Preliminary Inquiry* (Baton Rouge: Louisiana State University Press, 1969); R. Hummell, *The Bureaucratic Experience* (New York: Free Press, 1979); H. Kass and B. Catron, eds., *Images and Identities in Public Administration* (London: Sage, 1990); J. Handler, "Discretion: Power, Quiescence, and Trust," in Hawkins, ed., *The Uses of Discretion* (Oxford: Clarendon Press, 1992); and L. Sossin, "The Politics of Discretion: Toward a Critical Theory of Public Administration," *Canadian Public Administration* 36 (1993), 364.

8 M. Lipsky, *Street-Level Bureaucracy* (New York: Russell Sage, 1980), xii.

9 This is not an argument restricted to the charitable setting. Elsewhere, I have set out the importance of elucidating the purpose(s) of the tax system generally as a condition for the effective administration of the anti-avoidance provisions in the Income Tax Act. See L. Sossin, "Redistributing Democracy: Authority, Discretion and the Possibility of Engagement in the Welfare State," *Ottawa Law Review* 26 (1994), 1.

10 See OLRC, *Report*, 333–79; Panel on Accountability and Governance in the Voluntary Sector, *Helping Canadians Help Canadians: Improving Governance and Accountability in the Voluntary Sector*, discussion paper released May 1998, 31; P. Monahan, *Federal Regulation of Charities: A Critical Assessment of Recent Proposals for Legislative and Regulatory Reform* (Toronto: York University Centre for Public Law and Public Policy, 2000); and *Auditor General Report, 1990*. See also F. Woodman, "The Tax Treatment of Charities and Charitable Donations since the Carter Commission: Past Reforms and Present Problems," *Osgoode Hall Law Journal* 26 (1998), 539.

11 See Legislation Tabled to Create Canada Customs and Revenue Agency (Bill C-43). Revenue Canada, Customs, Excise and Taxation, News Release 25TC/98 (Ottawa, 4 June 1998).

12 See G. Jones, *History of the Law of Charity 1532–1827* (London: Cambridge University Press, 1969), 26.

13 Preamble to the Charitable Uses Act, 1601 (43 Eliz. I, c. 4). The categories include the relief of "aged, impotent, and poor people; the maintenance of sick and maimed soldiers and mariners, schools of learning, free schools, and scholars in universities; the repair of bridges, ports, havens, causeways, churches, seabanks, and highways; the education and preferment of orphans; the relief of stock, or maintenance of houses of correction; marriage of poor maids; supportation, aid, and help of young tradesmen, handicraftsmen, and persons decayed; the relief or redemption of prisoners or captives; and the aid or ease of any poor inhabitants concerning payment of fifteens, setting out of soldiers, and other taxes." The list was not intended to be exhaustive or exclusive. See Jones, *History of the Law of Charity*, 26.

14 The main prong of this response was the Poor Relief Act, 39 Eliz. I., c. 3.

15 As Jones emphasizes, "Public benefit was the key to the statute, and the relief of poverty its principal manifestation": *History of the Law of Charity*, 27. For a discussion of this purpose, see ibid., 16–22.

16 See F. More, *Reading*, C.U.L. Ms. Hh. III 2(c), cited in ibid., 27–9.

17 39 Geo. 3, c. 13 (UK).

18 Commencing with the outbreak of the First World War, the federal government offered tax incentives for charities supporting the war effort. The rationale appears to have been that such tax expenditures would reduce the obligation on the part of the government to finance humanitarian activities associated with the war. In the case of the first Canadian Patriotic Fund Act, 1914, 5 Geo. 5, c. 8 (Can.), this consisted of supporting soldiers through the Red Cross and similar humanitarian relief endeavours. The original Income War Tax Act exempted "religious, charitable, agricultural and educational institutions": see Income War Tax Act, 1917, 7–8 Geo 5, c. 28 (Can.), s. 5(d). All subsequent versions of income tax legislation retained this exemption in one form or another. For an excellent summary of the history of charitable regulation, see OLRC, *Report*, 249–86. See also R.M. Bird and M.W. Bucovetsky, *Canadian Tax Reform and Private Philanthropy* (Toronto: Canadian Tax Foundation, 1976).

19 See An Act to Amend the Income War Tax Act, 1917, 1920, 10–11 Geo. 5, c. 49 (Can.), s. 5.

20 See An Act to Repeal the War Charities Act, 1917, SC 1926–27, c. 39.

21 See An Act to Amend the Income War Tax Act, SC 1930, c. 24, s. 3.

22 See War Charities Act, 1939, SC 1939 (2d sess.), c. 10. A registration scheme set up to accompany the tax incentive for charities during the Second World War was repealed shortly after the end of the war. See An Act to Amend the Income War Tax Act, SC 1939 (2nd Sess.), c. 6.

23 See Act to amend the Income Tax Act, SC 1966–67, c. 47, s. 3.

24 These allegations implied that the charitable organizations were either complicitous or responsible for the abuse. See the summary of the parliamentary debates on this issue in OLRC, *Report*, 262–3.

25 Technically, the discretion provided in the act is ministerial. In this sense, it is not the CCRA nor particular officials in it that are authorized to make determinations; rather the minister is so authorized (and, by regulation, delegates certain kinds of authority to other officials in the ministry). In this chapter, however, I refer to decisions by variously "tax officials," "Revenue Canada officials," "Revenue Canada," and "the Minister."

26 See section 110(8) of the act. See also Revenue Canada, Information Circular 80-10R "Registered Charities: Operating a Registered Charity" (17 Dec. 1985).

27 Because private foundations are usually funded by a single family or organization, they are additionally subject to restrictions regarding non–arm's-length transactions between the foundation and its founders.

28 See section 149(1)(1) of the act. Revenue Canada, Interpretation Bulletin IT-496, "Non-Profit Organizations" (18 Feb. 1983).

29 See *L.I.U.N.A. Local 527 Members' Training Trust Fund v. Canada*, [1992] 2 CTC 2410 (TCC). However, an organization may always insert into its objects some activity or purpose that will disqualify it as a charity. In this fashion, organizations that have no interest in issuing tax receipts for donations can effectively avoid the added scrutiny that charitable registration may bring. See A. Drache, *Canadian Taxation of Charities and Donations* (Toronto: Carswell, 1994), 15–22.

30 See 1976–77, c. 4, s. 60(3)–(5).

31 See Drache, *Canadian Taxation of Charities*, 1–24.

32 Charitable Uses Act, 1601 (43 Eliz. I, c. 4).

33 [1896] AC 531 (HL)

34 See OLRC, *Report*, 167–8. See also *Human Life International in Canada Inc. v. Minister of National Revenue*, [1998] 3 FC 202 at 214: "One may observe in passing that that statute [*of Elizabeth*] does not purport to give an exhaustive definition of charity nor was that its purpose, and one may well question its relevance to Canadian society some four centuries later. This Court has however been obliged to develop principles appropriate for Canada particularly with respect to the open-ended fourth category of 'purposes beneficial to the community' and it is this jurisprudence to which we must give primary consideration. *It remains, nevertheless, an area crying out for clarification through Canadian legislation for the guidance of taxpayers, administrators, and the courts*" (emphasis added).

35 See, for example, *Native Communications Society of B.C. v. M.N.R.*, [1986] 3 FC 471 at 478 (CA), per Stone, JA.

36 Revenue Canada used to make this test explicit in Information Circular 77-14. However, in 80-10R, which superseded it, there is no mention of the *Pemsel* categories or of any other basis on which "charitable activities" will be defined. However, CCRA, Charities Division, *Employee Handbook* (May 1997), states, "It is still recognized that, in order to be charitable at law, a purpose must fall within one of [*Pemsel*]'s four heads of charity" (45).

37 See *Re Laidlaw Foundation* (1984), 48 OR (2nd) 549 at 582 (Div. Ct), per Southey, J.

38 See *Vancouver Society of Immigrant and Visible Minority Women v. Minister of National Revenue*, [1999] 1 SCR 10 at 107, in which Justice Iacobucci cited the following passage from *R. v. Salituro*, [1991] 3 SCR 654, at 670: "Judges can and should adapt the common law to reflect the changing social, moral and economic fabric of the country. Judges should not be quick to perpetuate rules whose social foundation has long since disappeared. Nonetheless, there are significant constraints on the power of the judiciary to change the law ... The judiciary should confine itself to those incremental changes which are necessary to keep the common law in step with the dynamic and evolving fabric of our society." See also Iacobucci, J., 135.

39 See Phillips, chapter 7 in this volume.

40 See *Vancouver Minority Women*, upholding dismissal of an appeal to the Federal Court of Appeal: [1996] 2 CTC 88 (FCA).

41 *Vancouver Minority Women*, 135.

42 See section 149.1(1)(6)(a) of the act. See also *Alberta Institute on Mental Retardation v. The Queen*, [1987] 2 CTC 70 (FCA.), leave to appeal to SCC denied 87 NR note (SCC). For further discussion, see Davis, chapter 15 in this volume.

43 See Information Circular 78-3 (27 Feb. 1978) [subsequently withdrawn]. See also *Positive Action against Pornography v. M.N.R.*, [1988] 1 CTC 232 (FCA); *Toronto Volgograd Committee v. M.N.R.*, [1988] 1 CTC 365 (FCA.); and *Briarpatch Inc. v. R.*, [1996] 2 CTC 94 (FCA). For more, see Drassinower, chapter 9 in this volume.

44 Whether this purposive vacuum is created by a legislative void or by a failure on the part of the courts, particularly the Federal Court of Appeal, to elucidate the purposes of the charitable subsidy remains an open question. For a discussion of this question, see Phillips, chapter 7 in this volume.

45 Canada, *Report of the Royal Commission on Taxation* (commissioner, K. Le M. Carter) (Ottawa: Queen's Printer, 1966), 135.

46 These figures come from correspondence from the CCRA dated 2 July 1998, on file with the author.

47 I draw these figures from Charities Division, *Employee Handbook*, 33.

48 For more on these jurisdictional boundaries, see OLRC, *Report*, 1–19.

49 The ministries of Finance and of Justice also help supervise charities: Finance drafts legislative provisions in the Income Tax Act relating to charities, and Justice undertakes the litigation arising from those provisions. The relationship between these ministries and its implications for the efficiency and accountability of the tax system and discussed in *Report of the Auditor General, 1998* (Ottawa, 1998), chap. 5.
50 OLRC, *Report*, 378.
51 Sharpe, chapter 2 in this volume.
52 See Information Circular 80-10R.
53 This list appears in a draft brochure issued by the CCRA entitled "Registered Charities: Operating outside Canada."
54 This list includes: a charity registered under the act; a Canadian amateur athletic association registered under the act; a national arts service organization registered under the act; a housing corporation resident in Canada and exempt from tax under Part I of the act because of paragraph 149.(1)(I); a municipality in Canada; the United Nations or an agency thereof; a university outside Canada that ordinarily includes students from Canada (listed in Schedule VIII); a charitable organization outside Canada to which Her Majesty in Right of Canada has made a gift during the taxpayer's taxation year or the 12 months immediately preceding that taxation year; and Her Majesty in Right of Canada or of a province.
55 Charities Division, *Employee Handbook*, 64.
56 Ibid., 63.
57 This apparent inconsistency may have resulted from a range of factors, including differences in objectives and in constituting documents. It could also result from the "grandparenting" of charities registered prior to 1977, discussed above. Thus a significant number of charities registered that would not qualify today. Organizations that are identical to registered charities may well be denied registration.
58 See J. Saunders and T. Appleby, "Scientology Seeks Tax Receipt Status," *Globe and Mail*, 19 Jan. 1998, A1, A6. For a discussion of religion, with obvious relevance to this case, see Phillips, chapter 10 in this volume.
59 Saunders and Appleby, "Scientology," A6.
60 On this point, Drache observed, "I mean, what they're saying is if it looks okay to us, we're going to register it, no matter what it is, and if it doesn't look okay to us, we're not going to register it": ibid., A6.
61 [1996] 3 CTC 102 (FCA).
62 *Vancouver FreeNet*, 118.
63 CCRA correspondence dated 2 July 1998.
64 Charities Division, *Employee Handbook*, 33.
65 (1985), 17 DLR (4th) 308 (FCA); leave to appeal to SCC refused 87 NR note (SCC).
66 *Scarborough Legal Services*, 323.

67 Ibid.

68 [1980] 2 SCR 735. In this case, the Supreme Court held that a duty of procedural fairness does not apply to the exercise of purely "legislative functions" by government.

69 *Scarborough Legal Services*, 317.

70 [1983] 1 FC 860 (CA).

71 *Scarborough Legal Services*, 313

72 See section 172(4) of the act.

73 CCRA correspondence dated 2 July 1998. Very few of these appeals result in decisions from the Federal Court of Appeal. According to Jim Phillips, since the 1970s, the Federal Court of Appeal has decided seventeen appeals from a denial of registration (see Phillips, chapter 7 in this volume). Thus, the majority of appeals commenced by unsuccessful applicants presumably are settled or abandoned.

74 Drache, *Canadian Taxation of Charities*, 6–13. It would appear that an incorporated charity must be represented by a lawyer should it seek judicial review of an adverse decision, even if it is impecunious: see *IAM Institute of Applied Methodology v. Canada*, [1991] 1 CTC 226 (FCTD).

75 See a brief discussion of these decisions in Drache, *Canadian Taxation of Charities*, 6–12.

76 See Phillips, chapter 7 in this volume.

77 Ibid.

78 See OLRC, *Report.*, 292, n18, noting criticism of the appeals procedures from both academic and judicial commentators.

79 Ibid, 341. The option of a more "robust internal administrative procedure within Revenue Canada" was also considered. The Tax Court reduced administrative costs and increased fairness, openness, and the ability to ensure a proper record. The OLRC further recommended that the appeal to the Tax Court would not be available only for adverse decisions but also for cases where no decision had been reached within 180 days, which would be deemed a refusal of registration.

80 *Auditor General Report, 1990*, 10.57.

81 See section 149.1(14).

82 See CCRA, "Guide to Charity Information Return"; see also Drache, *Canadian Taxation of Charities*, chap. 7.

83 CCRA correspondence dated 2 July 1998.

84 See OLRC, *Report*, 377–9. See also R. DeGaudenzi, "Tax-Exempt Public Charities: Increasing Accountability and Compliance," *Catholic Lawyer* 36 (1995), 203 (setting out a similar proposal for the American context).

85 Audits differ in scope, but most would involve independent verification of the key information provided on an organization's annual filings and disclosures. Pursuant to sections 230(2) and (4) and Regulation 5800(1)(d)–(g), all registered charities must have available sufficient

records to allow verification of donation receipts issued, income received, and disbursements made. The CCRA publishes a pamphlet explaining the audit process to registered charities. See T4118 Auditing Registered Charities, which can be located at www.rc.gc.ca/E/pub/gd/et4118w/3305e.w51.html. Charitable organizations are not required to file *audited* financial statements, though the Carter Commission and others have recommended this requirement, at least for larger charitable ones. See OLRC, *Report,* 264.

86 Assuming that an organization becomes a "registered charity," it must complete and file annually the Registered Charity Information Return (form T3010). Section I asks for details on how the charity is accomplishing its charitable goals. Based on these filings, the CCRA will target certain organizations for an audit.

87 CCRA correspondence dated 2 July 1998.

88 See Charities Division, *Employee Handbook,* Table 6.

89 See *Auditor General Report, 1990,* 265; and OLRC, *Report,* 312.

90 See Charities Division, *Employee Handbook,* Table 7.

91 Ibid., 34.

92 See sections 188(1) and (2) of the act. In such cases, the fair market is valued as of 120 days prior to the date on which the notice of the minister's intention to deregister was mailed.

93 *Renaissance International,* 864. Pursuant to this notification, the revocation would become effective when the notice is published in the *Canada Gazette,* which must be at least 30 days after the date the notification letter was mailed: see section 168 of the act.

94 The evidence indicated that the director had noticed a *Globe and Mail* article that cast doubt on Renaissance's charitable status: see *Renaissance International,* 869.

95 Justice Pratte concluded in his analysis of the act: "I have concluded after much hesitation that, contrary to what was argued by counsel for the respondent, the provisions of the *Income Tax Act* do not impliedly relieve the Minister from the duty to comply with the rules of natural justice and procedural fairness before sending a notice pursuant to subsection 168(1). On the contrary, those provisions, as I read them, rather suggest that the Minister, before sending the notice, must first give to the person or persons concerned a reasonable opportunity to answer the allegations made against them": ibid., 866.

96 See OLRC, *Report,* 340.

97 According to Phillips, only three decisions by the Federal Court of Appeal have resulted from appeals of deregistration: see Phillips, chapter 7 of this volume.

98 An annulment, see Drache, *Canadian Taxation of Charities,* 6–20.

99 Ibid.

100 The Department of National Revenue initiated a program in 1970 to provide interpretation bulletins and information circulars to the public. See Revenue Canada, Information Circular No. 70-1, "Announcements, Information Circulars, and Interpretation Bulletins," 25 Aug. 1970.

Interpretation bulletins are often written in technical language and tailored to the tax practitioner (lawyers, accountants, and financial advisers). Even more specialized technical explanations routinely accompany the Department of Finance's amendments to the Income Tax Act. The department has issued well over 500 interpretation bulletins since 1970, typically revealing its interpretation of a specific section or area of the act. These guidelines do not have the force of law, but they serve to structure the exercise of administration discretino and guarantee at least a measure of unifority and predictability in application of the act. It is a principle of administrative law that an administrative body may not bind itself to or fetter its discretion by non-statutory rules. See J.M. Evans, *de Smith's Judicial Review of Administrative Action*, 4th ed. (London: Stevens & Son, 1980), 311–17.

While interpretation bulletins clarify the department's interpretive judgments in particular areas of the act, information circulars are typically more general and oriented to procedure. They usually concern a certain class of taxpayer or realm of tax administration and tend to deal more with policy. Even more informal are pamphlets and brochures that offer general information to a large class of taxpayers, such as charities that engage in foreign operations. Additionally, when a new publication is contemplated, a draft is usually circulated for public comment: see, for example, a draft of the forthcoming brochure "Registered Charities: Operating outside Canada," available online at www.rc.gc.ca/E/pub/

Finally, the Charities Division of the CCRA publishes a newsletter that regularly updates registered charities on new developments in legal intepretations and administative practices. These publications provide practical and relevant guidance to the charitable sector and suggest the sense of balance and fairness that the division seeks to convey in its judgments. Typically, it provides examples of what would and would not be acceptable practice for charities.

101 See remarks by Carl Juneau, acting director, Charities Division, in *Canadian Not-for-Profit News* 5, no. 11 (Nov. 1997), 84. The division's move is not yet complete, and it is housed in two locations.

102 Section 241(3.2) was added by SC 1998, c. 19, s. 65(1).

103 This information was provided by Jayne Bell, Charities Division, CCRA, in a telephone conversation on 1 October 1998.

104 See L. Sossin, "Revenue, Legitimacy and Ideology: The Politics of Canadian Tax Administration," PhD dissertation, University of Toronto,

1993; L. Sossin, "Squeezing Blood from Stones: The Income Tax Industry in Canada," *Journal of Law and Social Policy* 8 (1992), 178; and L. Sossin, "Welfare State Crime: The Politics of Tax Evasion in the 1980s," *Windsor Yearbook of Access to Justice* 12 (1992) 98.

105 A. Drache, *The Charity and Not-for-Profit Sourcebook: Cases, Legislation and Commentary* (Toronto: Carswell, 1994), 2–12.

106 When an organization is told that its activities may be "charitable" in the popular sense but not in the legal sense because a court has so determined, it may have no alternative but to obtain legal assistance. For smaller bodies, this may foreclose the possibility of responding adequately to a negative decision. A 1994 study revealed that almost half of all charities in Canada have annual revenues of less than $50,000 and that 38 per cent of all charities are run entirely by volunteers and have no full-time staff. See Sharpe, chapter 2 in this volume.

107 *Vancouver Minority Women*, 135.

108 Ibid., 137.

109 OLRC, *Report*, 147–55.

110 *Helping Canadians Help Canadians*, 31; see also discussion in S. Greene, "A Crossroads for Canadian Charities," *Chronicle of Philanthropy* 10, no. 21 (27 Aug. 1998), 30.

111 *Helping Canadians Help Canadians*, 31. The panellists believe that flexibility could be preserved by having the statutory definition "reviewed" every 10 years.

112 *Vancouver Minority Women*, 88, 90.

113 See *Baker v. Canada (Minister of Citizenship and Immigration)* (1999) 174 DLR 4th 193 at 212 (SSC).

114 J. Evans et al., eds., *Administrative Law: Cases, Text and Materials*, 4th ed. (Toronto: Emond Montgomery, 1995), 479.

13 Charitable Contributions and the Personal Income Tax: Evaluating the Canadian Credit

DAVID G. DUFF

The last fifteen years has witnessed significant changes in the way in which charitable contributions by individuals are treated under the Canadian Income Tax Act.[1] In 1984, an optional standard deduction of $100, which taxpayers could claim irrespective of the amount that they actually contributed to charities, was repealed.[2] In the same year, rules governing the taxation year in which charitable contributions could be deducted were relaxed, permitting taxpayers to claim amounts up to five years after the year of the gift.[3] More recently, amendments have increased the maximum limit on charitable gifts eligible for tax assistance from 20 per cent of the taxpayer's annual income to 50 per cent for 1996 and 75 per cent for 1997 and subsequent taxation years[4] and reduced the taxable amount of any gain on charitable gifts of certain publicly traded securities made after 18 February 1997 and before 2002 from three-quarters of the gain to three-eighths.[5]

The most significant change, however, involves the conversion in 1988 of what had previously been a deduction for charitable contributions, whereby the value of the tax benefit depended on the donor's level of income,[6] into a tax credit, under which the value of this benefit depends on the total amount of charitable contributions claimed in the particular taxation year.[7] As a result of this amendment, Canada has become the only developed country that recognizes charitable contributions by individuals in the form of a tax credit rather than a deduction.[8]

This chapter evaluates the merits of this policy change and the structure of the Canadian charitable contributions tax credit in the light of alternative possible rationales for the recognition of these gifts in computing the amount of tax payable under an income tax. The first section reviews the history of Canadian income tax provisions regarding charitable contributions by individuals and explains the structure of the current tax credit and related provisions governing the tax treatment of charitable contributions by individuals. The second section examines four possible rationales and related tax designs for the recognition of these charitable gifts in computing the amount of tax payable under an income tax, rejecting the views that recognition is necessary to define income or reward altruism, but accepting the arguments that tax assistance may have a useful role to play in promoting pluralism by encouraging donations. The third section offers brief conclusions on the current Canadian tax credit in light of the rationales and design characteristics examined in the second.

HISTORY AND STRUCTURE

Although the Canadian income tax currently recognizes charitable contributions in the form of a credit against basic tax otherwise payable, not a deduction in computing taxable income, the basic structure of the credit and other provisions relating to charitable contributions dates back to 1930, when the Income War Tax Act[9] was amended by the addition of a deduction for charitable donations.[10] This part of the chapter examines the history of tax relief for charitable contributions in order to explain the current scheme of the act.

Deduction

When Canada adopted its first income tax in 1917, the act contained a limited deduction for "amounts paid by the taxpayer during the year to the Patriotic and Canadian Red Cross Funds, and other patriotic and war funds approved by the Minister."[11] While this provision was repealed in 1920,[12] a more general deduction was adopted in 1930, at which time a provision was introduced allowing taxpayers to deduct "... not more than ten per centum of the net taxable income of any taxpayer which has been actually paid by way of donation within the taxation period to, and receipted for as such by, any charitable organization in Canada operated exclusively as such and not operated for the benefit or private gain or profit of any person, member or shareholder thereof." Based on this provision, therefore, taxpayers could deduct receipted donations to qualifying "charitable organizations" up to an annual maximum of 10 per cent of their net taxable income, computed after deducting various costs of earning income and other personal amounts such as medical expenses and allowances for dependants. While subsequent amendments imposed a registration requirement on charitable organizations,[13] and increased the annual ceiling on deductible contributions to 20 per cent,[14] the deduction itself changed little until its conversion to a tax credit in 1988.[15] Indeed, the credit itself continues to contain an income-related ceiling on the extent to which charitable contributions qualify for the credit.[16]

Notwithstanding six printed pages of parliamentary debate, most of which centred on the kinds of organizations donations to which would qualify for the deduction,[17] there was remarkably little discussion of the purpose for which the deduction was introduced.[18] Referring to comments by Leader of the Opposition R.B. Bennett, however, one commentator concludes that "it was thought that the deduction would encourage wealthy taxpayers to contribute to 'useful, philanthropic and religious purposes' and that such contributions were laudable and deserving of encouragement in this fashion."[19]

In the United States, where a similar deduction was adopted in 1917,[20] four years after the introduction of its income tax in 1913, the deduction was designed to offset any discouragement to charitable contributions that might be caused by high tax rates needed to finance American participation in the First World War.[21] Similarly, as the Royal Commission on Dominion–Provincial Relations observed in 1940, the Canadian deduction was intended "to promote munificence or at least to protect charities against the indirect consequence of high rates of income tax on those who sustain them."[22]

More generally, the Canadian deduction, which was enacted in the early years of the Great Depression at a time when governments were increasingly pressed to provide relief to the unemployed, was a method whereby the federal government could "be seen to be assisting those in need" without itself assuming responsibility for relief or becoming involved in what was at the time a sphere of exclusive provincial jurisdiction.[23] In this respect, as another commentator has observed, the Canadian deduction was introduced in order to promote "public policy and the general good of the community."[24]

Qualifying Gifts

Among the early questions considered by Canadian courts in applying the deduction was whether it applied to gifts in kind as well as cash donations. In *Gaudin v. M.N.R.*,[25] where the taxpayer sold a house to a church for use as a rectory for half its value and claimed the other half as a charitable deduction, the court held that the contribution was not a "gift" within the meaning of then paragraph 27(1)(a) of the Income Tax Act of 1952.[26] Although the decision appeared to suggest that gifts-in-kind were not deductible,[27] a subsequent decision, in which a taxpayer was permitted to claim a deduction in respect of the value of a yacht donated to the University of Toronto, confirmed that the deduction applied to gifts in kind.[28] This result is now reflected in the language of subsection 118.1(1), which refers to "the fair market value" of gifts of various kinds.[29] As an administrative practice, however, the Canada Customs and Revenue Agency (CCRA) does not recognize gifts-in-kind of nominal value, such as gifts of used clothing of little value.[30] As well, gifts of services are not recognized as charitable contributions within the meaning of the act.[31]

Among tax theorists, non-recognition of gifts of services as charitable contributions is often explained on the basis that the donor obtains an implicit deduction through the non-taxation of the "imputed income" associated with the gift of services.[32] Indeed, to the extent that a person who contributes services is not subject to tax on the value of these services, while a person who works to earn the income to make a cash contribution is subject to tax on the earnings, it is often argued that a deduction for cash donations is essential to achieving equity between these two taxpayers.[33] More persuasively, it might be argued that non-recognition of the value of gifts of services is consistent with non-taxation of imputed income from self-performed services.[34] However, to the extent that tax assistance is designed to encourage charitable gifts and subsidize charitable activities, there seems little reason to limit this incentive to gifts of cash and property while excluding gifts of services.[35]

Optional Standard Deduction

The first significant amendment to the charitable deduction involved the enactment of an optional standard deduction in 1957, whereby taxpayers could claim a $100 deduction without submitting receipts in lieu of specific deductions for charitable contributions, medical expenses (which were deductible only to the extent that they exceeded 3 per cent of the taxpayer's net income[36]), and union, professional, or similar dues.[37] The reason for this standard deduction, which had been adopted in the United States in 1944,[38] was to limit paperwork both for the revenue authorities and for taxpayers. According to the minister of finance: "From a survey it has been established that for more than half of income taxpayers the combined claims for charitable contributions, medical expenses, union dues and professional fees of employees amount to less than $100 a year per taxpayer. In the light of this situation it is proposed to allow to every taxpayer the option of taking what might be called a 'standard deduction' of $100 a year in lieu of claiming actual deductions for the items just mentioned. Of course if the claims for these four items add up to more than $100 the taxpayer may obtain a deduction in the future just as he has in the past. For the majority of taxpayers, however, the standard deduction will prove more advantageous and will, for all concerned, eliminate handling millions of pieces of paper."[39]

While the optional standard deduction certainly reduced paperwork,[40] it also eliminated any tax incentive to make charitable contributions that, together with qualifying medical expenses and union, professional, or similar dues, did not exceed $100 per year – since this amount could be claimed in any event without submission of receipts. Indeed, although the effect of the optional standard deduction on amounts actually contributed to charities is uncertain, the percentage of taxfilers claiming charitable deductions decreased dramatically after 1956. According to one study published in 1976, total charitable donations of $284 million claimed in 1956, the year before the optional standard deduction was introduced, exceeded the total of itemized deductions for charitable contributions in each of the years from 1966 to 1971.[41] According to another study published in 1984, after increasing from 1951 to 1956, average amounts claimed as charitable donations as a percentage of average disposable personal income declined steadily from 1.9 per cent in 1956 to 0.54 per cent in 1974 before rising slightly to 0.61 per cent in 1980.[42] Similarly, the percentage of taxfilers claiming charitable donations decreased from 24.5 per cent in 1961 to 9.2 per cent in 1977 before recovering slightly to 10.3 per cent in 1980.[43]

Although it is unlikely that these declines were fully attributable to the optional standard deduction, which might have been expected to have its largest effects immediately after its enactment in 1956 and again in 1965 when the deduction was amended to exclude union, professional, or similar dues,[44] and a diminishing impact thereafter as the real value of the $100 deduction was eroded by inflation,[45] the measure was sharply criticized by advocates for voluntary organizations on the grounds that it lessened tax incentives to contribute to charities.[46] When the Royal Commission on Taxation (Carter Commission) delivered its final report in 1966, it accepted the optional standard deduction as "an administrative concession" but recommended that its dollar value be reduced.[47] According to the commission: "if an optional standard deduction, that is, a minimum amount that could be claimed instead of listing the actual donations and irrespective of the amount of actual donations, were too large, ... it would ... have a perverse incentive effect, discouraging those people from making moderate donations who could claim the standard deduction in any case. For this reason, we recommend that an optional standard deduction should be retained for charitable donations, but that it should be limited in size to the minimum amount necessary to achieve the desired administrative savings."[48] For this purpose, it recommended that "[a]n amount of not more than $50 would appear to be appropriate."[49]

Although the federal government did not act on the Carter Commission's recommendation when it amended the Income Tax Act in 1972, the optional standard deduction was eventually repealed effective for 1984 and subsequent taxation years.[50] According to documents released with the federal budget of 1983: "Representatives of voluntary associations have expressed concern that this deduction reduces the tax incentive for charitable giving since the deduction is not directly related to actual amounts given. The budget proposal to remove the $100 standard deduction for 1984 and subsequent taxation years responds to this concern."[51] Not surprisingly, the percentage of taxfilers claiming charitable contributions increased substantially following this amendment, rising from 10.3 per cent in 1980 to 25.7 per cent in 1984.[52] Since, then, however, the incidence of taxfilers claiming charitable contributions has remained relatively constant, rising to 29.5 per cent in 1990 and declining thereafter to 26.9 per cent in 1996.[53] As for dollar amounts, aggregate amounts claimed as charitable donations increased from slightly more than $1 billion in 1980 to more than $1.8 billion in 1984.[54] Since the aggregate amount claimed under the optional standard deduction was roughly $1.3 billion in 1980,[55] however, the information provided by this latter statistic is of limited value. More generally, whether the elimination of the optional standard deduction has had any impact on actual charitable contributions, as opposed to charitable contributions claimed for tax purposes, is uncertain.

Gifts of Appreciated Property

Among the many amendments to the Income Tax Act following the Carter Report, perhaps the most significant was the introduction of a tax on capital gains, one-half of which became subject to tax beginning in 1972.[56] This inclusion rate was increased to two-thirds in 1988 and 1989 and to three-quarters for 1990 and subsequent taxation years but was reduced by the most recent federal budget to two-thirds for dispositions of capital property made after 27 February 2000.[57] In addition to this measure, the federal government adopted the Carter Commission's recommendation to impose a tax on accrued gains when property is transferred by way of gift or at death[58] by enacting provisions deeming the donor to have received proceeds equal to the fair market value of the property so transferred.[59] As a result, while taxpayers making a charitable donation of capital property that had appreciated in value would be able to deduct the appreciated value of the property at the time of the gift, they would also have to include half the amount of any accrued gain in computing their income in the year of the gift.[60] Thus, for example, if a taxpayer acquired a capital asset for $1,000 and gave it to a charity when its value had risen to $5,000, the taxpayer would be able to claim a deduction for $5,000 (subject to the annual ceiling on deductible contributions) but be required to include $2,000 (half the gain) in computing his or her income for the year, resulting in a net deduction of $3,000.

Even before the amendments were enacted, concerns were expressed about imposing a tax on gifts of appreciated property to charities.[61] According to Commons and Senate committees examining the proposed legislation, gifts of appreciated property should be non-taxable but deductible only to the extent of their cost to the donor, not of their market value at the time of the gift.[62] In the above example, therefore, the taxpayer would not be taxable on any part of the $4,000 accrued gain but would be able to deduct only $1,000, representing the cost of the asset to the taxpayer.

Although the federal government initially rejected these proposals, the act was amended in 1972, shortly after the new rules came into effect, to allow taxpayers making a gift of appreciated property to elect any amount between the cost of the property and its fair market value at the time of the gift, which would apply to determining both the amount of any gain recognized for tax and the amount deductible as a charitable contribution.[63] As a result, the taxpayer in the above example could select any amount between $1,000 and $5,000, which would determine both the proceeds for the computation of any gain and the amount of the available deduction. Since only half the gain was taxable while the elected amount was fully deductible, however, the only circumstance in which it was not more advantageous to designate the full fair market value was where the ability to claim the deduction was limited by the 20 per cent ceiling.[64] Indeed, by including only one half of the capital gain in computing the donors income while permitting a deduction for the fair market value of the gift, the Canadian tax system created an added incentive for charitable donations of appreciated property.[65]

While this amendment was consistent with the recommendations of the Commons and Senate committees, it did not go as far as others, most notably representatives from private museums, recommended. Emphasizing the need to compete for donations with American museums, these representatives suggested that gifts of appreciated property should be non-taxable and fully deductible based on their fair market value at the time of the gift, as is the case in the United States.[66] On this basis, the taxpayer in the above example would be able to deduct the $5,000 value of the asset at the time of the gift (subject to the annual ceiling), without having to include any portion of the $4,000 accrued gain, resulting in a net deduction of $5,000.

Among U.S. tax theorists, the exemption from capital gains tax on gifts of appreciated property has been widely criticized.[67] According to William Andrews, for example, the additional "subsidy or artificial inducement" for philanthropic giving that is provided by this rule is both arbitrary and inequitable: "The magnitude of the subsidy is a function of the amount of unrealized appreciation in relation to the basis of the property and the taxpayer's rates of tax, being the greatest for taxpayers in highest brackets and with the most appreciation."[68] Moreover, as Richard Goode explains, this approach "tempts some donors to place excessive values on their gifts, occasionally with the collusion of recipient institutions."[69]

Notwithstanding these criticisms, subsequent amendments have introduced further incentives in Canada for gifts of appreciated property under limited circumstances. In 1977, the act was amended to exempt from capital gains tax any gain on a gift to designated institutions of "cultural property" certified under the Cultural Property Export and Import Act.[70] In this circumstance, therefore, the taxpayer in the above example would be able to deduct the full $5,000 value of the asset at the time of the gift (subject to the annual ceiling), without including any portion of the $4,000 accrued gain, resulting in a net deduction of $5,000. Although statistics on the value and frequency of donations of cultural property do not appear to be available, the extremely favourable tax treatment for gifts of this kind might be expected to produce a significant increase in donations of this kind. Indeed, by providing such favourable tax treatment, this provision has encouraged a number of questionable transactions, in which taxpayers (often with the encouragement of the recipient institution) have acquired property at a relatively low cost and donated this property immediately thereafter at an assessed value well in excess of its acquisition price, resulting in a net after-tax profit to the donor.[71] In response to these kinds of transactions, the

Income Tax Act was subsequently amended to authorize the Canadian Cultural Property Export Review Board to determine the fair market value of cultural gifts for which recognition is sought under the Income Tax Act.[72]

More recently, the act was amended effective 19 February 1997 to reduce the taxable amount of any gain on charitable gifts of certain publicly traded securities from three-quarters of the gain to three-eighths.[73] According to supplementary information released with the federal budget of 1997, this provision, which has a built-in "sunset clause" according to which the low inclusion rate applies only on gifts made before the year 2002, was enacted to "provide a level of tax assistance for donations of eligible capital property that is comparable to that in the U.S."[74] in order to "facilitate the transfer of appreciated capital property to charities to help them respond to the needs of Canadians."[75] Statistics are as yet unavailable to indicate the extent to which this measure has affected amounts donated to charities and amounts claimed for income tax purposes. By limiting this added incentive to publicly-traded securities, however, this measure may at least provide the secure basis for valuation that appears to have been lacking with respect to gifts of cultural property.

Credit

In the 1970s and 1980s, tax theorists increasingly came to question the merits of a deduction for charitable contributions.[76] Noting that a deduction is worth more to a high-income taxpayer under a progressive income tax than it is to a low-income taxpayer and is worthless to persons whose income is too low to pay any tax, critics argued that the deduction was a regressive method of encouraging charitable donations which provided a greater level of encouragement to charities favoured by high-income donors than low-income donors.[77]

In 1971, for example, when federal income tax rates ranged from 16 per cent on taxable income between $500 and $2,000 to 80 per cent on taxable income exceeding $400,000,[78] the value of the deduction for a dollar donated to charity was nil for taxpayers with taxable incomes of less than $500, 16 cents for taxpayers with taxable incomes between $500 and $2,000, and 80 cents for taxpayers with taxable incomes exceeding $400,000. As a result, the net after-tax cost of donating a dollar to charity was 20 cents for taxpayers with taxable incomes exceeding $400,000, 84 cents for taxpayers with taxable incomes between $500 and $2,000, and one dollar for taxpayers with taxable incomes less than $500. While top marginal rates of federal income tax were reduced significantly to 47 per cent in 1972,[79] 43 per cent in 1977,[80] and 34 per cent in 1982,[81] the difference between these rates and the lowest marginal rate, which was 6 per cent from 1976 to 1987,[82] continued to imply a regressive distribution of federal tax assistance to charitable giving.[83]

To the extent that high- and low-income taxpayers differ in the kinds of charities to which they contribute, moreover, this regressivity implied a greater level of encouragement to charities favoured by high-income donors than to those favoured by low-income donors. Indeed, studies indicating that high-income taxpayers tend to devote a larger proportion of charitable donations to hospitals, higher education, and culture (for example, museums and the arts), while low-income taxpayers are more likely to favour religious organizations and social welfare agencies,[84] suggest that a deduction provides greater encouragement for contributions to charitable organizations devoted to health, higher education, and culture than it does for contributions to charitable organizations devoted to religion and social welfare.

As an alternative to the deduction for charitable contributions, these critics suggested that charitable donations be encouraged by matching grants paid directly to the charitable organization[85] or by tax credits the value of which would depend not on the income level of the donor but on the total amount of charitable contributions claimed in the particular taxation year.[86] According to one study published in 1977, when federal income tax rates ranged from 6 per cent on the first $500 of taxable income to 43 per cent on taxable income exceeding $60,000,[87] a flat-rate credit set at 28 per cent of each taxpayer's charitable donations claimed in each year would result in a similar level of aggregate donations and a similar level of federal assistance to charitable donations in terms of forgone federal tax revenues.[88] As the authors noted, however, "such a rate would imply a shift in real income from high-income to low-income taxpayers, and probably a shift in the destination of donations."[89] More specifically, they explained: "Tax-credit schemes, since they can be expected to increase the percentage of charitable donations coming from low-income groups, will also increase the percentage going to religious institutions. Charitable organizations now heavily dependent on the wealthy would face difficult times under such a regime."[90]

Although any reduction in tax incentives for high-income taxpayers could be eliminated by setting the rate of the credit equal to the top marginal rate (47 per cent in 1977), this would provide even further encouragement to charitable contributions by low-income taxpayers and significantly increase the cost of the credit in terms of forgone tax revenues.[91]

When the Carter Commission examined the charitable deduction in 1966, it acknowledged the deduction's regressivity, explaining that "[i]f equity were the only consideration, we would propose a system of credits for charitable donations" so that "[t]he tax concession would ... be related only to the size of the donation and would not also depend upon the income of the taxpayer."[92] Emphasizing that "private philanthropy performs a worthwhile social purpose," however, the commission feared that "[t]he credit approach would ... tend to stifle charitable giving by upper income individuals and families"[93] – implicitly assuming that any credit would be set at a rate lower than the top marginal rate.[94] Consequently, it concluded, "the fundamental feature of the present system, the deduction of charitable donations from income, should be continued."[95]

Although the commission did not explain why the risk of a reduction in charitable giving by "upper income individuals and families" justified the continuation of a deduction which it itself considered inequitable, two arguments might be imagined. First, to the extent that high-income taxpayers are more responsive to changes in the after-tax cost of charitable giving than low-income taxpayers,[96] any reduction in the rate of tax assistance for high-income taxpayers would be expected to cause a greater reduction in charitable donations than any increase in charitable donations induced by a comparable increase in the rate of tax assistance for low-income taxpayers. On this basis, a deduction for charitable donations might be characterized as a more efficient method of encouraging charitable contributions than a credit. Indeed, a Canadian study published in 1986 estimated that a revenue-neutral tax credit of 29 per cent would cause aggregate donations to fall by $10 million, while a high-rate credit of 50 per cent would increase aggregate donations by only $6 million at a cost in terms of forgone revenue of $422 million.[97]

Alternatively, to the extent that charitable organizations which tend to be favoured by high-income taxpayers (i.e., hospitals, universities, and cultural institutions) are considered more deserving of public support than those favoured by low-income taxpayers (religious organizations and social welfare agencies), a deduction might be preferred to a credit on the grounds that it better targets tax assistance to these preferred organizations. As Faye Woodman has argued: "Simply, an argument may be made that some institutions are richer contributors to the social, cultural, and intellectual mosaic than others. Hence, it may be possible to justify a system of deduction that is skewed in the direction of the favourite charities of upper-income taxpayers."[98] Indeed, Woodman speculates that this was the key reason why the Carter Commission recommended that the deduction for charitable contributions be retained."[99]

Whatever reason or reasons caused the Carter Commission to recommend the continuation of the charitable deduction in 1966, the federal government ceased to be convinced by these arguments in 1987, at which time it announced that it would amend the Income Tax Act by converting the deduction to a credit designed to "increase fairness by basing tax assistance on the amount given, regardless of the income level of the donor."[100] Implicitly accepting the commission's concern that a credit might "stifle charitable giving by upper income individuals and families," however, the government also indicated that the credit would be designed to "maintain a substantial incentive for charitable giving."[101] Since a flat-rate credit could achieve this result only at a substantially increased cost in terms of forgone tax revenues,[102] moreover, the government settled on a "two-tier credit" equal to the lowest marginal rate of tax on charitable donations claimed up to $250[103] and the highest marginal rate of tax on amounts exceeding this threshold.[104] According to supplementary information accompanying the White Paper in which these reforms were announced, the proposed amendment was expected to cost an additional $80 million per year, increasing the aggregate level of federal tax assistance for charitable giving to $900 million in 1988.[105]

When the act was amended for 1988 and subsequent taxation years, the rates of federal income tax were set at 17 per cent on taxable income up to $27,500, 26 per cent on taxable income up to $55,000, and 29 per cent on taxable income exceeding $55,000.[106] As a result, under the formula enacted in 1988,[107] the credit for charitable contributions equalled 17 per cent on the first $250 claimed for the year and 29 per cent on amounts exceeding $250. For 1994 and subsequent taxation years, the credit equalled 17 per cent on the first $200 claimed for the year and 29 per cent on amounts exceeding $200. When federal surtaxes and provincial taxes are taken in to account, the credit is equal to roughly 25 per cent on amounts up to $200 and 50 per cent on amounts over this threshold. As a result, the after-tax cost of charitable gifts is approximately 75 cents for each dollar up to $200 and 50 cents for each dollar over $200.

For taxpayers paying tax at the lowest marginal rate, therefore, the credit functions as a deduction for annual contributions up to $200 and an additional incentive on charitable gifts exceeding these amounts. For taxpayers paying tax at the top marginal rate, the credit provides roughly half the assistance as a deduction for annual charitable gifts up to $200[108] but functions as a deduction for annual amounts exceeding $200. For taxpayers paying tax at the 26 per cent

Table 13.1 Charitable tax credit: average effective rates, by income class, 1996

Income class ($)	*Average donation for tax-filers claiming donations ($)*	*Average credit ($)**	*Average effective rate (%)*
1–10,000	196.12	33.34	17.0
10,000–30,000	468.08	111.74	23.9
30,000–60,000	617.80	155.16	25.1
60,000–100,000	939.23	248.38	26.4
100,000–250,000	2,177.05	607.34	27.9
Over 250,000	11,165.00	3,123.85	28.8

Source: Calculated from figures in CCRA, *Taxation Statistics on Individuals: 1996 Tax Year* (Ottawa: Minister of Supply and Services, 1998).
*Calculated as 17 per cent of the first $200 of average donations and 29 per cent of amounts exceeding $200.

rate, the credit is worth less than a deduction for amounts up to $200 but more than a deduction for amounts over this threshold.

Although the two-tier credit appears to be more equitable than the deduction, providing an "equal reward for effort in giving by donors in all income brackets in contrast to the ... deduction system which provides greater reward for those in higher income brackets,"[109] its distributional impact differs little from a deduction. On the contrary, since average contributions by low-income taxpayers are less than or not much greater than the $200 threshold, while average contributions by high-income taxpayers greatly exceed the $200 threshold, a significant proportion of charitable donations by low-income taxpayers is creditable at the 17 per cent rate, whereas most charitable contributions by high-income taxpayers are creditable at the 29 per cent rate. As Table 13.1 indicates, while the credit is on average somewhat more valuable than a deduction for claimants with incomes of $10,000 to $30,000 and slightly less valuable than a deduction for claimants with incomes of $60,000 to $100,000, its impact is indistinguishable from a deduction for claimants with incomes less than $10,000 and largely indistinguishable from a deduction for claimants with incomes from $30,000 to $60,000 or over $100,000. Since the credit is not refundable, moreover, it provides no assistance to charitable giving by taxpayers whose income is too low to pay any tax.

While these figures indicate that the two-tier credit has, as the government intended, preserved "a substantial incentive for charitable giving," particularly among high-income contributors, they also demonstrate that the level of tax assistance for charitable contributions continues to depend on the income level of the donor, as it did

Table 13.2 Distribution of tax-filers and charitable donations claimed, by income class, 1987, 1988

	1987		*1988*	
Income class ($)	*Percentage of tax-filers*	*Percentage of charitable donations claimed*	*Percentage of tax-filers*	*Percentage of charitable donations claimed*
1–10,000	31.3	2.5	29.1	2.2
10,000–30,000	44.6	33.4	44.6	31.1
30,000–60,000	21.0	37.7	22.3	37.8
60,000–100,000	2.3	10.9	3.0	12.0
100,000–250,000	0.7	8.5	0.9	8.9
Over 250,000	0.11	7.0	0.18	8.1

Source: Calculated from figures in Revenue Canada, *Taxation Statistics on Individuals: 1987 Tax Year* (Ottawa: Minister of Supply and Services, 1989); and Revenue Canada, *Taxation Statistics on Individuals: 1988 Tax Year* (Ottawa: Minister of Supply and Services, 1990).

under the deduction. Indeed, one commentator has suggested that the two-tier credit can be regarded as "a deduction masquerading as a credit."[110] Not surprisingly, therefore, the conversion from a deduction to a credit appears to have had little impact on the value of charitable donations claimed for tax purposes, which increased only slightly from 1987 to 1988.[111] Nor does it seem to have had much effect on the distribution of charitable donations by income group, which, as Table 13.2 demonstrates, changed very little from 1987 to 1988.

By adopting a two-tier credit rather than a flat-rate credit set at the top marginal rate of tax, however, the government was able to minimize the cost of the credit in terms of forgone revenues. In fact, despite the government's expectation that tax assistance for charitable giving would increase to roughly $900 million in 1988,[112] its figures indicate that the cost of the charitable credit was $670 million in 1988, $750 million in 1989, $815 million in 1990, $845 million in 1991, $865 million in 1992, $880 million in 1993, and $900 million only in 1994.[113] By lowering marginal rates of tax and the associated rates of the charitable credit, therefore, the 1987 tax reforms actually reduced federal assistance for charitable giving.

Ceilings

As I indicated above, the deduction for charitable contributions enacted in 1930 was limited to a maximum of 10 per cent of the taxpayer's income for the year. Although the U.S. provision on which the Canadian deduction was based contained a ceiling of 15 per cent of the taxpayer's income, a 10 per cent ceiling was selected in Canada on the basis that "it originated in the Mosaic Law and the practice of tithing."[114]

Although this rationale for a maximum ceiling on deductible contributions might suggest that contributions up to 10 per cent of a taxpayers annual income were regarded as in some sense obligatory and therefore meriting a deduction, while those exceeding 10 per cent were considered discretionary and non-deductible,[115] a more prevalent explanation involves the concern that without an income-related ceiling high-income taxpayers might be able to eliminate their tax liabilities altogether by making substantial charitable gifts.[116] As one American commentator has observed, although this outcome might be considered acceptable to the extent that donors contribute to various public purposes qualifying for a charitable deduction (or credit), it would enable large donors to avoid any obligation to support the cost of public goods and services determined by the elected representatives of the community as a whole.[117] Thus, he explains, the existence of a maximum limit on deductible (or creditable) contributions in any year "reflects a judgment ... that although charitable contributions are important and should be encouraged, every taxpayer should bear part of the burden of supporting the government."[118] In this respect, he adds, a maximum limit on deductible (or creditable) contributions functions as "a mechanism to effectuate an appropriately limited consumer sovereignty over social service expenditures."[119]

Consistent with the second rationale for a maximum limit on deductible (or creditable) donations, the ceilings in Canada and the United States have increased significantly since the deductions were enacted – well beyond the 10 per cent ratio established by the Mosaic law and the practice of tithing. In the United States, the ceiling was increased to 50 per cent, where it currently remains.[120] In Canada, the general ceiling was increased to 20 per cent in 1972,[121] 50 per cent in 1996,[122] and 75 per cent for 1997 and subsequent taxation years.[123] In each case, these amendments were designed to "encourage larger donations to charitable organizations."[124]

In addition to these increases in the general ceiling, as a further incentive for charitable giving, specific categories of gifts have been subject to higher limits or no limit at all. In 1939, for example, when the general ceiling on deductible contributions was 10 per cent of the donor's income, a separate ceiling of 50 per cent was enacted for donations to "any patriotic organization or institution in Canada which hereafter receives the written approval of the Secretary of State of the Dominion of Canada."[125] In 1941, this ceiling was replaced by a lower ceiling of 40 per cent applicable for donations to "the fund registered under *The War Charities Act, 1939*, under the name of The Canadian War Services Fund," provided that such funds were subscribed on before 7 April 1941 and paid before 31 December 1941.[126] Thereafter, the ceiling for all gifts returned to 10 per cent of the donor's income for the year.

In 1950, however, gifts to the federal government were made subject to a separate deduction without any limit.[127] For 1968 and subsequent taxation years, this provision was amended to include gifts to a province as well as the federal government.[128] In 1977, when the act was amended to exclude gifts of cultural property from capital gains tax,[129] a separate deduction without any ceiling was also enacted for gifts of this kind.[130] Although these specific deductions were repealed when the general deduction was converted to a credit in 1988,[131] the credit for these two categories of gifts continues to be available without any income-related limit.[132] In 1995, moreover, the act was amended yet again to exclude certain gifts of ecologically sensitive land from any income-related ceiling.[133] Noting that the value of such land "may often be high relative to the donor's income," supplementary information accompanying the announced reform indicated that the ceiling for gifts of this kind would be eliminated in order to "further encourage the conservation and protection of Canada's environmental heritage."[134]

In addition to these three categories of gifts, recent amendments have also increased the ceiling on creditable gifts to include the full amount of taxable capital gains from gifts of appreciated capital property[135] and increased the ceiling on creditable gifts made in the last two years of an individual's life to the individual's income for each of these two years.[136] While the former amendment is intended "to ensure that taxpayers making gifts of appreciated capital are able to claim tax credits for the full amount of the capital gain,"[137] the latter amendment is designed to "facilitate planned giving in circumstances where the gift is large relative to income in the last two years of life."[138] In more general terms, these amendments were enacted in order to eliminate "a serious impediment to charitable giving,"[139] both in the form of gifts of appreciated property, the tax on which might otherwise exceed the allowable credit,[140] and by way of bequests or legacies, which can be quite large relative to one's income in the last year of one's life.[141]

These increased ceilings, as well as recent increases in the general limit, appear to have had a dramatic impact on donations claimed for

Table 13.3 Distribution of tax-filers and charitable donations claimed, by income class, 1995, 1996

	1995		*1996*	
Income class ($)	*Percentage of tax-filers*	*Percentage of charitable donations claimed*	*Percentage of tax-filers*	*Percentage of charitable donations claimed*
1–10,000	24.0	0.97	24.1	0.76
10,000–30,000	43.5	25.6	42.9	23.2
30,000–60,000	25.5	36.5	25.5	34.9
60,000–100,000	5.5	16.6	5.9	17.0
100,000–250,000	1.3	10.6	1.4	11.3
Over 250,000	0.23	9.8	0.27	12.7

Source: Calculated from figures in Revenue Canada, *Taxation Statistics on Individuals: 1995 Tax Year* (Ottawa: Minister of Supply and Services, 1997); and CCRA, *Taxation Statistics on Individuals: 1996 Tax Year* (Ottawa: Minister of Supply and Services, 1997).

tax purposes. According to one recent study, the average inflation-adjusted value of donations claimed by taxfilers claiming charitable donations increased sharply from 1995 to 1996 by 11.7 per cent, after remaining relatively constant during the period 1984–95.[142] More significantly, as Table 13.3 indicates, increases in the maximum donations that can be claimed in a taxation year have altered the distribution of charitable donations claimed by income class, significantly increasing the percentage of charitable donations claimed by the highest income groups. The extent to which this increase reflects a change in actual donations or merely in donations claimed for tax purposes remains to be determined.

Carryovers

To the extent that the Income Tax Act limited deductions (and later credits) for charitable donations to a maximum percentage of the donor's annual income, it was inevitable that individuals with little or no taxable income and individuals who had made substantial charitable contributions relative to their annual incomes were likely to face limits on the extent to which otherwise eligible gifts would be recognized for tax purposes. In 1957, therefore, when the ceiling was 10 per cent of the donor's income for the year, the act was amended to permit taxpayers whose charitable donations were not deductible in the year of the gift to carry the excess forward to the next taxation year.[143] According to one commentator, this amendment was "a minor concession to supporters of the universities who were urging an increase in the 10 per cent limit."[144] Although the ceiling was increased to 20 per cent in 1972, the act was further amended in 1981 to allow taxpayers whose charitable contributions were not deductible in the year of the gift to carry the excess forward for five years.[145]

In 1984, this carryover was amended yet again to allow taxpayers to claim charitable contributions in the year of the gift or any of the following five taxation years, even if the amount could have been deducted in the year when the gift was made.[146] This amendment, which radically transformed the carryover from a "minor concession" to lessen the impact of the income-related ceiling into an instrument for tax planning, has enabled taxpayers to aggregate the value of their contributions over a six-year period and claim the value of these gifts in the year or years in which it is most advantageous to do so. Under the deduction available prior to 1988, the optimal strategy turned on the year in which the taxpayer expected to pay tax at the highest marginal rate, in which year the deduction would be most valuable, subject to the offsetting cost associated with a delay in obtaining the value of the deduction. Since the enactment of the two-tier credit in 1988, the optimal strategy may involve "bunching" claims in a single year, since taxpayers can thereby maximize the amount eligible for a credit at the higher rate, subject again to the offsetting cost associated with a delay in obtaining the value of the credit.

Although the impact of this optional carryforward on amounts actually donated to charities is uncertain, this amendment is likely to have decreased the incidence of claims made in any particular year and increased the average size of claims when made. In addition, by making the value of the deduction or credit depend not only on the amount contributed but also on the year in which the amount is claimed, this carryover has significantly increased the planning and record-keeping costs that taxpayers are likely to face in claiming charitable contributions for tax purposes. While at least some carryforward seems justified so long as the charitable credit is non-refundable, it is unclear why this carryforward should be optional and not limited to the amount of any excess that cannot be claimed in the taxation year of the gift.

In addition to this carryforward, the Income Tax Act also authorizes a limited carryback for charitable gifts made in the year of the taxpayer's death. According to subsection 118.1(4) of the act,[147] a gift made in the year in which the taxpayer dies may be claimed in the year preceding the taxpayer's death to the extent that it is not claimed in the year of the taxpayer's death. Since charitable gifts can be quite large relative to one's income in the last year of one's life, and obviously cannot be spread out over subsequent years, it seems reasonable to allow a limited carryback in this circumstance.

Transfer of Receipts

According to the act, charitable contributions must be claimed by the individual who makes the gift.[148] As an administrative practice, however, the CCRA allows either spouse to claim charitable donations made by either spouse or their dependants, regardless of the name to whom the receipt is issued. As a result, as Arthur Drache explains, "[u]nder the deduction system, it always made sense for the higher income spouse to claim the donations for tax purposes."[149] Likewise, under the two-tier credit introduced in 1988, it makes sense for one spouse to claim charitable contributions made by both spouses and their dependants in order to maximize the amount eligible for a credit at the higher rate.[150]

Since individual members of a family could easily arrange for only one member of the family to make all charitable donations, the CCRA's administrative practice makes sense as a way of extending the advantages of aggregation to less sophisticated taxpayers who might not adopt this behavioural response. If the credit were converted to a flat rate, however, much of the incentive to transfer receipts would disappear, although it would remain where the income of the actual donor is too low to pay tax or the aggregate amount of the actual donor's gifts exceeds the income-related ceiling for the year. In any event, the ability to transfer receipts, like the ability to carryover claims from one year to another, is likely to decrease the frequency of claims among taxfilers and increase the average size of claims made by each taxpayer claiming the credit.[151] As a result, statistics indicating that only 26.9 per cent of taxfilers claimed charitable contributions in 1996 cannot be read to suggest that only 26.9 per cent of individuals made charitable donations in 1996. Nor do statistics showing an average donation of $728 among taxfilers claiming charitable contributions in 1996 suggest that these individuals actually contributed an average of $728 to charities in 1996. Whether the CCRA's administrative practice affects either the frequency or amount of claims or (more importantly) the frequency and amount of charitable donations is uncertain.

RATIONALE AND DESIGN

Having examined the history and structure of the Canadian tax credit and related provisions governing the tax treatment of charitable contributions by individuals, I now consider the reasons why these gifts might be taken into account in computing a taxpayer's income tax and the resulting manner in which these gifts should be taken into account. This section evaluates four possible rationales for recognizing charitable contributions in the income tax – defining income, rewarding generosity, encouraging donations, and promoting pluralism. It considers possible design characteristics suggested by each of these rationales and develops a conceptual framework to evaluate the Canadian credit.

Defining Income

In computing an individual's income for the purposes of an income tax, deductions are generally allowed for reasonable expenses that must be incurred in order to produce the income. In computing a taxpayer's income from a business or property, for example, the Income Tax Act allows taxpayers to deduct outlays or expenses "made or incurred by the taxpayer for the purpose of gaining or producing income from the business or property."[152] In addition, income taxes often allow further deductions for involuntary expenses, such as necessary medical expenses,[153] which reduce the taxpayer's taxable capacity. These deductions ensure that tax burdens are distributed in an equitable manner, consistent with a reasonable measure of each taxpayer's ability to pay.

In this light, it would appear, provisions recognizing a taxpayer's charitable contributions cannot be justified as being necessary to the definition of an equitable measure of taxable income but must be explained on the basis of some extrinsic social or economic purpose that the provisions are designed to achieve.[154] Indeed, when the Canadian deduction was introduced in 1930,[155] its apparent purpose was not to ensure that each taxpayer's ability to pay would be defined in an equitable manner but to "encourage wealthy taxpayers to contribute to 'useful, philanthropic and religious purposes'"[156] and to promote "public policy and the general good of the community."[157] Likewise, the design of the two-tier credit and increases in the income-related ceiling for creditable donations were designed to "maintain a substantial incentive for charitable giving"[158] and to "encourage larger donations to charitable organizations."[159]

Notwithstanding this conclusion, advocates of a deduction for charitable contributions have advanced three reasons why such a deduction should be regarded as a necessary measure for defining taxable income. First, as U.S. tax theorist Boris Bittker has argued, "charitable contributions represent a claim of such a high priority" that they should be regarded as largely involuntary obligations that should be excluded "in determining the amount of income at the voluntary disposal of the taxpayer in question."[160] Alternatively, as U.S. tax theorist William Andrews has argued, to the extent that tax burdens are based on the aggregate of a taxpayer's personal consumption and accumulation,[161] they should not apply to charitable gifts that enter into the consumption of needy recipients (in the case of "alms for the poor") or provide non-exclusive or public goods and services (in the case of "philanthropy more broadly defined" to include contributions to hospitals, education, and culture).[162] Similarly, as one Canadian commentator has argued: "the tax deduction simply removes the tax penalty which would otherwise result if taxpayers had to pay taxes on income which they had voluntarily chosen not to receive personally but to redirect to registered charities or other qualified donees."[163] Finally, as Bittker has also argued, a deduction for charitable contributions maintains equity both between individuals who donate non-taxable services to charitable organizations and individuals who earn taxable income from which they make donations of cash or property[164] and between individuals who are able to make charitable gifts of large capital sums, the income from which is not subsequently subject to tax in their hand, and individuals who must make charitable contributions out of income as it is earned.[165]

With respect to the first argument, that charitable donations should be regarded as involuntary obligations, one may respond that whatever sense of obligation may underlie the motive to make charitable gifts is itself a matter of choice and not involuntary in any legal or practical sense.[166] In this respect, as several commentators have observed, charitable contributions can be characterized as a form of consumption expenditure much like any other, which is properly subject to tax.[167] Moreover, while the conception of charitable donations as involuntary obligations may have influenced the original design of the Canadian deduction, which was limited to 10 per cent of the taxpayer's income in accordance with "the Mosaic law and the practice of tithing,"[168] subsequent amendments increasing the level of this ceiling to 20 per cent, 50 per cent, and now 75 per cent suggest a very different rationale.

With respect to the second argument, that charitable donations are properly taxed in the hands of the recipients, rather than of the donors, for whom the money or property is "no longer available,"[169] one can respond that this conception of the income tax misconstrues both its purpose and its proper scope. As opposed to Andrews's view that the income tax is intended simply "to divert economic resources away from personal consumption and accumulation" to government uses,[170] for example, several tax theorists contend that the income tax is best understood as expressing a social claim to a share of each taxpayer's annual gains from participation in the market economy.[171] As a result, while Andrews argues that tax burdens should be allocated according to personal welfare as measured either by the aggregate of a taxpayer's personal consumption and accumulation[172] or by personal consumption alone (as he argued in a later article),[173] advocates of the income tax argue that tax burdens should be allocated according to each taxpayer's receipts over a specified accounting period, allowing deductions only for the costs of earning this revenue or for involuntary expenses that reduce the taxpayer's ability to pay.[174]

From this perspective, it follows, the argument that amounts donated by a taxpayer to charities are not the income of the donor ignores that fact that the donor is legally entitled to these amounts before making the voluntary choice to give to charity. To the extent that the income tax is based on amounts to which taxpayers are legally entitled, therefore, it is simply incorrect to view donations as the income of the recipient rather than of the donor. Indeed, as Bromley himself notes, "taxpayers are giving away their own money."[175] If the donation is, in fact, "their own money," it should be taxed in their hands and paid out of after-tax income, not in the hands of the recipient.[176]

As for the third argument, that a deduction for charitable contributions is essential to an equitable income tax, one can respond that donors who contribute money out of earned income are not similarly situated to donors to make gifts of services or contribute large capital sums, the subsequent income from which belongs to the charitable organization, not the donor. With respect to donations of services, time devoted to volunteer work may compete not with time devoted to taxable income-earning activities, but with time devoted to nontaxable leisure. More generally, while it is true that donors of services are not subject to tax on the imputed value of these services, this turns not on an implicit deduction for this imputed value, but on a more basic principle against the taxation of imputed income.[177] Indeed, to the extent that tax assistance is designed to encourage charitable gifts and subsidize charitable activities, it is arguable that it is inequitable for the income tax to recognize donations of cash and property but not gifts of services.[178]

With respect to donations of capital, it is worth noting that these donations may or may not be used by the recipient organization to derive a regular stream of income. Conversely, smaller donations made out of earned income may be added to the recipient's capital account to generate future income. As a result, the nature of the gift to the donor says nothing about its character to the donee. In any event, to the extent that the charitable recipient does use the charitable gift to derive subsequent income, it is clear that this income, unlike the income from which a donor makes annual gifts, is legally that of the charitable organization and no longer that of the donor. Since the donor of the capital gift has parted with his or her entitlement to the income from the capital, while the individual who makes annual donations out of earned income retains the legal right to contribute or not contribute in any year, it is odd to equate the position of the former with that of the latter.[179] Here too, therefore, tax equity does not require a deduction for charitable contributions.

Rewarding Generosity

If tax equity does not mandate a deduction for charitable contributions, tax recognition of charitable gifts must be justified, if at all, on the basis of some social or economic policy extrinsic to the equitable definition of taxable income. One such policy might be to reward generosity as a form of virtuous behaviour. Among other arguments for a charitable deduction, for example, Bittker suggests that "something can be said for rewarding activities that in a certain sense are selfless, even if the reward serves no incentive function."[180] Similarly, Richard Goode has referred to the charitable deduction in the United States as a "reward" for charitable giving.[181]

Although the goal of rewarding charitable donations might justify some method of recognizing the value of these donations in computing the donor's income tax, it is doubtful whether this recognition would take the form of a deduction, the value of which depends more on the donor's income than on the donor's relative generosity. On the contrary, as Paul McDaniel has argued, "if there is to be a reward for charitable giving, the incidence and amount of the reward should bear some rational relationship to the act of charitable giving. The reward should be the same for persons who make a similar sacrifice, however measured."[182] Indeed, since low-income people who give to charities tend to give a larger portion of their income than do high-income taxpayers,[183] this rationale suggests that a deduction, the value of which increases as the donor's income rises, has the reward structure backwards.

As opposed to a deduction, therefore, the reward rationale might suggest a credit that diminishes as the donor's income increases, on the basis that the sacrifice associated with a dollar contributed to charity by a low-income taxpayer is greater than the sacrifice of a one-dollar gift by a high-income taxpayer.[184] Neil Brooks, for example, suggests that a tax credit for charitable contributions "could be set at 30 per cent for those with incomes over $35,000; 40 per cent for those with incomes from $25,000 to $35,000, and so on, down to those with incomes under $10,000, where the credit might be set at 100 per cent."[185]

Alternatively, to the extent that the policy objective is to reward individuals based on the proportion of their income contributed to charities, a credit might apply at an increased rate based on the percentage of the donor's income contributed in each year.[186] On this basis, for example, McDaniel proposed a matching grant for charitable donations rising from 5 per cent of aggregate donations from donors contributing less than 2 per cent of their incomes to charities to 50 per cent of aggregate donations from donors contributing more than 10 per cent of their incomes to charities.[187] Similarly, some commentators have proposed an income-related floor, as opposed to a ceiling, below which charitable contributions would not be recognized for tax purposes.[188] In 1969, for example, the Treasury Department proposed that the charitable deduction in the U.S. Internal Revenue Code be available only for contributions exceeding 3 per cent of the donor's income.[189] Similarly, the Carter Commission in Canada considered, but rejected, a floor set at 1 per cent of the donor's income.[190] In addition to targeting the "reward" to the most generous contributors, such a floor might also be expected to reduce administrative costs associated with tax assistance for charitable giving.[191]

However, to the extent that low-income individuals who contribute to charities are able to finance these gifts from accumulated or inherited wealth, one might wonder whether the ratio between donations and income is a satisfactory measure of the donor's personal "sacrifice." If the goal is truly to reward individual generosity, therefore, one might imagine a credit based on the ratio between donations and a combined measure of income and wealth. Such a measure, of course, would be difficult to define and even more difficult to administer.

More generally, one might wonder why the tax system should be designed to reward persons for their generosity. Although generosity is undoubtedly worthy of praise, it is not clear that it merits monetary rewards. On the contrary, as critics from different perspectives have observed, to reward generosity through monetary means contradicts the spirit underlying the virtue of generosity, "corrupt[ing] the essential dignity and altruism of a simple gift"[192] and "accentuat[ing] the purely selfish goal of reducing one's own tax burden."[193]

Encouraging Donations

Another reason to allow taxpayers to claim a charitable deduction or credit is to encourage individuals to make donations to charitable organizations. As economic analysis suggests, a deduction or credit for charitable gifts increases the donor's after-tax income from which gifts may be made (the income effect) and decreases the after-tax cost or price of charitable gifts to the donor (the price, or substitution effect).[194] To the extent that charitable giving is what economists refer to as a "normal good," a decrease in its price will increase the quantity demanded and thus the aggregate level of charitable donations. The higher the rate of the deduction or credit, moreover, the lower the after-tax cost of charitable giving and the greater the encouragement to these kinds of gifts.

The extent to which donors increase the quantity of charitable giving in response to a decrease in its after-tax cost is defined as the "price elasticity" of giving.[195] A negative price elasticity, which is characteristic of a normal good, suggests that donations will increase in response to a decrease in their price. A low price elasticity indicates a slight increase in charitable giving in response to a decrease in its after-tax cost. A high price elasticity suggests that the quantity of charitable donations is highly responsive to changes in the after-tax cost of these gifts. A price elasticity of negative one indicates a corresponding increase in charitable giving in response to a given reduction in its after-tax cost.

Since reductions in the after-tax cost of charitable gifts are financed by forgone tax revenues, the price elasticity of charitable giving measures the cost-effectiveness of the tax incentive (whether a deduction or a credit) as a means of funding charitable organizations. While a price elasticity less then negative one indicates that the cost of the tax incentive in terms of forgone revenues exceeds the resulting increase in charitable donations, a price elasticity greater than negative one implies that the increase in charitable donations attributable to the tax incentive exceeds the resulting reduction in tax revenues.

A voluminous literature has developed over the past thirty years as economists have attempted to obtain reliable estimates of the price elasticity of charitable giving.[196] Although the earliest studies reported relatively low price elasticities of charitable giving,[197] suggesting that tax incentives are a relatively inefficient means of funding charitable organizations,[198] subsequent studies have reported price elasticities greater than negative one,[199] suggesting that tax incentives may be a cost-effective method of funding charitable organizations.[200] More recent studies using different methods have reported much lower estimates of price elasticities,[201] again calling into question the efficiency of tax incentives as a method of funding the charitable sector.[202]

With respect to the relationship between the price elasticity of charitable giving and other variables, early studies concluded that elasticity increases as income increases,[203] suggesting that a deduction is a more efficient method of encouraging charitable donations than a flat-rate credit.[204] Subsequent studies indicate that low- and middle-income taxpayers may be more responsive to the after-tax cost of charitable giving than previously thought,[205] suggesting that a deduction may be inefficient. Most studies, however, indicate that the price elasticity of charitable giving is much lower for donations to religious organizations than to other charities,[206] suggesting that tax incentives of any kind are an inefficient way to fund religious organizations. Finally, although empirical studies do not appear to have confirmed the result, one might expect that donations of capital property are more responsive to the price of giving than contributions out of annual income, which are more likely to reflect a sense of personal obligation.[207] Indeed, the assumption that donations out of capital are more price elastic than donations out of income appears to explain recent amendments to the Income Tax Act lowering the rate of capital gains tax on gifts of publicly traded securities.

To the extent that tax provisions recognizing charitable gifts are designed to encourage individuals to make charitable donations, economic analysis suggests that the most cost-effective method of so doing is to provide the greatest incentive to those categories of donors and/or donations for which the price elasticity of giving is greatest. While these efficiency considerations may suggest larger incentives for gifts of capital property and smaller incentives for gifts to religious organizations, they challenge the assumption that a deduction is more efficient than a credit in encouraging charitable donations.

Efficiency, of course, is only one goal of tax policy and must be weighed against other important values such as equity.[208] Although it might be more cost-effective to reduce or eliminate tax incentives for gifts to religious organizations, such an approach might be considered inequitable. Likewise, while lower capital gains taxes on gifts of appreciated property may be a cost-effective way to encourage gifts of capital property, this incentive is arguably inequitable and arbitrary, providing the greatest benefit to taxpayers in the highest tax brackets who have property that happens to have appreciated most in value.[209]

Moreover, the use of tax incentives to encourage donations to charitable organizations raises deeper questions as to the kinds of organizations donations to which should be encouraged and why these donations should be encouraged in the first place. As the final section of this chapter suggests, the ultimate rationale and the appropriate design of a tax incentive for charitable donations depend on the answers to these questions.

Promoting Pluralism

Among economists, the charitable sector is generally regarded as a provider of quasi-public goods and services – the key characteristics of which are non-rivalness, meaning that enjoyment by one person does not preclude enjoyment by another, and non-excludability, meaning that it is difficult or impossible to exclude a person from enjoying the benefit even if he or she refuses to pay for it.[210] To the extent that a good or service is relatively non-rival and/or non-excludable, economic analysis suggests that private markets will either oversupply the good or service (in the case of non-rival but excludable goods and services) or undersupply the good or service (in the case of non-excludable goods or services). In either case, the resolution of these "market imperfections" is the main economic justification for the existence of a public sector that provides these public goods and services directly, distributing their costs among individual beneficiaries through taxes and other levies.[211]

In addition to the public sector, the charitable sector represents another response to the existence of market imperfections, providing goods and services such as culture, education, health, and welfare, the benefits of which tend to be relatively non-rival and/or non-excludable.[212] Indeed, since charitable organizations enable individuals to select public goods and services according to their own values and preferences, this sector may have distinct advantages over the public sector in providing a mix of such goods and services more compatible with the demands of a diverse society.[213] Moreover, to the extent that the charitable sector is more innovative and service-oriented than the traditional public sector, it may provide a more efficient vehicle for the delivery of certain public goods and services.[214] As well, by relieving the public sector from sole responsibility for providing public goods and services, the charitable sector lessens the fiscal burdens of the public sector,[215] making it better able to perform the important redistributive, allocative, and stabilization functions that only it can effectively fulfil.[216] From this perspective, fiscal subsidies to the charitable sector may be justified on the grounds both that they increase the supply of public goods and services provided by this sector to levels reflecting their positive public benefits or "externalities" and that they finance alternative methods of delivering public goods and services vis-à-vis those employed by the traditional public sector.[217]

If one concludes that fiscal subsidies to the charitable sector are justified, however, it is not obvious why these subsidies should be provided indirectly to charitable *donors* in the form of credits or deductions rather than directly to charitable *organizations* in the form of sustaining grants or matching grants. Indeed, in one of his contributions to this volume, Neil Brooks offers a number of reasons why direct sustaining grants are generally preferable to direct matching grants and direct matching grants generally preferable to indirect tax expenditures as methods of subsidizing the charitable sector, emphasizing that sustaining grants allocate scarce public funds more rationally than matching grants or tax expenditures and are most consistent with the criteria that are normally applied to government funding, such as accountability, controllability, and transparency.[218]

While these arguments support a significant role for direct government grants in financing the voluntary sector,[219] they do not rule out direct matching grants or indirect tax expenditures as additional sources of fiscal support. Indeed, to the extent that these methods of financing allow individuals to select the charitable organizations to which they wish to direct public support without having to obtain the agreement of a political majority, they are preferable to direct sustaining grants in promoting the very diversity and innovation that underlie the charitable sector's unique advantages to the traditional public sector and are less susceptible to political manipulation by a governing party or coalition.[220] Moreover, although it might be argued that direct matching grants are as consistent with this objective as indirect tax expenditures,[221] the latter are more likely than the former to withstand the kinds of political controls that would undermine their effectiveness in promoting pluralism.[222] As a result, even if tax incentives were a less cost-effective method of subsidizing charitable organizations than direct government grants,[223] it is arguable that the former are preferable to the latter on broader policy grounds. As Harold Hochman and James Rodgers have written: "Public policy involves much more than whether an additional dollar of subsidies can generate more than a dollar of charity."[224]

As for the design of these tax incentives, the rationale of subsidizing charitable organizations that provide quasi-public goods and services suggests a structure of deductions or credits corresponding to the degree of "publicness" of the particular good or service provided by the charitable organization to which the donation is made.[225] Thus, as one Canadian commentator has suggested: "it would be desirable to disaggregate within an expenditure category and confer different rates of credit on items that contribute different amounts of social benefit. Not all charitable activities, for example, may yield the same degree of social value, in which case a policy of differentiated tax credits is called for."[226] Indeed, by exempting capital gains tax on gifts of cultural property,[227] the Income Tax Act, it might be argued, reflects an implicit judgment that gifts of this type provide greater social benefits than other charitable gifts. A similar distinction may underlie the absence of income-related ceilings on gifts to the Crown, gifts of cultural property, and gifts of ecologically sensitive land.[228]

With respect to the choice between a deduction and a credit, some have favoured a deduction on the grounds that it provides a larger tax subsidy to charitable organizations favoured by high-income donors (hospitals, higher education, and cultural institutions), which are assumed to be "richer contributors to the social, cultural, and intellectual mosaic" than the charitable organizations most favoured by lower-income donors (religious organizations and social welfare).[229] Faye Woodman, for example, suggests that a deduction "gives more support to charities that do what government would otherwise have to do" than does a credit.[230] To the extent that Canada's two-tier credit operates much like a deduction, the same argument might be made in its favour.

To others, however, it is unlikely that the charitable organizations generally favoured by high-income donors generate greater positive externalities than those more favoured by low-income taxpayers.[231] On the contrary, as a recent study concludes: "Available evidence ... seems to suggest that the activities of the nonprofit organizations and charities typically supported by the rich do not produce higher valued externalities than do those supported by lower income earners. In fact, the converse may be true: universities and cultural organizations are charities that may be viewed as more 'local' than churches and religious organizations. Thus larger giving by high income earners should be discouraged on efficiency grounds, while smaller gifts by low income earners should be encouraged."[232] Moreover, although lower-income donors tend to devote a larger share of their donations to religious organizations, U.S. studies suggest that 20 per cent of these funds go to non-sacramental purposes such as social welfare.[233] In a pluralistic society, moreover, who is to say that the public benefits associated with religious activities are any less than those associated with higher education?[234]

Indeed, to the extent that pluralism itself is regarded as a public good, it is arguable that a tax incentive for charitable contributions should not discriminate among different activities or organizations, except to deny charitable status to organizations advocating values contrary to those of a free and democratic society.[235] In any event, where a decision is made to discriminate in favour of certain kinds of charitable activities (such as higher education) and against others (such as religious organizations), this decision should be transparent, not concealed in the form of a deduction or the current two-tier credit.[236] As Neil Brooks has written: "If certain activities are to be favoured over others, that choice should be clearly reflected on the face of the instrument chosen."[237]

Finally, although a flat-rate credit might be regarded as more compatible with the goal of promoting pluralism than a deduction or the current two-tier credit, it is arguable that such a credit fails to take pluralism as seriously as it might. On the one hand, donors with little or no taxable income obtain no benefit from the non-refundable credit.[238] On the other hand, high- income donors who are able to contribute more to charities can obtain substantial tax assistance up to whichever income-related ceiling may apply. Though pluralistic in name, therefore, the distribution of charitable donations among income groups may foster a form of "philanthropic paternalism" in which the mix of goods and services provided by the charitable sector is shaped more by an affluent minority than by the community as a whole.

From this perspective, one might wonder whether recent increases in the income-related ceiling for allowable credits from 20 per cent to 50 per cent and now to 75 per cent are fully compatible with the goal of promoting pluralism.[239] In contrast, a more meaningful kind of pluralism might be fostered by restructuring the charitable credit along the lines of the tax credit for political contributions, which equals three-quarters of the first $100 contributed, half of the next $450, and one-third of the next $600, for a maximum credit of $500 on a contribution of $1,150.[240] Indeed, a recent Canadian study has considered this possibility, suggesting that "[a]ll gifts, whether to charities or political parties, should in principle be treated on the same basis."[241]

CONCLUSION

The design of any income tax provisions taking charitable gifts into account in computing a donor's tax liability should reflect the underlying purpose of the provisions, which should themselves be rationally related to the purposes of an income tax. This chapter has argued that a deduction for charitable contributions cannot be justified as a necessary provision to define income nor as a means of rewarding generosity, encouraging donations, or promoting pluralism. To the extent that Canada's current two-tier credit is little more than "a deduction masquerading as a credit,"[242] moreover, similar criticisms may be directed at this approach as well.

Having concluded that tax equity does not mandate a deduction for charitable contributions, this chapter considered three alternative reasons for recognizing charitable gifts in computing a donor's tax: rewarding generosity, encouraging donations, and promoting pluralism. While each of these goals suggest various characteristics for the design of specific tax provisions, a combination of the second and third provides the best rationale for a tax incentive for charitable giving.

Taking seriously the goal of promoting pluralism, finally, this chapter has argued that a refundable credit with a declining rate based on the amount claimed in each year would be preferable to a deduction, to the existing two-tier credit, or to a non-refundable flat-rate credit. From this perspective, recent amendments that have increased the annual ceiling on creditable gifts and decreased the rate of capital gains tax on gifts of appreciated property, though consistent with the goal of encouraging donations, are difficult to justify.

NOTES

I am indebted to Elizabeth Moore for research assistance in the preparation of this chapter. Bruce Chapman and Lisa Phillips provided helpful comments on an earlier draft.

1 RSC 1985, c. 1 (5th Supp.) as am.

2 SC 1984, c. 1, sec. 49(2), repealing former paragraph 110(1)(d). At the time of its abolition, this deduction, which was established in 1957, applied to charitable donations and medical expenses. Although it originally included union, professional, and other dues as well, these items were excluded from the standard deduction in 1965. On the history and rationale of this optional standard deduction, see below.

3 SC 1985, c. 45, s. 54(1), amending former paragraphs 110(1)(a), (b), and (b.1). Prior to 1984, individuals could deduct amounts up to five years after the year of the gift only when their net income did not exhaust the deduction. Before 1981, the carryforward was limited to the taxation year immediately following the year of the gift. On the history and structure of these carryovers, see below.

4 See SC 1997, c. 25, s. 26 (increasing the limit to 50 per cent), and SC 1998, c. 19, sec. 22(14) (increasing the limit to 75 per cent). These limits appear in the definition of "total gifts" in section 118.1(1). The limit is increased by 25 per cent of any taxable capital gain or recaptured depreciation resulting from a gift of appreciated property for which tax relief is claimed and rises to 100 per cent for the taxation year of the

donor's death and the subsequent taxation year. These limits do not apply with respect to qualifying gifts of cultural property designated under the Cultural Property Export and Import Act ("total cultural gifts"), gifts of ecologically sensitive land ("total ecoligical gifts"), or gifts to the Crown ("total Crown gifts"). On the history and structure of these ceilings, see below.

5 See paragraph 38(a.1), added by SC 1998, c. 19, s. 6. On the history and rationale for this provision, see below. With the reduction in the capital gains inclusion rate in the federal budget of 2000 from three-quarters to two-thirds, the taxable portion of gains on donations of publicly traded securities is reduced from three-eighths to one-third.

6 See former paragraphs 110(1)(a), (b), and (b.1), repealed by SC 1988, c. 55, s. 92. As I explain below, the value of a deduction under an income tax with graduated or progressive rates is worth more to a high-income taxpayer paying tax at a higher marginal rate than to a low-income taxpayer subject to tax at a lower marginal rate.

7 Subsection 118.1(3) (added by SC 1988, c. 55, s. 92) provides for a credit against tax otherwise payable equal to 17 per cent of the first $200 of total gifts for the year and 29 per cent of amounts exceeding $200. To the extent that the credit is not refundable and therefore of no value to donors whose income is such that they pay no tax, its value may also depend on the donor's level of income.

8 See S. Avrin McLean, R. Kluger, and R. Henrey, *Charitable Contributions in the OECD: A Tax Study,* (Alexandria, Va: Interphil, 1990). While some countries (such as Sweden) provide no tax recognition for charitable contributions by individuals, most countries (for example, France, Germany, Japan, and the United States) allow for a deduction in computing of the donor's income for the taxation year in which the contribution was made or certain other taxation years. In Spain, tax credits are available for a limited category of donations of heritage property to the Spanish government, to other public entities, or to qualified recipients.

9 SC 1917, c. 28.

10 See paragraph 5(1)(j) of the Income War Tax Act, SC 1917, c. 28, as amended by SC 1930, c. 24, s. 3.

11 Income War Tax Act, SC 1917, c. 28, paragraph 3(1)(c).

12 SC 1920, c. 49, s. 5.

13 SC 1966–67, c. 47, s. 3(1), amending then paragraph 27(1)(a) of the Income Tax Act of 1952, RSC 1952, c. 148.

14 See former paragraph 110(1)(a), enacted by SC 1970–71–72, c. 63, s. 1. The evolution of this ceiling is examined more fully below.

15 See subsection 118.1(3), added by SC 1988, c. 55, s. 92.

16 See paragraph (a) of the definition of "total gifts" in subsection 118.1(1). This ceiling is examined below.

17 See R. Watson, "Charity and the Canadian Income Tax Act: An Erratic History," *Philanthropist* 5, 3 (Spring 1985), 8–9. Although the initial amendment proposed that the deduction be available only for donations to "any church, university, college, school or hospital in Canada," the more general words "charitable organization" were substituted after concern was expressed that contributions to many worthy causes, such as the Red Cross and community funds such as the Federated Charities of Montreal, would not qualify.

18 R.M. Bird and M.W. Bucovetsky, *Canadian Tax Reform and Private Philanthropy*, Tax Paper No. 58 (Toronto: Canadian Tax Foundation, 1976), 17.

19 J.A. Rendall, "Taxation of Contributors to Charitable Organizations under the *Income Tax Act*," in *Report of the Proceedings of the Twenty-Fifth Tax Conference*, 1973 Conference Report (Toronto: Canadian Tax Foundation, 1974), 153.

20 Revenue Act of 1917, 73, s. 1201(2), 40 Stat. 300, 330, permitting a deduction for: "Contributions or gifts actually made within the year to corporations or associations organized and operated exclusively for religious, charitable, scientific or educational purposes, or to societies for the prevention of cruelty to children or animals, no part of the net income of which inures to the benefit of any private stockholder or individual, to an amount not in excess of fifteen per centum of the taxpayer's taxable net income as computed without the benefit of this paragraph."

21 See R. Goode, *The Individual Income Tax*, rev. ed. (Washington, DC: Brookings Institution, 1976), 160.

22 *Report of the Royal Commission on Dominion–Provincial Relations* (Rowell–Sirois Report) (Ottawa, 1940), vol. 2, 161.

23 Watson, "Charity," 9.

24 G. McGregor, "Charitable Contributions," *Canadian Tax Journal* 9 (1961), 441, 448.

25 55 DTC 385 (TAB).

26 RSC 1952, c. 148.

27 See Rendall, "Taxation," 155.

28 *Consolidated Truck Lines v. M.N.R.*, [1968] Tax ABC 472, 68 DTC 399.

29 See also Interpretation Bulletin IT-297R2, "Gifts in Kind to Charity and Others" (21 March 1990).

30 Ibid., para. 6.

31 See *Slobodrian v. The Queen*, [1998] 3 CTC 2654 (TCC), rejecting the taxpayers claim for a charitable contributions credit in respect of unpaid labour performed for the Université Laval on the grounds that a "gift" involves the transfer of property and services are not property. See also Interpretation Bulletin IT-110R3, "Gifts and Official Donation Receipts" (20 July 1997) para. 15(d): "A gift must involve property. Contributions

of services (that is, time, skills, effort) are not property and do not qualify." Since the act refers only to "the fair market value of a gift," not to "the fair market value of a gift *of property*," it is questionable whether this result is mandated by the words of the statute.

32 See, for example, Goode, *The Individual Income Tax*, 166.

33 See, for example, B.I. Bittker, "The Propriety and Vitality of a Federal Income Tax Deduction for Private Philanthropy," in *Tax Impacts on Philanthropy*, Symposium conducted by the Tax Institute of America (Princeton, NJ: Tax Institute of America, 1972), 166; and W. Andrews, "Personal Deductions in an Ideal Income Tax," *Harvard Law Review* 86 (1972), 309, 347–8. I return to this issue below.

34 The arguments against the taxation of imputed income are both ethical and administrative. First and foremost, to the extent that an income tax applies and should apply to market activities, it is inappropriate to subject non-market activities to tax. Moreover, since non-market activities are extremely difficult to value in any objective manner, it is difficult in practice to include such activities in an income tax. For an excellent presentation of the argument against taxing imputed income, see T. Chancellor, "Imputed Income and the Ideal Income Tax," *Oregon Law Review* 67 (1988), 561. For a persuasive response to the argument that a deduction for charitable contributions is necessary to equalize the position of taxpayers who contribute cash and those who contribute services, see M.G. Kelman, "Personal Deductions Revisited: Why They Fit Poorly in an 'Ideal' Income Tax and Why They Fit Worse in a Far from Ideal World" *Stanford Law Review* 31 (1979), 831, 838–44.

35 See, for instance, P.R. McDaniel, "Federal Matching Grants for Charitable Deductions: A Substitute for the Income Tax Deduction," *Tax Law Review* 27 (1972), 396, suggesting that "federal assistance could match contributions in services just as it could contributions in cash" if it is desired "to encourage volunteer work."

36 Although this deduction for medical expenses, like that for charitable contributions, was converted to a credit in 1988, it continues to apply only above a minimum amount, which is currently the lesser of $1,500 (adjusted for inflation after 1988) and 3 per cent of the taxpayer's income for the year. See subsection 118.2(1) of the act.

37 See paragraph 27(1)(ca) of the Income Tax Act of 1952, added by SC 1957, c. 29, s. 7(3). In 1972, this provision became former paragraph 110(1)(d.

38 M. Chirelstein, *Federal Income Taxation*, 5th ed. (Westbury, NY: The Foundation Press, 1988), 157.

39 Hon. W. Harris, Minister of Finance, *Budget Speech* (14 March 1957), 13.

40 According to McGregor, "Charitable Contributions," 449, 62 per cent of returns filed by taxable individuals claimed the standard deduction the

year after it was enacted. By 1980, the proportion had increased to 88.7 per cent. Calculated from Revenue Canada, *On Individuals: 1980 Tax Year* (Ottawa: Minister of Supply and Services, 1982).

41 Bird and Bukovetsky, *Canadian Tax Reform*, 8.

42 J.F. Deeg, "How and What Canadians Contribute to Charity," *Philanthropist* 2 (1984), 3, 11 (Table I).

43 Ibid., 11 (Table II).

44 SC 1965, c. 18, s. 7(1), repealing then subparagraph 27(1)(ca)(i).

45 Other more persuasive explanations for a long-term decline in the frequency and amount of charitable donations include an increasing proportion of younger taxpayers, rising personal incomes, and reductions in top marginal tax rates in 1972 and 1977, which increased the after-tax cost of making charitable donations. To the extent that charitable contributions correlate positively with age, increase less rapidly than growth in personal disposable income, and correlate negatively with the cost of giving, these developments are likely to have been as significant as the optional standard deduction, or more so. For a brief summary of empirical studies on the impact of age, income, and the cost of giving on charitable contributions, see K. Scharf, B. Cherniavsky and R. Hogg, *Tax Incentives for Charities in Canada*, Working Paper No. CPRN 03 (Ottawa: Canadian Policy Research Networks, 1997), 11–17.

46 See, for example, N. Carter, *Trends in Voluntary Support for Nongovernment Social Service Agencies* (Ottawa: Canadian Council on Social Development, 1974), 87.

47 *Report of the Royal Commission on Taxation* (Carter Report), vol. 3 (Ottawa: Queens Printer, 1966) 224. The commission considered, as an alternative to the optional standard deduction, allowing the deduction only on amounts exceeding 1 per cent of the donor's income. It concluded, however, that "a limit of this nature might tend to restrain charitable giving by upper income taxpayers that the allowance is designed to encourage."

48 Ibid., 224.

49 Ibid.

50 SC 1984, c. 1, s. 49(2), repealing former paragraph 110(1)(d) of the act.

51 Department of Finance, *Budget Papers* (13 April 1983), 30.

52 See M.H. Hall and S.L. Bozzo, "Trends in Individual Donations: 1984–1996," Canadian Centre for Philanthropy *Research Bulletin* 4, no. 4 (Fall 1997), 2 (Table 1).

53 Ibid., 2 (Table 1).

54 See Deeg, "How," 17 (Table IIIf); and Hall and Bozzo, "Trends," 2 (Table 1).

55 Calculated from figures presented in Deeg, "How," 17 (Table IIIf).

56 See paragraph 38(a) as it read prior to 1988. See also paragraph 39(1)(a), which defines a "capital gain," and paragraph 40(1)(a), which contains a verbal formula setting out the computation of a gain.

57 SC 1988, c. 55, s. 19. On the recent budget change, see Stikeman, Elliott, *Canadian Federal Budget, 2000* (Scarborough: Carswell, 2000).

58 Carter Report, 57.

59 See paragraph 69(1)(b), which applies to gifts *inter vivos*, and subsection 70(5), which applies to capital property transferred at death.

60 See Carter Report, 225–60.

61 See Bird and Bucovetsky, *Canadian Tax Reform*, 23–8.

62 Ibid., 25.

63 See former subsection 110(2.2), added by SC 1973–74, c. 14, s. 35(7). This rule is now subsection 118.1(6).

64 See Bird and Bucovetsky, *Canadian Tax Reform*, 26.

65 Ibid., 26–8.

66 Ibid., 24–5.

67 See, for instance, Andrews, "Personal Deductions," 371–7; and Goode, *Individual Income Tax*, 167–8.

68 Andrews, "Personal Deductions," 372.

69 Goode, *Individual Income Tax*, 167.

70 See paragraph 39(1)(a)(i.1), added by SC 1974–75–76, c. 50, s. 48, proclaimed in force from 6 September 1977.

71 See, for instance, *Friedberg v. The Queen*, [1989] 1 CTC 274, 89 DTC 5115 (FCTD), where the taxpayer claimed charitable deductions in respect of two textile collections acquired for $67,500 and $12,000 and donated to the Royal Ontario Museum immediately thereafter at average appraised values of $496,175 and $229,437. At a 50 per cent marginal tax rate, the tax value of the resulting deductions would have been roughly $250,000 for the first collection and $115,000 for the second, representing after-tax profit of 270 per cent on the first donation and 860 per cent on the second!

On appeal, [1992] 1 CTC 1, 92 DTC 6031 (FCA), the Federal Court of Appeal questioned the accuracy of the appraised values but found no basis to interfere with the trial judge's findings of fact in this respect. None the less, although it upheld the taxpayer's claim for the second donation, it rejected his claim in respect of the first, on the basis that he had never acquired title to the textiles, which were donated directly to the museum, though paid for by the taxpayer.

For other cases in which artworks have been purchased at one price and immediately thereafter donated to a charitable organization at appraised values significantly in excess of their acquisition price, see *Arvisais v. M.N.R.*, [1993] 1 CTC 2473, 93 DTC 506 (TCC); *Ball v. The Queen*, [1993] 2 CTC 2474 (TCC); *Ball v. The Queen*, [1993] 2 CTC 2475

(TCC); *Gardner v. The Queen*, [1993] 2 CTC 2480 (TCC); *Bouchard v. The Queen*, [1993] 2 CTC 2778 (TCC); *Whent v. The Queen*, [1996] 3 CTC 2542 (TCC); and *Paradis v. The Queen*, [1997] 2 CTC 2557 (TCC). For a critical evaluation of these kinds of transactions, see H. Erlichman, "Case Comment: Profitable Donations – What Price Culture?" *Philanthropist* 11 (1992), 3. Many of these transactions benefited from the rule under paragraph 46(1)(a) of the Income Tax Act deeming the adjusted cost base of personal-use property to be the greater of $1,000 and the amount otherwise determined. Following the most recent federal budget, this rule will no longer apply to property acquired after 27 February 2000 as "part of an arrangement in which the property is donated as a charitable gift."

72 See subsection 118.1(10), added by 1994, c. 7, Sch. II (1991, c. 49), s. 88(3), applicable to gifts made after 20 February 1990.

73 See paragraph 38(a.1), added by SC 1998, c. 19, s. 6. Following the most recent federal budget, this inclusion rate is reduced to one-third for donations of publicly-traded shares after 21 February 2000. The budget also proposes to extend this low inclusion rate to qualifying gifts of ecological property.

74 Department of Finance, *Tax Measures: Supplementary Information* (18 Feb. 1997). Although donations of appreciated property are fully exempt from capital gains tax in the United States, the Canadian Department of Finance explained that a three-eights inclusion rate for these capital gains would produce a comparable level of tax assistance in Canada because the top marginal rate of tax in Canada is greater than that in the United States, resulting in a lower tax price of donations in Canada.

75 Department of Finance, *Tax Measures: Supplementary Information* (18 Feb. 1997).

76 Among U.S critics of the charitable deduction, see McDaniel, "Federal Matching Grants," and D.B. Wolkoff, "Proposal for a Radical Alternative to the Charitable Deduction," *Law Forum* [1973], 279. For Canadian criticisms of the deduction, see W.R. Thirsk, "Giving Credit Where Credit Is Due: The Choice between Credits and Deductions under the Individual Income Tax in Canada," *Canadian Tax Journal* 28 (1980), 32; and N. Brooks, *Financing the Voluntary Sector: Replacing the Charitable Deduction* (Toronto: Law and Economics Workshop Series, Faculty of Law, University of Toronto, 1981). Much of this writing is based on "tax expenditure" theory, which views deductions that are not essential to the definition of the normative income tax base as a form of government spending to be evaluated as any other expenditure program. See S.S. Surrey, "Tax Incentives as a Device for Implementing Government Policy: A Comparison with Direct Expenditures," *Harvard Law Review* 83 (1970), 705; and

S.S. Surrey and P.R. McDaniel, *Tax Expenditures*, (Cambridge, Mass.: Harvard University Press, 1985).

77 See, for example Thirsk, "Giving Credit," 37: "Under the present system, the price of charitable donations is significantly cheaper if made by a wealthy donor rather than a poor one. Consequently, the charities favoured by the rich receive greater encouragement than those patronized by the poor." See also Wolkoff, "Proposal," 286–7.

78 See subsection 32(1) of the Income Tax Act of 1952, RSC 1952, c. 148.

79 See former subsection 117(1), enacted by SC 1970–71–72, c. 63, s. 1.

80 See former subsection 117(5.1), added by SC 1976–77, c. 10, s. 52(2).

81 See former subsection 117(5.2), enacted by SC 1980–81–82–83, c. 140, s. 75(2).

82 See former subsections 117(5), (5.1), and (5.2).

83 Since provincial income taxes increased these marginal rates, the differential in combined federal and provincial tax assistance for charitable giving was greater than that suggested by these federal rates alone.

84 Although many of these studies are American, Canadian studies have come to a similar conclusion. Among the leading U.S. studies, see M.K. Taussig, "Economic Aspects of the Personal Income Tax Treatment of Charitable Contributions," *National Tax Journal* 20 (1967), 1; and M. Feldstein, "The Income Tax and Charitable Contributions: Part II – The Impact on Religious, Educational and Other Organizations," *Natiomal Tax Journal* 28 (1975), 209. For a more recent Canadian study confirming a similar pattern, see H. Kitchen and R. Dalton, "Determinants of Charitable Donations by Families in Canada: A Regional Analysis," *Applied Economics* 22 (1990), 285.

85 See, for example, McDaniel, "Federal Matching Grants"; Wolkoff, "Proposal"; and Brooks, *Financing*.

86 See, for example, Thirsk, "Giving Credit." If the value of the credit is to depend solely on the amount donated to charity and not on the donor's income, the credit would have to be refundable so that individuals whose income is too low to pay tax would be eligible for a tax refund on a percentage of the value of their charitable donations. See Brooks, *Financing*, 23–4. See also Brooks, chapter 14 in this volume.

87 See former subsection 117(5.1), repealed by SC 1985, c. 45, s. 62(1).

88 R.D. Hood, S.A. Martin, and L.S. Osberg, "Economic Determinants of Individual Charitable Donations in Canada," *Canadian Journal of Economics* 10 (1977), 653, 667. The conclusion that aggregate donations and forgone tax revenues would change little appears to assume that low-income donors' responsiveness to a reduction in the after-tax cost of donations offsets that of high-income donors to an increase in after-tax costs. This issue is examined below. In addition, since the proposed tax credit on which this estimate is based appears to have been non-

refundable, a flat-rate refundable tax credit would have to be set at a lower rate in order to maintain a similar level of aggregate donations and a similar level of federal assistance to charities in terms of forgone tax revenue.

89 Hood et al., "Economic Determinants," 667.

90 Ibid.

91 Ibid.

92 Carter Report, 222.

93 Ibid., 222.

94 While the assumption that a credit would be set at a rate lower than the top marginal rate might have been reasonable – since the cost of federal assistance in terms of forgone revenues might have been expected to increase significantly otherwise – the commission might have made this assumption clear.

95 Carter Report, 222.

96 Until the mid-1970s, the prevailing view appears to have been that low-income taxpayers were largely unresponsive to changes in the after-tax cost of charitable giving. See, for example, H. Aaron, "Federal Encouragement of Private Giving," in *Tax Impacts on Philanthropy*, Symposium Conducted by the Tax Institute of America (Princeton, NJ: Tax Institute of America, 1972), 211. Subsequent studies are much less certain; for instance, C.T. Clotfelter, *Federal Tax Policy and Charitable Giving* (Chicago: University of Chicago Press, 1985), 66–71. I return to this issue below.

97 G. Glenday, A.K. Gupta, and H. Pawlak, "Tax Incentives for Personal Charitable Contributions," *Review of Economics and Statistics* 68 (1986), 688, 692.

98 See, for instance, F. Woodman, "The Tax Treatment of Charities and Charitable Donations since the Carter Commission: Past Reforms and Present Problems," *Osgoode Hall Law Journal* 26 (1988), 537, 575. I return to this issue below.

99 Ibid., 573–4.

100 Hon. M. Wilson, *Tax Reform 1987: White Paper* (Ottawa: Minister of Supply and Services, 1987), 32.

101 Ibid., 32.

102 See text accompanying notes 91 and 97.

103 For 1994 and subsequent taxation years, this threshold was lowered to $200. SC 1995, c. 3, s. 34.

104 Wilson, *Tax Reform 1987*, 32.

105 Department of Finance, *Supplementary Information Relating to Tax Reform Measures* (Ottawa: Minister of Supply and Services, 1987), 10.

106 See subsection 117(2), added by SC 1988, c. 55, s. 90(2). The rate brackets established by this provision are partially indexed by section

117.1 and are now $29,590 and $59,180, respectively. The most recent federal budget announced a return to full indexing of rate brackets beginning in the year 2000, and a gradual reduction in the middle rate to 25 per cent in 2000 and 24 per cent in 2001. For the 2000 tax year, therefore, the applicable rates are 17 per cent on taxable income up to $30,004, 25 per cent on taxable income between $30,004 and $60,009, and 29 per cent on taxable income exceeding $60,009.

107 See subsection 118.1(3), added by SC 1988, c. 55, s. 92.

108 While a $100 deduction would be worth roughly $50 to a taxpayer paying tax at the top marginal rate, for example, the credit is worth roughly $25 on an annual contribution of $100.

109 Department of Finance, *Supplementary Information Relating to Tax Reform Measures,* 10.

110 E.B. Bromley, "Charity, Philanthropy and Stewardship: A Philosophical Perspective on Tax Reform," *Philanthropist* 7 (Winter 1988), 4, 5.

111 See Hall and Bozzo, "Trends," 2 (Table 1).

112 See note 105 and accompanying text.

113 See Government of Canada, *Personal Income Tax Expenditures* (Ottawa: Department of Finance, 1992), 14; Government of Canada, *Personal and Corporate Income Tax Expenditures* (Ottawa: Department of Finance, 1993), 19; and Government of Canada, *Tax Expenditures* (Ottawa: Department of Finance, 1997), 29.

114 Watson, "Charity," 9, citing comments by Leader of the Opposition R.B. Bennett.

115 I return to this argument below.

116 See, for instance, Bird and Bucovetsky, *Canadian Tax Reform,* 17: "it seems highly probable that this limitation was motivated by the desire to reduce the possibility of abuse of the deduction for purposes of tax avoidance."

117 P.J. Wiedenbeck, "Charitable Contributions: A Policy Perspective," *Missouri Law Review* 50 (1985), 85, 115–7.

118 Ibid., 115.

119 Ibid., 117.

120 Ibid., 110–17.

121 See former paragraph 110(1)(a), enacted by SC 1970–71–72, c. 63, s. 1. This increase went beyond the recommendation of the Report of the Carter Commission (223–4), which suggested 15 per cent.

122 SC 1997, c. 25, s. 26.

123 SC 1998, c. 19, s. 22(14).

124 Department of Finance, *Tax Measures: Supplementary Information* (6 March 1996). See also Department of Finance, *Tax Measures: Supplementary Information* (19 Feb. 1997), suggesting that the increased

ceiling would "encourage more donations by providing an enhanced ability to claim tax assistance in the year of donation for the most generous donors."

125 SC 1939–40, c. 6, s. 1.

126 SC 1941, c. 18, s. 7.

127 See paragraph 26(1)(aa) of the Income Tax Act of 1948, added by SC 1950, c. 40, s. 10. This provision became paragraph 27(1)(b) of the 1952 act and former paragraph 110(1)(b) of the 1972 act.

128 SC 1967–68, c. 38, s. 1(2).

129 See subparagraph 39(1)(a)(i.1), added by SC 1974–75–76, c. 50, s. 48, proclaimed in force from 6 September 1977.

130 SC 1974–75–76, c. 50, s. 50, adding former paragraph 110(1)(b.1).

131 SC 1988, c. 55, s. 77(1). On the conversion from a deduction to a credit, see above.

132 See paragraphs (b) and (c) of the definition of "total gifts" in subsection 118.1(1), as well as the definitions of "total Crown gifts" and "total cultural gifts" in subsection 118.1(1).

133 See paragraph (d) of the definition of "total gifts" in subsection 118.1(1), as well as the definition of "total ecological gifts" in subsection 118.1(1), added by SC 1996, c. 21, ss. 23(3) and (4), applicable to gifts made after 27 February 1995.

134 Department of Finance, *Tax Measures: Supplementary Information* (27 Feb. 1995). The most recent federal budget provides further encouragement to these kinds of donations by reducing the inclusion rate on capital gains from the disposition of ecological gifts to half the rate otherwise applicable.

135 See subparagraph (a)(iii) of the definition of "total gifts" in subsection 118.1(1), as amended by SC 1997, c. 25, s. 26, applicable to 1996 and subsequent taxation years, and SC 1998, c. 19, s. 22(4), applicable to taxation years beginning after 1996.

136 See subparagraph (a)(ii) of the definition of "total gifts" in subsection 118.1(1), added by SC 1997, c. 25, s. 26, applicable to 1996 and subsequent taxation years.

137 Department of Finance, *Tax Measures: Supplementary Information* (6 March 1996).

138 Ibid.

139 Ibid.

140 For a useful demonstration of this point, at a time when half of each capital gain was taxable, charitable contributions were deductible, and the ceiling was 20 per cent of the taxpayers income, see W.D. Goodman, "The Impact of Taxation on Charitable Giving: Some Very Personal Views," *Philanthropist* (Fall 1984), 5, 7–8, explaining that if a taxpayer with annual income of $100,000 donated shares worth

$1 million acquired at a cost of $100,000, he or she would have to include an additional $450,000 (1/2 x $900,000) in computing income but be eligible for a deduction of only $110,000 (0.2 x ($100,000 + $450,000), creating a serious tax disincentive to the making of such a gift.

141 See, for instance, J.A. Langford, "The Tax Reform Bill and the Death of a Taxpayer," *Canadian Tax Journal* 19 (1971), 513.

142 See Hall and Bozzo, "Trends," 3.

143 SC 1957, c. 29, s. 7(1), amending then paragraph 27(1)(a) of the 1952 act.

144 Watson, "Charity," 11.

145 SC 1980–81–82–83, c. 140, s. 57(1), amending former paragraph 110(1)(a). See also SC 1980–81–82–83, c. 140, s. 65(2), amending former paragraphs 110(1)(b) and (b.1).

146 SC 1985, c. 45, s. 54(1), amending former paragraph 110(1)(a).

147 Added by SC 1988, c. 55, s. 92.

148 See the definitions of "total charitable gifts," "total Crown gifts," "total cultural gifts," and "total ecological gifts" in subsection 118.1(1), each of which refers to "a gift ... made by the individual."

149 A. Drache, *Canadian Tax Treatment of Charities and Charitable Donations* (Scarborough: Carswell, 1998), chaps. 11, 13.

150 If both spouses pay taxes, it does not matter which actually claims the credit. Since the credit is non-refundable, however, it is of no value to a spouse whose income is insufficient to pay any tax. In this circumstance, it makes sense for a spouse paying tax to claim the charitable donations.

151 Hall and Bozzo, "Trends," 1–2.

152 See paragraph 18(1)(a). As a general rule, deductions are allowed in computing the taxpayers "profit" from the business or property under subsection 9(1). See, for instance, *The Royal Trust Company v. M.N.R.*, [1957] CTC 32, 57 DTC 1055 (Exch. Ct). Limitations on allowable deductions in computing a taxpayer's income from an office or employment represent a departure from this general principle. See section 8(2) of the act, which limits allowable deductions in computing income from an office or employment to those specifically permitted by section 8.

153 Until 1988, the Canadian Income Tax Act permitted taxpayers to deduct these expenses to the extent that they exceeded 3 per cent of net income. See former paragraph 110(1)(c), repealed by SC 1988, c. 55, s. 77(1). As with the charitable deduction, this deduction was converted to a credit effective for 1988 and subsequent taxation years. See subsection 118.2, added by SC 1988, c. 55, s. 92. For a persuasive argument that necessary medical expenses should be recognized as a

deduction in computing taxable income, see R.W. Boadway and H.M. Kitchen, *Canadian Tax Policy,* 2nd ed. (Toronto: Canadian Tax Foundation, 1984), 69–71.

154 See, for example, McGregor, "Charitable Contributions," 441: "The allowance of a tax deduction for charitable contributions cannot be justified – and has not been justified – by any concept within an income tax system; any justification it has is social and economic." See also Rendall, "Taxation," 152, "the charitable deduction has a very uncertain, and uneasy rationale. It is not a deduction to recognize the cost of earning income, nor a hardship relief to recognize reduced ability to pay tax. Indeed, it really represents a consumption expense. Unlike other expenditures which result from consumption decisions, this one is encouraged by way of a tax deduction. Accordingly, it would seem to be indisputable that the relief should be subjected to some requirement to establish its continuing justification; at the very least, its proponents should be prepared to demonstrate its effectiveness if not to justify its purpose."

155 See above.

156 Rendall, "Taxation," 153.

157 McGregor, "Charitable Contributions," 448.

158 Wilson, *Tax Reform 1987,* 32.

159 Department of Finance, *Tax Measures: Supplementary Information* (6 March 1996). See also Department of Finance, *Tax Measures: Supplementary Information* (19 Feb. 1997), suggesting that the increased ceiling would "encourage more donations by providing an enhanced ability to claim tax assistance in the year of donation for the most generous donors."

160 Bittker, "Propriety," 165. For a similar argument, see also M.P. Gergen, "The Case for a Charitable Contribution Deduction," *Virginia Law Review* 74 (1988), 1393, 1426–33.

161 Andrews, "Personal Deductions," 317–31. This definition of the ideal personal income tax base is derived from H.C. Simons, *Personal Income Taxation: The Definition of Income as a Problem of Fiscal Policy* (Chicago: University of Chicago Press, 1938), 50: "Personal income may be defined as the algebraic sum of (1) the market value of rights exercised in consumption and (2) the change in the value of the store of property rights between the beginning and end of the period in question."

162 Andrews, "Personal Deductions," 344–70.

163 Bromley, "Charity," 5. See also W.D. Goodman, "Correspondence," *Canadian Tax Journal* 28 (1980), 399: "When a person makes a charitable donation, the money he parts with is no longer available for his use. ... In plain English, after a person makes a charitable donation, he has less money to live on."

164 Bittker, "Propriety," 166: "Side by side with taxpayers who can satisfy their charitable impulses by making a contribution of their time (from which they report no imputed income), are others who feel the same charitable impulse, but must discharge their moral obligation by contributing cash or property. This raises a question of equity between these two classes of taxpayers." See also Andrews, "Personal Deductions," 347–8, referring to a doctor who spends one day a week at a clinic without charging for his services and a lawyer whose skills "are not so directly useful to the poor as those of the doctor" who contributes "part of his fees for distribution among the poor or for the purchase of other services to meet their needs." Andrews concludes: "The charitable contribution deduction operates to treat the lawyer like the doctor, by taxing him only on the amount of personal consumption and accumulation he realizes from the practice of his profession, not on what he could have realized if he had not given part of his fees away."

165 Bittker, "Propriety," 166: "of two charitably minded persons, one may be able to satisfy his impulse by a transfer of inherited or accumulated property; once he has made his gift, whether in trust or outright, the income from that property is thereafter devoted to the charitable purpose and never again shows up in his tax return. The second person must rely upon contributions out of current earnings to discharge his moral obligation. The deduction helps to equalize their circumstances; its repeal would, in my opinion, create an inequitable disparity between them."

166 See, for example, McGregor, "Charitable Contributions," 442: "Charitable contributions ... are not a vital necessity of life and are voluntary"; and Boadway and Kitchen, *Canadian Tax Policy*, 71, contrasting medical expenses, "which are almost always involuntary," with charitable donations, which "are not a vital necessity of life and tend to be made on a voluntary basis."

167 See, for example, Rendall, "Taxation," 152; and Brooks, *Financing*, 4.

168 Watson, "Charity," 9, citing comments by Leader of the Opposition R.B. Bennett.

169 Goodman, "Correspondence," 399.

170 Andrews, "Personal Deductions," 325–6.

171 For a succinct statement of this position, see A. Warren, "Would a Consumption Tax Be Fairer Than an Income Tax?" *Yale Law Journal* 89 (1980), 1081, arguing, among other things, that this view is more consistent with liberal-egalitarian values than that advanced by Andrews. See also C.R. O'Kelley, "Rawls, Justice, and the Income Tax," *Georgia Law Review* 16 (1981), 1. As O'Kelley's title suggests, the basis for much of this thinking about the purpose of the income tax is J. Rawls, *A Theory of Justice* (Cambridge, Mass.: Harvard University Press, 1971).

172 Andrews, "Personal Deductions," 317–31.
173 W.D. Andrews, "A Consumption-Type or Cash Flow Personal Income Tax," *Harvard Law Review* 87 (1974), 1113.
174 See, for instance, Thirsk, "Giving Credit," 33.
175 Bromley, "Charity," 7.
176 This result is, of couse, subject to any reduction in the donor's tax that might be introduced for purposes extrinsic to the task of defining income. See the discussion below.
177 See the discussion at notes 32–5 and accompanying text. See also Brooks, *Financing*, 5–6.
178 See note 35 and accompanying text.
179 A possible exception to this conclusion might exist where the donor enters into a legally binding commitment to give a specific amount every year for a certain number of years. This view in fact appears to underlie the British "covenant" system, whereby donors are not taxable on amounts paid to a charity pursuant to a legal covenant that fulfils the requirements of the tax statute. It might be argued, however, that donors who enter into these arrangements are still giving away "their own money" (albeit prior to its actual receipt), which should therefore be taxed in their hands. For an explanation of this system, see McLean et al., *Charitable Contributions in the OECD*, 155–61.
180 Bittker, " Propriety," 166.
181 Goode, *Individual Income Tax*, 165.
182 McDaniel, "Federal Matching Grants," 394.
183 See Bird and Bucovetsky, *Canadian Tax Reform*, 18 (Table 18), reporting for the 1972 taxation year that, for taxpayers claiming charitable contributions, the percentage of average income among different income groups was 7.8 per cent for donors with incomes less than $5,000, 4.1 per cent for donors with incomes of $5,000–$10,000, 2.9 per cent for donors with incomes of $10,000–$20,000, 2.4 per cent for donors with incomes of $20,000–$50,000, 2.4 per cent for donors with incomes of $50,000–$100,000, and 3.6 per cent for donors with incomes over $100,000. More recent figures from the 1990 taxation year demonstrate a similar U-shaped ratio of charitable donations to income level of donors: 4.1 per cent for donors with taxable incomes less than $10,000, 2.1 per cent for donors with taxable incomes of $10,000–$30,000, 1.4 per cent for donors with taxable incomes of $30,000–$50,000, 1.3 per cent for donors with taxable incomes of $50,000–$100,000, 1.7 per cent for donors with taxable incomes of $100,000–$250,000, and 1.9 per cent for donors with taxable incomes exceeding $250,000. Calculated from figures in Revenue Canada, *Taxation Statistics on Individuals: 1990 Tax Year* (Ottawa: Minister of Supply and Services, 1992).

184 See, for example, McDaniel, "Federal Matching Grants," 383: it is "less burdensome for a person with $200,000 to give 10 per cent of his income to charity than it is for a $12,000 a year wage earner to give the corresponding 10 per cent."

185 Brooks, *Financing*, 24.

186 See, for instance, McDaniel, "Federal Matching Grants," 394, arguing that the reward rationale "appears to call for a system which increases the reward as the individual sacrifices a greater proportion of his income to charity."

187 Ibid., 397.

188 See, for instance, Bittker, "Propriety," 169. He suggests that the floor should exclude the least generous 10 or 20 per cent of donors. Goode, *Individual Income Tax*, 165, comments that such a measure would "focus the reward or incentive more sharply by withdrawing the deduction from persons whose contributions are small relative to income while continuing it for heavier contributions."

189 See the discussion of this proposal in McDaniel, "Federal Matching Grants," 387–8.

190 Carter Report, 224.

191 See, for instance, Rendall, "Taxation," 159; and Goode, *Individual Income Tax*, 165.

192 Bromley, "Charity," 12.

193 Brooks, *Financing*, 13. See also Brooks, chapter 14 in this volume.

194 See Taussig, "Economic Aspects," 3, who adds: "Only the price or substitution effect ... can be properly regarded as the result of ... the ... policy variable, since the income effect ... is incidental and could be achieved equally well by a cut in tax rates, an increase in personal exemptions, and by similar alternative devices."

195 For a useful introduction to this concept, see Scharf et al., *Tax Incentives*, 8–9.

196 For summaries of this literature, see J.A. Johnson, "The Determinants of Charitable Giving with Special Emphasis on the Income Deduction under the Income Tax – A Survey of the Empirical Literature," *Canadian Taxation* 3 (1981), 258; Clotfelter, *Federal Tax Policy*, 16–99; and Scharf et al., *Tax Incentives*, 11–17.

197 See, for example, Taussig, "Economic Aspects"; R.A. Schwartz, "Personal Philanthropic Contributions," *Journal of Poliical Economy* 78 (1970), 1264; and Hood et al., "Economic Determinants."

198 See, for example, Rendall, "Taxation," 158–9; Wolkoff, "Proposal," 291–3; and Brooks, *Financing*, 18–21.

199 See, for instance, M. Feldstein, "The Income Tax and Charitable Contributions: Part I – Aggregate and Distributional Effects," *National Tax Journal* 28 (1975), 81; C.T. Clotfelter and C.E. Steuerle, "Charitable

Contributions," in H.J. Aaron and J.A. Pechman, eds., *How Taxes Affect Economic Behavior* (Washington, DC: Brookings Institution, 1980), 403; Kitchen and Dalton, "Determinants of Charitable Donations by Families in Canada: A Regional Analysis"; and H. Kitchen, "Determinants of Charitable Donations in Canada: A Comparison Over Time," *Applied Economics* 24 (1992), 709.

200 See, for instance, Scharf et al., *Tax Incentives*, 9 and 14.

201 See, for example, W.C. Randolph, "Dynamic Income, Progressive Taxes, and the Timing of Charitable Contributions," *Journal of Political Economy* 103 (1995), 709; and K.S. Barrett, A.M. McGuirk, and R. Steinberg, "Further Evidence on the Dynamic Impact of Taxes on Charitable Giving," *National Tax Journal* 50 (1997), 321.

202 See, for example, Barrett et al., "Further Evidence," 332.

203 See, for instance, Aaron, "Federal Encouragement."

204 See, for instance, Glenday et al., "Tax Incentives."

205 See, for example, M.J. Boskin and M. Feldstein, "Effects of Charitable Deductions on Contributions by Low Income and Middle Income Households: Evidence from the National Survey of Philanthropy," *Review of Economics and Statistics* 59 (1978), 351; and Y.S. Choe and J. Jeong, "Charitable Contributions by Low- and Middle-Income Taxpayers: Further Evidence with a New Method," *National Tax Journal* 66 (1993), 33.

206 See, for example, Feldstein, "Income Tax"; Kitchen and Dalton, "Determinants."

207 For an argument to this effect, though not phrased in economic terms, see Bromley, "Charity," 14–16.

208 See, for instance, M. Feldstein, "A Contribution to the Theory of Tax Expenditures: The Case of Charitable Giving," in H.J. Aaron and M.J. Boskin, eds., *The Economics of Taxation*, (Washington, DC: Brookings Institution, 1980), 121.

209 See text accompanying note 68.

210 See, for example, Scharf et al., *Tax Incentives*, 4–5.

211 While market imperfections provide an *economic* justification for the existence of a public sector, there are non-economic rationales as well – for example, ensuring fair distribution of economic resources. The following analysis should not be read to suggest that charitable organizations should or can adequately fulfil this distributive role. On the contrary, as Will Kymlicka explains in chapter 4 of this volume, a liberal conception of justice casts these distributive considerations as matters of justice, not of charity. See also Brooks, chapter 6 in this volume.

212 This sector is often described as the "voluntary sector" to distinguish its method of finance from the public sector, which relies on compulsory

taxes and levies. See, for instance, B.A. Weisbrod, "Toward a Theory of the Voluntary Nonprofit Sector in a Three-Sector Economy," in S.R. Ackerman, ed., *The Economics of Non-Profit Institutions: Studies in Structure and Policy* (New York: Oxford University Press, 1986), 21.

213 See, for instance, L.M. Salamon, "Partners in Public Service: The Scope and Theory of Government-Non-profit Relations," in W. Powell, ed., *The Non-profit Sector: A Research Handbook* (New Haven, Conn.: Yale University Press, 1987), 99.

214 See, for example, Scharf et al., *Tax Incentives*, 5: "voluntary organizations foster a do-it- yourself culture, which can improve accountability, encourage technological innovation, and promote efficiency in the use of resources, which may be more desirable if government provision is encumbered with a lot of bureaucracy." See also R. Domingue, *The Charity "Industry" and Its Tax Treatment* (Ottawa: Minister of Supply and Services, 1995), 3: "At a time when attempts are being made to reinvent government, it should perhaps be recognized that social services could be provided much more efficiently by charitable organizations. It could be that communities and local agencies are in a better position to assess and meet these needs economically than government employees working in a capital city far removed from the people they serve."

215 See, for example, McGregor, "Charitable Contributions," 442, which notes that charitable contributions "relieve the government of some of its responsibilities, and make possible some activities, such as those of a cultural nature, which the government might not feel impelled, or be able, to afford to carry on."

216 For an introduction to these functions of the public sector, see R. Musgrave, P. Musgrave, and R. Bird, *Public Finance in Theory and Practice* (Toronto: McGraw Hill, 1987).

217 See H.M. Hochman and J.D. Rodgers, "The Optimal Tax Treatment of Charitable Contributions," *National Tax Journal* 30 (1977), 1, 2–3. See also Gergen, " Case," 1396–1414.

218 See Brooks, chapter 14 in this volume.

219 Indeed, a recent study indicates that direct government funding constitutes a much larger (and increasing) share of the revenues of charitable organizations as a whole than donations. See K.M. Day and R.A. Devlin, *The Canadian Nonprofit Sector*, Paper No. CPRN 02 (Ottawa: Canadian Policy Research Networks, 1997), 15–16, which reports that government funding decreased as a source of revenue for charities from 42.8 per cent in 1989 to 60.2 per cent in 1994, while revenues from donations decreased from 21.8 per cent in 1989 to 11.3 per cent in 1994.

220 Note the recent controversy in Ontario regarding control of the Trillium Foundation, which distributes roughly $100 million in funds

raised through provincially run lotteries and casinos. Brooks does not consider the controversy's implications for his argument in chapter 14 that direct sustaining grants are generally preferable to direct matching grants or indirect tax expenditures.

221 See, for example, ibid. Brooks claims that a system of direct matching grants would be more equitable than the current credit, more visible than a credit or deduction, administratively simpler than a credit or deduction, and more easily policed than a credit or deduction. Yet as he has acknowledged, to the extent that it is considered desirable to vary the rate of the fiscal subsidy with the amount contributed by individual donors, an indirect tax expenditure is preferable to a system of direct matching grants. I return to this point below, in notes 238–41 and accompanying text. See Brooks, *Financing the Voluntary Sector*, 32.

222 See, for instance, Bittker, "Propriety," 147–52. "I have very little confidence that a system of matching grants could be administered without administrative and congressional investigations, loyalty oaths, informal or implicit warnings against heterodoxy, and the other trappings of governmental support than the tax deduction has, so far, been able to escape."And see Goode, *Individual Income Tax*, 163, who considers it "unlikely" that direct matching grants "would be as free of undesirable controls or would serve the values of pluralism as well."

223 See text accompanying notes 196–202.

224 Hochman and Rodgers, "Optimal Tax Treatment," 11.

225 See, for example, ibid., 14: "The proper level of the tax credit depends ... on the 'external' content of the benefits that the charity-financed activities confer; it depends, in other words, on the relationship between the marginal evaluations of the primary sharing group, namely voluntary donors, and the community-at-large." See also Scharf et al., *Tax Incentives*, 9: "we should try to encourage donations to charities that provide goods or services to a large number of consumers."

226 Thirsk, "Giving Credit," 41–2.

227 See notes 70–72 and accompanying text.

228 See notes 127–34 and accompanying text.

229 Woodman, "Tax Treatment," 575.

230 Ibid., 574.

231 See, for instance, Hochman and Rodgers, "Optimal Tax Treatment," 13.

232 Scharf et al., *Tax Incentives*, 28.

233 Commission on Private Philanthropy and Public Needs (Filer Commission), *Giving in America: Toward a Stronger Voluntary Sector* (Washington, DC: Commission, 1975), 57.

234 See, for instance, Bromley, "Charity," 14: "Religious activities are justifiably 'charitable' on the basis that they are beneficial to the community

as a whole because they contribute to bettering the conduct and character of citizens." For a contrary view, see Wolkoff, "Proposal," 288. He argues that most religious gifts "help maintain the donors' congregations" and are "directed at satisfying the needs of the donor, not at satisfying the needs of society at large."

235 Although I have not examined the issue in detail, this argument suggests a much wider definition of "charity" than that currently accepted by the courts and the revenue authorities, which at the very least seems incompatible with the doctrine of political purposes. On the legal definition of charity, see Phillips, chapter 7, Moran, chapter 8, and Phillips, chapter 10 in this volume; on political purposes, see Drassinower, chapter 9, and Chapman, chapter 5; and on the administrative processes surrounding registration and deregistration, see Sossin, chapter 12. For an excellent example of a reasonable limit on acceptable pluralism in a free and democratic society, see the decision in *Bob Jones University v. United States*, 461 U.S. 574 (1983), in which the U.S. Supreme Court denied charitable status to a non-profit private school that had a racially discriminatory policy on admissions. For a more thorough examination of this issue, see Moran, chapter 8 in this volume.

236 See, for example, Wolkoff, "Proposal," 291. He concludes that "if some institutions are to be favored over others, the decision should be made democratically."

237 Brooks, *Financing*, 26.

238 See McDaniel, "Federal Matching Grants," 391, who suggests that society would be "greatly enhanced" by extension of this pluralism to all contributors. See also Brooks, *Financing*, who argues for a refundable tax credit; and Brooks, chapter 14 in this volume.

239 For a contrary view, see Brooks, *Financing*, 24, who emphasizes that "if the pluralism argument is to be taken seriously, the maximum tax credit available to each taxpayer should be limited."

240 See subsection 127(3). Bill C-2, which has passed the House of commons, and is before the Senate at the time of writing, proposes to increase the dollar amount eligible for a 75 per cent credit from $100 to $200 and to reduce the amount eligible for a 50 per cent credit from the next $450 contributed to the next $350.

241 Scharf et al., *Tax Incentives*, 35: "from an equity, efficiency, and simplicity point of view, the difference between the tax treatment of political donations and the tax treatment of charities could be viewed as undesirable."

242 Bromley, "Charity," 5.

14 The Tax Credit for Charitable Contributions: Giving Credit where None Is Due

NEIL BROOKS

Elsewhere in this volume (chapter 6) I argue that in a modern welfare state the voluntary sector should complement government activities and not attempt to replace them.[1] Its complementary role includes responding to local and minority interests, innovating and initiating new ideas, overseeing and monitoring the exercise of power by the state and other dominating institutions in society, and acting as venture capital for social change. I argue that these vital roles are placed at risk when the government "downloads" services to voluntary organizations or contracts with them for provision of public goods and services. In this chapter I argue that, to increase the voluntary sector's ability to perform these roles, Parliament should repeal the tax credit for contributions to charitable organizations. As a person interested in tax policy, I have tried to make a career out of one simple idea – namely, that the rich ought to pay their fair share of tax. Given this manifest bias – which some people regard as a serious character flaw – it is perhaps unsurprising that I take a somewhat critical view of the tax credit for charitable gifts.

As offensive as not requiring the rich to pay their fair share of tax is allowing them to direct where and on what government spends money – and that, of course, is exactly what the tax credit does. It allows high-income individuals to direct the spending of hundreds of millions of dollars of government money in a way over which neither government nor anyone else has any control, for which there is no public accountability, that is not transparent, and which allows them to buy public monuments and recognition for themselves and to give legitimacy to social indifference. The tax credit for charitable contributions is one of the most shameful tax concessions in the Income Tax Act.

The charitable tax credit is a system of indirect government matching grants, in which the government writes its cheque to the taxpayer who donates to a charity.[2] Taxpayers who donate, for example, $1,000 to a charity are able to claim a tax credit of about $500 when they file their tax return. Thus, in giving $1,000 to a charity, taxpayers give in effect $500 of their own money and act as a self-designated agent of the government in giving $500 of its money too. That is to say, a taxpayer's cheque to a charity represents two separate contributions: about one-half from the donor and the rest from the government's matching contribution. Although taxpayers are initially out of pocket for the full donation, when they file their tax returns and claim the charitable tax credit for their donations, the government essentially reimburses them for $500, in the example above, given to the charity on its behalf, by allowing them to offset this amount against their tax liability.

I develop my argument that the government should not finance the voluntary sector by matching donations in four related sections. First, I examine and critique the standard justifications for the tax credit for charitable donations. Observers have argued variously that the credit serves four principal purposes: promoting pluralism in the provision of public goods and services; encouraging innovation; maintaining independence in the voluntary sector; and promoting altruism. I suggest that it does none of these things. I argue that this method inhibits the attainment of each of these objectives. Second, I argue that the tax credit leads to a serious misallocation of government funds. Vital areas are left underfunded, while substantial sums go to areas that some wealthy individuals feel deserve private funding, whether or not these should have a priority claim on the public purse. Third, I postulate that the tax credit satisfies none of the evaluative criteria normally applied to government spending, such as controllability, accountability, and transparency. Its flaws are so serious that even if the arguments in favour of the credit had some force they could not rescue such a badly designed government instrument. Fourth, I argue that the tax credit represents an inefficient use of government resources. Some of its supporters claim that even though it has flaws as a spending program, it at least encourages philanthropy. Each dollar that government spends induces more than one dollar in private contributions that would otherwise not have been made. Thus the voluntary sector gains more in contributions than the government loses in revenue, and therefore overall more money is available to provide public goods and services. This argument is factually wrong. The best empirical evidence suggests that the government loses more revenue through the credit that the credit encourages in additional private monies.

Fifth and finally, I discuss two related issues: the ideal method of financing the voluntary sector and the relative efficacy of taxes and charitable donations as devices for promoting citizenship and furthering social cohesion. I make two points. First, a system of direct grants is a much better mechanism for increasing the funding of voluntary organizations than a system of matching grants, including the tax credit for charitable donations. The promotion of pluralism, innovation, altruism, and independence is often given as both the goal of the voluntary sector and the justification for subsidizing it by matching private donations. This represents a confusion of thought. A person might be prepared to accept these goals as justifications for encouraging formation of organizations in the voluntary sector, but not as justifications for this particular method of financing them. I concede that voluntary bodies play these essential roles but suggest that they are more likely to further these goals if the government subsidizes these organizations by direct grants instead of by matching private donations through the tax credit. Second, I suggest that as a nation we would all be much better off if, instead of relying on the rich for charity, we required them to pay their fair share of tax.

JUSTIFICATIONS FOR THE TAX CREDIT: PLURALISM, INNOVATION, ALTRUISM, AND INDEPENDENCE

Pluralism

Some supporters claim that subsidization of the voluntary sector by means of a tax credit for charitable donations promotes pluralism and dispersion of power through its provision of public goods and services. Citizens decide what institutions in society will receive subsidization for providing public goods and services by in effect voting with their donations. As the Filer Commission in the United States observed, "Governmental encouragements to giving are appropriate ... because giving provides an important mode of citizen expression. By saying with his or her dollars what needs should be met, what objectives pursued, what values served, every contributor exercises, in a profound sense, a form of self-government, a form that parallels, complements and enriches the democratic electoral process itself."[3] If this is the justification for government subsidization of the voluntary sector, it would seem imperative that a method of financing be chosen that permits as many citizens as possible to participate in the decision-making.[4]

As a mechanism for social choice used to determine government spending in a way that promotes pluralism, the tax credit effectively disenfranchises many low-income citizens who have no tax liability with which to offset their potential reimbursement. Thus it gives many of the young, the elderly, and the poor no ability to allocate government funds. This result is clearly unjustified: a taxpayer's status would not appear, on any political grounds – particularly in a society that purports to value equal participation and influence in the political process – to be a valid condition for eligibility in a scheme designed to allocate government funds to the voluntary sector.

The credit defeats the pluralist objective in other ways as well.[5] A feature that was designed deliberately to discriminate against low-income families limits the Canadian federal government's matching grant to only 17 per cent for the first $200 of total donations – donations in excess of $200 receive a federal matching grant of 29 per cent. Thus donations made by low-income Canadians, who will often not be able to give in excess of $200, will attract only slightly more than one-half as much government subsidy as donations from those with higher incomes, whose total donations will usually exceed $200. In a feature deliberately designed to benefit wealthy families, if the donor gives publicly traded shares that have accrued capital gains, the federal government's matching grant can often exceed 40 per cent of the donation. Under these rules, introduced in the 1997 budget, taxpayers are able to direct the spending of up to $650 of federal and provincial government money by giving only $350 of their own money to a charity, if they give eligible capital property that has appreciated in value. Again, since low-income individuals tend not to own a lot of stock that has appreciated in value, high-income individuals have even more ability to determine where government money will be spent.

Finally, the tax credit effectively prevents many lower-income citizens from directing government funds to particular charities, since they are less likely to ask for and keep receipts than high-income individuals and because if they want to direct the government funds they first must pay them to a charity and then wait for reimbursement when they file their tax return. This causes a financial hardship for many low-income families. Present tax laws, therefore, instead of promoting pluralism do just the opposite, concentrating the ability to direct government matching grants in the rich. But whatever the detailed rules of a scheme of matching grants, and even if a dollar contributed by a low-income person attracted the same matching percentage from the government as one given by someone with a high income, the latter would be able to control the disbursement of substantially more government money simply because they have more disposable income to donate.

Under matching grants, in 1996, the average person with income of $25,000 or less directed about $14 of federal money to some charity; by contrast, the typical Canadian with income over $250,000 determined which charities received about $2,830 of federal funds – over 200 times as much as those earning under $25,000.[6] Under this scheme, those earning over $250,000 – about 0.3 per cent of taxfilers in 1996 – directed about 14 per cent of allocated government funds. Those earning over $100,000 – about 2 per cent of those filing returns – allocated 25 per cent of the subsidy. Those earning under $25,000 – almost 61 per cent of taxfilers – allocated only 16 per cent of the government's subsidy. Thus, the top 2 per cent of income earners directed more than 1½ times as much government money as the bottom 60 per cent. Further, the rich will often control the funds even after they have donated the money because they will often be board members of the organizations or foundations to which they contribute. There seems little question that the charitable tax credit serves the process of elitism instead of the cause of democratic pluralism.

Although the rich allocate such a large share of government grants, low-income households donate a larger proportion of their incomes to charities. Thus the donations made by the poor represent a much greater commitment than those given by the rich. The most recent comprehensive survey of charitable giving in Canada found that donors with annual household incomes below $20,000 gave an average of 1.4 per cent of their income to charities and non-profits, while those who earned more than $60,000 donated only 0.4 per cent.[7] Thus poor families gave more than three times as much of their income to charities than the rich. But even these numbers understate the relative intensity of giving, since wealth also helps determine a person's ability to give. Households with greater income are likely to have substantially greater wealth than low-income families. The Mannix family was reported in 1998 to have made a donation of $100 million to its private foundation and to charities across the country.[8] This was one of the largest gifts ever made in Canada, and it received a good deal of publicity. But the family's fortune is estimated to be $10 billion. Thus, assuming that it is able to claim the tax credit for its contribution, the gift amounted to 0.5 per cent of its wealth. The bottom 40 per cent of Canadians have almost no wealth; their debts usually exceed their assets. Every time they make a charitable donation, no matter how modest, they give a greater percentage of their wealth than the Mannixes.

By any measure, it is clear that the matching-grant scheme inherent in the tax credit promotes a peculiar kind of pluralism. Control over government spending goes to the very rich. The credit could be changed so that, for example, donations by low-income families attracted a larger matching grant than equivalent donations by high-income families. But at this suggestion, high-income families and many charities begin to lose their enthusiasm for pluralism. It turns out that high- and low-income families do not give to the same type of charities. High-income families tend to give to universities, medical research, symphonies, and museums; those with low incomes to religious and social welfare organizations. Consequently, if the tax credit were made more equitable, universities, hospitals, and high culture would lose some government subsidies, and churches and social welfare organizations would gain substantially. This shift in the use of government funds is one that would simply have to be accepted if the pluralism argument were taken seriously, which is presumably why, although the pluralist rationale is often glibly recited as a justification for the tax credit, no one takes it seriously.

Although the argument for pluralism should not turn on how the funds are spent – pluralism refers to a process rather than to an outcome – letting the rich control a grossly disproportionate share of government funds would not be so objectionable if the expenditures by charities benefited all income groups. Rather surprisingly, no Canadian study of the incidence of charitable spending has been done. However, U.S. research has revealed that only a trivial amount of philanthropy in general goes to the poor.[9] Most, particularly that financed by the rich, went to cultural and educational activities that even the strongest proponent of the "trickle-down theory" would have to admit only remotely benefits the poor.

Innovation

Further essential roles for the voluntary sector – which might be affected by the way in which it is financed – are to foster constructive innovation, provide for diversity, and encourage challenges to established ways of thinking and doing things. Two reasons are often given for supposing that voluntary organizations financed by private donations will be more innovative than those financed by government.

First, some observers argue that voluntary bodies will be more innovative since they consist of people from across the country, with diverse backgrounds and experiences, working in different-size groups, in different circumstances, and, most important, in a form that is likely to be non-bureaucratic. As a result, as a landmark Canadian study on the voluntary sector phrased it, "they constitute a forum for initiating new ideas and processes, a place where people can take chances and experiment."[10] But this position misses the point, since it relates to the organizational form of charities, not their method of funding. Even if charities are funded solely by government, their form might be non-bureaucratic. Government funding ought not to be confused with government bureaucracy. Charities would be accountable to government for their expenditure of funds under direct grants, but the degree of government control would depend on the nature and needs of the organization. Thus, if innovation springs from the kinds of people involved in the activity and from the form of organization, this dynamic would not change if the credit for charitable contributions were repealed. Government agencies, instead of individual or corporate donors, would determine which groups received government funding.

Second, allocation by private donors allows voluntary organizations to escape government control and therefore renders them more willing to challenge prevailing political ideas and mores. If all of an organization's funding comes from government, so the argument goes, it will gradually accommodate itself to the wishes of government. However, if semi-autonomous government agencies allocate government funds, as occurs with most government subsidies to the voluntary sector now, they will be largely free of political control. Also, charities cannot escape some degree of control by donors. No organization that is dependent on outside financing can claim to be wholly autonomous.

The real issue therefore is whether the voluntary sector is more likely to be innovative if it must seek its funding from semi-autonomous government agencies rather than from individual donors and corporations? What is the record of private donors as innovators and harbingers of orderly social change? The conservatism and caution that corporations exercise in granting decisions are well known. Understandably, corporations, because they are accountable to a diverse group of shareholders, are unlikely to contribute to highly visible and controversial projects where the outcome or potential benefits are in doubt. They tend to give to familiar and well-established charities. If the object is to encourage the taking of chances in social reform or cultural expression, it strikes me as being quite naïve to allow business corporations to allocate the monies. In Canada, most of those bodies that have been confronting established ways of thinking, the marketplace and the media – such as those organizing communities, educating consumers, fighting poverty, and promoting women's rights, environmental action, and programs for Native Canadians – have been funded by government.

Altruism

A society in which strangers care about each other is presumably better than one in which each person's well-being does not affect the well-being of others. Therefore government policy should encourage, or at least not discourage, altruism. The voluntary sector, it is often said, strengthens the sense of community derived from sharing. When people involve themselves in the work of charitable organizations, this effort undoubtedly not only reflects a sense of altruism and of responsibility towards others but also strengthens these feelings.

Does simply giving money to a charity promote the same sense of altruism? And if so, does the fact that the donor is able to attract a matching government grant enrich that sense of altruism? It does seem unlikely that allowing taxpayers to direct government funding through their private donations is necessary to promoting a feeling of responsibility for others. Generally, people's perceptions of community expand through voluntary actions that they undertake on behalf of others and for which they assume personal responsibility. It would seem counterintuitive to believe that a person's sense of altruism and social responsibility will be increased only if they also allocate someone else's funds. A tax credit, rather than fostering a sense of altruism from giving, seems more likely to accentuate the purely selfish goal of reducing one's own taxes. Also, arguably, its availability obscures the donor's motives from the recipient and other citizens. It is not uncommon to hear the speculation that a particular charitable gift was motivated only by the tax write-off. Thus reciprocity and the sense of community that the gift might otherwise foster may be negated by the credit.

Independence

The independence of the voluntary sector is assumed to be one of its principal virtues. An automatic matching grant system for government financing, some say, allows charities to maintain their independence. However, no recipient of largesse can escape the donor's control. Any association looking for contributors is ultimately dependent on the goodwill of those from whom it receives donations, who thus exercise a degree of control over the organization. Is the voluntary sector more likely to be able to plan and act independent of donors if funded by a government agency or by private donors? Which source of funding is more likely to have strings attached?

Government funds in Canada generally come with fewer conditions attached than private donations. There is very little evidence of government interference with, for example, research undertaken at universities and hospitals or with the policies of cultural organizations. By contrast, there is a constant stream of news stories about the control that private donors attempt to exert over the institutions that they fund.[11] Cultural organizations in particular have often suffered because of donors' attempts at control. The most recent, notorious example is the attempt by Robert and Signe McMichael to prevent the McMichael Gallery in Kleinburg, Ontario, to which they donated their art collection of the Group of Seven, from purchasing and displaying contemporary art.[12] But even if there is no overt influence, when private donations fund the arts private donors set the direction in art funding.[13] When money comes from semi-autonomous government granting agencies, the arts community sets the direction, since the initiative for projects comes from the arts applicants and decision-making power about awards normally rests with review panels of peer experts.

Universities illustrate the effects of control by private donors, since arguably universities have the greatest need for independence of all non-profit organizations. Historically, even though governments have been the major source of university revenue, there has been little evidence of government interference in the research and educational mission of universities. Over the past decade, as universities have had to turn to private donors for gifts, even though their contributions make up a very small percentage of funding, the fact that their donations come with strings attached is evidenced everywhere on campuses.[14] Buildings, classrooms, chairs, and even courses[15] frequently bear the name of private donors. Although there has been little evidence of outside donors' overt influence over education and research,[16] the covert influence cannot help but be significant as universities increasingly seek private, usually business or business-related, contributions.

In an attempt to raise funds, universities might well be led to expand in a direction that they might not otherwise have chosen strictly on the basis of their educational mission and priorities. For example, almost every business school in the country is now named after a donor, yet few fine arts or humanities buildings bear the name of donors. In implementing their educational missions, would universities across the country have chosen to upgrade their business school facilities or programs in the absence of significant private donations? How does pursuit of private donations shape the programs of these schools? When York University's business school changed its name to the Schulich School of Business as a condition for receiving a donation from Toronto financier Seymour Schulich, the dean of the school, Dezso Harvath, was quoted as saying: "When you make programs relevant, when you are responsive, the business community is very responsive."[17] Inevitably, as universities rely more on private funding, scholarly activity that cannot, or whose practitioners refuse to, seek private funds will be downgraded.

Even the names attached to facilities can subtly affect a university's mission by apparently aligning it with the donor's interests. A university with buildings and classrooms named after large corporations or prominent business people hints at, at the very least, a sympathy with, if not an attachment to, corporate culture. It is more likely to begin to behave like a private-sector body. If a university chair is named the Arthur Andersen Professor of Taxation, for example, after one of Canada's largest accounting and management firms, whose clients include many of the country's largest corporations, can one easily imagine its holder taking a position opposed to the interests of those corporations? In an editorial entitled "The Public, Private University," which expressed concern about the restrictions attached to money donated to universities, the *Globe and Mail* noted that the 111 endowed chairs at the University of Toronto included chairs for "geo-technical mine design and analysis," "youth unemployment," and "medieval Jewish Studies." It went on to say, "There is nothing intrinsically wrong with any of these areas; it is just that their specificity clearly pushes the university down a certain intellectual track."[18]

In some of Canada's largest privately financed "think tanks," most of which are financed by the government's matching donations, the consistent, indeed blatant political bias of the research suggests that the research is undertaken with a view to maintaining sources of funding. Generally, the views represented range from the far right to the extreme right. In contrast, the one smallish research institute that relies on funding from trade unions – the Canadian Centre for Policy Alternatives – publishes only research with a left-wing bias. The record of privately financed think tanks would indicate that universities are being naïve if they think that research funds from the private sector come without strings attached.

The universities' mission may be affected in even more subtle ways by their reliance on private funding. For example, their administrators will increasingly be people who can raise private money, as opposed to being committed to an academic mission. In late 1998, when the University of Toronto announced that it would be looking for a new president, a newspaper headline predicted that "U of T job expected to go to one who knows a lot of people, not one who knows a lot."[19] One observer told the reporter that one candidate was particularly well placed since "she's well thought of among the horsey set." The reporter also noted that the present president "was seen as a great fundraiser rather than a brilliant thinker ... [who was able to turn] his political, business and social connections into big dollars for the university."

Aside from the subtle effects that it will have on universities' educational and research mission, this "monogrammed giving" is mildly irksome because when donors immortalize their names by getting a building, professorship, or classroom named after themselves or their firms the donation should be regarded as a price, not a gift. One can make a strong argument that it should not qualify for the tax credit subsidy at all. Moreover, in almost every case the costs of construction of a building, for example, will far exceed the size of the private gift. Often the university will leverage the gift with direct matching grants, and the tax credit means that the government is also paying for about one-half of the donor's contribution. At the very least, the business school at York, for example, should be called the Schulich and Canadian Taxpayers' School of Business.

THE MISALLOCATION OF GOVERNMENT RESOURCES

Even if a system of matching grants, like the tax credit, were more likely to promote pluralism, innovation, and the independence of the voluntary sector – since it allows taxpayers, rather than government officials or appointees, to make decisions concerning the allocation of government resources – we should still judge the credit in part on pragmatic grounds. That is, does it promote a rational allocation of government resources among competing claims?

It would be extraordinary if a scheme for allocating government funds based on private contributions resulted in a sensible allocation of resources. Let us look at a couple of examples. Under the present tax credit for charitable contributions, the total level of expenditures and the allocation of expenditures to various medical research projects depend largely on competing public fund-raising drives. One could hardly imagine a less appropriate way to decide between – for example, muscular dystrophy, cancer, heart and stroke, trauma, and mental disability, say, than to base the decision on the "pay-off" from competing publicity campaigns. Often the campaigns raise money through such community endeavours as walkathons and telethons unrelated to such criteria as the potential return from spending additional funds on research in particular areas. A charity may send out a letter that has been rewritten and tested countless times by public-relations and direct-mail people and couple it with a perhaps productive mailing list. In 1980 Terry Fox, who had lost part of one leg to cancer, ran half-way across Canada for cancer research, and in response to the extraordinary interest and fund-raising evoked by his effort and his untimely death, the government allocated millions of dollars to the Canadian Cancer Society.[20] However much one admires Terry Fox's courage, it does appear to be an odd basis for determining how much and where public money is spent on medical research.

More generally, people and corporations tend to give to charitable organizations in their own localities. Thus charities in communities with high per capita income or where corporations have their head offices will receive more government funding than those elsewhere. Hospitals in Toronto are able to attract considerably more private funding than those in smaller cities, which may not have sophisticated fund-raising facilities or a wealthy constituency.[21] In the last few decades an important objective of the federal government has been that public goods and services should be equally accessible to all Canadians, irrespective of region. If a member of Parliament were to suggest that government money for cultural activities, for example, should be allocated disproportionately to those cities in which corporations had their head office this would likely occasion some public debate. However, that is precisely what happens under the present scheme of matching grants without there being even public acknowledgment of that fact.

In the same way that big cities do better than smaller communities in attracting funds under a matching grant scheme, wealthy, high-profile institutions are able to attract a disproportionate amount of funds compared to smaller, less well-known institutions. Thus, when the Ontario government established the Student Opportunity Trust Fund for needy students, in which it agreed to match private donations, Ontario's 17 universities quite predictably, because of their knowledge, connections, and resources, raised $246.8 million, and its 25 community colleges only $18.2 million.[22]

Another reason why the tax credit results in inappropriate allocation of government funds is that few people plan their charitable giving. Instead they respond to family or friends' medical histories, door-to-door collections, the availability of raffle tickets, or the sponsoring of someone in an event without seriously weighing the relative seriousness of the cause or the effectiveness of the particular charitable organization. How could it be otherwise? Even when they are donating substantial amounts, people may give to causes or institutions about which they know personally. For example, in 1999, Vancouver businessman Jimmy Pattison donated $20 million to a research centre for prostate cancer at the Vancouver General Hospital.[23] He explained to a newspaper reporter that he knew and liked Dr Goldenberg, the head of the centre. Assuming that he obtains the full tax benefit for this gift, he gave in effect about $10 million of his own money and $10 million of the government's. Perhaps giving $10 million of government money to the centre was the most appropriate and effective use of this money in furthering medical research, but it does seem odd that one person, perhaps acting on a whim or as a favour to a close friend, should be able to divert this amount of government money.[24]

CONTROLLABILITY, ACCOUNTABILITY, AND TRANSPARENCY

Three of the most widely accepted criteria for judging government spending are controllability, transparency, and accountability. The matching grant scheme violates each of these criteria. First, the government ought to be able to exercise control over the expenditure of public funds so that it can be held accountable to the electorate for them and to ensure that expenditures reflect governmental priorities. By enacting a spending program through the Income Tax Act, it loses control over the resulting spending. It can never be sure how much it will have to spend. The amount will depend on, among other things, any changes in the marginal tax rates, the enactment of other tax incentives, and the success of charities' appeals. There is no annual appropriation of money for the program, and so Parliament has no opportunity to evaluate the estimates of the amount to be spent and assess them in the light of the government's spending priorities. In effect, the activities so financed are immune from evaluation and "prioritization." It is not obvious that charitable activities should be given this unassailable position.

Government spending should be, second, transparent and, third, accountable. The electorate should be able to determine easily how much a program costs, who is benefiting from it, and whether it is achieving its objectives. The charitable tax credit obscures not only the answers but even the questions themselves. Even the most basic question – how much government funding will each charity receive? – has no answer. Charities' activities are seldom subject to public scrutiny. In an extreme case, the Canadian Security Intelligence Service, for instance, suspects that about two dozen charitable groups in Canada are funding world-wide terrorism and ethnic conflict, yet the fact that they receive government money goes almost unnoticed under this scheme.[25]

Moreover, as Liberal MP John Bryden noted in his report on charities in 1996, the 66,000 registered charities included countless ones that, while they might be doing good work, would not appear to merit public funds.[26] He gave as an example the Quimby Foundation, which had issued tax receipts for $69,526 in 1994 and was dedicated to promoting the writing of an obscure 19th-century American spiritual leader. He also wondered about, among others, the Canadian Society for the Study of Names, the Canadian Naturopathic Education and Research Society, the American Civil War Reenactment Society, and the Back to the Farm Foundation. Information about direct government appropriations is readily available, their merits are frequently the subject of public debates, and the government is held accountable for them; however, when Ottawa gives money by means of the tax credit for charitable contributions, those grants are immune from public scrutiny.

Concern over government spending implicit in the tax concession for contributions to charities is not new. In 1863 William Ewart Gladstone introduced a resolution into the British House of Commons to repeal the income tax exemption for charities. Although the exemption was equivalent to a direct subsidy, because it was hidden in the income tax legislation the government had no control over it and could not be held accountable for it. After establishing that the tax exemption was conceptually equivalent to a direct government subsidy, he said:

> But if this latter is a portion of the State expenditure, I ask the Committee to consider why it is to be kept up in so strange a form? For many years, we have been passing Bills and adopting administrative provisions, with a view to bringing the whole expenditure of the State, from time to time, within the control, and under the eye, of the House of Commons. If this money is to be laid out upon what are called charities, why is that portion of the State expenditure to be altogether withdrawn from view, to be shrouded within the folds of the most complicated sections of our Act of Parliament, and to be so contrived that we shall know nothing of it, and have no control over it; so that, while to every other object recognized by the State as fit to be provided for

out of the public funds, we apply, and for the most part apply every year, a vigilant eye with a view to modification or retrenchment, here we maintain from year to year and from generation to generation what we are pleased to term an exemption, that is to say a public grant, but a public grant which we never investigate, and never weight. We plume ourselves upon our liberality; we leave this great expenditure entirely in the dark; we waive in favour of these institutions, not only the receipt of a certain sum of money, but the application of all those principles of philosophical and practical administration, and of constitutional control, which we consider necessary for the general government of the country and management of our finances? Ought we to act thus?[27]

Gladstone's resolution was defeated, but the concerns that he expressed about the lack of government accountability and control over the government spending inherent in the tax exemption for charities (and the tax credit for donations) remain valid today.

THE EFFICIENCY QUESTION: THE INCENTIVE EFFECT OF A MATCHING GRANT SCHEME

Some supporters of matching grants claim that, even though the spending program has design flaws, it is an efficient strategy for encouraging philanthropic contributions. They argue that each government dollar spent through such a program induces more than one dollar in private contributions. Thus the voluntary sector gains more in contributions than the government loses in revenue, and therefore overall more money is available for the provision of public goods and services.

Countless economists have studied the incentive effect of the charitable deduction and have summarized their findings in numerous publications.[28] The studies reach hopelessly irreconcilable results. Some suggest that its efficiency is near zero; for example, researchers at Canada's Department of Finance found that the government, to raise an additional $1 of private donations, had to spend $5.[29] Other studies find the incentive so efficient that each $1 of lost tax revenue raised $2 of private donations.

We can make some sense of the studies by dividing them into three chronological periods. The first round of empirical studies, in the late 1960s and early 1970s, tended to suggest that reducing the price of charitable giving by providing a tax concession for contributions did little to increase giving.[30] However, in the mid-1970s and the 1980s a series of studies, most notably those by Martin Feldstein[31] and Charles Clotfelter,[32] found tax deductions efficient, stimulating an increase in giving that exceeded the tax revenue forgone. These studies suggested that, as U.S. marginal tax rates declined dramatically in the 1980s, thus substantially increasing the price of giving to charities, charitable donations would drop. Just the opposite happened. Between 1980 and 1990 charitable giving increased. Intrigued by this fact, researchers undertook a new round of studies which, instead of looking at the cross-sectional data examined earlier, used longitudinal data relating to a panel of taxpayers and could determine whether tax changes affected only the timing of a person's donations or also the total over a lifetime. In a review of these new studies done in the late 1980s, Richard Steinberg concluded that the earlier consensus on efficiency "has been strongly questioned by recent progress in statistical techniques and by the availability of new data sets. Early analysis from panels of tax data indicate that giving is price inelastic, although further analysis is necessary."[33] Since then, other studies using panel data have also concluded that a tax concession is inefficient – that is, that governments lose substantially more tax revenue from such a concession than they generate in additional revenue for the voluntary sector.[34]

A tax credit undoubtedly stimulates some giving. However, the best evidence tells us that the amount is considerably less than the government loses in revenue. The tax credit is likely of little significance to most low- and middle-income earners, and most high-income earners probably receive some form of consideration for most of their contributions, if only some form of public acknowledgment. If the government were to repeal the tax credit and allocate the saved revenue through semi-autonomous government agencies to the voluntary sector, much of the charitable sector would have considerable additional revenue. Moreover, at present a substantial amount of money donated goes to religious organizations, which would probably not qualify for direct grants.[35] Consequently, this additional amount would be available for other organizations.

FINANCING THE VOLUNTARY SECTOR AND PROMOTING CITIZENSHIP THROUGH TAXES

Financing the Voluntary Sector

In this final section, I take a step back from detailed arguments and make two additional general points, closely related to the argument set out above. First, having maintained that matching grants, as represented by the tax credit for charitable donations, are not an effective way of financing the voluntary sector, I should state what the alternative should be. Aside from some form of contractual arrangement, there are essentially two possibilities – matching grants and direct grants. If the former are not effective, we are naturally left with the latter. Governments already use this technique in many areas. The federal government does so via agencies such as the Natural Sciences and Engineering Research Council of Canada, the Social Sciences and Humanities Research Council of Canada, and the Medical Research Council, or through programs in government departments. At the provincial level such granting agencies include the Ontario Arts Council and the Ontario Trillium Foundation.

I leave for another place discussion about the design and funding[36] of grant-giving, semi-autonomous government agencies. Such schemes permit allocation of funds to those areas considered most needy, in a way that allows for transparency of decision-making and effective accountability. It is difficult to imagine that the federal government could not make better use of the approximately $1.6 billion[37] it now gives each year to taxpayers who claim the credit by allocating it to granting agencies, however designed.[38] Funds would go to voluntary organizations according to predetermined criteria related in some way to their merits. This redirection of assistance would result in a more vibrant and relevant voluntary sector.

I am not suggesting that the voluntary sector should somehow be "squeezed out" of our national life. I accept completely the right of donors to give their own money or services to whatever organizations they choose. But should such donors also be able to compel others to contribute to that same group, which is the effect of the tax credit? Public funds are not limitless, and a scheme of matching grants must inevitably operate at the expense of some other, democratically determined public program or result in higher taxes.

Although the idea of bureaucrats' disbursing public finds to charities might seem anathema to some supporters of the private sector, bureaucrats, though not public bureaucrats, already disburse a good amount of charitable donations. Regional United Ways and other umbrella entities, which offer donors and constituents economies of scale in raising of funds and expertise in allocation of them among charities, operate like semi-autonomous government funding agencies. Whatever the advantages of having individuals choose the charities to which government subsidies go, they clearly do not apply when people give to umbrella organizations, in which a board of directors, often drawn from their own constituents, determines the annual grant to each constituent.[39] This is particularly the case now that their allocation of funds tends to be more program-related, is less discretionary, and gives greater priority to local needs. The same might be said of donations to large foundations in which boards of directors disburse grants to individual charities based on the bureaucratic judgment of the foundation's employees.

Comparing Taxes and Donations

Taxes are much more effective at promoting the values of democratic citizenship than are donations. No one can gainsay the extraordinary value of the work done by some charities and the significant contribution they have made to many areas of national life. However, as I argue elsewhere,[40] although charities play a vital role in a modern democratic welfare state, it is a somewhat restricted role: allowing citizens with common interests to come together to explore and enrich their experiences; defining and clarifying issues for public consideration and government action; ensuring that all members of society enjoy equal participation in government and society; improving the processes and competence of government; filling gaps in the delivery of social services in responsive and constructive ways; innovating with new ways for delivering public services and then urging governments to take over; monitoring, overseeing, and bringing to public attention abuses of power in the public or private sector; and advocating and working for social change.

Attempts to transfer to the voluntary sector responsibility for delivery of services traditionally discharged by the public sector will threaten not only the rights of citizenship that the recipients of these services should enjoy but also the unique and valuable characteristics of the voluntary sector itself as a form of social organization. In the words of Jennifer Wolch, "The rhetoric of social change and betterment, so pervasive in the nonprofit world, masks a reality in which the sector is increasingly expected to uphold dominant norms and values, protect existing resource distributions, and shield the state from attacks on legitimacy. Is this the center we would hold? ... Decentering the nonprofit sector [away from dominant institutions, powerful groups, and privileged places], and joining the margins therefore may stand as an alternative – and ultimately more viable – strategy for the weaving of a new, more humane and inclusive social contract."[41]

I underline this theme by comparing charitable donations and taxes. In recent years the backlash against the welfare state has resulted in denigrating the paying of taxes but glorifying the making of charitable donations. This is most unfortunate. As devices for promoting citizenship, taxes are superior to donations in almost every respect.[42] It is almost impossible to make any sense out of policy changes that would reduce government services and at the same time increase reliance on the voluntary sector except through the lens of class. After all, society's economic elite does not need social insurance, it has little to fear from cutbacks in social services, and liberalizing tax concessions for charitable gifts simply allows them more control over government funds and further disenfranchises low- and even middle-income families.

Other significant differences hold between taxes and donations. On average, charities spend 25 per cent of their revenue on raising funds; taxes are collected for little over 1 per cent of the revenue raised. Charitable contributions allow people to pursue their own personal predilections, without close regard to community needs. Conversely, by paying taxes, people contribute to the community without necessarily furthering their personal, perhaps idiosyncratic inclinations. They indicate their willingness to engage in public deliberation about the public good and ultimately to be bound by the judgment of the majority as to how it should be furthered. Paying taxes expresses a confidence in other citizens and acknowledges an intimate link with them.

Donors to charities frequently look for some recognition for their gift – a building bearing their name, a name plate on a seat, or a grateful smile. Citizens pay taxes without a strict accounting of what the bargain is worth for them personally. The only consideration they receive is the furtherance of the public good. In this respect paying taxes is true beneficence writ large.

Charity divides people into beneficent donors and grateful beneficiaries. Taxes, in contrast, erase differences. The services that taxes purchase, such as public education and health care, are available to everyone as members of the community. Social transfers financed by taxes provide entitlements to recipients that strengthen citizenship based on principles of mutual support and universal inclusiveness.

Contributions regarded as charitable imply that donors are sharing income to which they have an ethical claim and their giving an act of personal virtue. It therefore reinforces the justness of the existing social order. Progressive taxes, in contrast, imply that the distribution of income that results from market forces is ethically unjustifiable and socially unacceptable. They signal the intrinsically social nature of everyone's contributions to society; they underline the fact that what a person is able to earn in the market economy is dramatically affected by morally irrelevant factors such as the accident of being born into a family of wealth, the good luck of remaining able-bodied and working, or the chance event of having invested in growth securities. They emphasize that what people earn in the market economy bears no relationship to the value of their contribution to others.

By cutting programs and encouraging corporations to step into the breach, neo-conservative governments are taking social decisions away from the people and giving them to an unelected group of corporate officials. Taxes add democratic legitimacy to what individuals undertake together. In addition to demonstrating an undemocratic disposition, the suggestion that taxes should be cut and corporate charitable contributions increased also reflects a confused mind. To the shareholders of corporations, presumably there is little difference between paying taxes and having corporate executives siphon off shareholders' profits to their own favourite charities. As shareholders they can vote out the management if they think that it is being too generous, but as taxpayers they can do the same to the government.

Charities are unaccountable to their beneficiaries. Some groups who have been advocating devolving of more responsibilities from the government to the voluntary sector have appropriated the rallying cry, "Power to the People." Yet such devolution disempowers the people that they serve. The only people empowered are the charity givers. They can serve those whom they want to and attach whatever conditions they regard as appropriate. In contrast, those who receive benefits that are financed by taxes are empowered. They have the protections afforded by procedural due process and the Charter of Rights.

Charity deals with problems case by case and serves to reinforce society's narrowly defined idea of who is deserving. It implies that individual acts of charity can substitute for changing the underlying conditions that victimize vulnerable people. The assumption of appeals to help the needy, the homeless, or starving is that they will always be with us but at least a few can be helped. Only with taxes and government action can the conditions that place so many people at risk be eradicated.

Giving to charities is often seen as an act of generosity, while many regard having to pay taxes as an act of coercion, even oppression, on the part of government. This is an odd way to look at the world. Why is it an act of generosity to send a small cheque in a well-publicized case involving a starving child, for example, and yet a symbol of oppression to support a government program that will help all such children, whether publicized or not? Those who support the voluntary sector sometimes assert that it is necessary to rebuild notions of social obligations that have been eroded by the growth of government. It would be more accurate to say that government cutbacks reflect a complete abandonment of notions of social obligation.

When Ontario's Progressive Conservative government talked in 1995 about introducing dramatic tax cuts, which a majority of residents opposed, government spokespersons were fond of saying that if people did not really want the tax reduction they could give the money to a charity, a church, or some other group that they wished to support. But such a suggestion misconceives the problem of collective action. No one person, not even a large group of people, can solve the social problems facing Ontario. But lots of people might be willing to make a small sacrifice, if others did the same thing, so that together they might achieve some goal that benefits everyone, such as reducing child poverty or eradicating homelessness. This process of saying "I will if you will," so that the majority's preferences are respected, is what voting and taxes are all about.

In conclusion, the debate in Canada over tax cuts and the debate over enriching the tax credit for charitable contributions is not about "whether Canadians should be allowed to keep more of their hard earned income" or about "encouraging altruism." It is about the meaning of citizenship and about concepts of social rights, equality, and entitlement. Also, ultimately it is a debate about who will exercise power in Canadian society. Will the major sources of power be controlled by only a few people acting through private markets and through control of government funds allocated to the voluntary sector, or will they remain with the majority of Canadians, acting through democratically elected governments and their agencies in the public sector?

NOTES

1 See Brooks, chapter 6 in this volume.

2 I have not thought it necessary to detail here either the history or the current workings of the charitable tax credit. For a comprehensive review of both, see Duff, chapter 13 in this volume.

3 Commission on Private Philanthropy and Public Needs, *Giving in America: Toward a Stronger Voluntary Sector* (1975), 123.

4 A vast U.S. literature on the charitable tax deduction focuses on its role in an ideal income tax base and, if it is indeed a subsidy, whether it should give way to a scheme of direct matching grants. Leading articles include: W. Andrews, "Personal Deductions in an Ideal Income Tax," *Harvard Law Review* 86 (1972), 309 (deduction justifiable in calculating taxpayer's ability to pay); B.I. Bittker, "Charitable Contributions: Tax Deductions or Matching Grants?" *Tax Law Review* 28 (1972), 37 (refuting charges of its "impropriety," "inefficiency," and "inequity"); M.P. Gergen, "The Case for a Charitable Contributions Deduction,"

Virginia Law Review 74 (1988), 1394 (deduction both equitable and Kaldor–Hicks efficient); P.R. McDaniel, "Federal Matching Grants for Charitable Contributions: A Substitute for the Income Tax Deduction," *Tax Law Review* 27 (1972), 377 (replace it with direct matching grants); and M.G. Kelman, "Personal Deductions Revisited: Why They Fit Poorly in an 'Ideal' Income Tax and Why They Fit Worse in a Far from Ideal World," *Stanford Law Review* 31 (1979), 831 (no place for it in an equitable income tax).

I argue here that the government should repeal the tax credit and generally that it should not match private donations to charities. In a working paper that I wrote almost twenty years ago, which drew on some of these articles, I compared the merits of five possible policy instruments and concluded, by reference to almost every sensible criterion, that direct matching grants were preferable to a tax deduction or credit: see N. Brooks, "Financing the Voluntary Sector: Replacing the Charitable Deduction," Law and Economics Workshop Series, Faculty of Law, University of Toronto, 1981

5 For the design features discussed here, see Duff, chapter 13 in this volume.

6 Revenue Canada, *Tax Statistics on Individuals: 1996 Tax Year* (Ottawa: Revenue Canada, 1998), Table 2.

7 M. Hall et al., *Caring Canadians, Involved Canadians: Highlights from the 1997 National Survey of Giving, Volunteering, and Participating* (Ottawa: Statistics Canada, 1998), 16–17.

8 C. Howes, "To Say Thank You, Family Gives $100 M," *National Post*, 19 Dec. 1998, and M. Ingram and A. Picard, "Family Donates Record $100 million," *Globe and Mail*, 19 Dec. 1998.

9 E. James, "Commentary," in C.T. Clotfelter, ed., *Who Benefits from the Nonprofit Sector?* (Chicago: University of Chicago Press, 1992) 244–55. See also C. Jencks, "Who Gives to What?" in W.W. Powell, ed., *The Nonprofit Sector: A Research Handbook* (New Haven, Conn.: Yale University Press, 1987).

10 National Advisory Council on Voluntary Action, *People in Action* (Ottawa: Council, 1997), 29.

11 The most notorious story involved allegations that large donations from a drug company influenced the manner in which the University of Toronto's medical school dealt with a medical researcher, Dr Nancy Olivieri, who wished to publish data suggesting that a drug with which she was experimenting for the drug company was toxic. See B. Livesey, "Dollars and Drugs: The Corporate Takeover of Medical Research May Be Bad for Your Health," *Eye*, 7 Jan. 1999.

12 C. Hume, "Tyler, a Portrait of Patience: McMichael Director Has Weathered Cutbacks and an Unruly Founder Who Simply Wouldn't Let Go," *Toronto Star*, 22 Aug. 1999.

13 J.M.D. Schuster, "The Non-Fungibility of Arts Funding: Perspectives on Corporations and Foundations," in H. Hillman-Chartrand, ed., *The Arts: Corporations and Foundations*, Arts Research Seminar No. 4, Working Document 600–162. (Ottawa: Canada Council, 1985), 1–32; and M. Unseem and S.I. Kutner, "Corporate Contributions to Culture and the Arts," in P. J. DiMaggio, ed., *Nonprofit Enterprise in the Arts: Studies in Mission and Constraint* (New York: Oxford University Press, 1986) 93–112.

14 See T. McCausland, "Corporate Benevolence with Strings: Companies Donating to Universities Today Expect More Than a Plaque in Return," *Financial Post*, 30 Oct. 1996.

15 See J. Lewington, "Sponsors Invited to Name University Courses: Some Educators Uneasy about Growing Contact Between Institutions and Image-Conscious Corporations," *Globe and Mail*, 5 Feb. 1997.

16 At the University of Toronto, over the past few years a number of donations have been accepted that allegedly gave the donors some direct influence over the direction of university programs they were funding. The terms of these donations were changed after they became public. See T. Cole, "Ivy-League Hustle: The University of Toronto Fundraising Team Is Raking in both Cash and Controversy as They Put the Touch on Corporate Canada," in *Report on Business Magazine* (June 1999), 35, and Livesey, "Dollar and Drugs."

17 L. Kinross, "Business Schools Look to Private Funding Sources," *Financial Post*, 24 Apr. 1996. Also, in describing how a new program in the business school at York was initiated, he said, "You set up a steering committee with two or three major banks, insurance companies, and trust companies, and asked: 'How is the field changing, what are the new requirements, what kind of graduates would you like to see?' ... From there, it was a short distance to saying, 'We need some financial support to make it happen.'"

18 Editorial, "The Public, Private University," *Globe and Mail*, 21 May 1999.

19 *National Post*, 17 Dec. 1998.

20 His aborted run raised over $27 million. Since then, every year memorial runs take place in communities across Canada and raise millions more. Exactly how large a tax credit these donations attract is of course unknown, but it is reasonable to assume that it is significant.

21 See Editorial, "Private Money Distorts Public Priorities," *Toronto Star*, 27 June 1999.

22 J. Lewington, "Colleges Languish in the Minors on Fund Raising," *Globe and Mail*, 12 May 12 1997.

23 T. Mickleburgh, "Prostate Centre Gets $20 Million from Businessman," *Globe and Mail*, 27 May 1999.

24 His gift resulted in diversion of more government funds than was implicit in the tax credit. He insisted as a condition that the hospital

match his $20-million gift from its funding foundation and that the B.C. government spend $152 million to finish constructing a part of the hospital that it had put on hold.

25 K. May, "Ottawa Ready to Strengthen Charities," *National Post*, 12 Apr. 1999.

26 J. Bryden, *MP's Report – Canada's Charities: A Need for Reform* (Oct. 1996). For other critiques of the current definition of charity see Phillips, chapter 7, and Moran, chapter 8, in this volume.

27 W.E. Gladstone, *The Financial Statements of 1853, 1860–63 to which are added a Speech on Tax-Bills, 1861, and on Charities, 1861* (London: John Murray, 1864), 436–7.

28 See, most recently, K. Scharf, B. Cherniavsky, and R. Hogg, *Tax Incentives for Charities in Canada*, Working Paper No. CPRN O3 (Ottawa: Canadian Policy Research Networks, 1997) 11–17.

29 G. Glenday, A.K. Gupta, and H. Pawlak, "Tax Incentives for Personal Charitable Contributions," *Review of Economics and Statistics* 68 (1986), 688.

30 The study that was regarded as the leading one in the late 1960s concluded that the efficiency of the deduction was near zero. The author estimated that for every dollar lost in government revenue because of the tax deduction, charitable contributions increased by only five cents. The study found that the deduction cost the U.S. Treasury about $42.4 billion per year but increased charitable giving by only about $81 million over the level that would have prevailed in its absence. Taussig, "Economic Aspects of the Personal Income Tax Treatment of Charitable Contributions," *National Tax Journal* 20 (1967), 1.

31 See, for example, M. Feldstein, "The Income Tax and Charitable Contributions: Part I – Aggregate and Distributional Effects," *National Tax Journal* 28 (1975), 81.

32 C. Clotfelter, *Federal Tax Policy and Charitable Giving* (Chicago: University of Chicago Press, 1985).

33 R. Steinberg, "Taxes and Giving: New Findings," *Voluntas* 1 (1990), 76.

34 See, for example, W.C. Randolph, "Dynamic Income, Progressive Taxes, and the Timing of Charitable Contributions," *Journal of Political Economy* 103(1995), 709, and K. Stanton Barrett, A.M. McGuirk, and R. Steinberg, "Further Evidence on the Dynamic Impact of Taxes on Charitable Giving," *National Tax Journal* 50 (1997), 321. The results of these and other studies are discussed and summarized in E. Brown, "Taxes and Charitable Giving: Is There a New Conventional Wisdom?" *National Tax Association, Proceedings, Eighty-Ninth Annual Conference* (Chicago: National Tax Association, 1996), 153.

35 The fact that religious organizations qualify as charities and that donors thus qualify for a government subsidy is probably a reflection of the

unaccountability of the government for the spending implicit in the credit. It seems reasonably obvious that allowing a tax credit for contributions to religious bodies shifts the financing of churches from members to others. If separation of state and church means anything, it surely must include the notion that the state ought not compel those who do not belong to religious organizations to subsidize those who do.

36 See P. Leduc Browne, *Love in a Cold World? The Voluntary Sector in an Age of Cuts* (Ottawa: Canadian Centre for Policy Alternatives, 1996), 56–61, a "Community Benefit Tax," basically a small income surtax, would fund community councils that in turn would allocate funds to voluntary organizations.

37 This is the total projected cost to the federal government for 1998 of the tax concessions for charitable giving. The federal government's costs for the tax credit for individuals is estimated to be $1.3 billion. Government of Canada, Department of Finance, *Tax Expenditures 1999* (Ottawa: Finance Canada, 1999), Table 1, 16. The annual cost of the deductibility of charitable donations for corporations is estimated to be $300 million. Ibid., Table 2, 22. The tax credit for charitable contributions also costs the provincial governments approximately $650 million in lost tax revenues.

38 This is not an idea with which the wealthy, who benefit most from the tax credit, are likely to agree. In interviews with eighty-eight wealthy donors, Francie Ostrower found that almost all (over 90 per cent) "emphatically rejected a hypothetical proposal that would eliminate the incentive for giving, and have government use the increased revenue to support the types of cultural and welfare activity that have benefited from philanthropy." The interviewees added comments such as "'I'd absolutely hate that,' 'that would be awful,''I think it would be sad,' and 'that's socialism.'" F. Ostrower, *Why the Wealthy Give: The Culture of Elite Philanthropy* (Princeton, NJ: Princeton University Press, 1995), 114.

39 Just as bureaucrats at the United Way do not differ substantially from those in government, many employees probably regard the payroll deduction for their contribution to the United Way as little different from a tax.

40 See Brooks, chapter 6 in this volume.

41 J. Wolch, "Decentering America's Nonprofit Sector: Reflections on Salamon's Crises Analysis," *Voluntas* 10 (1999), 33.

42 A number of the following ideas probably had their source in Rick Salutin's weekly column on the media and culture in the *Globe and Mail*. Over the years, in various contexts, he has written perceptively about charity and collective responsibilities.

PART FOUR

Regulatory Challenges

15 The Regulation of Social Enterprise

KEVIN E. DAVIS

At one time it was convenient to divide society into three sectors: public, private, and "non-profit." In recent years, however, the distinctions between the sectors have become blurred, mainly because phenomena previously regarded as unique to the private sector have begun to emerge in the other two sectors. The public sector has introduced practices such as competition and reliance on financial incentives, and the non-profit sector, which includes the charitable sector, has experienced increased "commercialization," often in response to cuts in government grants to charities.

The term "commercialization" has a number of meanings, but in the charitable sector frequently refers to charitable entities' engaging in commercial activities – i.e., providing goods or services in exchange for valuable consideration. This phenomenon is sometimes called "social enterprise" and encompasses a wide variety of activities. Familiar forms of social enterprise include small-scale bake sales and car washes, the sale of Girl Guide cookies, the operation of gift shops and food stands by hospitals or museums, and the rental of unused real property by charities of all kinds. More innovative forms include charging user fees for social services, using a charity's staff to provide services to corporate clients at market prices, selling membership lists, and licensing trademarks to for-profit corporations.

This chapter focuses on the legal regulation of social enterprise.[1] The first section outlines the current legal regime.[2] The remainder of the chapter examines the benefits and the dangers associated with permitting charities to engage in social enterprise and the advantages and disadvantages of various methods of taxing the income that it generates. I conclude by outlining a proposal for reform of the current regime.

THE CANADIAN LEGAL REGIME

Overview

The legal rules that govern charities' commercial activities are actually quite complex. Like much of the law of charities, these rules seem to have evolved piecemeal over a long period in response to pressures created by specific abuses.[3] For instance, charities may engage in commercial activity either directly or indirectly (i.e., through the vehicle of a non-charitable intermediary), with differing legal consequences.[4] Moreover, both the federal and the provincial governments exercise jurisdiction in this area. The primary source of regulations concerning the commercial activities of charities is the federal Income Tax Act, but provincial legislation also contains important restrictions.[5]

The Income Tax Act

The Income Tax Act allows a charity that complies with certain regulations to become a registered charity and thereby entitled to an exemption from income tax and the right to issue donation receipts that in turn allow their holders to claim certain tax benefits. The Income Tax Act divides registered charities into two classes: charitable organizations, whose main purpose is to engage directly in charitable activities, and charitable foundations, which have greater latitude to disburse funds to charitable organizations.[6] There are both public foundations and private foundations, and the latter have particularly stringent rules governing their commercial and investment activities[7] because it has proven difficult to prevent them from distributing income or property to people who do not deal with them at arm's length.

The act restricts registered charities' commercial activities in two ways: by requiring that they be "exclusively charitable" and by explicitly restricting their business activities.[8] These rules bar private foundations from carrying on any kind of business.[9] However, charitable organizations and public foundations may engage in "related businesses." First, for the purposes of determining whether a charitable organization (but not a charitable foundation) has complied with the exclusively charitable standard, the organization is deemed to be devoting its resources to charitable activities to the extent that it carries on a related business.[10] Second, the act prohibits charitable organizations and public foundations from carrying on only businesses that are not related businesses.[11]

The act does not define "related business" other than to say that it "includes a business that is unrelated to the objects of the charity if substantially all persons employed by the charity in the carrying on of that business are not remunerated for their employment." In the leading case on point, *Alberta Institute on Mental Retardation v. The Queen*,[12] a majority of the Federal Court of Appeal suggested that an enterprise carried on by a charitable foundation was a related business because all of its income went to charitable purposes and the foundation was not "the vehicle of a substantial commercial business."[13] As Justice Pratte pointed out in dissent, the majority's definition of a related business would render the provision barring a foundation from carrying on an unrelated business virtually redundant. This is because, leaving aside cases involving substantial commercial businesses, the majority's "destination of profits" test would allow the minister to cancel a registration on the grounds that a business was not related only if the foundation were not using the income for charitable purposes. In that case, however, the foundation would have breached its obligation to operate exclusively for charitable purposes.

The Canada Customs and Revenue Agency (CCRA) has not fully accepted the *Alberta Institute* decision. Instead, it has suggested that it views an activity as a related business so long as it does not become a "substantial commercial endeavour" and the following conditions are substantially met: "the activity is related to the charity's objects or ancillary to them; there is no private profit motive since any net revenues will be used for charitable activities; the business operation does not compete directly with other for-profit businesses; and the business has been in operation for some time and is accepted by the community."[14] By including the first, third, and fourth conditions, the CCRA has adopted an interpretation of the act somewhat inconsistent with that taken by the majority in *Alberta Institute* (although those conditions were probably satisfied on the facts of that case). Consequently, it is unclear to what extent the act permits charities to engage in commercial activities directly.

By contrast, it seems relatively clear that the act contains few restrictions on charities' ability to undertake commercial activities indirectly, through a taxable, for-profit entity in which it has invested. In fact, the act contains only one explicit restriction on charities' investment activities: foundations that "acquire control" of a corporation may have their registration revoked.[15] Moreover, the act defines "control" narrowly as occurring when the foundation has acquired for consideration more than 5 per cent of the issued shares of any class of the corporation and, either alone or in concert with non-arm's-length persons, holds 50 per cent or more of its voting shares.[16] This suggests that foundations are permitted to acquire control of a corporation by way of receiving a gift. The act also seems to permit foundations to acquire control of businesses that are not organized as corporations with share capital.

The act provides only one penalty for a charity engaging in unauthorized commercial activities – deregistration. This draconian rule stands in sharp contrast to the prevailing U.S. rules, which simply require charities that engage in "unrelated" business activities to pay tax on the income from those activities.[17]

Ontario Law

In Ontario the most significant restriction on charities' ability to engage in commercial activity appears in the Charitable Gifts Act.[18] That act is triggered whenever an "interest in a business" is "given to or vested in a person in any capacity for any religious, charitable, educational or public purpose." Where that interest represents more than a 10 per cent interest in the business, section 2 of the act requires the holder to dispose of the excess.

There is some uncertainty regarding the scope of this ostensibly sweeping prohibition. For instance, at least one court has endorsed the view that the act does not prohibit a charity from acquiring a business that is directly related to its objects.[19] Moreover, some legal practitioners are of the view that section 2 does not apply when a charity receives a gift from a for-profit corporation that is indirectly controlled by the charity, so long as a non-profit corporation controlled by the charity serves as an intermediary. It has also been suggested that having a trustee acquire ownership of a business for the benefit of the charity may circumvent this provision.[20] However, both these tactics seem to be caught by section 2(5), which deems an interest in a business to have been vested in a person for a charitable purpose "so long as the interest or proceeds thereof or the income therefrom is to be used for any such purpose at any time and even though before any such use is made thereof the interest or the proceeds thereof or the income therefrom is to pass into or through the hands of one or more persons or is subject to a life or other intermediary interest."

Charities' investment activities may also be governed by the stipulations of trust law, as embodied in either the common law or the

Trustee Act.[21] Trust law will apply if the charity is organized as a trust, if the charity is organized as a corporation but holds specific funds on trust, or one adopts the somewhat controversial view that all the property of an incorporated charity is held subject to the requirements of trust law.[22] Most of the common law and statutory rules that govern trustees' investments are default rules that can be ousted by sufficiently explicit provisions in the charity's constating documents. However, no such provision can oust a trustee's duty to exercise sufficient care and prudence. A trustee is also barred from delegating responsibility for making investment decisions to others.[23]

THE BENEFITS OF SOCIAL ENTERPRISE

There are two potential benefits associated with permitting charities to engage in commercial activity. First, that activity might, either directly or indirectly, help the charity to fulfil its charitable purposes. Second, in some circumstances it may be efficient to have commercial activity conducted by charitable rather than by non-charitable entities. I assess each of these benefits in turn.

Facilitating Charitable Activity

There are two ways in which a charity may enhance its ability to fulfil its charitable purposes by engaging in commercial activity. First, some forms of commercial activity are intrinsically charitable. For instance, the provision of goods or services at a price that is less than or equal to their market price is both a form of commercial activity and a well-recognized form of charity. For example, a charity that provides psychiatric counselling to low-income people for a nominal charge is, at least according to the definition set out above, engaging in commercial activity, but it is probably doing charity at the same time. Generally, where a charity provides goods or services at a price that is below both their cost (to the charity) and their market price, the activity is likely to be intrinsically charitable. Second, commercial activity may be intrinsically charitable when it involves the use of inputs provided by members of a disadvantaged group. In this case, where the beneficiary of the charitable purpose is a supplier rather than a customer, the charitable purpose may entail providing goods or services to customers at a price that equals or exceeds their market price. As a general rule, however, when a charity provides goods or services to other parties at a price that exceeds their cost to the charity – i.e., with a view to making a profit – the activity is unlikely to be regarded as intrinsically charitable.[24] None the less, to the extent that the activity is ultimately profitable one might argue that it indirectly enhances the charity's ability to fulfil its charitable purposes by increasing the amount of funds that it has available to use for charitable purposes.

Promoting Efficient Commercial Activity

A second potential benefit of social enterprise is that it may be efficient. It is fair to presume that, all things being equal, the state has an interest in formulating legal rules that tend to encourage efficient and to discourage inefficient commercial activity. But what do we mean by "efficiency" in this context? One possible definition implies that individual charities would be better off (and no one else in society would be worse off) if charities were permitted to engage in commercial activity (Pareto efficiency). Another definition implies that society as a whole would do better under such a legal rule, even if some parties became worse off as a result (Kaldor–Hicks efficiency).[25] Any claim that it is Pareto efficient to permit charities to engage in social enterprise implies that charities' commercial activities are likely to be profitable. A claim that permitting social enterprise is efficient in the Kaldor–Hicks sense corresponds roughly to a claim that charities can provide certain products at lower cost than non-charitable entities.

The connection between these ideas is that if charities are relatively low-cost suppliers of a product, they are likely to provide it in a manner that is not only Kaldor–Hicks efficient but also lucrative. This is likely to occur if charities differ in some economically significant way from other entities and/or they enjoy economies of scope in certain commercial activities.

As for the first point, the most significant difference between charities and many other entities is that charities are non-profits. This means that they cannot use the money or property left over after they satisfy fixed claims for anything other than charitable purposes. Specifically, they may not distribute residual money or property to parties that supply them with either capital or labour. This "non-distribution constraint" is designed to ensure that the individuals who control charities actually use donated capital and labour to serve charitable purposes rather than their own.

A number of scholars have analysed whether non-profits are likely to perform certain commercial activities more efficiently than other entities. Most notably, Henry Hansmann has argued that they may be relatively well suited to mitigating the effects of information asymmetries between consumers and producers of certain goods or services. He reasons that the non-distribution constraint limits the incentives for non-profits' members to seek pecuniary benefits by exploiting informational asymmetries.[26] To the extent that customers are aware of this situation, non-profits will find it less costly to induce their customers to trust them than will for-profit organizations. Thus, for example, a non-profit ostensibly devoted to famine relief in developing countries may be trusted not to divert funds to other uses because its managers are relatively unlikely, compared to the managers of a for-profit firm, to benefit by diverting the funds.[27]

As useful as it may be in some contexts, Hansmann's theory is of limited utility for our purposes because it seems to apply only to charities that engage in commercial activities without any intention of earning a profit. This bodes well for charities that engage in commercial activities as a form of charity. However, for Hansmann's purposes, charities that engage in commercial activities with a view to earning a profit – even one to fund charitable activities – seem more analogous to for-profit organizations. For example, if the non-profit described above undertook famine relief solely to earn a profit to subsidize other charitable activities, then its managers might have an incentive to divert funds from famine relief to other purposes. In other words, the fact that the absence of a profit motive may enhance efficiency in providing certain goods or services is of little relevance when a profit motive is present.

Even if there are no economically significant innate differences between charities and non-charitable entities, some charities may enjoy economies of scope that make their commercial activities efficient. Such economies arise whenever it is less costly for an organization to perform both charitable and commercial activities than it would be for separate organizations to perform the same activities. Generally speaking, economies of scope are possible whenever there are common costs associated with fulfilling the charitable purpose and providing other goods or services. For example, the fixed costs required to construct both a museum and a gift shop or both a hospital and a parking lot may overlap. Similarly, the fixed costs of assembling a team of psychiatric counsellors to serve low-income persons may overlap with the costs of creating a similar group to service high-income customers.

Of course, some economies of scope are more apparent than real. Charities may incur greater fixed costs than are strictly necessary to fulfil their charitable purposes and then attempt to justify those costs as facilitating the performance of commercial activities. Take, for example, a charity whose object is to operate a museum but that owns a building larger than required to house its collection. It may be able to operate both a museum and a gift shop under the same roof at a lower aggregate cost than if it used the building solely to house its collection and another group operated a gift shop nearby. Its ability to spread the fixed costs of a building over both charitable and commercial activities seems to represent an economy of scope – but this economy might be illusory if the charity initially had the option of obtaining a smaller building. If the additional cost of obtaining the larger building exceeded the cost to any other organization of acquiring a structure suitable for use as a gift shop, then it would have been efficient for the charity to obtain a building just large enough to house its collection. Apart from such complications, however, there may sometimes be economies of scope between certain charitable and commercial activities that it is efficient, in any sense of the word, to permit charities to exploit.

THE DANGERS OF SOCIAL ENTERPRISE

The potential dangers associated with social enterprise have received as much as or more attention than the potential benefits. The most pressing concerns seem to be that permitting social enterprise is either unfair or inefficient or will compromise charities' ability to fulfil their charitable purposes.

Unfair Competition

One of the most frequent complaints about charities that engage in commercial activities is that they compete "unfairly" with for-profit entities. The putative unfairness arises from their exemption from many forms of taxation and their frequent reliance on donated capital and volunteer labour to conduct commercial activity. These factors seem to allow at least some charities to provide goods and services at a lower cost than for-profit entities, but it is less clear that they should worry lawmakers.

It is particularly difficult to argue that using donated capital or volunteer labour amounts to unfair competition. If it is unfair for a firm to rely on capital or labour supplied at below-market rates by arms'-length donors, then it should also be unfair for a firm to rely on capital or labour supplied by individuals who do not operate at arms' length, including blood relatives. Thus it would become unfair for a firm to rely on so-called love money or to employ family members at below-market rates. This change would entail a remarkable recharacterization of the practices of many small businesses. In addition, barring the use of donated capital or volunteer labour would be highly inefficient, because it would prevent many individuals from realizing non-pecuniary benefits from gratuitous or partially gratuitous transfers that they make.

By contrast, charities' exemption from many forms of taxation does seem to give them an unfair advantage.[28] In this context, opponents of the hybridization of charitable and commercial entities have made two distinct appeals to fairness. The first claim is that the state should treat similarly participants in for-profit enterprises and the beneficiaries of charities that raise funds through commercial activities. However, the two classes of individuals are not similarly situated and so do not require equal treatment.[29] One could in fact argue that the beneficiaries of charity are particularly deserving of subsidies from the state,[30] although those who disagree may argue that provision of assistance to the beneficiaries of a charity should not fall to the subset of society whose fortunes happen to be tied to the fortunes of the charity's competitors.

A second version of the complaint about unfair competition is that allowing charities to engage in commercial activity at a competitive advantage distributes economic opportunities unfairly among for-profit enterprises that compete with charities (at a disadvantage) and those that do not. This second claim has more merit than the first, because these classes of persons appear to be similar in all relevant respects and so it is difficult to justify a legal regime that allows them different economic opportunities. However, this claim seems valid only to the extent that some for-profit enterprises are more exposed to "unfair" competition from charities than others. Therefore, if all for-profits compete with charities at a disadvantage, then there can be no complaint about comparative disadvantage.

Although concerns about unfair competition may have legitimacy, Susan Rose-Ackerman suggests four reasons why they may be overblown. First, "if an industry were perfectly competitive with easy entry and exit of firms, complaints of 'unfair competition' would always be invalid. A for-profit firm that was losing money in competition with a non-profit would simply leave that industry and earn the competitive rate of return elsewhere."[31] Second, participants in for-profit enterprises who accurately anticipate the extent to which they will compete at a net disadvantage will probably take that fact into account when settling the terms on which they participate in the enterprise. It seems reasonable to assume that they will not participate in an enterprise that faces such competition unless they expect to receive the same benefits as they would have in one that did not face such competition. These particularly clairvoyant individuals will be unable to claim that they are any worse off than they would have been if they had chosen to participate in another enterprise.

Third, even if some charities have a competitive advantage, it is not clear that they will exploit that advantage in a way that harms some for-profits more than others. For-profit enterprises that compete with charities will be harmed only if the charitable entity uses its lower marginal costs to lower prices (and expand production) and thus reduce the profits of competitors. However, profit-seeking charities that have an absolute advantage over for-profit enterprises in a number of industries have an incentive to avoid entering any single industry on such a scale that they affect market prices. Instead, subject of course to any legal restrictions, those charities have an incentive to enter a number of industries on a relatively small scale and sell their products at the price that would prevail if only for-profit firms were to compete.[32]

Fourth, it is not clear how many charities have a significant net advantage over for-profit enterprises. Although charities sometimes enjoy competitive advantages as a result of their tax-exempt status and access to donated funds and volunteer labour, they may also face offsetting disadvantages. For instance, as I mention below, charities may generally be less efficient at providing goods and services than for-profit enterprises. In principle, these innate inefficiencies may completely offset the impact of the factors that give charities a competitive advantage.

Even if there is legitimate concern about unfair competition, the solution is not necessarily to exclude charities from commercial activity. In fact, removing rather than extending the prohibition on carrying on unrelated businesses should tend to mitigate the consequences of unfair competition by encouraging charities to enter a broader range of industries on a relatively small scale.[33] Ultimately, however, the only way to put to rest concerns about unfair competition is to "level the playing field" by denying charities that engage in commercial activity any special privileges.

Promoting Inefficient Commercial Activity

Another danger associated with allowing charities to engage in commercial activity is that they will do so inefficiently. Would restricting their commercial activities be efficient? The answer may depend on one's definition of efficiency. For Pareto efficiency, it is relatively difficult to justify any significant restrictions on commercial activities. Strictly speaking, it would be Pareto efficient to prohibit charities from engaging in commercial activity only if we could be confident that charities themselves were likely to be better off as a result. In other words, the Pareto standard justifies prohibiting charities only from engaging in commercial activities that are unlikely to be profitable. However, even if charities are capable of producing goods and services at a profit, restricting their commercial activities might be efficient in the Kaldor–Hicks sense if they can be expected to earn systematically lower profits than similar for-profit enterprises. In this second scenario one could argue that society as a whole would be better off if the prohibition were imposed, because this would maximize overall profits earned from commercial activity, even if the funds available to charities decreased as a result.[34]

As for Pareto efficiency, it is not completely implausible that charities might systematically tend to engage in unprofitable commercial activities. All charities are by definition non-profits, and so their managers are not accountable to a group of (presumably) self-interested residual claimants. The conventional wisdom is that in the absence of a class of residual claimants it is difficult to induce managers to maximize their employer's income from commercial activities,[35] mainly because there are few other private parties with either adequate resources or the appropriate incentives to make and follow through on threats to monitor managers and terminate or sue the ones who fail to maximize profits.[36] Charging a public official with the responsibility for disciplining the managers may overcome these problems to some extent. However, even if an obligation to maximize profits were a component of the fiduciary duties owed by charities' managers, it might be difficult for even a well-funded public agency to enforce that obligation, which is so difficult to define in any given context. For instance, it is reasonably clear that a charity should not engage in commercial activities that are expected to yield a lower return than it can anticipate obtaining by investing equivalent resources in risk-free, publicly traded securities. However, it also seems clear that, at least in some cases, any obligation to maximize expected financial returns should be qualified by an obligation to consider both the value of doing charity earlier rather than later and the riskiness of the activities in which the charity engages.[37] Therefore it will be very difficult for anyone who is not intimately familiar with a charity's operations to determine whether its employees are carrying on commercial activities so as to maximize its ability to fulfil its charitable purposes.[38]

The Kaldor–Hicks definition of efficiency provides a more compelling basis for restricting charities' commercial activities than does the Pareto definition. First, even if non-profits' relatively high agency costs are not so great as to prevent them from earning a profit, they may cause non-profits to be less profitable than for-profits that have access to equivalent amounts of capital and labour. Second, non-profits may also be unprofitable in relative as opposed to absolute terms because of their inability to issue equity. In some cases – for example, when expected cash flows are highly variable or debt levels are already high and the firm has few assets to offer as collateral – the marginal cost of equity financing is likely to be lower than that of debt financing.[39] Consequently, non-profits' average cost of external capital will be relatively high. This will tend to make them less profitable than for-profits unless they have sufficient internal – presumably donated – funds to finance their operations or can conduct commercial activities through a for-profit subsidiary that is able to issue equity to outside investors.

These efficiency-based arguments weigh in favour of restricting charities' commercial activities. However, they are subject to qualifications. First, there may be some goods or services that non-profit charities can produce at lower cost than for-profit firms, presumably because they can exploit economies of scope unavailable to for-profits. Second, it is difficult to see how agency costs could significantly impair charities' ability to make relatively low-risk passive investments. Third, the argument that Kaldor–Hicks efficiency is best served by restricting charities' commercial activities implicitly assumes that the stock of capital and labour in society does not vary according to whether non-profits are permitted to engage in commercial activity. That assumption may not be valid, however, vis-à-vis the stock of labour in society. Many people seem to derive greater satisfaction from donating labour to a charity than they would from donating, for example, its money equivalent. Thus if non-profits were barred from engaging in any commercial activities using volunteer labour, the displaced volunteers would not necessarily choose to supply the same amount of labour to a for-profit firm and then donate the resulting income to charity. Some might find an additional hour of volunteer work preferable to an additional hour of leisure, but an hour of leisure preferable to an additional hour of paid work, even if they would donate the income from that work to charity. Therefore barring charities from commercial activities, or at least those that rely on volunteer labour, might effectively reduce the amount of labour supplied in a society.[40]

Fourth, the claims that social enterprise is inefficient are based entirely on theoretical rather than on empirical analysis. It would be imprudent to base public policy on unsubstantiated theoretical claims, and so far empirical studies have failed to reveal significant differences between the performances of for-profit and of non-profit firms.[41] These findings may simply reflect shortcomings in the studies. However, the theoretical analyses may be deficient. A number of mechanisms probably reduce the impact of the absence of residual claimants in the non-profit sector. For example, both Henry Hansmann and Mark Schlesinger discuss how competition from for-profit firms disciplines managers of non-profit hospitals.[42] Bruce Chapman also considers the extent to which non-profits substitute screening mechanisms for monitoring by residual claimants – for instance, the low wages offered in the charitable sector probably attract managers who earn non-pecuniary benefits from pursuing the charities' mission and help screen out individuals likely to pursue other agendas.[43] Therefore, although concern about inefficiency should influence regulation of social enterprise, an outright prohibition seems inappropriate at this time.

Compromising Charitable Purposes

Although considerations of efficiency and fairness should affect the design of legal rules to govern charitable activity, it is not clear that either value ought to be a central concern. Rather, intuition suggests that the principal object of the law of charities, including the rules governing charities' commercial activities, should be to facilitate the doing of charity.

There are two ways in which charities' engagement in commercial activities might harm their charitable activities. First, it may unduly reduce the amount of resources – financial or otherwise – available for charitable purposes. This concern is essentially identical to the concern discussed above that charities will tend to engage in unprofitable commercial activities.

A second concern is that charities' commercial activities might be too profitable, rendering them less reliant on donated funds, so that they can "drift" away from the types of charitable activities preferred by donors. Fearing this sort of "mission drift,"[44] commentators such as Bruce Chapman support rules that force charities to return constantly to their donors for support by restricting commercial activities and mandating regular disbursements.[45]

One difficulty with Chapman's analysis, however, is that it blurs the distinction between malign and benign forms of mission drift. Some charities accept donations dedicated to one set of charitable purposes and then use them to fulfil different charitable purposes. Such opportunistic behaviour, if it became routine, would deter many potential donors from making donations or force them to take costly precautions. Either response would tend to reduce donations. Legal rules clearly ought to be designed to prevent this malign form of mission drift. However, restricting charities' commercial activities would overshoot that goal. Such limitations would prevent charities not only from using donations for unintended purposes, but also from using their original endowment as intended and applying new funds to new purposes.

This form of drift seems quite benign. Indeed, there is little evidence that the law of charities is designed to grant a charity's original set of donors such sweeping control of its affairs after its objects have been settled. For instance, donors generally do not have standing to enforce the fiduciary duties owed by the charity's managers. Furthermore, on Chapman's theory, granting managers the authority to attract funding from *any* new source would undermine the control of the original donors. However, neither Chapman nor anyone else seems willing to support a blanket prohibition on soliciting funds from new donors.

Not only would it be unorthodox to prohibit what I consider a benign form of mission drift, it would also be positively undesirable. Prohibition of this kind of mission drift would force managers to establish a new organization every time they wanted to pursue charitable purposes that diverged from the ones favoured by their original donors, even if they had spent all the previously donated funds in pursuit of the original purposes. Such a regime would entail significant transaction costs and would privilege the interests of one set of donors over a presumably more general public interest in having all sorts of charitable purposes fulfilled.

It also is not clear that Chapman's prescription is necessary to prevent the malign form of mission drift – namely, opportunistic alteration of purposes before donations have been used. First, the relative cost of developing new sources of funding as opposed to raising funds from previous donors would strongly discourage charities from abandoning previous donors. Even if charities are permitted to seek out new sources of funding, previous donors may have enough leverage to prevent opportunistic drift. In addition, concerned donors can protect themselves by making donations to a separate legal entity dedicated to their preferred purpose or purposes.[46] Alternatively, the "donor" could enter into a contract binding the charity to perform the specified charitable works in consideration for the donor's funds.

Although the need to control mission drift may not require limiting charities' commercial activities, it may justify some regulation. Specifically, the law should compel charities to disclose the extent to which they have used donated resources to support commercial activities and should forbid them to use donated resources to finance commercial activities unless the donor has explicitly consented. This requirement would prevent one type of malign mission drift – namely, use of donated funds to support commercial activities contrary to the donor's wishes.

Such a regime is necessary because donors' views may vary on how they wish their charitable donations to be used. Some may wish their donations to be used exclusively and directly to support charitable activities,[47] others may be willing to support commercial activity that will in turn finance charitable activities.[48] In order to cater to donors' varying preferences (and thus maximize donations) it seems appropriate to give donors the option of indicating whether they wish to support commercial activities.

This raises the issue of how to set the appropriate default rule – i.e., the rule that will apply unless donors indicate that they do not wish it to apply. If left to their own devices, many donors would be unaware of the default rule and would not think about the charity's supporting commercial activities. Many others might not know how to ensure that the charity complies with their wishes. Yet managers of charities are familiar with the intricacies of the law of charities and will presumably seek authority to allocate donated resources to commercial activities whenever this is in the best interests of the charity (and perhaps in other cases as well). Under these circumstances the appropriate default rule would bar use of donated funds to support commercial activities. Managers would have to request authority to do so. Simply by making such a request, the charity will inform donors of the possibility of their refusing.[49] By contrast, a default rule that permitted charities to use donations to support any commercial activities they saw fit would allow them to use funds contrary to the wishes of some unwitting donors.[50]

TAXATION OF CHARITIES THAT ENGAGE IN COMMERCIAL ACTIVITY

Even if we assume that charities ought to be permitted to engage in commercial activities, how should they be taxed? The answer depends heavily on the values that one hopes to promote through the tax system. For instance, if the sole purpose of the tax regime were to promote charity by maximizing the amount of wealth under the control of charitable entities, then it would be logical to exempt all charities from taxation. By contrast, eliminating unfair competition arguably requires taxing charities in exactly the same way as other entities.

The concept of Pareto efficiency is not helpful in this context because moving from one tax regime to another is almost certain to make some parties worse off.[51] Kaldor–Hicks efficiency is, however, relevant and supports taxing charities in much the same way as other entities, because the structure of the tax system can significantly affect the pattern, and thus overall efficiency, of economic activity. For instance, taxing charities' income from commercial activities less heavily than for-profit enterprises will encourage potential donors to give to charities (for investment in commercial activities) instead of investing in a for-profit enterprise and then donating the resulting income to charity. Similarly, if charities' income from some activities is taxed at lower rates than their income from other activities, they will have an incentive to invest in activities that generate the less heavily taxed type of income. In each case the regime in question is Kaldor–Hicks inefficient, because it tends to push capital towards entities or activities that attract preferential tax treatment, even if others would generate more pre-tax income and so create more wealth for society. The easiest way to avoid such distortions is to tax charities in the same way as other entities and to tax all income derived from commercial activity at the same rate.

There is one caveat: if it is efficient for a charity to invest in an activity that is taxed at a relatively low rate, then it may not be essential from an economic perspective to tax that activity more heavily. The relatively low tax rate simply gives the charity a potentially redundant incentive to take the efficient course of action. In principle therefore, lawmakers could attempt to identify a class of commercial activities in which it is efficient for charities to engage and tax those activities at a low rate without compromising efficiency. Presumably the class would be roughly coextensive with the class of activities in which charities appear to enjoy economies of scope or access to volunteer labour.

Given the inherent limitations of judicial and legislative processes, lawmakers are likely to find it difficult to legislate the class of commercial activities that can safely be taxed at a relatively low rate. Hence, whenever possible, it is best to tax charities in the same way as other entities and to tax the income that charities derive from all commercial activities at the same rate. However, it is difficult to tax charities' income from commercial activities efficiently, particularly ones in which charities can believably claim to enjoy economies of scope, which are most likely where certain common costs must be incurred to generate commercial income and to pursue charitable purposes. Taxation of commercial income will encourage charities to minimize their taxable income by allocating as much as possible of those common costs to their commercial rather than to their charitable activities.[52] However, refusing to permit charities to deduct such common costs would deter them from some efficient investments.[53] One way to address this problem is by requiring that charities' allocation of common costs be "reasonable."[54] But an even simpler solution would be not to tax income from activities in which a charity clearly enjoys economies of scope.[55]

RECOMMENDATIONS FOR REFORM

The preceding analysis illustrates the possibility of reconciling the values of charity, efficiency, and fairness in setting restrictions on charities' commercial activities. To the extent that a society wants to promote charity, it should permit charities to engage in any commercial activities that are either intrinsically charitable or likely to generate funds for charitable purposes. The only caveat should be a requirement that they obtain donors' consent before using donated resources to support commercial activities. Taking Pareto efficiency into account leads to a similar conclusion, but pursuing Kaldor–Hicks efficiency does not, since there may be activities that charities conduct profitably, but less profitably than do non-charitable entities. It is difficult, however, to identify with any confidence the commercial activities for which charities are relatively unsuited. Consequently, it is difficult to use the Kaldor–Hicks principle to justify restrictions on their commercial activities. Finally, although concerns about unfair competition might justify changes in taxation of charities that engage in commercial activities, they provide little basis for restricting such activities.

Unfortunately, it is more difficult to determine how charities' income from commercial activity ought to be taxed. As I indicated above, promoting charity is not compatible with taxing such income. Both Kaldor–Hicks efficiency and fairness, however, seem to require taxing it much like income earned by other entities. Where does this leave us? A partial solution is to exempt from taxation charities' income from commercial activities that appear to exploit economies of scope or make substantial use of volunteer labour and that, for whatever reason, do not unfairly compete with for-profit enterprises. All other income from commercial activities would be subject to taxation. Such a proposal might prove difficult and costly to administer and might tax commercial activities in which a charity has no apparent comparative advantage. However, other solutions seem to entail more significant compromises.

Building a workable legal regime based on these normative foundations is quite feasible. First, that regime would permit charities to engage in commercial activities that are intrinsically charitable. This rule may or may not be compatible with efficiency considerations – Hansmann's theory suggests that it is – but the fact that these sorts of activities are well-recognized forms of charity suggests that our society long ago decided that, in this area at least, the intrinsic value of charity outweighs other considerations. Second, as for other commercial activities, because of the agency problems arguably inherent in the non-profit form, it may be appropriate to take a cautious approach, except for activities that are highly likely to be profitable. This implies that charities ought to be routinely permitted to engage in activities in which they experience economies of scope or in which the majority of the participants are volunteers, so long as consent from the relevant donors is obtained.[56] However, attempts to engage in other sorts of activities should be subject to stricter scrutiny. Whether or not those activities are prohibited entirely ought to be dictated by experience. Third, as for taxation, the best, though not necessarily optimal, solution would exempt charities' income from commercial activities in which they are likely to enjoy economies of scope or they make significant use of volunteer labour and where there is no concern about unfair competition. This compromise would delineate a reasonably broad set of commercial activities in which charities could engage free from either significant regulatory scrutiny or taxation.

Adopting these recommendations would require a number of specific changes to the current legal regime. First, it would entail defining the term "related business" under the Income Tax Act to include only commercial activities that are intrinsically charitable or those that both are highly likely to be profitable, because they involve either economies of scope or the use of donated labour, and do not generate any concern about unfair competition. This may not require a significant departure from current practice, but other aspects of the foregoing analysis have more radical implications. For instance, adopting the principles set out above would require repealing the Charitable Gifts Act and amending the Income Tax Act to permit charities to participate in unrelated businesses, so long as those businesses are fully taxable and subject to oversight by either federal or provincial regulators.[57] Those regulators would have a role similar to that of Ontario's Public Trustee in ensuring that trustees' investments comply with the provisions of the Trustee Act. In addition, either federal or provincial regulators would have to enforce a requirement that charities obtain donors' explicit consent before using their donations to support commercial activity.

Charities subject to this kind of legal regime would always have the option of pursuing commercial ventures, but definitely would not be obliged to do so. Such a regime might deter many charities from unrelated commercial activity, which would expose them to additional regulatory scrutiny and the prospect of income taxation. Even related businesses might become relatively uncommon, given my proposal to ban the use of donations to sponsor for-profit ventures without donors' consent. In fact, it is difficult to predict whether implementing this proposal would accelerate or decelerate the widely noted erosion of the boundaries between the charitable and the for-profit sectors. This is just one of many intriguing questions that future research in this area might explore.

NOTES

I am grateful to Bruce Chapman, GuyLaine Charles, Jim Phillips, Alan Slivinski, participants in the conference on Charity and Charities Law, and to students in a class on Non-Profit Management and Leadership at the Schulich School of Business at York University for their comments on an earlier draft of this chapter. I have also benefited from helpful conversations with Brenda Gainer, Edward Iacobucci, and Arnold Weinrib. Any errors or omissions are my own.

1 For the sake of convenience, I focus on the laws applicable in Ontario.

2 For discussion of non-legal issues, please see B. Weisbrod, ed., *To Profit or Not to Profit: The Commercial Transformation of the Non-Profit Sector* (New York: Cambridge University Press, 1998). Other important contributions include J.G. Dees, "Enterprising Nonprofits," *Harvard Business Review* (1988), 55–67, and B. Shore, *Revolution of the Heart: A New Strategy for Creating Wealth and Meaningful Change* (New York: Riverhead, 1995). For a survey of the literature, see B. Zimmerman and R. Dart, *Charities Doing Commercial Ventures: Societal and Organizational Implications* (Toronto: Trillium Foundation and Canadian Policy Research Networks, 1998).

3 The history of the regime is discussed in Ontario Law Reform Commission (OLRC), *Report on the Law of Charities* (Toronto: Commission, 1996).

4 Some may distinguish these two sets of rules by claiming that only the former regulates charities' commercial activity, while the latter deals with their investment activities. However, while the activities addressed may differ in form, they are often functionally equivalent. Consequently, in the absence of a co-ordinated effort to regulate both activities, any attempt to regulate one activity may be subverted by actors who simply switch to the other.

5 For a discussion of the boundaries between federal and provincial jurisdiction over charities, see OLRC, *Report*, 1–19.

6 Charitable organizations, unlike charitable foundations, may not make grants to other qualified donees totalling more than 50 per cent of their income in any one year.

7 The makeup of their executive and the identity of their major donors distinguish charitable organizations and public foundations from private foundations. First, more than half of the executive of a charitable organization or a public foundation must deal with each other, and with each of the other members of the executive, only at arm's length. Second, not more than 50 percent of their capital may have been contributed by one person or by one group of persons who do not deal with each other at arm's length. See the Income Tax Act, section. 149.1(1), "charitable organization" and "public foundation." For public foundations created before 1984 or designated by the minister under sections 149.1(6.3), 110(8.1), (8.2) of RSC 1952, c. 148, the figure is 75 per cent.

8 The exclusively charitable rule takes slightly different forms for charitable foundations and for charitable organizations. A charitable foundation must be "constituted and operated exclusively for charitable purposes." By contrast, "all the resources" of a charitable organization must be "devoted to charitable activities carried on by the organization itself" – s. 149.1(1): "charitable organization" and "public foundation."

9 S. 149.1(6). Because this provision does not apply to charitable foundations it is theoretically possible for a foundation to breach the exclusively charitable standard by carrying on a related business.

10 S. 149.1(4)(a)

11 ss. 149.1(2)(a) and 149(3)(a).

12 87 DTC 5306.

13 *Alberta Institute,* per Heald, J.

14 *A Better Tax Administration in Support of Charities: A Discussion Paper* (Ottawa: Revenue Canada, 1990), reproduced in A. Drache, *Canadian Taxation of Charities and Donations* (Toronto: Carswell, 1994).

15 ss. 149.1(3)(c) and 149.1(4)(c).

16 S. 149.1(12)(a).

17 On the Canadian rule, see Sossin, chapter 12 in this volume. The American regime is briefly discussed in the *OLRC, Report,* 321–2.

18 RSO 1990, c. C.8.

19 *Re Centenary Hospital Association and Public Trustee* (1989) 69 OR (2d) 1 (HC) at 19.

20 See J. Burke-Robertson, "Charities Carrying on Business Activities: The Legal Considerations," Paper presented at Law Society of Upper Canada, Continuing Legal Education Programme, "Fit to Be Tithed 2: Reducing Risks for Charities and Not-for-Profits," Toronto, Nov. 1998).

21 RSO 1990, c. T.23.

22 OLRC, *Report*, 458–9; *Christian Brothers of Ireland in Canada* (Re) (1998), 37 OR (3d) 367 at 389–94.

23 See, generally, T. Youdan, "Investment by Charities," Paper presented at Law Society of Upper Canada, Continuing Legal Education Programme, "Fit to Be Tithed 2: Reducing Risks for Charities and Not-for-Profits," Toronto, Nov. 1998).

24 Charities that conduct commercial activity with a view to making a profit may still do so in ways that fulfil a charitable purpose. For example, they might set prices below profit-maximizing levels with a view to conferring a benefit on their customers. Alternatively, they may go out of their way to serve particular populations. To date these conjectures do not appear to have been tested empirically, and so the potential benefits remain highly speculative. See further R. Steinberg and B. Weisbrod, "Pricing and Rationing by Nonprofit Organizations with Distributional Objectives," in Weisbrod, ed., *To Profit or Not to Profit*, 65–82.

25 The conventional definitions of Pareto and Kaldor–Hicks efficiency are discussed in J. Coleman, *Markets, Morals and the Law* (New York: Cambridge University Press, 1988), chap. 4. The definitions employed in the text unconventionally use "charities" rather than individuals as the units of analysis and assume that the welfare of a charity is unambiguously improved by an increase in its wealth (and vice versa). This assumption obscures, among other things, the fact that individual members of a charity (such as its managers) may become better off if a charity is permitted to engage in an unprofitable commercial activity.

26 H. Hansmann, "The Role of Non-Profit Enterprise," *Yale Law Journal* 89 (1980), 835, and *The Ownership of Enterprise* (Cambridge: Belknap, 1996).

27 In this example, the organization's "customers" are donors who are characterized as purchasing famine relief.

28 On the effects of the exemption from corporate income taxation on non-profits' marginal costs of capital, see S. Rose-Ackerman, "Unfair Competition and Corporate Income Taxation," *Stanford Law Review* 34 (1982), 1017, 1025–8, nn 30–1. Certain charities also enjoy privileges other than the exemption from corporate income taxation, including exemption from certain property taxes. See OLRC, *Report*, 605–9.

29 Rose-Ackerman, "Unfair Competition," 1020.

30 This argument could be extended to justify the provision of a tax credit for charitable donations. For a critical discussion of such tax credits, see Brooks, chapter 14 in this volume.

31 Rose-Ackerman, "Unfair Competition," 1025.

32 Ibid., 1029; Hansmann, *Ownership*, 610–12. This analysis is valid only for charities that engage in commercial activities with a view to making a profit. Charities that do so with a view to conferring a benefit on their customers will typically sell their products at below-market prices.

33 In the American context, Rose-Ackerman, "Unfair Competition," argues that removing the tax on income from unrelated business activities would have a similar effect.

34 The increased profits resulting from a prohibition would be more than sufficient to pay charities the amount of money that they would have received if they had been allowed to engage in commercial activity. However, so long as we make the strong assumption that wealth generates the same amount of utility whether it is held by charities or other entities, the prohibition will be Kaldor–Hicks efficient even if charities do not receive this kind of compensation.

35 Why might managers of a charity not act in its best interests when making decisions about the extent and nature of the charity's commercial activities? Some might simply want a quiet life and so will be inclined to shirk their responsibilities altogether. Others might find commercial activity more glamorous and personally satisfying than charity. Still others might prefer to engage in commercial activities so as to ensure that the charity has sufficient income to continue to employ them. As for why some might not be capable of selecting profitable commercial ventures, it would not be surprising if managers selected for their ability to perform charitable activities were not ideally suited to engage in commercial activities.

36 See R. Atkinson, "Unsettled Standing: Who (Else) Should Enforce the Duties of Charitable Fiduciaries?" *Journal of Corporation Law* 23 (1998), 655; G. Manne, "Agency Costs and the Oversight of Charitable Organizations," *Wisconsin Law Review* (1999), 227.

37 This last point may require some clarification. Determining a charity's appropriate attitude towards risky opportunities is no easy task. To begin with, one must determine the nature of the relationship between a charity's income and its ability to carry out its charitable purposes. A charity's capacity for charitable activity will not necessarily be a constant function of the amount of its income from commercial activities. Take for example a charity formed for the sole purpose of providing room and board to a fixed number of individuals. Its ability to fulfil its charitable purpose may not increase constantly in proportion to the amount of income it earns from commercial activities, because it may need a certain minimum amount of income to provide an acceptable level of service to its beneficiaries. Reducing its income below that level will significantly reduce its capacity to fulfil its charitable purpose; an equivalent increase will not have a proportionate effect on its ability to do charity. Therefore, once its income exceeds the level required to provide the minimum acceptable level of service, its ability to engage in charity may be a concave function of its income from commercial activities. However, if the same charity's income is very low, its capacity for

charity may be a convex function of its income because a small increase in income may significantly increase its ability to do charity by making it functional, whereas an equivalent reduction would not affect its inability to function. Whether a charity's ability to do charity is a concave or convex function of its income will determine whether it should be averse to or prefer risky commercial activities. Another factor to consider is that a charity must assess the riskiness of a given investment opportunity in the context of all its other sources of income, paying due regard to the benefits of diversification. See further, M. Johnson, "Note, Speculating on the Efficacy of 'Speculation': An Analysis of the Prudent Person's Slipperiest Term of Art in Light of Modern Portfolio Theory," *Stanford Law Review* 48 (1996), 419.

38 Verifying compliance with such an obligation might be a daunting task. First, it is always difficult to obtain information about the rate of return and level of risk associated with engaging in a given commercial activity. Second, it will be difficult to calculate the appropriate rate at which to discount the expected returns from a project, because detailed knowledge of a charity's operations and values will be required to determine its appropriate stance towards risk and forgoing the opportunity to do charity immediately. Third, it may be difficult to determine what sort of non-financial resources, such as agents' labour, have been devoted to commercial rather than to charitable activities and how much charity those resources could have performed.

39 Under these circumstances it may be more costly to obtain financing through debt than through equity, because use of debt increases the likelihood of insolvency, with its attendant costs. See R. Brealey and S. Myers, *Principles of Corporate Finance*, 5th ed. (New York: McGraw-Hill, 1996), 484–98.

40 This may also occur if labour markets are such that people find it difficult to increase the amount of paid labour that they perform.

41 For instance, Hansmann concludes that managerial agency costs "do not seem to be exceptionally high" in non-profit firms with self-selecting boards of directors. See Hansmann, *Ownership*, 238. For a review and critique of the empirical literature, see M. Schlesinger, "Mismeasuring the Consequences of Ownership: External Influences and the Comparative Performance of Public, For-Profit and Private Non-Profit Organizations," in W. Powell and E. Clemens, eds., *Private Action and the Public Good* (New Haven, Conn.: Yale, 1998).

42 Schlesinger, "Mismeasuring," Schlesinger also discusses the impact of various forms of "institutional isomorphism."

43 Chapman, chapter 5 in this volume.

44 This is not the occasion to address the problems inherent in defining the mission of any given charity. In other words, how does one determine whether a charity has strayed from the pursuit of any given set of purposes?

45 See Chapman, chapter 5 in this volume.

46 That entity could even be an existing charity holding the property on trust for the specified purpose.

47 Some donors may see commercial activities *per se* as antithetical to the purposes that they wish to promote.

48 For an empirical analysis of the relationship between donations and commercial activity in the American context, see L. Segal and B. Weisbrod, "Interdependence of Donative and Commercial Revenues," in Weisbrod, ed., *To Profit or Not to Profit,* 105–27.

49 The law-and-economics literature refers to this sort of rule as a "penalty default." In a seminal article, Ayres and Gertner observed that in many contractual or quasi-contractual settings one party is better informed than the other and has an incentive strategically to withhold its superior information. In some of these cases it is possible to induce the better-informed party to reveal its private information by setting a "default rule" that the informed party does not favour. See I. Ayres and R. Gertner, "Filling Gaps in Incomplete Contracts: An Economic Theory of Default Rules," *Yale Law Journal* 99 (1989), 87.

50 In this scenario, the affected donors probably would not include large donors or donors who make regular contributions. Large donors would have an incentive to acquire better information about the ways in which their donations may be used. As for regular donors, charities may be unwilling to jeopardize future donations by having the donors discover that their donations have, contrary to the donor's wishes, been used to support commercial activities. Consequently, regardless of the default rule, charities may go out of their way to ascertain whether regular donors wish their donations to be used to support commercial activities.

51 For example, in Canada the income that charities earn from related businesses is exempt from taxation. However, the income earned by corporations in which charities have purchased shares is not exempt from taxation. This can cause charities to allocate inefficiently large amounts of resources to related businesses as opposed to portfolio investments. To see this, consider a charitable entity with excess funds that can use those funds either to purchase a minority stake in an existing spaghetti company, the income of which is subject to taxation, or to establish its own tax-exempt spaghetti company. Assume that the existing firm can be expected to use the funds to earn a before-tax rate of return of 12 per cent. By contrast, an investment in a new company can be expected only

to earn 10 per cent. However, the marginal tax rate on the income of the existing company is 25 per cent. In this case, the charity would do better to establish its own firm, with after-tax return of 10 per cent. If it invested in the existing company, it would get 9 per cent after tax. This last outcome is inefficient because the social rates of return on the two investments are 12 per cent for the existing company and 10 per cent for a new company.

52 For evidence that American non-profits respond to this incentive, see J. Cordes and B. Weisbrod, "Differential Taxation of Nonprofits and the Commercialization of Nonprofit Revenues," in Weisbrod, ed., *To Profit or Not to Profit*, 83–104.

53 See generally R. Sansing, "The Unrelated Business Income Tax, Cost Allocation, and Productive Efficiency," *National Tax Journal* 2 (1998), 291.

54 In principle, the allocation rule should ensure, with the common costs, deductibility of only the incremental costs of carrying on both the charitable activity and the taxable activity, as opposed to just the non-taxable activity. In practice, however, this principle will prove difficult to apply, as it requires the tax authority to determine a hypothetical value – namely, the costs that the charity would have incurred if it had engaged solely in the charitable activity. See Sansing, "Unrelated Business," 297–8.

55 Another difficulty arises where a charity engages in commercial activities that cause it to incur opportunity costs. Opportunity costs are often difficult to observe and verify, and so it may be difficult for charities to deduct them from their gross income. The inability to deduct opportunity costs can undermine charities' incentives to behave efficiently. For example, a charity that allows its name to be used to promote other firms' products may not incur any direct expenses but may incur a real opportunity cost in the form of reduced donations. Unless the charity is allowed to deduct that cost from its taxable income, any positive level of taxation will deter it from making certain efficient investments in commercial activity. See Sansing, "The Unrelated Business Income Tax," 298–301. Sansing's model allows him to identify the inefficiency that arises from the non-deductibility of both pecuniary and non-pecuniary opportunity costs. However, for practical purposes, only the non-deductibility of charities' pecuniary costs seems to be a pressing concern, as the entire tax system can be criticized for inefficiently failing to allow taxpayers – charitable or otherwise – to deduct non-pecuniary costs from their gross income.

56 Neither the presence of potential economies of scope nor the use of volunteers guarantees that a charity will actually conduct an activity profitably or even more profitably than a non-charitable entity. For example, economies of scope are obviously involved when a charity licenses its

name to a corporation for marketing purposes. However, a charity's managers may still enter into arrangements that so greatly dilute the value of their employer's name that the increased revenue does not compensate the charity for the loss of donated capital or labour.

57 Steps will also have to be taken to ensure that charities cannot escape taxation of their commercial income by having ostensibly taxable subsidiaries make large tax-deductible donations to the parent charity.

16 Flirting with the Devil while Doing God's Work: The Regulation of Charitable Fund-raising

RICHARD JANDA, CARA CAMERON, CHARLES-MAXIME PANACCIO, AND ANDRÉE LAJOIE

Recently heard at work: "Why don't we do old stuff anymore at McGill? Why did we hire a modernist for Art History and merge that department with the Communications Programme?" "The university received a substantial gift from a donor who wanted to highlight the quality of contemporary Chinese art, handicraft and cultural expression."

Some famous scepticism about fund-raising: "*Rendez-moi, lui dit-il, mes chansons et mon somme, / Et reprenez vos cents écus.* Jean de LaFontaine, "Le Savatier et le Financier"

We view our topic, the regulation of charitable fund-raising, as a mirror held up to the academic who works in a university. Over the last twenty years, fund-raising has become increasingly crucial to the continued existence of our universities. Its range and character have become staggeringly complex. The unadorned, unconditional gift now finds itself in the company of joint ventures, patent protection, consultancies, research grants, sponsorships, training contracts and partial privatizations. Today's university – a charitable non-profit institution – finds itself between state and market and is proliferating hybrid institutional forms apace. Whereas its setting may represent among the most elaborate examples of public–private partnership in the charitable sector, it is also part of a broader transformation of civil society. That sea change involves recharacterization of the role and ambitions of the state, renewed emphasis on charity as a means of assuring operation of public institutions, willingness to extend the ambit of markets, and high levels of tolerance for plural and overlapping normative orders – state, charity, market – within institutions.

As charity administrators come to embrace the new modes of funding, it is worth considering in what manner and to what degree these modes of funding will reshape the underlying activity of the charity. Our two introductory quotations sound a cautionary note that rings throughout this chapter. Gifts can change us, particularly if we seek them out. In the university, they can help set the agenda for teaching and research and on occasion can help redefine the contours of disciplines. LaFontaine's cobbler discovered that even a substantial gift with no strings attached changed his relationship to his work and created unforeseen anxiety.

This chapter develops the idea that the regulation of fund-raising should aim to ensure that charities continue to pursue charitable goals for their own sake and that funds facilitate rather than deflect them away from the accomplishment of those goals. The university remains the backdrop for this inquiry and provides a brief case study. The operative conception of regulation that we use is deliberately broad. We have in mind not only the formal state instruments of command and control but also, and principally, efforts by charities to put in place their own mechanisms for assessing whether gifts are changing them for good or for ill. The discussion also spills over into the subject of "social enterprise," since fund-raising for gifts in practice now includes discussion of joint projects with prospective donor-investors.

In pursuing this inquiry, we sketch out, in the first section, the resurgence of charity in Quebec as a means for fulfilling public purposes and examine, in the second, the tension between publicly identified goals of distributive justice and privately identified charitable purposes. The third section deals with the origins of secular fund-raising, using the emblematic example of Pierre Abélard's paradoxical vows of poverty when he established his university in Paraclete relying on students' gifts. This leads in the fourth section to a discussion of the transformation of the gift relationship into the fund-raising opportunity, where we examine the nature of attenuated or conditional altruism and describe the spectrum of fund-raising techniques, ranging from pure gift to pure bargain. We use principles of regulatory practice derived from the generally acknowledged characteristics of altruism to classify and characterize regulatory issues and traditional approaches. The tendency of the law to protect the donor rather than the charity focuses institutional regulation on the relationships between non-profit institution and donor almost to the exclusion of those within the non-profit institution and among non-profit institutions. Finally, in the fifth section, we test the proposed regulatory principles against the regulatory practice in all three loci of one reasonably sophisticated non-profit institution – McGill University – so as to draw general conclusions about the ideal orientation of fund-raising regulation within the non-profit institution and for the non-profit institution.

THE RESURGENCE OF CHARITY

La révolution tranquille

For someone living in Quebec, there is a special irony to stating that charity is resurgent and increasingly crucial to the funding of public institutions. Only one generation separates Quebec's effort to construct a modern welfare state from a time when social services were provided principally through charity. Schools, universities, hospitals, orphanages, and poor houses were operated in large part through churches – notably, the Catholic church. Central to *la révolution tranquille* was an effort to substitute professional, public-funded universal social services for the charity regime.[1] Given Quebec's history, it is not surprising that the reform of 1994 that produced the Civil Code of Quebec abandoned the nineteenth-century terminology of "charitable trust" in favour of an expansive notion of the "social trust."[2]

However, in Quebec, as elsewhere, successive cuts to governments' social spending budgets have produced renewed reliance on charity – in some instances, with explicit legislative support. For example, Quebec guarantees universal access to publicly funded elementary and secondary schools. However, budgets no longer permit the purchase of certain basic materials – paper, pencils, pens, books – and so parents now must purchase such items themselves. It is part of the routine business of *Conseils d'orientation* – parent–teacher school governing committees – to authorize fund-raising campaigns for a variety of school purposes. A provincially sanctioned mechanism allows for establishment of charitable foundations that work in tandem with the public school and fund special projects that budgets may not cover. This situation gives rise to difficult and complex debates about whether any particular foundation project – for example, the purchase of computers for classrooms – might simply allow the school board to redeploy funds that it would otherwise have to use for the purpose. This dilemma has led some people to oppose in principle the creation of school foundations.

If budget cuts to existing programs create pressure to supplement public spending with charitable gifts, so does creation of new programs. For example, the Quebec government, with some fanfare, has implemented a scheme of $5-a-day daycare so as to make child care accessible and affordable.[3] However, the limited public funds available to subsidize daycare constrain the quality of service, producing very high teacher–child ratios and very low wages for teachers. Consequently, parents who want high-quality service – typically levels of service that existed prior to the new scheme – are seeking to make charitable contributions to the daycare centre. Parent daycare administrators are now in the awkward position of soliciting additional funds from the very people who thought they were getting relief for child care expenses. However, the provincial government has been discouraging daycares from accepting charitable donations by threatening to reduce its contribution in proportion to the charitable contributions. Thus tight public budgets, combined with uncertainty surrounding charitable donations to daycare, have made certain daycare budgets more precarious than they were in the days of strict fee for service.

In both institutions – public school foundations and daycare centres – parents are in essence using charitable gifts to purchase personal services for their children. Non-parent donors are extremely rare. The purpose of fund-raising in these cases is to sell the higher-quality product – basic service, supplemented with charitable funds – and to overcome a significant and persistent "free-rider" problem by creating a bandwagon effect. The government justifies the use of charity to supplement universal, publicly funded programs by claiming that there is still a public funding dimension to the tax relief afforded to charitable donations and that donations are not mandatory or pegged at any particular level. However, what they leave without comment is the emergence of considerable variation in the resources available to individual schools or daycares as a result of differential success in fund-raising. The implication is that distributive justice, the *cri de cœur* of *la révolution tranquille,* can be achieved only in rudimentary form: that is, the provision of a minimum service baseline. The state deploys charity as a second-best outcome in order to extend service beyond that baseline, albeit unevenly.

The Unrealized Ambition of L'État providence

Here is one way of telling the story of the genesis of *la révolution tranquille.*[4] What Quebec did in the 1960s, and what took place elsewhere earlier and in varying degree, in effect substituted the state for the church, thereby secularizing and universalizing charity. The secularization of charity has a long and complicated pedigree. It is a reasonable shorthand statement that the early Christian church in a number of its manifestations reproduced the earlier, Jewish understanding of *Tsedakah* (charity). In practical terms, small church communities redistributed wealth among members and among churches. But very soon (inevitably?), the task of redistribution in the name of God was formalized in monastic institutions, which accumulated wealth for that purpose. This in turn produced the corruption of church luxury and the failure of church alms. Even assuming that the accumulation of property corrupts all human relations, not merely those involving a church, there is something particular about the devotion of property to God that undermines charity. Formulaic devotion to God obscured the doing of charity for other people and justified all manner of abomination in the name of rooting out heresy. This ultimately produced a response from that creation of human law, the state – for example, destroying the monasteries of England and favouring individual donations to state-sanctioned public purposes – grammar schools, hospitals, and poor houses.[5] Of course this was in large part an expropriation on behalf of the king's treasury and thus an equal and opposite form of corruption.

But the major transformation effected by this secularization was that it heightened personal responsibility for one's fellow citizens. And democratic accountability eventually came to constrain (in what measure?) use of the state's taxation power for the private gain of those controlling the state apparatus. As the state sought increasingly to fulfil the public purposes that it had identified for charitable gifts, secularization culminated in the universalization of charity as welfare.

The singular feature of Quebec's *révolution tranquille* is that it collapsed several stages of this transformation into a very brief period and with relative social peace. Thus, for example, the monasteries in Quebec were in effect "closed" by the state when they were allowed to languish. Those who, in an earlier generation, would have entered a religious order instead entered social work and other professions to help set up the expert bureaucratic agencies that replaced the church.[6] Some of the most magnificent empty buildings in Quebec are the old church properties.

Here is one way of telling the story of what happened to *la révolution tranquille*. The welfare state, *l'état providence*, had held out the promise that by designing the right set of formal legal instruments and setting them in motion, it could cure any social ill. Law had become programmatic: each legislative and regulatory social initiative required the state to deploy financial resources. The distributive function gained ascendancy over the state's narrow, corrective function.

The welfare state had notable successes attenuating social ills. But the more it became laden with expectations and claims for just distribution, the clearer the limits of its range of possible action became. Thus, for example, the war on poverty rechannelled but did not eradicate the problem of poverty. The bureaucracy and resources deployed to solve the problem became identified, tendentiously, as a significant cause of poverty. More significantly, the broader the social goals of the state, such as eradicating poverty, the broader and more complex the set of human relations the state had to steer. Many of these relations escaped the reach of formal, centralized law. The state's effort to steer them simply revealed the panoply of actors, institutions, and interactions implicated in the issues addressed. And the omniscient, omnipotent state, rich as it became, fell short of the resources needed to accomplish everything dreamed for it. The state came of age and started limiting its ambitions, privatizing and deregulating with a vengeance. It became generally accepted that the state was but one actor among others, and often not a very able one at that.[7]

The Problematic Return to Charity

The "hollowing out" of the state does not entail simply a return to older forms of charity that the state at its zenith had sought to supplant. Where the state had entered fields occupied under the traditional heads of charity – relief of poverty, advancement of education, or other beneficial public purposes (notably health care) – it has not simply departed.[8] It has instead more recently tolerated or even encouraged development of hybrid arrangements through which non-profit and even for-profit institutions work in partnership with the state to achieve public policy objectives.[9] This phenomenon transforms again the relationship between the state and charities when the welfare state itself became a major contributor of funds to charities. Whereas in the years of flush coffers, governments designed grants made through funding programs typically to pay fully for the service offered by the charity, today partnership leverages scarce government funds for services for which it can only partly pay.[10]

Fund-aising for charities in these hybrid relationships thus extends the state's purchasing power for social services. Yet some charitable community groups, notably those working with the poor, conclude that their central purpose should be to lobby for more government monies for services rather than to supply services themselves.[11] But the withdrawal or diminution of government grants necessarily changes the agency's orientation towards raising funds from private donors or from government. Health care is in some ways an exception, since the federal government's proclaimed effort to maintain universal service without user fees rules out some of the hybrid public–charity–private partnerships observable in education spending. Yet just as universities are selectively privatizating in the wake of budget cuts, so too removal of certain non-essential health services from public payment schedules effects a selective privatization.

A Provocative Characterization

As compared with the welfare state, which at once supplanted charities and co-opted them to government purposes, the state today is becoming a charitable intermediary or foundation and charities are becoming state actors. Where the state no longer views itself as sole or even principal provider of some public services, it becomes a part-supplier of funds for public purposes in a market of fund suppliers. Its role becomes indistinguishable from that of the charitable foundation, which attempts to prioritize and do distributive justice among a broad range of good causes soliciting its support. Contributions to the state "foundation" through taxes are compulsory, however, and this "foundation" is accountable to all citizens. Observe nevertheless that individuals increasingly change their residence or citizenship and thus choose where to direct their taxes – i.e., tax contibution to a particular state "foundation" is not strictly obligatory.[12] Some countries, such as Germany, still incorporate a residue of the "tithing" scheme into public taxation by providing a voluntary check-off for a charity contribution to a church on the tax return, and so many taxpayers do give to church foundations as part of paying taxes. Payroll deductions for "united fund" charities in Canada are arguably close cousins to taxation. In other words, it is not in principle inconsistent with foundation status that foundation funds be generated out of taxes. Furthermore, church foundations accountable to congregations or united funds accountable to a broad cross-section of the public face the same issues of accountability as does the state in its distribution of tax resources. Finally, taxpayers may choose to make contributions to state coffers in excess of their tax liability as a matter of charitable donation. In other words, the state is already explicitly characterizing itself as a charitable organization.

When the charity becomes a provider of a public service as well as the locus of collection and disbursement of public monies for that service, it becomes the way that the state acts. The "intermediation" of the state effects a shift towards charities as the ultimate state actors. With fully intermediated state funding, charities would no longer be supplementary, discretionary add-ons to state provision of services. They would instead become the executive arm of the state.

We intend this provocative characterization as a heuristic device to highlight the hybrid character of state–charity relations today. The state is taking on characteristics of charity and vice versa. This hybridization suggests that no actor, either the state or charities, will pay undivided attention to the identification and achievement of public purposes. The state will be too busy trying to leverage its limited funds through partnership with other donors, and the charity will be seeking to ensure that it is the final destination of funding. How and why priority should be given to any particular purpose will depend on what services emerge from the polycentric bargaining among funding agencies. The state will have attenuated influence as part-funder, and the charity may become rudderless, pulled in a variety of directions by contributors.

DISTRIBUTIVE JUSTICE VERSUS CHARITY

An Objection

The discussion above may give rise to the objection that the role of the state – to ensure distributive justice – cannot be placed on a continuum with the role of charity, which is to do good works for anonymous others out of altruism.[13] It is one thing to respond to claims of distributive justice, which will generate a relationship of entitlement, grounded in property rights, between the beneficiary and the state.[14] It is another to appeal to our better selves in the name of morality and to hope that some (or most) will want to do good. If one posits a priority of the right over the good, one will conclude that distributive justice must be the backdrop for any private choices to do good.[15] Distributive justice must be done for all. The charitable giver palliates extraordinary needs.[16] To use charity to meet the obligation to do distributive justice is to render distributive justice precarious, since justice will be done, or not, depending on willingness to give.[17] But this is no distributive justice at all, because precariousness cuts to the heart of what distributive justice must be: giving to all their due. Furthermore, to use charity to meet the obligation to do distributive justice is to drain charity of its virtue, since the givers are then doing only what is required, not something magnanimous. But this is no charity at all, because doing one's duty is not love of the other.[18] Thus to put the role of the state and the role of charity on a continuum is perverse, since it undermines what is essential to each.

Charity, Imperfect Distributive Justice, and Imperfect Social Solidarity

Yet to rule out state–charity "hybrids" and to insist on the pure form of distributive justice and the pure form of charity is to idealize human institutions and human behaviour in a way that fails to engage the workings of the world. Perfected distributive justice would eliminate the need for charity, because, once all have their due, no one can want. But this is not so and will not be. Perfected charity would eliminate the need for distributive justice, because if each cares fully for the other, no one can fail to have his or her due. But this is not so either, nor will it be. Thus the relationship between distributive justice and charity is better described as follows: Those who are altruistic despite limited social solidarity,[19] ought, in the name of the good, to supplement the state's only partly successful attempts to do distributive justice. Those whose magnanimity ought in conscience to be engaged most are those who are best off under the existing, imperfect scheme of distribution. This characterization acknowledges the precariousness of distributive justice without abandoning the state's obligation to do it equally for all at the same time as recognizing the mixed motivations for charity (duty/love) without draining it of virtue.

In addition, some have argued that not only is the state incapable of pursuing distributive justice perfectly, it ought not to try doing so. Godbout and Caillé claim that "the state is not competent to fill some of the roles it has inherited [from social networks], particularly those that owe most to gift."[20] Cohen and Arato postulate that the attempt to perfect distributive justice in the state, and thus to project social solidarity exclusively through the state, produces a "reification of human relations" that undermines civil society.[21] Civil society is composed of "self-limiting democratizing movements seeking to expand and protect spaces for both negative liberty and positive freedom and to recreate egalitarian forms of solidarity without impairing economic self-regulation" and is the locus par excellence of democracy.[22] According to this argument, it is illegitimate for the state to crowd out civil society, which is essential to human flourishing. If there is to be space for civil society, then there must be space for charity. Charity is one of the functions performed by the associations that arise within civil society, which should maintain its own integrity without becoming completely independent from the state or the economy.[23] The bonds of solidarity formed in civil society entail that "each must take responsibility for the other, because as consociates they all share an interest in the integrity of their common life context."[24]

The Trade-off

These critiques of efforts to replace charity by state-centred distributive justice suggest that there is a trade-off implicit in the attempt to reconcile distributive justice and charity. A heightened effort to pursue distributive justice through the state, consistent with the priority of the right over the good, will prompt an attempt to centralize the identification and pursuit of public purposes so as to effect the requisite distributive ranking among purposes. This effort will seek to achieve such a centralization with only moderate levels of bypass. That is, if charitable spending tends to bypass rather than align itself with the centralized ranking of priorities and substitutes other priorities significantly out of line with them, it too greatly weakens distributive justice. Thus distributive justice will require levels of centralized public spending that are credible enough to establish an overall ranking of priorities.[25] But private altruism will then tend to diminish because individual donors may see public spending effected through taxation (forced gift) not only as the means through which charitable goals are met but also as removing individuals' responsibility to identify and ameliorate social needs.

Public "overspending" will tend to require appeals to self-interest rather than to altruism for the purposes of eliciting public support. For example, health care, followed in descending order by primary and secondary education, by postsecondary education, and by relief of poverty, is now the implicit ranking of public purposes for "reinvestment" of government surplus monies. This may demonstrate the shift away from responsibility for others effected by a high-spending welfare state. That is, the public tends to believe that we should maintain as priorities those features of the welfare state on which each of us is most likely to draw personally. The hierarchy within the traditional judicially interpreted heads of charity is probably just the opposite.[26] As Weisbrod argues, a welfare state may thus justify charity on the grounds that only a minority is willing to pay for high levels of other-regarding social service.[27]

We can see the difficult search for an equilibrium point between public and charitable spending reflected in states' efforts to use public spending as leverage to gain matching charitable spending. What level of public taxation and spending, together with the residual willingess to give to charity, will produce the highest total levels of social spending to cure social ills?[28] The answer will probably vary from society to society and over time. However, the fact that willingness to give is elastic, except for the saintly or hardhearted few, places special emphasis on fund-raising. If successful raising of funds increases potential donors' willingness to part with their money, it becomes a way of offsetting individuals' diminished responsibility for others.[29] It thus becomes an important independent variable in achieving the appropriate equilibrium between state spending and charity. The next section explores the origins and nature of charitable fund-raising, and the section following it traces the uneasy transition from gift to fund-raising opportunity.

ABÉLARD'S PARADOXICAL VOW

The phenomenon of fund-raising, which emerges whenever good works are to be performed without full public funding (church or state), is wrapped in paradox. How can I claim that I am doing charity when I ask you for money? Pierre Abélard's efforts to do good works at his own school, Paraclete, which was unconnected with a church monastic order, provide an early example of the conundrum. Abélard vowed poverty – that is, to be utterly other-regarding and thus completely charitable, at least with respect to God. Yet, he writes, alluding to the parable of the unjust steward in the Gospel of Luke, that "unbearable poverty compelled me to run a school since 'to dig I was unable and to beg I was ashamed.'"[30] It may be shameful to beg for funds to do what is inherently good, but one needs to attract support to make it possible to do good. To avoid shame, one casts the good performed as a service to be paid for rather than as something that is in any event to be pursued for its own sake. Already Abélard, in his need for support of his true charity (to be a hermit), felt obliged to pursue another good purpose (education) in order to attract donors (his students). He was uncomfortable about and apologized for having to establish his school. This was because his teaching was an act of fund-raising that compromised his vow of poverty.

Abélard was arguably relying only minimally on fund-raising, since he expected that his students would spontaneously account for his needs and was not, as far as we know, organizing or directing the manner in which they would give of their time and resources. He had a face-to-face relationship with his students but did not cultivate a donor–donee relationship. However, there is historical record of at least one occasion on which they threatened to leave their "hard master," suggesting that he and they understood the relationship of dependence on funding. In the modern context, the non-anonymous, face-to-face relationship with donors that charities must cultivate produces explicit dependence for the charity and extends all the way towards outright bargaining with the donor for provision of services.

This is what Abélard, in uneasy fashion, strove to avoid. Abélard's solution was: do good; do not look at who gives; and allow yourself to be supported. His only solicitation was to engage in an activity (education) that givers could themselves decide was beneficial and to hold out that he was in need. This strict and principled solution to the paradox of charitable fund-raising would have to be loosened to accommodate the broad range of existing fund-raising practices today. Abélard's example thus puts before us the problem on which we want to focus: once we accept the need for charitable fund-raising as part of the state–charity relationship, how can the charity remain focused on a charitable purpose to be pursued for its own sake rather than drifting towards fulfilling the needs or wants of its donors?

FROM GIFT TO FUND-RAISING OPPORTUNITY

What then are the implications of constituting the relationship between donor and charity through fund-raising? On the one hand, raising of funds will tend to transform the charitable gift into a bargain and thus apparently taint its altruistic character.[31] If the gift is altruistic and thus purely charitable, it is made without expectation of recompense or reward, which fund-raising may, by contrast, trade on.[32] On the other hand, fund-raising organized by the donee may overcome some of the donee's dependence on altruistic charity. For the donor, in the "pure" gift relationship, it is the making of the gift, not so much its receipt, that is the virtuous act. The gift thus necessarily places the donee in a situation of dependence and potentially in a situation of humiliation or shame – at the mercy, if you will, of the donor.[33] Professional fund-raising would appear to eliminate the possibility of humiliation because the fund-raiser can be cast as an intermediary between the giver and the donee and by making a "case" for contribution can set the terms of the gift by specifying what is required, and for what purpose.[34] However, there are varying degrees to which the terms of the gift will be bargained. This can be the origin of the power that the donor can exercise over the donee.

Donor–Donee Relationships

Variable degrees of donees' bargaining with the donor emerge in the various forms of relationship that depart from the "pure," anonymous altruistic gift. Such relationships commonly aim at one or more of the following goals, ranging roughly from least to greatest dependence by the donee on the donor's approval of its activities:

- celebrate the donor or another in name
- reinforce the goodwill and reputation of donor and donee
- create social solidarity or pressure (giving to match what others are giving)
- provide against future possible needs of the donor[35]
- further the social agenda of the donor
- reorient the activities of the donee
- retain the donee to provide a service.

If the charity enters into any or all of these relationships as it seeks funds, it will find itself bargaining its "case" with the donor. If the donee adjusts its case so as to receive funds, the problem of mission drift arises. There may be instances in which a private benefactor assists a charity in staying truer to its mission by spurning a case that caters to specific narrow interests rather than to the broader purposes of a charity. However, the dynamic will often work in the opposite direction. In 1999 the Panel on Accountability and Governance in the Voluntary Sector characterized the problem this way:

> As governments have redefined and reduced their roles, new demands have been placed on voluntary organizations. They must not only deliver more services, but also serve new groups of people who often have more complex needs. New sources of funding have had to be found and, with more groups chasing private and corporate donations that are growing (but only modestly), competition in fundraising has become intense. Not only must voluntary organizations compete with each other, but with governments which increasingly are raising charitable dollars to pay for special projects, disaster relief and other public services. Corporate funding, although only a small part of the total income of the sector, has shifted to a large extent from unconditional philanthropy to philanthropy with conditions attached and, increasingly, 'cause marketing' – support or sponsorships tied to specific activities that help sell a product or build a positive image among a target group of potential consumers. The lack of stable funding often makes it hard for an organization to avoid being diverted by chasing project money, attached to priorities determined by the funder rather by than the organization or its constituency, and to stay true to its mission with the ability to undertake long term and strategic planning.[36]

Governments, Charities, and Corporations: Contrasting Sources of Funding

We can see the reconfiguration of the roles and responsibilities of governments, charities, and corporations to which the panel alludes if we

Table 16.1 Overlap of institutions and methods of funding

Method of funding	*Institution*		
	Government	*Charity*	*Corporation*
Taxation	Ordinary public taxation	Tithe	Fee collection (for example, road toll)
Gift	Donation (for example, towards debt)	Ordinary altruistic gift	Bailout
Investment	"Jurisdiction shopping"	Sponsorship	Ordinary business investment

contrast the traditional modes of funding for each institution and note the extent to which these now overlap. For governments it is taxation; for charities, the gift; and for corporations, investment (bargain). There are implications for governance in each of these traditional forms of funding – no taxation without representation, no gift without trust, and no investment without return.

Table 16.1 shows that taxation, gift, and investment are not the exclusive domain of politics, civil society, and markets, respectively. The general implication of overlapping funding techniques, which is outside the scope of this chapter, is that the actors in politics, in civil society, and in the market are in some measure and perhaps increasingly mutually substitutable.[37] The more specific implication, which we explore below, is that charities, as they depart from funding based on the pure form of altruistic gift, create significant regulatory problems.

REGULATORY PRINCIPLES

So as not to fall prey to Abélard's paradox, regulation of charitable fund-raising, whether internal or external to the charity, ought to reinforce altruistic giving and to monitor self-interested giving for compatibility with the charity's purpose. To work out the more detailed regulatory implications of this axiom requires a more complete account of altruistic giving, which we attempt to glean from a review of the relevant literature. In many ways the Canadian legal regime today aligns itself with principles of altruism. Our theme here, however, is that the regulatory regime and current reform initiatives emphasize transparency and accountability to protect the donor's gift – the supply side of the equation – rather than ensuring that the fund-raising charity remains true to its purpose – the demand side of the equation.

Altruistic Giving

Any attempt to account for altruistic giving must first face the objection that there may be no such thing. It is sometimes argued that what appears to be selfless is in fact motivated by an implicit *quid pro quo*. For example, Peter Hammond surmises: "Charitable behavior could be regarded as complying with a social contract. The egoist is worried that, if he breaks the contract, then many others may also decide to break the contract later on, with the result that the egoist's needs are not adequately met if he should ever require help in the future."[38]

Alternatively, psychological benefits of giving (such as affirmation by and respect from other people) may produce a "pay-off" that individuals can factor into their calculation of self-interest.[39] In the words of Laura Stoker, this perspective "rejects a narrow (and objective) version of self-interest, while retaining the premise that people do seek whatever it is that they find to be in their interest. It conceives of ... actors as egoists but not as egotistical."[40] Altruistic behaviour and self-interested behaviour accordingly collapse into a single category – rational egoism.

One could say much to counter this view – for example, to establish the existence of Bruce Chapman's *homo socioeconomicus*.[41] However, if the donor claims and appears to be acting selflessly, the charity receiving funds is concerned less with fathoming the donor's true, secret, and mixed motivations for any particular gift than it is with determining how and to what degree a donor's explicit self-interest might compromise the charity's purposes. The charity can usefully compare the form of a particular gift with an "ideal" type of altruistic gift. It can then accept non-altruistic gifts provided that it has shielded itself against the possible implications of an interested gift.

The literature on altruism suggests a number of characteristics of the ideal type or pure form of altruistic gift. Hong-Wen Chamg and Jane Allyn Piliavin, in a valuable review of theory and research on altruism, note that sociobiologists and game theorists tend to focus on the costs to the altruistic actor, whereas psychologists usually look at intentions. The authors' "largely motive-based definition of altruism" is a hybrid: "behavior costly to the actor involving other-regarding sentiments; if an act is or appears to be motivated mainly out of a consideration of another's needs rather than one's own, we call it altruistic."[42]

Kristen Renwick Monroe adopts a similar hybrid definition with emphasis on intention, concluding that an altruistic act must meet the following four conditions: it must entail action; its goal must be furthering the welfare of another; its intentions, not its consequences, are determinative; and it must carry some possibility of diminishing the actor's welfare.[43] Bar-Tal reviews the literature on altruistic motivations and concludes that altruistic intent "(a) must benefit another person, (b) must be performed voluntarily, (c) must be performed intentionally, (d) the benefit must be the goal itself, and (e) must be performed without expecting any external reward."[44] Karylowski distinguishes between "endocentric" altruism – a response to an internal moral imperative – and exocentric altruism – a desire to improve another's condition.[45] Robert Hancy Scott develops a more problematic account of altruistic motivations, arguing that they take their root in a "preference for inferiority."[46]

Other definitions consider the form taken by the altruistic gift relationship. Titmuss underlines its anonymity and independence, so that it is not paternalistic and must not place demands on those for whom it is performed.[47]

Derived Regulatory Principles

Each of the foregoing definitions of altruism helps to formulate regulatory principles governing fund-raising. Definitions of altruism that emphasize motivations suggest regulatory principles designed to monitor departures of donative from altruistic intent. Definitions of altruism that emphasize cost to the donor suggest regulatory principles designed to monitor cases in which benefits to the donor exceed the donor's costs. Definitions of altruism that emphasize the anonymous form of the gift relationship suggest regulatory principles designed to monitor the donor's control of the donee – or vice-versa.

We suggest the following compendium of regulatory principles applicable to charitable fund-raising, which should apply both to the donor and to the donee, since both ought to be engaged in altruistic behaviour (giving and doing good works, respectively). Yet, regulation of charities tends to focus on providing support to the donor vis-à-vis the charity, rather than vice versa.

There must be an intention to make a charitable contribution. We can see this characteristic of altruism reflected in the doctrine of certainty of intention applicable to charitable trusts: trust law will use only the explicit formulation of intention as a criterion and will not attempt to probe "true" or mixed intentions.[48] It does, however, insist on *charitable* intention. It thus assesses motivational elements of altruism only to ensure formal consistency with the idea of charity.[49] Having identified charitable intention, trust law then focuses on ensuring the fulfilment of donors' desires, not of recipients' needs.

In this respect it departs from the characteristics of altruism in a way that shapes how charities function. For example, Richard Bartlett argues that "[a]n efficient charity sector will produce precisely the charitable services that the donor population wishes, and as much of them as donations will cover."[50] Enforcement of donors' intentions assures the functioning of an efficient charity market. For Bartlett, competition here is positive, because it benefits donors and allows them control over how charities act.[51] He also argues that to the extent that large, united charities increase the efficiency of the execution of donors' wishes, they are more desirable than smaller organizations.[52] The united charity is thus an intermediary that faithfully matches donors' desires with agencies prepared to carry them out.[53] This is not mission drift; it is mission capture.

It must be voluntary. The concept of voluntariness is closely connected to intention and is reflected in judicial interpretation of the doctrine of certainty of intention applicable to charitable trusts. However, one can intend an act that one feels compelled to perform, such as paying taxes or tithes. Since "endocentric altruism" operates on an internally imposed obligation – do your duty to the other – high-pressure fund-raising can seek to transform the request for contribution into the recognition of an obligation. This is particularly so when what is at stake is a religious or social obligation, which is often accompanied by social pressure manifested in publicized comparisons of differing levels of donation.[54] The simplest form of this is the passing of the church collection plate.[55] Codes of conduct for fund-raising tend to address the problem of high-pressure solicitation.[56] Reinforcing voluntariness is also the goal of statutory disclosure requirements governing solicitation.[57] These measures all seek to protect the donor against the charity.

It must not be for profit. The law of charitable trusts will not recognize an institution operating for profit as a charity unless the for-profit purpose is merely ancillary to the charitable purpose. However, this principle is difficult to apply to fund-raising companies employed by the charity as well as to a wide range of promotional devices, such as token products and services exchanged for gifts. Statutory regulation and informal codes of conduct tend to deal with the role of fund-raising companies, principally to protect the donor.[58] Nevertheless, for example, a ban on commission payments for fund-raising protects the charity as well. Less attention has been paid to the donor fund-raiser, who sells a product or service with profits or part of the profits going to the charity, through which method it could exercise commercial control over the charity.[59] Even less attention has been paid to ancillary profit-making by individuals within the charity who, for example, engage in consulting activities related to the area of work of the charity and could therefore drift from their principal mission.

There must be benefit for another. The doctrine of public benefit, generally applicable to charitable trusts, has more particular application in regulatory efforts to monitor and control the proportion of funds that go towards charitable purposes, as opposed to paying the costs of fund-raising.[60] Section 149.1 of the Income Tax Act requires regular disbursement. However, the cy-pres doctrine allows charitable funds to be redirected away from the donee's preferred purpose only under very restricted circumstances, which do not include reorientation of the charity's own purposes and priorities. In other words, it is the donor who can determine which benefit to another ought to be pursued. Here again, the law errs on the side of protecting the donor against the charity. In cases of a clear personal nexus between the gift and the donor, no public benefit will be found.[61] Otherwise, gifts based on partly self-regarding and partly other-regarding motivations and that can push the charity to compromise its purposes will nevertheless be valid.

The giver should not place demands on those in need. The regulation of charitable fund-raising addresses this principle only indirectly, leaving it very much a matter of aspiration. For example, the Panel on Accountability and Governance in the Voluntary Sector notes: "an informed donor is one of the best ways of promoting ethical conduct" and cites the testimony of one group to the effect that "good charities want educated consumers, as they quickly become enthusiastic supporters of our work."[62] Implicit perhaps is the hope that information will breed allegiance to the charity's own definition of its work. Yet at least one code of conduct – *Model Standards of Practice for the Charitable Gift Planner* – emphasizes that donors should inform the charity of their purposes: "Although Gift Planners frequently and properly counsel donors concerning specific charitable gifts without prior knowledge or approval of the donee organization, the Gift Planners, in order to insure that the gift will accomplish the donor's objective, should encourage the donor, early in the gift planning process, to discuss the proposed gift with the charity [to whom] the gift is to be made."[63]

The activity must be conducted for its own sake. This principle is reflected indirectly in the doctrine that mixed and non-severable charitable and non-charitable purpose trusts are invalid. Furthermore, where a charity raises funds as an end in itself, it risks losing its charitable status and having control over its assets sought by the Public Trustee.[64] The Panel on Accountability and Governance drew on the public trust of voluntary associations to conclude that they were accountable for "establishing an appropriate mission and/or policy priorities and ensuring their relevance."[65] Establishing the mission and seeking a good governance structure and proper management techniques to implement it are analogous to pursuing the charitable end for its own sake. However, the panel's instrumental language, together with the notion that it be communicated to "stakeholders," suggests a kind of bureaucratic rationality rather than devotion to a goal. It is with respect to this principle that Abélard's paradox takes a more precise form: the charity must raise funds in order to do its charitable works; to be charitable is to pursue the good works for their own sake; fund-raising is not pursued for its own sake; and therefore the charity cannot be charitable. In a perverse way, the traditional common law governing charitable donations by corporations reinforces this paradox: corporate gifts to charity for the sake of the charity alone were *ultra vires*; such gifts had to involve the calculus that the gift would maximize shareholders' value.[66]

Six Axes of Analysis

These six regulatory principles, in the form of sets of axes (altruistic versus interested), can help to gauge departures from the pure form of gift:

- intended for charity versus not intended for charity
- voluntary versus compelled
- given versus bargained
- other-regarding versus self-regarding
- unconditional versus conditional
- devoted to the charitable purpose versus instrumental

This typology may help a charity to clarify the features of fund-raising that ought to attract higher levels of scrutiny as it assesses whether to engage in a particular fund-raising activity. Our working hypothesis is that fund-raising involving more of the first, or "altruistic" characteristics requires less internal scrutiny for mission drift than that involving more of the second, or "interested" characteristics. Table 16.2 gives examples of various possible combinations of these characteristics.

This table offers neither an exhaustive characterization of charitable funding nor a way to pigeon-hole any particular technique. The binary oppositions often involve differences of degree rather than of kind. For example, charitable gambling might be a token sale of a service or a business activity; the heavy regulatory burden on those

Table 16.2 Regulatory principles: sets of axes (altruistic versus interested)

	Altruistic						Interested						
Fund-raising method	*Intended for charity*	*Voluntary*	*Given*	*Other-regarding*	*Unconditional*	*Devoted*	*Not intended for charity*	*Compelled*	*Bargained*	*Self-regarding*	*Conditional*	*Instrumental*	*Principal regulatory concern*
Pure charitable gift	✓	✓	✓	✓	✓	✓							Truly settlor's intention?
Tithe	✓		✓	✓	✓	✓		✓					Abuse of power?
Alms-seeking	✓	✓	✓	✓	✓							✓	Pressured solicitation?
Token sale of product or service	✓	✓		✓	✓				✓			✓	Remains ancillary to charity?
Directed purpose gift	✓	✓	✓	✓							✓	✓	Direct relation to charity's purposes?
Donor fund-raiser	✓	✓	✓			✓				✓	✓		Co-opted to business?
Naming opportunity	✓	✓	✓										Over-deference to settlor?
Monitored grant	✓	✓				✓			✓	✓	✓		Charity remains autonomous?
Sponsorship	✓	✓							✓	✓	✓	✓	Significant business purpose?
Business activity							✓	✓	✓	✓	✓	✓	Only residual charitable purpose?

conducting it aims to keep it more in the nature of a token sale.[67] Furthermore, some of the broad types of fund-raising activity might be combined. For example, naming opportunities can be linked to monitored grants. The table does highlight the growing importance of protecting the charity's own purposes as the gift becomes more interested and less altruistic. It also suggests that a wide range of fund-raising techniques can compromise devotion to charitable purposes for their own sake. This is perhaps the regulatory principle both the least possible to enforce strictly and the one requiring most generalized monitoring.

Institutional Loci for Regulation

If both formal and informal regulatory regimes tend to protect the donor against the charity, rather than vice versa, this is because these regimes do not seek to deprive the charity of a gift that it could receive without prejudice to the donor. It is left for the charity alone to regulate the way it makes fund-raising consistent with its own purposes.

Alberta's Charitable Fund-raising Act illustrates this point neatly. Section 2 sets out the following two purposes for the legislation: "(a) to ensure that the public has sufficient information to make informed decisions when making contributions to a charitable organization or for a charitable purpose, and (b) to protect the public from fraudulent, misleading or confusing solicitations and to establish standards for charitable organizations and fund-raising businesses when making solicitations."

The legislation thus appears to suggest that the only fund-raising issues requiring a code of conduct arise as between the charity and donor and not within the charity or among charities.

Although the Panel on Accountability and Governance cast its own recommendations in the same manner, it did acknowledge other dimensions to the regulation of fund-raising. Thus it noted, for example, that it was unable to make detailed recommendations concerning the competition for donations among charities and with the government.[68] It also called for more emphasis on charities' articulating and staying true to their purposes. However, it did not seek to identify the link between modes of fund-raising and charities' missions.

For the charity, however, the implications of fund-raising for the donor–donee relationship are only part of the regulatory burden. Two other loci for regulation – within the charity and among charities – present significant concerns handled appropriately though internal charity directives. Within the charity, issues include who can ask for gifts? (centralized or decentralized); why can they ask? (strict adherence to mission); and whom can they ask (for example, is an armament manufacturer excluded)? As between charities, the issues include whether charities should "compete" to provide the same charitable service more effectively and whether they should "collude" to co-ordinate fund-raising schedules, "prices," and opportunities. We noted above some issues between the donor and the donee: Is there common cause? Is there sufficient information? Is there trust? Do donors have excessive control? A look at the practices of McGill University vis-à-vis these three loci of regulation can cast light on the neglected aspect of regulation – "demand-side" concern with avoiding mission drift.

THE CASE OF MCGILL UNIVERSITY

McGill University in Montreal was founded in 1821 and now has some 29,000 registered students. In 1999, its total annual operating revenues were $595 million, of which $224 million came from the provincial government grant, $61 million from tuition fees, $113 million from research, $41 million from endowment and investment revenues, and $39 million from gifts, grants, and bequests. Within McGill, broad policy decisions over fund-raising practices and needs are made by the McGill Fund Council, a subcommittee of the university's board of governors. The Annual Fund, which solicits gifts from every individual alumnus/a, was the main object of our investigations, although fund-raising practices differ only marginally in the other three channels for giving: major gifts, planned giving, and the alumni associations.

Our interviews reinforced two of the chapter's themes. First, fund-raising practices are tied to the more general problem of evolving state–charity–private sector relationships. "Downloaded" government deficits put further pressure on fund-raisers to make up shortfalls and to transform the university's relationship with government into a fund-raising relationship. Preparing the "case" for additional government funding is in effect a matter of going back to the biggest donor, which is not quite as prosperous as it once was. Second, fund-raising is increasingly wrapped up in Abélard's paradox: McGill will inevitably try to play to potential donors' interests in promoting its educational purposes. For example, one way of attracting gifts is to give potential donors a range of options, through different forms – or levels – of designation. Thus a gift can go to fund athletics, particular faculties or departments, libraries, scholarships, and so on, or simply remain undesignated. Fund-raisers have become quite sophisticated about discerning and playing to the different tastes of donors.

Nevertheless, McGill has developed broad internal standards limiting a donor's ability to impose his or her own personal tastes on the university, so that it has on a few occasions refused a gift that did not cohere with its objectives and priorities. In particular, in leading up to a major multi-year Advancement Campaign, the university goes through a general exercise of identifying goals and priorities linked to fund-raising targets. Martlet House, the fund-raising arm of the university, lines up potentially interested donors with the particular purposes identified, to cultivate a relationship and make the "ask." However, the donor's own interests and the university's differential success in raising funds for the various purposes mean that the original priority list is not necessarily the one finally implemented.

McGill provides a good illustration of the multiplicity of internal regulatory devices that constrain a fund-raising entity and a charitable community more generally, because McGill is both. In other words, not only is it a single fund-seeker, but it also needs to co-ordinate many potentially competing internal campaigns.

Within the Charity

In principle, Martlet House has a monopoly on the "ask." However, with the proliferation of needs, individual faculties, departments, and research centres have engaged in their own fund-raising activities. More than one unit may target the same donor, which undermines the relationship with the donor and may prevent securing of the maximum donation. Consequently, Martlet House has decentralized its operations and attached liaison officers to each faculty, allowing internal discussion, indeed competition, over which project will approach which donors. Martlet House informally reinforces its monopoly through internal conciliation and persuasion.

Martlet House's monopoly does not extend to those funding arrangements that are more in the nature of fee for service, such as the negotiation of overhead charges on projects and the planning of "fully funded" or "privatized" programs. There is an internal separation between the agency responsible for gifts and the agencies that enter into bargains. This separation has also permitted a proliferation of new ventures that by-pass the assessment of consistency with university purposes.

Regulations on research policy, on consulting and similar activities by academic staff, on inventions and patents, and on conflicts of interest in proprietary research establish loose limits on permissible research funding, on the amount of for-profit outside activity in which staff members individually can engage, on allocation of profit from research, and on separation of university activities and commercial development. The rules tend to be hortatory in character and, to the degree they are obligatory, focus on disclosure. For example, the regulations on consulting recognize that a "member of the academic staff may respond to the needs of society outside the University" while seeking to assure that levels of such service are disclosed as "appropriate" in keeping with "direct service to the University through teaching, research and administration."[69]

Although each donation for a larger project is scrutinized for consistency with university priorities and planning, some have been "fast-tracked" where funding was immediately available or available on a contingent basis. *Ex post facto* review by the Senate's Academic Planning and Policy Committee is in those cases *pro forma* at best.

Between Charity and Donor

McGill's annual operating budget for fund-raising (on the order of $450,000) is fixed by the McGill Fund Council at the beginning of every fiscal year. This means that McGill uses approximately ten cents of every dollar raised for fund-raising expenses, five cents for gift administration, and the rest (eighty-five cents) for the actual purpose of the gift. The university adheres broadly to the Canadian Centre for Philanthropy's Ethical Fund-raising and Financial Accountability Code, although it does not maintain strict scrutiny over compliance, on the view that its procedures are beyond reproach. Thus, for example, the Annual Fund broadly expressed the goal of ensuring that "people know where their money went." It does have a policy of sending tax receipts within five days of receipt of payment. However, solicitation agents will disclose financial information bearing on the gift only when it is expressly requested, and they do not elicit these requests. This practice is consistent with the letter of the Code but may be less so with its spirit – in particular the stipulation that "all fund-raising solicitations by or on behalf of the charity will disclose ... the purpose for which the funds are requested."[70]

One interviewee opined that "no extravagant expenses are tolerated; sobriety prevails in all aspects of the fund-raising campaigns." This was a matter of tradition and peer pressure rather than of any particular rule.

Martlet House does not employ outside professional fund-raisers, but did for a period report to a vice-principal who had been a professional fund-raiser. Although it now reports to an academic, it is best understood as an in-house professional fund-raising institution where fund-raisers are on salary, not on commission.

Among Charities

Although participants acknowledged the phenomenon of competition among campaigns, they mentioned no specific consultation mechanisms vis-à-vis other charities. This is a subject on which the Panel of Accountability and Governance specifically urges universities to work in the future.

Emerging Structural Problems

McGill's budget deficit has given rise to signs of slippage away from altruistic principles of charitable giving. Although there are mechanisms in place for academic oversight of most funding initiatives, some initiatives – notably joint ventures and contracts for service – are subject to only minimal scrutiny as long as they generate overhead monies. Increasingly as well, even the formal process of academic oversight is driven by the availability of funds for projects (see introductory quotation). What is too often missing is an *ex ante* test of each new funded activity for its relevance to scholarly and pedagogical objectives. On the contrary, approval is fast-tracked where funding is available, as in, ironically, the recent approval of the self-funded Voluntary Sector Management program. Furthermore, there is minimal oversight of individuals who trade on the reputation of the university to enhance their income. Indeed, this is sometimes encouraged, to compensate individuals for unavailable full-time positions or to address perceptions of inadequate remuneration. The emergence of a variety of part-time, non–tenure-track positions has opened the door to for-profit consultancy, in which the ability to raise project funds will compensate for part-time status. This amounts to a subtle undercutting of Martlet House's monopoly, since part-timers become fund-raisers for McGill. Once the door opens, even full-time staff go through it, loosely monitored and largely *sub rosa.*

CONCLUSION: BENIGN FLIRTATIONS WITH THE DEVIL?

The purpose of fund-raising regulation is not simply to enhance confidence in charities so as to maximize giving. That would lead us to a view of a charity as undertaking a contract to perform the service designated by the donor and thus to serve as the donor's agent. Fund-raising should rather seek to elicit gifts by virtue of a charity's purposes. From the standpoint of the charity, regulation should seek to channel administrative decision-making towards continued and principled elucidation of the goals of the charity and appraisal of success in meeting them. It should restrain the charity's temptation to set goals simply in response to funding opportunities. Self-regulation is the best instrument to achieve these ends, although public regulation, especially disclosure and monitoring, can encourage appropriate self-regulation. For the donor, regulation should facilitate publicly oriented magnanimity by permitting informed assessment of charitable purposes and their performance as well as of under-fulfilled needs consistent with those purposes. It should restrain the donor's temptation simply to project his or her will onto others. Public regulation is useful in rendering information comparable and accessible but must not be so administratively burdensome as to exclude smaller charities. For the community as a whole, regulation should promote an alignment between the capacity to solicit funds and the significance of the public purpose. It should avoid the contemporary libertarian temptation to view charities as so many conduits for private preferences. The burden of taxation and trust law rules is to fulfil this objective.

These regulatory criteria apply unobtrusively to the funding that made this volume possible. The research undertaken is valuable for its own sake and reflects a scholarly agenda that academics themselves have identified. Funds that were made available to us not only assisted us in the conduct of research – a principal purpose of the university – but also assisted students. In the absence of these funds, we might have established different priorities and research agendas. But the donor's role here was to signal a need otherwise consistent with the purpose of the university and, more specifically, with the scholarly orientation of those whose work forms the collection.

Unfortunately, one cannot be as sanguine about all the funding opportunities that have crossed university desks over the last few years and that have engaged the life of our faculties. Five features figure too strongly in many university fund-raising schemes:

- the desire to supplement professors' income
- the need to overinvest resources in donors' priorities, which brings accompanying opportunity costs
- the absence of strong linkage to scholarly or pedagogical goals
- the danger of participants' being "co-opted" to express donors' views or at least views not inconsistent with their preferences
- the marginalization of scholarly activity that cannot itself be cast as a fund-raising "profit centre"

These perverse incentives are all the more problematic in the absence of well-structured cross-subsidization of university priorities from overhead generated on non-governmental funds. A similar story emerges in the health sector as well and is characteristic of hybrid entities lying between state and market. When one raises funds conscious of these perverse incentives, one flirts with the devil.

As he thought about how to fund his monastic university, Pierre Abélard wished to exclude such flirtations categorically. Yet even he recognized that vows of poverty were something of a ruse as soon as donors' support became the condition for being able to do one's charitable work. It would be iconoclastic to turn one's back on fund-raising in the university or non-profit institution. This chapter has sought to identify the regulatory principles applicable within charities, between a charity and a donor, and among charities themselves that can help to keep flirtations benign.

NOTES

We acknowledge the invaluable scholarly assistance of Daniel Downes and Morella Saim and the financial assistance of the SSHRC.

1 For a critical appraisal, see J. Migué, *Étatisme et déclin du Québec: bilan de la Révolution tranquille* (Montreal: Les Éditions Varia, 1999).

2 Civil Code of Quebec, art. 1270: "A social trust is a trust constituted for a purpose of general interest, such as a cultural, educational, philanthropic, religious or scientific purpose." The Supreme Court of Canada's approach to the definition of charity in *Vancouver Society of Immigrant and Visible Minority Women v. M.N.R.* [1999] 1 SCR 10, rooted in the traditional four heads of charity developed in the *Pemsel* case, suggests that in Quebec the definition of social trust will work quite differently.

3 Loi sur les centres de la petite enfance et autres services de garde à l'enfance, LRQ 1997 c. c. S-4.1. See also Québec, Ministère de la Famille et de l'Enfance, Règlementation sur la contribution réduite, 22 Aug. 1997.

4 For more traditional accounts, see M. Fournier, *L'entrée dans la modernité* (Montreal: Éditions Saint-Martin, 1986), and H. Guindon, *Aspiration nationale de la societé québécoise* (Montreal: Éditions Saint-Martin, 1990). See also J. Gow, ed., *Administration publique québécoise* (Montreal: Beauchemin, 1970), and J. Robert, *Du Canada français au Québec libre* (Paris: Flammarion, 1975).

5 Notable in this regard is England's Statute of Charitable Uses, 1601 (Statute of Elizabeth). For a discussion of it, see S. Bright, "Charity and Trusts for the Public Benefit: Time for a Re-think?" *Conveyancer* (1989), 28. See also H. Berman, *Law and Revolution: The Formation of the Western*

Legal Tradition (Cambridge, Mass.: Harvard University Press, 1983), especially 165ff., on the religious origins of the state.

6 See G. Rocher, *Le Québec en mutation* (Montreal: Hurtubise HMH, 1973).

7 See, for example, Charles Murray, *Losing Ground* (New York: Basic Books, 1984), and the response by Christopher Jencks in *Rethinking Social Policy: Race, Poverty and the Underclass* (Cambridge, Mass.: Harvard University Press, 1990). For another stylized history of the decline of the welfare state, see A. Seldon, "The Idea of the Welfare State and Its Consequences," in S. Eisenstadt and O. Ahimeir, eds., *The Welfare State and Its Aftermath* (London: Croom Helm, 1985). However, relationships between the welfare state and the non-profit sector are more variegated: see T. Janoski, *Citizenship and Civil Society* (Cambridge: Cambridge University Press, 1998), 17–24, for a typology of welfare state regimes.

8 As for advancement of religion, the state undertook functions that had been performed by churches, which typically received charitable status on the strength not of their contribution to the salvation of souls but rather of their good works: see *Gilmour v. Coats* [1949] AC 426. The list of charitable purposes set out in the Statute of Elizabeth itself represented an effort to channel donations to the church for purposes preferred by the emergent state, such as development of infrastructure.

9 For an early treatment of this phenomenon, see R. Kramer, *Voluntary Agencies and the Welfare State* (Berkeley: University of California Press, 1981).

10 See F. Kaufmann, "Major Problems and Dimensions of the Welfare State," in S. Eisenstadt and O. Ahimeir, eds., *The Welfare State and its Aftermath* (London: Croom Helm, 1985): "Instead of the state as a singular actor, we have to consider, therefore, the production of welfare as a (partially contingent) result of networks of both governmental and non-governmental, formally public and private corporate actors."

11 Charitable organizations themselves depend significantly on government funding and so may not see themselves as competing with or substituting for the welfare state: see B. Gidron, R.M. Kramer, and L.M. Salamon, *Government and the Third Sector: Emerging Relationships in Welfare States* (San Francisco: Jossey-Bass, 1992), 15: "In short, the relationship between government and the nonprofit sector has not been static. To the contrary, it has changed significantly over time, reflecting the evolution of social policy generally. Far from competing with the state, nonprofit organizations were more often significant advocates of expanded state responsibilities and in many cases have themselves benefited from an expansion of state action."

12 See D. Downes and R. Janda, "Virtual Citizenship," *Canadian Journal of Law and Society* 13 (1999), 27. See also A. Ong, *Flexible Citizenship: The Cultural Logics of Transnationality* (Durham, NC: Duke University

Press, 1999).

13 See Kymlicka, chapter 4 in this volume, as well as Brooks, chapter 6. On the "deserving poor," see M. Valverde, "Moral Capital," *Canadian Journal of Law and Society* 9 (1994), 213.

14 C. Reich, "The New Property," *Yale Law Journal* 73 (1964), 733. Nancy Fraser and Linda Gordon note that the distinction between entitlement, modelled on contractual exchange (for example, industrial accident insurance), and non-contributory charity (such as mothers' pensions) has been strongly gendered: see "Contract versus Charity: Why Is There No Social Citizenship in the United States?," reprinted in G. Shafir, ed., *The Citizenship Debates* (Minneapolis: University of Minnesota Press, 1998), 113. See also L. Gordon, ed., *Women, the State and Welfare* (Madison: University of Wisconsin Press, 1991), and L. Gordon, "Social Insurance and Public Assistance: The Influence of Gender in Welfare Thought in the United States, 1890–1935," *American Historical Review*, 97 (1992), 97.

15 In *Political Liberalism* (New York, Columbia University Press, 1993), 173ff., John Rawls has clarified his famous defence of the priority of the right over the good (ibid., 174): "[T]he priority of the right means that the principles of political justice impose limits on permissible ways of life; and hence the claims citizens make to pursue ends that transgress those limits have no weight. But surely just institutions and the political virtues expected of citizens would not be institutions and virtues of a just and good society unless those institutions and virtues not only permitted but also sustained ways of life fully worthy of citizens' devoted allegiance." Rawls states the principle of distributive justice regarding social and economic inequalities as follows (291): "First, they must be attached to offices and positions open to all under conditions of fair equality of opportunity; and second, they must be to the greatest benefit of the least advantaged members of society." Thus, it could not be, for example, that social and material inequalities were maintained so as to allow some to pursue the good by being charitable to the disadvantaged. However, there might be some space for charity between the minimum level of material and social well-being *constitutionally* required to ensure that all can take part in social and political life and that level of material and social well-being that can assist people to flourish.

16 Michael Walzer would characterize this as involving a separate sphere of justice – namely, that of security and welfare: *Spheres of Justice: A Defence of Pluralism and Equality* (Princeton, NJ: Basic Books, 1983). See also B. de Souza Santos, *Toward a New Common Sense: Law, Science and Politics in the Paradigmatic Transition* (New York: Routledge, 1995), who writes of separate domains of justice. As Walzer himself acknowledges, the recognition of the duty to do distributive justice does not in itself identify the level of

needs that must be met (*Spheres,* 68): "But how much security is required? Of what sorts? Distributed how? Paid for how? These are serious issues and they can be resolved in many ways." If these issues can be resolved in a number of ways, or imperfectly addressed in any particular state, the need for supplementary charity arises. However, "in the West today, it seems to be a general rule that the more developed the welfare state, the less room there is and the less motivation there is for charitable giving" (91).

17 L.M. Salamon develops the idea of "voluntary failure" as parallel to "market failure" and "government failure": see "On Market Failure, Voluntary Failure, and Third Party Government: Toward a Theory of Government–NonProfit Relations in the Modern Welfare State," in S.A. Ostrander and S. Langton, eds., *Shifting the Debate: Public/Private Sector Relations in the Modern Welfare State* (New York: Transaction Books, 1987). This view contrasts with B.A. Weisbrod's account in *The Voluntary Non-Profit Sector: An Economic Analysis* (Lexington: Heath, 1977). See also L.M. Salamon, "The Voluntary Sector and the Future of the Welfare State," *Non-profit and Voluntary Sector Quarterly Review* (1989), 11.

18 But see Emmanuel Lévinas, for whom the obligation to the other becomes so absolute as to compel complete devotion: *Autrement qu'être; ou au-dela de l'essence* (The Hague: M. Nijhoff, 1974).

19 On charity as consisting of acting on an obligation to relieve suffering, humiliation, and distress of others, see J. Douglas, *Why Charity: The Case for a Third Sector* (London: Sage, 1983).

20 J. Godbout and A. Caillé, *The World of the Gift* (Montreal: McGill-Queen's University Press, 1998), 76.

21 J. Cohen and A. Arato, *Civil Society and Political Theory* (Cambridge, Mass.: MIT Press, 1992), 27.

22 Ibid., 17. See also J. Van Til, "The Three Sectors: Voluntarism in a Changing Economy," in S.A. Ostrander and S. Langton, eds., *Shifting the Debate: Public/Private Sector Relations in the Modern World* (New York: Transaction Books, 1987), and N. Gilbert, *Capitalism and the Welfare State* (New Haven, Conn.: Yale University Press, 1983). Cohen and Arato go on to assert (*Civil Society,* 27): "It is our central thesis that democracy can go much further on the level of civil society than on the level of political society or economic society, because here the coordinating mechanism of communicative interaction has fundamental priority ... It is indictively certain that the functioning of societal associations, public communication, cultural institutions and families allow for potentially high degrees of egalitarian participation and collegial decision-making." This begs the question as to the proper relationship between the state and civil society when those bodies become instead spheres of hierarchy and exclusion. Cohen and Arato attribute to civil society, the "medium" of which is soli-

darity, an absence of "a steering resource like money and power" (473). But honour or prestige is a "medium" of voluntary associations that can be a steering resource for them. Exemplary displays of solidarity merit honour and prestige. Honour can be made scarce and distributed unequally, creating levels of worth and excluding some. Indeed, there can often be a direct alignment between honour within the sphere of civil society, money in the economic sphere, power in the political sphere, and certainly an effort to accumulate all three. By underestimating the role of honour and prestige and idealizing solidarity in civil society, Cohen and Arato fail to identify the limits of civil society as a pure "steering mechanism" for the state and the economy. One could just as well idealize politics as the sphere of justice and the economy as the sphere of efficiency, with both needed to steer civil society. For further accounts of the relation between civil society and the state, see Andrée Lajoie, "Contribution à une théorie de l'émergence du droit : 1. Le droit, l'État, la société civile, le public, le privé: de quelques définition interreliées," *Revue juridique Thémis* 25 (1991), 103; and Danièle Lochak, "La société civile: du concept au gadget," in Jacques Chevallier et al. *La Société civile* (Paris: Presses universitaires de France, 1986).

23 See M. Lipsky and S.R. Smith, "Nonprofit Organizations, Government and the Welfare State," *Political Science Quarterly* 104 (1990), 625.

24 Ibid., 679.

25 There is empirical evidence that sectors receiving public spending will also receive non-governmental charitable spending, whereas sectors ignored by the state will also be ignored by civil society: see M. Sosin, *Private Benefits* (Orlando, Fla.: Academic Press, 1986).

26 However, Ware emphasizes the value of the welfare state, especially in assisting the poor, arguing that charity can in practice only play a secondary role: A. Ware, *Between Profit and State: Intermediate Organizations in Britain and in the United States* (Princeton, NJ: Princeton University Press, 1989).

27 B. Weisbrod, "Towards a Theory of the Voluntary Non-Profit Sector in a Three-Sector Economy," in E. Phelps, ed., *Altruism, Morality, and Economic Theory* (New York: Russell Sage Foundation, 1975), 121. See also J. Douglas, *Why Charity? A Case for the Third Sector* (Beverly Hills, Calif.: Sage Publications, 1983), and H. Hansmann, "The Role of the Nonprofit Enterprise," *Yale Law Journal* 89 (1980), 835.

28 In "On Market Failure," Salamon characterizes the requisite equilibrium as follows (43–5): "In view of their complementarity, neither the replacement of the voluntary sector by government nor the replacement of government by the voluntary sector, makes as much sense as collaboration between the two. This offers an opportunity to combine the service delivery of voluntary organizations with the revenue generating and democratic priority setting advantages of government [...] The key is to find a

balance that protects the legitimate public interest in accountability without undermining the characteristics that make nonprofits effective partners of government."

29 See N. Parry, M. Rustin, and C. Satyamurti, *Social Work, Welfare and the State* (London, 1979), 168: "a mobilization of altruistic capacities is essential if real help is to offered to those most in need."

30 *Historia Calamitatum*, lines 1110–11. Luke 16:3 (M.T. Muckle, trans.); see also M. Clanchy, *Abélard: A Medieval Life* (Oxford : Blackwell, 1997).

31 Note, however, that Marcel Mauss's famous "Essai sur le don, forme et raison de l'échange dans les sociétés archaïques," in *Sociologie et anthropologie* (Paris: Presses universitaires de la France, 1950), emphasizes the reciprocity of the gift relationship. See also Godbout and Caillé, *The World of the Gift*, especially the chapter "Gift, Market, Disinterestedness," 171.

32 See R. Schwartz, "Personal Philanthropic Contributions," *Journal of Political Economy* 78 (1970), 1264, defining "philanthropic transfer of wealth" as "a voluntarily generated, one-way flow of resources from a donor to a donee; the flow is one-way in the sense that it is based upon no donor expectation that an economic *quid pro quo* (in the usual sense of that term) will reward his act."

33 See A. Margalit, *The Decent Society* (Cambridge, Mass.: Harvard University Press, 1996). Margalit puts it this way: "Begging for alms is humiliating. In contrast, mercy is considered an ennobling emotion. The tension is palpable: on the on the one hand, mercy has an uplifting quality for the giver; on the other hand, being on the receiving end of mercy is humiliating."

34 See D. Bourgeois, *The Law of Charitable and Non-profit Corporations*, 2nd ed. (Toronto: Butterworths, 1995) 218–19, describing the elements of a good "case."

35 This is a version of what Tocqueville characterized as the American doctrine of self-interest properly understood: Alexis de Tocqueville, *De la démocratie en Amérique*, vol. 2, part II, chap. 8.

36 Panel on Accountability and Governance in the Voluntary Sector, *Building on Strength: Improving Governance and Accountability in Canada's Voluntary Sector*, Final Report, Feb. 1999, 5.

37 The panel reflects this overlap in its recommendations regarding strategic planning by the charity: ibid., 24ff. Mission statements and "results-based" management have become characteristic of "best practices" in both public and business administration. Furthermore, the panel – chaired by a former leader of a federal political party and including members from the voluntary sector, business, and government – exemplified the overlap of sectors. The fact that the voluntary sector could itself take the lead in setting up a body that acted very much like a commis-

sion of public inquiry – hearing evidence and making recommendations – is quite remarkable.

38 P. Hammond, "Charity: Altruism or Cooperative Egoism?" in E. Phelps, ed., *Altruism, Morality, and Economic Theory* (New York: Russell Sage Foundation, 1975), 116.

39 Weisbrod, "Towards a Theory," 187–8.

40 L. Stoker, "Interests and Ethics in Politics," *American Political Science Review* 86 (1992), 369.

41 See Chapman, chapter 5 in this volume. See also B. Bolnick, "Toward a Behavioral Theory of Philanthropic Activity," in E. Phelps, ed., *Altruism, Morality, and Economic Theory*, (New York: Russell Sage Foundation, 1975), 198.

42 H. Chamg and J. Piliavin, "Altruism: A Review of Recent Theory and Research," *Annual Review of Sociology* 16 (1990), 27, 30.

43 K. Renwick Monroe, "A Fat Lady in a Corset," *American Journal of Political Science* 38 (1994), 862–3.

44 D. Bar-Tal, "Altruistic Motivation to Help: Definition, Utility and Operationalization," *Humboldt Journal of Social Relations* 13 (1985–86), 3.

45 J. Karylowski, "Two Types of Altruistic Behavior," in V. Derlega and J. Grzelak, eds., *Cooperation and Helping Behavior* (New York: Academic Press, 1982), 396.

46 R. Haney Scott, "Avarice, Altruism and Second Party Preferences," *Quarterly Journal of Economics* 86 (1972), 5. See also Chapman, chapter 5 in this volume, who explores this idea.

47 R. Titmuss, *The Gift Relationship: From Human Blood to Social Policy* (London: George Allen & Unwin, 1970). He also notes (89) that while "[n]o donor type can, of course, be said to be characterized by complete, disinterested, spontaneous altruism," altruistic acts "are acts of free will; of the exercise of choice; of conscience without shame," thus emphasizing altruistic motivation as well.

48 Charities ought to view as suspect fund-raising that explicitly trades on mixed motivations. A recent example was the largest "Ponzi" scheme in U.S. history set up by Bennett Funding Group Securities to fund U.S. charities: *In re Bennett Funding Group Securities Litigation* (United States District Court, Southern District of New York).

49 This principle is reflected as well in various codes of conduct governing charitable fund-raising. For example, the Model and Standards of a Charitable Giver, adopted by the National Committee on Planned Giving and the Committee on Gift Annuities, 7 May 1991, sets out in article I: "Primacy of Philanthropic Motivation: The principal basis for making a charitable gift should be a desire on the part of the donor to support the work of charitable institutions." This statement of principle seems particularly well formulated, since it also preserves the autonomy of the chari-

table institution in identifying its own goals. However, see note and accompanying text.

50 R. Bartlett, "United Charities and the Sherman Act," *Yale Law Journal* 91 (1982), 1601.

51 Ibid., 1600.

52 Ibid., 1611.

53 For a sophisticated analysis of the intermediary function of united funds, see S. Rose-Ackerman, "United Charities: An Economic Analysis," *Public Policy* 28 (1980), 323.

54 See S. Long, "Social Pressure and Contributions to Health Charities," *Public Choice* (1976), 54.

55 See T. Ireland and D. Johnson, *The Economics of Charity* (Blacksburg, Va: Center for the Study of Public Choice, 1970).

56 At one end of the spectrum, the Code of Ethics of the Society of Fund Raising Executives contains only this general principle: "A member's public demeanor shall be such as to bring credit to the fundraising profession." At the other end, the Canadian Better Business Bureau's Standards for Charitable Solicitations contains a part on fund-raising practices, including a provision: "Fund raising shall be conducted without excessive pressure. Excessive pressure in fund raising includes but is not limited to solicitations in the guise of invoices; harassment; intimidation or coercion, such as threats of public disclosure or economic retailiation; failure to inform recipients of unordered items that they are under no obligation to pay for or return; and strongly emotional appeals which distort the organization's activities or beneficiaries." The Canadian Centre of Philanthropy's Ethical Fundraising and Financial Accountability Code, to which the Panel on Accountability and Governance recommends that charities adhere, lies somewhere in between. It announces a general principle and puts some onus on donors to articulate its application; "Donor will be treated with respect. Every effort will be made to honour their requests to limit the frequency of solicitations; not be solicited by telephone or other technology; receive printed material concerning the charity." Similarly, volunteers, employees, and hired solicitors who solicit or receive funds on behalf of the charity shall "cease solicitation or a prospective donor *who identifies* the solicitation as harassment or undue pressure" (emphasis added). Alberta's Charitable Fund-raising Act, SA 1995, c. C-4.5, ss. 29.1 and 29.2, provides for the promulgation of standards of fund-raising practice to be implemented by registered charities. This approach is recommended by the Ontario Law Reform Commission (OLRC), *Report on the Law of Charities* (Toronto: Commission, 1994), chap. 18.

57 See, for example, section 6 of Alberta's Charitable Fund-raising Act. For a thorough review of the various statutory regimes, see OLRC, *Report.*

U.S. developments are tracked in "Note: Developments in the Law – Nonprofit Corporations," *Harvard Law Review* 105 (1992), 1578, with emphasis on the problem of contingent-fee or commissioned fund-raising, and E. Harris, L. Holley, and C. McCaffrey, "Fund-raising into the 1990s: State Regulation of the Charitable Solicitation after *Riley*," *University of San Francisco Law Review* 24 (1990), 571. See also "Note: The Regulation of Charitable Fundraising and Spending Activities," *Wisconsin Law Review* (1975), 1158, for an account of the limited success of disclosure rules.

58 See, for example, sections 20–27.1 of Alberta's Charitable Fund-raising Act concerning "fund-raising businesses." The Panel on Accountability and Governance devotes much of its discussion of fund-raising to these questions: see *Building on Strength*, 46–7. The panel notes that it recommends adoption of the code of the Canadian Centre for Philanthropy largely because of how that code addresses fund-raising companies' practices (46): "It should be noted that adoption of the CCP code would prohibit two controversial practices: percentage based fundraising (ie., where the fundraising company takes a percentage of the money raised, rather than a flat fee) and the selling of donor lists."

59 See, for example, part III of Alberta's Charitable Fund-raising Act, which aims to facilitate acts of the donor fund-raiser by not subjecting him or her to the rules on solicitation. Thus, for example, it relaxes disclosure rules, since section 33 provides that a reasonable fee for providing information about the charity may be charged and information withheld if the fee is not paid.

60 The panel drew on figures prepared by Michael Hall of the Canadian Centre of Philanthropy to the effect that "[t]he average cost of fund-raising as a proportion of monies raised is 26 percent; however, 50 percent of charities have fund-raising costs of 12 percent or less of revenues raised." There is a rich literature on the pros and cons of controlling the proportion of spending by charities devoted to fund-raising. See S. Rose-Ackerman, "Charitable Giving and 'Excessive' Fund-raising," in S. Rose-Ackerman, ed., *The Economics of Nonprofit Institutions: Studies in the Structure and Policy* (New York: Oxford University Press, 1986), 333. See also R. Steinberg, "Should Donors Care about Fund-raising?" in ibid., 347, and "Economic Perspectives on Regulation of Charitable Solicitation," *Case Western Reserve Law Review* 39 (1989), 775. The article that arguably launched the contemporary discussion was K. Karst, "The Efficiency of the Charitable Dollar: An Unfulfilled State Responsibility," *Harvard Law Review* 73 (1960), 433. See also J. Harvey and K. McCrohan, "Fund-raising Cost–Societal Implications for Philanthropies and Their Supporters," *Business and Society* (1988), 15. More recently, the subject has been explored again by L. Espinoza, "Straining the Quality of

Mercy: Abandoning the Quest for Informed Charitable Giving," *Southern California Law Review* 64 (1991), 605.

61 The recent notorious case of Alexander Yashin, who made a gift to the National Arts Centre in Ottawa linked to the employment of his parents, illustrates the kind of quandary that can face charities.

62 Panel, *Building on Strength*, 48.

63 National Committee, Model and Standards, article VII.

64 See Bourgeois, *Law*, 222.

65 Panel, *Building on Strength*, 11; see also 24.

66 See, for example, *Dodge v. Ford Motor Company* 1709 NW 668 (1919).

67 See Bougeois, *Law*, 223ff., for an account of the regulation of charitable gaming.

68 Panel, *Building on Strength*, 49: "The second concern relates to direct competition from governments for fundraising dollars. The voluntary sector has long felt the impact of massive fundraising campaigns by the large institutional charities – hospitals and universities – that may scoop up millions of dollars from a community in a single campaign, earning them the reputation as fundraising 'trawlers' among a fleet of dinghies. We are not disputing that the needs of hospitals and universities are legitimate and are growing given the cutbacks in government support most have experienced, but we encourage them to discuss and coordinate in advance their major campaigns with other voluntary organizations in the community. In addition, governments themselves are turning to fundraising from the public, rather than using general tax revenues, to pay for special needs, such as ice storm relief, or particular projects, such as the Canada Innovation Foundation or wildlife conservation. Although the intent is not to undermine donations to the voluntary sector, such competition seems like a triple whammy given the simultaneous government downloading of services and funding cuts of recent years. As noted in our earlier discussion of capacity building, we urge governments to engage in a discussion and reach some understanding with sector leaders about direct government competition for fundraising."

69 McGill, *Handbook of Regulations and Policies for Academic Staff.* Staff members are not to undertake "substantial consulting" without the written approval of their chairs and deans. As a guideline, activity in excess of four working days per month is normally considered substantial.

70 Canadian Centre, Ethical Fundraising, s. 2.

17 Framing an Appropriate Corporate Law

DAVID STEVENS

Probably the predominant form of organization for charities in Canada is the non-profit corporation. It is not known how many organizations are constituted as unincorporated associations, so this form may be as common as or more common than the corporation. In the commercial sector its equivalents are the sole proprietorship and the partnership. The unincorporated association, like its two equivalents, is relatively easy to form and has few formalities concerning its governance. Its legal nature and its proper mode of governance however, are unclear. Its basic governing law is agency law. One might think that its articulation would replicate, with appropriate adaptations, the law of partnership, but it is not at all certain that such is the case. Like its two equivalents, the unincorporated association has no legal personality and therefore no civil capacity. Its members have no general protection against liability contracted or engaged on their behalf by their executive, so what limited liability protection they have must depend on the principles of agency law.

Despite the obvious deficiencies in the basic law governing the unincorporated association,[1] the focus of this chapter is the non-profit corporation.[2] Although both forms of organization badly need reform in almost all Canadian jurisdictions, the corporation is the more critical case.[3] For in both cases the legal framework is inadequate, but corporation law frequently gets in the way.[4] If, as this chapter argues, government's principal role in the sector is facilitative, then it not only fails to facilitate but actually frustrates.

The non-profit corporation has been the subject of several sustained efforts at reform in Canada.[5] One or two attempts have been successful;[6]

most have not.[7] Research on this form of organization and legal development in this area now lag far behind its business counterpart. The wave of reform of the business corporation that began with the Lawrence Report in Ontario in 1967[8] and ended with enactment of modern corporations statutes in almost all Canadian jurisdictions has been a major success.[9] Those reforms made the corporate form more accessible, principally by discarding many incoherent English legal doctrines and creating workable and responsive structures of governance. A similar reform is now long overdue in the non-profit sector.

In this chapter, I survey issues affecting the design of law for the non-profit corporation and suggest a framework for and some of the principles of reform. The desideratum should be a law that readily and clearly addresses the organizational needs (in a corporate form) of the sector. Surprisingly, very little theoretical writing on the corporation, in either its for-profit or its non-profit form, addresses normative questions with this goal in mind. If (as I assume) the main value of lawyers to society lies in their ability to design and implement workable and useful structures of co-operation and co-ordination (in both market and government), legal writing on the corporation ought to consider design of the appropriate corporate law.[10] It focuses instead on the subsidiary issue of fiduciary accountability.[11] Like much other writing in the social sciences, it concentrates on facts that fit the research paradigm rather than on how people actually live and work.

This chapter has two main sections – on barriers in the way of reform and on the design of a proper statute. The barriers are political (government inertia) and intellectual (poor conceptualization in English law, the perennial mix-up of trust law with corporate law, and overemphasis on fiduciary responsibility). Section 2 looks at definition and attributes, at formation, at governance, and at fundamental changes, including dissolution. Because of recent reform of U.S. law on non-profit corporations, I draw heavily on that experience. For reasons that I adduce in due course, I think that the *Revised Model Nonprofit Corporation Act* (*Revised Model Act*), published by the American Bar Association (ABA) in 1987, would be an excellent starting point for reform in Canada.[12] Even if many aspects of that act are not appropriate for Canada, there is much to learn from it and from the process that generated it.[13]

BARRIERS TO REFORM

Government Inertia

There needs to be greater understanding about the role of government, especially on the part of government, in the non-profit sector and clearer identification of what government can and cannot do and what it should and should not do. It should be possible to identify the nature of the relationship between government and the sector in such a way that policy can be expressed on key matters and at a level of generality that leaves open the perennial questions, while contributing concretely and positively to the work of the sector. Unfortunately there is very little writing on the relationship between the state and the "third" sector, and what little there is tends to place too great an emphasis on the sector's tax privileges.

I suggest the following as the four key elements of the government's role in the sector. The first two are based on the sector's interests, priorities, or objectives; the second two, on the state's interests, priorities, or objectives. First, government should do what it is capable of doing to facilitate charitable and other non-profit activity. Principally, this means providing clear, applicable legislative formulations of the basic association laws of the sector to the extent that either actors in the sector designing their own arrangements themselves or courts supplementing legislative activity by applying general rules in concrete contexts cannot do so more effectively. Given the complexity of association laws, it is fairly obvious that government should play a very substantial role here. These laws are the sector's legal infrastructure without which it would be virtually impossible for the sector to function. Second, government should do what it can to help the sector by also contributing to its work in non-intrusive ways. It could use its law-making and taxing powers to fund research and education, to provide infrastructure to encourage co-operation or co-ordination of activities (by funding umbrella organizations, for example), and to enhance the sector's credibility (by running appropriate licensing or certification regimes, for example). Third, government should protect the sector against fraudulent or deceptive activities by taking specific protective measures in line with the Crown's traditional *parens patriae* jurisdiction. Although the contours of such regulatory activity would be distinctive, it relates to government interest in detection and prevention of fraud generally. Fourth, government should police its own expenditures in the sector – tax deductions and exemptions and grants – to ensure that they remain properly targeted and effective.

Canadian governments, by and large, have seemed uncertain about their role in the sector. They have tended to *under*emphasize their facilitative, helping, and policing roles; they have tended to *over*emphasize their protective role. A few examples can serve to illustrate this claim.

- The Office of the Public Trustee in Ontario was involved in the 1980s in a series of high-profile cases involving difficult questions in the law of charity, many of which it lost because it took a position that, though technically reasonable, ran contrary to common sense (overemphasis on protective role).[14]

- The governments of Alberta and Canada developed and advanced reform proposals for non-profit corporation law in the 1980s and early 1990s, only to let them fail, for no apparent reason, in the very final stages (underemphasis on facilitative role).[15]
- Similarly, Ontario has not responded to the 1984 recommendations of the Ontario Law Reform Commission (OLRC) on the reform of charitable trust law (underemphasis of facilitative role).[16]
- The federal government brought down a budget in the early 1980s aimed at enhancing scrutiny of the charitable tax expenditure, only to retreat in the face of a substantial backlash (underemphasis on policing).[17]
- The statistical information on the sector available from traditional government sources is notoriously inadequate (underemphasis on helping).
- Many provinces lack an agency to supervise the sector, while those that have one, such as Ontario, divide the public authority over several branches and express the statutory mandate incoherently overemphasizing protection (underemphasis of facilitation and helping, overemphasis of protection).[18]
- The largest source of revenue for most categories of charity is government, yet supervision of government granting in all provinces is minimal (underemphasis on policing).[19]
- Revenue Canada's policing of the sector is notoriously understaffed (underemphasis of policing).

The overall impression created is one of awkwardness and ignorance. Why is this the case? There are perhaps three principal reasons. First, there is a lack of public consensus about the nature, meaning, and worth of the sector and, as a result, about its proper relationship with government.[20] Recently, there has been renewed interest in altruism in economics, philosophy, and sociology and in the non-profit and charity sector in law and political science.[21] Umbrella organizations, professional fund-raising companies, and university management programs have begun to flourish. These developments bode well.[22]

Second, the sector's vocation is to be, in a sense, the *antithesis* of government. Although it seeks to achieve many of the same goals as government – in education, health, research, and so on – it does so by using forms of co-operation that do not involve legal compulsion.

Moreover, because the sector usually acts on a more personal level, it is by nature particular, prejudiced, and discriminatory; it righteously acts on the basis of concrete value judgments or affiliations of an overtly religious, political, ethnic, or social nature. Government policy-makers naturally display little sympathy for this aspect, notwithstanding the current popularity of diversity and multiculturalism. Alternatively, government intervenes in a manner that is ill-informed and clumsy. There is very little of a direct nature that law can do to help working non-profits flourish, and almost nothing it can do to help the failures, yet there can be much harm in trying either.

Third, there is little of *political* value in government's exercising any part of its policy mandate. Few voters see or care about any of the legal infrastructure projects of government, let alone the ones that affect this sector,[23] and the policing and protective activities invariably seem to the sector – the electorate – intrusive and hostile. Why, politicians might wonder, take the chance? They have little to gain from facilitating and helping and much to lose by policing.

Reforming non-profit corporation law is a project that sits squarely within the facilitative mandate. It has surfaced many times. The Lawrence Report in 1967 said that the case for reform was strong and urgent. Yet very little has happened. Some mix of the three types of inertia explains this situation, but perhaps the third is the most important. The reform of law for non-profit corporations – a legal-infrastructure project *par excellence* – would leave completely open the selection of social goals to those who will use it. The new law merely facilitates the activity of others, often in ways that even they, as non-lawyers, do not appreciate. In a political culture where governments are encouraged to "achieve" and are rewarded for their "achievements," politicians may well feel that they have little to gain by devoting precious political capital to provide legal infrastructure for the projects of others,[24] especially in a way that only lawyers will really appreciate.

How to move forward? The only constituency with the resources to encourage governments to act is the legal profession. Only lawyers are fully aware that the current law is inadequate, can explain why it is so, have the influence to encourage its reform, and possess the skill to propose a replacement and the organizational resources to promote its adoption. This seems to have been the realization inspiring the *Revised Model Act*. The ABA's Business Law Section sponsored the process of revision. It commenced its work in 1979 and ended it in 1987, meeting 32 times and sending out over 1,000 exposure drafts for public comment. Michael Hone, reporter for the *Model Nonprofit*

Corporation Act, summarized the deficiencies of the earlier *Model Act* of 1964: "[I]t did not set forth standards of care or loyalty for directors or officers. It did not deal with statutory immunity or protection for directors who acted with due care and did not breach their duty of loyalty. Nor did it provide conflict of interest rules. It did not deal with derivative suits, transfer and purchase of memberships, or the resignation or termination of members. It did not mention delegates or deal explicitly with self-perpetuating boards of directors. It had not been amended to reflect the numerous changes that had occurred in state statutory and case law since its adoption."[25]

These are all defects that typically only a lawyer would see and be able to describe and remedy. The processes of adoption in several states has also been led mainly by lawyers. Invariably, the state bar associations or their committees take up the challenge of moving governments. So perhaps the problem in Canada is that the legal profession has not really done what it should do for the non-profit sector.

Poor Conceptualization

The objective in this section is to clear away some of the clutter in the way of reform so that the goal and means of reform come more clearly into view. First, I described the clutter, and second, I propose a simpler model of the corporation. What I say applies to the concept "corporation" generally, both profit and non-profit, since it is the concept itself that needs clarification.[26] Since most of our experience with the concept is in its commercial instantiation, that is where courts and writers have done most of their thinking. Hence, in what follows, I emphasize examples from that context, but the same points apply to the non-profit corporation.

In summary, my argument is that the corporation is simply a structure of governance created by its participants to facilitate co-operation and co-ordination in the pursuit of a common purpose. It exhibits one important private law feature – limited liability – which does not, contrary to the clutter, require a very complex intellectual apparatus to derive or explain. In particular, it does not require that the corporation be a person or that personhood and limited liability be benefactions of the state.

With those false ideas out of the way, a corporation statute becomes just another codification of a special contract that facilitates the activity of those who choose to enter it. I apply this general argument in generating ideas for reform in the second section of the chapter – for example, by suggesting that it is obvious that incorporation should be available as of right.

The English Model of the Corporation: The Clutter Described The inheritance of Anglo-Canadian legal thinking on the nature of the corporation is pretty close to a disaster.[27] This was perhaps realized, even if left largely unsaid, in Canada's reforms of business corporation law in the 1970s and 1980s. The difficulty that English law had in conceptualizing the corporation is the result in part to its origin in the joint-stock company and, prior to that, in the partnership.[28] Partnership is a centuries-old private-law institution; the limited liability corporation is relatively new. As the latter emerged out of the former, it carried with it inappropriate concepts.

Another element inhibiting conceptualization was overuse of the legal fiction of corporate personality to express the effects of incorporation. This reliance has added a layer of concepts – such as *ultra vires* and piercing the corporate veil – that are both irrelevant and misleading.

A third contributing element is the process of law making in the common law tradition. Generally speaking, the tradition is not capable of defining complex concepts clearly, since neither the courts nor reforming/responding legislators are often asked to think about and define all the necessary elements of the concept at once. The method instead is incremental and unsystematic in its process and external and consequentialist (rather than internal and coherentist) in its normativity. The result is that complex concepts, such as "corporation," are badly defined, and the poor definition becomes embedded deeply in legal thinking, on the odd principle that the older the precedent, the stronger its value. Paradoxically, if not unexpectedly, the result is a body of law that frustrates the very activity it is, in theory, intended to facilitate.

If one compares the state of conceptualization of the corporation to modern accounting techniques, the contrast in methods and definitions is remarkable. The comparison is apt. Lawyers and accountants belong to "helping" professions, so it is useful to see how they construct their tools. The law attempts to state the formal or legal relationship among the participants in the corporation, and accountancy, the financial state of the underlying business, both with a view to facilitating the co-operative activity. In the mid-18th century, accounting standards "were inconsistent to the point of chaos."[29] Companies, for example, created opportunities for dividends by simply not depreciating their assets. The British Parliament intervened in 1868 with a modest and specific reform, but chaos continued until the development of professional accounting standards by professional associations in the United States, the United Kingdom, and eventually Canada. The Generally Accepted Accounting Principles (GAAP) that emerged, articulated systematically in Canada in the Canadian Institute of Chartered Accountants' *CICA Handbook* as either basic principles or specific rules, is a highly rational system; while it is not perfect or complete, it is as free as possible, intentionally and by great effort, from irrelevant or irrational concepts. The drafters of this statement, like the drafters of a civil code, tried to be as conceptually rigorous and simple as the subject matter permitted in order to state as clearly as possible the governing norms. In the process, they discarded old conceptualizations that did not work.

Conversely, in a precedent-based conceptual system, the old ideas retain their normative status, and ancient, irrational ideas at the foundation retain their influence. In such a system, there really is no hope of ever stating the formal relationships succinctly and clearly. As good (conceptually) as the modern Canadian business corporation statutes are, most of them still prevent a clear statement of the internal legal relations in the corporation by imposing the greatest possible judicial discretion on the participants in the form of the oppression remedy. The same failure can be seen in modern corporate litigation, which leaves many elementary questions of corporate law unanswered:

- We do not know what a share is.[30]
- We do not know what obligations directors owe.[31]
- We do not know who the creditor(s) of these obligations are.[32]
- We are not certain whether "stakeholders" other than shareholders are also beneficiaries of legal claims against the corporation.[33]
- We are not certain what is meant by "corporate personality" and in what circumstances it can be ignored.
- We are unsure whether shareholders have rights against each other.[34]

I describe the basic confusion in order to contrast it with a much simpler and, I believe, more accurate conceptualization in the next section. Since the inheritance is largely English, it is simplest to do this by examining corporations in what might be called the "English model."[35] Corporation statutes in that tradition provide typically that the memorandum of association and the articles, when registered, bind the company and its members "as though each had signed them." This allusion to agreement establishes a contractual basis for the corporation.[36] This foundation in contract, first, allocates powers between the shareholders and directors, as subject to the terms and conditions of the memorandum of association, not of the statute;[37] and, second, it vests residual authority in the corporation with the shareholders.[38]

This contractual basis, however, exists alongside four other foundational rules, established in a series of well-known decisions. The effect of the rules is to make the contract characterization seriously misleading and to make the ultimate conceptualization completely and utterly confusing.

Foss v. Harbottle[39] held that the corporation was not the same thing as the aggregate of its members and that a wrong done to it – such as misapplication of funds by directors for their own benefit, as in that case – had to be vindicated by the corporation, not by individual shareholders suing on behalf of the shareholders. Later cases extended the holding to a range of corporate irregularities, which, construed exclusively as wrongs to the corporation, were held to be under the ultimate control of the corporation. There are two rules in this line of jurisprudence – first, the corporation is a separate legal person from its shareholders, and, second, shareholders, as shareholders, have no standing to sue for wrongs done to the separate legal person.[40] The second rule does not necessarily follow from the first – it depends on the rights constituting a share. I leave that issue aside for the moment and observe only that the fiction of legal personality (the first rule) was used in this line of cases to reason, inappropriately, to the second result.[41]

Northwest Transportation v. Beatty[42] held that a majority of shareholders is able to ratify a voidable transaction entered between the company and a director. *Burland v. Earle* affirmed and extended the holding.[43] In *Burland,* Lord Davey formulated an "internal management rule" pursuant to which courts must eschew interference with the internal management of the corporation. In *Pender v. Lushington,*[44] Lord Jessel, MR, articulated the same principles as a "selfish ownership rule," so that shareholders may vote their shares as they please, without regard to the interests of other shareholders. Recent decisions have continued in this line. The courts in *Hogg v. Cramphorn*[45] and *Bamford v. Bamford,*[46] for example, held that the general meeting could ratify directors' breaches of their duty.

These and other cases imply a third rule: all aspects of the contract establishing the corporation, except any possible public-order provision, are amendable by majority vote or, in some circumstances, by special or extraordinary resolution. This means that the majority constitutes the will of the corporation and, therefore, that the directors of the corporation are, in some sense, agents of that majority.[47] A fourth and final rule, first articulated in *Percival v. Wright,*[48] states that the director owes his or her duty directly and exclusively to the corporation.

These in essence are the elements of the English model. There is an obvious logical tension here between its claims variously that the corporation is a contract, that it is the majority, and that it is a separate person with a will.[49] In fact the model is radically incoherent. For example, if the corporation is a contract, then why doesn't the minority shareholder who is harmed by the director's breach have a right to enforce it? Or, if the corporation is a separate person from the shareholders for the purposes of limited liability, then how can the shareholders ratify – as though they were principals – the wrongs of the directors?[50]

It is not possible, and therefore not advisable, for a legislature enacting an infrastructure law to facilitate for-profit or not-for-profit co-operative activity not to challenge these elements. The reform has to start from the ground up, with reconceptualization of what is happening juridically in the concept "corporation." I suggest the following model as a start.

The Revised Model The revised model proposed here (which we might call "legal" because of its emphasis on coherent legal analysis) presents all five principal attributes of the modern business corporation – perpetual existence, limited liability, separation of ownership and management, free transferability of shares, and legal personality – together with all the accompanying rights and duties as the outcome of contracts between real persons. The institution has certain essential elements, the absence of which renders what has been created by the parties or by the governing statute not a "corporation." Although this "legal model" would shape corporation statutes, like the special-contracts provisions of civil codes, the statutes may also contain a wide variety of other imperative and suppletive provisions.

The basic concept would work out a little differently for non-profit corporations. Although I seek here to apply this basic analysis to the non-profit, I start with the business corporation, which drives all the precedents, fix it at the foundational level, and then adapt it to the non-profit context. So, in the arguments that follow, I refer to "shares" and "shareholders," not "members" and "membership."

Of the five attributes of the modern corporation, limited liability is the most central. It legaly obliges the corporate patrimony to answer for obligations incurred by others, and renders other apparent candidates for the liability, such as shareholders, directors, and employees, not as such liable. The proposed new definition must therefore provide a coherent and accurate account of limited liability. That concept can be constructed out of simple contracts between real persons as follows.

The first shareholders of the corporation contract with each other in order to establish and dedicate a patrimony in which each has a "share" but no direct right of ownership or extensive power of administration. The contract dedicates the patrimony to the capitalization of a defined business administered by "directors," selected in accordance with the contract. The contract establishes that the shareholders are not agents of each other: no shareholder, *as shareholder*, need answer for the civil obligations incurred by any other shareholder, and no *shareholder* is a fiduciary of any other shareholder. The shareholders, in short, are not mutual agents, as they would be if the contract were a contract of partnership. Interpreted strongly, the absence of a fiduciary relationship renders the identity of a holder of a share irrelevant to the determination of his or her rights.

The directors are elected by the shareholders and appointed under a (second) contract that obliges and benefits only the corporate patrimony. The directors promise to manage the patrimony with care and loyalty; to distribute the patrimony in accordance with the "share" entitlements established; to abide by all the other terms and conditions of the shareholders' contract; and, in managing the patrimony, to act to maximize its net present value within a given range of risk.[51] The contract establishes that the directors are not agents of the shareholders or of each other and therefore that no juridical act or fact of the directors legally obliges or benefits the shareholders or other directors. The contract also provides that the directors have full power to incur civil obligations for which the corporate patrimony alone is charged or benefited.

These two contracts contain all the elements required to establish a corporation. They are entered simultaneously[52] at incorporation in a "bootstrap" operation – the certificate of incorporation – that establishes shares and shareholders, the separate patrimony, and the administrators of that patrimony simultaneously. With the two contracts in place, limited liability works as follows.

Contract creditors of the corporation contract with the directors or with others authorized by the directors to enter contracts charging or benefiting the corporate patrimony. The contracts provide that only the corporate patrimony, not the director(s) or the corporate agent,[53] is charged with or benefits from the contractual obligation. Hence limited liability in respect of the corporation's contractual obligations. If an agent of the corporation commits a tort in the performance of his or her duty, the tort creditor, of course, may sue the agent. The tort creditor may also, pursuant to the legal doctrine *respondeat superior*, recover from the corporation. This is because the ultimate liability of any principal for the torts of their agent arises out of the principal's promise to indemnify the agent (in the contract of agency) for losses that he or she suffers in the course of his employment. The claim by the tort creditor against the principal can be derived as follows: if the agent is liable, the tort creditor is entitled to be compensated out of the agent's patrimony; one element of value in that patrimony is the principal's promise to indemnify the agent against harm arising from that precise claim; and the agent can compensate the tort creditor, in part, by transferring that promise.

It is a small, but conceptually difficult step from this deduction to conclude that the tort creditor can sue the principal directly. We do not need to develop the remainder of that argument here, however, since our present objective is to understand limited liability. Whatever the further argument may be, a tort creditor cannot recover against the directors or shareholders, since no agent of the corporation is by virtue of that fact an agent of the directors or of the shareholders, and therefore there is no promise by directors and shareholders to indemnify the tortfeasor/agent. Hence limited liability in respect of the tort obligations of the corporation.

In summary, the first two contracts create a separate patrimony with administrators. The incidents of ownership of the property in the patrimony are distributed between the directors, who have the power to administer, and the shareholders, who have supervisory rights and a residual proprietary interest. All four elements of the argument together show that the separate patrimony may be charged with civil obligations, as though it were a principal, a real person. Because of the two effects – separate patrimony and status of principal – the network of contracts establishes a juridical operation that manifests the main attributes of civil personality. Consequently, it makes sense to use the fictional expression "corporate personality" and to speak of "the corporation" as though it were a real person. The expressions substitute for the more complex legal description just sketched. However, because they are fictions, they cannot serve as the basis for analysis in any seriously difficult case.

The other two incidents of incorporation flow from what is established above. Transferability of shares follows from the not–mutual-agent provision of the first contract. Partnership statutes typically state, as suppletive rules, that new partners may not be introduced without the consent of all[54] and that assignees of partnership interests may not exercise the full rights of partners.[55] The restrictions on admission to membership in the partnership are established, suppletively, because the legislator presumes that people do not enter contracts of mutual agency with just anyone. However, since shareholders are not mutual agents, there is no reason why admission to that status should depend on anything other than the desire to pay the price of admission. The first contract, I suggest, thus establishes free transferability as being of the essence of the corporation. This conclusion may be too strong, however, since many corporation statutes permit the articles of incorporation to restrict transferability.[56] There are two ways to accommodate this reality: do not interpret the not–mutual-agents term so strongly, and thereby relax the status of the free transferability rule to suppletive or partially suppletive; or, as I prefer, establish some other juridical basis for the statutory rules that permits restrictions on transfer. One such formula would be to construe restrictions on transfer of shares as akin to restrictive covenants – restrictions on ownership, created by contract, but binding on third parties with notice.[57]

Perpetual existence also tends to follow from what is established above. If the shares are freely transferable, and if the administrators are replaceable by simple election, the continued "existence" of the corporation is not contingent on the life of any real person and therefore may, just like a purpose trust, be perpetual.

At the foundation of this conceptualization is the claim that the corporation is a voluntary co-operative endeavour that deploys a patrimony for defined purposes. Directors or fiduciaries manage the patrimony under the supervision of shareholders. Limited liability ends up not being the puzzle that economists portray it to be; juridically, it is the basic regime, since no one is responsible for the juridical acts or facts of another, unless there is a legal reason to shift liability. Agency and master–servant contracts contain the legal apparatus that do this in some cases – the promise to indemnify – but few if any other legal relationships do. The corporation certainly does not.

The reorientation that this model provides to legislators is quite fundamental. First, it says that they are not engaged in an act of state benefaction of some special privilege of limited liability or, what is worse, of personhood. Second, it says rather that their task is to discern the elements of this contract – its imperative and suppletive terms – so that what they come up with can serve private purposes on an off-the-shelf, ready-to-use-basis. The imperative terms are those that flow from the essence and/or that the state imposes for purposes of public order. Usually the suppletive terms identify typical intentions of the parties to this type of contract. Occasionally terms are suppletive in that they provide guidance for a court intervention in a usual kind of case. Third, it tells us that the lawyers who engage in the drafting of this foundational contract will have to have great familiarity with how these co-operative endeavours typically work so that they can define the elements at the right level of detail, in the correct normative – imperative or suppletive – voice. In sum, the legislator can do this job properly only if there is no irrelevant historical legal baggage attached, so that people with vast experience of how things typically work can construct the real contract.

Mix-up of Corporate and Trust Law

The third significant barrier in the way of proper reform is again legal in nature. Some of non-profit corporation law is or has been too much influenced by the law of trusts.[58] Courts have felt compelled to refer to trust law in order to find norms to govern charitable non-profit corporations in the apparent absence of appropriate norms in some situations.[59] In particular, in the absence of an appropriate set of rules governing self-interested transactions (and of a public administration with a coherent mandate), Canadian courts treat directors as trustees, then apply the severe trustee rule, which requires prior court approval for all self-interested transactions.

In *Toronto Humane Society*, Justice Anderson said: "Whether one calls them trustees in the pure sense (and it would be a blessing if for a moment one could get away from the problems of terminology), the directors are undoubtedly under a fiduciary obligation to the Society and the Society is dealing with funds solicited or otherwise obtained from the public for charitable purposes. If such persons pay themselves, it seems only proper that it should be upon terms which alone a trustee can obtain remuneration, either by express provision in the trust documents or by the order of the court. The latter would appear to be the only practical mechanism." Likewise, a leading American authority on trust law prevaricates: "The truth is that it cannot be stated dogmatically that a charitable corporation either is or is not a trustee ... Ordinarily the rules that are applicable to trusts are applicable to charitable corporations ... although some are not. It is probably more misleading to say that a charitable corporation is not a trustee than to say that it is, but the statement that it is a trustee must be taken with some qualifications."[60]

Although the main problem involves self-interested transactions, there are other areas that may require supplementary principles from trust law. For example, an improper expenditure of corporate funds would put the directors in breach of their duty and render them liable to reimburse the corporation for the loss caused by the breach. It is often said that this liability originates in trust law, but it actually derives from corporate law. The reference to trust law is redundant.

A second set of problems arises when the corporation dissolves or undergoes fundamental change. Trust law controls the disposition of property devoted to charitable purposes in these circumstances, but the corporate law statutes often do not, sometimes leaving apparently no restriction on rededication of the charitable property. Here the observed deficiency is real, and the solution must originate in a better-drafted corporate statute appropriate to the needs of the sector.

Properly formulated corporate law has no need of concepts from trust law. Borrowings only confuse lay users of the statute, who have difficulty enough grasping their responsibilities as directors, without being told that they are also, in some unspecified sense, trustees. This is just sloppy law-making – an example of the facilitating law getting in the way. To be sure, the legislator should heed analogies to other pertinent institutions of private law, but the final expression should use concepts appropriate to the association being designed.

Distracted by Subsidiary Issues

A good deal of contemporary academic writing on the corporation deals with the responsibility of fiduciaries. Questions relating to the design of governing structures of private institutions, both profit and non-profit, focus on the identification of the constituency to which corporate fiduciaries should answer and on the legal and market techniques of their accountability.[61] This strain of analysis seeks to minimize the costs of agency, which consist of the cost of monitoring the agent's performance, the cost to the agent of making his or her promises to perform credible, and the residual cost to the principal of the agent's shirking and looting.

Agency cost theory recognizes that design is crucial, since its explicit aim is to reduce the costs of co-operation and co-ordination. But the theory does not give design adequate attention, since it ignores the fact that people come together in associations to pursue *purposes*. It would seem obvious that the purposes pursued should shape the design of any organizational structure, as constrained by (the limited number of) basic forms of co-operation and co-ordination available. Those designing an associational law should therefore first identify the categories of purposes that are to be served. The old non-profit corporation statutes fail to differentiate intelligently among non-profit purposes, a point to which I return in the second section. The weakness of much economic writing on the corporation is its inability to differentiate at all. This failure is characteristic of consequentialist moral theories, which tend to collapse all value into a single fungible or commensurable unit – here, "non-profit." This reductionism derives from the logic of economics itself. At its core, economics is a science of waste reduction. Thus the usual form of a good economic argument is: given goal "x," the cheapest way to pursue it is ... The inherent desirability and therefore the nature of goal "x" are irrelevant, since "x" is always assumed or given in the analysis.

The economic reduction of all purposes to the placeholder "non-profit" is really rather stunning, if the value of the sector lies in its value judgments, prejudices, and affiliations and if the point of the discussion is to discover the corporate law regime that facilitates pursuit of these values. Investigations must consider the costs of agency, but they have to be far more comprehensive than that. Ultimately, successful design must pursue those values effectively. No discussion can succeed that ignores them completely by reducing them to "non-profit."

The peculiarly non-economic dimensions of altruistic behaviour (charitable non-profits) and of co-operative behaviour (political and mutual-benefit non-profits) compound this initial error. The economic approach assumes that rational behaviour consists in maximizing some (assumed) good for oneself – that it is self-interested in a selfish, possessive way.[62] Of course people do behave this way much of the time, so that it is often a useful starting point for social analysis. Altruistic behaviour, however, is its antithesis, since it seeks the maximization of some good for someone else. Co-operative behaviour – the mutual pursuit of a common purpose – is also fundamentally different. Instead of adjusting the social analysis to accommodate distinctive types of behaviour or distinctive motivational frameworks, economic analysis of the non-profit frequently simply assumes away their existence. It frequently assumes that *all* behaviour must be self-interested so that altruism is merely a "consumption preference" and co-operation is merely exchange.

Henry Hansmann provides an illustration of the economic approach: "[T]he charter of a nonprofit corporation serves a rather different purpose than does the charter of a business corporation. In a business corporation, the charter, and the statutory and decisional law in which it is embedded, serves primarily to protect the interests of the corporation's shareholders from invasion by those immediately in control of the corporation, including management and other shareholders. In a nonprofit corporation, on the other hand, the restrictions imposed on contracting individuals by the charter and the law are primarily for the benefit of the organization's patrons. As a consequence, business corporation law is often a poor model for nonprofit corporation law."[63]

Both of the erroneous tendencies are on display here – the assumptions, first, that the objective of corporate law is to reduce agency costs and, second, that the material difference between shareholders and patrons is that the former are providers of capital and the latter are consumers of the good of their (inscrutable) choice, altruism. My alternative suggestion is, first, that corporate law facilitates the co-operative pursuit of a common purpose, and second, that, despite important differences between the non-profit corporation and its for-profit counterpart, construing patrons as consumers does not identify the relevant point of distinction. To the contrary, patrons *give* and in so giving provide the capital for the altruistic endeavour. They are thus exactly analogous to shareholders, since they are the primary source of "equity" capital. Hansmann eschews the patron–shareholder analogy in favour of the patron–consumer equivalence, presumably because he rejects the concept "altruism": his patron is a customer, a purchaser of the commodity altruism, presumably because he cannot conceive of anybody's financing the well-being of others. Imagine! What they really must be doing is buying some commodity.

The altruism-as-commodity model distorts much of the subsequent analysis. Hansmann argues, for example, that in the case of non-profit entities that provide services for the needy or public goods, "the need for fiduciary organization is so obvious that for-profit firms are virtually unheard of."[64] Donors need reassurance that their donations are actually purchasing (the commodity) "poor-relief," and such like. The alternative analysis is that the "profit" is simply "competed" away, since the most successful altruistic organization is the one that gives the most it possibly can. The objective of the donor is to maximize altruism, not profit on a capital investment. Or, to put it another way, the altruism is, in a sense, the profit, and the donor the investor. A companion error in the analysis is the suggestion that there is any choice about the fiduciary obligation of the fiduciary *once* it is decided to engage in any co-operative pursuit, including the co-operative pursuit of altruism. In every co-operative enterprise, tasks will be distributed or delegated; fiduciaries are obliged to do only what they have undertaken, just like leftwingers, goalies and defencemen in ice hockey. It is the objective or purposes of the co-operative effort that define the tasks, and it is the agreement of the parties that distributes them.

THE ELEMENTS OF AN APPROPRIATE DESIGN

Having identified four significant barriers in the way of reform, I now seek to identify some of the main principles of that reform. My discussion is at the level of principles, or basic elements, not of details and is therefore more of an agenda for reform than a prescription for specific statutory rules. The first subsection sets out four design principles for drafting the statute; the remaining four subsections take up the specific issues of definition and attributes, of formation, of governance, and of fundamental changes, including dissolution.

Design Principles

I suggest four design principles, some of which flow out of the previous discussion and all of which I intend to aid in the implementation of the state's objective of facilitating non-profit activity by providing an appropriate corporate law.

Different Types of Statutory Rules Common lawyers tend to write and read statutes as though the law speaks a kind of monotonic normativity. Rules in statutes drafted in the common law tradition are written and read as though they express norms of the same type and more or less at the same level of generality. Even in statutes in which there is quite evidently a structure provided by chronology, concept, or other ordering principles, the writer or reader may not be aware that this is the case. This normative flatness results from the tradition's empirical and pragmatic mentality: common law norms are almost always first articulated in a factual, not a conceptual setting (in judicial decisions, as opposed to a professor's study), and its statutes are drafted as compilations of these rules or responses to or remediations of them, as opposed to attempts to articulate sound juridical concepts. Some of the more successful statutes in recent years, such as the personal property security statutes, work precisely because they ground the legislative product in rigorously defined general concepts, which in turn determine or control the expression of the specific rules. These statutes show a conceptual awareness that is new to the tradition.

Statutes that establish an organic law of a type of association should be grounded in explicit awareness of the essence of the juridical entity that they instantiate. There will thus be rules in the statute that define the association and that state its characteristic attributes. There must also be rules governing the three stages of its "existence": its creation, its governance, and its reorganization and dissolution. This division of subject mater supplies the basic structure of the statute.

The rules in each of these parts, in turn, will be of four types: imperative as a matter of public policy, imperative as a matter of essence or real definition, suppletive for the members of the institution, and suppletive for adjudicators called on to resolve conflicts that arise during the entity's "existence." Some of these rules will be general, and some, very specific. The drafter must be sensitive to this variety of rule types in a way that common law drafting, compared to the drafting of civil codes, typically is not. He or she will also have to be careful to identify both rules that are regulatory – that is, that seek to constrain the behaviour of the entity or its members for reasons unrelated to organic law – and rules that pertain to the object at hand – that is, that identify and state the imperative and suppletive rules. The former will typically appear in a law applicable to the sector as a whole, not in the associational law.

Several Types of Corporation Private law institutions are related hierarchically. The general idea "contract" is related to the ideas "contract of sale" and "contract of lease" as general to specific. However, although the specific participates in the essence of the general, it also has imperative (essential) elements of its own. The common law tends to collapse these hierarchies *and* to overlook specificity. The law of contract, for example, has no notion of special contract and thus no explicit doctrinal awareness of the hierarchy, and it is reluctant to recognize that each of the special contracts – sale and lease, for example – has imperative (essential) elements of its own. The latter failing emerges in the poor definitions of the relevant private law institution and is of a piece with general reluctance to state real definitions.

Awareness of hierarchy and specificity is also missing in Canadian corporate law. In the legislation of Canada, Ontario, and Quebec, for example, the current non-profit corporation law appears in short parts of a general statute applicable to all types of corporation. These older statutes express a few non-profit rules in a separate part, relying on a general part to be read, *mutatis mutandi*.[65] They thus assume that individual variations are all contingent, like the difference between the corporation General Motors and the corporation Sears, as opposed to the essential, as in the difference between sale and lease.

The facilitative objective requires clear articulation of the distinctive essential rules of the non-profit form. This difference is located mostly in the difference between the juridical interest of the participant in a for-profit corporation – the "share" – and that of a participant in a non-profit – "membership." Although the golf course and IBM are both corporations, a person who is both a member of the first and a shareholder of the latter does not regard that sameness to express the whole truth on the juridical logic of his or her participation. Implications flow from the basic distinction between a membership and a share that reverberate through the whole statute. Therefore separate statutes are required.

As an aside, the distinctiveness of these forms of association may also have implications for other areas of private law that apply to them. For example, many non-profits rely on the services provided by volunteers, and volunteering, as a social phenomenon, is largely restricted to non-profits. People lend a hand in circumstances calling for altruism, and non-profits provide them with the means to do so. These are important social facts, which may imply that the private law which expresses this relationship has to be distinctive. What is the private law relationship between the organization and the volunteer? The private law categories that come to mind are employment, agency and/or the contract for services. Are the rules on *respondeat superior* in these special contracts applicable to the organization–volunteer relationship? Are the rules of civil responsibility applicable to the actions of volunteers in the way that they apply to employees, agents, and providers of services? Recent developments in the United States suggest that they may not be. The U.S. Congress "immunized" volunteers from tort liability in certain circumstances.[66] Several state legislatures have done the same.[67]

Various Activities The law should be designed with the unique non-profit characteristics in mind. As one commentator noted many years ago: "An evaluation of the legal framework for not-for-profit corporations therefore invokes different considerations from those relevant to the business corporation for three reasons. First, there is a fundamental difference in purpose between a corporation formed for a non-pecuniary purpose as compared to one formed for a pecuniary purpose which calls for essentially different statutory provisions. Secondly, the uses to which not-for-profit corporations as a group are being put are considerably more varied than the uses of business corporation. Thirdly, the functional distinctiveness of the non-pecuniary purpose corporation calls for statutory language suitable to its unique non-commercial charities."[68]

The majority of the rules in the statute will be suppletive, and, of the suppletive rules, the majority will be suppletive for the parties. The juridical logics of "corporation" and "membership" will inform the design of many rules and will feature prominently in some parts of the statute. There are likely to be few public order rules, as most such issues pertain to the sector as a whole and therefore should be the subject of separate regulatory instruments. Therefore the main contribution of the statute will be its suppletive rules, and their quality will be a function mainly of the drafter's awareness of the patterns of activity in the sector that bear on the creation, governance, and reorganization and dissolution of this type of entity.

The Ideal "Informed User" Most statutes address exclusively persons with legal training, because of their complex subject matter (tax law) and sometimes merely because of their (unnecessarily) complex legal thought (the sale of goods). The non-profit corporation's statute should address principally the ideal "informed user," who need not be a lawyer. People conducting associational activity may not have easy access to lawyers with expertise in the area or may have access only to a lawyer-member of the association, who has no specialist knowledge. The typical informed user has no legal education but sufficient sophistication to manage the process of incorporating and launching an organization. As much as possible, the statute should be addressed to that person. To the extent that rules relating to corporate law or non-profit corporate law have to be drafted for the legal specialist, the specialist should be the generalist lawyer and, for some provisions, the generalist corporate lawyer.

Thus the statute should have a clear structure and accessible language. It should not leave the user to design organizational rules on any key or complex question but should provide these clearly in a set or sets of suppletive rules. The older statutes are often silent on matters on which they should say something, if only of a suppletive nature. For example, the current federal statute leaves matters dealing with election of directors to be established in by-laws, since the analogous rules applicable to the other types of corporation covered by the statute – sections 86–92 and 94–7 – do not apply to non-profits.[69] These rules must be set out in a by-law, which then requires ministerial approval both on the initial application for incorporation and upon subsequent amendment. This approach, characteristic of the older statutes, violates the principle that the statute should be "user friendly."

Definition and Attributes

Purposes and the Non-profit Principle Economic analysis reduces much of the variety in the sector into a single identifying characteristic, "non-profit." Although that is a valid and useful principle, it is not the only one. Here we look at the relationship between the non-profit principle and the purposes that non-profit corporations pursue.

Statutes for non-profit corporations typically contain three types of rules that touch on or regulate the purposes for which non-profits may be formed. There is, first, the "non-distribution constraint." It prohibits uncompensated distribution of value to members or fiduciaries. Its two elements deal with distributions of benefits both from the corporation during its existence and on dissolution. Second, restrictions on purposes include a prohibition on profit-motivated activity as a principal, as opposed to a subsidiary activity. Often they include more. Third, and closely related to the second, is permission to pursue various purposes, sometimes listed in detail, sometimes left implicit. If a statute lists a set of purposes, then presumably it is forbidding what it omits. All three approaches define or give some content to the term "non-profit."

In keeping with putting purposes first, I look at permitted purposes, then at prohibited purposes, and finally at the non-distribution constraint. The economic approach mistakenly puts this last concept first because of its narrow focus on agency cost – it is the only set of rules that deals with agency cost. In what follows I suggest that permitted purposes must come first in design of the law and that non-distribution is merely one of many implications that flow from the proper identification and articulation of the permitted purposes.

The lists of permitted purposes found in most non-profits' statutes serve two functions. First, it identifies the sectors of society entitled to use this form; second, it provides a technique for varying treatment in the statute for non-profits of the different types identified. Some observers think the first function pointless. Although several U.S. statutes use it,[70] there appears to be a "trend ... in favour of liberalization of purposes."[71] The second function has come into its own only with the third generation of American model acts. It allows for variation in the formulation of rules in four main areas: the fiduciary obligations of directors; the rules governing fundamental changes; the formulation of the non-distribution constraint; and members' rights.

The *Revised Model Act* provides a good illustration of the technique. It uses a three-fold classification of non-profit corporations: public benefit, mutual benefit, and religion.[72] Public benefit corporations purport to act for the public good. For the purposes of corporate law, as opposed to tax law, the category "public benefit" under the *Revised Model Act* includes entities that may not be charitable but which, like a lobbying organization, pursue their version of the public good. The theory of the statute is that all organizations of this type share or should share common structural features. So, for example, membership interest, unlike a share, cannot be sold and cannot be repurchased by the corporation; members' governance rights are not as robust as those of shareholders in a modern for-profit corporation's statute; since public benefit–type corporations attract financing and membership largely on the basis of their specific purposes and projects, rules governing fundamental changes and dissolution are more restrictive (compared to other non-profits), so that the donated property remains dedicated to the specific purposes and projects; and, a higher standard governs directors in regard to their transactions with the organization.

Mutual benefits are, in the theory of the statute, substantially different from public benefit organizations. They are organized for the common advantage of their members. Social clubs, fraternal organizations, and trade associations are the most common examples. Its members often have a significant economic interest at stake in their memberships and hence an enhanced interest to monitor activities. Their governance rights are more substantial, and the controls on fundamental changes and dissolution less restrictive. Religion is obviously distinctive and may even, as in California and New York law, merit its own statute.

The list of permitted purposes turns out to be quite important. If done properly, it serves well *both* functions mentioned above: it both delimits the scope of the statute, by implicitly or explicitly excluding what is off the list, and it provides a framework for rule variations throughout the statute. Older statutes listed items randomly and inclusively, rather than (as the *Revised Model Act* does) conceptually and exhaustively: public benefit, mutual benefit, and religion, the statute claims, is all there is. And, the statute claims, this division is the most appropriate, all things considered, to serve the rule-variation function.

Although I believe the *Revised Model Act*'s list is quite good, my suggestion is not necessarily that it should be adopted. Rather, identifying an exhaustive list of purposes should serve the first function and assist the second. If that is done, and done well, the next two rules are subsidiary.

If the categorization of permitted purposes exhausts the field of non-profit purposes, as some claim, then we are at the boundary between non-profit and for-profit. For the sake of clarity the statute could, and probably should, describe the prohibited areas. The most obvious outsider is commercial or for-profit activity. The statute should therefore probably prohibit pursuit of profit as a principal (though not necessarily as a subsidiary) activity. The statute would be stating the second of two obvious implications of the non-profit principle. Its proper and clear expression requires articulation of the first, more general proposition. Those permitted purposes, in other words, have to be primary in the normative framework of the statute.

Economists identify the non-distribution constraint as the primary norm. The constraint prohibits the non-profit form of organization from distributing its net earnings to its members or fiduciaries. The *second* rule prohibits it from operating at a profit or from engaging in commercial activities aimed at earning a profit. The constraint means only that the beneficiary of any profit may not include the members or fiduciaries. Moreover, it does not prohibit them from earning reasonable remuneration or compensation for services that they provide to the non-profit. Almost all non-profit statutes in Canada express this requirement in one way or another.[73] Any organization that wants to make pecuniary distributions to members should be organized as a co-operative (producer or consumer) or business corporation.

Although this too is an important rule and requires clear statements, like the rule on prohibited purposes it is merely an implication of the larger idea that the organization may pursue only a permitted purpose. The rule on prohibited purposes says "no commercial activity"; this rule says "no selfish pecuniary purposes." These two sets of purposes are outside the permitted purposes.

To articulate the non-distribution constraint properly, one must place the rule on permitted purposes in the normative framework of the statute. Generally speaking, public benefits and religions, to use the scheme of the *Revised Model Act*, should be subject to a general prohibition against either (temporal) type of distribution; mutual benefits, only during their existence. Permitted purposes come first in the normative scheme given their function of facilitating meaningful variation of rules throughout the statute. Moreover, although the non-distribution constraint just stated is generally true, it requires some nuancing, again according to purposes. Religions, for example, should be able to distribute to less well-off members, and a national, umbrella, public benefit organization, to its local or provincial chapters, each individually incorporated. The Saskatchewan statute, for example, negotiates the difficulties well, explicitly excepting this type of distribution in section 31(2). The key point, however, is that all of this requires clear statement of and normative primacy for permitted puposes.

In sum, drafters of the older statutes had none of these three rule types clearly in view. Much less did they recognize the normative primacy of permitted purposes. Consequently, their formulation of the non-profit principle is often a disaster. The current federal and Ontario laws, for example, prohibit "pecuniary gains" by members. What precisely did the legislators mean by this?

Civil Capacity and Powers It is common for corporations' statutes to limit the powers of a corporation. The most fundamental limitation is found in the *ultra vires* doctrine, which restricts a corporation's exercise of civil capacity to its objects, on pain of nullity. The exact import of this type of rule depends on the theory of the corporation informing the statute. There are two basic views: the corporation gets its capacity either on a delegation from its original incorporators with the imprimatur of the state (the English contract model) or from a pure benefaction of the state (the letters patent model).[74] In either case, the "originator" or "creator" of capacity may withhold certain elements. The English model looks at the corporation the first way and interprets the *ultra vires* doctrine as a withholding of capacity by the originators. The English model here slips into a principal–agent characterization of the incorporators–corporation relationship and therefore naturally perceives the objects clauses as stating the agent's mandate (power) in respect of the patrimony. The capacity granted by the state has traditionally been regarded as wider, on the view either that the state is more powerful and/or liberal or that no, or not many powers in respect of the patrimony can have been withheld, because there is no principal or no residual authority to withhold them.[75] However, an *ultra vires* doctrine still occasionally applies to corporations of this type too.

Additional specific restrictions on investment activities and ownership powers also appear in some corporation statutes. Such rules restrict use of a specific power, even for a legitimate object. For example, Ontario used to limit investment activity and land ownership in its corporations law and still does so in its Charitable Gifts Act and its Charities Accounting Act (section 8). Even if it is thought advisable to regulate the investment decisions of non-profit fiduciaries, that regulation should probably not be in the organic law, since it presumably ought to apply to all non-profit fiduciaries, not just those in the corporate context.

The revised theory regards the corporation juridically as a nexus of contracts and not in any sense as a person. The old way, since it regarded the corporation as a person, naturally fell into the view that restrictions on activities should be formulated in terms of civil capacity, as a question of legal power. The only logical sanction for an act in excess of power is nullity. Regarding the corporation instead as essentially an institution of private law, founded in real contracts, facilitates a move away from power–nullity logic to a wider and more reasonable logic of prohibited activity and penalty. If the state, for good or bad, wants to regulate the activity of these people, then let it deploy the latter logic, not the former. There are several practical merits to this approach, in addition to the old theory's falsity. This move also facilitates a shift of this type of regulation out of the corporation statute and into collateral regulatory statutes. (Of course, members or the corporation could still sue directors for breach of their obligation to comply with the constitution.) Henceforth, only those prohibitions that correlate to or reflect rights of members should continue to be expressed in the organic law.

The Corporate Constitution The basic law of the non-profit must have three distinct elements to facilitate activity: the document(s) of its expression (statute, by-laws, articles, and so on); the required and permitted organs (board of directors, officers, members, and so on); and the basic structures of governance and accountability (meetings, elections, and so on). Because the statute is dealing with the structure of a purposive community, it is in essence a constitutional law. How or where should this basic law be expressed? The concern is "constitution" in the sense merely of its mode(s) of expression, not of its substance.

If one refers first to the business context, the constitutional law embodied in the Canadian Business Corporations Act (CBCA) is expressed in the articles of incorporation, in the imperative provisions of the statute, and in the by- laws. The first element establishes only the name, the share structure, the number of directors, and the location of the head office. The second and third are quite extensive. The second, the statute, sets out the imperative rules and facilitates the remainder with optional suppletive rules. The third, by-laws, deals with internal matters such as the frequency and timing of membership meetings, the notice and quorum requirements for such meetings, the election procedures for the board of directors and for the officers of the company, the constitution and mandate of the committees of the board, and amendment procedures.

How does the distinctiveness of the non-profit form play out in the modes of expression of this constitutional law?[76] If we think in terms of the ideal user described above, the statute should require, as a minimum, establishment of the basic organizational structure in the articles of incorporation. Using the *Revised Model Act,* the incorporators indicate which type of corporation they intend – public benefits, mutual, or religious – thereby opting into the imperative and suppletive structures provided in the statute. For similar reasons, the articles or accompanying documents might also require that everything necessary to make the corporation operational, such as appointment of the initial board, be a condition of incorporation. The statute or the regulations under it might also make available several general by-laws, from which the incorporators might select one or be presumed to select one in the absence of some contrary indication. Constitutional law is not as accessible to lay users of a statute, or even to most lawyers, as is, for example, contract law, so that the state might play a greater facilitative and helping role here.

Formation

Discretionary Grant Some degree of regulation of the sector is imposed at the incorporation stage. In Ontario, for example, the Office of the Public Guardian and Trustee and, in some instances, ministries such as Housing, in the case of non-profit housing corporations, routinely review applications for letters patent.[77] The federal practice is for the receiving ministry (Industry) to forward applications to other relevant ministries for review and comment. This all happens because, under the statute, the grant is discretionary.

Its discretionary nature is a remnant of the theory of the corporation as a subject of law created by the state. If this theory is discarded, does reservation of a discretion continue to serve any useful purpose? On the theory of the corporation proposed here, the state is merely facilitating an organizational form by stipulating the conditions for, and elements of, civil capacity and limited liability, and so there does not seem to be any reason (relating to organic law) to issue corporate charters on a discretionary basis. There may, however, be a regulatory objective – for example, restricting use of the word "charity" or ensuring that charitable corporations are subject to some regulatory authority. If so, would this objective find better expression in the corporate law or in a general statute applicable to charities? Should withholding corporate capacity be the consequence of failing to satisfy any relevant condition?

The current administrative regime in Ontario aims at more than protecting the name of charity. Its rationale relates to the protective role of the state. Presumably, no non-profit that purports to be charitable can become incorporated unless it satisfies certain minimum conditions, such as directors' serving without remuneration, and certain minimum standards on dissolution. This type of regulation ought to apply to the sector in general, not just to corporations, and therefore should not usually appear in the corporation statute. That general statute could begin by restricting the use of the word "charity."

The Name Statutes on corporations address the issue of the legal element of the corporate name by prohibiting the use of certain words ("limited" in Manitoba [section 10(1]) and by requiring others ("incorporated" or "corporation" in Saskatchewan [section 10(1)] and Newfoundland [section 421(1]) and "society," "association," or "club" in British Columbia [section 6]). Probably the name should contain an element that identifies the corporation either as a non-profit or as a non-profit of the relevant type, since the name should give the public a sense of its purpose and of its structure of governance. A distinctive element in the name informs persons who see or hear it that the entity is subject to the provisions of the relevant statute of non-profit corporations. That would be a useful rule of public order.

The Number of Incorporators Sometimes one (Saskatchewan section 5[1]), sometimes five (British Columbia section 3[1], Alberta section 3[1], and Nova Scotia section 1), and sometimes three persons are required as initial incorporators. There may be some difficulty in theory with one-person corporations, but the juridical operation described above can easily be adjusted to accommodate unilateral acts. If there is to be any requirement as to the number of incorporators, it probably has to be based on regulatory considerations. It may be that the requirement of several incorporators, several continuing members, and/or several continuing directors will reduce the possibility of fiduciary breach and fraudulent use of the form. More probably, like much of the older corporate law, it is an empty formality.

Governance

The older statutes are deficient in numerous ways, resulting from failure to adjust to modern conditions or to modern corporate practices and from failure to adapt the corporate form to the specific needs of this type of organization. I investigate some of the main deficiencies here.

Membership and Affiliate Structures Non-profit corporations develop unique and perculiar relationships with other organizations, both profit and non-profit. Consider three examples, and contrast them with typical affiliate structures in the profit sector. First, an operating non-profit, no longer content to rely on donors' annual giving, might set up a fund-raising foundation. In this structure, the "parent–subsidiary" control is from operating to financing, not, as is typical in the for-profit sector, vice versa. The foundation is more like a bank account than a bank or a venture capitalist. This type of structure is not uncommon. An operating charity might establish a foundation to receive and administer a ten-year gift. Or a foundation might be established to engage in planned giving, such as charitable remainder trusts, charitable gift annuities, and gifts of life insurance. In these cases, the operating charity may want some veto control over basic changes or may want some automatic representation – perhaps even by appointing the chair – of the foundation. Alternatively, arrangements may be required to provide for an element of protection against too large a call on the foundation's resources by the operating organization, in which case the direction of control may be more ambiguous. For example, the board of an operating charity might, after a successful fund-raising campaign, shift the funds into a related foundation, beyond the direct reach of future boards. Foundations are also useful for segregating funds to acknowledge separate donors or to insulate the operating charity in the grant application process to government, vis-à-vis other charities, or in future appeals for funds to the public.

Second, a charity decides to put profit-making commercial activities into a related entity – a for-profit corporation or a business trust – in order to maintain its charitable status under the Income Tax Act. Third, large multi-member organizations may require a variety of membership structures. These can be of two main kinds: a federated structure to accommodate different structures of membership (perhaps on a regional) basis, delegate voting, and so on; and an affiliate structure both to insulate participating entities from each other's liability risks and to allow for some degree of control of one by the other.

These examples indicate that membership structures in this sector are quite different from those in the profit sector. The legislator must take this into account in the design of the law. A good facilitative law should provide the concepts and the framework to permit these structures. The CBCA's concepts of affiliate, subsidiary, and control are probably not adequate to the task.

Membership Rights The theme of most reforms of the business corporation statutes was the enhancement of shareholders' governance rights and increased protection for their pecuniary entitlements. Reform of these areas of the law in non-profit corporations is significantly different for a variety of reasons. Certainly, those reforms, such as the derivative action, that are grounded in a more accurate appreciation of the juridical nature of the corporation would apply with few changes to the non-profit. In two areas, however, the shape of the law should be considerably different: governance is substantially different, as is members' inclusion and expulsion.

Governance rights in the non-profit sector do not aim to protect a pecuniary interest. The point of members' involvement may be variously to allow pursuit of the common purpose and to hold the organizations's executive accountable for its performance in that regard (for example, a humane society); to permit deliberation on tactics and strategy in the pursuit of common purposes (as in a political advocacy group); to express the common purpose (for instance, a congregational religion); or to oversee or decide on the quality of the service provided by the non-profit to its members (such as a golf course or daycare). Many organizations, especially religious ones, already have a good deal of structure provided by their internal law. Thus the drafting of the law will have to accommodate a wide range of organizational types. The *Revised Model Act* provides a useful starting point, as it makes a significant distinction between religious and other non-profit organizations in this regard and alternates the legislative voice between imperative and suppletive.

The personal identity and behaviour of individual and group members are of concern in the non-profit in a way that they typically are not even in the case of the closely held for-profit corporation. Members of a religion have to at least profess the religion. Boors are unwelcome in the curling club's dining-room, as are infiltrators and usurpers in the political advocacy group. Given a legitimate common purpose, however, it cannot hurt most non-profits to decide issues of expulsion, if not inclusion, in a manner that is fair. Provisions in the statute should require some sort of valid fact-finding process and some manner of unbiased decision-making applicable to most non-profits. Religious groups might again be exempted on the basis that enforcing a member's right to natural justice in expulsion would involve a court in argument about truth in doctrinal matters.

Directors' Duties Boards of directors in all corporate sectors have at least five key functions: to select and supervise the performance of the chief executive officer; to establish and supervise implementation of long-term or strategic objectives; to facilitate obtaining of resources sufficient to implement these objectives; to supervise management's performance; and to reproduce themselves.[78] But there are important differences between profit and non-profit boards. Fishman and Schwarz outline some of the differences: "For-profit boards concentrate on developing and carrying out board strategies for enhancing shareholder value while non-profit boards are more committed to the organization's mission. While a business board may have an obligation to divest itself of unprofitable activities, a non-profit board has a greater duty to stay the course if it is to be true to its mission. Corporate boards devote much more time to review of performance than the typical non-profit. The bottom-line, the talisman of profit-seeking activity is easier to measure than non-profit effectiveness."[79] Another commentator says: "it is especially hard to be an effective director of a non-profit organization. The very mission of the enterprise can be difficult to define with precision and subject to intensive debate. It is often seen differently by various influential participants and supporters. Relevant data and analyses are frequently either unavailable or, if available, tricky to interpret. Performance often defies easy assessment and lack-luster leadership can go unnoticed, or at least uncorrected, for considerable periods of time. Resources are almost always scarce and problems often appear intractable. Creative solutions can be elusive and, if identified, hard to put into effect – in part because of the lack of ready access to the kind of "buy–sell" mechanisms provided by markets."[80] Another has observed that the non-profit boards tend to be larger (relative to assets), to be dominated by outsiders (as opposed to insiders), and to function more through a committee structure than their for-profit counterparts.[81]

The situation regarding modes of accountability is also distinctive, if somewhat paradoxical. The non-profit sector receives its funding almost entirely from the public or the government, and the task of a director is more complex than that of his or her for-profit counterpart. Yet its formal and informal modalities of accountability are far more lax than anything encountered in the profit sector, and there is nothing in it equivalent to the "market" modes of accountability – takeover, product, and manager markets. Its distinctiveness, which flows from its peculiar purposes, requires the legislator's special attention in the design of the general and specific rules governing the duties of directors. The place to begin thinking about this is in the formulation of directors' duties. I examine first the logic of the rule and then its content.

The codification of directors' duties in Canadian law is a recent project. Unfortunately, the current statements are exceptionally weak conceptually. In theory, the duty of a director has three components: a duty to act prudently (with care) and a duty to act loyally, both in pursuit of a specified purpose, with prudence (or care) further divided into competence or skill and attention or diligence. This whole package expresses the logical components of all fiduciary duties and is sometimes called (correctly, in my view) "fiduciary duty," which term sometimes refers to only loyalty.

The CBCA's codified formulation states: "Every director and officer of a corporation in exercising his or her powers and discharging her or her duties shall, (a) act honestly and in good faith with a view to the best interests of the corporation; and (b) exercise the care, diligence and skill that a reasonably prudent person would exercise in comparable circumstances." Note at least four significant conceptual deficiencies. The specified purpose is "the best interests of the corporations." The duties of loyalty and prudence are formulated as "honestly and in good faith" and "care, diligence and skill," respectively. And the level of skill required is that of a "reasonably prudent person."

As far as the first goes, the formulation "best interests of the corporation" is imponderable, since only entities with a will or desires can have interests. Here, the corporation-as-person metaphor surfaces again. One is forced either to identify some human constituency that is "the" corporation or "unpack" the metaphor to discover the true legal reality. Most observers would probably agree that what the drafters really meant was that the directors must prudently and loyally pursue "the maximization of the net present value of the corporate assets, within a given range of risk," as suggested above in section 1. For non-profits, the analogous objective can be only the "mission" or common purpose of the organization. In the jurisprudence of the for-profit sector, as I noted above, the meaning of this objective is a source of considerable controversy. It probably does not make sense to import that controversy to the non-profit context by using the same phrase. In any event, it is probably better to state much more clearly what the objective is and not to resort to a metaphor for such an important rule. Even though this rule is probably imperative (essential), its proper expression is facilitative, because it tells our ideal reader as plainly as possible what his or her duties are as a director.

As for the second aspect of the formulation, one can ask whether "honestly and in good faith with a view to" clearly and adequately expresses the idea of loyalty? What, in particular, does "good faith" mean – that the actor really intends what the actor purports to intend? Thus the director must "really intend" the best interests of the corporation. What does "honestly" add to that? At most the requirement that the director must not, in "really intending," be fooling himself or herself. If the director *is* loyal, then he or she must intend loyalty, since loyalty is a virtue, a subjective state. This is what the concepts "honestly" and "in good faith" are aiming at. If so, which is more readily intelligible to the ideal reader – the current formulation or to "be loyal" or "act loyally" in the pursuit of the common purpose? "Good faith" and "honestly" are just fragments of the larger concept of "loyalty."

On the third aspect, there is less of a problem with prudence. One might quibble that "care" and "diligence" say the same thing. But, with regard to the fourth, what does it mean to exercise the skill of a "reasonably prudent person"? Do all reasonably prudent people have the same level of skill? This formulation attempts to state the duty of prudence in too short a compass. A better approach might be to identify the components and then, for each one, the relevant standard. If the components are diligence and skill, as suggested in the statute and in the definition, then we can and probably should require a uniform standard of diligence (go to meetings, pay attention, do the reading, and so on) and a varying standard of skill (the skill of a lawyer for lawyers, the skill of a housewife for housewives, and so on). After all, the point of having a board of directors, as opposed to a single person, is to allow for deliberative decision-making. It must be assumed that the directors will not and should not share the same social, economic, or professional make-up. It must be assumed that their skills will be complementary. Alternatively, the standard of skill might be uniform, but, if so, it cannot be the skill of a reasonably prudent person, since the concept "skill" implies a craft, calling, or profession, and persons as such have none of these. Maybe what was meant was "reasonably prudent director."

In sum, to clarify these conceptual difficulties, the essential elements of the director's duty may be stated as follows: the director of a non-profit corporation must pursue the common purpose loyally and with prudence (diligence and skill). Now the question is: to what standard must he or she fulfil this duty?

First, much ink has been spilt over whether the standard of diligence and the standard of skill are higher or lower than those that apply to trustees or those that apply to directors of for-profits. This discussion is sometimes confused with a parallel debate on the duty of loyalty. The expression "fiduciary duty" is ambiguous – used to refer to the duty of loyalty and to both the duty of loyalty and the duty of prudence. The first step in clarification is to separate diligence and skill for independent analysis.

The duty of diligence turns out to be the more important. In fact, I do not know of a case where a court said that the directors lacked the requisite level of skill. Even in cases where there was an implicit finding of fact that they did lack the skill, the easier and more obvious conclusion was that they lacked the diligence, under the circumstances, to acquire the skill, to delegate appropriately, or to resign. In most cases, however, the problem was simple inattentiveness. And in a large number of these, the lack of attentiveness is related to a breach of the duty of loyalty.[82]

One could argue that the duty of diligence should be high, on the basis that the director of a charitable non-profit is analogous to the trustee of a charitable purpose trust. His or her position carries a very large social responsibility. Conversely, perhaps a standard set too high will simply scare people away.[83] Or perhaps the formulations available say pretty much the same thing, and anyway this question is seldom litigated. I take this last view. My preference would be "diligence of a reasonably prudent person in the same circumstance." Everybody understands that.

Second, because it makes no sense to talk about a level of skill without identifying a craft, the standard applicable to the duty of skill must be stated either in the context of a craft or not at all. Therefore, it appears that the choice is the "reasonable director" or no standard and therfore no duty of skill. Another option in the for-profit context is the business judgment rule. For non-profits, it has been referred to as the "best judgment rule."[84] The U.S. business judgment rule is a standard that courts use to police their own involvement in enforcing the accountability of directors. It is a standard, in effect, of judicial review. It has been stated in numerous cases and was most recently and usefully codified in the American Law Institute's Principles a formulation. Some U.S. jurisdictions have applied it in the non-profit context.[85] In general terms, the rule provides that, if directors take a decision in a good faith and in a disinterested manner, and if they have taken the proper steps to inform themselves of the matter to be decided, no court will subsequently review the decision for breach of the duty of care. In essence, the skill with which the decision has been made or its wisdom will not be questioned if the directors have made it with proper diligence.

Second, besides stating the general rule governing the behaviour of directors, a statute might also identify norms that apply in particular areas of activity. Corporate statutes address this issue in a number of ways besides simply imposing a particular duty in a specific context. For example, many contain rules that restrict the power of directors or of a corporation to borrow, to invest, or to own land. I argue above against rules that use a capacity–nullity logic. Are such restrictions, stated directly as specific duties in particular contexts, desirable at all?

These types of rules make sense only if the prohibited activity would probably or too frequently be carried on in some undesired way if it were permitted. In theory, there are only two justifications for any rule imposing specific duties on a fiduciary or prohibiting certain intrinsically unobjectionable behaviour. Either the specific duty is an application of the general duty in a defined circumstance, or it is too difficult for interested persons, including adjudicators, to apply the general rule accurately. If that is true, the rule would rarely if ever say: "You have a duty to invest in X, Y, Z, but not anything else," because this rule may not always instantiate what is prudent. Rather it would say either: "Be prudent, and, if you want to be safe from a judge's second guessing, then invest in XYZ"; or "Judge: In this type of case the usual solution is XYZ."

There cannot be too many instances in which such rules are appropriate. Since prudence depends very much on circumstances, it is hard to see how this type of legislative strategy would get the rule right often enough. All such rules are susceptible to the following criticism: "But what the prudent man [or woman] should do at any time depends on the economic and financial conditions of that time – not on what judges of the past, however eminent, have held to be the prudent course in the conditions of 50 or 100 years before".[86]

Finally, let us consider the content of the duty of loyalty. Its positive content is clear – the director must use his or her powers in the pursuit of the common purpose. The negative content is also clear – no stealing. Difficulties arise in two related areas: conflicts of interest and self-dealing transactions. Trustees may not deal with the trust at common law; they may not place themselves in a situation where their interest conflicts with their duty. This rule works reasonably well where the fiduciary really has no need and no occasion to deal with the trust. The activity of a fiduciary is to manage passive investments. In an operational setting, such as the typical for-profit or non-profit corporation, there is a need for fiduciaries to deal with the corporation: they may require remuneration; they will want or require indemnification; and they may have skills or assets needed by the corporation that the corporation should purchase. Therefore the absolute prohibition against conflicts of interest is not generally appropriate in the corporate context, and the legislator should design rules regulating self-dealing transactions so that they meet the loyalty requirement. These rules, moreover, like the specific context rules in the duty of prudence, will take the form of "safe harbour" rules or suppletive rules for judges.

Fundamental Change and Dissolution

American studies show that non-profits, compared to their for-profit counterparts, tend to resist fundamental changes. For-profits in financial difficulty may seek to take advantage of tax and economic benefits available on amalgamations and dissolution, whereas financially stressed non-profits with a large asset base, including a strong reputation, often seek to maintain their existence at the expense of not seeking new opportunities. In the absence of economic incentives, the negative factors inhibiting merger – such as cultural barriers, management's hubris, and inertia – are just overwhelming.

Non-profits are also distinctive in the types of considerations that they face on dissolution. The reasons for dissolution may vary – assets or funds may be insufficient for stated purposes, or stated purpose may have become redundant, or the board or the members may be deadlocked ideologically.

Although these differences are important and may shape the rules governing decision-making on fundamental changes and dissolution, the most critical consideration is disposition of the assets of corporations that have raised money for some public purpose. What is required therefore is some corporate law version of the cy-pres doctrine.

CONCLUSION

My main argument has been that designing a good law for non-profit corporations requires a great deal of thinking on the purposes for which the statute will be used. This turns out to be a difficult task because of the incredible variety of non-profit purposes. Still, that is the work that has to be done, because those purposes play out all the way through the statute. I suggest that this is a task that (probably) only lawyers with great experience in the sector can do well, but that even they are handicapped by the old, familiar models of corporate law. I believe that the *Revised Model Act* is a very good start and speculated above that its virtues derive from the fact that it is the third or fourth such attempt, and involved a lengthy, collegial process. I sought to contribute to reform by looking at design principles, while downplaying my favoured solutions. This is a useful level for the lawyers to begin thinking about the issues. I aimed at stating more an agenda of issues than a list of answers. But I do suggest one answer: the objective is a law appropriate to the purposes.

NOTES

1 The basic law of the unincorporated association has been reformed in several American states, based on National Conference of Commissioners on Uniform State Laws, Unincorporated Associations Act, 1992, (draft act). The Uniform Act has been adopted in Colorado (Colo. Rev. Stat., 17-30-101–9), Idaho (Idaho Code, 53701–7), Wisconsin (1997 Wisc. Stat. 140) and Wyoming (Wyo. Stat. 1977, 17-22-101–15). The Uniform Act provides that members, officers, and directors of unincorporated associations are not, as such, liable for the torts or contracts of the association; it defines and states the legal implications of membership; and it gives the association the capacity to own property.

2 On non-profit corporation law, U.S. writing includes: D. Barrett, "A Call for More Lenient Director Liability Standards for Small, Charitable Non-profit Corporations," *Indiana Law Journal* 71 (1996), 967; W. Bowen, T. Nygren, S. Turner, and T. Boyd, "A Call to Reform the Duties of Directors under State Not-for- Profit Corporation Statutes," *Iowa Law Review* 72 (1987), 725; B. Boykin, "The Non-profit Corporation in North Carolina: Recognizing a Right to Member Derivative Suits," *North Carolina Law Review* 63 (1985), 94; R. Boyle, "Non-profit Corporation Act of 1991: Introduction to Significant Changes," *Res Gestae* 35 (1992), 462; R. Dart, P. Bradshaw, V. Murray, and J. Wolpin, "Boards of Directors in Non-profit Organizations: Do They Follow a Life-Cycle Model?" *Non-profit Management & Leadership* 6 (1996), 367; D. DeMott, "Self-Dealing Transactions in Nonprofit Corporations," *Brooklyn Law Review* 59 (1993), 131; I. Ellman, "Another Theory of Nonprofit Corporations," *Michigan Law Review* 80 (1982), 999; J. Fishman, "The Development of Nonprofit Corporation Law and an Agenda for Reform," *Emory Law Journal* 34 (1985), 617; P. Galanti, "Indiana Nonprofit Corporation Act," *Indiana Law Review* 25 (1992), 999; H. Hansmann, "Reforming Nonprofit Corporation Law," *University of Pennsylvania Law Review* 129 (1981), 497, "The Role of Non-profit Enterprise," *Yale Law Journal* 89 (1980), 835, and "The Evolving Law of Nonprofit Organizations: Do Current Trends Make Good Policy?" *Case Western Reserve Law Review* 39 (1989), 807; H. Henn and M. Pfeiffer, "Nonprofit Groups: Factors Influencing Choice of Form," 1 *Wake Forest Law Review* 11 (1975), 181; P. Kay, "Director Conflicts of Interest under the Model Business Corporation Act: A Model for all States," *Washington Law Review* 69 (1994), 207; B. Kirschten, *Non-profit Corporation Forms Handbook* (1993); L. Moody, "State Statutes Governing Directors of Charitable Corporations," *University of San Francisco Law Review* 18 (1984), 749; L. Moody, "The Who, What, and How of the Revised Model Non-profit Corporation Act," *Northern Kentucky Law Review* 16 (1989), 251; and H. Oleck, *Non-Profit Corporations and Associations*, 3rd ed., (1975), and "The Nature of Nonprofit Organizations in 1979," *University of Toledo Law Review* 10 (1979), 962.

Canadian writings include: R. Cudney, "Corporation without Share Capital," *Canadian Bar Review* [1951], 846; P. Cumming, "Corporate Law Reform and Canadian Not-for-Profit Corporations Statute" *Philanthropist* 1, no. 2 (1973), 10; J. Gibson, "Liability of Directors of Ontario Charitable Corporations," *Estates and Trusts Quarterly* (1979–81), 71; J. Hodgson and A. McNeely, "Directors and Trustees: The Charitable Corporation and Trusteeship," in *Charitable Mosaic* (Toronto: Canadian Bar Association – Ontario, 1983) [unpublished]; W. Hurlburt, "Towards a Reformed Non-Profit Corporations Statute," *Philanthropist* 7 No. 3 (1988), 17; W. Innes, "Liability of Directors and Officer of Charitable and Non-profit

Corporations (Part 1 and 2)," *Estates and Trusts Journal* 13 (1993), 1, 151; D. Roberts, "Charitable and Non-profit Corporations in Alberta: An Update on Legal and Tax Issues," *Alberta Law Review* 27 (1989), 476. For general surveys of the law governing charities, see Ontario Law Reform Commission (OLRC), *Report on the Law of Charities* (Toronto: Ontario Law Reform Commission, 1996), and D. Bourgeois, *The Law of Charitable and Non-profit Organizations*, 2nd ed. (Toronto: Butterworths, 1995)

3 Most commentators agree that the current statutory framework is sorely inadequate. "Much of the confusion in this area evidently originates from the lack of any coherent conception of the basic purposes served by the non-profit form of organization ... [E]xisting non-profit corporation law, including the various recent efforts of statutory reform, is, in fundamental respects, misconceived and badly flawed": Hansmann, "Reforming," 500. "[The] present [federal] Act is ... awkward, confusing and functionally unsuitable": Cumming "Corporate Law Reform," 13. See also H. Henn and J. Boyd, "Statutory Trends in the Law of Non-profit Organizations: California, Here We Come!" *Cornell Law Review* 66 (1981), 1103; they note that non-profit corporate law is the "neglected stepchild" of corporate law receiving the latter's "hand-me-downs," as opposed to the distinctive treatment that it deserves.

4 Canadian laws form the background to this study: British Columbia: Society Act RSBC 1996, c. 433; Alberta: Societies Act RSA 1980, c. 5–18; Saskatchewan: The Non-profit Corporations Act, 1995, s. 5 1995, CN-4.2; Manitoba: The Corporations Act RSM 1987, c. C225; Ontario: Corporations Act RSO 1990, c.C-38; Quebec: Companies Act RSQ 1977, c. C-38; New Brunswick: Companies Act, RSNB 1973, c. C- 13; Nova Scotia: Societies Act RSNS 1989, c. 435; Prince Edward Island: Companies Act, RSPEI 1988, c. C-14; Newfoundland: The Corporations Act, RSN 1990, c. C-36; Canada: Canada Corporations Act RSC 1970, c. C-32.

5 There have been reform efforts federally, in Alberta, and in Saskatchewan. For the federal effort, see Canada, *Proposals for a New Not-for-Profit Corporations Law for Canada* (Ottawa: Department of Consumer and Corporate Affairs, 1974). The last version of the federal proposal was Bill C-10; it died on the order paper in 1980. For Alberta, see Alberta Institute of Law Research and Reform, *Proposals for a New Alberta Incorporated Associations Act*, Report No. 39 (Edmonton: March 1987), Alberta, Task Force on the Volunteer Incorporations Act, *Toward New Non-profit Legislation: Report of the Task Force on the Volunteer Incorporations Act* (Edmonton: Minister of Consumer and Corporate Affairs, January 1990); and Volunteer Incorporations Act, Bill 54, Alta. 1987 (21st Leg., 2nd Sess.). For Saskatchewan, see The Non- Profit Corporations Act, SS 1979, c. N-4.1. Now, see Non-Profit Corporations Act, 1995, SS 1995, c. N-4.2.

6 A newly revised statute, the Society Act RSBC 1979, c. 390, was enacted in 1977 in British Columbia. Saskatchewan reformed its law in 1979.

7 *The Interim Report of the Select Committee on Company Law* (Chair: A.F. Lawrence, QC) (Toronto: Ontario Legislative Assembly, 1967) had recommended a study and revision of Ontario's non-profit corporation law, but nothing came of the recommendation. The Alberta and federal efforts described in note 4 also did not result in legislation.

8 Ibid.. The report led to adoption of a new law for corporations in 1970. See Business Corporations Act, RSO 1970, c. 53.

9 See *Proposals for a New Business Corporations Law in Canada* (Ottawa, 1971), prepared by a federal task force (Dickerson Committee) led by Robert Dickerson, John Howard, and Leon Getz. Legislation implementing its recommendations was enacted in 1975; see Canada Business Corporations Act, SC 1974-75-76, c. 33. The federal statute was adopted almost *verbatim* in Alberta (Business Corporations Act, SA 1981, c. B-15), Manitoba (Corporations Act, RSM 1987, c. C225), and Saskatchewan (Business Corporations Act, RSS 1978, c. B-10), and substantially influenced new legislation in Ontario (Business Corporations Act, RSO 1990, c. B.16), Quebec (Companies Act, RSQ, c. C-38, Part IA, as en. by SQ 1980, c. 28, s. 14), New Brunswick (Business Corporations Act, SNB 1981, c. B-9.1) and Nova Scotia (Investor Protection Act, SNS1990, c. 15).

10 There has not been much writing on the non-profit corporation. See note 1 above. One author noted in 1973: "Not-for-profit corporations have received considerably lessattention than the business corporation. This is readily evidenced by a significantly less developed statutory framework, very few judicial interpretations through the case law, little attention from the academic world and general disinterestedness on the part of the legal profession as a whole": Cumming, "Corporate Law Reform," 14.

11 F. Easterbrook and D. Fischel, *The Economic Structure of Corporate Law* (Cambridge, Mass.: Harvard University Press, 1991), is the most comprehensive application of the approach.

12 See M. Hone, *Revised Model Nonprofit Corporation Act*, adopted in 1987 by the Subcommittee on the Model of Nonprofit Corporation Law, Business Law Section, American Bar Association (Englewood Cliffs, NJ: Prentice-Hall Law & Business, 1988). Two previous versions influenced the design of first- and second-generation reform statutes: American Law Institute and American Bar Association, *Model Nonprofit Corporations Law* (Philadelphia, 1952), and *Model Nonprofit Corporation Act*, rev. ed. (Philadelphia, 1964). Independent reform initiatives were taken in California and New York, the former serving as a model for the *Revised Model Act*. See California, Nonprofit Corporation Law, 1978 Cal. Stats., c. 567, operative 1 Jan.

1980 and New York, Not-for-Profit Corporation Law, ch. 35 (Consol. 1969), Chap. 1066, effective 1 Sept. 1970.

13 In the United States, a majority of states still use the *Model Act* of 1952, as revised in 1957 and 1964. Some apply, with adaptations, a general corporations statute. See, for example, Delaware, Code, Title 8; Kansas, Statutes; Maryland Code 5-202–8; and Oklahoma, General Corporation Act. New York implemented a major reform in 1969, and California, in 1980. Their non-profit corporation laws were original and innovative. Their interpretation and administration over the past 15 to 20 years provide a wealth of experience for Canadian legislators. Numerous U.S. states have adopted the Revised Model Act, which appears to be growing in popularity. The following jurisdictions have adopted it to date: Idaho, Code 30-3-1–145; Arkansas, Code Ann. 54-28-201–6 and 4-28-209-223; Colorado, Code 7-121-101–301; Mississippi, Code 79-11-101–399; Montana, Code 35-2.112–1402); Oregon, Revised Statutes 65.001–990; Tennessee, Code 48-51-101–105; and Wyoming, Statutes 17-19-101 –18070. Some jurisdictions have implemented portions of the statutes. For example, Texas uses the Revised Model Act's rule for a director's fiduciary duty. See, Texas Revised Civil Statutes s. 1396-3.02.

14 See: *Re Centenary Hospital Association and Public Trustee* (1989), 69 OR (2d) 1 (HCJ); supplementary reasons 69 OR (2d) 447 (HCJ); *Re Faith Haven Bible Training Centre* (1988), 29 ETR 198 (Ont. Surr. Ct); *Re David Feldman Charitable Foundation* (1987), 58 OR (2d) 626 (Surr. Ct); *Re Harold G. Fox Education Fund and Public Trustee* (1989), 69 OR (2d) 742 and 748 (HCJ); and *Re Public Trustee and Toronto Humane Society* (1987), 60 OR (2d) 236, (HCJ) *Re Laidlaw Foundation* (1984), 48 OR (2d) 549 (Div. Ct); *Re Incorporated Synod of the Diocese of Toronto and HEC Hotels Ltd.* (1987), 61 OR (2d) 737 (CA).

15 See Society Act and The Non-Profit Corporations Act.

16 OLRC, *Report on the Law of Trusts* (Toronto: Ministry of the Attorney General, 1984).

17 See ibid., 277–84.

18 Ibid., chap. 17.

19 See Sharpe, chapter 2 in this volume.

20 I do not intend to address that question, which many contributions to this volume consider. A recent statement by an American author suggests the elements of an answer in the U.S. context: "[T]he non-profit sector makes a significant, probably pivotal, contribution to the American form of representative democracy in at least three respects. First, the non-profit sector teaches the skills of self-government. Second, it inculcates the habits of tolerance and civility. Finally, it mediates the space between the individual and the other two sectors of society, that is, the 'public' or governmental sector and the 'private' or 'entrepreneurial' or 'propri-

etary' sector. Thus, the non-profit sector acts as a counterpoise against excessive displays of power emanating from the public or private sectors. Consequently, any legislative attempt to change the way the non-profit sector is regulated should preserve its capacity to play these three political roles effectively." See B. Bucholtz, "Reflections on the Role of Non-profit Associations in a Representative Democracy," *Cornell Journal of Law and Public Policy* 7, (1998), 555, 556. See also C. Taylor, "Modes of Civil Society," *Public Culture* 3 (1990), 95, and A Seligman, *The Idea of Civil Society* (Princeton, NJ: Princeton University Press, 1995).

21 For surveys, see OLRC, *Report*, chap. 9, and K. Monroe *The Heart of Altruism* (Princeton, NJ: Princeton University Press, 1996), chaps. 6–9.

22 Some lobbying efforts of the sector in recent years have been successful, but relatively minor. For example, the standard $100 deduction for charitable donations was repealed in 1987, and the deduction was converted to a credit in 1988.

23 The OLRC was abolished in 1996. Few of its private law projects have been acted on in the last 20 years.

24 This may explain why so little of the OLRC's private law work has been implemented.

25 *Revised Model Act*, xxix–xxx. This list of deficiencies mentions fiduciary responsibility implicitly only once (when it lists derivative suits), and all the others relate to whether the statute addresses organizational needs.

26 This section draws on arguments that I made in "The Regulation of Takeovers and the Idea of the Corporation," *Meredith Lectures* (Montreal, 1994–95), 371, 418–27.

27 England no longer exports its corporate law. More and more, common law jurisdictions seeking to reform their corporate law go to other jurisdictions for inspiration. See L. Gower et al., *Principles of Modern Company Law*, 5th ed. (London: Sweet & Maxwell, 1992), 70, which laments this "sad conclusion."

28 On the development of the legal concept of the corporation in common law, see M. Lizée, "Le principe du meilleur intérêt de la société commerciale en droits anglais et comparé," *McGill Law Journal* 34 (1989), 653; Gower et al., *Modern Company Law*, chap. 2; T. Hadden, R. Forbes, and R. Simmonds, *Canadian Business Organizations Law* (Toronto: Butterworths, 1984); E. LaBrie and E. Palmer, "The Pre-Confederation History of Corporations in Canada," in J. Ziegel, ed., *Studies in Canadian Company Law*, vol. 1 (Toronto: Butterworths, 1967) chap. 2; F. Wegenast, *The Law of Canadian Companies* (Toronto: Carswell, 1979) chap. 2; and B. Welling, *Corporate Law in Canada: The Governing Principles*, 2nd ed. (Toronto: Butterworths, 1991).

29 R. Skinner, *Accounting Standards in Evolution* (Toronto: Holt Rhinehart and Winston, 1987), cited in G. Webb, "GAAP and the Canadian Income

Tax Act," in *1997 Conference Report* (Toronto: Canadian Tax foundation, 1998) 10:1, 10:2.

30 The leading cases are recent, contradictory, and not exhaustive: *Sparling v. Caisse de dépôt et placement* [1988] 2 SCR 1015; *Bowater Canadian Ltd. v. RL Crain Inc.* (1987), 62 OR (2d) 752 (OCA); *Jacobsen v. United Canso Oil & Gas Ltd.* (1980), 11 BLR 313 (Alta. QB); and *Jacobsen & United Canso Oil & Gas Ltd.* (1980), 12 BLR 113 (NS SCTD).

31 Are directors obliged to maximize shareholders' value or the value of the corporate patrimony?

32 Do they owe their duty to the corporation, to society at large, or to the shareholders?

33 Hence the "stakeholders" debate. See generally the essays collected in *University of Toronto Law Journal* 43 (1993), Special Issue on the Corporate Stakeholder Debate: The Classical Theory and Its Critics.

34 J. MacIntosh, J. Holmes, and S. Thompson, "The Puzzle of Shareholder Fiduciary Duties," *Canadian Business Law Journal* 19 (1991), 86.

35 There is an American model as well, which has a proliferation of fiduciary duties among all the constituents of the corporation. The leading U.S. cases on director–shareholder and shareholder–shareholder fiduciary duties are *Jones v. H.F. Ahmanson & Co.*, 460 P.2d 464 (Cal. 1969); *Pepper v. Litton,* 308 U.S. 295 (1939) and *Donahue v. Rodd Electrotype Co. of New England Inc.*, 328 NE 2d 505 (Mass. 1975). See also *Hanson Trust PLC v. MLSCM Acquisition Inc.*, 781 F.2d 264 (2d. Cir. 1986); *Radol v. Thomas,* 772 F.2d 244 (6th Cir. 1985); *Samuel F. Feinberg Testamentary Trust v. Carter,* 652 F Supp. 1066 (SDNY 1987); and *Panter v. Marshall Field & Co.*, 486 F Supp. 1168 (ND Ill. 1980) aff'd. 646 F.2d 271 (7th Cir. 1981) cert. denied 454 U.S. 1092 (1981).

36 The thing created by the contract – the company – is also a party to it in many versions of this provision.

37 This suggests that statutory rules allocating the power to manage are suppletive. Query whether the obligation of whoever manages to maximize the net present value is also suppletive. I would suggest not; I would suggest that it is either essential or at least of public order.

38 See Gower, *Modern Company Law.*

39 (1843), 2 Hare 461, 67 ER 189.

40 There are four exceptions to this rule. Shareholders may sue: when it is complained that the company is acting ultra vires: (*Yorkshire Miners' Asscn. v. Howden,* [1905] AC 256 (HL)); when the act complained of is one that could be done validly or sanctioned not by a simple majority vote but only by some special majority: *Baillie v. Oriental Telephone Co.*, [1915] 1 Ch. 503 (CA); *Edwards v. Halliwell,* [1950] 2 All ER 1064 (CA); when the personal rights of the plaintiff shareholder have been infringed: *Johnson v. Lyttle's Iron Agency* (1877), 5 Ch. D. 687 (CA); and

when those who control the company are perpetrating a fraud on the minority: *Menier v. Hooper's Telegraph Works* (1874), 9 Ch. 350 (CA); *Mason v. Harris* (1879), 11 Ch. D. 97 (CA).

41 *Mozley v. Alston* (1847), 1 Ph. 790, 41 ER 833; *MacDougall v. Gardiner* (1875), 1 Ch. D. 13.

42 (1887), 12 App. Cas. 589 (JCPC).

43 [1902] AC 83 (PC).

44 (1877), 6 Ch. D. 70 (CA).

45 [1967] Ch. 254.

46 [1970] Ch. 212 (CA).

47 There is no precedent for this idea in partnership law. Major elements of the partnership contract, such as admitting new partners, changing the business, and modifying the mutual rights and duties of the partners, require unanimous approval.

48 [1902] 2 Ch. 421.

49 An Ontario case, *Craik v. Aetna Life Insurance company of Canada* [1995] OJ No. 3286 (Gen. Div.), at para. 5, captures the conventional picture: "A corporation is an artificial entity. That is, it is a juristic person whose reality arises because the law recognizes it as a separate person. It can only function and act through human beings acting on its behalf ... That is, the corporation acts through individuals who form its directing mind and management. A director or officer who carries on discussions and makes decisions relating to the business carried on by the corporation, if acting within the scope of his/her authority as a human agent for the corporation, is simply causing the corporation to act and form legal relationship."

50 There is English authority for the proposition that the corporation is variously the shareholders, as in *Allen v. Gold Reefs of West Africa*, [1900] 1 Ch. 656 (CA); *Brown v. British Abrasive Wheel*, [1919] 1 Ch. 219; and *Greenhalgh v. Arderne Cinemas Ltd.* [1951] Ch. 286, [1950] 2 All ER 1120 (Eng. CA); the majority of shareholders, as in the ratification cases; and a separate person, as in (*Salomon v Salomon* [1897] AC 22 (HL); and *Macaura v. Northern Assurance Co.*, [1925] AC 619 (HL).

51 It is critical that their promise is to maximize corporate wealth, not shareholders' wealth. It is well-known that the two criteria diverge at insolvency: the residual claimants at that point have every incentive to choose higher variance and lower net-present-value investment opportunities – or, in other words, to "bet the farm." See S. Myers, "Determinants of Corporate Borrowing,"*Journal of Finance and Economics* 5 (1977), 147; J. Ziegel, "Creditors as Corporate Stakeholders: The Quiet Revolution – an Anglo-Canadian Perspective," *University of Toronto Law Journal* 43 (1993), 511. See also *Kinsela v. Russell Kinsela Pty.* (1986), 4 NSWLR 722 (court).

52 In many corporation statutes, the articles appoint the first directors.

53 "Corporate agent" is a fiction. The "agent" cannot really be that because the corporation cannot be a principal; only real persons can be principals. However, the fiction is a perfectly accurate description of the *effects* of the contracts described in the text, and the juridical mechanics are easily "unpacked." See Lord Diplock's discussion of corporate agents in *Freeman & Lockyer* v. *Buckhurst Park Properties*, [1964] 2 QB 480 (CA).

54 See Ontario, Partnerships Act, RSO 1990, c. P.5 at s. 24 (7).

55 Ibid., s. 31.

56 Delaware General Corporation Law, s. 202; CBCA, ss. 6(1)(d) and 49(8); Business Corporations Act, RSO 1990, c. ss. 5(1)(d) and 56(3).

57 The restrictive covenant interpretation might explain why some statutes tie permitted restriction to some concrete benefit in the corporation and why UCC Article 8–style statutes do not bind restrictions on purchasers without notice if the share certificate does not mention it. This construal might also suggest that the restrictions should not be capable of amendment without the consent of the person(s) who benefit from it. So, for example, where the restriction creates a right of first refusal in other shareholders, an amendment should require the consent of the class. *Contra*: *Greenhalgh v. Arderne Cinemas Ltd.*, [1951] Ch. 286.

58 E. Mockler, *Charitable Corporation: A Bastard Legal Form* (1966): "As the common law has developed, numerous situations have arisen in which legal forms have been interbred; purity has been lost to expediency and the needs of the day have spawned some curious results. Forms, once strangers to each other, have been joined out of wedlock and the result has been the birth of a 'nullius filius.' Of all the bastard legal forms it is my contention that the charitable corporation ranks close to the top of the list. It has strains of both corporation law and trusts and on the paternal side one sees shades of the Chancellor's foot!"

59 The main cases are *Faith Haven Bible Training Centre; Re David Feldman Charitable Foundation, Re Harold G. Fox Education Fund*; *Toronto Humane Society*; and *Re Incorporated Synod of Toronto*; as well as *Roman Catholic Archiepiscopal Corp. of Winnipeg v. Ryan* (1957), 12 DLR (2d) 23 (*sub nom. Canada Trust Co. v. Roman Catholic Archiepiscopal Corp. of Winnipeg*) 26 WWR 69 (BCCA); *Re French Protestant Hospital and Attorney General*, [1951] Ch. 567; and *Liverpool & District Hospital for Diseases of the Heart v. Attorney General*, [1981] 1 Ch. 193.

The American situation is much the same. See *Somerland of Santa Barbara, Inc. v. County of South Barbara*, 31 Cal. Rptr 131 (Cal. Dist. Ct App., 1963) ("[A]ll property held by a benevolent corporation is impressed with the charitable trust"), cited in "Developments in the Law:

Nonprofit Corporations," *Harvard Law Review* 105 (1992), 1578, 1593. The *Model Act*, however, states unequivocally that directors are not trustees: 8.30(e). See also L. Sealy, "The Director as Trustee," *Cambridge Law Journal* [1967], 83.

60 W. Fratcher, *Scott on Trusts*, Vol. IV A. 4th, 1989 – 348.1 at 23.

61 On non-profits, see Hansmann "Reforming." On for-profits, see Easterbrook, *Economic Structure.*

62 Albert O. Hirschman has complained about the parsimony of the postulates of economics as follows: "Economics as a science of human behaviour has been grounded in a remarkably parsimonious postulate, that of the self-interested, isolated individual who chooses freely and rationally between alternative courses of action after computing their prospective costs and benefits." And Thomas Schelling has noted likewise: "The human mind is something of an embarrassment to certain disciplines, notably economics .... that have found the model of the rational consumer to be powerfully productive." See A. Hirschman, "Against Parsimony: Three Ways of Complicating Some Categories of Economic Discourse," *Economics and Philosophy* 1 (1987), 7. Hirschman provides the quote from Schelling, *Choice and Consequence* (Cambridge, Mass.: Harvard University Press, 1984) 342. Among the many modes of behaviour that this model excludes is love. Hirschman points out that things such as love and skill and civic spirit should be modelled not as scarce resources but as abilities or dispositions that grow or increase in value as they are used or practised. So any economics – any science of efficient resource use – in the charity sector or civil society in general would have to accommodate the different logics of these types of resources into its basic model.

63 Hansmann, "Reforming," 507.

64 Ibid., 508.

65 See sections 133 of the Ontario act and 157(1) of the federal act, which now make the general part applicable to the non-profit, subject to necessary modifications. This was not always the case. See Cumming, "Corporate Law Reform," 11.

66 See the Volunteer Protection Act, PL 104-19, 42 U.S.C. 14051. The act was signed by President Clinton on 18 June 1997.

67 Similarly, it has been argued that non-profits should not be subject to punitive damage awards: D. Barfield, "Better to Give Than to Receive: Should Nonprofit Corporations and Charities Pay Punitive Damages?" *Valparaiso University Law Review* 29 (1995), 1193.

68 Cumming, "Corporate Law Reform," 20.

69 See ibid., 12: "[T]he absence of statutory standards results in a lesser knowledge and appreciation of duties, responsibilities, powers, etc. on the part of directors than would be so if there were statutory provisions

present as enabling provisions and standards. It further results in an unnecessary expenditure of time and energy through the supervisory administrative role of the Department."

70 Alaska, Statutes 10.20 005; Florida, Statute 617.03101; and Illinois, Comprehensive Statute 805 101/103.5.

71 Fishman and Schwarz. Indiana's statute provides: "Corporations may be organized or re-organized for not-for-profit under this chapter for any lawful purposes consistent with the provisions of this chapter and regardless whether any other law is available which specifically provides for the incorporation of a corporation for the purposes sought to be accomplished by the incorporations." Indiana, Code 23-7-1.1-3.

72 Some states have used the *Revised Model Act*'s tripartite classification; others have not. Even some that do have reduced the significant differences in treatment. For example, the *Revised Model Act* imposes a stricter conflict-of-interest approval process on public benefit and religious corporations, but the additional requirement – that the directors bona fide believe that the transaction is fair to the corporation – is not imposed under the Arkansas law.

73 There is no statement of the non-distribution constraint in New Brunswick's statute. Some provinces' laws prohibit "pecuniary gain," others "monetary gain" (Newfoundland, s. 421). Saskatchewan's law contains perhaps the clearest expression of the constraint: "30(1) Subject to subsection (2), any profits or accretions to the value of the property of a corporation shall be used to further its activities, and no part of the property or profits of the corporation may be distributed, directly or indirectly, to a member director or officer of the corporation except as permitted pursuant to sections 111, 112, 169, 177, 209, 225 and 227. Where a member of corporation is a body corporate or association that is authorized to carry on activities on behalf of the corporation, the corporation may distribute any of its money or property to carry out those activities."

74 Canada, Ontario, Quebec, Prince Edward Island, and New Brunswick are letters-patent jurisdictions. Saskatchewan, Manitoba, and Newfoundland use articles of incorporation. British Columbia, Alberta, and Nova Scotia incorporate "societies" by "certificate of incorporation." Some of these jurisdictions require the filing of a "memorandum of association": Quebec section 6, Nova Scotia section 4, and New Brunswick section 7(1).

75 Letters patent statutes contain lists of powers usually complemented by the power to things incidental to or conducting to achieving their objects. These in turn are supplemented by provisions in the relevant interpretation acts. See section 27, Interpretation Act, RSO 1990 c. I 11].

76 Canada section155(2), British Columbia section 3(1)(a), Alberta section 5(1), Prince Edward Island section 90(2), and Nova Scotia section 4

require filing of by-laws with the application for incorporation. The federal (section155) and Alberta (section 5[1]) statutes require that by-laws be submitted with the application for letters patents, and these are occasionally returned by the relevant minister for deficiencies. Organizations can avoid this delay by using the by-law (annotated) provided by the ministry in its information kit. The Ontario statute (section 29) contains a list of items that may be included in the by-laws; Saskatchewan's contains neither a list nor a requirement to file by-laws.

77 See Housing Development Act, RSO 1990, c. H-18. Applications are also sent to the legal services branch of the Ministry of Consumer and Commercial Relations in the case of corporations pursuing objects relating to education, social welfare, health, and fitness.

78 See W. Bowen, *Inside the Boardroom: Governance by Directors and Trustees* (New York: J. Wiley, 1994), 18–20. American Law Institute (ALI), *Principles of Corporate Governance,* establishes the following specific responsibilities for directors of public corporations: "3.02. The Board of directors of a publicly held corporation should perform the following functions:(1) Select, regularly evaluate, fix the compensation of, and, where appropriate, replace the principal senior executives; (2) Oversee the conduct of the corporations business to evaluate whether the business is being properly managed; (3) Review and, when appropriate, approve the corporation's financial objectives and major corporate plans and actions; (4) Review and, where appropriate, approve major changes in, and determinations of other major questions of choice respecting the appropriate auditing and accounting principles and practices to be used in the preparation of the corporation's financial statements; (5) Perform such other functions as are prescribed by law, or assigned to the board under a standard of the corporation."

79 G. Overton, ed., *Guidebook for Directors of Non-profit Corporations* (American Bar Association, Section of Business Law, 1993), 151.

80 W. Bowen, *Inside the Boardroom: A Reprise in Non-profit Governance* (New York: J. Wiley, 1996), 9. H. Goldschmid, "The Fiduciary Duties of Non-profit Directors and Officers: Paradoxes, Problems and Proposed Reforms," *Journal of Corporation Law* 23 (1998), 632.

81 See L Moody, "Book Review: Guide for Non-profit Directors, by Daniel Kurtz," *Business Law* 43 (1998), 1605, 1606.

82 The U.S. jurisprudence provides an instructive illustration. In the *Sibley Hospital* case, a finance committee had directed that large sums of money be held on deposit with defendant banks with no or inadequate interest being paid in return. Each director on the committee held a position on the board of a defendant bank. In respect of the duty of diligence, the allegation was that the directors failed to exercise any of their responsibilities as members of any of the board committees (000): "[T]he Court

finds that each of the defendant trustees has breached this fiduciary duty to supervise the management of Sibley's investments. All except Mr. Jones were duly and repeatedly elected to the Investment Committee without ever bothering to object when no meetings were called for more than ten years. Mr. Jones was a member of the equally inactive Finance Committee, the failure of which to report on the existence of investable funds was cited by several other defendants as a reason for not convening the Investment Committee. In addition, Reed, Jones and Smith were, for varying periods of time also members of the Executive committee, which was charged with acquiring at least enough information to vote intelligently on the opening of new bank accounts. By their own testimony, it is clear that they failed to do so ... [T]hese men have ... failed to exercise even the most cursory supervision over the handling of Hospital funds and failed to establish or carry out a defined policy."

83 The standard might also vary with the size of the non-profit. See D. Barrett, "A Call for More Lenient Director Liability Standards for Small, Charitable Nonprofits," *Indiana Law Journal* 71 (1996), 967, suggesting a lower standard for small charities to increase rates of volunteering.

84 See *Beard v. Achenbach Memorial Hospital,* 170 F. 2d 859 (10th Cir. 1948).

85 *Brand v. Achenbach Memorial Hosp. Ass'n.* 170 F. 2d 859 (10th Cir. 1948); *John v. John,* 450 NW 2d 795 (Wis. Ct App. 1989); *Yarnall Warehouse Transfer, Inc. v. Three Ivory Bros. Moving Co.,* 226 So 2d 887 (Fla Dist. Ct App. 1989).

86 Dillon, LJ, in *Nestlé v. The National Westminster Bank Plc* [1994] 1 All ER 118 at 126 (CA). See also S. Rodgers, "Not-for-Profit: Caught in a Crossfire between the Payoffs of Portfolio Diversification and the Law That Restricts It," *Canadian Investment Review* 8, no. 2 (1995), 39.